Modern Research Methods for the Study of Behavior in Organizations

The goal for the chapters in this SIOP Organizational Frontiers series volume is to challenge researchers to break away from the rote application of traditional methodologies and to capitalize upon the wealth of data-collection and analytic strategies available to them. In that spirit, many of the chapters in this book deal with methodologies that encourage organizational scientists to reconceptualize phenomena of interest (e.g., experience sampling, catastrophe modeling), employ novel data-collection strategies (e.g., data mining, Petri nets), and/or apply sophisticated analytic techniques (e.g., latent class analysis). The editors believe that these chapters provide compelling solutions for the complex problems faced by organizational researchers.

Jose M. Cortina is a Professor in the Industrial/Organizational Psychology program at George Mason University. His recent research has involved topics in meta-analysis, structural equation modeling, significance testing, and philosophy of science, as well as predictors and outcomes of emotions in the workplace. He currently serves as Editor of *Organizational Research Methods* and is a former Associate Editor of the *Journal of Applied Psychology*. Dr. Cortina was honored by SIOP with the 2001 Ernest J. McCormick Award for Distinguished Early Career Contributions, by the Research Methods Division of the Academy of Management with the 2004 Robert O. McDonald Best Paper Award, and by the *Organizational Research Methods* Editorial Board with the 2012 Best Paper Award. He was also honored by George Mason University with a 2010 Teaching Excellence Award and by SIOP with the 2011 Distinguished Teaching Award.

Ronald S. Landis is Nambury S. Raju Endowed Professor in the College of Psychology at Illinois Institute of Technology. He has also served on the faculty at Tulane University, where he was awarded the Tulane President's Award for Excellence in Graduate and Professional Teaching in 2004. He is a Fellow of SIOP and was honored by the *Organizational Research Methods* Editorial Board with the 2012 Best Paper Award. He has primary research interests in the areas of structural equation modeling, multiple regression, and other issues associated with measurement and the prediction of performance. He is currently an Associate Editor of the *Journal of Business and Psychology* and a former Associate Editor of *Personnel Psychology*.

The Organizational Frontiers Series

SIOP Organizational Frontiers Series

Series Editor

Eduardo Salas
University of Central Florida

Weekley/Ployhart: (2006) *Situational Judgment Tests: Theory, Measurement, and Application*

Dipboye/Colella: (2005) *Discrimination at Work: The Psychological and Organizational Bases*

Griffin/O'Leary-Kelly: (2004) *The Dark Side of Organizational Behavior*

Hofmann/Tetrick: (2003) *Health and Safety in Organizations*

Jackson/Hitt/DeNisi: (2003) *Managing Knowledge for Sustained Competitive Knowledge*

Barrick/Ryan: (2003) *Personality and Work*

Lord/Klimoski/Kanfer: (2002) *Emotions in the Workplace*

Drasgow/Schmitt: (2002) *Measuring and Analyzing Behavior in Organizations*

Feldman: (2002) *Work Careers*

Zaccaro/Klimoski: (2001) *The Nature of Organizational Leadership*

Rynes/Gerhart: (2000) *Compensation in Organizations*

Klein/Kozlowski: (2000) *Multilevel Theory, Research and Methods in Organizations*

Ilgen/Pulakos: (1999) *The Changing Nature of Performance*

Earley/Erez: (1997) *New Perspectives on International I-O Psychology*

Murphy: (1996) *Individual Differences and Behavior in Organizations*

Guzzo/Salas: (1995) *Team Effectiveness and Decision Making*

Howard: (1995) *The Changing Nature of Work*

Schmitt/Borman: (1993) *Personnel Selection in Organizations*

Zedeck: (1991) *Work, Families, and Organizations*

Schneider: (1990) *Organizational Culture and Climate*

Goldstein: (1989) *Training and Development in Organizations*

Campbell/Campbell: (1988) *Productivity in Organizations*

Hall: (1987) *Career Development in Organizations*

Modern Research Methods for the Study of Behavior in Organizations

Edited by

Jose M. Cortina
George Mason University

Ronald S. Landis
Illinois Institute of Technology

Routledge
Taylor & Francis Group

NEW YORK AND LONDON

First published 2013
by Routledge
711 Third Avenue, New York, NY 10017

Simultaneously published in the UK
by Routledge
27 Church Road, Hove, East Sussex BN3 2FA

Routledge is an imprint of the Taylor & Francis Group, an informa business

Library of Congress Cataloging in Publication Data
Modern research methods for the study of behavior in organizations /
  edited by Jose M. Cortina, Ronald S. Landis.
  p. cm.—(SIOP organizational frontier series)
  1. Organizational behavior—Research.   2. Psychology,
  Industrial—Research.   I. Cortina, Jose M.   II. Landis, Ronald S.
  HD58.7.M6273 2013
  302.3′5072—dc23   2012035472

ISBN: 978-0-415-88559-1 (hbk)
ISBN: 978-0-203-58514-6 (ebk)

Typeset in Minion
by Florence Production Ltd, Stoodleigh, Devon, UK

Printed and bound in the United States of America by Sheridan Books, Inc. (a Sheridan Group Company).

The Editors dedicate this book to their advisor, Neal Schmitt. Many people rave about their advisors. Actually, most complain, but a few rave, and with good reason. A good advisor gives time and expertise without any expectation of receiving anything in return. But Neal wasn't a good advisor. He wasn't a great advisor. Neal Schmitt was simply the best possible advisor. He was (and is) a great scholar and teacher to be sure, but the quality that distances him from all others was his absolute commitment to putting students first. Neal has had dozens and dozens of advisees (he is quite old, you know), and every single one of them that we know felt that Neal ALWAYS prioritized them over all of his many other commitments. We can never pay you back Neal. We can only offer our gratitude and esteem.

Plus the occasional book dedication.

Jose M. Cortina
Fairfax, Virginia

Ronald S. Landis
Chicago, Illinois

Contents

About the Editors

Jose M. Cortina is a Professor in the Industrial/Organizational Psychology program at George Mason University. Professor Cortina received his Ph.D. in 1994 from Michigan State University. His recent research has involved topics in meta-analysis, structural equation modeling, significance testing, and philosophy of science, as well as predictors and outcomes of emotions in the workplace. His work has been published in journals such as the *Journal of Applied Psychology, Personnel Psychology, Psychological Bulletin, Organizational Research Methods*, and *Psychological Methods*. He currently serves as Editor of *Organizational Research Methods* and is a former Associate Editor of the *Journal of Applied Psychology*. Dr. Cortina was honored by SIOP with the 2001 Ernest J. McCormick Award for Distinguished Early Career Contributions, by the Research Methods Division of the Academy of Management with the 2004 Robert O. McDonald Best Paper Award, and by the *Organizational Research Methods* Editorial Board with the 2012 Best Paper Award. He was also honored by George Mason University with a 2010 Teaching Excellence Award and by SIOP with the 2011 Distinguished Teaching Award.

Ronald S. Landis is Nambury S. Raju Endowed Professor in the College of Psychology at Illinois Institute of Technology. Prior to IIT, he was Professor of Psychology and founding Director of the University of Memphis Center for Organizational Research and Effectiveness (UMCORE) at University of Memphis. He has also served on the faculty at Tulane University, where he was awarded the Tulane President's Award for Excellence in Graduate and Professional Teaching in 2004. He is a Fellow of SIOP and was honored by the *Organizational Research Methods* Editorial Board with the 2012 Best Paper Award. He has primary research interests in the areas of structural equation modeling, multiple regression, and other issues associated with measurement and the prediction of performance. His work has been published in several leading journals, including *Organizational Research Methods*, *Organizational Behavior and Human Decision Processes*, *Personnel Psychology*, and the *Journal of Applied Psychology*. He is currently an Associate Editor of the *Journal of Business and Psychology* and a former Associate Editor of *Personnel Psychology* and serves on the editorial boards of *Organizational Research Methods*, *Journal of Management*, *Personnel Psychology*, *Human Performance*, and the *Journal of Applied Psychology*. He received his Ph.D. from Michigan State University in 1995.

About the Contributors

Cory S. Adis is a researcher at PDRI, Inc., in the Military Research Division. His many research interests currently include cognitive training, adaptability and resilience, and cross-cultural competence. He is presently engaged in research to evaluate training using neuroimaging techniques. The present work was completed at George Mason University, where Mr. Adis is finishing a Ph.D. in Industrial/Organizational Psychology.

Wendy L. Bedwell is a doctoral candidate in the Industrial/Organizational Psychology program at the University of Central Florida (UCF). Ms. Bedwell earned a BA in Psychology with a minor in Business from James Madison University and a Masters in Distance Education (MDE) from the University of Maryland. As a graduate research associate at the Institute for Simulation and Training, her research interests focus on enhancing adaptive performance through individual and team training, especially technology-based training. Her emphasis is on team membership fluidity and its effects in teamwork KSAs, such as adaptation and collaboration in collocated and distributed teams.

Michael T. Braun, MA, is a doctoral candidate in the Organizational Psychology program at Michigan State University. His research interests are in the areas of team knowledge building and decision-making, team collaboration and effectiveness, longitudinal data analysis, and dynamic modeling. He is currently a member of the Society for Industrial Organizational Psychologists and the Academy of Management. He received his BA in psychology from Purdue University (2006) and his MA (2009) from Michigan State.

Robert Cookson is currently working toward a Ph.D. in Industrial and Organizational Psychology at the Georgia Institute of Technology.

Michael D. Coovert, upon completing his doctorate at the Ohio State University, joined the industrial/organizational faculty at the University of South Florida, where teaching factor analysis and structural equation modeling are among his responsibilities. One summer, when working as part of a research team whose purpose was modeling behavior and interactions in combat information centers on Naval warships, he was stumped, as none of his traditional methodological tools could capture behavior across time and at multiple levels of abstraction. Not wanting to pump gas for the summer, he reached back into his training in computer science and pulled out graph theory and Petri nets to apply to the problem.

Richard P. DeShon, Ph.D., is Professor and Chair of Organizational Psychology at Michigan State University. His research interests are in the areas of dynamic models, motivation and self-regulation, measurement theory, performance measurement, and selection and classification based on individual differences. He is currently an Associate Editor for the *Journal of Applied Psychology* and is on the Editorial Boards for *Psychological Methods* and the *Journal of Management*. He is a Fellow of the Association for Psychological Science and winner of the Ernst J. McCormick award for early career contributions to industrial and organizational psychology. He received his Ph.D. from the University of Akron.

Justin A. DeSimone has a BA in Psychology from Duke University and an MS in Psychology from the Georgia Institute of Technology. He is currently working toward a Ph.D. in Industrial and Organizational Psychology. Justin's research interests include statistical and psychometric issues, as well as the development and validation of new personality measures.

Aaron S. Dietz is a doctoral student in the Applied Experimental and Human Factors Psychology program at the University of Central Florida (UCF). He currently works as a graduate research associate at the Institute for Simulation and Training (IST), Department for Human Systems Integration Research, where his research interests include teamwork, training, performance measurement, and advanced training technologies. Mr. Dietz earned his bachelor's degree in Psychology and Economics from the University of Washington. Prior to enrolling at UCF, Mr. Dietz worked as a program analyst at the National Transportation Safety Board.

Nikolaos Dimotakis is an assistant professor in the Department of Managerial Sciences at Georgia State University. His research focuses on the ways employees experience their work, and how these experiences affect the way they feel, behave, and interact with others around them. His work has been published or is forthcoming in journals such as the *Journal of Applied Psychology*, the *Academy of Management Journal*, and *Personnel Psychology*.

Nikki Dudley-Meislahn is a senior consultant and partner at Shaker Consulting Group. Current research interests include innovative measurement methodologies for knowledge, skills, and personality, high-fidelity simulations, "day in the life" assessments, and applicant reactions. She has worked with numerous Fortune 100 clients and has also received the Edwin A. Fleishman award for her dissertation and the G. Klopfer Award for distinguished contribution to the literature in personality. She received her Ph.D. from George Mason University.

Robert P. Gephart, Jr. is Professor of Strategic Management and Organization at the University of Alberta, School of Business. Dr Gephart is the author of *Ethnostatistics: Qualitative Foundations for Quantitative Research* and a co-editor of *Postmodern Management and Organization Theory*. His research has appeared in a number of journals, including the *Administrative Science Quarterly* and the *Academy of Management Journal*. Dr. Gephart's current research interests include qualitative research methods, ethnostatistics, risk sensemaking and deliberative democracy. He received his Ph.D. from the University of British Columbia.

Stephen J. Guastello is a Professor of Psychology at Marquette University in Milwaukee, Wisconsin, where he specializes in industrial–organizational psychology and human factors. He received his Ph.D. in Industrial–Organizational Psychology from the Illinois Institute of Technology in 1982, his MA in Psychology from Washington University, St. Louis, and BA in Psychology from the Johns Hopkins University. He is the author or co-editor of four books on applications of nonlinear dynamics in psychology, author of a textbook on human factors and numerous articles in the same topic areas, and Editor-in-Chief of *Nonlinear Dynamics, Psychology, and Life Sciences*.

Remus Ilies is Professor of Management and Organization at the National University of Singapore (NUS). Before moving to NUS in 2011, he was the Gary Valade Research Fellow and Professor of Management at Michigan State University. His research focuses on individual differences, employee well-being, work–family processes, attitudes, leadership and motivation, and on understanding the role of emotional processes in explaining outcomes relevant to these research topics.

Lawrence R. James is a leading researcher in industrial–organizational psychology and organizational behavior. Dr. James has been active in building new measurement systems for personality and in studying the effects of organizational environments on individual adaptation, motivation, and productivity. His statistical contributions have been designed to make possible tests of new models in areas such as organization climate, leadership, and personnel selection.

Timothy A. Judge is the Franklin D. Schurz Professor of Management at Notre Dame. He received his Ph.D. from the University of Illinois at Urbana–Champaign in 1990. In his career, he has published 130 articles in refereed journals, including 82 articles in top-tier journals. Judge is a fellow of the Academy of Management, the American Psychological Association, and the American Psychological Society. His research interests are in the areas of personality, leadership, moods and emotions, and career and life success.

Yuval Kalish is Assistant Professor at the Leon Recanati Graduate School of Business Administration, Tel Aviv University, Israel. He received his Ph.D. in Organizational Psychology from the University of Melbourne. His research links psychology with social network analysis. In particular, he examines the psychological antecedents to, and consequences of, different positions in leadership, friendship, communication, and negative-tie networks.

Kathryn E. Keeton is a Senior Scientist at NASA Johnson Space Center, working as the Team Risk Manager in the Human Research Program's Behavioral Health & Performance (BHP) Research Element Division at EASI, Inc. The research that Dr. Keeton manages is shaping how NASA and others interested in high-performing teams define, think about, and

study collective behavior and performance—particularly for planned long-duration space-flight missions. Dr. Keeton earned her Ph.D. in Industrial/Organizational Psychology from the University of Houston.

Youngsang Kim is a doctoral student in management at the Moore School of Business, University of South Carolina. His primary research interests include strategic human resource management (staffing), human capital, and green organizational behavior. He received his MS in Human Resource Management at the School of Management and Labor Relations, Rutgers University.

Goran Kuljanin, MA, is a doctoral candidate in Organizational Psychology at Michigan State University. He researches individual and team performance dynamics, explores and develops quantitative methods to model the dynamics of human behavior, and seeks computational understanding of psychological phenomena. His work appears in *Psychological Methods*, and he serves as a reviewer for *Methodology*, *Psychological Assessment*, and *Organizational Research Methods*.

James M. LeBreton is an Associate Professor of Psychological Sciences at Purdue University. He earned his Ph.D. in Industrial/Organizational Psychology with a minor in Statistics from The University of Tennessee. His research focuses on personality assessment and the application of personality assessment in personnel selection and work motivation contexts.

Hye Joo Lee is an instructor in the School of Psychology and Social Welfare at Handong Global University in Pohang, South Korea. She received her Ph.D. from Georgia Institute of Technology in Industrial Organization Psychology in May 2012.

Terence R. Mitchell received a BA from Duke, in 1964, and a Ph.D. from Illinois in 1969. He is currently the Carlson Professor of Management at the University of Washington. He is a fellow of AOM and SIOP. His research focuses on the topics of turnover, motivation, leadership, and decision-making.

James M. Oglesby is a doctoral student in the Applied Experimental and Human Factors Psychology program at the University of Central Florida

(UCF). Mr. Oglesby received a BS in Psychology from UCF and is a graduate research assistant at the Institute for Simulation and Training. His research interests include team cognition and performance in extreme environments.

Robert E. Ployhart is the Bank of America Professor of Business Administration at the Darla Moore School of Business, University of South Carolina. He received his Ph.D. from Michigan State University. His primary interests include human capital, staffing, recruitment, and advanced statistical methods.

Eduardo Salas is Trustee Chair and Professor of Psychology at the University of Central Florida, where he also holds an appointment as Program Director for the Human Systems Integration Research Department at the Institute for Simulation and Training. Dr. Salas has co-authored over 300 journal articles and book chapters and has co-edited 19 books. His expertise includes assisting organizations in how to foster teamwork, design and implement team training strategies, facilitate training effectiveness, manage decision-making under stress, and develop performance measurement tools. Dr. Salas is a Fellow of the American Psychological Association and the Human Factors and Ergonomics Society and a recipient of the Meritorious Civil Service Award from the Department of the Navy.

Marisa A. Seeds is a Senior Consultant with Shaker Consulting Group. Her research interests center primarily on selection in the areas of high-fidelity job simulations and applicant reactions. She received her Ph.D. from the University of Akron.

Daniel R. Smith, Ph.D., is a Lieutenant Colonel in the U.S. Army and an Assistant Professor in the Department of Behavioral Sciences and Leadership at the United States Military Academy, West Point. He has spent 20 years studying leadership and leading people in diverse settings, ranging from academia to active combat zones.

Jeffrey M. Stanton is an Associate Dean for Research and Doctoral Programs and Professor at the School of Information Studies at Syracuse University. Dr. Stanton's research focuses on the intersection of organizational behavior and technology, with recent projects examining how organizational behavior affects information security in organizations. His work has been published in top behavioral science journals, such as the *Journal of Applied Psychology*, *Personnel Psychology*, and *Human Performance*. He received his Ph.D. from the University of Connecticut in 1997.

Eric J. Sydell is a Senior Consultant and Principal with Shaker Consulting Group. His research interests include legal issues in employee selection, applicant faking on, and reactions to, selection tools, and creating/ researching new technology-based methods of assessment. He received his Ph.D. from the University of Akron.

James C. Thompson is a faculty member in the Department of Psychology at George Mason University. He received his BA and Ph.D. from Swinburne University of Technology, Melbourne, Australia. His primary research interest is the neural basis of the perception and understanding of human actions. This includes studying basic visual perceptual mechanisms, how we map our bodies in relation to the external world, and how we make inferences about the actions of others.

E. Daly Vaughn is a Senior Consultant with Shaker Consulting Group. He has developed numerous custom knowledge measures for a variety of clients across a broad range of industries. His research interests include implicit attitude measurement, personality, training, legal issues, and the use of social media within a selection context. He received his Ph.D. from University of Connecticut in 1997.

Mo Wang, an Associate Professor at the University of Florida, specializes in research areas of retirement and older worker employment, occupational health psychology, cross-cultural HR management, leadership, and advanced quantitative methodologies. He has received the Academy of Management HR Division Scholarly Achievement Award (2008), Careers Division Best Paper Award (2009), and Erasmus Mundus Scholarship for Work, Organizational, and Personnel Psychology (2009) for his research in these areas. He also received the Early Career Achievement Awards from SIOP (2012), Academy of Management's HR Division (2011), and Research Methods Division (2011), and the Society for Occupational

Health Psychology (co-sponsored by the APA, NIOSH, and SOHP, 2009). He currently serves as an Associate Editor for the *Journal of Applied Psychology* and also serves on the editorial boards of five other academic journals.

Le Zhou is a Ph.D. student at the University of Florida. Her research interests include leadership, team, and employee training and development. She is also interested in quantitative methods in organizational behavior research (e.g., longitudinal data analysis, computational modeling).

Series Foreword

Know thy methods! It's a must. We all need them—an indispensable tool of our profession. If there is something we all use, need, and apply as scientists and practitioners, it is methods. Methods are what make or break our studies, experiments, interventions, or practical actions in the labs and the field. Methods are at the core of our science and practice—that is why we all should know our methods. We need to know their strengths, limitations, and applicability. We need to know what they do for us, as well as what they won't do. We need to know how they help us with external and internal validity of our studies and interventions. We need to learn new and emerging methods to deal with our ever-changing research and practice. And so this volume is much welcomed and, more importantly, much needed.

Jose and Ron have rightfully described this volume as "transforming our field by transforming methods" and have assembled a set of chapters illustrating that. Our theories and constructs are changing, and so our methods must change as well. Topics range from longitudinal growth modeling to qualitative research to Petri nets to synthetic environments. This volume contains a set of transforming chapters to help us answer questions about our science and practice and to increase our methodological toolbox. There is food for thought and tools for graduate students and for seasoned scientists and practitioners, something for all of us. Remarkable.

On behalf of the Editorial Board of the SIOP Organizational Frontiers Series—thank you Jose and Ron (as well as your collaborators) for creating this one-of-a-kind addition to our series. A much needed volume that will enhance how we think and execute our science and practice. Well done Jose and Ron!

Eduardo Salas, Ph.D.
SIOP Organizational Frontier Series Editor
University of Central Florida

Preface

We wanted to create this volume because we believe that advances in research methodology play a crucial role in the development of our field. Cutting-edge methods can, and should, invigorate and inform our science. For many researchers, applying newer, and often more sophisticated, techniques can be daunting. This, in part, arises from trying to understand the "guts" of a particular analysis from the rather limited information often provided in typical journal articles. Along with this, researchers may not see how particular techniques can be used to study their particular substantive questions. In that spirit, we challenged our contributors to provide specific, detailed examples that will give researchers the confidence to use techniques that they might otherwise avoid.

Descriptions of each contribution are contained in our introductory chapter, but it suffices to say that we were lucky enough to have contributors not only accept our invitations to explain these vanguard methods, but also to provide clear road maps for those interested in applying said techniques to their own research. In short, the chapters in this volume provide fabulous treatments of a variety of measurement, design, and statistical topics. We are supremely confident that these chapters will stimulate the enhanced use of the focal techniques and be a wonderful reference source for interested researchers.

If you find one or more chapters to be especially useful to you and/or your students, we would be thrilled to hear from you. If you have complaints, contact the authors.

1

Introduction: Transforming Our Field by Transforming its Methods

Jose M. Cortina and Ronald S. Landis

Those who study human behavior in organizations confront a plethora of challenges. In order to meet these challenges, researchers sometimes employ complex measurement or analytic techniques, without necessarily knowing how, or even if, they serve the researcher's purposes. Although there are many ways in which human–computer interaction has changed for the better, the ability to collect or analyze data without knowing what one is doing is not one of them. What we need is a sort of methodological prism that breaks our techniques into their component parts, allowing us to understand how they fit together.

Our goal for the chapters in this book is to challenge researchers to break away from the rote application of traditional methodologies and to capitalize upon the wealth of data-collection and analytic strategies available to them. In that spirit, many of the chapters in this book deal with methodologies that encourage organizational scientists to reconceptualize phenomena of interest (e.g., experience sampling, catastrophe modeling), employ novel data-collection strategies (e.g., data mining, Petri nets), and/or apply sophisticated analytic techniques (e.g., latent class analysis). We believe that these chapters provide compelling solutions for the complex problems faced by organizational researchers, problems that, if left unaddressed, might leave us on the dark side of the moon.

TOO MANY COOKS, TOO FEW APPLIANCES

The methods that we use to collect data necessarily influence (and constrain) the way that we conceptualize organizational phenomena. As a result, scientific advancements are limited, to the extent that we continue to rely on the same old methods to study new problems. Imagine a chef who wishes to make a tasty meal. If the chef is given only, say, a deep fryer with which to work, culinary options become necessarily limited. Although it is certainly true that the deep fryer will be useful for making some dishes, the chef will be in trouble if he or she would like to poach an egg [Editor's note: *Do not* drop an egg into a deep fryer unless you enjoy third-degree burns]. As anyone who grew up in the deep south can tell you, the chef operating in the deep fryer-only kitchen will come to view available dishes primarily through the lens of this tool [Editor's note: If you find yourself in Louisiana, avoid the fried green salad]. On the other hand, if the chef is provided with a range, oven, grill, wok, etc., a much wider variety of dishes can be conceptualized and executed. The same is true for the organizational researcher who operates in, say, the "OLS regression kitchen." If ordinary least squares (OLS) serves as the only methodological tool, the researcher will come to view organizational problems through the OLS lens. Although many wonderful dishes can be made with OLS regression, many others cannot. One must limit oneself to the prediction of continuous dependent variables whose errors are uncorrelated, using variables that are, or can be, converted into interval level variables. One must restrict oneself to the study of phenomena that change in a continuous fashion over time. At a broader level, one must restrict oneself to phenomena that are sufficiently understood that one knows which questions to ask (i.e., quantitative as opposed to qualitative research). It is only when the list of tools is augmented that the list of topics can be expanded.

Of course, we have no desire to denigrate OLS regression. Indeed, there are still many social scientists who work in the even more rustic analytic kitchen in which analysis of variance (ANOVA) is the technique of choice. When confronted with the horror that is a continuous predictor, these poor devils either artificially categorize it, resulting in nonlinear, non-random measurement error, or relegate it to (additive) covariate status in ANCOVA. They need their blender to frappé, but, alas, it only has on/off. And don't get us started on what is happening in the t-test galley.

The chapters compiled in this book help organizational researchers to become aware of, and appreciate, the tools that are hiding in the methods pantry. The authors of these chapters not only provide descriptions of these contemporary methodologies, but also provide examples of how they may be applied to organizational phenomena. In particular, we believe this latter aspect of each chapter may be this volume's greatest asset. Frequently, we see researchers get excited by particular techniques, only to become frustrated because they do not see how the methods can be applied to their own work. The authors of the chapters in this volume have taken care to provide this information.

A second theme that we have attempted to integrate in the current collection of chapters is that of organizational research as increasingly complex and challenging. As a field, we study phenomena that are typically directly unobservable, temporally volatile, and in contexts that often do not permit tight, experimental control. Thus, despite the claim that ours is a field of "soft" scientists, we hope that the current chapters convince you that our field can apply rigorous methodologies for studying organizational behavior, and that, through the use of these methods, our field can further develop as an applied science that meaningfully contributes to the understanding of modern organizational phenomena and problems.

We also want to emphasize that statistics and methods are as vibrant and vital a research area as any substantive one. Both of us have had interactions with colleagues, the nature of which will be familiar to many readers of this book:

Colleague: So, tell me, what is your primary research area of interest?
Jose/Ron: Research methodology.
Colleague: That isn't an area of research.

To us, this type of interchange reflects a conceptualization of methods as immutable (read: stagnant) and leads to a cookbook application of old techniques that constrains theoretical development and knowledge creation. We believe the chapters in this volume challenge that view of methodology and, instead, convey the important contributions made by those working in the area.

ADVANCED, NOT MAGICAL

In choosing authors and topics for this particular volume, we had certain principles in mind. First, we wanted chapters on cutting-edge topics and authors with the expertise to write them. Second, we wanted the chapters to inform and educate readers about the nature and relevance of particular techniques and tools through clear summaries and reviews. Third, we wanted the chapters to provide sufficient information to allow the reader to adapt the techniques to his or her own research. All too frequently, beneficial methodological techniques are not adopted, because researchers don't have a clear road map for application. Finally, we wanted the chapters to prompt researchers, not only to apply newer techniques (when appropriate), but also to challenge status quo thinking about particular organizational phenomena. As a result, we specifically asked the contributors to identify cutting-edge issues with respect to particular methods that will serve to stimulate future substantive research. Our contributors have provided such a resource, and we trust that the following chapters will serve as catalysts for significant advances in the organizational sciences.

CONNECTING THE PRESENT (AND FUTURE) TO THE PAST

More than a decade has passed since the publication of the most recent volume in the *Organizational Frontiers Series*, devoted to research methods. Since the publication of that volume (Drasgow & Schmitt, 2002), our field has seen an explosion of interest in, and use of, advanced measurement, design, and analysis techniques. At the time that Drasgow and Schmitt went to press, many of the techniques that now seem common were either in their infancy (e.g., latent growth modeling (LGM), grounded theory, response surface methodology) or so uncommon in the organizational sciences as to be unworthy of inclusion in a volume on methodology (e.g., catastrophe modeling, latent class analysis, experience sampling). Indeed, the Drasgow and Schmitt volume was instrumental in solidifying researchers' understanding of many advanced methodological techniques, which in turn led to these techniques being more commonly and appropriately used.

We believe that our field is now poised to take another important step down the path of sophisticated methodological techniques. In recent decades, techniques have emerged that, not only improve our ability to collect data and to evaluate the data that we collect, but also provide researchers with the freedom to develop more nuanced theory. Instead of exploring LGM at a broader level, as did David Chan in his excellent and crucial chapter from the Drasgow and Schmitt volume, we assert that our field is ready to explore extensions of LGM (Ployhart and Kim), as well as pitfalls that are well understood in other fields but new to ours (Braun, Kuljanin, and DeShon). We must go beyond a descriptive treatment of grounded theory and explore the latest in case studies, textual analysis, and other quantitative methods (Gephart). We must acknowledge the existence of nonmonotonic relationships and more explicitly consider discontinuous relationships with techniques such as catastrophe modeling (Guastello) and discontinuous growth modeling (Ployhart and Kim). We should move beyond recognizing that some organizational phenomena involve hierarchical structures and parallel processes and more appropriately model these contexts (Coovert), as well as more explicitly consider individuals as part of larger systems (Kalish). In short, it is time for our field to explore the next frontiers of research methodology. Some of these frontiers may represent fine-tuning of our techniques, but others (e.g., catastrophe modeling, experience sampling) have the potential to turn our field on its ear and, indeed, have already done so (e.g., Guastello, 1988; Ilies, Scott, & Judge, 2006; Guastello, 2007).

ORGANIZATION OF THE VOLUME

This book is divided into two parts: *Statistical Analysis* and *Research Design and Measurement*. In the first chapter of the *Statistical Analysis* part, Guastello describes catastrophe theory and the analyses that accompany it. Many of us have heard of catastrophe theory (or at least have heard of related concepts such as chaos theory), but few of us have taken steps toward applying it to our research in organizations. This is a terrible shame, because so many organizational phenomena are likely to conform to catastrophe models. In fact, we believe that our field is on the cusp (if you will) of a "catastrophe revolution," and those who join it early

6 • *Jose M. Cortina and Ronald S. Landis*

will be remembered for (and credited with) having changed our field for the better.

Catastrophe models describe discontinuous phenomena, that is, phenomena that involve sudden "catastrophic" change. For example, Guastello (1987) suggested that, for low levels of task variety, there is a monotonic, positive relationship between ability and performance, whereas, for high levels of task variety, there is a discontinuous relationship between ability and performance such that performance is stable and low for lower ability levels but tends to jump "catastrophically" at some middle level of ability, with the jump point being tied to the reward system. The jump is consistent with the tenets of insight learning, in which an "a-ha moment" creates a qualitative change in knowledge. As another example, Guastello (1988) showed that, for large workgroups, accidents are monotonically and positively related to environmental hazards. For small workgroups, however, accidents are discontinuously related to hazards, such that accident rates are stable and low for low-hazard groups, stable and high for high-hazard groups, and jump catastrophically at some mid level of hazard. One reason for this is that small groups tend to be more cohesive, and this cohesiveness creates a cyclical process that causes accident rates to "shift gears" at some level of environmental hazard.

Guastello and his colleagues have used catastrophe theory to explain a wide variety of organizational phenomena, and yet few other researchers have done so. We suspect that the reason is that most organizational researchers are intimidated by the abstruse mechanics of catastrophe modeling. In Guastello's chapter in the current volume, he provides a detailed and approachable description of catastrophe modeling and its application. We cannot imagine a better presentation of this material and believe the chapter will serve as foundation for "catastrophically" influencing our field for the better.

In the second statistical-analysis chapter, Ployhart and Kim tackle random coefficient models (RCMs). These authors focus their attention on a surprisingly underutilized application of RCM, namely *dynamic* or *time-varying predictor models*. Although RCM and LGM have become quite common in organizational research, it is relatively rare to see research in which Level 1 predictors vary over time. And yet, as Ployhart and Kim put it, "wouldn't it be exciting to see research showing how changes in knowledge acquisition relate to changes in job performance over time?" We know from cross-sectional research that those with greater amounts of knowledge tend to have better performance evaluations, but, because dynamic predictor models have not been applied to the problem, we don't actually know if one's performance increases as one's knowledge increases! Ployhart and Kim explain the mechanics of dynamic predictor models (including latent growth models), their data requirements, the pitfalls associated with such models, and the strategies that can be used to avoid these pitfalls.

These authors also discuss extensions of the standard dynamic predictor RCM. First, they discuss *lagged growth models*, in which data points are lagged in time to reflect hypothesized causal sequences. Collecting data in this way, as the authors explain, allows one to address problems that are common to dynamic models, such as reciprocal causation and spurious relationships. Second, these authors describe *autoregressive latent trajectory (ALT) models*. In ALT models, change over time in a given variable is estimated after controlling for previous levels of the variable (i.e., the autoregressive element). As the authors point out, ALT models reflect the axiom that the best predictor of future behavior is past behavior.

Third, Ployhart and Kim discuss *nonlinear* and *discontinuous growth models*. Nonlinear growth models capture change over time as a nonlinear function of time. For example, we know that knowledge acquisition does not change in a linear manner over time, so why should its effects be modeled as if it did? Discontinuous growth models can be used to model phenomena that do not change in a monotonic manner. Indeed, discontinuous growth models are very similar to the catastrophe models described in the Guastello chapter.

Finally, Ployhart and Kim describe *between groups change models*. In such models, grouping variables are used to distinguish different clusters of change patterns. For well-defined groups, multiple group LGM is quite useful. For less defined or unknown groups, latent class analysis or, more broadly, mixture modeling can be used. In short, if you want to understand the latest in RCM with time-varying predictors, this chapter is a must.

Social network analysis, as described in the third statistical chapter, by Kalish, holds great promise for researchers interested in modeling social influence and communication in organizational contexts. No matter their formal structures, services provided, or products generated, organizations are fundamentally social systems. Individual employees interact with customers, colleagues, subordinates, supervisors, and myriad others through the formal and informal aspects of contemporary jobs.

Unfortunately, we organizational scientists frequently choose to simplify these complex relationships and, all too frequently, study individuals in isolation, or at best as members of collectives, and attempt to explain behavior through a somewhat static lens. Social network analysis provides us with opportunities to uncover how individual relationships (dyads, triads, etc.) are formed, influence individual behavior, and ultimately change and dissolve.

One would not likely choose to study a family by individually survey-ing the children and presuming that these individual perceptions fully capture the complexity of the family dynamic. Even if we were to take a higher-level perspective and consider the children as a "team," we are still likely to miss important dyadic relationships between the children and/or the parents. Similarly, organizational researchers should not ignore the contextual aspects of modern organizations. These contexts shape indi-viduals and their interactions with one another through formal policies, structures, rules, and informal norms. Social network analysis allows researchers the opportunity to more fully model such contexts and to capture important, "bottom-up" processes that are not easily assessed through traditional techniques (e.g., hierarchical linear modeling (HLM)).

Upon reading the Kalish chapter, one will have a clear understanding of why social network analysis is an important tool. One is also left with a profound appreciation of the tremendous research opportunities that await those interested in studying networks. Of equal importance, Kalish provides user-friendly examples of how to apply social network analysis that will provide the necessary grounding for individuals interested in applying these techniques. Advances in theory are, to some degree, constrained by available methodological and analytic tools. Kalish demon-strates this by illustrating how social network analysis, not only allows researchers to more accurately model individual processes, but also allows for, and encourages the development of, more sophisticated theories about how individuals within a system are connected with one another.

Wang and Zhou explore the latest issues and applications of *latent class analysis* (LCA) in the fourth statistical-analysis chapter. As mentioned earlier in this chapter, variable-centered statistical methods such as multiple regression have been, and continue to be, invaluable tools for organizational researchers. Despite the wide applicability of these analytic techniques and their obvious relevance for answering particular research questions, variable-centered methods are ill equipped to answer questions of intraindividual differences. For such questions, researchers instead rely on person-centered approaches, such as cluster analysis. As Wang and Zhou's chapter points out, our ability to answer more sophisticated research questions is greatly expanded when the variable-centered and person-centered approaches are combined in latent class procedures. More recently, LCA has been extended further so that class membership can be based, not only on patterns of scores on variables, but also on factors such as item response patterns and changes over time.

The extensions of LCA discussed in this chapter are *mixed-measurement item response models, growth mixture modeling,* and *mixture latent Markov modeling.* Wang and his colleagues have written some of the seminal work on these procedures (e.g., Wang & Bodner, 2007; Wang & Chan, 2011). This chapter not only explains the nuts and bolts of these procedures, but also illustrates why and how they are applied. After a discussion of LCA and how it differs from more traditional clustering techniques (i.e., theory driven, ML estimation), Wang and Zhou describe mixed-measurement item response models (MM-IRT), which are combinations of LCA and IRT models. In traditional IRT models, variability in item parameters between specified groups can be examined by testing for measurement equivalence among pre-specified groups. MM-IRT can be used to identify heterogeneity in item parameters, which can then be attributed to membership in latent classes. The technique can also be used to compare models with different numbers of latent classes.

Wang and Zhou then discuss growth mixture modeling (GMM). LGM typically involves the identification of growth parameters that describe the growth curves that exist for a given set of data. GMM is a combination of LGM and LCA that allows for the identification of groups of subjects that have similar growth curves. Latent class variables can then be used to explain this variability in growth curves. These authors also describe mixture latent Markov modeling (MLMM). The term "Markov chain" is used to describe response patterns on a categorical variable across time. As the authors put it, a Markov chain reflects the changing status of a respondent on a discrete variable, which is traditionally modeled with latent transition analysis. Of course, just as is the case with growth curves, it is possible for different groups of respondents to have different transition patterns over time. MLMM can be used to identify such groups and to link latent classes to other covariates, thus providing the categorical variable analog to GMM.

For each of these three extensions of MCA, Wang and Zhou provide the mathematical underpinnings of the approach, parameter estimation methods, and model testing methods. Any researchers who are interested in identifying latent classes of item responses or response patterns over time, and/or who wish to link such class membership to other covariates will find this to be an indispensable chapter.

In the fifth statistical analysis chapter, Braun, Kuljanin, and DeShon describe their work on some of the pitfalls of growth modeling. For reasons also discussed in relation to the Ployhart and Kim chapter, growth modeling has become increasingly common, as our field has come to recognize the importance of intraindividual variability and individual trends over time. Although growth modeling is relatively new to the organizational sciences, it has been common in other fields (e.g., economics) for some time. These fields have discovered important dangers associated with growth modeling research of which the organizational sciences are relatively unaware. In the present chapter, Braun et al. investigate stochastic trends in growth models, focusing particularly on the "random walk."

A random walk is a longitudinal trend that is comprised entirely of random error that cumulates over time. The problem is that random walks are very difficult to distinguish from the deterministic trends that we typically hypothesize and hope to find in our growth models. That is, it is entirely possible to hypothesize a certain trend, collect longitudinal data, and find evidence of trends that seem to be deterministic and supportive of hypotheses, but are in fact due only to the cumulative effect of errors across time. The authors explain the nature of these random walks and describe the various techniques that allow one to identify, and to some degree correct for, them.

The final chapter of the first section, by Jeff Stanton, examines the use of data mining techniques in organizational research. Is there truth in the sentiment that one can have "too much of a good thing?" We suspect that the answer when the good things are data is, generally, "No." In fact, many of us pine for larger samples. Increased access to large datasets affords organizational researchers with opportunities that have traditionally been unavailable. These opportunities, however, are accompanied by challenges that many of us have not been trained to confront. Stanton's chapter describes the opportunities and problems associated with extremely large datasets and provides a road map for researchers interested in studying organizational phenomena using these resources.

Given the nature of data mining, many of us may be wary of, if not hostile toward, the application of such exploratory techniques. We have been conditioned to view confirmatory techniques as "real" science and are all too happy to leave exploratory techniques to the tea-leaf readers. We do this, however, to our own detriment. Although criticisms of "dust-bowl empiricism" are well targeted to particular elements of our scientific history, we must be careful to distinguish the practice of drawing confirmatory conclusions through exploratory, bottom-up techniques from using such techniques to generate research questions that can be used as jumping-off points for future studies.

Indeed, it has been argued quite convincingly that our obsession with developing and "confirming" novel theories has damaged the field. For example, Gray and Cooper (2010) suggest that this obsession has led to an incoherent literature. In a related vein, Edwards and Berry (2010) commented that increases in methodological precision have led, not to a refinement of hypotheses, but merely to an increased capacity for confirming that which we want to confirm. Gephart (this volume) urges us to explore, to learn before we set about confirming anything.

Exploratory techniques, in particular the types of analysis described by Stanton, afford us the opportunity to base our theories, in part, on observation. As Stanton notes, "there could be important reservoirs of social and behavioral knowledge that remain untapped unless more organizational researchers become comfortable with data mining tools." We couldn't agree more. Perhaps there is a researcher out there right now who, through data-mining techniques, is poised to uncover "Moneyball"-type principles applied to traditional organizational settings. The possibilities are certainly exciting, and, when the movie rights are sold, we will all wish that we had the foresight to take advantage of this underutilized methodology.

Of course, data analysis of any kind is pointless without good research design. The first chapter in the *Research Design and Measurement* section, by James, LeBreton, Mitchell, Smith, DeSimone, Cookson, and Lee explores the latest in personality-measurement techniques. Personality measurement is a cornerstone of research in organizational settings. Despite the widely acknowledged limitations of self-report measures, surprisingly few alternatives are available for assessing personality. For almost two decades, research has been building on a promising alternative to self-report measurement: conditional reasoning. James and colleagues' chapter provides another success story for conditional reasoning, with this one having as its focus the measurement-of-power motive.

For more than a decade, James and colleagues have reported successful development of personality measures based on principles of conditional reasoning. In short, conditional reasoning is based on the notion that people want to believe they make choices rationally (James, 1998). In order to accomplish this, people rely on reasoning processes (i.e., justification mechanisms (JMs)). People tend to favor certain types of behavior and, in turn, develop JMs that support these behaviors. In turn, because individuals differ on various personality dimensions, people express different behaviors across situations. Further, even when the same behavior is expressed, individuals will have different reasons (JMs) as a function of individual differences on various latent variables. The term "conditional" reflects the idea that what is justifiable behavior in a particular situation is fully dependent upon the person choosing the behavior.

In the present chapter, James and colleagues apply principles of conditional reasoning to the general area of leadership, and the power motive in particular. Of particular interest, James et al. carefully distinguish the power motive from "toxic" applications of power. One can certainly appreciate that a given individual may have a desire for power, but not abuse that power if given the opportunity to do so. Alternatively, another individual with the same motive may act aggressively when given the chance. As the authors note, it is truly unfortunate that the power motive has been cast as the villain in the latter case above. Doing so has retarded research progress in this area.

One might well ask the question, "Why are there not more examples of conditional reasoning measures in our literature?" The answer is not that such measures are unreliable, invalid, or in any way psychometrically weak. Instead, the reason would appear to be the heavy lifting required to develop such tools. We find this to be an unfortunately reality. Our field should not be daunted by the time commitment required for the development of conditional reasoning measures. Indeed, we hope this chapter serves as a stimulus for personality researchers in our field to devote time and effort to the development of similar measures.

In the second research-design chapter, Gephart offers a modern review of qualitative methods. This is certainly not the first treatment of qualitative methods, but it is one of the best in terms of explaining (to those who might otherwise be skeptical) why qualitative methods represent a valuable class of methodologies and how they should be used. Specifically, Gephart discusses the various paradigms that underlie qualitative research, such as post-positivist, critical theory/research, and interpretive and offers organizational science applications of case studies, interviews, observational approaches, document analysis, computer-aided interpretive textual analysis, and grounded theory from each paradigmatic perspective (insofar as this is possible).

Several of the studies described by Gephart are particularly noteworthy as exemplars of applications of qualitative techniques in the organizational sciences. For instance, Graham (1995) and Barker (1998) reported ethnographic studies that explored different aspects of team-based management systems. In a nutshell, through interviews and observations, both authors found that team-based systems were associated with many counterintuitive consequences, not the least of which was less individual agency than is typically the case in traditional top-down systems. These sorts of finding certainly might pave the way for targeted quantitative research, but they would have been difficult to produce with quantitative research, because such research requires one to know which questions to ask ahead of time. The ethnographic approaches of Graham and Barker allowed the nature of the phenomena under observation to emerge as the phenomena unfolded naturally, and this nature turned out to be rather different than anyone (including Graham and Barker) might have expected. Ethnography also requires a level of immersion by the researcher that is seldom present in quantitative research (e.g., Graham was at a West Lafayette automobile plant for 6 months), without which the requisite detail is unlikely to be apparent.

As examples of grounded-theory applications, Gephart describes some of his own work (Gephart, 1975, 1978). These papers describe a grounded theory exploration of a graduate student organization in turmoil. Gephart used initial observations of interactions among organization members to form initial questions that he then addressed by searching through records of prior organization activities. The answers to these questions provided the basis for more targeted data collection, with the result being a deep understanding of the genesis of the forced removal of the organization's leader.

As with the previously mentioned ethnographic examples, the Gephart examples show how a grounded theory approach can yield detailed information about a specific phenomenon, and do so in a way that wouldn't be possible with a quantitative study. In particular, one wouldn't know which questions to ask, and of whom. It would be difficult to argue that there are no organizational phenomena about which we know very little. Indeed, new phenomena are frequently identified. For example, two of our students are examining cell-phone-app usage in the workplace as a coping mechanism for workplace stress (Kim & Niu, in progress). The present chapter does an excellent job of explaining how qualitative methods can set us on the road to understanding hitherto unseen phenomena, as workplaces change, new technologies emerge, and organizational systems evolve.

The next research-design chapter, by Dimotakis, Ilies, and Judge, describes the use of *experience sampling methodology* (ESM) in organizational research. A theme from several chapters in this volume is that the previous decade has seen a dramatic shift from cross-sectional to longitudinal designs. One of the most prominent approaches has been ESM, in which measurements of variables thought to vary within persons are taken at regular intervals, at specific times, or in response to environmental triggers.

Dimotakis et al. explain the various types of ESM design (signal based, interval contingent, and event contingent), as well as the ways that these different types can be combined. The authors are able to do this in a particularly compelling way because they can use examples drawn from their own work for nearly every sort of design. They also discuss the technologies that can be used to implement these designs, as well as the difficulties that must be overcome for various design–technology combinations.

Through reading this chapter, one certainly learns a great deal about using ESM designs. Perhaps more importantly, however, the authors' use of examples demonstrates the degree to which the results of ESM studies force us to look at even the most mainstream phenomena in a completely novel way. Until relatively recently, our field conceptualized many variables as between-person variables (i.e., stable within person), even though an argument could be made that they are more appropriately conceptualized as within-person variables. Thanks to applications of ESM designs by the authors and their colleagues, we now know that much of the variance in variables such as job satisfaction (Judge & Ilies, 2004), quality of co-worker interactions (Ilies, Johnson, Judge, & Keeney, 2011), organizational citizenship (Ilies et al., 2006), workplace deviance (Judge, Scott, & Ilies,

2006), workload (Ilies, Dimotakis, & De Pater, 2010), work–family conflict (Ilies et al., 2007), and emotional labor (Judge, Woolf, & Hurst, 2009) is within-person variance, and that this variability overlaps with within-person variance in other important variables.

To take one example, Ilies et al. (2006) reported that (1) nearly one third of the variance in organizational citizenship was within person; (2) slightly more than one third of the variance in job satisfaction was within person; (3) within-person variability in satisfaction explains within-person variability in citizenship; and (4) agreeableness, a stable trait, moderated this relationship such that agreeable people were more consistent in their citizenship, with the result being that their citizenship was less influenced by their job satisfaction. In retrospect, these results make perfect sense. A person tends to be a better citizen on days on which the person is satisfied with his or her job, agreeable people are more likely to engage in citizenship, and their citizenship is less governed by their ephemeral job attitudes than is the case for those low in agreeableness. Prior to this study, citizenship was almost always studied as a between-person variable (i.e., a person is a good citizen or not). Through the use of ESM, Ilies et al. showed that people who are typically good citizens could, on some days, be bad citizens, and that this within-person variability can be explained by job attitudes. What does this mean for the hundreds of primary studies and dozens of meta-analyses in which citizenship was treated as a between-person variable? At the very least, it means that those studies missed part of the story. How many more organizational variables are out there waiting for their within-unit components to be discovered via ESM?

In the next chapter in the research-design section, Dietz, Bedwell, Oglesby, Salas, and Keeton describe *synthetic task environments* (STEs). An STE is a combination of task and medium in which fidelity is higher than in a typical lab task, but control is higher than in a typical field study. Although it is possible to design an STE oneself, significant investments and resources are required in terms of programming skill (for computer tasks), construction (for noncomputerized tasks), or both. As a result, adaptation or customization of off-the-shelf tasks (COTS) to one's purposes is far more common. For this reason, Dietz et al. devote most of their attention to these COTS tasks.

STEs come in many different forms. After describing the principles that determine the quality of STEs in general, Dietz et al. discuss *games*, *simulations*, *microworlds*, and *virtual worlds*. For each form of STE, the authors describe how they have been, and can be, used to study organizational phenomena, as well as the challenges posed by the use of each form.

A *game* in this context is an artificial, interactive activity and has a specific, goal-driven purpose in a specific context. Alternatively, a *simulation* is also interactive, goal-driven, and contextualized, but involves more realistic activities and/or more complex process models. Because the distinction between games and simulations is not always clear, the authors treat them together. An example of a game/simulation that can be used to study organizational phenomena is *SimCity*. *SimCity* is a decision-making game in which the participant plays the role of city planner, using survey data, crime data, etc. to make decisions about the city's development. Games/simulations such as *SimCity* are especially useful for studying contexts that are generally unavailable (the authors give the example of landing on the moon) or contain too much danger to study directly (such as reacting to a nuclear plant emergency or flying a plane). Thus, they can be used to study, for example, shared mental models in dangerous contexts without putting individuals at risk.

The authors next discuss microworlds, which are "computer-based platforms that simulate a complex work environment" and permit the active exploration of that environment. Microworlds differ from games/simulations in that the activities that they offer are less regimented, allowing the participant more freedom regarding what they do and how they do it. This makes them especially useful for the study of emergent phenomena. For example, the microworld *C3 Fire* requires teams of participants to execute the extinguishing of a wildfire, but does so in a relatively unstructured environment in which team members must gather information without even knowing which pieces of information are needed. In this way, phenomena such as norm formation, emergent leadership, and development of shared mental models might be studied.

Finally, the authors discuss virtual worlds. Virtual worlds typically have the structure of games, but they are unique in that they can allow entry through the Internet from anywhere in the world, by as many people as required. Moreover, the virtual world continues to function and change, even if a participant leaves. Thus, if that person returns, s/he returns to a different world. Virtual worlds such as *Second Life* are used by many organizations for various functions, and they should be particularly useful for studying complex, long-term phenomena. For example, many organizations use virtual worlds for recruiting purposes. They allow job seekers to acquire information, either directly or through an interview with a virtual representative. Thus, virtual worlds can be used to identify the information sources that job seekers find most useful at various stages of the recruitment process, and to do so in an environment that has fewer demand characteristics than a typical lab study. The applications are virtually (pun intended) limitless.

After reading the Dietz et al. chapter, one is left with two lasting conclusions. The first is that STEs offer enormous advantages over more traditional data-collection platforms and provide unlimited possibilities that have yet to be fully explored. The second is that relatively few organizational scientists are using STEs to study organizational phenomena. Given the first conclusion, the lack of application is truly unfortunate. We are confident that this chapter will encourage researchers to more fully exploit this largely untapped methodological resource.

Perhaps no technique in the industrial and organizational (I/O) psychology literature is as well established as job analysis. Most of us received extensive exposure to job analysis through graduate training and are well versed in the benefits of a high-quality job analysis. One may, in fact, reasonably argue that job analysis represents one of the most important contributions of I/O psychology to contemporary organizations. Given this state of affairs, there are obviously no methodological frontiers or challenges for job analysts. Or are there?

Despite the notable strengths of job analytic methods for identifying critical job tasks and required individual attributes (i.e., knowledges, skills, abilities, and other characteristics (KSAOs)), such information often cannot fully capture the complexity of contemporary jobs. In Chapter 12, Coovert describes how the application of *Petri nets* provides an opportunity to model tasks that occur in an asynchronous fashion, incorporate hierarchical job structures that involve parallel activities, and include both individuals and collectives (e.g., teams). Such dynamism and complexity are neither well captured through traditional job analysis nor well described graphically through traditional flowcharts.

Coovert provides a brief summary of the historical background of Petri nets that provides a clear sense of why this method has been more commonly applied in the study of chemical processes and software design, but explains why organizational researchers should more seriously consider applying these tools. Through his examples, Coovert refers to successful applications of Petri nets to organizational settings in his own work (e.g., Coovert, Salas, Cannon-Bowers, Craiger, & Takalkar, 1990) and identifies opportunities for other applications. Similar to how structural equation modeling (SEM) has forced researchers to be more specific with regard to expected relations and nonrelations between variables of interest, Petri nets allow researchers to propose and test models with even greater complexity. Also similar to SEM, the quality of the inferences drawn from Petri nets is fully dependent upon the components included (and not included) in the model. Because the visual palette for creating Petri nets may not be known to many organizational researchers, Coovert provides an invaluable and accessible primer for developing models.

Coovert also explicitly describes the application of Petri nets to two common organizational contexts. In the first example, he describes how Petri nets can be used to represent a three-person team operating in a dynamic environment in which individuals have unique expertise and access to information and must make decisions in parallel. The second example describes how Petri nets can be used to understand a team working aboard an air force AWACS. Because this team performs missions that have identifiable stages, the individual members have well-defined roles and responsibilities, and events may necessitate reacting to unexpected events, so that traditional workflow or job analytic methods are likely to provide an incomplete picture of the crew's task performance. As Coovert notes, Petri nets are not just useful for describing particular systems, but also provide information that can be used to redesign any aspect of the system.

When organizations update technology or workflow, or otherwise redesign jobs, great care and attention are frequently given to the process or program itself. Such redesign efforts, however, are not as frequently accompanied by an understanding of how the technology will in fact be used by individuals. Petri nets would appear to be a promising tool that could be used in conjunction with traditional job analysis techniques to develop a more thorough understanding of job demands, individual skills required, and processes through which individuals currently interact. Perhaps even more interesting are those applications in which jobs do not yet even exist. This methodology would appear well suited for assisting with such future-oriented job analysis efforts (Schneider & Konz, 1989; Landis, Fogli, & Goldberg, 1998). After reading this chapter, the reader is left with an enthusiasm for using Petri nets when traditional methods provide an incomplete picture, and, in the words of the author, "watch your model come to life!"

In Chapter 13, Adis and Thompson discuss the application of neuro-imaging techniques to organizational research. Our field generally claims to be less interested in scores on manifest variables than in the latent factors that cause them, and yet we pay little attention to the neurological causes of the cognition and behaviors that drive our field. In fact, there has long been hostility in our field toward neuroimaging techniques, just as there seems to have been hostility in the neuroscience community toward behavioral research. We tend to see neuroimaging researchers as being obsessed with pretty color images, while they see behavioral researchers as ignoring the root causes of the very things that they purport to care about. It is long past time for this rift to close, and the Adis and Thompson chapter shows us why and how to do it.

These authors explain how three neuroimaging techniques can be used to study behavior and cognition in the workplace. Although there are many neuroimaging techniques, Adis and Thompson focus on *structural MRI* (MRI), *functional MRI* (fMRI), and *electroencephalography* (EEG). The two MRI techniques are based on the observation that different parts of the brain have not only different functions but also different magnetic properties, owing to differences in water concentration (MRI) or oxygen-rich blood (fMRI). MRI uses differences in magnetic properties to assess the volume of different types of brain matter. These differences, in turn, can be linked to different behavior patterns. For example, DeYoung and colleagues have linked differences in gray-matter density in areas associated with reward sensitivity to extraversion (DeYoung & Grey, 2009; DeYoung et al., 2010). Others have linked creativity to the dopamine systems of the prefrontal cortex (Takeuchi et al., 2010). This work moves us toward brain-based theories of many of our most important individual-difference variables.

One of the limitations of MRI is that it is not dynamic in nature. fMRI, on the other hand, can be used to examine neurological responses to stimuli. Active neuronal cells use oxygenated blood, and this blood usage (or, rather, its immediate consequences) is detected in an fMRI. In other words, fMRI detects the parts of the brain that are particularly energized at any given point in time. Although fMRI has not really been used in organizational studies, many researchers have suggested that it might be used to identify the parts and actions of the brain that distinguish effective leaders from ineffective leaders (e.g., Rock & Schwartz, 2006; Peterson, Walumbwa, Byron, & Myrowitz, 2009) or to uncover the driving forces behind organizational citizenship behavior (OCB) (e.g., empathy; Marsh, Kozak, & Ambady, 2007).

Two nontrivial problems with MRI and fMRI is that they are physically cumbersome and very expensive. A single scan costs about $500 (at least currently) and requires that the subject lie motionless in an enclosed space. Although EEG is not as precise, more freedom of movement is allowed, and it costs about $10 per subject and tracks neuronal activity in real time. Again, various possibilities exist for the use of EEG in organizational research. The authors explain, for example, that EEG can be used to detect neuronal responses to errors and goal interference. Thus, EEG might be useful in providing feedback to participants in error-based training (i.e., where the committing of errors is desirable).

The authors provide many examples of areas of interest to organizational scientists that are appropriate for study through neuroimaging. We suspect that the reader will be able to imagine applications in his/her own areas of interest. In any case, I/O will have to come to the party sooner or later. Why wait?

The final chapter, by Dudley-Meislahn, Vaughn, Sydell, and Seeds, may strike some readers as the most heretical of all. If one were to suggest to organizational scientists that they rethink the measurement of knowledge, they might very well react with, "If it ain't broke, don't fix it." As Dudley-Meislahn et al. recognize in this chapter, knowledge-based assessments have been largely unchanged for many decades. This is owing, in part, to the relative ease of use and generally strong psychometric properties of existing measures. Although many traditional measures have been refined to take advantage of technological innovations (e.g., computer-based administration and/or adaptive testing formats), the fundamental approach to knowledge assessment has been quite consistent since at least the time of Goddard and his immigrant screening tools at Ellis Island.

The ideas presented in the Dudley-Meislahn et al. chapter do not offer a condemnation of traditional knowledge measures. Instead, these authors advocate the possible benefits of expanding our methodological toolkit when assessing knowledge. Dudley-Meislahn et al. first provide a summary of how and why we measure knowledge using the methods that we do. This brief review provides a foundation upon which they propose two alternative techniques. Drawing from research in other areas, Dudley-Meislahn et al. then describe the *construct-generation* and *idea-generation* methodologies.

Construct generation is predicated on the assumption that individuals construct, and continually revise, personal theories that help them make sense and meaning of the world around them. The complexity of one's personal construct theory relative to a particular domain should, therefore, be useful in predicting how that person will behave in that domain. Although much of the reviewed research in support of this methodology is drawn from clinical researchers, the constructs that are targeted by these measures (e.g., interpersonal skills) are often highly relevant for organizational scientists. For example, interpersonal construct complexity has been empirically linked with communication skills (e.g., Burleson & Caplan, 1998), perspective-taking ability (e.g., Kline, Pelias, & Delia, 1991), nonverbal decoding ability (e.g., Woods, 1996), and social perception skills (e.g., Burleson, 1994). Construct complexity has also been related to effectiveness on the job, particularly for those in management-level positions (e.g., Sypher, 1984).

Because this method has often been applied with a focus on interpersonal constructs in general, Dudley-Meislahn et al. caution that tailored applications may be necessary when interest is related to other knowledge domains. Indeed, one of the presented examples, based on the lead author's own work, describes the adaptation of construct generation to measuring interpersonal construct knowledge specific to Reserve Officers' Training Corps (ROTC) cadets. Along with the clear review and summary of research using this technique, this example serves as a road map for how one can apply construct generation to similar knowledge domains.

A related methodology that Dudley-Meislahn et al. review is idea generation. Although this technique has often been applied in the measurement of divergent thinking, examples of the application of idea generation by organizational scientists, though encouraging, are still rather limited. As a field, we may be conditioned to view measures of divergent thinking as exclusive to situations in which creativity is the primary construct of interest. As noted by Dudley-Meislahn et al., however, such measures may also be linked to organizationally relevant variables such as sales strategies and performance (e.g., Sujan, Sujan, & Bettman, 1988), leadership knowledge (Mumford, Marks, Connelly, Zaccaro, & Johnson, 1998), and helping behavior (Dudley & Cortina, 2008).

If the only benefit of applying idea generation were to increase the pallet of alternative formats for knowledge assessment, we would certainly do well to explore this method in more depth. On top of this, however, Dudley-Meislahn et al. also present some evidence (Dudley & Cortina, 2008) that, at least in one context, this technique provides incremental validity beyond more traditional measures of helping behavior. If altering our conceptions of what knowledge measures "should" look like allows us to explain even more variance in important criterion variables, we should be eagerly exploring methods such as idea generation.

SUMMARY

The request that we made to the authors of the chapters in this book was to explain and justify the use of a particular methodological technique. Further, we asked each author to illustrate the technique through examples that would easily allow a reader to see how the technique could be applied to her or his own work. We believe the authors have responded to both of these requests even better than we dared hope. In isolation, each of the chapters should serve as a fantastic resource for those interested in learning more about these techniques.

Taken as a set, several common themes emerge from these chapters. First, our interest in intraindividual change has been, and will continue to be, buoyed by advances in analytic techniques such as LGM. Several chapters (Wang and Zhou, Ployhart and Kim, Dimotakis, Ilies, and Judge, and Braun, Kuljanin, and DeShon) provide excellent treatments of associated techniques, advances in knowledge that have accrued through their use, and potential issues to which we should be attentive when modeling change. Second, we see parallels between the ideas presented in the Dudley-Meislahn et al. chapter and those presented by James et al. In both of these chapters, the authors' challenge the inertia that, in one case, seems to keep our personality measurement constrained to self-reports and, in the other, cultivates the belief that the methods we use to assess knowledge cannot be improved.

Third, our methodological pantry is greatly enhanced when we look outside the boundaries of our field to work performed in other areas. Several of the contributions (Dudley-Meislahn et al., Adis and Thompson, and Coovert) describe methodologies with roots clearly outside of traditional organizational research. Additional chapters (Guastello, Kalish, and Stanton) describe methods that, though slightly more familiar to organizational researchers, are still not widely used by our field. In an increasingly multidisciplinary world, we hope that our field continues to adapt techniques and philosophies that have proven successful in others.

Finally, from these chapters, it is clear that most of our contemporary analytic techniques require advanced statistical software and/or modeling tools. Although these tools are not necessarily intuitive for many researchers, the examples provided in the included chapters should give researchers a resource upon which to build. Related, widespread accessibility of computing technology has been, unfortunately, underutilized in organizational research. The chapters by Dietz et al. and Stanton, in particular, describe methodological tools that more fully exploit these technological opportunities and advances. We will certainly not be able to put the computing genie back in the bottle, nor would we want to. Instead, we should follow the lead of these authors and fully embrace what the virtual world has to offer for our field.

In conclusion, we could not be more pleased with the contributions contained in this volume. We believe they summarize the current, and future, methodological tools that will play an important role in shaping our field in the coming decade. We hope that these chapters encourage organizational scientists to continue to push boundaries, challenge conventional thinking, and view our methodologies as vibrant and evolving.

REFERENCES

Barker, J. R. (1998). Tightening the iron cage: Concertive control in self-managing teams. In J. Van Maanen (Ed.), *Qualitative studies of organizations* (pp. 126–158). Thousand Oaks, CA: Sage.

Burleson, B. R. (1994). Friendship and similarities in social–cognitive and communication abilities: Social skill bases of interpersonal attraction in childhood. *Personal Relationships, 1*, 371–389.

Burleson, B. R., & Caplan, S. E. (1998). Cognitive complexity. In J. C. McCroskey, J. A. Daly, M. M. Martin, & M. J. Beatty (Eds.), *Communication and personality: Trait perspectives* (pp. 230–286). Cresskill, NJ: Hampton Press.

Coovert, M. D., Salas, E., Cannon-Bowers, J. A., Craiger, J. P., & Takalkar, P. (1990). Understanding team performance measures: Application of Petri nets. *Proceedings* of the 1990 IEEE International Conference on Systems, Man, and Cybernetics (pp. 387–393). Washington, DC: IEEE Computer Society Press.

DeYoung, C. G., & Grey, J. R. (2009). Personality neuroscience: Explaining individual differences in affect, behavior, and cognition. In P. J. Corr & G. Matthews (Eds.), *The Cambridge handbook of personality psychology* (pp. 323–346). New York: Cambridge University Press.

DeYoung, C. G., Hirsh, J. B., Shane, M. S., Papademetris, X., Rajeevan, N., & Grey, J. R. (2010). Testing predictions from personality neuroscience: Brain structure and the Big Five. *Psychological Science, 21*(6), 820–828.

Drasgow, F., & Schmitt, N. (2002). *Advances in measurement and data analysis.* San Francisco, CA: Jossey-Bass.

Dudley, N. M., & Cortina, J. M. (2008). Knowledge and skills that facilitate the personal support dimension of citizenship. *Journal of Applied Psychology, 93*, 1249–1270. doi:10.1037/a0012572

Edwards, J. R., & Berry, J. W. (2010). The presence of something or the absence of nothing: Increasing theoretical precision in management research. *Organizational Research Methods, 13*, 668–689.

Gephart, R. P. (1975). *The development of a graduate students' centre.* Unpublished master's thesis, University of Calgary, Alberta, Canada.

Gephart, R. P. (1978). Status degradation and organizational succession: An ethnomethodological approach. *Administrative Science Quarterly, 23*, 553–581.

Graham, L. (1995). *On the line at Subaru-Isuzu: The Japanese model and the American worker.* Ithaca, NY: Cornell University Press.

Gray, P. H., & Cooper, W. H. (2010). Pursuing failure. *Organizational Research Methods, 13*, 620–643.

Guastello, S. J. (1987). A butterfly catastrophe model of motivation in organizations: Academic performance. *Journal of Applied Psychology, 72*, 165–182.

Guastello, S. J. (1988). Catastrophe modeling of the accident process: Organizational subunit size. *Psychological Bulletin, 103*, 246–255.

Guastello, S. J. (2007). Nonlinear dynamics and leadership emergence. *Leadership Quarterly, 18*, 357–369.

James, L. R. (1998). Measurement of personality via conditional reasoning. *Organizational Research Methods, 1*, 131–163.

Ilies, R., Dimotakis, N., & De Pater, I. E. (2010). Psychological and physiological reactions to high workloads: Implications for well-being. *Personnel Psychology, 63*, 407–436.

Ilies, R., Johnson, M. D., Judge, T. A., and Keeney, J. (2011). A within-individual study of interpersonal conflict as a work stressor: Dispositional and situational moderators. *Journal of Organizational Behavior, 32*, 44–64.

Ilies, R., Scott, B. A., & Judge, T. A. (2006). The interactive effects of personal traits and experienced states on intraindividual patterns of citizenship behavior. *Academy of Management Journal, 49*, 561–575.

Judge, T. A., & Ilies, R. (2004). Affect and job satisfaction: A study of their relationship at work and at home. *Journal of Applied Psychology, 89*, 661–673.

Judge, T. A., Scott, B. A., & Ilies, R. (2006). Hostility, job attitudes, and workplace deviance: Test of a multilevel model. *Journal of Applied Psychology, 91*, 126–138.

Judge, T. A., Woolf, E. F., & Hurst, C. (2009). Is emotional labor more difficult for some than for others?: A multilevel, experience-sampling study. *Personnel Psychology, 62*, 57–88.

Kim, S., & Niu, Q. (in progress). Microbreaks as a coping mechanism for occupational stress.

Kline, S. L., Pelias, R., & Delia, J. G. (1991). The predictive validity of cognitive complexity measures on communication-relevant abilities. *International Journal of Personal Construct Psychology, 4*, 347–357.

Landis, R. S., Fogli, L., & Goldberg, E. (1998). Future-oriented job analysis: A description of the process and its organizational implications. *International Journal of Selection and Assessment, 6*(3), 192–197.

Marsh, A. A., Kozak, M. N., & Ambady, N. (2007). Accurate identification of fear facial expressions predicts prosocial behavior. *Emotion, 7*, 239–251.

Mumford, M. D., Marks, M. A., Connelly, M., Zaccaro, S. J., & Johnson, J. F. (1998). Domain-based scoring of divergent-thinking tests: Validation evidence in an occupational sample. *Creativity Research Journal, 11*, 151–163.

Peterson, S. J., Walumbwa, F. O., Byron, K., & Myrowitz, J. (2009). CEO positive psychological traits, transformational leadership, and firm performance, in high technology start-up and established firms. *Journal of Management 35*(2), 348–368.

Rock, D., & Schwartz, J. (2006). The neuroscience of leadership. *Strategy + Business, 43*, 72–83.

Schneider, B., & Konz, A. M. (1989). Strategic job analysis. *Human Resource Management, 28*, 51–63.

Sujan, H., Sujan, M., & Bettman, J. R. (1988). Knowledge structure differences between more effective and less effective salespeople. *Journal of Marketing Research, 25*, 81–86. doi:10.2307/3172927

Sypher, B. D. (1984). The importance of social-cognitive abilities in organizations. In R. N. Bostrom (Ed.), *Competence in communication* (pp. 103–127). Beverly Hills, CA: Sage.

Takeuchi, H., Taki, Y., Sassa, Y., Hashizume, H., Sekiguchi, A., Fukushima, A. *et al.* (2010). Regional gray matter volume of dopaminergic system associate with creativity: Evidence from voxel-based morphometry. *NeuroImage, 51*, 578–585.

Wang, M., & Bodner, T. E. (2007). Growth mixture modeling: Identifying and predicting unobserved subpopulations with longitudinal data. *Organizational Research Methods, 10*, 635–656.

Wang, M., & Chan, D. (2011). Mixture latent Markov modeling: Identifying and predicting unobserved heterogeneity in longitudinal qualitative status change. *Organizational Research Methods.*

Woods, E. (1996). Associations of nonverbal decoding ability with indices of person-centered communicative ability. *Communication Reports, 9*, 13–22.

Part I

Statistical Analysis

2

Catastrophe Theory and Its Applications in Industrial/ Organizational Psychology

Stephen J. Guastello

INTRODUCTION

Imagine a group of people doing 2 hours of the same strenuous work of the type that one might encounter in a steel mill. Imagine further that they are all measured on dynamometer arm strength and retested after the 2 hours of work. Many show a sharp drop in strength, but some show a sharp increase, as though they were just getting warmed up.

A manufacturing company experienced a sudden shift in economic conditions, resulting in the first layoff in its 60-year history. The morale of those who remained was not good, and the production efficiency (the inverse of the work time required to do standard jobs) had dropped to a 30-year low. The surprise was not the drop, but that production efficiency hit a 30-year high 12 weeks later.

A group of policymakers held a meeting to discuss a topic that they all agree is very important and for which they need an action plan. As the discussion ensues, the opinions and preferences drift further apart than they were when the meeting started. Although most of the group was polarized, there were some people whose opinions swayed in both directions during the discussion, before they came down on one side or the other.

Tourists in Southeast Asia thought the seawater was acting a bit strange as it receded far back from its usual shoreline, exposing the ocean bed underneath. Hundreds ran up to the guardrail to see more, while a few started to back away. Within minutes, a wall of seawater rushed forward. Most of the crowd ran away after varying seconds of delay, but some still stood there, holding umbrellas while the water rushed over them.

The foregoing stories have several things in common: The events produced at least two diverging reactions, and most of the reactions were sudden when they occurred. In each case, there was a variable that made the differences in outcomes large and small (but I didn't tell you what it was), and, in each case, there was a variable that could shift the system closer to the critical point where it would change from one extreme reaction to the other (but I didn't tell you about that either yet). Each of these events was an example of a *catastrophe*—a sudden and discontinuous change of events.

In its mathematical definition, a catastrophe depicts a sudden change in a system's state. The change can occur between two or more qualitatively different states, or from an ambiguous condition to one of the clearly defined states. The central proposition of catastrophe theory is the classification theorem (Thom, 1975), which states (with qualifications) that, given a maximum of four control parameters, all discontinuous changes of events can be described and predicted by one of seven elementary topological models. The models can be tested with real data using readily available software for polynomial (multiple) regression and nonlinear regression (NLR). Applications in psychology over the last three decades have included problems in learning theory (Frey & Sears, 1978; Guastello, 1995; Mayer-Kress, Newell, & Liu, 2009), multistable perception (Stewart & Peregoy, 1983), creative problem solving (Guastello, 1995; Stamovlasis, 2006), human development (van Geert, 2009), work motivation (Guastello, 1981, 1987, 1995), personnel selection (Guastello, 1982a, 2002), accident analysis and prevention (Guastello, 1995; 2003), risk perception (Guastello et al., 2008), stress and performance (Guastello, 1982b, 2003; Thompson, 2010), perception of work performance (Hanges, Braverman, & Rentch, 1991), group polarization and conflict (Latané, 1996; Guastello, 2009a; Vallacher, Coleman, Nowak, & Bui-Wrzosinska, 2010), attitude–behavior relationships (Flay, 1978; Smerz & Guastello, 2008), leadership emergence (Guastello, 1998, 2007, 2009b), organizational development (Bigelow, 1982; Gresov, Haveman, & Oliva, 1993; Guastello, 2002), and clinical applications. The foregoing list is not intended to be all-inclusive and does not begin to describe the applications outside of psychology.

Catastrophe theory is part of a broader spectrum of nonlinear dynamical systems (NDS) processes that explain and predict the temporal unfolding of events. NDS offers a rich lexicon of constructs such as attractors, bifurcations, saddles, chaos, fractals, self-organization, emergence, and, of course, catastrophes. Some of the simpler elements in the foregoing list are inherent in catastrophe models and are explained in the next section of this chapter. Importantly, catastrophe theory, and NDS more generally, can be regarded as a scientific paradigm because: (a) They offer new perspectives on both new and old problems that could not be resolved otherwise. (b) They build on the dynamic character of phenomena that was already thought to exist before the necessary concepts and tools became available. (c) They reconcile controversial issues by integrating related theories and disparate areas of knowledge. (d) They resolve analytically what cannot be accomplished with linear models (Koopmans, 2009). Once again, the applications of the broader range of NDS in psychology are extensive and growing (Guastello, 2009c; Guastello, Koopmans, & Pincus, 2009). Interestingly, the development of catastrophe theory and other NDS subgroups such as chaos and complexity theory grew in parallel and converged further as the processes of self-organization and emergence became better understood.

The central principles of catastrophe theory are explained next, followed by descriptions of two statistical methods for testing and building catastrophe models. Next, four application areas in I/O are described that illustrate the analytic methods: stress, fatigue, and performance; occupational accidents; leadership emergence; and personnel selection, work motivation, and performance. Koopmans' four points above are evident in these applications.

CATASTROPHE THEORY

The seven elementary models are hierarchical in the sense that the topologies of the more complex models subsume the simpler models as subsets. The models vary in the complexity of the behavior spectrum they encompass. The models describe change between (or among) qualitatively distinct forms for behavior, such as remaining on a job versus quitting; they do not necessarily infer any notion of desirable or undesirable outcome. Steady states and changes in behavior are governed by between one and four *control parameters*, depending on the complexity of the behavior spectrum under consideration. It is important to remember that control variables play specific functional roles in a nonlinear model and are not interchangeable in function like variables that are used in the myriad uses of additive general linear models.

The elementary catastrophe models fall into two groups: the cuspoids and the umbilics. The four *cuspoid* models involve one dependent measure, have potential functions in three to six dimensions and response surfaces in two to five dimensions. They are the fold, cusp, swallowtail, and butterfly. The names reflect fanciful interpretations of what parts of their geometry resemble. The three *umbilic* models involve two dependent measures, three or four control parameters, and response surfaces whose dimensionality totals to five or six dimensions.

Only the three models that are most commonly used are included in this chapter. The cusp is the most popular and is discussed next; the swallowtail and butterfly models are introduced later in the context of relevant applications. An important feature of the theory is that Thom's (1975) taxonomy of models allows us to reduce the plethora of possible discontinuous change functions to a small number of distinct possibilities.

Cusp Catastrophe Model

The cusp surface is three-dimensional (3D) and describes two stable states of behavior (Figure 2.1). Change between the two states is a function of two control parameters, *asymmetry* (a) and *bifurcation* (b). At low values of b, change is smooth, that is, y is a continuous and monotonic function of a. This is the sort of bivariate relationship with which we are all most familiar, where the y variable changes by an amount that is proportional to a change in a.

At high values of b, the relationship between a and y is potentially discontinuous, depending on the values of a. At the lower end of the a scale, y is generally unresponsive to changes in a. Something similar occurs at the upper end of the a scale. In the middle of the a scale, however, y changes suddenly (i.e., catastrophically) as a function of a. Said another

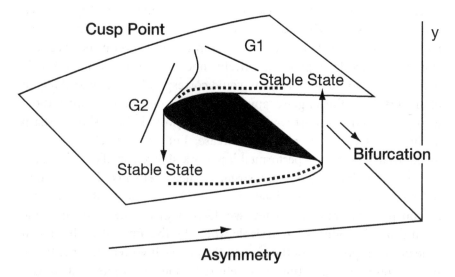

FIGURE 2.1
The cusp catastrophe response surface.

way, at low values of *a* when *b* is high, changes occur around the lower mode and are relatively small in size. At middle values of *a*, changes occur between modes and are relatively large, assuming *b* is also large. At high values of *a*, changes occur around the upper mode and are again small.

The cusp response surface is the set of points where

$$(2.1)$$

Change in behavior is denoted by the path of a control point over time. The point begins on the upper sheet denoting behavior of one type and is observed in that behavioral modality for a period of time. During that time, its coordinates on *a* and *b* are changing when suddenly it reaches a fold line and drops to the lower value of the behavior, which is qualitatively different, where it remains. Reversing direction, the point is observed in the lower mode until coordinates change to a critical pair of values; at that moment, the point jumps back to the upper mode. There are two thresholds for behavior change, one ascending and one descending. The phenomenon of *hysteresis* simultaneously refers to relatively frequent changes between the two behavioral states and the two different thresholds for change.

The shaded area of the surface is the region of inaccessibility in which very few points fall. Whereas the stable states are *attractors*, the inaccessible region is a *repellor*: Points are deflected in any direction if they veer too close to the repellor region. Statistically, one would observe an antimode between the two stable states that would correspond to the shaded region of the surface. In the fatigue example at the beginning of the chapter, those who performed the most work (bifurcation) would either show a sharp decline in strength or a sharp increase, but are unlikely to remain unchanged. Those who performed less work showed smaller differences between the first and second strength measurements. In the group polarization example, the individuals would be clearly aligned with the pro or con position, but only a few would remain on the fence after the discussion. The bifurcation variable would be the amount of discussion time or the importance of the issue to the people involved (Latané, 1996). If the group were debating in an effort to solve a problem, such as a courtroom jury's deliberation, the asymmetry variable would be whether the weight of the evidence supports one position more decisively than it supports the other (Guastello, 1995). If the group were debating to make a political point, the asymmetry variable could be an ideology that individuals had previously formed, such as a political "left" or "right" (van der Maas, Kolstein, & van der Plight, 2003).

The cusp bifurcation structure induces two diverging response gradients on the response surface, which are joined at a *cusp point*. The diverging gradients are labeled *G1* and *G2* on the cusp surface in Figure 2.1. Behavior at the cusp point is ambiguous. The cusp point is the most unstable point on the surface. This type of point is a saddle: Control points, which designate the behavior of the system, are drawn to it, but they are quickly deflected in the direction of one of the stable states. Analogous points exist in other catastrophe models as well.

The cusp model has a potential function also:

$$f(y) = \frac{y^4}{4} - \frac{by^2}{2} - ay \qquad (2.2)$$

as do all the catastrophe models. The potential functions, which are the integrals of the response surface functions, represent the catastrophe models in static form. The distinctions should become clearer when the two methods of catastrophe analysis are described.

Thus, there is a close relationship between self-organizing systems, phase shifts, and cusps. Equation (2.2) is often used to represent phase transitions that arise from self-organizing or emergent processes. Systems in a state of far-from-equilibrium conditions self-organize into structures by building feedback loops among the subsystems, thereby shaping their own structures and stabilizing the system in a state of lower entropy. The emergence of structure, or changes from one structure to another, is characterized as a *phase shift*. There are a few different processes of self-organization, but the common feature is that information flow patterns arise from local interaction among agents (Guastello & Liebovitch, 2009; Haken, 1988; Holland, 1995; Sawyer, 2005).

Polynomial Regression Method

The polynomial regression method for assessing catastrophe models makes use of the response surface equation and data that are collected at two points in time. It is an extension of the general linear model and can be executed on popular statistical programs such as SPSS. The most essential details of the procedure are recounted here. Readers who would like to dig more deeply into the broader scope and theory of nonlinear systems analysis for the behavioral sciences, computer programs, and execution commands, including this particular method, should see Guastello and Gregson (2011).

The first step in the analysis is to convert the order parameter (or dependent measure *y*) and the control parameters (or predictors *a* and *b*) to standardized scores with respect to location and scale. The *location* (λ) parameter fixes the zero-point where the function is going to start, which is not necessarily the mean of the function, as in Gaussian distributions. The probability density function (*pdf*) for NDS processes a member of an exponential family of distributions and is asymmetrical, unlike the so-called normal distribution. Thus, the location parameter for Equation (2.3) is the lower limit of the distribution, which is the lowest observed value in the series. For the dependent variable *y*, the standardization equation is:

$$z_y = \frac{(y - \lambda)}{\sigma_s} \tag{2.3}$$

where *y* is the raw value of the dependent variable, λ is the lowest observed value of *y*, and σ_s is the scale parameter for *y* (described in the next paragraph). The transformation in Equation (2.3) has the added advantage of fixing a zero point and thus transforming measurements with interval scales (common in the social sciences) to ratio scales. A fixed location point defines where the nonlinear function is going to start. The same transformation is made on the variables that are going to be asymmetry and bifurcation variables in the cusp model.

The *scale* parameter usually refers to the standard deviation of the distribution. The standard deviation is also used here. The use of the scale parameter when testing structural equations serves the purpose of eliminating bias between two or more variables that are multiplied together. Although the results of ordinary linear regression are not affected by values of location and scale, nonlinear models are very often affected by the transformation.

Occasionally one may obtain a better fit using alternative definitions of scale for y in Equation (2.4) below. Interested readers should see Guastello and Gregson (2011). The standard deviation of y, however, solves most problems well, most of the time, for analyses reported in this chapter. Next, we take the deterministic equation for the cusp response surface and insert regression weights and a quadratic term:

$$\Delta z = \beta_0 + \beta_1 z_1^3 + \beta_2 z_1^2 + \beta_3 b z_1 + \beta_4 a \qquad (2.4)$$

From a practical standpoint, the quadratic term assesses the extent that the cusp response surface is lopsided, such that shifts upward dominate shifts downward, or vice versa. The dependent measure Δz denotes a change in behavior over two subsequent points in time; it is the difference in standardized y between Time 1 and Time 2 and is used in place of the differential shown in the left-hand side of Equation 2.1; b and a are the two predictors in standardized form; and z_1 is the standardized value of y at Time 1. The term bz_1 is the product of the predictor that represents the bifurcation parameter and standardized y at Time 1.

Several hypotheses are being tested in the power polynomial equation (Equation 2.5). There is the F test for the model overall: retain the R^2 coefficient and save it for later use. There are t tests on the beta weights: they denote which parts of the model account for unique portions of variance.

Some model elements are more important than other elements. The weight for the cubic term expresses whether the model is consistent with cusp structure; the correct level of complexity for a catastrophe model is captured by the leading power term. In order for there to be a cusp structure, there should also be a significant bifurcation variable, as represented by the term bz_1. The weight for the asymmetry term a is important in the model, but failing to find one does not negate the cusp structure if the cubic and bifurcation elements are present. The lack of a significant weight for an asymmetry term only means that the model has not been adequately specified, and the researcher should continue to look for an asymmetry variable. The quadratic term is the most expendable, however, for reasons stated earlier: it is not part of the formal deterministic cusp structure. In the event that unique weights are not obtained for all model components, delete the quadratic term and test the remaining elements again.

Note the procedural contrast with common practice in linear regression analysis: in common linear regression, when a variable does not attain a significant weight, we simply ignore that variable. In NDS analyses, we delete variables based on their relative importance to the structure. In linear analyses, there is only a linear structure under consideration, and so particular variables are then kept or discarded. In nonlinear analyses, different variables may be playing different structural roles, and sometimes even multiple roles, which have a hierarchy of importance.

Next, we construct comparison models. The objective is to compare the cusp *model* with an alternative *model*. The alternative model should reflect current thinking on the subject matter, which involves strictly linear structures most often. Log-linear relationships pop up occasionally as alternatives. Occasionally, the contrast is made between one nonlinear model and another with very different properties; for an example, see Guastello, Nathan, and Johnson (2009). If the alternatives are linear models, construct Equations (2.5) and (2.6) and compare their R^2 coefficients against the R^2 that was obtained for the cusp:

$$\Delta y = B_0 + B_1 a + B_2 b \tag{2.5}$$

$$y_2 = B_0 + B_1 y_1 + B_2 a + B_3 b \tag{2.6}$$

The linear models involve the same variables that are used for cusp control variables, but without the nonlinear structures. Equation (2.5) states the relationship as a prediction of change in the dependent measure. Equation

(2.6) describes the subsequent performance as a function of prior performance and the research variables; it is essentially the same as Equation (2.5), except that y_1 has been moved from the left-hand side to the right-hand side of the equation.

Ideally, the R^2 for the cusp models should exceed the R^2 for their linear counterparts. This is a Bayesian type of hypothesis testing, where the set of elements that comprise one intact model are compared against another intact set (Rodgers, 2010; Guastello & Gregson, 2011). There is no significance test to compare the other two coefficients; in principle, the accuracy of the cusp model only needs to be equal to that of the alternative model in order to conclude that the cusp is a viable explanation for the observations in the data. The cusp contains explanatory power that is not afforded in the alternative model. Ultimately, researchers should conduct several studies to decide whether the additional increment of variance accounted for and the heuristic value of the theory warrant further development of the model in question. Better control variables and a more dramatic exposure that produces the catastrophe are two avenues for improving results, rather than a wholesale rejection if all its features do not work out as planned on the first pass.

Next, evaluate the elements of the cusp model. If all the necessary parts of the cusp are significant, and the R^2 coefficients compare favorably, then a clear case of the cusp has been obtained.

Sometimes, several psychological variables contribute to an underlying control parameter. Equation (2.4) can be expanded to include multiple bifurcation and asymmetry terms, each with its own regression weight. The alternative models would be expanded similarly. If the set of possible variables is relatively large, it can be factor analyzed, and a smaller number of variables can be made from the factors. The solution to a complex problem is more direct if the research has a well-reasoned catastrophe model to use as a starting hypothesis.

Note that the cusp and alternative models are tested separately and compared, and they are not tested in a hierarchical fashion where the cusp elements are piled on top of a linear model. The primary reason for the strategy that is advocated here is topological in origin, rather than statistical. Nonlinear functions have regions that are linear, and it is not until you see enough of the whole function that the nonlinearities become apparent (Wiggins, 1988; Guastello & Gregson, 2011). Local linearity is particularly prominent in the neighborhood of an attractor center. Those linear segments are thus *part of* the nonlinear function. Removing them prior to analysis of the target model (a process that is sometimes known as "detrending" or "bleaching") will degrade the degree of fit and distort the assessment of dimension in the model (cusps are cubic); this problem can also be severe when the underlying model involves noninteger dimensions. The statistical implication, nonetheless, is that variance stealing would occur between the linear and nonlinear components in a hierarchical test. To do so would compromise the nonlinear model, because variance would end up being assigned to the comparison model, where it should be assigned to the target model.

Critics have questioned whether the polynomial regression method could distinguish a cusp if one were present in the data from a linear function, or whether the analysis would produce a cusp from random numbers (Alexander, Herbert, DeShon, & Hanges, 1992). Analyses of their arguments, simulations to the contrary, and further developments in nonlinear statistics since that time indicated several important points: there were some serious errors in the critics' arguments and their supporting simulation. Numbers produced by random-number generators have structure, but the structure is not cuspoid, nor does it contain any semblance of control parameters. The polynomial regression method does exactly what it purports to do. The R^2 associated with it conveys all the same meaning as R^2 associated with any other multiple regression model. Least-squares solutions are perfectly acceptable for nonlinear functions (Guastello, 1992a, 2011a). Maximum likelihood alternatives do exist for several types of NDS analysis, but they can be clumsy to implement (Guastello & Gregson, 2011).

Static Nonlinear Regression Method

The polynomial regression method has been used mostly for applications where many people have been observed and measured at two points in time, before and after a significant event such as a training program, physical work-out, tsunami, or group discussion. Common candidates for bifurcation variables include the amount of exposure to the event, such as being in the training group or control group, or some other variable that modulates the impact of the event. The polynomial regression method can also be used for a time series where one entity is observed many times. The limitation in the latter case is that two points that are observed too closely in time can be locally linear, and the nonlinearities do not become apparent until a sufficient amount of time elapses (and, hence, elapses in measurement space) are observed (Wiggins, 1988).

The researcher might then prefer the static method of analysis, which is indifferent to that particular problem. By doing so, however, one gives up the intuitive appeal of watching differences in observations directly. Instead, the analysis fits the data to a probability density function that is uniquely associated with the cusp catastrophe model. Fortunately, any integratable differential function can be expressed as a unique *pdf*. If the model holds true, one can then infer all the temporal dynamics that are associated with the cusp model. This procedure actually allows the researcher to draw inferences about within-person change from cross-sectional data. In the case of an extended time series, the procedure essentially freezes the time series so that it looks like a cross-sectional dataset.

The static method was first introduced by Cobb (1981), and some variations have been introduced over the years. The variation presented here provides the most direct means of testing hypotheses concerning the control parameters and involves the simplest computations and the smallest number of regression weights. It is a least-squares solution that can be executed in SPSS. For comparisons with the other options, see Guastello (2011b). The analysis is conducted through NLR, which is computationally different from multiple linear regression. Granted NLR is not yet popular in psychology, but those who would like to pursue the technique further should see Guastello (2011c).

The first step in the analysis is, once again, to transform measurements for location and scale into z form (Equation 2.3). The second step is to define the model that NLR is going to resolve. Equation (2.7) is the *pdf* for the cusp:

$$Pdf(z) = \xi \exp\left(\theta_1 z_1^4 + \theta_2 z_1^3 + \theta_3 B z_1^2 + \theta_4 A z_1\right) \tag{2.7}$$

where θ_i and ξ are nonlinear regression weights; ξ is a proportionality constant that does not impact on the elements of the cusp that appear within the square brackets. $Pdf(z)$ is the cumulative probability of the dependent variable; it needs to be defined and included in the database prior to NLR analysis, which one can do by employing a probit transformation on y, or relying on a frequency distribution of y to substitute the cumulative probability of y for each value of y; z is the dependent variable (i.e., the order parameter) that has been corrected for location and scale; B and A are bifurcation and asymmetry variables, respectively. The argument to the exponent is the potential function for the cusp, with the regression weights and a cubic term added.

NLR produces significance tests on all the regression weights and an overall R^2. The cubic term in Equation (2.7) does the same job as the quadratic in Equation (2.4). Once again, if significance is not obtained on the important parts of the cusp—quartic and bifurcation, primarily—drop the cubic term and try it again. Sometimes it is necessary to drop ξ also.

STRESS AND HUMAN PERFORMANCE

This section of the chapter recounts three related models that describe different types of stress and performance dynamics: the diathesis-stress model, the buckling model, and the fatigue model. Importantly, they all share the same cusp structure, but the control variables are different.

Diathesis Stress

In the diathesis-stress model (Guastello, 1982b), there is an underlying level of attentiveness on the part of the operator that varies by work shift. A dataset would be constructed so that difference scores (per Equation 2.5) are comparisons between a task done under favorable conditions (e.g., between 7 a.m. and 3 p.m.) with a very similar task done under unfavorable conditions (e.g., between 3 and 11 p.m. or 11 p.m. and 7 a.m.). Difference scores would be large or small, depending on the other two control variables.

Larger cognitive loads (or challenges) that are inherent in the job specifications themselves predispose the person–machine system to larger variations in work-performance time across work shifts. That is, the difference in time-to-completion between one work shift and another will be larger for cognitively loaded tasks than for simpler tasks. Cognitive load is thus the bifurcation parameter. Here, it also helps the research design if the participants work rotating shifts rather than one shift only.

Management policies, which involved some human-relations improvements during the time period of the study, also biased performance times to relatively lower or higher levels of efficiency. The management influence was thus the asymmetry parameter. During management's darker period, performance varied around the lower stable state—from bad to worse. During periods of mediocre management, large swings were visible. During periods of good management, performance exhibited small variations again, but around the higher stable state—from very good to really excellent.

Buckling Stress

The buckling model is analogous to Euler buckling of an elastic beam as larger loads are placed on the beam. A more elastic beam will waffle when heavily loaded, but an inelastic beam will snap under the same conditions. Inelasticity or rigidity corresponds to the high bifurcation side of the cusp surface, where the discontinuous changes occur.

The first application of the model (Guastello, 1985) arose from a study of physical labor, where the participants completed a wheelbarrow obstacle course. Employees in a steel-manufacturing facility completed the obstacle course three times with increasing loads in their wheelbarrows. The addition of weights had the effect of separating people who displayed no slowing in their response times as loads were added from people who exhibited a sharp increase in their response times under the same conditions. The amount of change in response time was governed by a group of physiological variables, which, when taken together, indicated a condition comparable to elasticity in materials science. In the buckling model, the amount of weight on the proverbial beam was the asymmetry parameter, and the elasticity measurement was the bifurcation parameter.

Karwowski, Ostaszewski, and Zurada (1992) used essentially the same concept to study the incidence of low-back injury. The lifting load was the asymmetry parameter, and variables related to the elasticity of the spinal column comprised the bifurcation parameter.

The buckling model also applies to cognitive workload. Several problems in the literature on cognitive-workload phenomena remain unresolved: (a) The measurement of workload is relative to the task situation and not particularly generalizable (Lin & Cai, 2009). (b) Empirical evidence supports both a fixed and a variable upper limit on cognitive channel capacity (Kantowitz, 1985); in other words, there are times when people cannot take on any more tasks without incurring a balloon in errors or delays, and there are occasions, such as we see in emergencies sometimes, when they can push themselves beyond the usual limits. (c) However we now know that, when two or more tasks are performed simultaneously, their impact on channel utilization is not additive, and their impact on performance depends on whether the tasks draw from the same mental resources (Wickens, 2008); adaptation, coping, or resilience are further possible explanations for variable upper limits (Hockey, 1997; Sheridan, 2008; Matthews & Campbell, 2009). (e) The conceptual separation of the effects of work overload and the effects of fatigue has not been clear (Hancock & Desmond, 2001).

The apparent solution to the cluster of problems takes the form of two cusp catastrophe models: one for the effect of workload on performance, and one for the effects of fatigue. They have similar structures, but derive from different underlying dynamics. Contributing variables play different roles in each model. For load stress, the asymmetry parameter is once again the load amount, and the bifurcation parameter is the elasticity variable, which takes the form of "coping strategies" (Guastello, Boeh, Shumaker, & Schimmels, 2012). The role of coping strategies or elasticity as the bifurcation factor, which could vary across individuals and perhaps situations, explains why both variable upper limits and fixed upper limits have been reported in the experimental literature.

Thompson (2010) used essentially the same cusp model to describe the possible results of high-impact decisions that are made under conditions of stress. He observed that otherwise capable leaders sometimes make disastrous decisions. Any of the load or environmental stressors that are known in stress research could be part of the asymmetry parameter. He recommended emotional intelligence as the primary variable that captures the elasticity that is needed to respond to the load demands. The notion of coping strategies in the face of severe stress has also been interpreted as resilience in sociotechnical systems (Seligman & Matthews, 2011), and the connection between catastrophes and resilience is now crossing over into clinical psychology and medicine (Pincus 2010; Guastello, in press).

Fatigue

The fatigue model was based on the classical phenomenon of work-capacity loss over time worked. The study (Guastello & McGee, 1987) was conducted in a primary steel-manufacturing facility. Employees participated in a 2-hour work simulation involving common labor tasks. Dynamometer measures of static arm and leg strength were measured before and after the sequence of work activities, along with measurements of height, weight, and percentage of body fat. Most workers showed a decline in strength over time, although some showed strength increases; the latter were interpreted as exercise effects. The bifurcation parameter contained several variables that had positive or negative deflections on strength: the amount of work produced (–), weight (+), body fat (-), and labor experience (–). Leg strength acted as a compensation strength factor and functioned as the asymmetry variable: people with stronger legs did not fatigue so much in their arms.

Guastello and McGee also noted that an equation that was very similar to the cusp catastrophe was published in the fatigue literature (Ioteyko, 1920), long before catastrophe theory actually existed. The model captured, not only the most common trajectory of decline of work capacity, but also some less common trajectories, such as actually improving over time as if the exercise helped, or not changing work capacity at all. The improvement in capacity was labeled anti-fatigue: fatigue and anti-fatigue constituted the two stable states. The conditions of not changing work capacity were interpreted as movements around one of the two stable states. An analogous model was later developed for mental fatigue (Guastello, 1995).

Table 2.1 depicts the essential data from a recent experiment on cognitive fatigue (Guastello et al., 2012). In their experiment, 73 undergraduates completed a task that was intensive on nonverbal episodic memory and had an automatically speeded component. Performance was measured over a 20-minute period along with measures of spelling and arithmetic ability and anxiety. Changes in task performance from the first three minutes to the last three minutes were characterized well by the catastrophe models. There were two bifurcation factors; one was the total work accomplished, and the other was the peak score obtained by the participant before making an error. An arithmetic test score, which was tested as a compensatory ability, was the asymmetry parameter.

In the example shown in Table 2.1, the R^2 for the cusp model was somewhat greater than that obtained for the linear alternative model based on Equation (2.6). The R^2 for the alternative model based on Equation 2.5 was .02 and not significant. The cubic term, which characterizes the cusp function, was significant. Both bifurcation variables were significant, such that larger amounts of work accomplished and lower peak scores

TABLE 2.1

Cusp and Linear Models for Fatigue on an Episodic Memory Task

Element	β	t
Cusp Model ($R^2 = .55$)		
z_1^3	−1.38	−5.19****
Total work*z_1	0.98	3.80****
Max score*z_1	−0.20	−1.88*
Arithmetic	−0.15	−1.82*
Linear Pre-post Model ($R^2 = .50$)		
Arithmetic	−0.19	−2.12**
Total work	0.82	4.74****
Max score	−0.06	−0.42
y_1	−0.33	−2.68***

Notes: * $p < .10$; ** $p <. 05$; *** $p < .01$; **** $p < .001$

Source: From Guastello et al., 2012.

contributed to the discontinuity of the cusp response surface. The compensatory ability was significant also. The quadratic term was dropped, indicating that the shifts to higher or lower performance were about equal.

ACCIDENT ANALYSIS AND PREVENTION

Given the impact of stress and cognitive functioning, it is not a big leap to surmise that stress has a substantial impact on industrial accident rates. Of course, if we all worked in rubber rooms, the consequences of stress would be limited. As the hazard level of the environment becomes greater, however, the impact of stress is more visible. Ironically, the mainstay of research in accident analysis and prevention research through the mid 1980s focused *either* on the ambient hazards *or* the psychosocial contributions, and for the most part it still does. The two were put together in a dynamical cusp model nonetheless (Guastello, 1988, 1989), such that hazard levels contributed to the asymmetry parameter, and a variety of psychosocial variables, collectively labeled *operator load*, contributed to the bifurcation parameter. The cusp model for occupational accidents has been illustrated in manufacturing (Guastello, 1988, 1989; Guastello & Lynn, 2010), public transportation (Guastello, 1991, 1992a), and health-care settings (Guastello, Gershon, & Murphy, 1999). The salient hazard and operator load variables can be different in each type of setting. Settings also differ in the relative amounts of group dynamics that are involved in the accident process (Guastello, 2003).

Safety climate, which was a novel idea at the time (Zohar, 1980), was part of the operator load variable and tended toward a positive (low-accident shift) deflection in risk levels for an individual or group. Operator load also included stress indicators, anxiety, beliefs in accident control, work-group size, and work pace. Reason (1999) noted that work pace by itself can have what amounts to a hysteresis effect on accident rates: An organization might make concerted efforts to reduce accidents, including adjusting the work pace demands. Eventually, however, the organization starts to demand higher production output, and, as a result, the accident rates start to zigzag up and down until the control point lands on "up" (i.e. higher risk). Figure 2.2 is a stylized rendition of Reason's illustration (p. 5). It is a view of the cusp surface from the top down. The point of the "<" is the cusp point, and the open side of the "<" is the high bifurcation side of the surface. Although Reason did not invoke catastrophe models as part of his exposition, movement across the bifurcation manifold is essentially what he was describing.

In a most recent study with the accident cusp, Guastello and Lynn (2010) responded to a report (Clarke, 2006) that safety climate, as defined by Zohar (1980 et seq.), had a generalizable relationship to safety behaviors but not to actual accident incidences or rates. Several things were thought to be missing from the simplistic correlation data: the cusp structure with hazards as the asymmetry parameter, the characterization of safety climate as a bifurcation variable, and anxiety as another bifurcation variable. Anxiety could have either a positive or negative impact on safe outcomes. It could interfere with response time to emergency situations and interfere with clear decisions, or it could be symptomatic of hypervigilance for unsafe conditions.

The participants were 1,262 production employees of two steel-manufacturing facilities who completed a diagnostic survey that measured safety management (akin to safety climate), anxiety, and two types of hazard that were salient in that industry. The accident variable was also

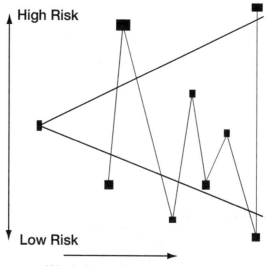

FIGURE 2.2
Hysteresis of risk levels across the cusp manifold as work pace increases.

collected by a survey item in which the individual gave the number of (OSHA-reportable) accidents they had in the preceding 3 years. Because the survey was given at only one point in time, the static cusp model was used for the analysis.

Nonlinear regression analyses showed, for this industry, that the accident process could be explained by safety management, anxiety, hazards, and age and experience within the cusp structure ($R^2 = .72$). The alternative model, which used a log-transformation on the accident criterion and multiple linear regression with anxiety, safety management, hazards, and age and experience, was substantially less accurate ($R^2 = .08$).

All parts of the cusp model were sustained; results of the tests on the regression weights are given in Table 2.2. The quartic term, which characterizes the cusp shape, was significant. The two bifurcation variables were significant, such that low ratings of safety management and high anxiety levels were associated with the high-bifurcation side of the surface. There were two significant asymmetry variables also. The hazards variable listed in the table was a combination of a particular group of tools and lifting and carrying tasks; high hazards were associated with the greater numbers of accidents. The age–experience variable was the other asymmetry

TABLE 2.2

Cusp Catastrophe Analysis for the Accident Model

Element	Parameter[a]
Cusp ($R^2 = .72$)	
x	0.82*
z_1^4	−0.54*
Safety mgmt*z_1^2	−0.70*
Anxiety*z_1^2	0.55*
Hazards*z_1	0.10*
(Age–experience)*z_1	2.38*
Stepwise linear regression ($R^2 = .08$)	
Anxiety	.19***
Safety mgmt	−.10**
Lift and carry	.11**
Tools 1	−.08*

Note: (a) In the culture of NLR users, more extreme *p*-values are not considered interesting. * $p < .05$; ** $p < .01$; *** $p < .001$

Source: From Guastello & Linn, 2010.

variable. Ordinarily, one would expect more accidents among younger and inexperienced workers, but in this situation the opposite was true: the more experienced people were incumbent in the more hazardous jobs.

LEADERSHIP EMERGENCE

A series of studies on the emergence of leaders from leaderless groups made use of the swallowtail catastrophe model (Guastello, 1998, 2010, 2011d; Zaror & Guastello, 2000; Guastello, Craven, Zygowicz & Bock, 2005; Guastello & Bond, 2007). The swallowtail response surface (Figure 2.3) contains two stable states, an unstable state, and two antimodes with amount of leadership as an individual-level dependent variable. The asymmetry control parameter (*a*) distinguishes all leaders from non-leaders; the non-leaders comprise the unstable state. The bifurcation parameter (*b*) controls the extent to which the leaders stabilize into

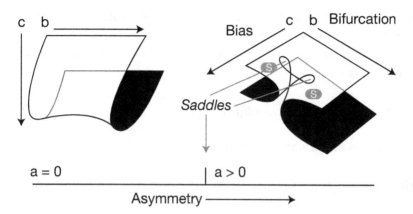

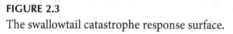

FIGURE 2.3
The swallowtail catastrophe response surface.

either primary or secondary roles, which are the two stable states. The bias control parameter (*c*) distinguishes the primary from the secondary leaders. The bias factor bears some similarity to the asymmetry parameter, but it specifically distinguishes the two stable states.

The equation for the response surface is:

$$\frac{\delta f(y)}{\delta y} = y^4 - cy^2 - by - a \qquad (2.8)$$

The response surface is four-dimensional, and so it is shown in two 3D sections in Figure 2.3. On the left, asymmetry, which in this application is a set of social skills that are visible to the group members, is low. Group members are located in the non-leader state, which is not stable. As the asymmetry variable increases, the group members can pass through the dark-shaded region to the right-hand portion of the surface, where the two stable states are located. They do not lock into one of the stable states, however, unless the bifurcation variable is high. If it is high, then the individuals can lock into either of the stable states, which correspond here to primary and secondary leadership roles. The bias or swallowtail variable distinguishes whether the person does indeed land in the primary or secondary role.

As in the case of the cusp, the process can be reversible. Primary leaders can retrench into secondary roles, and leaders in secondary roles can become primary. Primary or secondary leaders can go off the map, so to speak, into the non-leader region of the surface.

Swallowtail models can be tested using an extension of the polynomial regression equation:

$$\Delta z = \beta_0 + \beta_1 z_1^4 + \beta_2 z_1^3 + \beta_3 c z_1^2 + \beta_4 b z_1 + \beta_5 a \qquad (2.9)$$

or an extension of the static *pdf* method:

$$Pdf(z) = \zeta \exp\left(\theta_1 z_1^5 + \theta_2 z_1^4 + \theta_3 c z_1^3 + \theta_3 b z_1^2 + \theta_4 a z_1\right) \qquad (2.10)$$

Inasmuch as the value of leadership behavior for everyone in a group starts, in principle, at 0.00, the polynomial regression method would not be useful, because there would not be any variance of z_1. Thus, the *pdf* method was used instead.

The quartic term in Equation (2.9) and the quintic term in Equation (2.10) are the signature shapes of the swallowtail response surface. They are as important to the swallowtail as the cubic (in the difference Equation 2.4) and quartic (in the static Equation 2.7) terms are to the cusp. The cubic term in Equation (2.9) and the quartic term in Equation (2.10) account for imbalances in the "ups" and "downs" in the data. It is as useful or disposable as the quadratic (in the difference Equation 2.4) and cubic (in the static Equation 2.7) terms are to the cusp.

In the leader emergence data, the asymmetry variable is probably the strongest effect, or perhaps the easiest to find, of the three control variables, because it runs along the long axis from non-leaders to primary leaders. The bias factor has, to date, been the most challenging of the three to identify, probably because there is some functional overlap with part of the range of the asymmetry parameter; the two tend to separate better if the leadership experiment involves more demanding tasks (Guastello, 2011d). The bifurcation variable is an important feature of the swallowtail manifold, and so it is important to find it, particularly if the bias factor is not cooperating. Note here that I am advocating an orientation toward building and improving models.

The research program on leadership emergence has been summarized in other publications recently (Guastello, 2007, 2009b), and so only a quick synopsis is warranted here. The central idea is that the members of a leaderless work group all interact with each other, and eventually patterns of interaction tend to form and stabilize. A social structure emerges that includes, not only the leader, but also a social system supporting the leader (sometimes the support is not unanimous, of course). A portion of the social system is occupied by secondary leaders, who play more specific roles. There was a precedent for distinguishing primary and secondary leaders that dated back to Cattell and Stice (1954), although the idea seemed to have been forgotten for a while. Nonetheless, the cusp would only have permitted two stable states—non-leaders and leaders, and would not accommodate the possibility of distinguishing secondary from primary leaders. Thus, the swallowtail was a better model for the job.

So far, the swallowtail structure has been illustrated for leaders emerging from creative problem solving, production, coordination-intensive, and emergency-response groups. (The latter can be coordination intensive also, but in a different way.) The leadership criterion in these studies was composed of ratings of amount of leadership. These ratings were given by group members to all other groups members after the work period; the ratings for each person were summed or averaged across raters. The control variables are different in each case, but the underlying common themes are consolidated as follows: Both primary and secondary leaders exhibit a broad repertoire of social and conversational skills relevant to the task, e.g., the asymmetry parameter that separates them from the non-leaders. The bifurcation factor is a task-relevant attribute, e.g., producing useful, creative ideas in an engineering design team, or the ability to talk (experimentally manipulated) in a coordination-intensive group. The bifurcation factor brings people who are high on the asymmetry factor into either the primary or secondary roles. The bias parameter, which distinguishes the primary from secondary leaders, tends to be more specific to the task, e.g., facilitating the creative contributions of others in engineering design, task control in coordination-intensive groups, and group performance in emergency response.

In the quest to build the models and define the right control parameters, a few other interesting points came to light. First, large portions of the social dynamics that result in a particular leader emerging involve control issues—control of the task or control of the conversation. Second, it is more likely that strongly endorsed leaders would arise from high-performing groups, rather than that strongly endorsed leaders would produce high-performing groups. Similarly, if the goals appear impossible to reach, potential leaders can be expected to hide under their desks; no one wants to be the leader of a losing cause. Third, it is possible to see combinations of task-relevant behaviors and process-relevant behaviors in some of the control parameters; primary and secondary leaders do not necessarily separate between task leaders and process leaders.

WORK MOTIVATION

Psychological theories of motivation have taken many forms. One important theme that pervades many social and organizational theories of motivation is the distinction between intrinsic and extrinsic motivation. Extrinsic motivation and extrinsic reward describe situations where the agent receives reward from an outside source. It contrasts with intrinsic motivation, where the agent receives reward, usually intangible, from the activity itself. Examples of intrinsic motivation also include the motives for achievement, affiliation, and power.

The butterfly catastrophe model of motivation in organizations draws together many of the previously known dynamics affecting personnel selection and training, motivation, and work performance, absenteeism, and turnover (Guastello, 1981, 1987, 1995, 2002). The butterfly catastrophe model consists of three stable states of performance and four control parameters. Its response surface is shown in Figure 2.4. Because it involves a five-dimensional response surface, it is shown in 3D sections. The sectioning in the center is perhaps the most widely replicated image of the butterfly model. The uppermost stable state is characterized by high performance and is also associated with low absenteeism and low probability of turnover from either a voluntary or involuntary origin. The middle stable state is characterized by adequate performance relative to the job requirements and is also associated with normative levels of absenteeism and a somewhat higher probability of turnover. The lower stable state is characterized by actual turnover, or performance levels that are sufficiently low to warrant termination. In the latter case, absenteeism could become so frequent that the individual does not show up for the job ever again. Similarly, if the person quits, their performance level would be a zero-contribution to the organization.

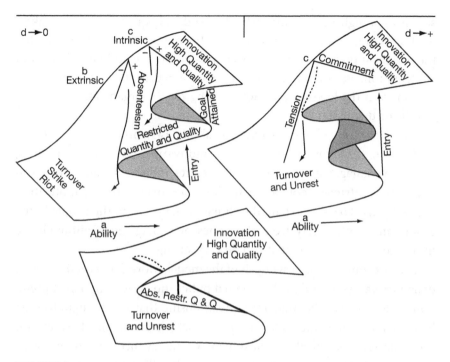

FIGURE 2.4
The butterfly catastrophe response surface for motivation and performance in organizations. (Reprinted from Guastello (1987), with permission of the American Psychological Association.)

The butterfly response surface is shown in Figure 2.4. Its equation is:

$$\frac{\delta f(y)}{\delta y} = y^5 - dy^3 - cy^2 - by - a \tag{2.11}$$

Butterfly models can be tested using an extension of the polynomial regression equation:

$$\Delta z = \beta_0 + \beta_1 z_1^5 + \beta_2 z_1^4 + \beta_3 dz_1^3 + \beta_4 cz_1^2 + \beta_5 bz_1 + \beta_6 a \tag{2.12}$$

In principle, they can also be tested as an extension of the static *pdf* method, but no such examples have been reported yet.

The control point can move anywhere along the surface, as with the other catastrophe models. Discontinuous change can occur between the contiguous stable states, or between extreme states. In one of the latter scenarios, a high-performing individual suddenly quits, perhaps to take a job that is more rewarding in some way. In another, someone who has left the organization is readily hired back because of their solid past history of contribution. Personnel selection is represented by the movement of a person from the lowest state (not working for the organization) into the middle or upper state.

The four control parameters are ability (asymmetry, *a*), extrinsic motivation (bifurcation, *b*), intrinsic motivation (swallowtail or bias, *c*), and a management climate that tolerates individual differences and encourages intrinsic motivation to dominate over extrinsic motivation (butterfly, *d*). To some extent, the climate emerges from the people in the group, and not entirely from the antics of management, although the influence of the management can be very strong.

The foregoing is a brief synopsis of the model. More details of the system dynamics can be found in the original publications. An important point, nonetheless, is that the moderating relationship that was thought to exist between motivation and ability in a personnel selection context, which also shows up as a theoretical relationship in expectancy theory (Vroom, 1964), is incorporated here as a bifurcation relationship. The difference, however, is that, instead of motivation interacting with ability, it interacts with previous levels of performance to produce the new observation of performance. The separation of extrinsic and intrinsic motivation, besides being consistent with earlier research that noted the distinctions initially, also accounts for the well-known relationships between motivation or satisfaction and turnover: absenteeism is associated with intrinsic, but only much less often with extrinsic, satisfaction; turnover is explained by both forms.

All parts of the model have been empirically verified; for summaries, see Guastello (1995, 2002). Some applications encompassed the entire butterfly structure, and others encompassed only subsets of the butterfly dynamics. The cusp model for two-stage personnel selection and turnover is one such subset; for an illustrative example involving performance and turnover among U.S. Air Force recruits, see Guastello (2002).

FUTURE RESEARCH

The models presented in this chapter in conjunction with the five application areas resolve theoretical problems and provide insights in ways that are not afforded by ordinary linear models or the style of reasoning that typically goes with them. The emphasis through the research paradigm is to compare *models*—explanations for processes that go beyond simple significance testing or effect sizes, or even generic nonlinearities. Rodgers (2010) reported that comparisons of models have become increasingly frequent in the past 30 years, a phenomenon that he called "a quiet methodological revolution." In cases where the catastrophe or other NDS model was considered the favored alternative, the NDS model accounted for more criterion variance by a 2:1 margin, in studies that were analyzed in a manner that allowed for the comparison of R^2 coefficients (Guastello, 1995, 2002).

As a good rule of thumb, greater levels of accuracy can be expected to the extent that the events that are supposed to be inducing the catastrophe are more powerful, and if the sampling captures enough hysteresis around the manifold relative to the steady states. A strong and well-reasoned hypothesis concerning the control variables will have an impact on the results also. There are no hard and fast rules for determining optimal sample sizes for NDS models, mostly because of the variability in the dynamics that could be involved and the range of large and small effect sizes for components of a model. The interested reader should consult Guastello and Gregson (2011) for further expansion regarding the state of the science on this matter. One preview, however, is that a smaller sample that represents the full scope of the contributing dynamics trumps a larger sample that captures only a portion of them; this principle has been called *restriction of topological range.*

The prevailing limitation of the models that have been reported in this chapter is that they have only been studied in a small number of applications each. The extensiveness of the applications requires further study. Some suggestions are outlined below.

The buckling-stress models can be expanded into a broader family of models for cognitive workload that encompass different types of load manipulation, task types, and dual-task or multitasking scenarios. Research has only scratched the surface of possible variables that act as elasticity effects, although some viable possibilities can be found in the psychological literature. Cognitive fatigue is a growing concern in the information age. How can tasks with different properties be combined or sequenced to minimize fatigue effects? Is it possible to build an extensive map, so to speak, of abilities that act as compensation abilities against fatigue while doing some kinds of task?

The accident studies lend themselves to expansions in the direction of risk analysis for more specific unwanted events. Importantly, the cusp offers an explicative mechanism that captures a broader picture of the system than what is obtained from single-cause, domino, or factorial models of risk (Guastello, 1989). In the course of developing the accident model, the concept of safety climate was expanded beyond Zohar's (1980) original concept to a broader range of psychosocial variables and hazards. This version of the social picture could withstand more research in many directions pertaining to stress, health, anxiety, and technologies for hazard control.

The leadership-emergence studies identified the swallowtail structure early on (Guastello, 1988; Zaror & Guastello, 2000). It was a bit of a struggle to identify all the control parameters, but they were eventually found for most task situations studied so far; the search for parameter c in production tasks is still on the agenda, however.

The work-motivation model contains the largest number of variables in any one model of those mentioned in this chapter. It would make an ideal basis for new organizational development studies where individuals' behaviors are a concern, and in conjunction with cusps for organizational change at the organizational level of analysis (Bigelow, 1982; Gresov et al., 1993; Guastello, 2002).

Finally, this chapter could provoke a temptation to make a wholesale connection between any form of "tipping point" that might have appeared in the popular press and the formalities of catastrophe models that are described here. There are probably many such connections between critical points and catastrophe models that should be explored further. By the same token, bifurcation theory extends beyond the catastrophe models, and bifurcations of different sorts can be found in other nonlinear dynamical processes that are distinct from the catastrophe models (Guastello & Liebovitch, 2009; Guastello & Gregson, 2011). Similarly, leadership-emergence and catastrophe models work well together, but there are other types of emergent phenomenon that lend themselves to other model structures (Guastello, 2002; Goldstein, 2011). So here, as with any other research program, the structure of the dynamics of the dependent measure needs to be well reasoned for the application, the contributing variables need to be well defined and associated with the correct control variables, and the empirical study needs to connect all the features of the theory with the features of an appropriately chosen method. The situation is more challenging than a simple multiple linear regression, but the payoff is in a cogent and accurate explanation for the phenomenon.

REFERENCES

Alexander, R. A., Herbert, G. R., DeShon, R. P., & Hanges, P. J. (1992). An examination of least-squares regression modeling of catastrophe theory. *Psychological Bulletin, 111*, 366–374.

Bigelow, J. (1982). A catastrophe model of organizational change. *Behavioral Science, 27*, 26–42.

Cattell, R. B., & Stice, G. F. (1954). Four formulae for selecting leaders on the basis of personality. *Human Relations, 7*, 493–507.

Clarke, S. (2006). The relationship between safety climate and safety performance: A meta-analytic review. *Journal of Occupational Health Psychology, 11*, 315–327.

Cobb, L. (1981). Parameter estimation for the cusp catastrophe model. *Behavioral Science, 26*, 75–78.

Flay, B. R. (1978). Catastrophe theory in social psychology: Some applications to attitudes and social behavior. *Behavioral Science, 23*, 335–350.

Frey, P. W., and Sears, R. J. (1978). Model of conditioning incorporating the Rescorla–Wagner associative axiom, a dynamic attention process, and a catastrophe rule. *Psychological Review, 85*, 321–340.

Goldstein, J. (2011). Emergence in complex systems. In P. Allen, S. Maguire, & B. McKelvey (Eds.), *The Sage handbook of complexity and management* (pp. 65–78). Thousand Oaks, CA: Sage.

Gresov, C., Haveman, H. A., & Oliva, T. A. (1993). Organizational design, inertia, and the dynamics of competitive response. *Organization Science, 4*, 181–208.

Guastello, S. J. (1981). Catastrophe modeling of equity in organizations. *Behavioral Science, 26*, 63–74.

Guastello, S. J. (1982a). Moderator regression and the cusp catastrophe: Application of two-stage personnel selection, training, therapy and program evaluation. *Behavioral Science, 27*, 259–272.

Guastello, S. J. (1982b). Color matching and shift work: An industrial application of the cusp-difference equation. *Behavioral Science, 27*, 131–137.

Guastello, S. J. (1985). Euler buckling in a wheelbarrow obstacle course: A catastrophe with complex lag. *Behavioral Science, 30*, 204–212.

Guastello, S. J. (1987). A butterfly catastrophe model of motivation in organizations: Academic performance. *Journal of Applied Psychology, 72*, 165–182.

Guastello, S. J. (1988). Catastrophe modeling of the accident process: Organizational subunit size. *Psychological Bulletin, 103*, 246–255.

Guastello, S. J. (1989). Catastrophe modeling of the accident process: Evaluation of an accident reduction program using the Occupational Hazards Survey. *Accident Analysis and Prevention, 21*, 61–77.

Guastello, S. J. (1991). Psychosocial variables related to transit accidents: A catastrophe model. *Work & Stress, 5*, 17–28.

Guastello, S. J. (1992a). Clash of the paradigms: A critique of an examination of the polynomial regression technique for evaluating catastrophe theory hypotheses. *Psychological Bulletin, 111*, 375–379.

Guastello, S. J. (1992b). Accidents and stress-related health disorders: Forecasting with catastrophe theory. In J. C. Quick, J. J. Hurrell, & L. M. Murphy (Eds.), *Work and well-being: Assessments and interventions for occupational mental health* (pp. 262–269). Washington, DC: American Psychological Association.

Guastello, S. J. (1995). *Chaos, catastrophe, and human affairs: Applications of nonlinear dynamics to work, organizations, and social evolution.* Mahwah, NJ: Lawrence Erlbaum.

Guastello, S. J. (1998). Self-organization in leadership emergence. *Nonlinear Dynamics, Psychology, and Life Sciences, 2*, 303–316.

Guastello, S. J. (2002). *Managing emergent phenomena: Nonlinear dynamics in work organizations.* Mahwah, NJ: Lawrence Erlbaum Associates.

Guastello, S. J. (2003). Nonlinear dynamics, complex systems, and occupational accidents. *Human Factors in Manufacturing, 13*, 293–304.

Guastello, S. J. (2007). Nonlinear dynamics and leadership emergence. *Leadership Quarterly, 18*, 357–369.

Guastello, S. J. (2009a). Chaos and conflict: Recognizing patterns. *Emergence: Complexity in Organizations, 10*(4), 1–9.

Guastello, S. J. (2009b). Group dynamics: Adaptability, coordination, and leadership emergence. In S. J. Guastello, M. Koopmans, & D. Pincus (Eds.), *Chaos and complexity in psychology: Theory of nonlinear dynamical systems* (pp. 402–433). New York: Cambridge University Press.

Guastello, S. J. (2009c). Chaos as a psychological construct: Historical roots, principal findings, and current growth directions. *Nonlinear Dynamics, Psychology, and Life Sciences, 13*, 289–310.

Guastello, S. J. (2010). Self-organization and leadership emergence in emergency response teams. *Nonlinear Dynamics, Psychology, and Life Sciences, 14*, 179–204.

Guastello, S. J. (2011a). Discontinuities: SETAR and catastrophe models with polynomial regression. In S. J. Guastello & R. A. M. Gregson (Eds.), *Nonlinear dynamical systems analysis for the behavioral sciences using real data* (pp. 251–280). Boca Raton, FL: C R C Press/Taylor & Francis.

Guastello, S. J. (2011b). Catastrophe models with nonlinear regression. In S. J. Guastello & R. A. M. Gregson (Eds.), *Nonlinear dynamical systems analysis for the behavioral sciences using real data* (pp. 305–318). Boca Raton, FL: C R C Press/Taylor & Francis.

Guastello, S. J. (2011c). Nonlinear regression and structural equations for nonlinear phenomena. In S. J. Guastello & R. A. M. Gregson (Eds.), *Nonlinear dynamical systems analysis for the behavioral sciences using real data* (pp. 281–304). Boca Raton, FL: C R C Press/Taylor & Francis.

Guastello, S. J. (2011d). Leadership emergence in engineering design teams. *Nonlinear Dynamics, Psychology, and Life Sciences, 15,* 89–104.

Guastello, S. J. (in press). *Modeling illness and recovery with nonlinear dynamics.* In J. Sturmberg & C. M. Martin (Eds.), *Handbook on complexity and health.* New York: Springer.

Guastello, S. J., Boeh, H., Shumaker, C., & Schimmels, M. (2012). Catastrophe models for cognitive workload and fatigue. *Theoretical Issues in Ergonomic Sciences, 12,* "ahead of print."

Guastello, S. J., & Bond, R. W. Jr. (2007). A swallowtail catastrophe model of leadership in coordination-intensive groups. *Nonlinear Dynamics, Psychology, and Life Sciences, 11,* 235–351.

Guastello, S. J. Craven, J., Zygowicz, K. M, & Bock, B. R. (2005). A rugged landscape model for self-organization and emergent leadership in creative problem solving and production groups. *Nonlinear Dynamics, Psychology, and Life Sciences, 9,* 297–333.

Guastello, S. J., Gershon, R., & Murphy, L. (1999). Catastrophe model for the exposure to blood-borne pathogens and other accidents in health care settings. *Accident Analysis and Prevention, 31,* 739–750.

Guastello, S. J., & Gregson, R. A. M. (Eds.) (2011). *Nonlinear dynamical systems analysis for the behavioral sciences using real data.* Boca Raton, FL: C R C Press/Taylor & Francis.

Guastello, S. J., Koehler, G., Koch, B., Koyen, J., Lilly, A., Stake, C. *et al.* (2008). Risk perception when the tsunami arrived. *Theoretical Issues in Ergonomic Science, 9,* 95–114.

Guastello, S. J., Koopmans, M., & Pincus, D. (Eds.) (2009). *Chaos and complexity in psychology: Theory of nonlinear dynamical systems.* New York: Cambridge University Press.

Guastello, S. J., & Liebovitch, L. S. (2009). Introduction to nonlinear dynamics and complexity. In S. J. Guastello, M. Koopmans, & D. Pincus (Eds.), *Chaos and complexity in psychology: Theory of nonlinear dynamical systems* (pp. 1–40). New York: Cambridge University Press.

Guastello, S. J., & Lynn, M. (2010, March). *Catastrophe model of the accident process, safety climate, and anxiety.* Paper presented to the 4th International Nonlinear Science Conference, Palermo, Italy.

Guastello, S. J., & McGee, D. W. (1987). Mathematical modeling of fatigue in physically demanding jobs. *Journal of Mathematical Psychology, 31,* 248–269.

Guastello, S. J., Nathan, D. E., & Johnson, M. J. (2009). Attractor and Lyapunov models for reach and grasp movements with application to robot-assisted therapy. *Nonlinear Dynamics, Psychology, and Life Sciences, 13,* 99–121.

Haken, H. (1988). *Information and self-organization: A macroscopic approach to self-organization.* New York: Springer-Verlag.

Hancock, P. A., & Desmond, P. A. (Eds.) (2001). *Stress, workload, and fatigue.* Mahwah, NJ: Lawrence Erlbaum Associates.

Hanges, P. J., Braverman, E. P., & Rentch, J. R. (1991). Changes in raters' perception of subordinates: A catastrophe model. *Journal of Applied Psychology, 76,* 878–888.

Hockey, G. R. J. (1997). Compensatory control in the regulation of human performance under stress and high workload: A cognitive–energetical framework. *Biological Psychology, 45,* 73–93.

60 • *Stephen J. Guastello*

Holland, J. (1995). *Hidden order*. Reading, MA: Addison-Wesley.

Ioteyko, J. (1920). *La fatigue* [Fatigue] (2nd ed.). Paris: Flammarion.

Kantowitz, B. H. (1985). Channels and stages in human information processing: A limited analysis of theory and methodology. *Journal of Mathematical Psychology, 29*, 135–174.

Karwowski, W., Ostaszewski, K., & Zurada, J. M. (1992). Applications of catastrophe theory in modeling the risk of low back injury in manual lifting tasks. *Le Travail Humain, 55*, 259–275.

Koopmans, M. (2009). Epilogue: Psychology at the edge of chaos. In S. J. Guastello, M. Koopmans, & D. Pincus (Eds.), *Chaos and complexity in psychology: Theory of nonlinear dynamical systems* (pp. 242–281). New York: Cambridge University Press.

Latané, B. (1996). Dynamic social impact: The creation of culture by communication. *Journal of Communication, 46*, 13–25.

Lin, Y., & Cai, H. (2009). A method for building a real-time cluster-based continuous mental workload scale. *Theoretical Issues in Ergonomic Science, 10*, 531–544.

Matthews, G., & Campbell, S. E. (2009). Sustained performance under overload: Personality and individual differences in stress and coping. *Theoretical Issues in Ergonomics Science, 10*, 417–443.

Mayer-Kress, G., Newell, K. M., and Liu, Y.-T. (2009). Nonlinear dynamics of motor learning. *Nonlinear Dynamics, Psychology, and Life Sciences, 13*, 3–26.

Pincus, D. (2010). Self-organizing biopsychosocial dynamics in resilience and wellness: Many methods, one process. *Nonlinear Dynamics, Psychology, and Life Sciences, 14*, 353–380.

Reason, J. (1999). *Managing the risks of organizational accidents*. Brookfield, VT: Ashgate.

Rodgers, J. L. (2010). The epistemology of mathematical and statistical modeling: A quiet methodological revolution. *American Psychologist, 65*, 1–12.

Sawyer, R. K. (2005). *Social emergence: Societies as complex systems*. New York: Cambridge.

Seligman, M. E. P., & Matthews, M. D. (Eds.) (2011). Special issue: Comprehensive soldier fitness. *American Psychologist, 66*, 1–87.

Sheridan, T. B. (2008). Risk, human error, and system resilience: Fundamental ideas. *Human Factors, 50*, 418–426.

Smerz, K. E., & Guastello, S. J. (2008). Cusp catastrophe model for binge drinking in a college population. *Nonlinear Dynamics, Psychology, and Life Sciences, 12*, 205–224.

Stamovlasis, D. (2006). The nonlinear dynamic hypothesis in science education problem solving: A catastrophe theory approach. *Nonlinear Dynamics, Psychology, and Life Sciences, 10*, 37–70.

Stewart, I. N., & Peregoy, P. L. (1983). Catastrophe theory modeling in psychology. *Psychological Bulletin, 94*, 336–362.

Thom, R. (1975). *Structural stability and morphegenesis*. New York: Benjamin-Addison-Wesley.

Thompson, H. L. (2010). *The stress effect: Why smart leaders make dumb decisions—and what to do about it*. San Francisco, CA: Jossey-Bass.

Vallacher, R. R., Coleman, P. T., Nowak, A., & Bui-Wrzosinska, L. (2010). Rethinking intractable conflict: The perspective of dynamical systems. *American Psychologist, 65*, 262–278.

van der Maas, H. L. J., Kolstein, R., & van der Plight, J. (2003). Sudden transitions in attitudes. *Sociological Methods and Research, 32,* 125–152.

van Geert, P. (2009). Nonlinear complex dynamical systems in developmental psychology. In S. J. Guastello, M. Koopmans, & D. Pincus (Eds.), *Chaos and complexity in psychology: Theory of nonlinear dynamical systems* (pp. 242–281). New York: Cambridge University Press.

Vroom, V. H. (1964). *Work and motivation.* New York: Wiley.

Wickens, C. D. (2008). Multiple resources and mental workload. *Human Factors, 50,* 449–455.

Wiggins, S. (1988). *Global bifurcations and chaos.* New York: Springer-Verlag.

Zaror, G., & Guastello, S. J. (2000). Self-organization and leadership emergence: A cross-cultural replication. *Nonlinear Dynamics, Psychology, and Life Sciences, 4,* 113–119.

Zohar, D. (1980). Safety climate in industrial organizations: Theoretical and applied implications. *Journal of Applied Psychology, 65,* 96–102.

3

Dynamic Longitudinal Growth Modeling

Robert E. Ployhart and Youngsang Kim

If one looks back over the last 100 years of longitudinal research in the social and organizational sciences, one finds that 1987 was a seminal year. Prior to that time, there was relatively little attention paid to conceptualizing and modeling change in constructs and processes over time. However, in 1987, two articles introduced to the masses statistical models capable of studying change. Bryk and Raudenbush (1987) introduced growth modeling via hierarchical linear modeling (HLM), and McArdle and Epstein (1987) introduced latent growth modeling (LGM) via structural equation modeling (SEM). These models are referred to generically as "growth models" because they originated from methods used in developmental and educational psychology (e.g., the study of human growth and development), which in turn adopted methods from biology and agriculture (e.g., the study of plant growth).

Since the publication of these two articles, researchers have increasingly adopted growth models to study change in a variety of phenomena, and many new insights have been uncovered. However, the applications of growth models in the organizational sciences have remained largely unchanged from the original models proposed by McArdle and Epstein (1987) and Bryk and Raudenbush (1987), which in turn trace their origins to Rao (1958) and Tucker (1958). As will be discussed shortly, most models are still parameterized using a linear coding of time as a predictor, and then try to explain variance around this linear trend using time-invariant predictors. This is in contrast to more sophisticated ways of theorizing change that emphasize dynamic relationships among constructs and processes (e.g., Marks, Mathieu, & Zaccaro, 2001; Mitchell & James, 2001; DeShon, in press). Thus, as theoretical attention has evolved to increasingly dynamic, multivariate, and complex forms of change, the application of growth models itself has, ironically, scarcely changed in 20 years. Indeed, the lack of change in growth-modeling methodology may now be constraining our thinking on change processes.

The purpose of this chapter is to introduce several extensions and modifications to the basic growth models we already know and love. We suggest that the "typical" growth model is still very useful, but, as theories become more dynamic, it becomes important to model these increasingly complex forms of change. Fortunately, the basic growth models dominating the last 20 years can be extended in relatively straightforward ways to model more dynamic forms of change. This chapter begins by first attending to some basic theoretical issues surrounding change and dynamicism. We then briefly summarize the "traditional" growth model using HLM and SEM conventions, concluding with similarities and differences between the two approaches. We further contrast the evolution of theory to the basic growth-curve model, so that one may see how the basic model is strained to accommodate theoretical advancements. Next, we introduce several extensions to the growth model capable of modeling more complex forms of change. These extensions offer many directions for future methodological and substantive research.

Throughout the chapter, we try to maintain a nontechnical treatment of these topics as much as possible, so that the material will be meaningful to the largest number of readers. There are already many overviews of longitudinal modeling that we cite in relevant places below. We will assume a basic understanding of growth modeling to focus on ways of extending these models to provide more rigorous tests of change processes.

THEORETICAL BACKGROUND

Most theories in the organizational sciences give little explicit consideration of temporal issues. This point has been made very clearly in George and Jones (2000), Mitchell and James (2001), and Roe (2008). With few exceptions (Keil & Cortina, 2001; Kanfer & Ackerman, 2004), if one were to take a hypothesized relationship from a theory and ask the following questions, one would be hard pressed to find answers:

- How long should the effect occur?
- Will the strength of the effect change over time?
- Why should the strength of the effect change?
- What is the process of change?

An example may be helpful to illustrate these theoretical limitations. Consider that there are approximately 100 years of research linking individual differences in knowledge, skills, abilities, and other characteristics (KSAOs) to individual job performance. In the personnel-selection literature, the primary goal is to identify those KSAOs that will predict performance on the job. Rarely in this research is there any consideration for how long the predictive relationship will hold, even among the studies that look at the prediction of dynamic performance. Job performance may consist of maintenance and transition stages (Murphy, 1989). Transition stages occur when new tasks are being learned, and, hence, performance during these periods is determined mainly by cognitive ability. Maintenance stages occur when mastery of the tasks has been achieved, and, hence, performance during these periods is determined mainly by personality. Such propositions are helpful, but are vague with respect to (a) how long transition and maintenance stages last, (b) when the relationships between cognitive ability and personality should change, and (c) the specific form of the performance trend (linear, nonlinear). Of course, no theory can account for all the specific nuances of a particular context or study, but, for scholars wishing to apply Murphy's theory, it would be helpful to provide theoretical arguments for these questions (not to mention that answering questions about duration, timing, and so on, offer much more prescriptive advice to practitioners). To illustrate the value of such an approach, Keil and Cortina (2001) undertook a large-scale study of these issues and found that cognitive-ability validity decayed over time in a nonlinear fashion, providing more specific guidance to researchers and practitioners about how long they can expect cognitive ability to be predictive of performance.

Our point is that theories, and the research that tests those theories, rarely give careful consideration to temporal issues. The consequence is that theories remain vague with respect to time and change (Mitchell &

James, 2001), hypotheses are weak and difficult to falsify (Pitariu & Ployhart, 2010), and the study of change is limited to linear forms (George & Jones, 2000).

Ployhart and Vandenberg (2010) recently discussed a variety of theoretical issues relating to the study of change that should be considered. Among these are: the theoretical explanation for why change should occur, specification of the form of change (including timing and duration), and emphasis on the distinctiveness of longitudinal predictions from cross-sectional predictions. This last point is an important one. Too often we see longitudinal studies where the longitudinal hypothesis is identical to the cross-sectional hypothesis, with the additional caveat of "over time" added. For example, the cross-sectional hypothesis of "Cognitive ability is positively related to performance" is adapted to a longitudinal hypothesis of "Cognitive ability is positively related to performance over time." If one takes the longitudinal hypothesis literally, then there is no reason to conduct this study or test this question, because it is nearly identical to the cross-sectional hypothesis. It would be much more informative, interesting, and insightful to instead hypothesize, "Performance increases but with diminishing returns over time" and "The relationship between cognitive ability and performance change is positive, but weakens over time." Even these hypotheses can be made more precise to be explicit about duration. Notice that, in these more precise hypotheses, we learn much more about the change process and also develop more refined tests of theory (see Keil & Cortina, 2001; Pitariu & Ployhart, 2010).

Of course, for many constructs and phenomena, we know so little about how they change over time that even a simple, descriptive study of change can be informative and enlightening. Indeed, there is compelling evidence to suggest that cross-sectional relationships may not hold to the same degree or even direction when examined longitudinally. For example, Maxwell and Cole (2007) show that cross-sectional tests of mediation may be severely biased and should be tested longitudinally. In our own research, we have seen many instances where the relationship between a static (time-invariant) predictor and some outcome is trivial, but, when examined longitudinally, the relationship is stronger and significant. For example, Chen, Ployhart, Cooper-Thomas, Anderson, and Bliese (2011) found that change in job attitudes was a stronger predictor of turnover intentions than job satisfaction at any given point in time. Likewise, Ployhart, Weekley, and Ramsey (2009) found that change in human capital was predictive of change in unit sales, even though the cross-sectional relationships were close to zero and nonsignificant. Empirically then, change variability is often substantively different from static variability, and, hence, requires different theory rather than simply applying cross-sectional theory.

Therefore, the theoretical goals for a longitudinal study should be to specify the form of change, how long the change will last, and why the change occurs. Such specificity pushes the boundaries of existing theories, which give little attention to these issues. Although challenging, developing such theory is also likely to produce significant theoretical insights. The work by Vancouver, Thompson, and Williams (2001) is an excellent example, where they show that modeling goal setting and self-efficacy dynamically over time can lead to different predictions (and actual empirical support) than cross-sectional research suggests. In answering these kinds of question, researchers will increasingly recognize that they must theorize and model change in the predictors as well as change in the criteria. Scholars must recognize that dynamic relationships, or relationships that exist between two or more variables that are themselves changing, are likely the norm in organizational phenomena.

One final point before moving to methodology: the study of change requires at least three repeated waves of data (Rogosa, 1995). More repeated observations are better, because they allow one to model more complex forms of change (e.g., nonlinear), better distinguish true change from error, and provide greater reliability. Ployhart and Vandenberg (2010) review these benefits in detail and, hence, define longitudinal research as, "research emphasizing the study of change and containing at minimum three repeated observations (although more than three is better) on at least one of the substantive constructs of interest" (p. 97). We also adopt this definition.

TRADITIONAL GROWTH MODELS

There are a variety of approaches that can be used to model change. In most of the organizational and social sciences, these approaches fall under the general label of "growth models." There are two broad classes of such models: random coefficient (HLM) models and latent growth structural equation models (SEM). Again, we assume readers have a basic familiarity with these models, but those wanting more foundational information are referred to the following sources: for random coefficient (HLM) models, see Bliese (2002), Bliese and Ployhart (2002), Bryk and Raudenbush (1987), Hofmann (1997), and Raudenbush and Bryk (2002); for latent growth SEM, see Bollen and Curran (2006), Chan (1998), Meredith and Tisak (1990), McArdle and Epstein (1987), and Tisak and Meredith (1990); for broad introductions, see also Ployhart and Vandenberg (2010) and Singer and Willett (2003).

In our goal of keeping this chapter as nontechnical as possible, we will introduce graphical conventions to describe different forms of change. These conventions do not replace the graphical conventions in SEM, for example. Rather, we introduce these as a way to better understand conceptually how change is being theorized, and how random coefficient models (RCM) and SEM are similar. Figure 3.1 shows these conventions and different types of change process. The capital letters X, M, and Y refer, respectively, to predictor (or independent) variables, mediating variables, and outcome or dependent variables. The capital letter T has a specific meaning in longitudinal studies: it refers to time and the metric used to code time. For example, with four repeated observations, time may be coded simply 0, 1, 2, 3 (the reason the first time period is coded zero will be explained shortly). Subscripts are used to denote different variables as relevant (e.g., X_1 and X_2 suggests there are two different independent variables). Superscripts are used to denote different levels of analysis, where 1 refers to the lower level (e.g., individual), 2 refers to the next higher level (e.g., group), and so on. In a group study, for example, $X_1^{(2)}$ and $X_1^{(1)}$ refer to an independent variable at the group level and the same independent variable at the individual level, respectively. If no superscripts are used, then all variables exist at the same level. A delta symbol (Δ) before X, M, or Y suggests that the variable is expected to change over time. One-headed arrows denote a hypothesized causal direction. If an arrow points directly to another variable, it means it has a direct effect on it. If an arrow points to another arrow, it means there is a moderation effect. Therefore, $\Delta X^{(2)} \rightarrow \Delta Y^{(1)}$ hypothesizes that changes in the higher-level independent variable X directly cause changes in the lower-level dependent variable Y.

Note that $\Delta X^{(2)} \rightarrow \Delta Y^{(1)}$ is not the same as $X^{(2)} \rightarrow Y^{(1)}$. The former relationship is one that is dynamic; the latter relationship is one that is static. For example, we may want to study how change in group cohesion is related to change in individual job performance ($\Delta X^{(2)} \rightarrow \Delta Y^{(1)}$). The

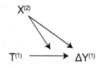

(a) Traditional Growth Model

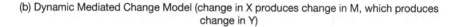

(b) Dynamic Mediated Change Model (change in X produces change in M, which produces change in Y)

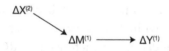

(c) Multilevel Dynamic Mediated Change Models

FIGURE 3.1
Illustration of graphical conventions for describing change processes.
(Note: X = independent or predictor variable; M = mediator variable; Y = dependent or outcome variable; T = coding for time. Delta (Δ) indicates the variable or construct changes over time. Superscripts refer to level of analysis. One-headed arrows refer to theoretical directions of causality.)

emphasis is not in how group cohesion is related to individual performance at any given point in time, but rather is how *changes* in group cohesion contribute to *changes* in job performance dynamically over time. The psychological "meaning" of belonging to a group whose cohesion is increasing may give group members a sense of optimism and, hence, a renewed commitment to performing better. Those in a group whose cohesion is declining may begin to distrust other group members and withdraw from their responsibilities. It is worth emphasizing that, even if we measured group cohesion at Time 1 and individual performance at Time 2, it is still a static relationship and does not capture a dynamic process of change. Instead, we are merely examining the degree to which individuals in cohesive groups tend to have high performance scores.

Figure 3.1 provides several illustrative types of longitudinal model. The traditional growth model is presented in Figure 3.1a. Note that this model is representative of how change is modeled in either RCM or SEM. Conceptually, Figure 3.1a suggests that there is change only on the dependent variable Y. A variable for time, T, is used to provide a metric for scaling change on Y. Both T and Y are at the lower level. A static predictor at a higher level, X, has two potential effects. First, X may moderate the relationship between T and Y, such that change in Y may be greater or weaker for different scores on X. Second, X may directly influence the starting point or initial score on Y (this will be more obvious after discussing the specifics of growth modeling below). For example, X may be cognitive ability, Y may be job performance, and T is time scaled linearly (0, 1, 2, 3, etc.). Figure 3.1a suggests that individual differences in cognitive ability explain change in performance over time (i.e., the moderated effect) and initial performance (i.e., the direct effect of X on Y). Note that this is a two-level model, because within-person change occurs at level 1, and individual differences exist at level 2. We now show how this conceptual model is parameterized in RCM and SEM growth models.

Random Coefficient Models (HLM)

Random coefficient growth models (RCM) are conceptual extensions of the general linear model (GLM), although from a technical perspective HLM and GLM are entirely different animals. Note that HLM is actually the name of a software package, and, hence, the more appropriate name for this type of statistical model is the random coefficient model. For the remainder of this chapter, we shall use the label RCM to keep the software distinct from the statistical model. The groundbreaking work of Bryk and Raudenbush (1987) laid the foundation for RCM models as they are used today. We shall adopt their notation and conventions in this chapter.

RCM growth models may be conceived as having two types of systematic variance: within-person variance (intraindividual change) and between-person variance (interindividual differences in intraindividual change). Of course, these models are not limited to individuals, as one might study firm-level change, and the model would account for intrafirm change and interfirm differences in intrafirm change. Recognizing this distinction, the following parameterize the basic growth model:

Level 1: $\quad Y_{ti} = \pi_{0i} + \pi_{1i}T_{ti} + e_{ti}$ \hfill (3.1)

Level 2: $\pi_{0i} = \beta_{00} + \beta_{01}X_i + r_{0i}$ (3.2)

$\pi_{1i} = \beta_{10} + \beta_{11}X_i + r_{1i}$ (3.3)

In this model, the Level 1 equation, Y is the dependent variable measured repeatedly t times, and i is a subscript representing differences across observations. The terms in the model include an intercept π_0, a slope π_1, the time variable T, and a residual term. Notice that, unlike the traditional regression model, there are i subscripts for each term, suggesting that the intercept and/or slope may differ across observations. That is, each person may have a different starting point (intercept score) and rate of change (slope). The label RCMs comes from the fact that the intercept and slope terms (coefficients) may vary across observations. The intercept, slope, and residual term can be random effects in this model because they vary across observations.

The coding of time is important for the estimation and interpretation of the parameters (Biesanz, Deeb-Sossa, Papadakis, Bollen, & Curran, 2004). Recall that, in regression, the intercept refers to a score when all the predictors are zero. Therefore, in growth models, the intercept refers to the point where time equals zero. Suppose one has five repeated observations reflecting measurements taken in January–May. If we code time such as 0, 1, 2, 3, 4, then the intercept will refer to the score at the first time period (January). If, instead, we code the data 1, 2, 3, 4, 5, then the intercept will refer to an estimated point where time = 0 (e.g., December). If we coded time such as 4, 3, 2, 1, 0, then the intercept would refer to the score in May. Thus, for interpretational convenience, it is best to code time such that the first time period is zero. Biesanz et al. (2004), Singer and Willett (2003), Rogosa (1995), and Ployhart, Holtz, and Bliese (2002) provide much more information about the choices and consequences of using different time-coding structures.

The Level 2 equations contain the between-observation effects. The overall average intercept (β_{00}) and overall slope (β_{10}) are known as fixed effects, because they are constant across observations. These are the estimates one would obtain from a typical ordinary least squares (OLS) regression analysis. The Level 2 residual terms for the intercept (r_{0i}) and slope (r_{1i}) are random effects and represent the variance in these terms across observations. These terms are also known as variance components. If these variance components are nonzero, then one may wish to try to explain variability in intercepts and/or slopes. In the intercept model (Equation 3.2), a predictor X_i is included in the model. If the slope term β_{01} is statistically significant, it means there is a relationship between the predictor X and variability in intercepts. That is, scores on X are related to Time 1 scores on Y. The reduction in r_{0i} between the model that includes X and a model that does not is an indication that X is related to intercept variability and can be used to construct pseudo estimates of variance explained. In the slope model (Equation 3.3), the same predictor X_i is included to explain differences in slopes (or rate of change) across observations. Again, if β_{11} is statistically significant, then the predictor X is associated with change in Y, and reductions of r_{1i} can be used to provide pseudo estimates of variance explained.

Returning to the cognitive ability and performance example presented earlier, overall average change in performance is represented by β_{10}, and first-period performance is represented by β_{00}. Individual differences in performance change over time are represented by r_{1i}, and individual differences in performance at time one are represented by r_{0i}. The effect of cognitive ability on performance change is represented by β_{11}, and the effect of cognitive ability on initial performance is represented by β_{01}. Mapping this back to Figure 3.1a, it is seen that the relationship $T^{(1)} \rightarrow \Delta Y^{(1)}$ is denoted by π_{1i}; the moderating effect of $X^{(2)}$ is denoted by β_{11}; the direct effect of $X^{(2)}$ on $\Delta Y^{(1)}$ is denoted by β_{01}. Details on the benefits of RCM can be found in Bliese and Ployhart (2002), Littell, Milliken, Stroup, andWolfinger (1996), Raudenbush and Bryk (2002), and Singer and Willett (2003).

Latent Growth Structural Equation Models

LGM are a powerful means for analyzing change because they can model many different types of change in X, M, and/or Y, can model measurement error variance, and allow very precise testing of theoretical questions using a model comparison process (see Singer & Willet, 2003). SEM uses a graphical convention that corresponds to equations, so it is possible to describe LGM models graphically instead of through equations. Boxes refer to manifest measures, circles or ellipses refer to latent constructs, one-headed arrows refer to theorized causality, and two-headed arrows refer to covariances. Figure 3.2 shows an LGM that is identical to the RCM model in Equations (3.1)–(3.3) and Figure 3.1a.

In Figure 3.2, change in the repeatedly measured variable Y is modeled through two latent endogenous factors: an intercept factor (ηI) and a time (slope) factor (ηT). Notice the factor loadings (λs) for the intercept and slope. The intercept is a constant, and, hence, the factor loadings are all 1s. The slope factor loadings are fixed to represent the coding for time (T) and, hence, are 0, 1, 2, etc. Further, both factors have a mean estimate (MI and MT) and variability around these means (UI and UT). These mean and variance estimates correspond directly to the fixed and random RCM intercept and slope effects described above. That is, the mean intercept and mean time estimates refer to the overall average score at Time 1 and average slope or rate of change, respectively. The variability in intercepts and slopes refers to interindividual differences in intercepts and intraindividual change.

There is also a time-invariant independent variable, ξ_X, that is hypothesized to causally relate to the latent intercept and time factors (γ_I and γ_S, respectively). However, the latent independent variable is based on three manifest indicators, and, hence, by modeling the indicators, it is possible to remove error variance due to item content away from the latent exogenous independent variable factor (see DeShon, 1998). To the extent there is measurement error in X, the paths (γ_I and γ_S) between the latent independent variable ξ_X and the intercept and slope factors will be larger than what one would find in RCM.

Finally, this basic LGM can be mapped back onto the cognitive ability–performance example and conceptual model of change in Figure 3.1a. Overall average change in performance is represented by MT, and first-period performance is represented by MI. Individual differences in performance change over time are represented by UT, and individual differences in performance at Time 1 are represented by UI. The effect of cognitive ability on performance change is represented by γ_T, and the effect of cognitive ability on initial performance is represented by γ_I. Linking back to Figure 3.1a, it is seen that the relationship $T^{(1)} \rightarrow \Delta Y^{(1)}$ is denoted by MT; the moderating effect of $X^{(2)}$ is denoted by γ_T; the direct effect of $X^{(2)}$ on $\Delta Y^{(1)}$ is denoted by γ_I. Although not shown in Figure 3.2, it is possible to introduce other parameters into the model. For example, correlated residuals or uniquenesses are the norm in longitudinal research, and so it is possible to correlate uniquenesses among the errors for Y (εs). For some excellent references on LGM, please see Bollen and Curran (2006), Chan (1998), and Meredith and Tisak (1990).

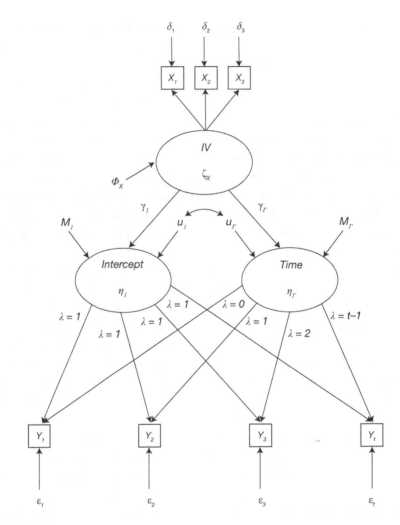

FIGURE 3.2
Simple latent growth model.

LIMITS OF THE BASIC GROWTH MODEL[1]

The basic growth model, described above via RCM and LGM, presents the dominant approach for modeling change in the social and organizational sciences. The model has been applied to socialization (e.g., Chan & Schmitt, 2000), commitment (e.g., Vandenberg, 2002), goal setting (e.g., Vancouver et al., 2001), and job performance (Hofmann, Jacobs, & Baratta, 1993; Ployhart & Hakel, 1998). RCM and LGM have some important differences, but are more similar than many people realize (Bollen & Curran, 2006). For the simple growth model expressed in Figure 3.1a, both RCM and LGM are appropriate and will provide identical estimates (unless measurement error is considerable with the predictor variable X and is modeled and removed within the LGM framework). These models have found widespread appeal with researchers and have led to many important insights. However, it is important to recognize that, as we have discussed them so far, both models share a fundamental assumption that limits their ability to test more complex forms of change. The nucleus of this assumption is about the role of time in the models and its substantive interpretation.

First, when the growth model is specified with no predictor and time as the independent variable, the model posits that change in the dependent variable is caused by time. That is, the coding for time is operationalized within the models as the cause for change in the dependent variable. This is referred to as "descriptive" longitudinal research by Ployhart and Vandenberg (2010), or an "unconditional growth model" by Singer and Willett (2003). Although this model provides a valuable description of change, it is unlikely that time is the cause of any particular phenomenon or construct of interest. For example, performance doesn't change because of time, but owing to changes in other constructs (e.g., knowledge) and environmental factors. Knowledge doesn't change because of time, but owing to changes in learning opportunities and experiences. Time is the metric upon which to scale change on the dependent variable, but, lacking any predictors of change, the growth models implicitly assume that time is the cause of change in the dependent variable (just as any predictor in a regression model is implicitly assumed to be the cause of Y).

Second, adding predictors of slope variability may lead to the broader expectation that the predictor explains change within the dependent variable. Ployhart and Vandenberg (2010) refer to this as "explanatory" longitudinal research, and Singer and Willett (2003) refer to this as a "conditional" growth model. Yet, even in this model, notice how the predictor has been specified as time-invariant (or static, in that there is only one score on the predictor, regardless of time). Time-invariant predictors make sense when the predictor is generally stable across time and situations, such as with many individual differences, such as cognitive ability and personality. When the predictor constructs are stable, the basic growth model is appropriate. However, when the predictors are themselves malleable over time (i.e., time-varying), or when there are dynamic relationships among variables and processes, the traditional growth model is mis-specified.

Thus, the traditional growth model works reasonably well when the predictors of change are time-invariant, but the model does not estimate time-varying predictors and/or dynamic relationships. Fortunately, it is possible to extend the basic growth model to include time-varying predictors and study dynamic relationships. Thus, the problem lies not in the model but with the dominant application of the model. We suspect many researchers are unfamiliar with the numerous variations that exist among different types of growth model, and so, for the remainder of this chapter, we explore ways in which RCM and SEM can be extended to model more complex and dynamic forms of change. We start by exploring the meaning of time-varying predictors.

TIME-VARYING PREDICTORS AND DYNAMIC RELATIONSHIPS

Time-varying predictors are constructs or variables that can change over the course of a study's investigation. Examples include mood, emotions, attitudes, beliefs, knowledge, skill, and expertise. Time-varying predictors may occur at any level (e.g., change in individual climate versus change in organizational climate), and they may be psychological or environmental (e.g., change in unemployment rates). Like the variable time, time-varying predictors can either be constant across all observations (a fixed effect), or allowed to vary across observations (a random effect).

When there are relationships among two or more constructs or variables that are changing over time, it becomes possible to study dynamic relationships. *Dynamic relationships* are relationships where the variables change over time, and/or the strength of the relationship changes over time. For example, Vancouver et al. (2001) showed how the relationships among self-efficacy and goal setting could change over time, and Ployhart, Van Iddekinge, and MacKenzie (2011) showed how changes in generic and firm-specific human capital translated into changes in service behavior and, ultimately, changes in unit effectiveness.

Singer and Willett (2003) describe four types of time-varying predictor. *Defined* time-varying predictors are those where the scores on the predictor are predetermined and cannot be manipulated by participants or researchers. The way we have treated time so far, such as a nominal coding of weeks, months, quarters, or years, is an example. *Ancillary* time-varying predictors are caused by random or erratic factors, but are not under the direct control of participants. Changes in the economy, such as national GDP or regional unemployment rates, are examples. *Contextual* time-varying predictors are similar to ancillary predictors, except that there is a potentially stronger relationship between the predictor and the outcome. For example, a person's turnover in a small team will affect other team members. Finally, *internal* time-varying predictors are those that can be influenced by a study participant or manipulated by an experimenter. Examples include physical states (e.g., body mass index), psychological states (e.g., attitudes), or social states (e.g., friendships). Keep in mind that these examples are illustrative, and the same issues apply for the study of constructs at other levels. For example, suppose one is studying the relationship between local unemployment rates and organizational hiring rates. Obviously, a large employer in a particular region can have a profound effect on the local unemployment rate.

The reason it is important to understand the nature and characteristics of time-varying predictors is that, to the extent participants or researchers can influence scores on the predictor, it becomes difficult to distinguish cause and effect, and to rule out reciprocal causation and endogeneity. Longitudinal studies can offer greater inferences of causality, but, if the predictors and outcomes are measured concurrently at any given time period, *and* the scores on the predictors are malleable, then it becomes very difficult to ignore such concerns. Ironically, the same challenges in separating cause from effect in cross-sectional research reappear with the longitudinal study.[2] For example, if job satisfaction is measured at the same times as turnover intentions, and one regresses the vector of turnover-intention scores over time onto the vector of job-satisfaction scores over time, the slope represents the relationship between the two sets of scores over time, but we don't know which variable causes the other. We also can't very effectively rule out "third-variable" influences. In such situations, a very serious concern is whether the relationship is contemporaneous.

The four types of time-varying predictor presented by Singer and Willett (2003) provide a ruler for gauging concerns about endogeneity and reciprocal causation. The key issue is whether participants or observations in the study can influence the scores on the predictor. We suggest this issue can be better understood by a broader understanding of multilevel issues. Simon (1973) introduced the concept of *bond strength* to describe the extent to which two different levels are mutually related. Relationships among variables within a level are nearly always stronger than relationships among variables between levels (Kozlowski & Klein, 2000). As the "distance" between the levels increases, the strength of the relationship decreases. Thus, the four types of time-varying predictor really fall on a continuum of bond strength. Viewed from this perspective, defined time-varying predictors have no bond strength, because time (i.e., days, weeks, months) cannot be changed or altered (although we recognize that theoretical physicists may not agree!). It is for this reason that defined time-varying predictors have no reciprocal-causation concerns (e.g., the month of May doesn't "occur" because of sales in April). On the opposite extreme, internal time-varying predictors are within the same level, and, hence, reciprocal-causation concerns are serious (e.g., April showers bring May flowers). Between these two extremes, it is only a matter of degree, and a difference in bond strength, between ancillary and contextual time-varying predictors, as the former have less bond strength than the latter. To summarize: if the time-varying predictor and outcome are measured at the same level, reciprocal-causation concerns are relevant. Such concerns become less relevant as the bond strength between the predictor and outcome decrease (i.e., as they are separated by more levels). Table 3.1 provides an overview of these issues.

TABLE 3.1

Different Types of Time-Varying Predictor

Type	Reciprocal-causation concerns?	Bond strength	Examples
Defined	No	Nonexistent	Milliseconds, days, weeks, quarters, years
Ancillary	Little	Low	Unemployment rates
Contextual	Potential	High	Team or group composition and processes
Internal	Yes	Within-level	Attitudes, emotion, stress, knowledge

It is our belief that the inclusion of time-varying predictors will provide a significant advancement to the study of change. It will allow researchers to move from testing descriptive or static explanatory growth models, to testing dynamic explanatory models linking change in multiple constructs and variables. For example, wouldn't it be exciting to see research showing how changes in knowledge acquisition relate to changes in job performance over time? Are the relationships found with cross-sectional research likely to be stronger or weaker? Prior research has found that some relationships, particularly those at the unit level, are only likely to be found when both predictors and outcomes are linked over time (Ployhart et al., 2009). Likewise, cross-sectional mediator models may grossly mis-estimate the size and even direction of relationships (Maxwell & Cole, 2007).

We do not present concerns over reciprocal causation to discourage researchers from using time-varying predictors. Rather, we want researchers to understand that there are important substantive and methodological issues that must be considered if such predictors are going to provide stronger tests of theory. We don't want researchers to simply include time-varying predictors because they are available in a dataset. Obviously, the successful resolution of all such issues starts with good theory. Is there a solid theory of the change process? Are the functional forms of change in the time-varying predictors understood? If the time-varying predictor changes in a different form over time (e.g., curvilinear) than the outcome (e.g., linear), concerns that the relationship is a result of a third variable seem less likely. Theory is best tested with appropriate designs and analyses. As we shall see in a later section, it is possible to reduce concerns of reciprocal causation by using temporal lags between the predictors and outcomes.

We conclude this section by returning to the concern that prompted it: the role of time in growth models. If one believes the inclusion of a time-varying predictor is important, then the question becomes whether the variable time should be included in the model. Including both time and a time-varying predictor will, in theory, allow one to explain change in the outcome with two terms, and the effect for time is conditional on the time-varying predictor, and the effect for the time-varying predictor is conditional on time. This type of model has been used in some studies (e.g., Pitariu & Ployhart, 2010), but does it make sense? If time is only the metric used to code change with the dependent variable, and theoretically the time-varying predictor is the presumed cause of change, are both terms necessary? Singer and Willett (2003) suggest that, if the time-varying predictor scores are not monotonic over time, then it is necessary to have time in the model. From a substantive perspective, we are not so sure.

Consider a study that links change in job performance to change in knowledge. If one includes time in the model, then change in knowledge can only explain performance variance that remains after controlling for time, and vice versa. All else equal, the time variable will account for more variance than a time-varying predictor such as knowledge, because time is measured with perfect reliability, and the scores are spaced to represent linear change. To be comparable to, or better than, the time predictor, the knowledge measure would need perfect reliability and scores more closely synchronized to change in performance. Both possibilities seem unlikely, given the reliability and strength of relationships typically found in the social sciences. In general, including time in the model will make it very difficult for any time-varying predictor to significantly explain variance in Y. This will be even more true to the extent the time-varying predictor follows a trend similar to the time variable (e.g., both are linear). Theoretically, such a model says that change on a substantive variable can only explain change on a dependent variable after controlling for the effects of time. This seems unrealistic and gives time too much explanatory power.

It is our position that whether one includes time in a growth model along with substantive time-varying predictors needs to be balanced against a variety of theoretical and practical issues. We are aware of no empirical or methodological research that informs this question, and so, until such research is available, we propose the following set of model comparisons, based on our experience.

Step 1: Is the form of change in the predictor monotonic? If the change present on the predictor and/or mediator is monotonic, then it seems that including time in the model is unnecessary (Singer & Willett, 2003). Time is also usually coded in a manner that is monotonic, and so time and the predictor are redundant and testing highly similar "forms" of change. For example, if the scores on the predictor and/or mediator are linear, and one includes a linear term for time, then the two variables will be very highly related. On the other hand, if the predictor and/or mediator are not monotonic, then one should proceed to the next step.

Step 2: Adopt methodological safeguards. If the predictor and/or mediator are not monotonic, then one should consider the following methodological safeguards.

First, lag the timing of the measurement occasions, so that scores on the predictor are followed by scores on the outcome. For example, if one has a measure of job satisfaction and turnover intentions, one can lag the scores such that turnover intentions are measured at a time period after job satisfaction, and this is done for each measurement occasion. This is conceptually similar to separating the timing of cause and effect in cross-sectional research, except that here it is done on a series of repeated measures data, so that there is still an ability to study dynamic relationships. Lagging the predictor and criterion scores makes it less likely that scores on the criterion can influence the predictor, but raises a different concern about the optimal length of the time lags. We will discuss this issue in detail in the section on "Lagged Growth Models."

Second, include a product term between time and the time-varying predictor. In this manner, one is basically testing whether the predictor—structured linearly to time—is related to change in the outcome. The moderator thus captures whether the linear portion of the predictor's change is related to the dependent variable. However, this moderator is different from the moderating term (β_{11}) in Equation (3.3) above. The moderating term in the time-varying predictor model exists at Level 1, whereas the moderating term in the basic growth-curve model is a cross-level moderator. Thus, they are conceptually very different and likely also differ in their statistical power.

Third, switch the order of entry of time and the time-varying predictor and, using sequential (Type I) sums of squares, determine whether the effect sizes and significance tests differ. That is, examine the incremental validity of the time-varying predictor over time, and vice versa. If the time-varying predictor is a strong predictor when entered first in the model, but is no longer a strong predictor after modeling of the time variable, it suggests that the predictor is redundant with the time variable (perhaps because the predictor is itself changing linearly). On the other hand, if time is a strong predictor when entered first in the model, and still is when entered after the time-varying predictor, it suggests that there is not much systematic relationship between the time-varying predictor and time.

Fourth, compare models that include only time, only the time-varying predictor, a moderator term between time and the time-varying predictor, and where the order of entry differs for time and the time-varying predictor. This is a model-comparison approach and is not done to conduct a "search and seek" mission on the data, but rather to understand the nature of the relationships present. Evaluate the different models in terms of fit, effect sizes, statistical significance of terms, and bottom-line conclusions. It will often be the case that these models all point to the same bottom-line conclusion, even if the effect sizes differ a bit across the models. However, if there are discrepancies, they should be described, and one should ultimately choose the model most consistent with the theory (regardless whether the results support the theory!). If there are no discrepancies, make a brief note that you ran such models and no differences existed, and just report the model most consistent with the theory.

Step 3: Use a growth model that allows the most direct test of the hypothesized change process. Because of their flexibility, LGMs may offer a means of modeling time-varying predictors without some of the concerns raised by the use of RCM growth models. We consider such differences in the following subsections. To help illustrate these models, we will use a common example that builds from the prior cognitive ability–performance example. One of the main reasons cognitive ability is expected to relate to job performance is because those with greater ability are able to acquire knowledge more quickly, and apply it and generalize it more broadly (Jensen, 1998). Cognitive ability is stable, but knowledge is clearly malleable, and, hence, it is quite likely that cognitive ability influences the development and acquisition (change) in job knowledge, which in turn contributes to improvements (change) in job performance.

Dynamic RCM

In RCM, time-varying predictors are incorporated into the Level 1 equation. This can be seen in Equation (3.4) below, where time (T) is still included in the model, as is the time-varying predictor Z (knowledge). Changes in the time-varying predictor X are related to changes in the outcome variable Y (performance). Further, one may allow variation in the relationship between the time-varying predictor Z and Y, just as can be done for the intercept and slope (see Equation 3.5 below). Substantively, the Level 1 model suggests that changes in job performance are regressed on time and changes in job knowledge. Time is included in the model because job knowledge may not be monotonic over time. Equation (3.5) also allows individual differences in the relationship between job knowledge and performance. Finally, one may include time-invariant predictors of such variability (X in Equation 3.5). For example, those with greater cognitive ability (X) may have a stronger relationship between knowledge change (Z) and performance change (Y).

Level 1: $\quad Y_{ti} = \pi_{0i} + \pi_{1i}T_{ti} + \pi_{2i}Z_{ti} + e_{ti}$ $\hspace{3cm}$ (3.4)

Level 2: $\quad \pi_{2i} = \beta_{20} + \beta_{21}X_i + r_{2i}$ $\hspace{4cm}$ (3.5)

It is worth emphasizing that, because the time-varying predictor is at Level 1 (i.e., intraindividual change), it can explain variance in Y directly (and, hence, reduce the residual in the Level 1 equation). On the other hand, a time-invariant predictor cannot explain any variance in Y directly, but will potentially explain variance in the variability around the Level 2 intercept and slope (and, hence, reduce the Level 2 residual terms for those equations). Thus, only a time-varying predictor can directly explain variance in Y, whereas a time-invariant predictor can only explain variance in the relationship between time and Y. This is a very important distinction.

Including time-varying predictors is relatively straightforward but is rarely done (see Pitariu & Ployhart, 2010). Note that, in this example, we have modeled the relationships with both time and the time-varying predictor Z in the model simultaneously. As noted above, it may not be necessary to also include time (T) in the model, in which case only the time-varying predictor Z is included. Or, as also noted, one could include the interaction between time (T) and the time-varying predictor (Z), such as $\pi_{3i}TZ_{ti}$. Singer and Willett (2003) provide an excellent introduction to such models.

Neglecting to include time in the model raises concerns about whether the relationship between changes in Y and Z (estimated by π_{2i}) is contemporaneous. Estimating the relationship between Y and Z over time can be highly informative, but there is no specific form of change imposed on Z. That is, Z is not structured to change linearly, nonlinearly, or in any other specific function. For example, if one speaks to the acquisition of knowledge, one should expect to find a learning curve. In such instances where theory provides strong evidence for a particular trend for the time-varying predictor, one could impose such structure via a product term, but the variance attributable to the product term can only contain variance left unexplained by the main effects for time (T) and the predictor (Z). So long as change is monotonic, there are lags introduced between the predictor and outcome, and/or there is little chance scores on the time-varying predictor are manipulated by participants, then use of time-varying predictors in RCM provides a powerful and simple platform for the study of change.

Dynamic LGM

Alternatively, if a specific form of change for the time-varying predictor is hypothesized to relate to a specific form of change on the outcome variable, then use of LGM may be preferable. For example, perhaps one proposes that knowledge increases over time, but to some asymptote where it starts to level off—the classic learning curve. This curvilinear form of change is then expected to produce the same function for performance over time. In such a model, it is a *specific* form of change in the predictor that is related to a *specific* form of change in the outcome. Or, consider a researcher wishing to test a longitudinal, mediated model, where changes in X relate to changes in M, which in turn relate to changes in Y. For example, perhaps one studies cognitive ability over the lifespan, finding that declines in cognitive ability (e.g., processing speed) are compensated with increases in knowledge, thereby offsetting age-related declines in performance (Kanfer & Ackerman, 2004). In this example and other complex change models, LGM is often preferred over RCM, because of its flexibility and ability to estimate or constrain specific paths.

Figure 3.3 shows an example of what the SEM literature refers to as a "cross-domain LGM," which is simply a growth model with a time-varying predictor (and, for this reason, we will not use the "cross-domain" language further because it is limiting). In this figure, one sees that change in the independent variable is hypothesized to cause change in the dependent variable. The LGM in Figure 3.3 is not the same as the RCM growth model with a time-varying predictor (regardless of whether time is or is not included). A specific functional form of change is hypothesized for the predictor in LGM, and this specific form of change is hypothesized to lead to a specific form of change in the outcome (through γSXSY). For example, change in job knowledge (the exogenous variable) is hypothesized to occur linearly, as is job performance. In turn, linear change in knowledge is predicted to explain linear change in performance (through γXSY). One could expand this model by instead proposing different types of change for knowledge, such as a learning curve, a forgetting curve, or any other curve of theoretical interest.

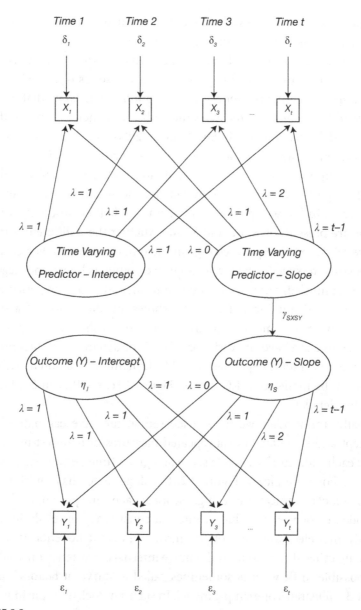

FIGURE 3.3

Dynamic mediated latent growth model. (Note that latent means, variances, and covariances are not shown.)

Figure 3.4 shows an LGM that involves mediated dynamic relationships. For example, one may examine whether changes in intelligence across adulthood relate to changes in knowledge, which in turn relate to changes in performance. In LGM, it is possible to test a series of nested models, for example, to compare models specifying full or partial mediation. One simply adds or removes the relevant paths, and then compares the fit of the models (see James, Mulaik, & Brett, 2006). With the performance example, one might compare fully versus partially mediated models. Finding support for a partially mediated model relative to a fully mediated model suggests performance may yet decline with ability, irrespective of increases in knowledge. One can also test whether different forms of change are present for X, M, and Y, and whether these different forms of change relate to subsequent change in the other constructs. For example, it is possible to specify change in cognitive ability as linear and negative, change in knowledge as positive and nonlinear, and change in performance as positive and nonlinear. Figure 3.4 shows an illustration of a simple (linear-only) model manifesting a change process shown in Figure 3.1b. However, one can have any variation of static or dynamic variables present, including even a static dependent variable. Dynamic mediation models can, to a point, be modeled in RCM (e.g., Figure 3.1c; see Pitariu & Ployhart, 2010, for details).

Finally, the models we have discussed so far have estimated latent intercept and slope factors via repeated measures of manifest indicators, where each indicator is a single score at a given time period (e.g., Figures 3.2–3.4). For example, in Figure 3.2, the slope factor has multiple indicators, but each indicator is a single score at each time period. In this type of model, error variance due to internal consistency unreliability is not directly modeled, and one of the most important benefits of SEM is not being utilized. To model and remove internal consistency unreliability, it is possible to fit what is sometimes called a "curve of factors" model. Figure 3.5 illustrates one simple model. In such a model, multiple indicators (j) are used at each time period to estimate a latent factor at each time period. For example, suppose one administers a five-item job knowledge test quarterly for 1 year. Given such data, it is possible to estimate a latent knowledge factor for each of the 4 quarters, and then estimate the latent intercept and slope using the four repeated latent factors. This model will thus remove error due to item content from the latent intercept

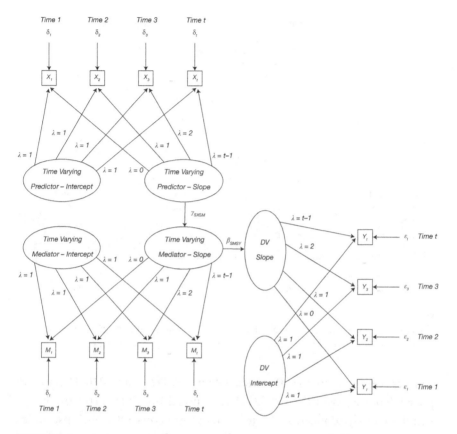

FIGURE 3.4

Dynamic mediated latent growth model. (Note that latent means, variances, and covariances are not shown.)

and slope. These models also allow one to test for invariance longitudinally, to ensure that factor loadings for the performance dimensions do not change over time (and, hence, rule out concerns of shifting factor structures and a loss of configural or metric invariance). Chan (1998) provides an excellent introduction to these models.

LGM provides a powerful approach for modeling complex change processes. LGM's flexibility makes it easier to model complex change processes than through RCM. However, it is important to recognize that, in LGM with time-varying predictors (e.g., Figures 3.3–3.5), the same concerns expressed with RCM time-varying predictors apply. Only a few

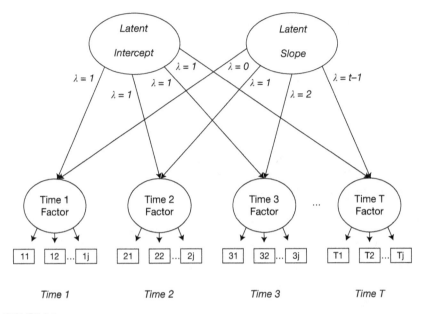

FIGURE 3.5

Curve of factors model. (Note that latent means, variances, and covariances, and manifest uniquenesses, are not shown; T = time period; j = item number.)

sources seem to recognize this issue (Pitariu & Ployhart, 2010; DeShon, in press). That is, even though LGM can model multiple forms of change simultaneously, concerns about contemporaneous relationships, endogeneity, and reciprocal causation still remain. These concerns are lessened by LGMs' ability to parameterize specific forms of change in X, M, and Y, but they are not eliminated. We find it surprising that there is so little treatment of this issue within the SEM literature. Rather, the SEM literature has seemed to have evolved into the study of autoregressive models as a means to control for endogeneity, as we see in the next section.

EXTENSIONS TO THE BASIC GROWTH MODEL

Thus far, we have discussed the inclusion of time-varying predictors into RCM and LGM. Such models offer a significant evolution of the basic growth model dominating research for the last 20 years. However, there are other variations of growth models that are even more radical. In this section, we provide a broad introduction to several models likely to be most relevant to organizational researchers.

Lagged Growth Models

Concerns with using time-varying predictors in both RCM and LGM involve ruling out endogeneity, reciprocal causation, third variables, and contemporaneous relationships. Perhaps the most straightforward way to reduce all such concerns is to introduce a temporal lag between the timing of the measures. For example, suppose one has a model specified such as shown in Figure 3.1b, where change in X leads to change in M, which leads to change in Y. Substantively, such a process could occur when changes in group cohesion lead to changes in individual motivation, which may in turn lead to changes in individual job performance. A cross-sectional study that measured all constructs simultaneously would raise immediate (and fatal) concerns about method bias. A study that separated the timing of these three constructs, but used only a single measurement occasion for each, would reduce concerns about method bias, but say little about how the constructs evolve over time and how their relationships change over time. This is important because cohesion, motivation, and performance are all highly malleable and dynamic. Hence, modeling the change in these constructs makes it possible to study their dynamic relationships. Yet, if one does not lag the measurement occasions for each variable, then concerns about contemporaneous relationships become appropriate, and the method-bias issues of the cross-sectional study actually become relevant again. The solution is to lag the measurement occasions, hence preserving the benefits of the longitudinal study but reducing concerns of method bias. Provided there are enough repeated observations, one might lag the data as shown in Table 3.2.

Notice that X at Time 1 is linked to M at Time 2, which is linked to Y at Time 3, and so on. Besides reducing concerns about method bias, introducing lags recovers the temporal separation of cause from effect, and allows stronger inferences of causality than the contemporaneous relationships we have discussed so far (see DeShon, in press; Singer & Willett, 2003). Clearly, there must be multiple waves of repeated-measures data for such models to be feasible.

The obvious question is how far the lags should be spaced. Should lags be separated by one time period (as illustrated above), or multiple time

TABLE 3.2

Illustration of Temporal Lags Among Predictors (X), Mediators (M), and Dependent Variables (Y)

Time period	X	M	V
1	1	2	3
2	2	3	4
3	3	4	5
4	4	5	6
T . . .	5 . . .	6 . . .	7 . . .

periods? There is little methodological guidance for answering this question. Lags that are too short or too long could result in inaccurate estimation. In general, as the lags increase, the effect sizes will decrease, but how far is too far? Gollob and Reichardt (1987; 1991) and DeShon (in press) discuss issues with lags, and potential ways to estimate how long the lags should be. In practice, the most important place to start is by developing a theory to specify how long the lags should be, and then testing the consequences on model fit and estimation using lags of different lengths. Let us reconsider the example of dynamic group cohesion–individual motivation–individual performance relationships. If the lag between cohesion and motivation is too short, then, to the extent method bias is an issue, the effect size will be inflated. If the lag between cohesion and motivation is too long, the effect size is likely to be depressed, perhaps even to the point where the relationship ceases to exist or reverses direction (Maxwell & Cole, 2007)! Despite such ambiguity with specifying the length of lags a priori, there is little question that using lags is an improvement over the contemporaneous relationship between two variables. We encourage researchers to adopt lagged growth models when using time-varying predictors whenever possible, and devote the time to presenting a strong theoretical justification for the length of the lags (which, by itself, could be an important contribution).

Autoregressive Latent Trajectory Models

The growth models we have discussed in this chapter have not considered autoregressive structures among the substantive variables. Autoregressive structures are those where the hypothesized determinant of a variable at time T + 1 is a function of the same variable at time T. That is, the score on a variable at a later time is regressed on itself from an earlier time. In this manner, autoregressive models are consistent with the notion that "the best predictor of future behavior is past behavior." Note that we are not referring to autoregression among the residuals, but rather autoregression among the substantive variables or constructs.

Bollen and Curran (2004) introduced a class of models capable of incorporating autoregression within LGM. These models, referred to generically as autoregressive latent trajectory (ALT) models, synthesize the autoregressive tradition with the growth modeling tradition. In doing so, they provide a means to control for autoregression among variables while simultaneously estimating change. That is, change over time is estimated after controlling for the effects of the same variable at a prior time period. Zyphur, Chaturvedi, and Arvey (2008) illustrated the utility of such models for understanding dynamic performance. They showed that the fit of an ALT model was better than the fit of an LGM, suggesting that performance contains both growth and autoregressive elements.

Incorporating an ALT model is fairly straightforward. One simply takes the Time 1 measurement indicator, and treats it as an exogenous variable that (a) correlates with the latent intercept and slope factors, and (b) is a determinant of the Time 2 manifest indicator score. Additionally, the Time 2 indicator score is a determinant of the Time 3 indicator score, and so on. Thus, the main difference between an ALT model and an LGM is that the manifest indicators "cause" each other sequentially through time. Of course, given that causal relationships are hypothesized among the manifest variables, one may no longer need to allow covariances among the uniquenesses (residuals).

A far-reaching substantive area where ALT models could offer powerful insight is in the area of strategic human resources, and, in particular, the connection between organizational human capital resources and firm performance. Firm performance is affected by many factors and is expected to be path dependent. The creation and maintenance of human-capital resources is likewise expected to be path dependent. Path dependency is thus a form of endogeneity, and it becomes vital to control for "prior" levels of performance and human capital. Traditional growth models may not provide a sufficiently strong means of modeling such variability, and yet ALT models could do so through their modeling on autoregressive relationships. Indeed, ALT models may help close the gap between growth models and econometric models and, in turn, between psychology and strategy.

The ALT model offers an opportunity to study a variety of different features of change and causality, and the autoregressive feature provides a strong degree of control of the change process. Bollen and Curran (2004) provide many extensions to the basic ALT model that should prove highly relevant to organizational scholars.

Nonlinear and Discontinuous Growth Models

We tend to treat time linearly in the organizational sciences, and every model discussed in this chapter has been a linear model. But what, in reality, truly operates in a linear manner? Changes in height, weight, stock markets, and performance are sure to develop over time in a nonlinear manner. Yet, even when faced with obviously nonlinear relationships, researchers tend to use linear models to approximate the change. For example, most of the dynamic-performance literature finds that performance increases positively over time, but with a decreasing slope to the point where it levels off (i.e., a negatively accelerated curve). Most researchers that study dynamic performance approximate this nonlinear curve with a linear growth curve methodology by using polynomials (e.g., linear, quadratic, cubic) to approximate the curve. These linear approximations are wonderfully simple, but they do not model the curve exactly. For example, if using a true nonlinear model, it would be possible to fit a negatively accelerated curve with only two parameters rather than three required polynomials (intercept, linear, and quadratic terms).

A second form of nonlinearity can occur when there are dramatic breaks or tipping points in a curve. Discontinuous models may involve a change in slope (magnitude or direction), or an abrupt shift in level. In these situations, an otherwise smooth linear or nonlinear curve "moves." For example, Keil and Cortina (2001) show that the validity of cognitive ability tests follows many "breaking points," where the direction of the relationship changes rather dramatically. One might be content to know that validity decays, but it is much more informative for theory, and useful for practice, to know when validity is likely to change. Knowing where the "breaking points" are in the curve help one understand the duration of an effect or relationship.

We believe that many real-world phenomena likely exhibit discontinuous breaks and, most certainly, nonlinear relationships. A major hurdle to discovering such relationships is the quality of our measures. Self-report measures, and measures with adequate (but not high) reliability, can obscure nonlinear relationships. However, a more serious hurdle to discovering such relationships is the quality of our theories. If scholars begin to theorize about duration and timing as we suggested earlier, they will soon also be confronted with a need to specify nonlinearity, as most everything in the natural world is finite (despite William Blake's famous quote!). Burchinal and Appelbaum (1991), DeShon (in press), Singer and Willett (2003), and Ployhart and Vandenberg (2010) discuss these and other forms of nonlinear growth model. Even more powerful approaches to model nonlinear relationships are provided in the chapter by Guastello (this volume). We believe the catastrophe approach to modeling nonlinear data is a fascinating one, and perhaps those who study growth models can extend their reach to adopt catastrophe models and develop much richer portrayals of dynamic longitudinal data.

Between Groups Change Models

Growth models obviously allow variation among observations over time, but the models we have discussed do not consider whether there are different groups of people who have similar trends over time. That is, given variability in growth curves, are there subgroups that exhibit more similar curves than different subgroups? For example, is it possible that different demographic groups manifest different performance trajectories over time because of subgroup differences in cognitive ability? There are two main ways that such subgroups might be examined.

The first approach is to use multiple-group LGM (MGLGM). When there are existing, easily identifiable subgroups, and only a few subgroups, MGLGM is an effective means to test whether the change process is identical across subgroups. For example, if one had a sample of white, black, Hispanic, and Asian workers, one could fit different growth models (with or without predictors), and determine whether the type of change, variability in change, and predictors of change were identical across groups. MGLGMs are a simple extension of the single-group LGM.

The second approach is to use latent class analysis (LCA) or, more broadly, mixture models. In this framework, the number and nature of the subgroups are not known, and so the model estimates different numbers of subgroups that exhibit similar curves. Continuing our example, if cognitive ability drives performance change, then Asians may have a stronger linear performance trend than whites, who in turn have a stronger trend than Hispanics and blacks. However, it may also be possible that all subgroups ultimately reach similar levels of performance after a period of time on the job (as is typically the case, subgroup performance differences are smaller than subgroup predictor differences).

Both MGLGM and LCA could offer a nuanced approach for understanding change, potentially leading to important refinements to theory. However, the challenge with both is to ensure the subgroups are reasonable and there is good theory to identify subgroup differences a priori. This is particularly a concern with LCA, because the nature and number of subgroups are not known in advance, and so must be estimated from the data.

CAVEATS

A few caveats are in order before we conclude. First, we have scarcely addressed the issue of correlated residuals within growth models. This neglect is intentional, because it is not critical to the points we want to emphasize in this chapter, and discussions exploring different error structures are already available. However, readers should understand that appropriately modeling the error structure (e.g., degree and structure of intercorrelations among residuals) is important for accurate effect-size testing. Second, we did not directly deal with issues of reliability, statistical power, missing data, or sample size. These are vitally important topics in longitudinal modeling. Attrition always occurs with real-world data, we frequently have fewer measurement occasions than we hoped, and the reliability of our measures may be adequate but not desirable. As with cross-sectional research, these factors lead to the underestimation of effect sizes and confusing patterns of findings. Finally, we have avoided an in-depth discussion of how to code time in different ways, and the consequences of different time codings. Because growth or change is dependent upon how time is coded, it is paramount that researchers choose the appropriate coding scheme for their questions and data. For discussions of these various issues, see Biesanz et al. (2004), Bliese and Ployhart (2002), Littell et al. (1996), Ployhart and Vandenberg (2010), and Singer and Willett (2003).

A CALL FOR ACTION

Longitudinal growth models have been around a long time, but have only become popular in the social sciences in the last 20 years. Although it is encouraging that more scholars are examining longitudinal questions and adopting growth models, the vast majority of this research has only used the basic growth model. There are many extensions and variations to the basic growth model that can be used to test more complex theories of change. Examples of such extensions include mediated growth models, growth models using time-varying predictors, and discontinuous growth models. In this chapter, we have presented a variety of such models, using random coefficient modeling and LGM to illustrate how future research can provide more sophisticated tests of theory. It is our hope that researchers will adopt more sophisticated growth-modeling approaches, with the broader goal of improving our theoretical understanding of how and why phenomena change over time.

NOTES

1. Let us emphasize up front that the limits we discuss with the basic growth model are limits only in terms of how researchers have applied the model; they are not limits of the model itself.
2. Interestingly, this is less of a concern with the basic growth model when the predictor is measured prior to the dependent variable, compared with a model where a time-varying predictor and an outcome are measured at the same times.

REFERENCES

Biesanz, J. C., Deeb-Sossa, N., Papadakis, A. A., Bollen, K. A., & Curran, P. J. (2004). The role of coding time in estimating and interpreting growth curve models. *Psychological Methods, 9*, 30–52.

Bliese, P. D. (2002). Using multilevel random coefficient modeling in organizational research. In F. Drasgow & N. Schmitt (Eds.), *Advances in measurement and data analysis* (pp. 401–445). San Francisco, CA: Jossey-Bass.

Bliese, P. D., & Ployhart, R. E. (2002). Growth modeling using random coefficient models: Model building, testing, and illustration. *Organizational Research Methods, 5*, 362–387.

Bollen, K. A., & Curran, P. J. (2004). Autoregressive latent trajectory (ALT) models: A synthesis of two traditions. *Sociological Methods & Research, 32*, 336–383.

Bollen, K. A., & Curran, P. J. (2006). *Latent curve models: A structural equation perspective*. Hoboken, NJ: John Wiley & Sons.

Bryk, A. S., & Raudenbush, S. W. (1987). Application of hierarchical linear models to assessing change.*Psychological Bulletin, 101*, 147–158.

Burchinal, M., & Appelbaum, M. I. (1991). Estimating individual developmental functions: Methods and their assumptions. *Child Development, 62*, 23–43.

Chan, D. (1998). The conceptualization and analysis of change over time: An integrative approach incorporating longitudinal mean and covariance structures analysis (LMACS) and multiple indicator latent growth modeling (MLGM). *Organizational Research Methods, 1*, 421–483.

Chan, D., & Schmitt, N. (2000). Interindividual differences in intraindividual changes in proactivity during organizational entry: A latent growth modeling approach to understanding newcomer adaption. *Journal of Applied Psychology, 85*, 190–210.

Chen, G., Ployhart, R. E., Cooper-Thomas, H. D., Anderson, N., & Bliese, P. D. (2011). The power of momentum: A new model of dynamic relationships between job satisfaction change and turnover intentions. *Academy of Management Journal, 54*, 159–181.

DeShon, R. P. (1998). A cautionary note on measurement error corrections in structural equation models. *Psychological Methods, 3*, 412–423.

DeShon, R. P. (in press). Multivariate dynamics in organizational systems. In S. W. J. Kozlowski (Ed.), *Handbook of industrial and organizational psychology*. New York: Oxford University Press.

George, J. M., & Jones, G. R. (2000). The role of time in theory and theory building. *Journal of Management, 26*, 657–684.

Gollob, H. F., & Reichardt, C. S. (1987). Taking account of time lags in causal models. *Child Development, 58*, 80–92.

Gollob, H. F., & Reichardt, C. S. (1991). Interpreting and estimating indirect effects assuming time lags really matter. In L. M. Collins & J. L. Horn (Eds.), *Best methods for the analysis of change: Recent advances, unanswered questions, future directions* (pp. 243–259). Washington, DC: American Psychological Association.

Hofmann, D. A. (1997). An overview of the logic and rationale of hierarchical linear models. *Journal of Management, 23*, 723–744.

Hofmann, D. A., Jacobs, R., & Baratta, J. E. (1993). Dynamic criteria and the measurement of change. *Journal of Applied Psychology, 78*, 194–204.

James, L. R., Mulaik, S. A., & Brett, J. M. (2006). A tale of two methods. *Organizational Research Methods, 9*, 233–244.

Jensen, A. R. (1998). *The g factor*. Westport, CN: Praeger.

Kanfer, R., & Ackerman, P. L. (2004). Aging, adult development, and work motivation. *Academy of Management Review, 29*, 440–458.

Keil, C. T., & Cortina, J. M. (2001). Degradation of validity over time: A test and extension of Ackerman's model. *Psychological Bulletin, 127*, 673–697.

Kozlowski, S. W., & Klein, K. J. (2000). A multilevel approach to theory and research in organizations: Contextual, temporal, and emergent processes. In K. J. Klein & S. W. J. Kozlowski (Eds.), *Multilevel theory, research, and methods in organizations: Foundations, extensions, and new directions* (pp. 3–90). San Francisco, CA: Jossey-Bass.

Littell, R. C., Milliken, G. A., Stroup, W. W., & Wolfinger, R. D. (1996). *SAS system for mixed models*. Cary, NC: SAS Institute.

Marks, M. A., Mathieu, J. E., & Zaccaro, S. J. (2001). A temporally based framework and taxonomy of team processes. *Academy of Management Review, 26*, 356–376.

Maxwell, S. E., & Cole, D. A. (2007). Bias in cross-sectional analyses of longitudinal mediation. *Psychological Methods, 12*, 23–44.

McArdle J. J., & Epstein, D. (1987). Latent growth curves within developmental structural equation models. *Child Development, 58*, 110–133.

Meredith, W., & Tisak, J. (1990). Latent curve analysis. *Psychometrika, 55*, 107–122.

Mitchell, T. R., & James, L. R. (2001). Building better theory: Time and the specification of when things happen. *Academy of Management Review, 26*, 530–547.

Murphy, K. R. (1989). Is the relationship between cognitive ability and job performance stable over time? *Human Performance, 2*, 183–200.

Pitariu, A. H., & Ployhart, R. E. (2010). Explaining change: Theorizing and testing dynamic mediated longitudinal relationships. *Journal of Management, 36*, 405–429.

Ployhart, R. E., & Hakel, M. D. (1998). The substantive nature of performance variability: Predicting interindividual differences in intraindividual performance. *Personnel Psychology, 51*, 859–901.

Ployhart, R. E., Holtz, B. C., & Bliese, P. D. (2002). Longitudinal data analysis: Applications of random coefficient modeling to leadership research. *Leadership Quarterly, 13*, 455–486.

Ployhart, R. E., Van Iddekinge, C., & MacKenzie, W. (2011). Acquiring and developing human capital in service contexts: The interconnectedness of human capital resources. *Academy of Management Journal, 54*, 353–368.

Ployhart, R. E., & Vandenberg, R. J. (2010). Longitudinal research: The theory, design, and analysis of change. *Journal of Management, 36*, 94–120.

Ployhart, R. E., Weekley, J. A., & Ramsey, J. (2009). The consequences of human resource stocks and flows: A longitudinal examination of unit service orientation and unit effectiveness. *Academy of Management Journal, 52*, 996–1015.

Rao, C. R. (1958). Some statistical methods for comparison of growth curves. *Biometrics, 14*, 1–17.

Raudenbush, S. W., & Bryk, A. S. (2002). *Hierarchical linear models: Applications and data analysis methods.* Thousand Oaks, CA: Sage.

Roe, R. A. (2008). Time in applied psychology: The study of "what happens" rather than "what is." *European Psychologist, 13*, 37–52.

Rogosa, D. R. (1995). Myths and methods: "Myths about longitudinal research" plus supplemental questions. In J. M. Gottman (Ed.), *The Analysis of Change* (pp. 3–66). Mahwah, NJ: Lawrence Erlbaum Associates.

Simon, H. A. (1973). The organization of complex systems. In H. H. Pattee (Ed.), *Hierarchy theory* (pp. 1–27). New York: Braziller.

Singer, J. D., & Willett, J. B. (2003). *Applied longitudinal data analysis.* New York: Oxford University Press.

Tisak, J., & Meredith, W. (1990). Descriptive and associated developmental models. In A. von Eye (Ed.), *Statistical methods in longitudinal research* (Vol. 2, pp. 387–406). San Diego, CA: Academic Press.

Tucker, L. R. (1958). Determination of parameters of a functional relation by factor analysis. *Psychometrika, 23*, 19–23.

Vancouver, J. B., Thompson, C. M., & Williams, A. A. (2001). The changing signs in the relationships between self-efficacy, personal goals, and performance. *Journal of Applied Psychology, 86*, 605–620.

Vandenberg, R. J. (2002). Toward improving measurement invariance methods and procedures. *Organizational Research Methods, 5,* 139–158.

Zyphur, M. J., Chaturvedi, S., & Arvey, R. D. (2008). Job performance over time is a function of latent trajectories and previous performance, *Journal of Applied Psychology, 93,* 217–224.

4

Harnessing the Power of Social Network Analysis to Explain Organizational Phenomena

Yuval Kalish

The past decade has witnessed an increased call for incorporating context into the study of organizations in an attempt to fill the micro–macro gap in organizational scholarship . For example, Kilduff and Tsai (2003, p. 3) argue that the field of organizational behavior, and specifically, organizational decision-making, portrays individual actors making decisions "in splendid isolation of the force-field of influences that surround them." Rousseau and Fried (2001, p. 1; *italics added*) argue that, to make our models more accurate, scholars of organizational phenomena should link their observations "to a set of relevant facts, events or *point of view*."

Bamberger (2008) recently noted, with some satisfaction, that contextual influences are now more often incorporated into organizational research through the use of hierarchical linear models (HLM; Raudenbush, Bryk, & Congdon, 2005). HLM, a regression technique that separates group-level and individual-level variance, allows for an examination of contextual (group-level) effects and their relationship to individual-level effects. However, HLM analyses suggest that top–down effects (e.g., from teams to individuals) are generally more powerful than bottom–up effects (i.e., from individuals to teams; Kozlowski & Klein, 2000). Yet, the theoretical arguments often used to explain various phenomena such as emotional convergence (Kelly & Barsade, 2001), crossover of stress (e.g., Bakker, Westman, & van Emmerick, 2009), and leadership emergence (e.g., Lord & Maher, 1991) often start at the individual level and build up to the group level—a bottom–up approach. Second, HLM posits the formal team as a unit of analysis. Yet we know that formal and informal team structures often do not concur, and that informal team structure—for example, the pattern of friendship ties between individuals—has a greater impact on outcomes compared with formal structures (e.g., Krackhardt & Hanson, 1993). Although analysis at the (formal) team level provides useful information, the analysis of informal team structure may provide researchers with more relevant contextual information, particularly as different subgroups (cliques) of individuals may be differently influenced by context. Third, the assumption of independence of observations underlying traditional ordinary least squares (OLS) (and somewhat relaxed in HLM) regressions is often not met when examining teams, yielding incorrect results (Krackhardt, 1987).

In the current chapter, I introduce social network analysis (SNA) and argue that it is a fruitful way of incorporating social influences into organizational studies. SNA assumes that actors are interdependent, it gives precedence to bottom–up processes, and it accounts for informal team structure (Wasserman & Faust, 1994; Kilduff, Tsai, & Hanke, 2006). It therefore allows the research to "capture the interactions of any individual unit within a larger field of activity to which that unit belongs" (Kilduff & Tsai, 2003, p. 13), incorporating an individual's immediate context into data analysis. In fact, with recent developments in SNA, we now have models that provide us with direct tests of different, often competing, social processes that may give rise to network structure and outcomes (Monge & Contractor, 2003; Robins, Pattison, Kalish, & Lusher, 2007). These models greatly expand on the results that can be obtained from HLM (or OLS) regression analyses.

The chapter is structured as follows. I first introduce SNA and work through some key definitions. Next, I examine some techniques often used in SNA and introduce exponential random graph (ERG) models, a recent development in SNA that holds great promise for modeling networks (Snijders, Pattison, Robins, & Handcock, 2006). I then provide a small example of an ERG model of leadership emergence and compare it with more traditional network analytic methods. I close with a brief discussion of extensions to the ERG models.

WHAT ARE SOCIAL NETWORKS?

A social network is defined as "a finite set or sets of actors and the relation or relations defined on them" (Wasserman & Faust, 1994, p. 20). Thus, *actors* are often individuals, and the *relations* between them can range from formal reporting lines, to physical distance and email exchanges, to more subjective relationships, such as friendship, advice, conflict, and emotional or instrumental support. Actors are considered to have *attributes*, which can be stable or changing characteristics (e.g., intelligence, turnover intention, performance indicators, traits, states, and demographic variables). Traditional OLS regressions examine the relationship between attributes (e.g., whether demographic variables are related to turnover; Morrell, Loan-Clarke, & Wilkinson, 2001). The network approach, in comparison, examines whether relationships are related to dependent variables (e.g., is centrality in the friendship network related to turnover?) or links attributes to other attributes through relationships (e.g., are demographic variables related to turnover through centrality in the friendship network?; see Feeley, Hwang, & Barnett, 2008). Thus, the network approach both incorporates and expands on the more traditional statistical approach, yielding a more comprehensive and statistically sound story.

The organizational-network perspective has a long history: seminal studies of social behavior utilized network ideas. Moreno (1934) and Lewin (1943) used network approaches to predict turnover and attitudes toward change, respectively. The Hawthorne studies (Roethlisberger & Dickson, 1939) examined how different relations were related to performance and to the development of group norms. The Robbers' cave experiment (Sherif, Harvey, White, Hood, & Sherif, 1961) and Whyte's (1941) "corner boys" studies utilized network insights to explain identity, norm, and leadership emergence. Newcomb's (1961) study on the development of friendship in a fraternity highlighted how friendship relates to attitudes (see Borgatti & Foster, 2003, for a review and typology of more recent research). Theoretically, these and other network studies were often based on three major social–psychological theories: balance theory (Heider, 1946), social comparison theory (Festinger, 1954), and theories of homophily (McPherson, Smith-Lovin, & Cook, 2001; for a review of the theoretical underpinnings of the network approach, see Kilduff & Tsai, 2003, Chapter 3).

What make the network approach a unique research paradigm are four interrelated principles: the importance of relations, actors' embeddeness in the social field, the social utility of network connections, and the structural patterning of social life (Kilduff et al., 2006). The network paradigm assumes that relations are important for individual and group outcomes. Thus, for example, the network approach can be utilized to examine questions relating to leadership, emotional contagion, identity, and attitudes (for a list of references on network studies in organizational contexts, see Dan Brass's homepage).[1] The second core idea of network analysis is that actors are embedded in the social world through different types of relationship, and that this embedding (at least partly) shapes actors' behavior and attitudes, ultimately leading to outcomes (Granovetter, 1985; Uzzi, 1997). Thus, for example, peoples' perceptions of "who has power" in the organization are embedded in their friendship and advice networks (Krackhardt, 1990). The third and fourth core ideas of SNA are that actors' relations are a form of social capital, and that the structure of relationships provides actors with opportunities and constraints, leading to increased power, innovation, reputation (Burt, 2005), control over misbehavior (Krackhardt, 1999), and norms and identity (e.g., Kalish & Robins, 2006; Kalish, 2008).

WHAT ARE NETWORK DATA?

Network data differ from more "traditional" data in that they consist of at least one relationship between actors. Data are depicted in a matrix, whereby rows and columns represent actors, and the cell (i, j) depicts the existence of a relationship between actors i and j. Relationships can be binary (for example, 1 "is a friend of" or 0 "is not a friend of") or valued (for example, 1–5, representing "level of support given"). Matrices are called adjacency matrices (or "one-mode networks") when rows and columns represent a similar set of actors, and affiliation matrices (or "two-mode networks") when rows and columns represent different sets of actors (for example, rows represent people, and columns represent participation in organizational events). Appendix A presents a binary adjacency matrix of leadership nominations in a group of 12 recruits, and it contains the data that will be used throughout this chapter.

Once network data are collected, researchers can utilize different techniques for analyzing them (see Wasserman & Faust, 1994, for a comprehensive list of techniques). Basically, there are three ways of analyzing network data. The first is to derive network statistics for each actor (for example, an actor's centrality score in the network), and utilize this score as a variable in traditional statistical analyses. This approach has been shown to yield incorrect standard errors, because the assumption of independence of observations is not met (Krackhardt, 1987). A second, more appropriate statistical technique is to use quadratic assignment procedures (QAP) to correlate networks, or multiple regression quadratic assignment procedures (MRQAPs) to regress networks onto each other.[2] The third technique, which will be the focus of this chapter, is ERG models.

EXPONENTIAL RANDOM GRAPH MODELS

ERG models are a relatively new network methodology and are considered be the most promising method for modeling networks (Snijders et al., 2006). The methodology differs significantly from most other network techniques in three important ways (Robins et al., 2007). First, ERG models yield statistical (as opposed to descriptive) results regarding network properties and actor attributes; second, these properties are assumed to reflect underlying forces that drive the formation of networks (and/or attributes); third, these models enable researchers to understand how underlying social processes combine to form global patterns, therefore assisting in bridging the micro–macro gap in organizational research. As a result, these models can be used to test hypotheses that relate to social processes, providing a robust test of competing theories that relate to macro processes and their emergence (Monge & Contractor, 2003).

There are two main classes of ERG model: social selection models (Robins, Elliott, & Pattison, 2001) and social influence models (Robins, Pattison, & Elliott, 2001). Although they share a similar logic, described below, the main difference between them is in what they are trying to explain. Social selection models assume that actor attributes precede network relationships, whereas social influence models assume that network relationships precede actor attributes. Thus, in social selection models, we are trying to explain the development of relationships based on the characteristics of actors (for example, who emerges as a leader in a group, and how leadership emergence is related to intelligence). In social influence models, we are trying to explain actor attributes based on network relationships (for example, how an actor's perceived stress is related to his/her relationships). In many instances, social influence models seem more appropriate to organizational research questions; however, their analysis is more complex. Therefore, the focus of the current chapter will be social selection models.

The underlying idea of social selection ERG modeling is simple. It assumes that the pattern of ties in the *observed network*, the network the researcher has collected, is explained by the prevalence of overlapping *network configurations* and *actor attributes* (for a nontechnical introduction, see Robins et al., 2007). These network configurations can be very simple (e.g., a relationship between two actors, an *edge*), or more complex (e.g., three edges between three actors, a *triangle*; or two edges between three actors, a *2-star*; see Appendix B). "Overlapping" means that configurations can be embedded within each other. Thus, for example, one triangle in the network is also counted as three edges and as three 2-stars.

The logic behind ERG models is to examine whether the observed network has more or fewer of each of these configurations, compared with networks that are generated randomly. If, for example, the observed network has more "triangle" configurations than would be expected by chance (conditional on all other configurations), we can deduce that there is a force driving actors to form "triangle" structures in this network—for example, there are pressures towards balance (e.g., to become friends with friends' friends) in the network. For example, if a positive and significant "triangle" structure emerges in the network of a minority in an organization, we can deduce that pressures towards in-group selection are operating (e.g., Mehra, Kilduff, & Brass, 1998).

Each configuration in the model has an associated parameter (and standard error). These parameters are similar to parameters in regression, in that each parameter describes the net effect of a configuration controlling for all other parameters in the model. As with any statistical test, a given parameter is statistically significant if it is twice (actually, 1.96 times) the size of its standard error. A positive (negative) parameter estimate indicates that, controlling for all other configurations in the model (e.g., the number of edges), a configuration (e.g., number of triangles) is more (less) frequent than would be expected by chance.

Fitting a model to an observed network involves three steps. The first step involves estimation, the second involves simulation, and the third involves testing for goodness of fit of the observed and simulated networks. The process of estimation starts with the observed network, which is assumed to be just one possible realization from a large population of networks on the same number of actors. Thus, for example, the network in Figure 4.1 (the observed network) is considered to be one instance of a large sample-space of networks, all of which have 12 actors (and similar actor attributes). The first step in estimation involves measuring (counting) the numbers of each configuration in the network. These counts are called *graph statistics*. For example, in the observed network (Appendix A and Figure 4.1), there are six mutual arcs (lines in which both sender and receiver chose each other). Note that graph statistics for higher-order configurations include lower-order configurations. Thus, for example, the mutual arc referring to the two-headed arrow between Actors 11 and 12

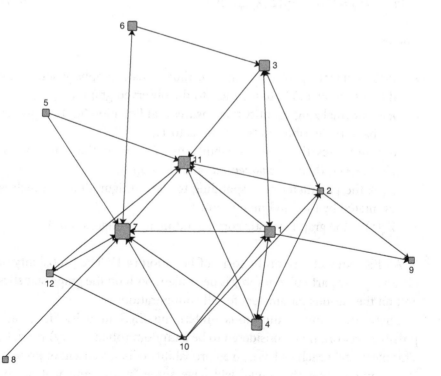

FIGURE 4.1

Observed network of leadership nominations between 12 recruits. Node size represents score on general intelligence (*g*).

in Figure 4.1 is counted three times: once as a mutual arc, and also as two separate arcs (an arc from 11 to 12, and an arc from 12 to 11). Note also that the "count" is blind to where in the graph the configuration occurs (i.e., it makes no difference whether the mutual arc is between Actors 11 and 12 or between Actors 4 and 1). This is called the homogeneity constraint (Robins et al., 2007) and is used to simplify the number of parameters in the model. Graph statistics are used to estimate parameter values for each configuration. The estimation of parameter values is based on simulating thousands of graphs based on parameter values, and comparing the simulated graph statistics with the graph statistics counted on the observed network (more on this below).

An understanding of the estimation of parameter values requires an understanding of the ERG model formula. ERG models have the following form:

$$\Pr(Y = y) = (1/\kappa) \exp\{\Sigma_A \lambda_A z_A(y)\} \tag{4.1}$$

where:

- $\Pr(Y = y)$ is the probability that the thousands of graphs generated by the ERG model (Y) are identical to the observed graph (y);
- κ is a normalizing quantity that ensures that Equation (4.1) is a proper probability distribution (i.e., it sums to 1);
- exp indicates that the probability of $(Y = y)$ is the exponent of $\{\Sigma_A \lambda_A z_A(y)\}$ (hence, *exponential* random graph);
- λ_A is the parameter corresponding to the configuration A, which is estimated by the ERG model; and
- $z_A(y)$ is the graph statistic corresponding to configuration A.

All ERG models are of the form of Equation (4.1). The probability of observing any particular graph y is dependent both on the graph statistics and on the various parameters for all configurations A.

There are some assumptions underlying ERG models. First, each possible network tie is considered to be a random (often binary) variable. This means that each tie has a given probability of being absent or present. It also means that the model will have some "noise" and will not be perfectly deterministic. The probability for each tie being present or absent is based on the dependence assumptions the researcher makes. Formally, the dependence assumption is represented by a dependence graph (Frank & Strauss, 1986) and implies the possible configurations in Equation (4.1), so that each configuration in the dependence graph is represented by a parameter in the model. Typical configurations used to estimate ERG models are shown in Appendixes B, C, and D (depending on the dependence assumption the researcher makes), together with their interpretation. Homogeneity constraints are then imposed to obtain a manageable number of parameters, which are then interpreted (for a more technical explanation, see Robins et al., 2007).

To clarify the processes described above, I will illustrate the ERG model through a (relatively simple) example that incorporates only six structural configurations: arc, mutual arc (reciprocity), in-2-star, out-2-star, mixed-2-star, and transitive triad. These are all part of the Markov dependence assumptions for directed networks, which assume that two ties are conditionally dependent on each other if they share an actor (Frank & Strauss, 1986; Table 4.1). Given Markov dependence assumptions and the selection of these six parameters, the ERG model in Equation (4.1) will have the following form:

$$Pr(Y = y) = (1/\kappa) \exp\{\theta L(y) + \rho M(y) + \sigma_{2i}S_{2i}(y) + \sigma_{2o}S_{2o}(y)$$

$$+ \sigma_{2m}S_{2m}(y) + \tau T(y)\} \tag{4.2}$$

where L is the count (graph statistic) for arcs (directed arrows) in graph y, M is the graph statistic for mutual arcs, s_{2i}, s_{2o} and s_{2m} are the graph statistics of in-, out- and mixed-2-stars, respectively, and T is the count of transitive triads in the observed graph. θ, ρ, s_{2i}, σ_{2o}, σ_{2m}, and τ represent the parameter estimates for the arcs, mutual arcs, in-2-star, out-2-star, mixed-2-star, and transitive triad configurations, respectively. These parameters model the number of ties, the level of reciprocity, whether some actors are popular in the network, whether some actors are expansive in their choices, whether there is a correlation between the incoming choices and outgoing choices of actors, and the level of transitivity in the network, respectively. The aim when attempting to generate an ERG model is to find the set of parameters (in this case, six parameters) that maximizes the probability that thousands of random graphs generated by simulating the model based on these parameter values will be identical (i.e., have similar graph statistics) to those of the observed network.

TABLE 4.1

(Markov) ERG Model Parameter Estimates for the Leadership Network, Their Interpretation, and Graph Statistics in the Observed Graph

	Graphical representation	Interpretation	Graph statistic (count)	Parameter estimate (SE in brackets)	t-statistic
Necessary controls					
Arcs		Baseline tendency to nominate leaders	32	-4.46* (1.13)	0.01
Out-2-stars		Tendency of actors to nominate multiple others as leaders, representing expansiveness in leadership nominations	40	0.40 (0.24)	0.02
Mixed-2-stars		Tendency for actors to be nominated and nominate others in return (control for the correlation between in-degree and out-degree distributions)	67	-0.18 (0.17)	0.01
Sender effect for g		Tendency for people higher on g to nominate more leaders	163.5	0.06 (0.13)	0.01
Direct hypotheses tests					
Receiver effect for g (H1)		Tendency for people high in g to receive more nominations	216.5	0.33** (0.17)	0.03
Dissimilarity effect for g (H2)		Tendency for people to choose dissimilar others on g as leaders	95	-0.02 (0.13)	0.05
Reciprocity (H3)		Tendency to reciprocate leadership choices given	6	1.87* (0.94)	0.03
In-2-stars (H4)		Tendency for two individuals to nominate a third as leader (popularity)	68	0.39* (0.17)	0.03
Transitive triads (H5)		Tendency to also directly nominate nominated leaders' leaders	25	-0.27 (0.23)	0.04

* $p < .05$; ** $p < .06$

Equation (4.1) is solved using Markov chain Monte Carlo maximum likelihood estimation (MCMCMLE; see Snijders, 2002, for a technical explanation). Basically, the procedure constantly refines the set of parameter estimates by comparing the graph statistics obtained from thousands of simulated graphs with those of the observed graph, until parameter estimates stabilize. The result of MCMCMLE estimation is a set of parameter estimates and standard errors. These values can be read like parameters in regression; thus, if a parameter estimate is positive (negative) and twice the size of its standard error, we can say that the specific configuration that the parameter estimates is observed more (less) often than expected by chance, given all other configurations in the model. We can then argue for an underlying social process that "generates" this tendency in the network (Robins et al., 2007). For example, if we find a positive and significant parameter estimate for mutual arcs (ρ), we could deduce that, given the number of arcs in the network (represented by the θ parameter), there is a force driving actors to reciprocate choices sent to them. If we also find a positive and significant parameter estimate for the in-2-star parameter (σ_{2i}), we would deduce that, given all other parameters in the model, some actors receive a disproportionately large number of incoming choices (i.e., there are hubs in the network).

Once parameter estimates are obtained, they are tested for adequacy. This is achieved through simulating graphs (typically 1,000) based on the parameter values obtained from the model, and comparing the simulated graphs with the observed graph through goodness of fit (GOF) statistics (for a technical introduction, see Goodreau, 2007). GOF statistics are based on comparing the mean and standard error of generated graph statistics in the 1,000 simulated graphs with those of the observed graph, using the following *t-statistic*:

$$t \text{ statistic}(A) = \frac{GS(A) - \overline{GS}(A)}{SE(A)} \tag{4.3}$$

where $GS(A)$ is the graph statistic for configuration A in the observed network, (A) is the mean graph statistic for configurations A obtained from 1,000 simulated graphs, and $SE(A)$ is the standard error obtained for the graph statistic of configuration A across 1,000 simulated graphs. It is important to note that the t-statistic defined in Equation (4.3) is *not* a test of the parameter value (whether there are more or fewer of a configuration than expected by chance), but rather a test of how well a configuration is reproduced by the simulated graphs, given the observed graph.

Adequate models should have very small t-statistics ($t < .1$) for the parameters that are in the model. This means that the simulated networks are very similar to the observed network in terms of the configurations directly modeled (i.e., they have similar graph statistics for all configurations A directly modeled). However, in order to argue that the model is a good fit to the data, we want to be certain that the model also captures *other* important characteristics of the observed graph, which may not have been directly modeled. For example, while the ERG model in Equation (4.2) only directly models six parameters (arcs, mutual arcs, in- out- and mixed-2-stars, and transitive triads), we want to be sure that the model captures, for example, the level of clustering in the network or the skewness of the distribution of incoming choices (in-degree distribution) in our observed network. Thus, GOF statistics are performed on 51 network configurations that are typically used to describe network characteristics (see Appendix A for these 51 configurations). A model is said to be a good "fit" to the observed network if, for all configurations directly modeled, t-statistics are smaller than $|.1|$, and, on all other configurations, t-statistics are smaller than $|2|$ (Goodreau, 2007).

Adding actor attributes to the model is important because we often want to test (at least, in social selection models) whether network relationships are formed because of attributes. For example, we may want to ask whether leaders get nominated because of their intelligence. As opposed to the structural parameters (e.g., arcs), attributes have more complicated graph statistics. Briefly, attribute values are summed across the network, to generate one graph statistic per attribute. Traditional attributes for directed networks include a sender effect (representing the tendency for a person high on an attribute to send more ties), a receiver effect (representing the tendency for a person high on an attribute to receive more ties), and a heterophily effect (representing the tendency for people to select others who are dissimilar to them on the attribute; see Appendix D).

New Specification Parameters for ERG Models

It is often the case (especially for large networks) that models do not converge. Such models are called degenerate and are indicated by t-statistics (Equation 4.3) that are very large, suggesting that it is impossible to get consistent parameter estimates across simulations. This could be the result of failure to model a significant effect in the data (for example, failing to model the fact that there are many isolates—unconnected individuals—in the observed network), or it could be the result of significant clustering (e.g., dense areas) and variability (e.g., a few hubs, people who are extremely well connected, and many others who are significantly less connected) in the data. In such cases, the simple Markov parameters fail to adequately capture the clustering or degree distribution.

A significant step forward in estimating and simulating ERG models to avoid degeneracy problems included new specifications for parameters (Snijders et al., 2006; Robins, Snijders, Wang, Handcock, & Pattison, 2007; Robins, Pattison, & Wang, 2009). These often yield more satisfactory results, but are less intuitive to interpret. They are all based on an expansion of Markov dependence assumptions (through an assumption called "partial conditional dependence"; Snijders, 2005), and they allow the modeling of denser regions in the network and more extreme degree distributions. Snijders et al. (2006) proposed three new parameters (alternating-k-triangle, alternating-k-stars, and alternating-k-2-paths), described below.

The alternating-k-star parameter is basically a weighted average of the 2-star, 3-star, k-star parameters that were part of the Markov dependence assumption. It therefore serves as an indicator of popularity, the tendency for actors to have multiple partners. It can be shown that the alternating-k-star parameter is related to the degree distribution, so that a positive alternating-k-star parameter indicates that the degree distribution is positively skewed—there are hubs in the network, whereas a negative alternating-k-star parameter indicates that the degree distribution is "flat"—the network is decentralized. The mathematical formula for the alternating-k-star parameter is:

$$s = \sum_{k=2}(-1)^k \frac{s_k}{\lambda^{k-2}} \tag{4.4}$$

where s is the graph statistic for the alternating-k-star configuration, k is the order of the star configuration (for 2-star, $k = 2$; for 3-star, $k = 3$, etc.), $(-1)^k$ gives negative weighting to odd-number star-configurations and positive weighting to even-number star-configurations (hence, "alternating"), (s_k) is the graph statistic for the star configuration of order k, and (λ^{k-2}) is a constant (typically, $k = 2$). Because λ^{k-2} is the denominator in Equation 4.4, higher-order stars have a lower impact on the graph statistic *s*.

The alternating-k-triangle parameter follows a similar logic. It is a combination of *k* individual triangles that share one edge (share a common base). A 1-triangle is similar to the triangle configuration in Markov dependence assumptions; a 2-triangle indicates that the same dyad is connected to two different actors, etc. The alternating-k-triangle parameter measures the extent to which triangles cluster together. In the presence of all other parameters, a positive alternating-k-triangle parameter indicates a core–periphery structure, in which the core consists of a large "clump" of triangles (as opposed to a few hubs, in which case the alternating-k-star parameter is positive). The mathematical formula for the alternating-k-triangle parameter is:

$$v = \sum_{k=2}(-1)^k \frac{T_k}{\lambda^{k-2}} \qquad (4.5)$$

where T_k is the graph statistic (the count) of k-triangles in a graph.

The alternating-k-2-paths parameter is a lower-order configuration for the alternating-k-triangle parameter. It represents the number of distinct 2-paths between two actors, and can be thought of as the number of k-triangles without the base (Equation 4.6). The exact interpretation of this parameter is still being investigated; however, for some data, its inclusion is important to obtain good convergence. We do know, however, that, together with the alternating-k-triangle parameter, the alternating-k-2-paths parameter indicates whether the pressures toward clustering in a network result from the base (in which case the alternating-k-triangle parameter is positive and significant) or from the addition of edges to the sides of the triangle (in which case the alternating-2-paths parameter becomes significant). The mathematical formula for the alternating-k-2-path parameter is:

$$u = \sum_{k=2}(-1)^k \frac{u_k}{\lambda^{k-2}} \qquad (4.6)$$

where u_k is the graph statistic (the count) of k-2-paths in a graph.

A final parameter that is often important for inclusion in estimation of ERG models is the *isolates parameter*. The isolate parameter counts the number of actors who have 0 degrees and are, therefore, not connected to anyone in the network. The isolates parameter is basically modeled by the same formula as the alternating-k-star parameter (Equation 4.4), when $k = 1$. For some network data for which there are many isolates, the inclusion of this parameter is important to avoid model degeneracy problems (Snijders et al., 2006).

Basic configurations for new specifications are presented in Appendix C, along with their interpretation. The interested reader is strongly encouraged to examine Snijders' and Robins' work (Snijders et al., 2006; Robins et al., 2007; Robins et al., 2009).

Recently, the nondirected new specifications have been expanded to model directed networks (Robins et al., 2009). These are not discussed in the current paper. I note, however, that the alternating-k-star parameter is "broken down" into alternating-k-in-star (indicating popularity), alternating-k-out-star (indicating activity, the tendency for some individuals to choose many others), and alternating-k-mixed-star (the tendency for some individuals to receive many choices while sending many choices; in effect, this parameter controls for the correlation between the in- and out-degree distributions, which is often a problem for modeling networks). It is also possible to model sources, sinks, and isolates (actors who only choose others, actors who only receive choices, and actors who neither receive nor choose others, respectively). Appendix D provides a summary of these new specification parameters, which may be useful for the modeling of directed networks, together with their interpretation. The interested reader is strongly encouraged to read Robins et al., 2009.

AN EMPIRICAL EXAMPLE: WHAT SOCIAL PROCESSES GIVE RISE TO EMERGENT LEADERSHIP?

Traditional leadership research has tended to focus on the traits and behaviors of formal, appointed leaders. As a result, relatively little is known about the distribution of leadership potential within a group, or about the emergence of informal leadership (Kickul & Neuman, 2000). Emergent leaders, people who exert significant influence over other members of their group despite having no formal authority (Goktepe & Schneier, 1989), have recently received increasing research attention (Neubert & Taggar, 2004).

Research on emergent leadership branched into two separate streams. The first, more developed stream focused on traits and behaviors that cause leaders to emerge; the second focused on the social topology (social structure) of emergent leadership. The following example illustrates how ERG models can be used to simultaneously answer both questions and provides a more complete (and somewhat surprising) description of the processes that give rise to emergent leadership, thus integrating previously contradictory research results.

Recall that ERG models for social selection are used to answer questions about forces that create the networks. Research suggests that people choose as emergent leaders individuals who fit their leadership prototype (Implicit Leadership Theory (ILT); Lord & Maher, 1991). As general cognitive ability (g) is part of the universally held leadership prototype (den Hartog et al., 1999), ILT theory would suggest that people who have greater g will receive more leadership nominations.

Hypothesis 1: People with greater g will be selected as leaders more frequently than those with lesser g

Because leadership research has tended to focus on the traits associated with leaders, less is known about how leader traits interact with follower traits. We know from theories of homophily that people tend to choose similar others (McPherson et al., 2001). Leader–member exchange (LMX) suggests that high-quality LMX is associated with similarity on attributes (for a review, see Graen & Uhl-Bien, 1995). If these theories are correct:

Hypothesis 2a: People with similar levels of g will select each other as leaders

Alternatively, theories of charismatic leadership suggest that people may select dissimilar others as leaders (for a review, see House & Aditya, 1997). Similarly, social comparison theory (Festinger, 1954) suggests that people select others who are higher on an attribute for comparison. Based on these theories, the competing hypothesis is, therefore:

Hypothesis 2b: People with lower g will select people with higher g as leaders

A third, well-documented force driving leadership nominations may be the tendency to reciprocate leadership choices (Mehra, Smith, Dixon, &

Robertson, 2006). There could be many reasons why leaders select each other. It may be the case that each emergent leader is an expert in a different field, and all of them are necessary for successful team performance (e.g., Howell & Boies, 2004); that they divide the labor between themselves (see Gronn, 2002, for a complete discussion); or that one is responsible for emotional and the other for task-related components of team performance (Pescosolido, 2001). Thus, the existence of several leaders may be beneficial for each of them, and therefore they may acknowledge and support each other.

Hypothesis 3: The emergent leadership network will exhibit reciprocation
However, there is an overall consensus that leadership is hierarchical. Evidence suggests that only a very small proportion of group members emerge as leaders at any point in time (Krackhardt, 1994; Guastello, 2007). These ideas resonate with Whyte's (1941, p. 656) observation that, "the social structures vary from group to group, but each one may be represented in some form of hierarchy."

Hypothesis 4: The emergent leadership network will exhibit a hierarchical structure such that a few individuals will be selected by many others
Festinger's (1954) social comparison theory suggests that people compare themselves on relevant attributes with people who are higher on those attributes. If these people are considered experts, their expert opinion (their leadership choices) should have greater weight and should, therefore, influence the focal individual. In other words, if individual B is judged by individual A as higher on leadership (i.e., individual A compares himself with individual B), and individual C is judged by individual B as higher on leadership (i.e., B compares himself with C), individual A should also nominate individual C as leader, because he views individual B's opinion as expert opinion: we expect to find transitivity (Luria and Kalish, forthcoming).

Hypothesis 5: The emergent leadership network will exhibit transitivity
Note that these driving forces for leadership emergence yield different network structures. Forces for reciprocity and similarity in g in leadership nominations will create a network with less hierarchy (a "shared-

leadership" network), whereas forces for dissimilarity in g, transitivity and hierarchy, will lead to a hierarchical network. ERG models test these hypotheses against each other within the one analysis.

Data for the current example were collected as part of a larger study (Kalish & Luria, 2013). For the purpose of this chapter, I examine one all-male team, consisting of 12 18-year-old recruits,[3] who were undergoing a 48-hour selection process to an elite military unit. Prior to entering the selection process, recruits were given IQ tests, with scores standardized on a 10-point scale. On the second day of the selection process, recruits were administered a network questionnaire, requesting them to nominate the people they viewed as leaders in the team. Recruits could write as many names as they wanted, but self-nominations as leader were not allowed (the ERG framework precludes self-nominations). Appendix A presents the matrix of leadership nominations in the team, as well as the actors' scores on intelligence tests.

The analysis will be performed twice. First, using "traditional" network approaches (i.e., deriving an individual network centrality score for each recruit, and correlating these scores with their scores on g), then by fitting a social selection ERG model to the data. The model that I fit is based on the (simpler) Markov assumptions for directed networks and is, overall, similar to the model in Equation (4.2). The only different between the model in Equation (4.2) and the current model is the inclusion of three attribute parameters: a sender effect (representing the tendency for people who are higher on g to select more others as leaders, used as a control), a receiver effect (representing the tendency for people who are higher on g to be selected more often as leaders, Hypothesis 1), and a dissimilarity effect (representing the tendency for people to select others who are dissimilar to them on g as leaders, Hypothesis 2). Hypothesis 3 is directly modeled by the reciprocation parameter, Hypothesis 4 is directly modeled by the in-2-star parameter, and Hypothesis 5 is directly modeled by the transitive-triad parameter.[4] All other parameters in the model serve as (structural and attribute-based) controls.

Analysis 1: For this analysis, I will focus on in-degree centrality (Freeman, 1978), one of the simplest measures that can be derived for an actor in a network. In-degree centrality is simply the number of nominations received from others. An actor's in-degree centrality is therefore a simple summation of all the scores he/she received from others— a summation of his/her column. For example, Actor 1 (Appendix A, column 1) has an in-degree centrality of three: he received nominations from Actors 4, 5, and 10 (fourth, fifth, and tenth rows, respectively). Using a program such as UCINet (Borgatti, Everett, & Freeman, 2002), we can calculate in-degree centralities for each actor (see Appendix A) and correlate these centrality measures with the actors' attributes. As these data are not normally distributed, a Spearman correlation was performed. The Spearman correlation for in-degree centrality and g was .62 ($p < .05$), providing support for Hypothesis 1. As stated earlier, it is important to note that this analysis may be inappropriate because it yields incorrect standard errors (Krackhardt, 1987).

Analysis 2: The social selection ERG model examines the underlying forces that drive the formation of the leadership network. The model starts with a count of the different configurations. For this analysis, I have chosen the standard (and easier to interpret) Markov configurations for directed networks, represented in Table 4.1. An examination of GOF statistics reveals that all t-statistics are less than the established 0.10 cutoff, suggesting that the simulated networks and the observed network concur on parameter values (i.e., the model is a good fit to the data). Further, all 51 parameters examined in the complete GOF analysis (Appendix A) have t-statistics less than the required 2, as recommended by Goodreau (2007). We can therefore conclude that our model captures the network well.

Hypothesis 1 suggested, based on implicit leadership theory, that leadership nominations will be positively related to g. Recall that results from Analysis 1 provided strong support for this hypothesis. In the current, more appropriate, analysis, the tendency for people who are high on g to receive more leadership nominations is captured by the receiver effect. The parameter for this effect was 0.33 (SE = 0.17, $p < .06$). Thus, controlling for all other effects (including structural effects and behavioral tendencies to nominate others based on g), results from the current analysis do not reach traditional standards for support of Hypothesis 1. For present purposes, the important message in these data is that the two analyses lead to different results and, therefore, different conclusions.

Hypothesis 2a suggested that people will choose others with similar cognitive ability as leaders, whereas Hypothesis 2b suggested that people with lower g would choose others with higher g as leaders (i.e., they will choose dissimilar others). The ERG model captures choosing similar or dissimilar others through the dissimilarity effect, which was nonsignificant (parameter = –0.02, SE = 0.13, ns). Therefore, there was no evidence for either Hypothesis 2a or 2b, and the jury is still out on whether social comparison or similarity on g drives leadership nominations.

Hypothesis 3 suggested that there will be reciprocity in leadership nominations. The positive, significant mutual arc parameter (parameter = 1.87, SE = 0.94, $p < .05$) captures this effect and provides support for this hypothesis.

Hypothesis 4 suggested that there will be hierarchy in the leadership network. This hypothesis is captured by the in-2-star ("popularity") effect, which was positive and significant (parameter = 0.39, SE = 0.17, $p < .05$) and provides support for Hypothesis 4.

Hypothesis 5 posited the existence of transitivity in leadership nominations. The hypothesis was not supported, with a nonsignificant transitive triad parameter (parameter = −0.27, SE = 0.23, ns).

To summarize, although Analysis 1 suggested that leadership nominations were clearly related to g, the more comprehensive Analysis 2, which controls for network structure and its relation to actor attributes, suggested that there were forces that drive the leadership network to exhibit both reciprocity and hierarchy at above-chance levels, but there was only a trend to suggest that people who are higher on g emerge as leaders more often. Thus, results from Analysis 1 differ from those of Analysis 2, leading to different conclusions regarding the relationship between leadership emergence and intelligence.

How do these competing forces play out in the leadership network? In interpreting these results as a whole, it is important to remember that parameter estimates obtained for each configuration represent net effects, given all other configurations in the model. As a whole, the analysis suggests that leadership exhibits reciprocation above what is expected by chance. Thus, there was evidence for the idea of shared leadership. However, above and beyond this effect, there are people who are popular (the positive and significant 2-in-star effect). Moreover, these individuals do not select each other (otherwise they would have been counted by the reciprocity graph statistic). This indicates that the structure of emergent leadership involves two tiers: on the lower tier, there is reciprocation in leadership nominations, but, on the top tier, there are individuals who are nominated by others and do not reciprocate leadership choices. The contradictory findings in the literature are therefore integrated, by suggesting that, at different levels of leadership, different phenomena occur.

Results also suggest a nearly significant effect for people who are higher on *g* to be nominated as leaders more often, but no effect for similarity (or dissimilarity) in *g*. This indicates that the two-tier structure of leadership defined above has, at the higher (top) tier, people with greater scores on a measure of *g*. The hubs of the leadership network (the emergent leaders) are the recruits with higher general cognitive ability who do not reciprocate leadership choices. At a lower level are people with lesser scores on a measure of intelligence, who reciprocate leadership nominations.

To summarize, results from Analysis 1 and those from the more comprehensive ERG model (Analysis 2) would lead researchers to different conclusions regarding the relationship between intelligence and leadership emergence. The ERG model is to be preferred, as it provides accurate standard errors, controls for more (structural and attribute-related) effects, and provides a more complete analysis of how micro-processes (leadership selection) lead to macro-structure (two-tier structure of leadership emergence). Further, interpreting the ERG model integrates previously contradictory results (e.g., is there hierarchy or reciprocity in emergent leadership, e.g., see Mehra et al., 2006, and Guastello, 2007, respectively) by suggesting that different social processes occur at different levels of the leadership hierarchy. The added value of ERG model fitting is, I believe, apparent in this example.

OTHER NETWORK MODELS

Two additional models worth mentioning are also likely to have relevance for organizational research (references are provided in Appendix F). The first is the extension of ERG models to multiple networks. These models have additional parameter estimates for the relationship, not only within, but also between, networks. They allow, for example, a statistical test of whether people seek work-related advice from their friends, and how individual attributes (e.g., seniority) influence this relationship (Lazega & Pattison, 1999). These models have been applied to interorganizational research questions (Lomi & Pattison, 2006; Rank, Robins, & Pattison, 2010), and they provide a valuable tool for innovative research.

The second model is well suited for evaluating the co-evolution of network ties and actor attributes (Snijders, 1996, 2001, 2005). It allows researchers to unpack network contagion (the idea that, over time, an individual's attributes become more similar to those of the people they have relationships with) from network selection (the idea that people select others who are similar to them, and then form a relationship with them), and is therefore extremely useful for the modeling of emotional convergence, crossover, attitudes and attitude change, etc.

CONCLUSIONS

As Krackhardt and Hanson (1993, p.104) wrote: "if the formal organization is the skeleton of a company, the informal is the central nervous system driving the collective thought processes, actions and reactions of its business units." SNA, and especially the developments in network modeling presented in this chapter, can greatly enhance understanding of organizational phenomena precisely because they allow for an examination of these informal processes. Further, if organizational researchers take Rousseau and Frieds' (2001) call to better integrate contextual influences into theories seriously, SNA will certainly prove to be an important analytic tool, because it assumes and directly tests such influences on the individual.

The benefits of network analysis are many. It provides a clearer conceptualization of constructs that are often used in organizational scholarship. Instead of giving participants questionnaires (thus enhancing single-source biases), the same constructs can be directly measured by using network questionnaires, eliminating single-source bias. For example, team cohesion can be directly operationalized by examining the density of a network: the denser the network, the more cohesive it is. The construct of "social support" can be directly measured by in-degree centrality of the network question "who do you give support to?". The job embeddeness construct (Mitchell, Holtom, Lee, Sablynski, & Erez, 2001) can be directly measured using the number of ties to people in the community and in the organization. Organizational power (especially referent and expert power) can be directly measured using the number of incoming friendship and advice ties, respectively (or more complex measures of power; see Wasserman & Faust, 1994). There are also unique research questions that the modeling of networks can greatly expand. As previously suggested, any studies that test forces underlying the formation of network relationships and their relationship to attributes will benefit from ERG models.

Although data collection and analysis are slightly more complex than in "traditional" analytic methods, the benefits of utilizing SNA approaches more than overcome the increased complexity. Moreover, the use of SNA approaches does not preclude the use of traditional data-analytic approaches. The researcher still collects individual attribute information and can always revert to running (less-than-optimal) techniques that assume independence of observation (e.g., regressions or ANOVAs). The hallmark of the SNA approach is that, by collecting relational data in addition to the attribute data, researchers can better unpack social context, team processes, and group dynamics, which may lead to a better formulation of theories that link micro- (individual) and macro- (team/group-level) processes through social networks.

APPENDIX A: DATA FOR THE ANALYSIS

Matrix of Leadership Nominations Between Recruits

```
0 0 1 1 0 0 1 0 1 0 1 0
0 0 1 1 0 0 0 0 1 0 1 0
1 1 0 0 0 0 1 0 0 0 1 0
1 1 0 0 0 0 1 0 0 0 1 0
0 0 0 0 0 0 1 0 0 0 1 0
0 0 1 0 0 0 1 0 0 0 0 0
0 0 0 0 0 1 0 0 0 0 0 0
0 0 0 0 0 0 1 0 0 0 0 0
0 0 0 0 0 0 0 0 0 0 0 0
1 1 0 0 0 0 1 0 0 0 1 0
0 0 0 0 0 0 1 0 0 0 0 1
0 0 0 0 0 0 1 0 0 1 1 0
```

Vector of *g*

6.5, 3, 6.5, 6.5, 4.5, 5.5, 9.5, 3.5, 3, 1, 7.5, 5

Analysis 1: In-Degree Centralities for Leadership Nominations (Number of 1s in Each Column)

3, 3, 3, 2, 0, 1, 8, 0, 2, 1, 6, 1

Analysis 2: GOF Statistics for the ERG

GOF statistics for the data (parameter name, graph statistics in the observed network, mean graph statistic in 1,000 simulated networks (with standard error) and t-statistic for GOF):

*   Arc: 32.0000 Mean = 31.8730 (5.1853) t = 0.0245
*   Reciprocity: 6.0000 Mean = 6.0080 (2.5488) t = −0.0031
*   2-in-star: 68.0000 Mean = 66.5220 (19.3186) t = 0.0765
*   2-out-star: 40.0000 Mean = 39.8470 (14.0690) t = 0.0109
\#   3-in-star: 122.0000 Mean = 112.8570 (52.5772) t = 0.1739
\#   3-out-star: 27.0000 Mean = 31.7580 (20.6965) t = −0.2299
*   Mixed-2-star: 67.0000 Mean = 66.8780 (25.1632) t = 0.0048
\#   T1: 0.0000 Mean = 0.1570 (0.4296) t = −0.3655
\#   T2: 0.0000 Mean = 2.8340 (3.5035) t = −0.8089
\#   T3: 2.0000 Mean = 6.0590 (5.4302) t = −0.7475
\#   T4: 0.0000 Mean = 5.1730 (4.0602) t = −1.2741
\#   T5: 7.0000 Mean = 4.2120 (3.2248) t = 0.8645
\#   T6: 4.0000 Mean = 7.1160 (6.1136) t = −0.5097
\#   T7: 28.0000 Mean = 38.7620 (20.5874) t = −0.5227
\#   T8: 30.0000 Mean = 28.1170 (16.7782) t = 0.1122
*   T9(030T): 25.0000 Mean = 24.1710 (12.1349) t = 0.0683
\#   T10(030C): 2.0000 Mean = 3.6630 (2.9020) t = −0.5730
\#   Sink: 1.0000 Mean = 0.4860 (0.7087) t = 0.7252
\#   Source: 2.0000 Mean = 2.3290 (1.3523) t = −0.2433
\#   Isolates: 0.0000 Mean = 0.0990 (0.3087) t = −0.3207
\#   K-in-star(2.00): 33.5391 Mean = 34.0190 (7.8009) t = −0.0615
\#   K-out-star(2.00): 28.6250 Mean = 27.6741 (7.7859) t = 0.1221
\#   K-in-star(2.00): 33.5391 Mean = 34.0190 (7.8009) t = −0.0615
\#   K-out-star(2.00): 28.6250 Mean = 27.6741 (7.7859) t = 0.1221
\#   K-1-star(2.00): 39.1953 Mean = 35.2197 (11.1760) t = 0.3557
\#   1-L-star(2.00): 42.3125 Mean = 41.7336 (12.4135) t = 0.0466
\#   K-L-star(2.00): 21.9609 Mean = 21.0848 (4.9769) t = 0.1760
\#   AKT-T(2.00): 19.2500 Mean = 19.2976 (8.5520) t = −0.0056
\#   AKT-C(2.00): 6.0000 Mean = 9.7236 (7.1518) t = −0.5206
\#   AKT-D(2.00): 15.7188 Mean = 17.5115 (7.5747) t = −0.2367
\#   AKT-U(2.00): 22.0000 Mean = 20.4627 (9.1648) t = 0.1677
\#   AKT-TD(2.00): 17.4844 Mean = 18.4046 (7.9782) t = −0.1153

\#   AKT-TU(2.00): 20.6250 Mean = 19.8801 (8.8042) t = 0.0846

\#   AKT-DU(2.00): 18.8594 Mean = 18.9871 (8.2460) t = −0.0155

\#   AKT-TDU(2.00): 18.9896 Mean = 19.0906 (8.3142) t = −0.0122

\#   A2P-T(2.00): 55.5000 Mean = 56.6568 (19.4361) t = −0.0595

\#   A2P-D(2.00): 26.2188 Mean = 29.6743 (9.6230) t = −0.3591

\#   A2P-U(2.00): 53.0000 Mean = 53.9996 (13.0347) t = −0.0767

\#   A2P-TD(2.00): 40.8594 Mean = 43.1655 (13.6261) t = −0.1692

\#   A2P-TU(2.00): 54.2500 Mean = 55.3282 (14.1326) t = −0.0763

\#   A2P-DU(2.00): 39.6094 Mean = 41.8370 (9.2644) t = −0.2404

\#   A2P-TDU(2.00): 44.9063 Mean = 46.7769 (11.7599) t = −0.1591

*   Sender for Attribute1: 163.5000 Mean = 162.9820 (28.1047) t = 0.0184

*   Receiver for Attribute1: 216.5000 Mean = 214.8820 (32.3984) t = 0.0499

\#   Single sum for Attribute1: 380.0000 Mean = 377.8640 (57.5878) t = 0.0371

*   Single difference for Attribute1: 95.0000 Mean = 94.4850 (16.8549) t = 0.0306

\#   Single product for Attribute1: 1104.7500 Mean = 1078.1488 (165.1056) t = 0.1611

\#   Mutual sum for Attribute1: 223.0000 Mean = 225.6690 (31.9296) t = -0.0836

\#   Mutual difference for Attribute1: 48.0000 Mean = 49.5890 (8.1730) t = −0.1944

\#   Mutual product for Attribute1: 679.7500 Mean = 697.9160 (101.0147) t = −0.1798

\#   Two-in-stars for Attribute1: 557.0000 Mean = 518.1560 (154.9375) t = 0.2507

\#   Two-out-stars for Attribute1: 199.5000 Mean = 204.7365 (74.8533) t = −0.0700

\#   Mixed-two-stars for Attribute1: 411.5000 Mean = 444.5825 (173.9432) t = −0.1902

\#   StdDev in-degree dist: 2.6247 Mean = 2.5109 (0.4445) t = 0.2561

\#   Skew in-degree dist: 1.3048 Mean = 1.0537 (0.5151) t = 0.4876

\#   StdDev out-degree dist: 1.4907 Mean = 1.3975 (0.3212) t = 0.2904

\#   Skew out-degree dist: −0.1733 Mean = 0.3508 (0.5626) t = −0.9315

\#   CorrCoef in-out-degree dists: −0.1349 Mean = −0.1582 (0.3484) t = 0.0668

\# Global clustering Cto: 0.3125 Mean = 0.2975 (0.0940) $t = 0.1596$
\# Global clustering Cti: 0.1838 Mean = 0.1755 (0.0564) $t = 0.1475$
\# Global Clustering Ctm: 0.3731 Mean = 0.3649 (0.1314) $t = 0.0627$
\# Global clustering Ccm: 0.0896 Mean = 0.1469 (0.0865) $t = -0.6625$
\# Global clustering AKC-T: 0.3468 Mean = 0.3464 (0.1185) $t = 0.0041$
\# Global clustering AKC-D: 0.2998 Mean = 0.2930 (0.0817) $t = 0.0822$
\# Global clustering AKC-U: 0.2075 Mean = 0.1842 (0.0568) $t = 0.4112$
\# Global clustering AKC-C: 0.1081 Mean = 0.1542 (0.0856)
  $t = -0.5385$

Note how all t-statistics for the parameters directly estimated are smaller than .1 in absolute value, and all t-statistics for the other parameters are smaller than 2 in absolute value. This indicates good fit for the model—our model, with its nine parameters (indicated with *), captures all other aspects of the observed network (indicated with #) well.

APPENDIX B

TABLE 4.B

Recommended Initial Parameters for the Modeling of Networks With Their Explanation: Markov Dependence Assumptions for Nondirected Graphs

Parameter name		Parameter meaning (and interpretation for a significant positive parameter estimate, in brackets)
Edge		Tendency to form relationships (the density of the network is higher than 0.5)
2-star		Tendency to form structural holes (some people are hubs in the network—they are more popular than expected by chance)
3-star		

TABLE 4.B *continued*

Recommended Initial Parameters for the Modeling of Networks With Their Explanation: Markov Dependence Assumptions for Nondirected Graphs

Parameter name	Parameter meaning (and interpretation for a significant positive parameter estimate, in brackets)
Triangle	Tendency to form cliques (pressures toward closure)
Isolates	Tendency for individuals to have no ties at all (there are people who are unconnected to anyone in the network)

Binary attributes

Popularity	Tendency for people with the attribute to have more ties (a person with the attribute has more ties)
Similarity	Tendency for people with the attribute to connect with each other (pressures toward homophily)

Continuous attributes

Sum	Tendency for people high on the attribute to have more ties
Difference	Tendency for people high in the attribute to have more ties with dissimilar others (pressures toward heterophily)

Categorical attribute

Same category	Tendency for people within the same category to have ties to each other (pressures toward homophily)

Note: The 3-star parameter has a similar interpretation to the 2-star parameter and is often included to assist in model convergence, especially when the network is hierarchical. The isolate parameter should only be incorporated into analyses if there are isolates in the data.

APPENDIX C

TABLE 4.C

Recommended Initial Parameters for the Modeling of Networks With Their Explanation: New Specifications Dependence Assumptions for Nondirected Graphs

Parameter name	Parameter meaning (and interpretation for a significant positive parameter estimate, in brackets)
Arc	Tendency to form relationships (the density of the network is higher than 0.5)
Alternating k-stars	Tendency for actors to have multiple partners (the degree distribution is positively skewed—there are hubs in the network)
Alternating k-triangles	Tendency to form cliques (pressures toward dense cliques in the network)
Alternating k-2-paths	Tendency to 2-paths, situations in which to people are unconnected to each other, but connected to multiple others
Isolates	Tendency for individuals to have no ties at all (there are people who are unconnected to anyone in the network)

Attributes are incorporated into the analysis similarly to Table 4.B.

Note: The interpretation of the alternating k-2-paths is usually made given the alternative k-triangle parameter. If an alternating k-triangle parameter is positive given the existence of an alternating 2-path parameter, this means that the formation of connections between multiple nodes is increased if they are connected directly to each other.

APPENDIX D

TABLE 4.D

Recommended Initial Parameters for the Modeling of Networks With Their Explanation: New Specifications Dependence Assumption Parameters for Directed Graphs

Parameter name		Parameter meaning (and interpretation for a significant positive parameter estimate, in brackets)
Arc		Tendency to form relationships (the density of the network is higher than 0.5)
Reciprocity		Tendency to form reciprocated ties (pressures toward reciprocity)
Isolates		Tendency for individuals to have no ties at all (there are people who are unconnected to anyone in the network)
k-in-stars		Tendency for actors to be nominated by multiple others (the in-degree distribution is positively skewed—there are hubs in the network)
k-out-stars		Tendency for actors to nominate multiple partners (the out-degree distribution is positively skewed—some people are expansive in their choices)
Alternating k-triangles-transitive		Tendency to form dense cliques based on transitivity cliques (pressures toward transitivity in the network)

TABLE 4.D *continued*

Recommended Initial Parameters for the Modeling of Networks With Their Explanation: New Specifications Dependence Assumption Parameters for Directed Graphs

Parameter name		Parameter meaning (and interpretation for a significant positive parameter estimate, in brackets)
Alternating k-2-paths-transitive		Tendency to form multiple, transitive 2-paths, situations in which people select multiple others, who select a third individual (interpretation in relation to the alternating k-triangle-transitive above)

(*Note*: The interpretation of the alternating k-two-paths is usually made given the alternative k-triangle, as described in Table 4.B.)

Attributes for directed networks

Sender effect		Tendency for people with the attribute to send more ties (people with the attribute are more expansive in their choices)
Receiver effect		Tendency for people with the attribute to receive more ties (people with the attribute are more popular)
Dissimilarity effect		Tendency for people to select others dissimilar to them on the attribute (heterophily)

APPENDIX E: STEPS FOR FITTING AN ERG MODEL TO SOCIAL NETWORK DATA USING PNET

The following brief tutorial (based on "Pnet for dummies," by Nick Harrigan) assumes you have already collected network and attribute data:

1. Prepare your data files:

   (a) Both files should be .txt (notepad) files, one file for the network data, the second file for the attribute data. Each row in both files represents the same actor. Columns represent other actors to whom the row actor sent a tie (in the network data file), or the value for the row actor on an attribute (in the attribute file). Entries in both files are separated by spaces, and cases (lines) are separated by carriage returns.

(b) Make sure the diagonal on your network file is 0 (Pnet has a curious tendency to crash if it is not).

(c) Place both files in the same folder.

2. Obtain graph statistics from your observed network. You will receive a count for all 51 available structural configurations. Pay attention to configurations with 0 (or very low, 1–2) frequencies. These should NOT be modeled, as they will cause the model to degenerate (more on this in Step 7).

3. Start by fitting an ERG model with Markov assumptions and the recommended initial configurations (presented in Table 4.1 for directed networks, or Appendix B for nondirected networks).

4. Run your estimation.

5. Examine your t-statistics:

(a) If all t-statistics are smaller than |.1|, you just hit the jackpot (unfortunately, this rarely happens on the first estimation). Continue to step 9.

(b) If all t-statistics are lower than |4| and some are lower than |2|, and the current t-statistics are better (i.e., smaller in absolute value) than the ones obtained from the previous estimation, use the parameters from the current estimation as the starting parameters for your next estimation (basically, this means that the program starts the next search for parameter estimates based on a model that is not entirely "off," and that you are heading toward the "true" parameter estimate. In Pnet, you do this by hitting the "update" button).

(c) Return to Step 4.

6. If, after about 50–100 estimation runs, the model still does not converge, do the following (start with option (a), continue to option (b); after each step, return to Step 4):

(a) Increase the multiplication factor in the program to about 400 (this basically means that the program searches for parameter estimates in a larger range. It also means that each estimation will be much longer).

(b) Start over by setting all parameter values to 0.

(c) Fit the model using new-specification ERG models (recommended initial configurations are presented in Appendixes C and D for nondirected and directed networks, respectively).

7. If your model still does not converge after Step 6 (a–c):

(a) Make sure you are not directly modeling a low-frequency configuration (make sure your model does not have any of the configurations you found in Step 2).

(b) Try to think whether you need to add more configurations to the model. For example, if there is a lot of clustering in the network (i.e., the graph statistics for all triads in Step 2 are extremely high), you might want to introduce other triadic structure to the model (see Robins et al., 2009).

(c) Consult an expert on model fitting. It is probably the case that you have complete or quasi-complete separation in your data. Basically, this means that your dependent variable (i.e., tie formation) is completely predicted by one of your independent variables (i.e., one of your configurations). The solution to the problem is to remove parameters from the model, based on theoretical reasoning.

8. Run GOF statistics on your final model. A model has good fit to your observed network if all directly modeled configurations have t-statistics that are smaller than $|.1|$, and configurations not directly modeled have t-statistics that are smaller than $|2|$. It may be the case that one or two configurations that you did not model directly are slightly larger than $|2|$. If, after attempting to re-fit the model (Step 4), this does not improve, it means that the model fails to capture that particular characteristic of your network well. Unless that particular characteristic of the network is important for your analyses or theory, state this as a caveat, and continue to Step 9 with a more cautious interpretation.

9. Interpret parameter estimates.

APPENDIX F: FURTHER READING AND PROGRAMS
FOR THE ESTIMATION OF ERG MODELS

For a more complete introduction to ERG models, readers are referred to the Robins et al. (2007) article, and to the entire issue 29 of *Social Networks*. A new book, edited by Dean Lusher, Johan Koskinen and Garry Robins, called "Exponential Random Graph Models for Social Networks" includes an excellent introduction to, and application of, all types of ERG models.

For researchers who are interested in fitting ERG models, Pnet (Wang, Robins, & Pattison, 2006) is a program for estimating and simulating ERG models for social selection. It is accompanied by an excellent beginners' tutorial on how to model networks, written by Nicholas Harrigan ("Pnet for dummies").[5] Stochastic actor-oriented models and ERG models can also be estimated using the SIENA program (Snijders, Steglich, & Schweinberger, 2007b). Tom Snijders' website[6] has useful information, tutorials, articles, and examples of how to estimate ERG models and stochastic actor-oriented models in the SIENA framework. Finally, the R package now has modules for both ERG models and stochastic actor-oriented models.

NOTES

1. gatton.uky.edu/Faculty/brass/ConsequencesofSocialNetworks.doc
2. Briefly, a correlation coefficient is calculated from two matrices. The rows and columns of one of the matrices are then permuted, and a new correlation coefficient is calculated. The process is repeated many times (typically 1,000), and each time a correlation coefficient is calculated between the (newly) permutated matrix and the other matrix. At the end of the process, the actual correlation between the original two matrices is compared with the distribution of correlation coefficients. If fewer than 5 percent of the correlations derived from this distribution are larger than the observed correlation, the correlation is considered to be significant at the $p < .05$ level. MRQAP extends this logic to multiple networks (see Kilduff & Tsai, 2003, Appendix 2, for a complete explanation). QAPs and MRQAPS address the issue of interdependence of observations at the dyadic level, but, as they do not account for triadic and higher-level effects, such as the use of centrality scores, they too may provide inappropriate results.
3. I note that an added benefit of ERG models is that power analysis is not based on the number of actors in the network (in our example, 12 actors), but rather on the number of possible ties between actors (in our case, 132 potential ties). Therefore,

ERG models have more statistical power than "traditional" models that posit the individual as a unit of analysis.

4. The model presented above converged (see the t-statistics in Appendix A). Had the model not converged, as is very often the case when attempting to initially fit ERG models to observed networks, the researcher should shift to the new specifications for ERG models (see Appendix E for troubleshooting of model-fitting). An isomorphic model using new specifications would include the arc, reciprocity, k-in-star parameter (testing Hypothesis 4, replacing the in-2-star parameter in Equation 4.2), the k-out-star (replacing the 2-out-star in Equation 4.2), the k-mixed-star (replacing the mixed-2-star parameter in Equation 4.2), and the transitive-k-triangle parameter (testing Hypothesis 5 and replacing the transitive triad parameter in Equation 4.2).

5. www.sna.unimelb.edu.au/pnet/pnet.html

6. http://stats.ox.ac.uk/~snijders/siena

REFERENCES

Bakker, A. B., Westman, M., & Van Emmerik, I. J. H. (2009). Advancements in crossover theory. *Journal of Managerial Psychology, 24*, 206–219.

Bamberger, P. A. (2008). Beyond contextualization: Using context theories to narrow the micro–macro gap in management science. *Academy of Management Journal, 51*(5), 839–846.

Borgatti, S. P., Everett, M. G., & Freeman, L. C. (2002). *Ucinet for Windows: Software for Social Network Analysis* (Version 6.64) [Computer software]. Harvard, MA: Analytic Technologies.

Borgatti, S. P., & Foster, P. C. (2003). The network paradigm in organizational research: A review and typology. *Journal of Management, 29*(6), 991–1013.

Burt, R. S. (2005). *Brokerage and closure: An introduction to social capital.* Oxford, UK: Oxford University Press.

den Hartog, D. N., House, R. J., Hanges, P. J., & Ruiz-Quintatanilla (1999). Culture specific and cross-culturally generalizable implicit leadership theories: Are attributes of charismatic/transformational leadership universally endorsed? *Leadership Quarterly, 10*(2), 219c256.

Feeley, T. H., Hwang, J., & Barnett, G. A. (2008). Predicting employee turnover from friendship networks. *Journal of Applied Communication Research, 36*(1), 56–73.

Festinger, L. (1954). A theory of social comparison processes. *Human Relations, 7*(2), 117–140.

Frank, O., & Strauss, D. (1986). Markov Graphs. *Journal of the American Statistical Association, 81*(395), 832–842.

Freeman, L. C. (1978). Centrality in social networks: Conceptual calrification. *Social Networks, 1*, 215–239.

Goktepe, J. R., & Schneier, C. E. (1989). Role of sex, gender roles, and attraction in predicting emergent leaders. *Journal of Applied Psychology, 74*(1), 165–167.

Goodreau, S. M. (2007). Advances in exponential random graph (p*) models applied to a large social network. *Social Networks, 29*(2), 231–248.

Graen, G. B., & Uhl-Bien, M. (1995). Relationship-based approach to leadership: Development of leader-member exchange (LMX) theory of leadership over 25 years: Applying a multi-level multi-domain perspective. *Leadership Quarterly, 6,* 219–247.

Granovetter, M. (1985). Economic action and social structure—the problem of embeddedness. *American Journal of Sociology, 91*(3), 481–510.

Gronn, P. (2002). Distributed leadership as a unit of analysis. *Leadership Quarterly, 13*(4), 423–451.

Guastello, S. J. (2007). Non-linear dynamics and leadership emergence. *Leadership Quarterly, 18*(4), 357–369.

Heider, F. (1946). Attitudes and cognitive organization. *Journal of Psychology, 21,* 107–112.

House, R. J., & Aditya, R. N. (1997). The social scientific study of leadership: Quo vadis? *Journal of Management, 23*(3), 409–473.

Howell, J. M., & Boies, K. (2004). Champions of technological innovation: The influences of contextual knowledge, role orientation, idea generation, and idea promotion on champion emergence. *Leadership Quarterly, 15,* 130–144.

Kalish, Y. (2008). Bridging in social networks: Who are the people in structural holes and why are they there? *Asian Journal of Social Psychology, 11*(1), 53–66.

Kalish, Y., & Luria, G. (2013). Brain, brawn, or optimism? Structure and correlates of emergent military leadership. In D. Lusher, J. Koskinen & G. Robins (Eds.), *Exponential Random Graph Models for Social Networks: Theory, Methods, and Applications.* Cambridge, UK: Cambridge University Press.

Kalish, Y., & Robins, G. L. (2006). Psychological predispositions and network structure: The relationship between individual predispositions, structural holes and network closure. *Social Networks, 28*(1), 56–84.

Kelly, J. R., & Barsade, S. G. (2001). Mood and emotions in small groups and work teams. *Organizational Behavior and Human Decision Processes, 86*(1), 99–130.

Kickul, J., & Neuman, G. (2000). Emergent leadership behaviors: The function of personality and cognitive ability in determining teamwork performance and KSAs. *Journal of Business and Psychology, 15*(1), 27–51.

Kilduff, M., & Tsai, W. (2003). *Social networks and organizations.* London: Sage.

Kilduff, M., Tsai, W., & Hanke, R. (2006). A paradigm too far? A dynamic stability reconsideration of the social network research program. *Academy of Management Review, 31*(4), 1031–1048.

Kozlowski, S. W. J., & Klein, K. J. (2000). A multilevel approach to theory and research in organizations: Contextual, temporal, and emergent properties. In K. J. Klein & S. W. J. Kozlowski (Eds.), *Multilevel theory, research, and methods in organizations: Foundations, extensions, and new directions* (pp. 3–90). San Francisco, CA: Jossey-Bass.

Krackhardt, D. (1987). QAP partialling as a test of spuriousness. *Social Networks, 9*(2), 171–186.

Krackhardt, D. (1990). Assessing the political landscape—structure, cognition, and power in organizations. *Administrative Science Quarterly, 35*(2), 342–369.

Krackhardt, D. (1994). Graph theoretical dimensions of informal organizations. In K. M. Carley & M. Prietula (Eds.), *Computational organizational theory* (pp. 89–111). Hillsdale, NJ: Erlbaum.

Krackhardt, D. (1999). The ties that torture: Simmelian tie analysis in organizations. In S. B. Andews & D. Knoke (Eds.), *Networks in and around organizations* (Vol. 16, pp. 183–212). Stamford, CT: JAI press.

Krackhardt, D., & Hanson, J. (1993). Informal networks: The company behind the chart. *Harvard Business Review, 71*(4), 104–111.

Lazega, E., & Pattison, P. E. (1999). Multiplexity, generalized exchange and cooperation in organizations: A case study. *Social Networks, 21*(1), 67–90.

Lewin, K. (1943). Defining the "Field at a Given Time". *Psychological Review, 50*, 292–310.

Lomi, A., & Pattison, P. (2006). Manufacturing relations: An empirical study of the organization of production across multiple networks.*Organization Science, 17*(3), 313–332.

Lord, R. G., & Maher, K. J. (1991). *Leadership and information processing:Linking perceptions and performance.* NY: Routledge.

McPherson, M., Smith-Lovin, L., & Cook, J. (2001). Birds of a feather: Homophily in social networks. *Annual Review of Sociology, 27*, 415–444.

Mehra, A., Kilduff, M., & Brass, D. J. (1998). At the margins: A distinctiveness approach to the social identity and social networks of underrepresented groups. *Academy of Management Journal, 4*, 441–452.

Mehra, A., Smith, B. R., Dixon, A. L., & Robertson, B. (2006). Distributed leadership in teams: The network of leadership perceptions and team performance. *Leadership Quarterly, 17*(3), 232–245.

Mitchell, T. R., Holtom, B. C., Lee, T. W., Sablynski, C. J., & Erez, M. (2001). Why people stay: Using job embeddedness to predict voluntary turnover. *Academy of Management Journal, 44*(6), 1102–1121.

Monge, P. R., & Contractor, N. S. (2003). *Theories of communication networks.* New York: Oxford University Press.

Moreno, J. L. (1934). *Who Shall Survive?* New York: Beacon House.

Morrell, K., Loan-Clarke, J., & Wilkinson, A. (2001). Unweaving leaving: The use of models in the management of employee turnover. *International Journal of Management Reviews, 3*(3), 219–244.

Neubert, M. J., & Taggar, S. (2004). Pathways to informal leadership: The moderating role of gender on the relationship of individual differences and team member network centrality to informal leadership emergence. *Leadership Quarterly, 15*(2), 175–194.

Newcomb, T. (1961). *The acquaintance process.* New York: Holt, Rinehart & Winston.

Pescosolido, A. T. (2001). Informal leaders and the development of group efficacy. *Small Group Research, 32*(1), 74–93.

Rank, O., Robins, G., & Pattison, P. (2010). Structural logic of interorganizational networks. *Organization Science, 21*(3), 745–774.

Raudenbush, S. W., Bryk, A. S., & Congdon, R. (2005). HLM 6.0: Hierarchical Linear and Non-linear Modeling (Version 6.0) [Computer software]. SSI.

Robins, G., Elliott, P., & Pattison, P. (2001). Network models for social selection processes. *Social Networks, 23*(1), 1–30.

Robins, G., Pattison, P., & Elliott, P. (2001). Network models for social influence processes. *Psychometrika, 66*, 161–190.

Robins, G., Pattison, P., Kalish, Y., & Lusher, D. (2007). An introduction to exponential random graph (p*) models for social networks. *Social Networks, 29*(2), 173–191.

Robins, G., Pattison, P., & Wang, P. (2009). Closure, connectivity and degree distributions: Exponential random graph (p*) models for directed social networks. *Social Networks, 31*(2), 105–117.

Robins, G., Snijders, T. A. B., Wang, P., Handcock, M., & Pattison, P. (2007). Recent developments in exponential random graph (p*) models. *Social Networks, 29*(2), 192–215.

Roethlisberger, F. J., & Dickson, W. J. (1939). *Management and the worker.* Cambridge, MA: Harvard University Press.

Rousseau, D. M., & Fried, Y. (2001). Location, location, location: Contextualizing organizational research. *Journal of Organizational Behavior, 22*(1), 1–13.

Sherif, M., Harvey, O. J., White, B. J., Hood, W. R., & Sherif, M. (1961). *Intergroup conflict and cooperation: The Robbers Cave experiment.* Normal, OK: University of Oklahoma Book Exchange.

Snijders, T. A. B. (1996). Stochastic actor-oriented models for network change. *Journal of Mathematical Sociology, 21*(1–2), 149–172.

Snijders, T. A. B. (2001). The statistical evaluation of social network dynamics. In *Sociological methodology* (Vol. 31, pp. 361–395).

Snijders, T. A. B. (2002). Markov chain Monte Carlo estimation of exponential random graph models. *Journal of Social Structure, 3*(2).

Snijders, T. A. B. (2005). Models for longitudinal network data. In P. Carrington, J. Scott, & S. Wasserman (Eds.), *Models and methods in social network analysis.* New York: Cambridge University Press.

Snijders, T. A. B., Pattison, P., Robins, G. L., & Handcock, M. (2006). New specifications for Exponential Random Graph models. *Sociological Methodology, 36*, 99–153.

Snijders, T. A. B., Steglich, C., & Schweinberger, M. (2007b). SIENA: Simulation Investigation for Empirical Network Analysis (Version 3.11) [Computer software]: ICS Netherlands.

Uzzi, B. (1997). Social structure and competition in interfirm networks: The paradox of embeddedness. *Administrative Science Quarterly, 42*(1), 35–67.

Wang, P., Robins, G., & Pattison, P. (2006). PNet: Program for estimation and simulation of p* exponential random graph models (Version 1.0) [Computer software].

Wasserman, S., & Faust, K. (1994). *Social network analysis: Methods and applications* (Vol. 8). Cambridge, UK: Cambridge University Press.

Whyte, W. F. (1941). Corner boys: A study of clique behavior. *American Journal of Sociology, 46*(5), 647–664.

5

Latent Class Procedures: Recent Development and Applications

Mo Wang and Le Zhou

Statistical methods commonly used in organizational research usually either take a variable-centered approach or a person-centered approach (Wang & Hanges, 2011). Methods taking a variable-centered, or dimension-centered, approach are used in research to capture the interrelatedness (often in the form of covariance or latent factor) between or among different variables and using it to infer the underlying processes or causes. The typical variable-centered methods used in organizational research include ANOVA, regression analysis, and structural equation modeling, just to name a few. However, sometimes, organizational researchers are interested in classifying individuals into subpopulations that differ from each other in patterns of variables (e.g. Mumford et al., 2000). Statistical methods taking a person-centered approach are used in these studies, which include cluster analysis and latent class analysis. Recent development in quantitative methods has extended the latent class analysis to integrate variable-centered and person-centered analytical approaches (Langeheine & van de Pol, 2002; Muthén, 2004). Specifically, the newly developed latent class procedures (e.g., mixed-measurement item response models, growth mixture modeling, and latent mixture Markov modeling) classify individuals into subpopulations, conditional not only on their similarities in patterns of variables, but also on various types of interrelatedness among variables (e.g., item response patterns and longitudinal quantitative and qualitative changes). These recently developed methods have been used in research areas such as developmental psychology (e.g., Schaeffer, Petras, Ialongo, Poduska, & Kellam, 2003) and consumer behavior (e.g., Varki & Chintagunta, 2004), and have started to be applied to organizational research (e.g. Zickar, Gibby, & Robie, 2004; Wang, 2007).

Another perspective to appreciate the integration of the variable-centered approach and the person-centered approach is that this integration allows researchers to test the assumption of population heterogeneity/homogeneity in the interrelatedness among variables. The populations studied in organizational research can be assumed to be homogeneous or heterogeneous. When homogeneity is assumed, a single set of parameters can be used to describe the phenomena of interest, which are usually estimated via the variable-centered approach. However, homogeneity might not hold, and population heterogeneity might be of theoretical interest to researchers. When subpopulation membership is observed, values of the observed categorical variable (e.g., gender) can be used to represent the subpopulation memberships (e.g., "male" and "female"). Consequently, research questions can be asked about the observed heterogeneity regarding the interrelatedness among variables—for example, whether a theoretical model of measurement is shared by different subpopulations (e.g. measurement equivalence across gender). Population heterogeneity can also be unobserved, and thus can be represented by a latent categorical variable (also called a latent class variable), the parameters of which can be estimated based on the observed data and the theoretical model specified. For example, responses to a personality measure might reflect two subpopulations that use the response scale systematically differently: those who avoid using the middle category and those who use the full range of the scale (Hernández, Drasgow, & González-Romá, 2004). In this case, subpopulations cannot be observed directly, but can be inferred from their different response patterns by using latent class procedures.

In general, latent class procedures have the following features. First, latent class procedures are based on the assumption that unobserved subpopulations exist within the target population. Therefore, variable-centered methods can be considered as special cases in the latent class framework where the number of latent classes is restricted to one. Second, latent class procedures are model-based methods that are different from methods that cluster data with arbitrary data-driven criteria (e.g., K-means cluster analysis). Specifically, latent class procedures specify model parameters, including number of latent classes and relationships among variables within subpopulations, a priori. Moreover, model estimation in latent class procedures involves maximizing likelihood functions based on the model specified. Therefore, the statistical likelihood can be used as a consistent criterion for evaluating different models. Furthermore, as compared with traditional cluster analysis techniques, there are more formal criteria developed to evaluate and compare different models in latent class procedures (e.g., information criteria, the Lo–Mendell–Rubin test, and bootstrapped likelihood ratio test). Therefore, latent class procedures can avoid the "dustbowl empiricism" criticism usually associated with traditional cluster analysis techniques. Third, latent class procedures can estimate the posterior probabilities of individuals belonging to each latent class. Therefore, classification uncertainty can be taken into consideration when interpreting classification results from a certain sample. It is also possible to use model parameters to predict new observations' subpopulation membership, whereas, in traditional cluster techniques, the classification results are always sample-specific. Finally, latent class procedures can be used to test the mechanisms underlying the effects from the observed population heterogeneity (e.g., gender, race, or culture). When explaining the effects of observed heterogeneity, researchers often face the question regarding how well the differences as hypothesized by theoretical mechanisms map to the categories of observed grouping variables. For example, for some scale measures, there are gender differences in item response functions that are explained by different response strategies used by men and women. Although measurement equivalence analysis can evaluate the effect of this observed heterogeneity, it cannot answer to what extent gender is associated with different response strategies, because different response strategies cannot be observed directly. Latent class procedures solve this issue by identifying subpopulations with different item response patterns using the latent class variable and estimating the extent to which gender is associated with this latent class variable. Thereby, it directly examines to what extent the observed grouping variables are associated with the systematic heterogeneity in item responses.

In the following sections, we introduce three recently developed latent class procedures in detail. They are mixed-measurement item response models, growth mixture modeling, and mixture latent Markov modeling. For each modeling technique, we first discuss which research questions can be addressed by the technique and then introduce model specification, model estimation, and model selection procedures.

MIXED-MEASUREMENT ITEM RESPONSE MODELS

Item response theory (IRT) has been applied in organizational research for measurement development of a variety of variables, including personality (e.g., Stark, Chernyshenko, Drasgow, & Williams, 2006), job attitudes (e.g. Collins, Raju, & Edwards, 2000), and job performance (e.g., Craig & Kaiser, 2003). Traditional IRT models assume that a single set of parameters (e.g., ability, difficulty, discrimination, and guessing parameters) can describe how all examinees respond to items in a test. This assumption can be relaxed by allowing parameters specified in IRT models to vary across groups when researchers are interested in studying whether item functioning differs across observed grouping variables, which essentially tests the measurement equivalence for the items across those groups (Vandenberg & Lance, 2000; Stark, Chernyshenko, & Drasgow, 2006). However, there are also situations in which researchers are interested in identifying and understanding unobserved subpopulations that differ in their response patterns to the items. For example, research on personality measures has hypothesized that there exist two subpopulations that differ in their rating strategies to the items: one subpopulation responds honestly, and the other fakes the responses (Zickar et al., 2004). Traditional IRT models, which either assume population homogeneity or examine differences across observed grouping variables, are not able to test this hypothesis about unobserved heterogeneity in item functioning. Instead, mixed-measurement IRT (MM-IRT) is the newly developed latent class procedure that directly addresses this need.

MM-IRT combines features of latent class analysis and traditional IRT models. First, MM-IRT identifies unobserved heterogeneity in item response patterns without relying on information on any specific observed grouping variable. Therefore, the unobserved heterogeneity may result from various underlying mechanisms that do not exactly map onto any particular observed grouping variable. MM-IRT allows the inclusion of observed grouping variables as covariates of the unobserved heterogeneity (modeled as the latent class variable), estimating the association between the observed grouping variables and the mechanisms underlying the heterogeneous item response patterns (Tay, Newman, & Vermunt, 2011). Second, MM-IRT is flexible, because different traditional IRT models with different numbers of response parameters or models for different response formats can be adapted similarly according to a general form of MM-IRT (Rost, 1997), as we will demonstrate in greater detail below. Third, as model-based procedures, MM-IRT can compare models with different numbers of latent classes and select the best-fitting model based on multiple statistical criteria. Finally, MM-IRT models follow the general latent variable analysis framework. Therefore, MM-IRT models can be extended to incorporate multilevel modeling features (Cho & Cohen, 2010; Tay, Diener, Drasgow, & Vermunt, 2011) and be estimated by general latent variable analysis programs (e.g., Mplus; Muthén & Muthén, 2007). For example, multilevel MM-IRT modeling can estimate unobserved heterogeneity at both individual and group level. Individual-level latent classes may differ in response strategies, while group-level latent classes may differ in terms of proportions of individual-level latent classes in observed groups (Tay et al., 2011).

Based on the above technical features, MM-IRT can be applied to a variety of organizational research topics. First, a direct application of MM-IRT would be to check whether the same item response functions can be applied to all examinees. For example, MM-IRT can be used to test whether there are unobserved subpopulations that systematically differ in response-scale use, such as a preference for using extreme response categories in job attitude measures (e.g., Eid & Rauber, 2000; Carter, Dalal, Lake, Lin, & Zickar, 2011). If a difference between unobserved subpopulations exists, it is necessary to adjust the scoring method to make the test scores comparable across subpopulations. Second, when researchers are interested in examining the cognitive mechanisms underlying different response strategies among examinees, MM-IRT can be used to identify unobserved subpopulations that systematically use different response strategies. Therefore, theories on measurement process can be empirically tested and developed (Rost, 1997). For example, by identifying multiple faking patterns via MM-IRT modeling, extended theories on faking were tested (Zickar et al., 2004). Third, covariates of the latent class variable can be included in MM-IRT models to enable further understanding of antecedents and outcomes of the unobserved heterogeneity in measurement functioning. For example, demographic, organizational (Eid & Rauber, 2000), and personality (Hernández et al., 2004) variables can be investigated as predictors of the membership of unobserved subpopulations. Fourth, relationships between observed and unobserved grouping variables can be examined to enable further understanding of issues related to measurement equivalence (Tay et al., 2011). It is possible to examine whether the differential item functioning between observed groups may hold across different unobserved subpopulations. For example, items may function differently for male and female. However, it is possible that gender difference only exists for subpopulations that respond to the items using a certain strategy. MM-IRT models can be used to test such a hypothesis (e.g. Cohen & Bolt, 2005). Finally, by incorporating features of latent class analysis and multilevel modeling, multilevel MM-IRT can be used in research that takes a pattern-centered approach to understanding multilevel phenomena. For example, group-level latent classes identified by MM-IRT may reflect structural differences among observed groups. Therefore, examining the covariates of group-level latent class can help with understanding of the emergence of group structure in different organizational settings (e.g., self-management teams or downsizing organizations; Tay et al., 2011).

Mixed-Measurement Item Response Model Specification

MM-IRT models can be summarized in a common form as follows (Rost, 1997):

$$p(\mathbf{u}) = \sum_{g=1}^{G} \pi_g p(\mathbf{u} \mid g) \tag{5.1}$$

where $p(\mathbf{u})$ denotes the probability of the response vector $\mathbf{u} = (u_1, u_2, \ldots, u_n)$ for n items, G denotes the number of latent categories, π_g is called mixing proportions or mixing parameter, which is the parameter representing the proportion of individuals belonging to class g and is restricted as:

$$\sum_{g=1}^{G} \pi_g = 1 \tag{5.2}$$

and $p(\mathbf{u} \mid g)$ denotes the probability of response vector $\mathbf{u}$ under the condition of group membership being g.

Different IRT models can be adapted to the above general formula. In MM-IRT model estimation, the computation load increases greatly as the number of parameters increases. We will use a partial credit model in the following illustration. A partial credit model is a generalized one-parameter IRT model (i.e., Rasch model) for items scored by successive integers. The probability of a response vector is modeled as a function of latent trait, θ, and item difficulty, σ, which is defined as:

$$p\left(U_{ij} = h\right) = \frac{\exp\left(h\theta_j - \sigma_{ih}\right)}{\sum_{s=0}^{m} \exp\left(s\theta_j - \sigma_{is}\right)} \quad \text{for } h = 0,1,2,\ldots,m \tag{5.3}$$

where U_{ij} is the response of individual j on item i ($i = 1, 2, \ldots, n$), h is the possible response option, θ_j is individual j's standing on the latent trait, and σ_{ih} is a parameter representing cumulated threshold on the continuum of the latent trait, which is defined as:

$$\sigma_{ih} = \sum_{s=1}^{h} \tau_{is}, \quad \sigma_{i0} = 0 \tag{5.4}$$

where τ_{is} is the location of threshold s on the continuum of the latent trait. Substituting Equation (5.3) in place of the $p(\mathbf{u} \mid g)$ term in Equation (5.1), the marginal response probability of individual j to item i is defined as:

$$p\left(U_{ij} = h\right) = \sum_{g=1}^{G} \pi_g \frac{\exp\left(h\theta_{jg} - \sigma_{ihg}\right)}{\sum_{s=0}^{m} \exp\left(s\theta_{jg} - \sigma_{isg}\right)} \quad \text{with } \sigma_{ihg} = \sum_{s=1}^{h} \tau_{isg} \tag{5.5}$$

and, with normalization conditions:

$$\sum_{g=1}^{G} \pi_g = 1, \sum_{i=1}^{n}\sum_{h=1}^{m} \tau_{ihg} = 0 \text{ for all } g, \text{ and } \sigma_{i0g} = 0 \text{ for all } i \text{ and } g$$

As can be seen from this mixture model specification, in MM-IRT models, each individual and each item will have g sets of parameters, instead of a single set of parameters associated with traditional IRT models that assume population homogeneity. Other IRT models can also be generalized to MM-IRT models similarly by substituting an original response function in place of the $p(\mathbf{u} \mid g)$ term in Equation (5.1) (see Rost, 1997, for examples).

Mixed-Measurement Item Response Model Estimation

In order to estimate the model parameters, further assumptions need to be made about the latent trait parameters in each class (i.e., θ_{jg}). Different estimation methods have different assumptions about the distribution of θ, and, based on their assumptions, different estimation procedures are used (Rost, 1997). Here, we follow Rost's (1990, 1997) approach, which reparameterizes the mixture Rasch model so that item parameters within each class are estimated without conditioning on latent trait parameters, and then, based on the conditional item parameter estimates, the latent trait parameters are estimated for each individual.

For the partial credit model, or its restricted two-response category model, an extended expectation-maximization (EM) algorithm can be used for estimation of item parameters and sizes of latent classes. In the expectation step, starting values or preliminary estimates of model parameters are used to estimate the portions of the observed frequency of response vector **u** in each latent class. In the maximization step, based on the estimated portions from the expectation step, item parameters within each class are estimated by maximizing the log-likelihood function. Class sizes are also estimated in the EM procedures. After EM procedures provide final conditional item parameter estimates, these estimates are used for estimating individuals' latent trait parameters in each class by maximizing conditional intra-class likelihood functions. For each individual, the estimates of latent trait parameters for each latent class all depend mainly on the individual's total number of response vector **u** in all classes. Therefore, the latent trait parameter estimates typically do not differ much across classes for each given individual (Rost, 1997).

It is important to note that, although the mixing proportions (i.e., π_g) are estimated as model parameters, the number of latent classes (i.e., G) is not estimated but should be set by researchers according to theories. When multiple models with different numbers of latent classes are estimated, the model selection procedures (as we describe below) should be carried out to help decide which model fits the data best. With regard to software to achieve these estimations, WINMIRA (von Davier, 2001), Latent GOLD (Vermunt & Magidson, 2005), and Mplus (Muthén & Muthén, 2007) can all be used to estimate the MM-IRT models. Estimates reported usually include maximum likelihood (ML) estimates of conditional item parameters, probabilities of each individual belonging to each latent class, and estimates of individuals' latent trait parameters.

Mixed-Measurement Item Response Model Selection

Theoretically, the log-likelihood ratio statistic can be used to compare a model with G classes with a model with $G+1$ classes. However, the log-likelihood ratio statistic is only asymptotically chi-square distributed when all possible response patterns have a reasonable chance to be observed. When measures include more than eight dichotomous items or four items with four response categories (i.e., more than 256 possible response patterns), a huge sample, frequently not available to organizational researchers, will be needed to estimate MM-IRT models. Therefore, model fit criteria that do not assume a particular statistical distribution for drawing inferences can be used as alternatives for evaluating MM-IRT models. These information criteria include Akaike's information criterion (AIC) $= -2 \ln(L) + 2k$, Bayesian information criterion (BIC) $= -2 \ln(L) + k \ln(N)$, and consistent Akaike's information criterion (CAIC) $= -2 \ln(L) + 2k[\ln(N) + 1]$, where L is the likelihood, k is the number of parameters in the model, and N is the sample size. The smaller the values of the information criteria, the better the model fits the data. As can be seen from the equations, AIC, BIC, and CAIC all penalize overparameterized models. As compared with AIC, BIC and CAIC also adjust for sample size.

Another alternative for evaluating model fit of sparse categorical data is to use parametric bootstrap procedures to generate an empirical distribution of the model fit statistic and use this distribution to test the fit statistic from the original data. Similar to hypothesis testing for other statistics, it is assumed that, if the model fits the original data well, then the fit statistic calculated from the original data should fall into a certain range (e.g. 95 percent confidence interval) of the empirical distribution of the fit statistic. Based on a Monte Carlo study, von Davier (1997) concluded that bootstrap procedures work adequately for the Pearson chi-square statistic and the Cressie–Read (CR) fit statistic (Cressie & Read, 1984). Moreover, for Rasch models, the Q-statistic proposed by Rost and von Davier (1994) can be used for inspecting item-level fit within each latent class.

GROWTH MIXTURE MODELING

Conventional latent growth modelling (LGM) has been used to model the growth curve of a variety of organizational variables, such as newcomer adaptation (e.g. Chan & Schmitt, 2000) and job performance (e.g., Ployhart & Hakel, 1998), and to model the relationships between the growth curves of variables (e.g., Jokisaari & Nurmi, 2009). Conventional LGM assumes that a single set of growth parameters can be used to describe the growth curves of all individuals. However, qualitatively different growth curves might exist in the population, therefore requiring different sets of growth parameters for subpopulations. When subpopulation membership can be observed, multi-group LGM can be estimated to compare the growth parameters across groups. However, sometimes, researchers are interested in identifying unobserved subpopulations whose growth trajectories might differ systematically to reconcile inconsistent empirical findings and integrate different theoretical perspectives (e.g., Wang, 2007). Growth mixture modeling (GMM) can be used for identifying unobserved subpopulations that differ in growth trajectories and estimating the relations between covariates and unobserved subpopulation membership at the same time.

GMM has the following technical features, based on which it can help answer certain change-related questions in organizational research. First, GMM can identify unobserved subpopulations that differ in growth-curve patterns. Therefore, it can be used to test whether the change of interest manifests in unitary or multiple paths (Chan, 1998). Second, within the general latent variable analysis framework, different types of covariates (e.g., observed or latent, continuous or categorical) of growth factors and latent class variables can be included in the model (Muthén, 2001). For example, different growth-curve patterns can result in a different development status, which is a categorical outcome variable (e.g. Muthén, 2004). Further, different growth-curve patterns might result from another dynamic process (i.e., covariates can be growth parameters of other change processes). Therefore, theories about antecedents or outcomes of different growth patterns can be tested using GMM. Finally, because a growth model is inherently multilevel in nature, GMM can be seen as a multilevel modeling technique as well. Therefore, it can be extended to model mixed growth curves of individuals nested in higher grouping levels. For example, it is possible to test how different work units may differ in the number and shape of newcomer adaption patterns.

Growth Mixture Model Specification

The growth curves of outcome variable Y in K latent classes (as illustrated in Figure 5.1) can be presented by the following formulae:

$$y_{itk} = \eta_{Iik} + \eta_{Sik}\lambda_{Stk} + \varepsilon_{itk} \tag{5.6}$$

$$\eta_{Iik} = \mu_{Ik} + \gamma_{Ik}x_i + \zeta_{Iik} \tag{5.7}$$

$$\eta_{Sik} = \mu_{Sk} + \gamma_{Sk}x_i + \zeta_{Sik} \tag{5.8}$$

where, for individual i in latent class k, y_{itk} is the observed score at time t, η_{Iik} is the intercept factor, η_{Sik} is the growth-rate factor, λ_{Stk} is the factor loading, ε_{itk} is the measurement errors of the outcome variable, μ_{Ik} and μ_{Sk} are the means of intercept factor and growth-rate factor of individuals belonging to the same latent class k, x_i is individual i's score on a time-invariant covariate X. The residual variances of intercept and growth-rate factor are σ_{Ik}^2 and σ_{Sk}^2 (i.e., the variances of ζ_{Iik} and ζ_{Sik}), and the covariance of ζ_{Iik} and ζ_{Sik} is σ_{ISk}. Different shapes of growth curves are specified for different latent classes by having different sets of loadings on growth factors (i.e., λ_{Stk}). Different latent classes can also differ on the means (i.e., μ_{Ik} and μ_{Sk}) and variance–covariance (i.e., σ_{Ik}^2, σ_{Sk}^2, and σ_{ISK}) of growth factors, and measurement errors of outcome variables (i.e., ε_{itk}). The growth factors can vary as functions of time-invariant covariates across individuals within subpopulations, and the effects of covariates can differ between subpopulations (i.e., γ_{Ik} and γ_{Sk}).

For the prediction of subpopulation membership, a multinomial logistic-regression model can be defined as:

$$p\left(c_{ik} = 1 \mid x_i\right) = \frac{\exp(a_k + b_k x_i)}{\sum_{k=1}^{K} \exp(a_k + b_k x_i)} \tag{5.9}$$

where $p(c_{ik} = 1 \mid \mathbf{x}_i)$ is the probability that individual i belongs to latent class k ($c_{ik} = 1$ if individual i belongs to class k, otherwise $c_{ik} = 0$) given covariate x_i. For the reference class K, a_K and b_K can be standardized to 0. Therefore, the logit of the odds of belonging to class k relative to class K is:

$$\operatorname{logit} = \ln \frac{p\left(c_{ik} = 1 \mid x_i\right)}{p\left(c_{iK} = 1 \mid x_i\right)} = a_k + b_k x_i \tag{5.10}$$

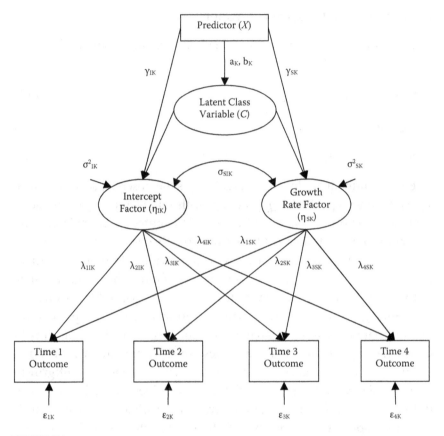

FIGURE 5.1

An illustration of a growth mixture model with covariate X.

The interpretation of the effect of covariates is similar to interpreting multinomial logistic-regression models. For example, for the effect of gender (male scored as "1" and female scored as "0") in a two-class latent model, Equation (5.10) provides the odds of belonging to the first class versus belonging to the second class (i.e., the reference class). Specifically, it follows that e^b is the odds ratio for being in the first latent class versus being in the reference latent class when comparing males with females.

The above equations specify a basic growth mixture model, which can be extended in various ways. Time-varying covariates of outcome variables can also be included in the growth models (Muthén, 2004). Moreover, as GMM is within the framework of latent variable modeling, categorical or continuous, latent or observed outcomes of latent class variables can also be included in the model (Muthén, 2001).

Growth Mixture Model Estimation

Maximum likelihood using an EM algorithm can be used to estimate growth mixture models (Muthén & Shedden, 1999; Muthén, 2001). In the expectation step, individuals' latent class memberships (i.e., scores on c_{ik}) are considered as missing values. The posterior probabilities of c_{ik} conditional on data for the outcome variable and covariates can be calculated. In the maximization step, the conditional expectations for c_{ik} are used to form the expected complete-data log-likelihood, which is maximized to provide an estimation of means and variances–covariances of the growth factors, factor loadings of observed outcomes on growth factors, logistic-regression coefficients of covariates, and residuals.

In GMM, missing data on the outcome variable can be modeled by a full-information maximum-likelihood (FIML) method assuming that data are missing at random (MAR; Little & Rubin, 2002). Newman (2003) showed that, in estimation of longitudinal models, FIML performs better than listwise deletion, pairwise deletion, and stochastic regression imputation. Estimation of growth mixture models and modeling of missing data assuming MAR can be conducted in Mplus (Muthén & Muthén, 2007) and SAS quite easily.

Growth Mixture Model Selection

Statistically, the following issues should be considered when selecting the best-fitting growth mixture model to the data. First, when maximum likelihood using an EM algorithm is used for model estimation, it is very likely to produce a distorted estimation of class memberships if the effects of covariates on growth factors are not included in the model (an unconditional growth model). This is because, when forming the posterior probabilities of latent class variables in the expectation step, the information on covariates is left unconsidered in the unconditional growth model. Consequently, the parameter estimates obtained from the maximization step, including latent class membership and growth parameters, are based on distorted expectations (Muthén, 2004). Therefore, in GMM, it is not very meaningful to compare the fit between unconditional and conditional models. Although an unconditional model might have better fit in terms of information criteria values, owing to model misspecification it is very likely to give less accurate classification results and obscured growth parameter estimates than conditional models.

Second, when comparing different models with different numbers of latent classes, conventional chi-square tests for log-likelihood ratio of $k-1$ and k-class models cannot be used, because the ratio does not follow a chi-square distribution. Instead, evaluating information criteria values of different models is an option for model comparison. Another option is to use the Lo–Mendell–Rubin likelihood ratio test (LMR or adjusted LRT; Lo, Mendell, & Rubin, 2001). The LMR method is also based on the likelihood ratio of models to be compared, but is based on the correct distribution of the likelihood ratio. If the p value of the test statistic is low, it suggests that the k-class model should be rejected to allow at least $k+1$ classes in the model. Because this test is still based on a likelihood ratio, the magnitude of the test statistic tends to be inflated by sample size, like other likelihood ratio-based tests (Lo et al., 2001). Moreover, the bootstrap approach introduced previously in the MM-IRT model selection section can also be applied in GMM (Nylund, Asparouhov, & Muthén, 2007). Nylund et al.'s simulation study compared the performance of information criteria and likelihood-based methods in deciding the number of latent classes in latent class methods, including GMM. Their results showed that, compared with other methods, a bootstrap likelihood-ratio test is a consistent indicator of number of latent classes.

Third, certainty in classification of a model can be evaluated by an entropy index (Jedidi, Ramaswamy, & Desarbo, 1993), which can also be used to compare models. When examining individuals' posterior probabilities of belonging to each latent class, it is possible to compare the average probabilities of individuals whose highest probability falls into the same class with the average probabilities of these same individuals in other classes. If the difference is large, the classification is more certain. Entropy measures such differences, ranging from .00 to 1.00. The higher the value, the more certain the classification results are. Previous research has used .80 as an acceptable value of entropy to suggest good classification quality (e.g. Muthén, 2004; Lubke & Muthén, 2007; Wang, 2007).

Given that there has not yet been a systematic comparison of the performance of all the available fit criteria, we recommended that researchers consider multiple criteria when deciding upon an optimal model. Apart from the above statistical concerns, it is also necessary to consider theoretical interpretability and practical usefulness when evaluating GMM results (Muthén, 2004; Wang & Bodner, 2007).

MIXTURE LATENT MARKOV MODELING

In organizational research, another interesting question to ask about change is how individuals transition between discrete statuses over time (e.g. employment status change in career, promotion history in an organization, development of withdrawal or rule-breaking behaviors, and skill acquisition–attrition–relearning process; Wang & Chan, in press). Empirically, these questions can be examined by measuring a categorical variable repeatedly across time and modeling the change pattern. The data from multiple time points on the same categorical variable can be viewed as manifesting a Markov chain. Statistical methods for analyzing longitudinal categorical data from a latent variable modeling approach are known as latent transition analyses (i.e., latent Markov modeling; Wiggins, 1973). Basic latent Markov modeling assumes that a single Markov chain can describe the transition of all individuals. However, similar to other organizational phenomena we have discussed so far, the population homogeneity assumption does not always hold. In other words, subpopulations can have different change patterns across discrete statuses. When population heterogeneity in the change patterns of qualitative variables can be predicted by observed grouping variables, multiple-group analysis procedures can be used to compare model parameters across observed groups (Muthén & Muthén, 2007). When population heterogeneity in a transition pattern cannot be observed directly, mixture latent Markov modeling can be used to identify subpopulations that have different qualitative change patterns and to model the relations between covariates and subpopulation membership.

Mixture latent Markov modeling combines the features of latent Markov modeling and latent class analysis (Langeheine & van de Pol, 2002). In mixture latent Markov modeling, as in latent Markov modeling, categories at each particular time point are considered as levels of a latent variable, and the observed category might be influenced by noise (i.e., measurement error). Based on this assumption, observed change patterns can be modeled as the reflection of latent patterns manifested by latent categorical variables. For example, minor discrepancy between similar observed patterns can be modeled as fluctuation in measurement. Therefore, a large number of observed patterns can be summarized by a lower number of latent patterns. Moreover, modeling qualitative change at the latent level also makes it possible to capture information in patterns observed at lower frequency. Therefore, it is possible to examine whether the low-frequency patterns are reflecting a unique latent pattern or just a reflection of similar latent patterns resulting from measurement error. Finally, as within the latent variable analysis framework, multiple types of covariate can be modeled as antecedents or outcomes of the unobserved heterogeneity in latent transition patterns (Wang & Chan, 2011).

Based on these technical features, mixture latent Markov modeling can help answer research questions regarding qualitative changes in organizational phenomena. For example, researchers focusing on career issues (e.g. job search, turnover, and retirement) are usually interested in identifying and explaining differences in individuals' employment status change patterns. By examining the relations between covariates and latent class membership, different theoretical mechanisms of the transition process in career development can be clarified. It is also possible to apply mixture latent Markov modeling in research on withdrawal behaviors in organizations. Specifically, the withdrawal process can be represented by categorical variables (e.g., present versus absent at work) over time. As such, we could model subpopulations with different profiles of status changes in discrete withdrawal variables and examine correlates of these withdrawal profiles. We can also use withdrawal behavior change profiles identified via mixture latent Markov modeling to predict the ultimate employee turnover outcomes. Other examples for using mixture latent Markov modeling include modeling profiles of changes in recidivism status in addiction research, profiles of changes in pass–fail status in skills test in skill-acquisition research, profiles of changes in performance award status (e.g., receiving versus failing to receive an excellence employee award) in customer-service research, and profiles of changes in organizational status on the annual listing of "employers of choice" (in versus out of the list) in organizational attractiveness research.

Mixture Latent Markov Model Specification

For a categorical outcome variable measured at four equally spaced time points, $g = 1, 2, \ldots, G$, $h = 1, 2, \ldots, H$, $i = 1, 2, \ldots, I$, and $j = 1, 2, \ldots, J$, represent the observed category at each time point. Each possible observed pattern can be labeled as a cell (g, h, i, j). Each individual's observed categories at all four time points fall into one cell. The total number of possible cells equals $G*H*I*J$. For the population of interest, the latent Markov model is defined as:

$$P_{ghij} = \delta_{1a} \cdot \rho_{1(g|a)} \cdot \tau_{12(b|a)} \cdot \rho_{2(h|b)} \cdot \tau_{23(c|b)} \cdot \rho_{3(i|c)} \cdot \tau_{34(d|c)} \cdot \rho_{4(j|d)} \tag{5.11}$$

where P_{ghij} is the expected proportion of individuals whose observed categories are in cell (g, h, i, j). For each time point, we can also have $a = 1, 2, \ldots, A$, $b = 1, 2, \ldots, B$, $c = 1, 2, \ldots, C$, and $d = 1, 2, \ldots, D$, to represent the categories of the latent variable. δ_{1a} is the proportion of individuals in latent category a at Time 1. Parameter $\rho_{1(g|a)}$ is the probability of observing status g given that latent status is a at Time 1, which is called response probability or reliability probability. It is similar for $\rho_{2(h|b)}$, $\rho_{3(i|c)}$, and $\rho_{4(j|d)}$. $\tau_{12}(b|a)$ is the probability of transiting from latent status a at Time 1 to latent status b at Time 2. Parameters $\tau_{23}(c|b)$ and $\tau_{34}(d|c)$ have similar meaning and are also called transition probabilities. Usually, the response probabilities are constrained to be equal across all time points, assuming that the measurement errors are equal across time.

Extending from the above model, a mixture latent Markov model with K latent classes (as illustrated in Figure 5.2) is defined as:

$$P_{ghij} = \pi_k \cdot \delta_{1a|k} \cdot \rho_{1(g|a,k)} \cdot \tau_{12(b|a,k)} \cdot \rho_{2(h|b,k)} \cdot \tau_{23(c|b,k)} \cdot \rho_{3(i|c,k)} \cdot \tau_{34(d|c,k)} \tag{5.12}$$
$$\cdot \rho_{4(j|d,k)}$$

where π_k is the mixture parameter that denotes the proportion of individuals in latent class k. The other parameters in this model are then all conditional on the latent class membership k. Therefore, in mixture latent Markov model, each individual will have K times as many as the number of parameters in the basic latent Markov model. Further, similar

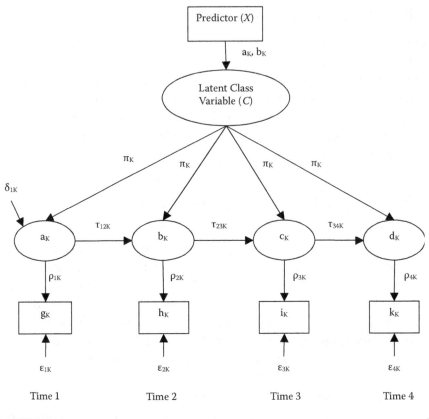

FIGURE 5.2
An illustration of a mixture latent Markov model with covariate X.

to GMM, the effect of covariates on latent class variable can be defined by a multinomial logistic-regression model, as represented in Equation (5.9) and Equation (5.10).

Mixture Latent Markov Model Estimation

Similar to GMM, a mixture latent Markov model can also be estimated by maximum likelihood methods using an EM algorithm (Langeheine & van de Pol, 2002). In the expectation step, individuals' latent class variable is considered as having missing values, and its posterior probability is calculated. In the maximization step, the posterior probabilities of individuals' latent class memberships are inserted into the expected complete-data log-likelihood function, which is maximized to provide estimation of a mixture parameter, reliability parameters, transition parameters, and the regression coefficients of covariates on latent classes. In mixture latent Markov modeling, missing data on the outcome variable can also be modeled by an FIML method, assuming that data are MAR (Little & Rubin, 2002). With regard to software, both Mplus (Muthén & Muthén, 2007) and Latent GOLD (Vermunt & Magidson, 2005) can be used to estimate mixture latent Markov models.

Mixture Latent Markov Model Selection

When there are no missing values in the data, a Pearson chi-square test can be used to evaluate absolute model fit. For each cell (g, h, i, j), an observed frequency, O_{ghij}, can be calculated from the data, and a model-based frequency, E_{ghij}, can be calculated using individuals' latent class membership. The chi-square statistic is defined as:

$$\chi^2 = \sum_{ghij} \frac{\left(O_{ghij} - E_{ghij}\right)^2}{E_{ghij}} \tag{5.13}$$

If the test is not significant, the null hypothesis is not rejected, which suggests that the model-based frequencies are not significantly different from the observed frequencies (i.e., the model fits the data well).

To determine the number of latent classes, information criteria (e.g., AIC, BIC, and sample-size adjusted BIC) can be used to compare the fit of models with different numbers of latent classes. Entropy can also be used in selecting mixture latent Markov models. Because the log-likelihood ratio of models with k and $k-1$ latent classes is not distributed as a chi-square distribution, the conventional log-likelihood ratio test is not appropriate for comparing fit of mixture latent Markov models. Although previous studies have shown that likelihood-based tests, such as adjusted LRT and the bootstrap likelihood ratio test, perform well in comparing mixture models with one latent categorical variable (e.g., growth mixture model and latent class model), it is not known yet whether they perform adequately for comparing models with multiple latent categorical variables (e.g., mixture latent Markov model). When deciding the number of latent classes, it is also important to consider whether the estimates of the model parameters have interpretable, substantive meaning. Further, to improve classification accuracy, one potential approach is to include covariates of latent classes to provide additional information for estimating conditional probabilities of latent class memberships (Muthén, 2004; Wang & Bodner, 2007).

CONCLUSION

In this chapter, we introduced three latent class procedures that hold promise for addressing important organizational research questions. We would like to end this chapter by discussing several further thoughts regarding their use in organizational research. First, to apply latent class procedures appropriately, researchers must rely on substantive theories related to the phenomena of interest, and model specification in latent class procedures should be theory driven. For example, in growth mixture modeling, the shape of longitudinal change patterns for each latent class should be specified according to the theoretical mechanisms underlying the changes (e.g., Wang, 2007). Moreover, in the model selection process (e.g., determining the appropriate number of latent classes), theories can provide additional diagnostic information to statistical indices. It is possible that two models fit the data equally well from a statistical sense, but only one of them can be interpreted according to current theories. Furthermore, a misspecified model can fit the data well and cannot be distinguished from the correct model by statistical means. For example, there was no agreement reached by methodologists about how to distinguish between heterogeneous mixtures of normal distributions and homogeneous nonnormal distributions in data (for a detailed discussion, see Bauer & Curran, 2003a, 2003b; Cudeck & Henly, 2003; Muthén, 2003; Rindskopf, 2003). Based on these reasons, we recommend using the latent class procedures in a confirmatory, rather than exploratory, manner.

It should also be noted that there are infinite ways to look at the same reality (Wang & Hanges, 2011). Through the lens of statistics, the same set of data can be fit by different statistical models. Derived from different statistical approaches, these models might be parameterized differently, but fit the data equally well. For example, the same covariance matrix can be fit equally well by a latent class model or a factor analysis model (Molenaar & von Eye, 1994; Bartholomew & Knott, 1999). Latent class analysis takes the person-centered approach and answers questions about how individuals stand as subgroups in the variable space. Latent factor analysis takes the variable-centered approach and answers questions about how variable vectors relate to each other in the person space. Depending on a researcher's perspective and which substantive theories he/she endorses, different statistical models can be used to answer different questions. Therefore, whether to use latent class procedures should be decided by the substantive research questions and theories.

Further, appropriate use of latent class procedures has several requirements for research design. The identification of the latent class memberships depends on the information available from the data of a particular sample. Therefore, classification results from representative samples would be especially informative for making inferences about latent class and its relationships with covariates. When random sampling is not possible, cross-validation is strongly recommended. In addition, a large sample size may be necessary to identify some models estimated by latent class procedures (e.g. MM-IRT models).

Finally, by introducing latent class procedures in this chapter, we hope to broaden ways for researchers to generate ideas and develop new theoretical models from a person-centered perspective, thereby promoting theoretical development in organizational research. When raising research questions, organizational researchers are sometimes limited by the availability of means to answer the questions. Therefore, the introduction of these advanced latent class procedures may direct organizational researchers' attention to developing better, or more comprehensive, theories in terms of helping to recognize the potential unobserved heterogeneity in measuring organizational phenomena and capturing organizational dynamic processes. This may also help organizational researchers to reconcile and connect theories, which may lead to different predictions by providing a way to examine whether different theories may correspond to different subpopulations.

REFERENCES

Bartholomew, D. J., & Knott, M. (1999). *Latent variable models and factor analysis* (2nd ed.). London: Arnold.

Bauer, D. J., & Curran, P. J. (2003a). Distributional assumptions of growth mixture models: Implications for overextraction of latent trajectory classes. *Psychological Methods, 8,* 338–363.

Bauer, D. J., & Curran, P. J. (2003b). Overextraction of latent trajectory classes: Much ado about nothing? Reply to Rindskopf (2003), Muthén (2003), and Cudeck and Henly (2003). *Psychological Methods, 8*, 384–393.

Carter, N. T., Dalal, D. K., Lake, C. J., Lin, B. C., & Zickar, M. J. (2011). Using mixed-model item response theory to analyze organizational survey responses: An illustration using the job descriptive index. *Organizational Research Methods, 14*, 116–146.

Chan, D. (1998). The conceptualization and analysis of change over time: An integrative approach incorporating longitudinal mean and covariance structure analysis (LMACS) and multiple indicator latent growth modeling (MLGM). *Organizational Research Methods, 1*, 421–483.

Chan, D., & Schmitt, N. (2000). Interindividual differences in intraindividual changes in proactivity during organizational entry: A latent growth modeling approach to understanding newcomer adaptation. *Journal of Applied Psychology, 85*, 190–210.

Cho, S., & Cohen, A. S. (2010). A multilevel mixture IRT model with an application to DIF. *Journal of Educational and Behavioral Statistics, 35*, 336–370.

Cohen, A. S., & Bolt, D. M. (2005). A mixture model analysis of differential item functioning. *Journal of Educational Measurement, 42*, 133–148.

Collins, W. C., Raju, N. S., & Edwards, J. E. (2000). Assessing differential functioning in a satisfaction scale. *Journal of Applied Psychology, 85*, 451–461.

Craig, S. B., & Kaiser, R. B. (2003). Applying item response theory to multisource performance ratings: What are the consequences of violating the independent observations assumption? *Organizational Research Methods, 6*, 44–60.

Cressie, N., & Read, T. R. C. (1984). Multinomial goodness-of-fit tests. *Journal of the Royal Statistical Society, Series B, 46*, 440–464.

Cudeck, R., & Henly, S. J. (2003). A realistic perspective on pattern representation in growth data: Comment on Bauer and Curran (2003). *Psychological Methods, 8*, 378–383.

Eid, M., & Rauber, M. (2000). Detecting measurement invariance in organizational surveys. *European Journal of Psychological Assessment, 16*, 20–30.

Hernández, A., Drasgow, F., & González-Romá, V. (2004). Investigating the functioning of a middle category by means of a mixed-measurement model. *Journal of Applied Psychology, 89*, 687–699.

Jedidi, K., Ramaswamy, V., & Desarbo, W. S. (1993). A maximum likelihood method for latent class regression involving a censored dependent variable. *Psychometrika, 58*, 375–394.

Jokisaari, M., & Nurmi, J. (2009). Change in newcomers' supervisor support and socialization outcomes after organizational entry. *Academy of Management Journal, 52*, 527–544.

Langeheine, R., & van de Pol, F. (2002). Latent Markov chains. In J. A. Hagenaars & A. L. McCutcheon (Eds.), *Applied latent class analysis* (pp. 304–341). New York: Cambridge University Press.

Little, R. J., & Rubin, D. B. (2002). *Statistical analysis with missing data* (2nd ed.). New York: John Wiley & Sons.

Lo, Y., Mendell, N. R., & Rubin, D. B. (2001). Testing the number of components in a normal mixture. *Biometrika, 88*, 767–778.

Lubke, G., & Muthén, B. (2007). Performance of factor mixture models as a function of model size, covariate effects, and class-specific parameters. *Structural Equation Modeling, 14*, 26–47.

Molenaar, P. C., & von Eye, A. (1994). On the arbitrary nature of latent variables. In A. von Eye & C. C. Clogg (Eds.), *Latent variable analysis: Applications for developmental research* (pp. 226–242). Thousand Oaks, CA: Sage.

Mumford, M. D., Zaccaro, S. J., Johnson, J. F., Diana, M., Gilbert, J. A., & Threlfall, K. V. (2000). Patterns of leader characteristics: Implications for performance and development. *Leadership Quarterly, 11*, 115–133.

Muthén, B. (2001). Second-generation structural equation modeling with a combination of categorical and continuous latent variables: New opportunities for latent class-latent growth modeling. In L. Collins & A. Sayer (Eds.), *New methods for the analysis of change* (pp. 291–322). Washington, DC: American Psychological Association.

Muthén, B. (2003). Statistical and substantive checking in growth mixture modeling: Comment on Bauer and Curran (2003). *Psychological Methods, 8*, 369–377.

Muthén, B. (2004). Latent variable analysis: Growth mixture modeling and related techniques for longitudinal data. In D. Kaplan (Ed.), *Handbook of quantitative methodology for the social sciences* (pp. 345–368). Thousand Oaks, CA: Sage.

Muthén, B., & Shedden, K. (1999). Finite mixture modeling with mixture outcomes using the EM algorithm. *Biometrics, 55*, 463–469.

Muthén, L. K., & Muthén, B. O. (2007). *Mplus User's Guide* (5th ed.). Los Angeles: Muthén & Muthén.

Newman, D. A. (2003). Longitudinal modeling with randomly and systematically missing data: A simulation of ad hoc, maximum likelihood, and multiple imputation techniques. *Organizational Research Methods, 6*, 328–362.

Nylund, K. L., Asparouhov, T., & Muthén, B. O. (2007). Deciding on the number of classes in latent class analysis and growth mixture modeling: A Monte Carlo simulation study. *Structural Equation Modeling, 14*, 535–569.

Ployhart, R. E., & Hakel, M. D. (1998). The substantive nature of performance variability: Predicting interindividual differences in intraindividual performance. *Personnel Psychology, 51*, 859–901.

Rindskopf, D. (2003). Mixture or homogeneous? Comment on Bauer and Curran (2003). *Psychological Methods, 8*, 364–368.

Rost, J. (1990). Rasch models in latent classes: An integration of two approaches to item analysis. *Applied Psychological Measurement, 14*, 271–282.

Rost, J. (1997). Logistic mixture models. In W. J. van der Linden & R. K. Hambleton (Eds.), *Handbook of modern item response theory* (pp. 449–463). New York: Springer.

Rost, J., & von Davier, M. (1994). A conditional item fix index for Rasch models. *Applied Psychological Measurement, 18*, 171–182.

Schaeffer, C. M., Petras, H., Ialongo, N., Poduska, J., & Kellam, S. (2003). Modeling growth in boys' aggressive behavior across elementary school: Links to later criminal involvement, conduct disorder, and antisocial personality disorder. *Developmental Psychology, 39*, 1020–1035.

Stark, S., Chernyshenko, O. S., & Drasgow, F. (2006). Detecting differential item functioning with confirmatory factor analysis and item response theory: Toward a unified strategy. *Journal of Applied Psychology, 91*, 1292–1306.

Stark, S., Chernyshenko, O. S., Drasgow, F., & Williams, B. A. (2006). Examining assumptions about item responding in personality assessment: Should ideal point methods be considered for scale development and scoring? *Journal of Applied Psychology, 91*, 25–39.

Tay, L., Diener, E., Drasgow, F., & Vermunt, J. K. (2011). Multilevel mixed-measurement IRT analysis: An explication and application to self-reported emotions across the world. *Organizational Research Methods, 14*, 177–207.

Tay, L., Newman, D., & Vermunt, J. K. (2011). Using mixed-measurement item response theory with covariates (MM-IRT-C) to ascertain observed and unobserved measurement equivalence. *Organizational Research Methods, 14*, 147–176.

Vandenberg, R. J., & Lance, C. E. (2000). A review and synthesis of the measurement invariance literature: Suggestions, practices, and recommendations for organizational research. *Organizational Research Methods, 3*, 4–70.

Varki, S., & Chintagunta, P. K. (2004). The augmented latent class model: Incorporating additional heterogeneity in the latent class model for panel data. *Journal of Marketing Research, 41*, 226–233.

Vermunt, J. K., & Magidson, J. (2005). *Latent GOLD 4.0 user's guide.* Belmont, MA: Statistical Innovations Inc.

von Davier, M. (1997). Bootstrapping goodness-of-fit statistics for sparse categorical data: Results of a Monte Carlo study. *Methods of Psychological Research Online, 2*, 29–48.

von Davier, M. (2001). *WINMIRA 2001: Windows mixed Rasch model analysis* [Computer software and user manual]. Kiel, The Netherlands: Institution for Science Education.

Wang, M. (2007). Profiling retirees in the retirement transition and adjustment process: Examining the longitudinal change patterns of retirees'psychological well-being. *Journal of Applied Psychology, 92*, 455–474.

Wang, M., & Bodner, T. E. (2007). Growth mixture modeling: Identifying and predicting unobserved subpopulations with longitudinal data. *Organizational Research Methods, 10*, 635–656.

Wang, M. & Chan, D. (2011). Mixture latent Markov modeling: Identifying and predicting unobserved heterogeneity in longitudinal qualitative status change. *Organizational Research Methods.*

Wang, M., & Hanges, P. (2011). Latent class procedures: Applications to organizational research. *Organizational Research Methods, 14*, 24–31.

Wiggins, L. M. (1973). *Panel analysis.* Amsterdam: Elsevier.

Zickar, M. J., Gibby, R. E., & Robie, C. (2004). Uncovering faking samples in applicant, incumbent, and experimental data sets: An application of mixed-model item response theory. *Organizational Research Methods, 7*, 168–190.

6

Spurious Relationships in Growth Curve Modeling: The Effects of Stochastic Trends on Regression-based Models

Michael T. Braun, Goran Kuljanin, and Richard P. DeShon

Growth is fundamental to understanding phenomena in all scientific disciplines. Fascination with explaining how things change over time has dominated scientific investigations for hundreds of years (McArdle & Nesselroade, 2003). Learning, memory, intelligence, development, personality, mood, and motivation are just a few of the topics that psychologists study that exhibit changes over time. Examining the dynamics of these processes can yield insights that are not apparent in static research. One such discovery is that, frequently, a great deal of heterogeneity exists in the growth process of individuals (Collins & Horn, 1991; Collins & Sayer, 2001). Interest in explaining these interindividual differences in intraindividual change has led to an increase in the number of longitudinal studies in recent years (Collins, 2006).

Unfortunately, the very thing that makes growth interesting and pivotal to scientific investigations—understanding change over time—is the very thing that makes it complex and extremely difficult to study and analyze appropriately. Growth, by definition, is a nonstationary process. Nonstationary processes create trends that reveal themselves in longitudinal data. These underlying trends can take on two distinct forms: deterministic trends, which result from consistent, substantive processes that can be measured and predicted, and stochastic trends, which result from an accumulation of mathematically random shocks or errors that, although measurable, are impossible to predict. Frequently, it is extremely difficult to distinguish between these two types of trend in longitudinal data. However, the accuracy of statistical results and appropriateness of scientific inferences rely on the ability to do so.

Each of these types of trend has distinct, unique mathematical properties that must be accounted for by statistical models. Failure to properly account for these unique mathematical properties can result in biased statistical results and mistaken scientific inferences. Psychologists typically model longitudinal data as the result of a noisy, purely deterministic trend by utilizing regression-based models, such as random coefficient or LGM. Using regression to analyze data that result, at least partially, from a stochastic trend results in greatly inflated Type I errors, called spurious regression (Granger & Newbold, 1974). As random coefficient and LGM are generalizations of the regression model, they also perform poorly in the presence of stochastic trends, resulting in systematic biases (Braun, Kuljanin, & DeShon, in press; Kuljanin, Braun, & DeShon, in press). These biases permeate almost all aspects of random-coefficient and latent-growth models and leave psychological researchers extremely susceptible to making inaccurate statistical and scientific inferences if stochastic trends are present.

To demonstrate this problem, the chapter is organized in the following manner: First, a brief overview of current trends in psychological longitudinal data collections and longitudinal modeling is discussed, ending with a brief mathematical and conceptual synopsis of random coefficient modeling (RCM), the most common analytic strategy. Then, the distinction between deterministic and stochastic trends is explained, and the potential problems resulting from analyzing longitudinal data with stochastic trends with regression (spurious regression) are highlighted. The phenomenon of spurious regression is then expanded to RCM, and results are given from a number of common random coefficient models, highlighting the spurious effects caused by the presence of stochastic trends. The implications of ignoring stochastic trends are discussed for each type of model, focusing on the potential mistaken scientific inferences researchers can make when using regression-based models to analyze longitudinal data resulting from stochastic trends. Finally, recommendations are given by providing methods for identifying stochastic trends in longitudinal data and by providing potential alternative statistical methods to analyze data with stochastic trends.

PSYCHOLOGICAL LONGITUDINAL DATA COLLECTION

The evaluation of longitudinal data structures allows researchers to model and predict the dynamics of psychological processes. Longitudinal data often reveal complex relationships over time that are not easily identified in cross-sectional analyses (e.g., Block, 1995; Mitchell & James, 2001; Vancouver, Thompson, & Williams, 2001; Molenaar, 2004; Vancouver, More, & Yoder, 2008). Therefore, many psychological methodologists have called for the expansion of models, research designs, and theoretical frameworks to incorporate the dynamics of psychological processes (e.g., McGrath & Rotchford, 1983; George & Jones, 2000; Ancona, Okhuysen, & Perlow, 2001; Mitchell & James, 2001). Similarly, there is a push from substantive researchers to understand the dynamic nature of psychological processes and, thus, include time in more theories and models. For example, research on teams is one of the most predominant areas in organizational psychology where this has taken place (e.g., Kozlowski & Klein, 2000; Kozlowski & Ilgen, 2006; Mohammed, Hamilton, & Lim, 2008). Not surprisingly, then, the number of longitudinal data collections has increased (Collins, 2006).

Along with the increased frequency of studying psychological processes over time, technological advancements made it easier to collect and store data over a larger range of time points, resulting in longer series for each individual. This shift is most evident in studies utilizing event/experience sampling methodology. In experience sampling studies, each individual can have anywhere from fewer than 10 (e.g., Sonnentag, 2003) to more than 70 (e.g., Ilies & Judge, 2002) time points. In economics, time series typically have between 5 and 100 time points, very similar to the numbers being collected in event/experience sampling studies in psychology (Bhargava & Sargan, 1983; Hsiao, Pesaran, & Tahmiscioglu, 2002). With this increase in series length, psychological longitudinal data start to mirror the structure and properties of time series that can be seen in the biomedical and economic literature, resulting in intensive longitudinal designs (Walls & Schafer, 2006).

CURRENT TRENDS IN LONGITUDINAL MODELING

Recent advances in the development of longitudinal data analysis techniques provide researchers with multiple statistical tools to choose from when analyzing longitudinal data. Repeated measures analysis of variance (ANOVA) and regression provide researchers with the average trajectory over time across multiple individuals. However, recent interest in interindividual differences in intraindividual change led to the development of more complex analytic methods, such as random coefficient models (also known as growth curve models, multilevel models, hierarchical linear models, mixed effects models, latent growth models). Random coefficient models both provide the average trajectory across multiple individuals and capture any heterogeneity in individual trajectories if it exists. Regardless of whether trajectory heterogeneity is substantively interesting or thought of as nuisance variance, it must be represented in the model to avoid statistical biases (Barcikowski, 1981; Winer, Brown, & Michels, 1991; Kreft & De Leeuw, 1998; Molenaar, 2004). Therefore, RCM is currently the dominant approach to longitudinal data analysis in psychology. Although RCM has substantially advanced psychological longitudinal data analysis, the validity of the statistical results and scientific inferences depend on the applicability of the model assumptions to the longitudinal processes under investigation.

MATHEMATICAL AND CONCEPTUAL OVERVIEW OF RCM

RCM is an extension of the regression model that uses maximum likelihood estimation to estimate hyperparameters for each variable in the model to maximize the fit between the observed and expected variance–covariance matrices. Hyperparameters are the mean and variance of each parameter across all individuals in the sample (Gelman & Hill, 2006). RCM is typically used to analyze longitudinal data through a stepwise process of nested model testing (Kreft & De Leeuw, 1998; Snijders & Bosker, 1999; Raudenbush & Bryk, 2002; Singer & Willett, 2003). The first recommended step is to analyze two unconditional models as a baseline for all future analyses. These two models are the unconditional means model and the unconditional growth model (Singer & Willett, 2003). They are used to analyze the variance components and determine the trajectories of the growth curves. The unconditional means model, as represented by Singer and Willett (2003), is specified as:

$$Y_{ij} = \pi_{0i} + \varepsilon_{ij}$$
$$\pi_{0i} = \gamma_{00} + \zeta_{0i}$$

(6.1)

where it is assumed that:

$$\varepsilon_{ij} \sim N\left(0, \sigma_\varepsilon^2\right) \text{ and } \zeta_{0i} \sim N\left(0, \sigma_0^2\right)$$

Y_{ij} is the dependent variable measured for each individual i and each occasion j, π_{0i} is the mean of Y for individual i, γ_{00} is the mean of Y across everyone in the population, ε_{ij} is the residual for individual i at occasion j, σ_ε^2 is the pooled variance of each individual's data around his/her mean, ζ_{0i} is the random effect for individual i, and σ_0^2 is the variance of the random effect.

The unconditional means model splits the total variance into within- and between-person variance components. These variance components are then frequently used to compute the intraclass correlation coefficient (*ICC(1)*). The *ICC(1)* indicates the proportion of total variance residing between individuals. From this, researchers typically evaluate whether a substantial amount of variance exists within and between individuals. If it is determined that there is a significant amount of unexplained variance, either within or between individuals, then it is suggested that the researcher search for predictors to explain the remaining variance. However, before adding substantive predictors, the researcher is recommended to run an additional baseline model, the unconditional growth model, to determine the shape and trajectory of the growth curves. The unconditional growth model, as represented by Singer and Willet (2003), is specified as:

$$Y_{ij} = \pi_{0i} + \pi_{1i}\text{Time}_{ij} + \varepsilon_{ij}$$
$$\pi_{0i} = \gamma_{00} + \zeta_{0i}$$
$$\pi_{1i} = \gamma_{10} + \zeta_{1i}$$

(6.2)

where it is assumed that:

$$\varepsilon_{ij} \sim N\left(0, \sigma_\varepsilon^2\right) \text{ and } \begin{bmatrix} \zeta_{0i} \\ \zeta_{1i} \end{bmatrix} \sim N\left(\begin{bmatrix} 0 \\ 0 \end{bmatrix}, \begin{bmatrix} \sigma_0^2 & \sigma_{01} \\ \sigma_{10} & \sigma_1^2 \end{bmatrix}\right)$$

Y_{ij} is the dependent variable measured for each person i and each occasion j, π_{0i} is the initial status (intercept) of Y for individual i, γ_{00} is the fixed effect for the intercepts and is the initial status of Y across everyone in the population, π_{1i} is the rate of change (slope) of Y for individual i, γ_{10} is the fixed effect for the slopes and is the rate of change of Y across everyone in the population, σ_ε^2 is the pooled variance of each individual's data around their linear change trajectory, ζ_{0i} is the intercept random effect, ζ_{1i} is the slope random effect, σ_0^2 is the variance component of the random effect of the intercepts and is the unpredicted variability in initial status, σ_1^2 is the variance component of the random effect of the slopes and is the unpredicted variability in rate of change, and σ_{10} is the population covariance between intercepts and slopes, and all other terms are defined as above.

If the unconditional growth model has a large amount of unexplained variance in either initial status (intercept) or rate of change (slope), it is recommended that investigators search for additional predictors to explain the heterogeneity (Snijders & Bosker, 1999). Singer and Willet (2003) echo this notion by saying that researchers need to look at the variance components to "assess whether there is hope for future analyses" (p. 99).

There are many routes that researchers can explore to explain additional variance, and it is recommended that theory guide the choice of all subsequent predictors. When using RCM to analyze longitudinal data, predictors can take on two forms: Level 2 and Level 1 predictors. Level 2 predictors vary between individuals but are constant within individuals. They are often grouping variables such as gender, race, or religion, but can also be variables such as salary, personality, or intelligence, which remain constant over the time frame of the study. Level 2 predictors are used to form conditional models by entering them as fixed effects to test both main effects and cross-level interactions. On the other hand, Level 1 predictors (also known as time-varying covariates) vary both within and (on average) between individuals over time. Some examples are fatigue, self-efficacy, and mood. It is recommended that Level 1 predictors are added to the model as fixed effects first, and then a log-likelihood ratio test is used to determine whether additional variance is explained. Then, if it makes conceptual sense that the substantive predictor varies systematically across people, and if the researcher has the degrees of freedom to estimate the additional parameters, the predictor is allowed to vary as a random effect (Singer & Willett, 2003).

POTENTIAL PITFALLS IN USING RANDOM COEFFICIENT MODELS

As mentioned above, as psychologists collect a greater number of time points for each individual, psychological longitudinal data structures become intensive longitudinal designs, similar to those found in economics. It is important to note that the increase in series length comes with an increase in the complexity of the components of the data that need to be addressed by statistical models (Walls & Schafer, 2006). It is easy to ignore the increased complexity because the statistical packages psychological researchers typically use, such as HLM, easily handle the increased number of time points. However, by ignoring these increased complexities, researchers could get an inaccurate representation of the underlying psychological relationships.

A model fit to a longitudinal process results in one or more trajectories. In psychological research, the observed trajectories are typically modeled as though they are the result of a noisy, purely deterministic process. Although not widely recognized in psychology, it is well known in other disciplines (e.g., physics, computer science, and economics) that the observed trends in these trajectories may be due, at least in part, to a stochastic, or random, process. Regression and generalizations of the regression model such as RCM require the assumption that all trends present in the dependent variable are the result of solely deterministic processes (Nelson & Kang, 1984). If regression models are used to analyze data containing a stochastic trend, a serious inflation of Type I error rates, called spurious regression, is frequently observed (Granger & Newbold, 1974; Nelson & Kang, 1984; Phillips, 1986, 1987; Durlauf & Phillips, 1988). To make matters worse, as the number of time points collected increases, the effects of spurious regression are exacerbated, resulting in even greater Type I error rates (Phillips, 1986, 1987; Durlauf & Phillips, 1988). Psychological researchers typically use RCM, an extension of the regression model, to analyze longitudinal data and frequently collect a greater number of time points. Therefore, they are extremely susceptible to the statistical and inferential problems that result from spurious regression, if the trends present in their dependent variable result, at least partially, from a stochastic trend.

RANDOM WALKS AND STOCHASTIC TRENDS

A purely deterministic model is one in which all observed changes in the dependent variable are due to systematic changes in the independent variable, without any error. Conversely, a stochastic model is one in which observed changes in the dependent variable are due, at least in part, to error. In psychology, almost all models are considered to be stochastic, or include error. It is important to distinguish between a stochastic model and a stochastic trend. The important distinction between a stochastic model and a stochastic trend lies in the properties of the error structure. Processes in psychology are typically modeled as being the result of a deterministic trend and an error process, where errors are independent of one another and the errors do not have a cumulative effect over time. An example of this is the standard regression equation:

$$Y_t = \alpha + \beta t + \varepsilon_t \tag{6.3}$$

where the dependent variable at time t (Y_t) is the result of an initial value (α), a deterministic trend (βt), and an error at time t (ε_t). In regression-based models, it is possible to estimate alternative error structures such as errors that are correlated within-person over time. All such examples are considered stochastic models, because they include error terms but do not contain any stochastic trends. All growth in the dependent variable is due solely to the deterministic trend (βt).

Unfortunately, one alternative error structure that is not commonly considered is one in which the error term has a cumulative effect over time. Modeling a cumulative error structure changes the regression model in Equation (6.3) to:

$$Y_t = \alpha + \beta t + \sum_{i=1}^{t} \varepsilon_t \tag{6.4}$$

In Equation (6.4), the dependent variable at time t (Y_t), is the result of an initial value (α), a deterministic trend (βt), and the cumulative effect of a series of errors from Time 1 to time t ($\sum_{i=1}^{t} \varepsilon_t$). This cumulative error term creates a growth process that is comprised entirely of error, called a stochastic trend. In Equation (6.4), growth in the dependent variable is not solely attributable to the deterministic trend, as in Equation (6.3), but rather is a combination of the deterministic and stochastic trends. Additionally, it is possible that the dependent variable is due entirely to a cumulative error process and does not contain any deterministic trend. This latter model is called a random walk and is defined by the equation:

$$Y_t = \alpha + \sum_{i=1}^{t} \varepsilon_t \tag{6.5}$$

Random walks are the most commonly encountered and studied example of a stochastic trend. They are prevalent in virtually all scientific disciplines, including computer science models of information search (Tang, Jin, & Zhang, 2008), ecological models of biodiffusion (Skellam, 1951) and population dynamics (Wang & Getz, 2007), economic models of real gross national product (GNP) and employment (Nelson & Plosser, 1982), genetic models of genetic drift (Wright, 1931), and physics models of Brownian motion (Uhlenbeck & Ornstein, 1930). Random walks are less studied in psychology than in other fields but are fundamental to the study of consumer behavior such as new product adoption (Eliashberg & Chatterjee, 1986), diffusion models of decision processes (Busemeyer & Townsend, 1993), neuronal firing (Gerstein & Mandelbrot, 1964), and speeded categorization (Nosofsky & Palmeri, 1997). The simplest form of a random walk is described by the equation:

$$Y_t = Y_{t-1} + \varepsilon_t \tag{6.6}$$

where Y_t is the value at time t, Y_{t-1} is the value at time $t-1$, and ε_t is a random error term from a normal distribution that has a mean of zero and a constant variance, σ_{ε}^2. As seen in Equation (6.6), each value of a random walk is derived from the value of the data point directly preceding it, in addition to some random error term (Enders, 1995). Therefore, a random walk is created by an accumulation of random occurrences (i.e., error) and can be thought of as a series that is created by taking successive random steps. This can most easily be seen using the alternative equation for a random walk given in Equation (6.5). As random walks are simply an accumulation of error, it is impossible to predict future values. This means that the best guess or expected value for any time point is the value directly preceding it. This eventually reduces down so that the initial condition (i.e., intercept), Y_0, becomes the expected value for all future time points, as can be seen in the following equation:

$$E(Y_t) = E(Y_{t-1}) = E(Y_0) \tag{6.7}$$

As the intercept becomes the expected value for all time points, the long-run mean of a random walk is time-invariant. However, the variance–covariance matrix of a random walk follows the equation:

$$\Omega_{j,k} = \min(j,k)\sigma_\varepsilon^2 \tag{6.8}$$

where j and k are the number of time points, causing the variance of a random walk to follow the equation:

$$\text{Var}(Y_t) = \text{var}(\varepsilon_t + \varepsilon_{t-1} + ... \varepsilon_1) = t\sigma_\varepsilon^2 \tag{6.9}$$

As a result of Equations (6.8) and (6.9), the variance is time-varying, meaning that the variance at any one time point is not equal to the variance at any other time point. Figure 6.1 shows a random walk that appears to be a positively directed growth process.

As seen in Figure 6.1, although the long-run mean of a random walk is the initial condition (i.e., intercept), random walks frequently appear to be stable growth processes when measured over short durations. Not surprisingly, then, it is often nearly impossible to distinguish between series that result from purely deterministic trends and ones that result from purely stochastic trends. To demonstrate this, Figure 6.2 plots a regression line on data generated by a purely deterministic (Equation 6.3) or purely stochastic (Equation 6.5) trend. Without the labels, it would be impossible to tell them apart, and yet it is imperative that researchers are able to do so to make correct statistical and scientific inferences.

Both of the series in Figure 6.2 appear to be positively trending growth processes. The regression lines fit both sets of data quite well, potentially fitting the stochastic trend better. Despite the fact that regression appears to accurately reflect the trend in both sets of data, there are problems that arise when utilizing regression-based methods to model data containing

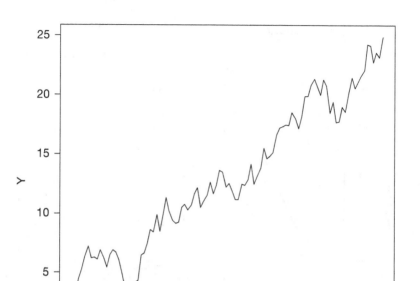

FIGURE 6.1
Random walk.

stochastic trends. First, inferential problems arise when researchers want to talk about prediction. A deterministic series is created from a consistent trend so that researchers are able to gain insight into future realizations based on previous measurements. A series resulting from a stochastic trend, on the other hand, is made up of a collection of random errors, and so having information about prior measurements is useless in trying to predict future outcomes. Likewise, because random walks are created only by an accumulation of errors, no true predictive relationship can exist between them and any other variable. Therefore, if the series under investigation results from a stochastic trend, finding predictors of that process as well as making accurate scientific inferences around future events is impossible. The second problem that arises when using regression-based methods to model data with stochastic trends is that statistical results are systematically biased. This phenomenon is called spurious regression and will be discussed in the following section.

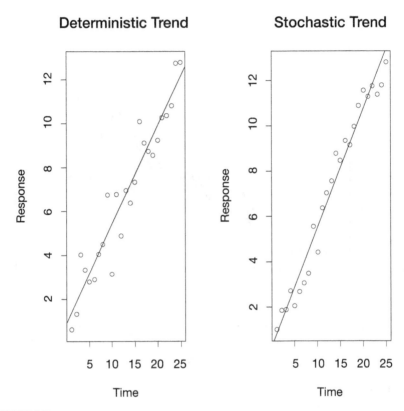

FIGURE 6.2
Regression lines fit to deterministic and stochastic trends.

Conceptualizing a series created entirely by error is difficult. To do so, it is easiest to think of error as unpredictable environmental shocks that are mathematically random. If these environmental shocks have a cumulative effect on a psychological process, they create a stochastic trend. For example, consider Muraven and Baumeister's (2000) theory of self-regulatory depletion. The theory states that self-regulation is like a muscle that can become fatigued with repeated use. It further states that individuals self-regulate to events in the environment, and that people have a limited pool of self-regulatory resources. As individuals continually self-regulate to environment events, their resource pool becomes depleted. Thus, individuals are less able to self-regulate in the future. It is generally accepted that environmental events occur in a random and unpredictable (i.e., stochastic) fashion. If the effect of these unpredictable environmental events is, as the theory states, cumulative on people's self-regulatory resources, then it creates a stochastic trend. Similarly, it is possible that, over time, measurement error is being compounded, also creating an accumulation of errors, resulting in a stochastic trend.

Self-regulatory depletion is just one area of research that has the potential to be impacted by the presence of stochastic trends in longitudinal data. Any research area that postulates unpredictable events impacting a psychological process or utilizes multiple self-report measures over time is susceptible. Two other examples are theories of emotional labor (e.g., Ashforth & Humphrey, 1993) and Affective Events Theory (AET; Weiss & Cropanzano, 1996), the dominant approach to the study of affect in organizational psychology. Focusing on AET, the theory states that mood and emotions fluctuate over time, and that events in the environment are proximal causes for affective reactions. If the effect of these unpredictable environmental events is cumulative on people's affective responses, then it creates a stochastic trend. These examples are worrisome, because many longitudinal studies focus on self-regulation, emotional labor, and affect, and almost all longitudinal designs in the organizational sciences utilize repeated self-report measures over time.

SPURIOUS REGRESSION

Dealing with spurious relationships has been a persistent problem in psychological measurement over the years. Yule first pointed out in 1926 that any two series that exhibit growth over time can appear statistically related, even if no true relationship between them exists. Similarly, Barcikowski (1981) and, later, Kreft and De Leeuw (1998) showed that, if clustering (nonindependence) exists in data, then Type I error rates dramatically increase, making it more likely to find relationships among variables that are not truly related. These issues have received significant attention in the literature and, for the most part, have been effectively dealt with. However, one potential cause of spurious relationships that has received significantly less attention in psychology is spurious regression due to stochastic trends.

Random walks and stochastic trends are found in almost all fields and are frequently encountered in economics, where spurious regression due to stochastic trends was first documented by Granger and Newbold (1974). They observed that, in the economics literature, regression coefficients were almost always significant, and the amount of variance explained (R^2) was extremely high whenever regression was used to determine the relationship between time series. They suggested that, in the presence of stochastic trends, the regression model inaccurately overestimates the true relationships between series. To demonstrate this, they regressed one independent random walk on another. As previously mentioned, as random walks are created only by an accumulation of errors, no true predictive relationship can exist between them. Therefore, the regression coefficient should be significant at the nominal rate ($\alpha = 0.05$), and the proportion of variance explained should be approximately zero ($R^2 = 0$). Any significant deviation from these expected results is due to problems with the estimation method. They found that, when stochastic trends are present in the dependent variable, for series with 100 time points, the Type I error rate of the regression coefficient is dramatically inflated, leading the parameter to be significant approximately 76 percent of the time (for $\alpha = 0.05$), well beyond the nominal rate. Similarly, they found that the variance explained was greatly overestimated. The model R^2 was found to be 0.47, indicating that 47 percent of the variance in the dependent random walk was accounted for by the predictor random walk, even though no true relationship existed between the series. These results supported Granger and Newbold's hypothesis that regression overestimates true relationships between series in the presence of stochastic trends.

Nelson and Kang (1984) expanded on the findings of Granger and Newbold (1974) by examining how spurious regression manifested in the presence of a purely stochastic trend (random walk) being regressed on a deterministic, linear time index, *Time*, and an independent stochastic trend (random walk). As in Granger and Newbold (1974), all stochastic trends were created only from an accumulation of errors, so that all significant results for any predictor beyond the nominal rate are due to faulty estimation. As adding a predictor to a model never results in a decrease in R^2, it is not surprising that the addition of *Time* as a predictor increased R^2 from 0.47 in the prior case to 0.50 when the length of the series was 100 time points. The addition of *Time* as a predictor decreased the Type I error on the slope parameter for the predictor random walk from 76 percent in the prior case to 64 percent (for $\alpha = 0.05$). However, the Type I error rate for the slope of *Time* increased beyond that of the predictor random walk, resulting in the regression coefficient being significant approximately 83 percent of the time. This means that, once again, both predictors were found to be significant well above the nominal rate.

When regression is used to analyze data containing stochastic trends, a number of systematic statistical biases, such as the ones just presented, occur, resulting in faulty estimation. For example, when regression is applied to longitudinal data containing stochastic trends, the variance of R^2 becomes inflated, causing the distribution to no longer be unimodal around the origin. This results in R^2 being consistently overestimated, where the expected value diverges from the true value of zero as the number of time points increases (Granger & Newbold, 1974; Nelson & Kang, 1984). Also, as the number of time points collected increases, the predicted error covariance matrix from the regression model increasingly misestimates the true covariance matrix of a random walk given by Equation (6.8) (Nelson & Kang, 1984). This results in the standard errors of the regression coefficients being increasingly underestimated relative to their standard deviations, leading to significance tests that are too liberal. This bias results in grossly inflated Type I errors for all continuous predictors. However, the regression coefficients themselves are unbiased and, thus, correctly estimated to be approximately zero in all cases (Granger & Newbold, 1974; Nelson & Kang, 1984; Phillips, 1986, 1987).

The consistent pattern of statistical biases is the result of the unique distributional properties of the regression coefficients in the presence of purely stochastic trends in the dependent variable. Phillips (1986, 1987) and Durlauf and Phillips (1988) mathematically derived the distributions of the regression parameters when a purely stochastic trend was the dependent variable and both deterministic (*Time*) and stochastic (random walk) variables were inserted as predictors. The means for the intercept, the deterministic predictor, *Time*, and the stochastic predictor were all shown to be approximately zero (Nelson & Kang, 1984; Durlauf & Phillips, 1988). This is consistent with the findings in Nelson and Kang (1984) and Granger and Newbold (1974) that empirically show that the intercept, the slope of *Time*, and the slope of the predictor random walk parameter estimates are correctly estimated at zero.

The variance components of the distributions also have very consistent properties. The variance of the intercept parameter was proven to increase linearly as a function of the number of time points, defined by the equation, $2T/15$ However, the variance of the parameter estimate on the slope of the deterministic predictor, *Time,* converges toward its true value of zero as a function of the number of time points, defined by the equation, $6/5T$. The variance of the stochastic predictor was shown to converge weakly to a distribution, meaning that the variance will converge to some value as the number of time points increases and remain at approximately that value for all additional numbers of time points.

The effects of spurious regression due to stochastic trends in data are quite dramatic and could lead to many incorrect statistical and scientific inferences if they are not accounted for. To make matters worse, the spurious regression effects are exacerbated as the number time points or the number of additional continuous predictors increases (Granger & Newbold, 1974; Nelson & Kang, 1984; Phillips, 1986, 1987). To complicate matters even further, two unrelated series can often appear to covary, thus making their true relationship harder to detect. This has been documented

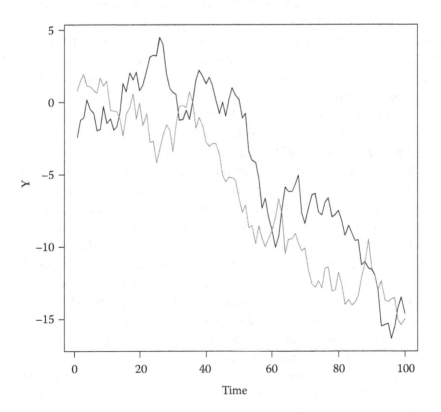

FIGURE 6.3
Seemingly related independent random walks.

many times using random walks, and an example of such a case can be seen in Figure 6.3.

SPURIOUS REGRESSION IN RCMS

The effects of data containing stochastic trends on the regression model presented above are well known in economics and are directly applicable to psychological researchers. However, significantly less is known about how stochastic trends in longitudinal data will affect the results from RCMs, the dominant approach to the analysis of longitudinal data in psychology. As an RCM is a generalization of the regression model, it follows that the results will be biased when stochastic trends are present in the dependent variable. The distributional properties derived by Durlauf and Phillips (1988) described above, along with Monte Carlo simulation results from two recent papers, provide insight into the exact nature and scope of the biases in RCM caused by the presence of stochastic trends in longitudinal data. The statistical biases present in the unconditional models, conditional growth models with Level 2 predictors, and growth curve models with Level 1, time-varying covariates will be presented, ending with a brief discussion of the general patterns of biases. Finally, the results will then be generalized to latent growth models.

Unconditional Models

Unconditional Means Model

As previously mentioned, RCM is typically run by analyzing a series of nested models. The first recommended model is the unconditional means model, as described by Equation (6.1). The primary purpose in running the unconditional means model is to determine the proportion of variance that exists between individuals by calculating the *ICC(1)*. The *ICC(1)* is calculated by taking the amount of variance between individuals, σ_0^2, divided by the total variance of the system ($\sigma_0^2 + \sigma_\varepsilon^2$). Kuljanin and colleagues (in press) combined the equation for calculating the *ICC(1)* with the mathematical expectations of each component when stochastic trends are present. They derived that the *ICC(1)* will consistently overestimate the true amount of variance that exists between individuals and will always produce a value of approximately 0.67 if the dependent variable is a purely stochastic trend. They empirically demonstrated this phenomenon using Monte Carlo simulations and showed that, regardless of sample size or number of time points, the value of *ICC(1)* was approximately 0.66. Thus, researchers would incorrectly conclude that 66 percent of the variance in the dependent variable was attributable to between-person variance, even though the data-generating mechanism for all individuals was exactly the same.

Unconditional Growth Model

After determining that a significant amount of variance exists, either within or between individuals, the next recommended step in RCM is to run the unconditional growth model, specified as:

$$Y_{ij} = \left[\gamma_{00} + \gamma_{10} Time_{ij}\right] + \left[\zeta_{01} + \zeta_{1i} Time_{ij} + \varepsilon_{ij}\right] \tag{6.10}$$

This model includes fixed effects for the intercept and slope of *Time*, γ_{00} and γ_{10}, respectively, as well as random effects for the intercept and *Time*, ζ_{0i} and ζ_{1i}, respectively, along with variance components for the random effects for the intercept and *Time*, σ_0^2 and σ_1^2, respectively, and a variance component for the residual error term, σ_ε^2.

Kuljanin et al. (in press) found that, for the unconditional growth model, regardless of sample size or the number of time points, the average intercept and slope (i.e., fixed effects) are all close to the true value of zero, and the observed rejection rates approximately maintain the nominal 5 percent significance level. Consistent with the mathematical proofs by Durlauf and Phillips (1988), as the number of time points increases, the intercept variance increases at the approximate rate of $2T/15$, while the slope variance decreases at the rate of approximately $6/5T$. The intercept and slope variance, along with the deviance statistic between the unconditional means and the unconditional growth model, is always significant, regardless of sample size or number of time points. Although this is not surprising for the intercept variance, because its value becomes increasingly large, it is surprising that the slope variance is significant even when the value approaches zero. This happens because the chi-squared tests on the variance components increase with time, thus always indicating significance, regardless of the actual value of the variance estimate (Kuljanin et al., in press).

All of these results follow the mathematical expectations of Durlauf and Phillips (1988), and, without regard to the size of the longitudinal dataset, these results indicate that statistics from random coefficient models would mislead researchers into believing that there is significant variation in intercepts and slopes. However, the true slope for each person in every simulation and replication was set to zero. Thus, there is no variability in true slopes. In a literature review by Kuljanin et al. (in press), it was found that substantive researchers frequently follow the advice of methodologists and use the variance components as a justification to search for predictors. Therefore, the observed variance in intercepts and slopes would lead researchers to model explanatory variables of this variance. If the underlying data-generating mechanism were generated entirely by a stochastic trend, this would only result in the identification of correlates of intercepts and slopes that are entirely spurious.

Conditional Growth Models With Level 2 Predictors

The findings above highlight the consequences of fitting unconditional models to data containing a stochastic trend. The results from these models indicate that the variance-component estimates and tests are biased, while the fixed-effect estimates and tests are accurate. Although exploring the effects of stochastic trends on the unconditional models is an excellent first step, the focus of most research studies is on predictors of growth. Frequently, these investigations focus on predictors of heterogeneity in the random effects, and the predictors are modeled as fixed effects. The fact that the fixed-effects estimates and tests are unbiased in the unconditional models may result in a mistaken belief that RCMs protect against finding spurious predictors of random-effect heterogeneity. Unfortunately, this is not the case. Results from the conditional models are still biased in systematic ways, depending on what parameters are modeled.

Kuljanin et al. (in press) identified two distinct ways substantive researchers model Level 2 predictors. Researchers either build upon the unconditional growth model and simply add a predictor as a fixed effect, or remove the random effect of *Time* from the unconditional growth model and then add a predictor as a fixed effect. The specific nature of the biases due to the presence of stochastic trends depends on whether the random effect for *Time* is modeled. Both types of conditional model will now be discussed.

Conditional Growth Model Without a Random Effect for Slopes

Typically, when researchers examine the impact of a Level 2 predictor (L2P), they model both the main effect and moderating effect of the predictor on the dependent variable. They do this by inserting the predictor into the Level 2 equation for both intercepts and slopes. Based on the results of the unconditional growth model, the Level 2 equation for slopes can either include or exclude a random effect. If it is determined that little or no variance in slopes exists, then researchers can remove the random effect from the model. The equation takes the form:

$$Y_{ij} = \left[\gamma_{00} + \gamma_{01} L2P + \gamma_{10} Time_{ij} + \gamma_{11} L2P_i * Time_{ij} \right] + \left[\zeta_{01} + \varepsilon_{ij} \right] \quad (6.11)$$

This model includes fixed effects for the intercept, slope of *Time*, main effect of the Level 2 predictor, and moderating effect of the Level 2 predictor, γ_{00}, γ_{10}, γ_{01}, and γ_{11}, respectively, as well as an intercept random effect, ζ_{0i}, along with variance components for the random effect and the residual error term, σ_0^2 and σ_ε^2, respectively.

When a Level 2 predictor is added to the model and the slope random effect is removed, a number of problems exist if the data being analyzed result from a stochastic trend. Consistent with the results from the unconditional models, the random effect of the intercept once again increases drastically as the number of time points increases and is found to always be significant, regardless of the number of time points or sample size (Kuljanin, et al., in press). Similarly, all fixed-effect estimates are accurate and estimated to be approximately zero. However, contrary to the results from the unconditional models, the fixed-effect significance tests become biased when the random effect for slope is removed. The significance tests for the fixed effect for the intercept (γ_{00}) and main effect of the Level 2 predictor (γ_{01}) become increasingly conservative with increased numbers of time points. More specifically, for as few as five time points, the rejection rate for the intercept and main effect is as low as 0.7 percent (for $\alpha = 0.05$). Conversely, the significance tests for the slope (γ_{10}) and moderating effect of the Level 2 predictor (γ_{11}) become increasingly liberal with greater numbers of time points (Kuljanin et al., in press). For example, the rejection rate for the slope of *Time* and moderating effect increases to as high as 23 percent for only five time points. This finding is particularly interesting because there are no true slope differences in the data-generating mechanism. Hence, if researchers correctly model the stochastic trend by identifying the lack of variance in growth and removing the random effect for slopes, they become extremely susceptible to biased results on both the fixed and random effects.

Conditional Growth Model With a Random Effect for Slopes

If researchers determine that significant variance in slopes exists and choose to model a corresponding random effect, then the equation takes the form:

$$Y_{ij} = \left[\gamma_{00} + \gamma_{01}L2P + \gamma_{10}Time_{ij} + \gamma_{11}L2P_i * Time_{ij} \right] + \qquad (6.12)$$
$$\left[\zeta_{01} + \zeta_{1i}Time_{ij} + \varepsilon_{ij} \right]$$

This model includes fixed effects for the intercept, slope of *Time*, main effect of the Level 2 predictor, and moderating effect of the Level 2 predictor, γ_{00}, γ_{10}, γ_{01}, and γ_{11}, respectively, as well as intercept and slope random effects, ζ_{0i} and ζ_{1i}, respectively, along with variance components for the intercept and slope random effects and residual error term, σ_0^2, σ_1^2, and σ_ε^2, respectively.

When the slope random effect is included in the model, then the pattern of results is identical to those of the unconditional models. All four fixed effects are well behaved and accurately estimated to be approximately zero. Similarly, the significance tests on those fixed effects approximately maintain the nominal rate ($\alpha = 0.05$). However, the random effects and their corresponding significance tests are biased. The intercept random effect once again increases by the function of $2T/15$ as the number of time points increases, while the slope random effect decreases toward its true value of zero at the rate of $6/5T$. The significance tests for the random effects were found to be significant in every replication of every condition, regardless of sample size or number of time points (Kuljanin et al., in press).

The patterns of results across these two types of conditional model are troubling, because, if the underlying data-generating mechanism is a random walk, the slope variance decreases toward zero with increased time points. Therefore, if researchers correctly identify that there is no variance in slopes and remove the random effect, they become susceptible to bias in both the fixed and random effects. As part of this bias, results indicate the presence of significant moderators of slope heterogeneity, despite the fact that no true relationships exist. This could lead researchers to incorrectly identify substantive predictors of heterogeneity.

Conversely, if researchers ignore the lack of variance in slopes and keep the random effect in the model, they are still likely to encounter bias in the random-effect estimates and significance tests and are still susceptible to finding spurious predictors of heterogeneity. As the primary focus of conditional models is on the fixed-effect tests of predictors, the behavior of the fixed effects may lead researchers to incorrectly believe that the RCM behaves well as long as all random effects are included. Although the probability of a Type I error for a single predictor is approximately nominal when all random effects are modeled, Kuljanin and colleagues' (in press) literature review indicates that researchers typically include as many as eight predictors of intercept or slope heterogeneity. Also, those are only the predictors that researchers reported. In reality, it is likely that other predictors were examined and left out of the final manuscript. Thus, the probability of obtaining at least one Type I error for the model is $(1 - (1 - 0.05)^8) = 0.34$, or 34 percent. Therefore, as each examined predictor increases the risk of finding at least one spurious relationship, researchers cannot rely on RCMs to protect against the inferential mistakes that result from stochastic trends in the dependent variable, even when all random effects are modeled. As a result, if stochastic trends are present in the dependent variable, researchers are extremely susceptible to finding spurious predictors of heterogeneity, regardless of what other variables are included in the model.

Growth Curve Models With Time-Varying Covariates

Another common method researchers use to explain variance in the dependent variable is to insert Level 1 time-varying covariates into the model. There are once again two distinct ways that researchers commonly model time-varying covariates. One method is to build upon the unconditional growth model and simply include an additional Level 1 predictor. The other method is to remove the variable *Time* from the model and then insert the Level 1 predictor. Either way, the recommended practice is to first insert the predictor as only a fixed effect, and then, if there is still additional variance to be explained, let it vary as a random effect as well (Singer & Willett, 2003). Much like in the case of the conditional models, the exact nature of the estimation bias in RCM depends on what variables and parameters are modeled.

Growth Curve Models With Time and Time-Varying Covariates

Quantitative methodologists recommend that researchers first run the unconditional models and determine the proportion of within- and between-person variance to be explained and the trajectories of the growth curves. Then, researchers should build upon the unconditional growth model and insert any time-varying predictors. The rationale of this approach is that the predictor *Time* will account for any linear trend in the dependent variable not attributed to the independent variables (i.e., time-varying predictors), leading to unbiased estimates of the predictors of interest (Nelson & Kang, 1984). It is recommended to begin by inserting the predictors as only fixed effects (Kreft & De Leeuw, 1998; Snijders & Bosker, 1999; Raudenbush & Bryk, 2002; Singer & Willet, 2003). The model takes the form:

$$Y_{ij} = \left[\gamma_{00} + \gamma_{10} Time_{ij} + \gamma_{20} TVC_{ij}\right] + \left[\zeta_{01} + \zeta_{1i} Time_{ij} + \varepsilon_{ij}\right] \tag{6.13}$$

This model includes fixed effects for the intercept, slope of *Time*, and the time-varying predictor (TVC), γ_{00}, γ_{10}, and γ_{20}, respectively, as well as random effects for the intercept and *Time*, ζ_{0i} and ζ_{1i}, respectively, along with variance components of the random effects of the intercept and *Time*, σ_0^2 and σ_1^2, respectively, and a variance component for the residual error term, σ_ε^2.

The pattern of results for models with time-varying predictors is very similar to those exhibited in the conditional models with Level 2 predictors. Braun et al. (in press) used Monte Carlo simulations to demonstrate that the fixed-effect estimates are once again accurate, regardless of sample size and number of time points. However, when the random effect for the TVC is not included, the significance tests on the fixed effects are not as well behaved. The intercept and slope tests maintained the nominal rate, regardless of sample size or number of time points, but the time-varying predictor's rejection rate exploded with increased time points to well beyond the nominal level. In fact, the Type I error rate becomes greater than 60 percent for long series, meaning that more than 60 percent of the time, researchers would inaccurately conclude that adding a predictor explained significant variance. The random effects exhibited the same problems seen in both the conditional and unconditional models. The intercept variance increased, and the slope variance decreased, with increased time points, and the significance tests rejected the null 100 percent of the time, regardless of sample size or number of time points. All of these results lead researchers to believe that they have identified a significant predictor and that they should continue searching for predictors, even though, if the data result from stochastic trends, all relationships, current and future, are entirely spurious.

The results above would likely lead researchers to continue testing additional models, and the next recommended step would be to include the random effect for the TVC, so long as it makes conceptual sense that the TVC will vary across people, and if researchers have the sample size required to estimate the additional parameters. If researchers do this, the model takes the form:

$$Y_{ij} = \left[\gamma_{00} + \gamma_{10} Time_{ij} + \gamma_{20} TVC_{ij}\right] + \left[\zeta_{0i} + \zeta_{1i} Time_{ij} + \zeta_{2i} TVC_{ij} + \varepsilon_{ij}\right] \tag{6.14}$$

This model includes fixed effects for the intercept, slope of *Time*, and the time-varying predictor (*TVC*), γ_{00}, γ_{10}, and γ_{20}, respectively, as well as random effects for the intercept, *Time*, and *TVC*, ζ_{0i}, ζ_{1i}, and ζ_{2i}, respectively, along with variance components of the random effects of the intercept, *Time*, and *TVC*, σ_0^2, σ_1^2, and and σ_2^2, respectively, and a variance component for the residual error term, σ_ε^2.

The biases in this model are very similar to those of the unconditional growth model and the conditional model with the random effect for *Time* included. All of the fixed-effect estimates and tests are well behaved and maintain nominal rejection rates. The intercept and slope variance components exhibit the exact same trends, although, because the variance of the system is further divided up from the addition of a predictor, the effects are somewhat ameliorated. The intercept variance still increases toward infinity as the number of time points increases, just at a slightly slower pace than the $2T/15$ documented in the unconditional growth model. Likewise, the variance of slopes decreases toward its true value of zero, but at a slower pace than 6/5*T*. Despite the fact that the observed trends of the variance components are weakened, the significance tests on both the intercept and slope variance components is significant always, regardless of sample size or number of time points. The variance of the additional predictor, *TVC*, weakly increases with an increased number of time points. Despite the fact that no true relationship exists between the TVC and dependent variable, the variance component is found to be increasingly significant with increased number of time points. With as few as 10 time points, the variance becomes significant 100 percent of the time (Braun et al., 2011). These results would likely lead researchers to believe they have found a substantive predictor of growth and would encourage them to search for additional predictors. Unfortunately, if the underlying data-generating mechanism is the result of a stochastic trend, all predictors are entirely spurious.

Growth Curve Models With Only Time-Varying Covariates

When testing the impact of Level 1 time-varying covariates, some researchers opt to remove *Time* from the model, after testing the unconditional growth model. Although this decision may be theoretically valid, it does not eliminate the effects of spurious regression due to analyzing data with stochastic trends. Typically, when researchers choose this route, they analyze the unconditional means model to assess the *ICC(1)*, and then test the unconditional growth model to determine the average effects and shape of the growth trajectories. Researchers then generally remove *Time* from the model and insert the time-varying predictor as only a fixed effect first, as was done in the previous models, and then allow it to vary if it makes conceptual sense and researchers have adequate sample size to estimate the additional parameters.

The models are identical to those seen in Equations (6.13) and (6.14), with the variable *Time* removed. The pattern of biases is exactly the same as demonstrated above for the growth-curve models, with a TVC and *Time* included (Braun et al., in press).

General Results

Across the three general types of model described, a number of distinct patterns emerge. The fixed-effects estimates are well behaved and accurately estimated in all cases. When a corresponding random effect is modeled, the fixed-effect significance tests are also well behaved and stay approximately at the nominal rate in most conditions. The only exception is in conditional models when the random effect for *Time* is removed. In this case, the fixed effects of the other variables become overly conservative and do not maintain nominal rates. Similarly, in all types of model, if a corresponding random effect is not modeled, the fixed-effect significance tests of that variable diverge with increased number of time points, leading to a serious inflation of Type I error rates and rejection rates well beyond the nominal level (upward of 70 percent).

The variance components of the random effects also follow very distinct patterns across all the models. The variance component of the intercept increases toward infinity as the number of time points collected increases across all models. Similarly, in all models, the variance component of the slope random effect decreases toward its true value of zero as the number of time points increases. The variance component of the random effect of a TVC slightly increases as the number of time points increases. When a large amount of information is present (i.e. large number of people or time points), all the variance components are always significant. For a few models, when information is limited (small sample size and number of time points), the rejection rates of the variance components can drop slightly below 100 percent, but are still much greater than the nominal level ($\alpha = 0.05$). This is troubling, because, typically, having more information (in terms of time points and sample size) is considered advantageous, because it increases statistical power. However, in the case of spurious regression due to stochastic trends in longitudinal data, having more information makes researchers more susceptible to finding spurious relations.

Although not highlighted earlier, the deviance statistics between the models presented also follow a specific pattern. When the only difference between models is the addition of a fixed effect, the deviance statistic becomes another significance test on that parameter; therefore, as the number of time points increases, the rejection rate between models increases toward 100 percent. When the difference between models was multiple parameters resulting from the addition of a random effect, the deviance statistics closely mirror the rejection rates of the variance components of the inserted random effect. The correlations among variance components are often small and nonsignificant, and so, once again, the deviance statistic essentially becomes a single parameter test for the variance component of the inserted random effect. As such, as the variance components are almost always significant, so are the deviance statistics (Braun et al., in press; Kuljanin et al., in press).

Application to Latent Growth Models

All of the models shown and results provided from prior studies were done using RCM. The other dominant method used to analyze longitudinal data and answer questions about dynamics is a structural equation modeling approach called LGM. To the extent that latent growth models mirror the structure and properties of RCMs, they suffer from exactly the same estimation biases of spurious regression owing to the presence of stochastic trends in longitudinal data. More specifically, the fixed- and random-effect estimates are identical, and their corresponding significance tests exhibit the same pattern of biases as documented above. Also, the deviance tests on latent growth models become increasingly significant with increased number of time points, leading to 100 percent rejection rates for significance tests between nested models and on individual parameters (e.g., variance components) (Braun et al., in press).

One benefit to the use of latent growth models is that global fit indices may be used to evaluate overall model fit. Three of the most common global fit indices are the model chi-squared, the Comparative Fit Index (CFI), and the Root Mean Squared Error of Approximation (RMSEA) (Hu & Bentler, 1999). Unfortunately, these fit indices also suffer from estimation bias and behave in systematic ways when longitudinal data with stochastic trends in the dependent variable are analyzed. The model chi-squared test is heavily biased by the presence of stochastic trends and increases toward infinity with increased time points, thus always indicating poor model fit. This occurs for the same reason that the chi-squared tests on the variance components and nested models in RCM diverge and always indicate significance. As both the CFI and RMSEA are functions of the model chi-squared, they indicate increasingly worse model fit as the number of time points increases (Kline, 2005; Braun et al., in press).

The fact that these common global fit indices indicate poor model fit may be mistakenly seen as an advantage of LGM over RCM and a way of protecting against the biases due to the presence of stochastic trends in the data. However, it does not actually alleviate any of the problems caused by analyzing data resulting from a stochastic trend. Researchers may wish to attempt to explain additional variance or improve overall model fit by adding predictors. However, if they do this, they will be engaging in the proverbial snipe hunt, because no true predictive relationships can exist, and any significant predictors found (due to the biases presented above) would be due solely to Type I error.

DEALING WITH STOCHASTIC TRENDS

As previously mentioned, random walks and stochastic trends are encountered in virtually all scientific disciplines. Although it is unclear as to the exact prevalence of stochastic trends in psychology, it is likely that they exist in the psychological sciences, and it is important to be able to identify and analyze them. It is, therefore, important to look to other fields for guidance on how to effectively deal with stochastic trends in longitudinal data, to avoid the statistical and inferential problems that arise in regression models when they are present. Perhaps most similar to psychology is the field of economics.

Economists have adopted the practice of first attempting to identify whether the trends present in the dependent variable are stochastic, before selecting an analytic strategy. To do so, economists typically begin their analyses by using one or more statistical tests known as unit root tests. If a unit root test indicates that all trends in the dependent variable are distinguishable from a random walk and thus deterministic, then economists frequently utilize regression models similar to those found in psychology. However, if a unit root test indicates that the dependent variable is indistinguishable from a random walk and thus stochastic, then economists utilize an alternative class of statistical method that can model the stochastic trends in the data. Further research is needed to determine whether the practice of using unit root tests as a precondition of applying regression-based models is appropriate for psychological data structures. In the meantime, it is recommended that researchers familiarize themselves with unit root tests and report the results of one or more of these tests when analyzing longitudinal data. This will help to identify potential stochastic trends in psychology, and help researchers appropriately qualify their inferences from regression-based models, if it is found that the trends present in the data are stochastic.

Unit Root Tests

In economics, the most commonly used unit root test is the Augmented Dickey Fuller (ADF) test (Dickey & Fuller, 1979; Said & Dickey, 1984). For a single series, the ADF is

$$\Delta Y_t = \alpha + \gamma Y_{t-1} + \sum_{i=1}^{p} \delta_p \Delta Y_{t-p} + \varepsilon_t \qquad (6.15)$$

where Y_t is the series, $\Delta Y_t = Y_t - Y_{t-1}$, α is the drift parameter, p is the lag order of the autoregressive process, δ_p are the structural autoregressive effects, and ε_t is the error term. The null hypothesis associated with this test is $\gamma = 0$, indicating that a series is indistinguishable from a random walk and, thus, is likely the result of a stochastic trend. To properly run the ADF, researchers first need to determine whether the series contains a drift and determine the lag structure of the time series. To evaluate the existence of a drift, researchers typically visually assess the series to determine if the mean of the series changes over time. If it appears that there is growth, then it is recommended to include the drift parameter when running the ADF. To determine the lag structure of the series, researchers evaluate the autocorrelation and partial autocorrelation functions (see Enders, 1995). The ADF is a low power test, and estimating unnecessary parameters for long lags and drift wastes degrees of freedom. Therefore, to get the most accurate results, it is important that researchers only include the appropriate number of lags and the presence of a drift if it is necessary.

One important difference between economic and psychological research is that, in economics, researchers commonly collect only one or two series of data. Conversely, in psychology it is common to collect data on many individuals, resulting in panel data. The standard ADF test can only be used to evaluate the trends present in a single trajectory. Therefore, for psychological longitudinal data, a panel version of the ADF is needed to determine whether the sample of trajectories as a whole is distinguishable from multiple random walks. To use the panel ADF test, researchers must set up a common model across all of the series. As a result, it is necessary to examine each series to determine whether a drift exists in the majority of the series and to evaluate the autocorrelation and partial autocorrelation functions of each series, to determine the most common lag structure across the sample. This process is described in most introductory time-series texts (e.g., Enders, 2004). Once the appropriate parameters are determined, the panel version of the ADF test developed by Im, Pesaran, and Shin (2003) is computed by applying the standard ADF on each series in the sample and then taking the average value of γ in Equation (6.15). This average value is then compared with a percentile (e.g., 90th or 95th) from the distribution of estimated unit roots (i.e., γ) on random walks for the specified drift, lag order, length of series, and size of the sample (see Im et al., 2003). The free statistical software, R, includes the ADF in its set of analytical techniques, as well as the autocorrelation and partial autocorrelation functions. An example of running the panel ADF on psychological longitudinal data in R, complete with the necessary code, can be seen in Kuljanin et al. (in press).

Although the ADF test is the most common unit root test in economics, it is generally recommended to run multiple unit root tests before deciding on the structure of the data, owing to the low power of each of these tests. As a result, a number of other unit root tests exist. For example, Elliott, Rothenberg, and Stock (1996), Kwiatkowski, Phillips, Schmidt, and Shin (1992), Phillips and Perron (1988), Schmidt and Phillips (1992), and Zivot and Andrews (1992) all developed slightly different unit root tests to deal with small samples, fewer time points, and other design issues that can impact the power of unit root tests. The statistical program R has all of these techniques available for researchers to use. Most relevant to psychological researchers, there are also a number of other panel unit root tests available. The two most commonly run are the Multivariate Augmented Dickey–Fuller test (Taylor and Sarno, 1998) and the Johansen (1988) likelihood ratio test. Osterholm (2004) provides a good example of how to interpret the results and qualify scientific inferences when using these two additional panel unit root tests along with the panel ADF test described above.

Despite some of the low-power issues associated with these tests, they do provide good insight into the underlying structure of the data. By running multiple unit root tests, as well as using panel versions of the tests, researchers can achieve greater statistical power to distinguish deterministic and stochastic trends in their data (Osterholm, 2004). Further research is needed to determine the applicability of some or all of these tests to psychological data structures, and to examine the necessary parameters (sample size and time points) needed to achieve appropriate statistical power.

Alternative Statistical Techniques

If one or more unit root tests indicate that the trends present in the dependent variable are indistinguishable from random walks, then RCM results are almost certainly biased. In that case, it is important to utilize an alternative class of statistical method that can model stochastic trends and produce unbiased results. In economics, there are a number of commonly applied models that researchers can choose from when analyzing data resulting, at least partially, from stochastic trends. The two most common and promising analytic strategies are autoregressive-integrated-moving average (ARIMA) models and structural time-series models. These approaches will be briefly explained, focusing on how they work, their common applications, and potential usefulness to psychological longitudinal data analysis.

ARIMA Models

The dominant approach to the analysis of data containing stochastic trends in economics is the use of ARIMA models. ARIMA models take the difference of the dependent variable by subtracting each data point from the data point directly preceding it $(t_n - t_{n-1})$ an appropriate number of times until the resulting trends are solely deterministic. Then, they allow researchers to input variables into the model to predict the resulting deterministic series (Enders, 1995, 2004). Although this method is the most commonly used in economics, it has a number of flaws that make it less applicable to psychological data structures. First, ARIMA models can only be used to analyze a single time series. For economists, this rarely poses a problem, as they often deal with single series; however, for psychologists who deal with longitudinal panel data, this is a major limitation. Second, this method is often criticized because differencing the data many times produces a deterministic series that may be nothing like the original data. This creates the potential for researchers to make inferential mistakes by determining relationships among types of data that do not exist in the real world. Therefore, despite their prevalence in economics, ARIMA models are not particularly useful for analyzing typical psychological longitudinal data structures.

Structural Time-Series Models

Less common in economics, but perhaps more promising, is the use of structural time-series models to analyze data with stochastic trends. Structural time-series models allow researchers to insert a stochastic component into the model to filter out any stochastic trends, while simultaneously allowing researchers to insert predictors of any remaining deterministic trends. This allows researchers to more accurately model the true underlying data-generating mechanism by simultaneously modeling deterministic and stochastic trends, along with predictors of the deterministic trends (Harvey, 1989, 1997; Harvey and Shephard, 1993). Like ARIMA models, structural time-series models are typically applied to single time series. However, a panel version has been created to handle the types of longitudinal data structure commonly found in psychology (Harvey & Koopman, 1996; Chu & Durango-Cohen, 2008). Structural time-series models provide a general longitudinal modeling framework that psychologists might find useful, regardless of whether stochastic trends are present. These models can be computed in many different statistical programs, for example, using the StructTS package in R. Further research is needed to determine the applicability of these methods to psychological longitudinal data structures, but they do provide a solid foundation on which to begin to analyze data containing stochastic trends.

Limitations and Future Directions

Using economics as a foundation is a good start to identifying and dealing with stochastic trends in psychology. However, a number of limitations exist that could potentially hinder the use of the unit root tests and alternative analytical strategies presented here. As previously stated, the ADF test and other unit root tests are low-power tests. Therefore, a relatively large number of time points are needed to properly distinguish between series resulting from deterministic and stochastic trends. If researchers have an insufficient number of time points, the test will always fail to reject the null hypothesis, thus indicating that all series likely contain stochastic trends. Similarly, the proposed alternative analytic methods to handle data with stochastic trends also require a relatively large number of time points to function properly. Unfortunately, as the presence of stochastic trends can impact statistical results and scientific inferences with as few as five time points, all longitudinal studies are potentially susceptible to bias, even if detecting and analyzing stochastic trends is extremely difficult. Analyzing panel data does increase the power of unit root tests and could increase the power of structural time-series models as well. However, further research is needed to determine the adequate parameters (sample size and number of time points) needed to properly run the ADF and to apply ARIMA or structural time-series models to psychological longitudinal data.

Just as further research is needed on the proposed data-analysis methods, more research is needed to identify the prevalence of stochastic trends in psychology. One possible method of discovering series resulting from stochastic trends is analyzing previously published longitudinal studies and testing the data for the presence of stochastic trends. Finally, this chapter has only dealt with purely stochastic dependent variables, but it is possible that both deterministic and stochastic trends may be present in the dependent variable, and more work is needed to determine how much relative influence stochastic trends need to have before their presence is problematic. Despite the fact that more work is needed to determine the exact scope of the problem and what the best solution is, it is important to recognize that stochastic trends exist and could bias statistical and scientific inferences when regression-based models are used to analyze longitudinal data.

SUMMARY

Longitudinal data structures are becoming more common and more intense as researchers focus attention on the dynamics of psychological processes. Growth processes are typically modeled as resulting from solely deterministic trends by utilizing random coefficient or latent growth modeling. If the process results, at least partially, from a stochastic trend, then results from regression-based models are biased, leading to incorrect statistical results and scientific inferences. It is important to identify and understand the underlying data-generating mechanism to determine an appropriate analytic strategy and form sound and accurate conclusions. This chapter highlights the sources and prevalence of the bias, as well as providing multiple potential strategies for distinguishing between deterministic and stochastic trends and analyzing data containing stochastic trends. Although this chapter does provide a solid foundation for understanding the nature of spurious regression due to stochastic trends in longitudinal data, further research is needed to identify the prevalence of stochastic trends in psychology and understand the necessary conditions needed to properly utilize the proposed analytic methods for identifying and analyzing stochastic trends.

REFERENCES

Ancona, D. G., Okhuysen, G. A., & Perlow, L. A. (2001). Taking time to integrate temporal research. *Academy of Management Review, 26,* 512–529.

Ashforth, B. E., & Humphrey, R. H. (1993). Emotional labor in service roles: The influence of identity. *Academy of Management Review, 18,* 88–115.

Barcikowski, R. S. (1981). Statistical power with group mean as the unit of analysis. *Journal of Educational Statistics, 6,* 267–285.

Bhargava, A., & Sargan, J. D. (1983). Estimating dynamic random effects models from panel data covering short time periods. *Econometrica, 51,* 1635–1659.

Block, J. (1995). A contrarian view of the five-factor approach to personality description. *Psychological Bulletin, 117,* 187–215.

Braun, M. T., Kuljanin, G., & DeShon, R. P. (in press). Spurious results in the analysis of longitudinal data in organizational research. *Organizational Research Methods.*

Busemeyer, J. R., & Townsend, J. T. (1993). Decision field theory: A dynamic cognition approach to decision making. *Psychological Review, 100,* 432–459.

Chu, C., & Durango-Cohen, P. L. (2008). Estimation of dynamic performance models for transportation infrastructure using panel data. *Transportation Research, 42,* 57–81.

Collins, L. M. (2006). Analysis of longitudinal data: The integration of theoretical model, temporal design, and statistical model. *Annual Review of Psychology, 57,* 505–528.

Collins, L. M., & Horn, J. L. (1991). *Best methods for the analysis of change: Recent advances, unanswered questions, future directions.* Washington, DC: American Psychological Association.

Collins, L. M., & Sayer, A. G. (2001). New *methods for the analysis of change.* Washington, DC: American Psychological Association.

Dickey, D. A., & Fuller, W. A. (1979). Distribution for the estimators for autoregressive time series with a unit root. *Journal of the American Statistical Association, 44,* 427–431.

Durlauf, S. N., & Phillips, P. C. B. (1988). Trends versus random walks in time series analysis. *Econometrica, 56,* 1333–1354.

Eliashberg, J., & Chatterjee, R. (1986). Stochastic issues in innovation diffusion models. In V. Mahajan & Y. Wind (Eds.), *Innovation diffusion models of new product acceptance* (pp. 151–199). Massachusetts: Nallinger Publishing Company.

Elliott, G., Rothenberg, T. J., & Stock, J. H. (1996). Efficient tests for an autoregressive unit root. *Econometrica, 64,* 813–836.

Enders, W. (1995). *Applied econometric time series*. New York: John Wiley & Sons.

Enders, W. (2004). *Applied econometric time series* (2nd ed.). Hoboken, NJ: Wiley.

Gelman, A., & Hill, J. (2006). *Data analysis using regression and multilevel/hierarchical models*. Cambridge: Cambridge University Press.

George, J. M., & Jones, G. R. (2000). The role of time in theory and theory building. *Journal of Management, 26*, 657–684.

Gerstein, G., & Mandelbrot, B. (1964). Random walk models for the spike activity of a single neuron. *Biophysical Journal, 4*, 41–68.

Granger, C. W. J., & Newbold, P. (1974). Spurious regression in econometrics. *Journal of Econometrics, 2*, 111–120.

Harvey, A. (1989). *Forecasting, structural time series models, and the Kalman filter*. Cambridge, UK: Cambridge University Press.

Harvey, A. C. (1997). Trends, cylces, and autoregressions. *The Economic Journal, 107*, 192–201.

Harvey, A. C., & Koopman, S. J. (1996). Structural time series models in medicine. *Statistical Methods in Medical Research, 5*, 23–49.

Harvey, A. C., & Shephard, N. (1993). Structural time series models. In G. S. Maddala, C. R. Rao, & H. D. Vinod (Eds.), *Handbook of statistics* (Vol. 11, pp. 261–302). Amsterdam: Elsevier Science.

Hsiao, C., Pesaran, M. H., & Tahmiscioglu, A. K. (2002). Maximum likelihood estimation of fixed effects dynamic panel data models covering short time periods. *Journal of Econometrics, 109*, 107–150.

Hu, L., & Bentler, P. M. (1999). Cutoff criteria for fit indices in covariance structure analysis: Conventional criteria versus new alternatives. *Structural Equation Modeling, 6*, 1–55.

Ilies, R. & Judge, T. A. (2002). Understanding the dynamic relationships among personality, mood, and job satisfaction: A field experience sampling study. *Organizational Behavior and Human Decision Processes, 89*, 1119–1139.

Im, K. S., Pesaran, M. H., & Shin, Y. (2003). Testing for unit roots in heterogeneous panels. *Journal of Econometrics, 115*, 53–74.

Johansen, S. (1988). Statistical analysis of cointegration vectors. *Journal of Economic Dynamics and Control, 12*, 231–254.

Kline, R. B. (2005). *Principles and practice of structural equation modeling* (2nd ed.). New York: Guilford Press.

Kozlowski, S. W. J., & Ilgen, D. R. (2006). Enhancing the effectiveness of work groups and teams. *Psychological Science in the Public Interest, 7*, 77–124.

Kozlowski, S. W. J., & Klein, K. J. (2000). A multilevel approach to theory and research in organizations: Contextual, temporal, and emergent processes. In K. J. Klein & S. W. J. Kozlowski (Eds.), *Multilevel theory, research, and methods in organizations: Foundations, extensions, and new directions* (pp. 3–90). San Francisco, CA: Jossey-Bass.

Kreft, I., & De Leeuw, J. (1998). *Introducing multilevel modeling*. London: Sage.

Kuljanin, G., Braun, M. T., & DeShon, R. P. (in press). A cautionary note on modeling growth trends in longitudinal data.*Psychological Methods*.

Kwiatkowski, D., Phillips, P. C. B., Schmidt, P., & Shin, Y. (1992). Testing the null hypothesis of stationarity against the alternative of a unit root. How sure are we that economic time series have a unit root? *Journal of Econometrics, 54*, 159–178.

McArdle, J. J., & Nesselroade, J. R. (2003). Growth curve analysis in contemporary psychological research. In J. A. Schinka & W.F. Velicer, *Handbook of psychology: Vol. 2. Research methods in psychology* (pp. 447–480). Hoboken, NJ: Wiley & Sons, Inc.

McGrath, J. E., & Rotchford, N. L. (1983). Time and behavior in organizations. In L. L. Cummings & B. M. Staw (Eds.), *Research in organizational behavior* (Vol. 5, pp. 57–101). Greenwich, CT: JAI Press.

Mitchell, T. R., & James, L. R. (2001). Building better theory: Time and the specification of when things happen. *Academy of Management Review, 26*, 530–547.

Mohammed, S., Hamilton, K., & Lim, A. (2008). The incorporation of time in team research: Past, current, and future. In E. Salas, G. F. Goodwin, & C. S. Burke (Eds.), *Team effectiveness in complex organizations: Cross-disciplinary perspectives and approaches.* Mahwah, NJ: LEA.

Molenaar, P. C. M. (2004). A manifesto on psychology as idiographic science: Bringing the person back into scientific psychology, this time forever. *Measurement, 2,* 201–218.

Muraven, M., & Baumeister, R. F. (2000). Self-regulation and depletion of limited resources: Does self-control resemble a muscle? *Psychological Bulletin, 126,* 247–259.

Nelson, C. R., & Kang, H. (1984). Pitfalls in the use of time as an explanatory variable in regression. *Journal of Business and Economic Statistics, 2*, 73–82.

Nelson, C. R., & Plosser, C. I. (1982). Trends and random walks in macroeconomic time series: Some evidence and implications. *Journal of Monetary Economics, 10*, 139–162.

Nosofsky, R. M., & Palmeri, T. J. (1997). An exemplar-based random walk model of speeded classification. *Psychological Review, 104*, 266–300.

Osterholm, P. (2004). Killing four unit root birds in the US economy with three panel unit root test stones. *Applied Economics Letters, 11*, 213–216.

Phillips, P. C. B. (1986). Understanding spurious regressions in econometrics. *Journal of Econometrics, 33*, 311–340.

Phillips, P. C. B. (1987). Time series regression with a unit root. *Econometrica, 55*, 277–301.

Phillips, P. C. B., & Perron, P. (1988). Testing for a unit root in time series regression. *Biometrika, 75*, 335–346.

Raudenbush, S. W., & Bryk, A. S. (2002). *Hierarchical linear models: Applications and data analysis methods.* Newbury Park, CA: Sage.

Said, S. E., & Dickey, D. A. (1984). Testing for unit roots in autoregressive-moving average models of unknown order. *Biometrika, 3*, 599–607.

Schmidt, P., & Phillips, P. C. B. (1992). LM tests for a unit root in the presence of deterministic trends. *Oxford Bulletin of Economics and Statistics, 54*, 257–287.

Singer, J. D., & Willett, J. B. (2003). *Applied longitudinal data analysis modeling change and event occurrence.* New York: Oxford University Press.

Skellam, J. G. (1951). Random dispersal in theoretical populations. *Biometrika, 38*, 196–218.

Snijders, T., & Bosker, R. (1999). *Multilevel analysis. An introduction to basic and advanced multilevel modeling.* Thousand Oaks, CA: Sage.

Sonnentag, S. (2003). Recovery, work engagement, and proactive behavior: A new look at the interface between nonwork and work. *Journal of Applied Psychology, 88*, 518–528.

Tang, J., Jin, R., & Zhang, J. (2008). A topic modeling approach and its integration into the random walk framework for academic search. In *Proceedings of the 2008 18th International Conference on Data Mining* (pp. 1055–1060).

Taylor, M. P., and Sarno, L. (1998) The behaviour of real exchange rates during the post-Bretton Woods period, *Journal of International Economics, 46*, 281–312.

Uhlenbeck, G. E., & Ornstein, L. S. (1930). On the theory of Brownian motion. *Physics Review, 36*, 823–841.

Vancouver, J. B., More, K. M., & Yoder, R. J. (2008). Self-efficacy and resource allocation: Support for a nonmonotonic, discontinuous model. *Journal of Applied Psychology, 93*, 35–47.

Vancouver, J. B., Thompson, C. M., & Williams, A. A. (2001). The changing signs in the relationships among self-efficacy, personal goals, and performance. *Journal of Applied Psychology, 86*, 605–620.

Walls, T. A., & Schafer, J. L. (2006). *Models for intensive longitudinal data.* New York: Oxford University Press.

Wang, G., & Getz, L. L. (2007). State–space models for stochastic and seasonal fluctuations of voles and shrews in east central Illinois. *Ecological Modelling, 207*, 189–196.

Weiss, H. M., & Cropanzano, R. (1996). Affective events theory: A theoretical discussion of the structure, causes, and consequences of affective experiences at work. In B. M. Staw & L. Cummings (Eds.), *Research in organizational behaviour (Vol. 18).* Greenwich, Connecticut: JAI Press Inc.

Winer, B. J., Brown, D. R., & Michels, K. M. (1991). *Statistical principles in experimental design.* New York: McGraw-Hill.

Wright, S. (1931). Evolution in Mendelian populations. *Genetics, 16*, 97–159.

Yule, G. U. (1926). Why do we sometimes get nonsense-correlations between time-series? A study in sampling and the nature of time-series. *Journal of the Royal Statistical Society, 89*, 1–63.

Zivot, E. & Andrews, D. W. K. (1992). Further evidence on the great crash, the oil-price shock, and the unit-root hypothesis. *Journal of Business & Economic Statistics, 10*, 251–270.

7

Data Mining: A Practical Introduction for Organizational Researchers

Jeffrey M. Stanton

As organizational researchers, many of us received methods training at a time when datasets were time consuming and expensive to obtain, and, as a result, petite. We coveted our carefully gleaned dozens of survey responses and celebrated our acquisition of hundreds of records from an HR database, but we rarely, if ever, had access to thousands or millions of data records. The evolution of information technology and the Internet, however, has generated the opposite problem: datasets so large and unruly that our normal methods of thinking about data analysis break down. To illustrate, the federal government has established a site called data.gov, where it publishes the raw data from thousands of agency-conducted studies. In one small category with relevance to organizational research, "Labor Force, Employment, and Earnings," there are 32 data sources, where a typical data source contains 150,000 records obtained from a careful, representative sampling process of U.S. businesses. We might choose to ignore these data sources, because the variables are questionable or because there are no multi-item scales or because we feel that the dataset won't match to our theory very well, or because it is just too big a job to tackle. Even without a good match to theory or exactly the right variables, however, there might be something important to learn from this or some other large dataset.

Such a situation lends itself to the application of data mining. Data mining is a term that refers to the use of algorithms and computers to discover novel and interesting structure within data (Fayyad, Grinstein, &

Wierse, 2002). Data mining typically consists of four processes generally familiar to all statistical analysts: (1) preprocessing/data preparation, (2) exploratory data analysis/dimension reduction, (3) model exploration and development, and (4) interpretation. Within these four areas, the activities that are most likely to be unfamiliar to organizational researchers comprise the techniques from the second and third processes of exploratory data analysis and dimension reduction: the multiple correspondence analysis, semi-automated classifiers, clustering techniques, and nonlinear regression strategies that are only infrequently taught in a standard applied statistics curriculum. In this chapter, I introduce data mining for organizational researchers based on a case study that includes an exploratory analysis and model-building activity on a large government dataset. Later, I briefly review software tools, both commercial and open source. Throughout the chapter, I refer to books and articles of interest to those who want to get started with data mining. I hope that this chapter will pique your interest in data mining sufficiently so that you become energized to experiment with one or more of these techniques. The general trend toward greater availability of large, poorly structured, noisy datasets seems likely to continue; there could be important reservoirs of social and behavioral knowledge that remain untapped unless more organizational researchers become comfortable with data-mining tools.

BACKGROUND

A distinctive area of algorithmic research emerged in the 1950s and 1960s. At that time, statisticians and computer scientists began addressing problems that required many repetitive calculations by developing algorithms that could perform those calculations in a reasonable amount of time (e.g., March & Gray, 1969). During the same time period, early explorations of ideas in artificial intelligence spawned an area of research now referred to as *machine learning*, which focuses on creating algorithms that can use pre-existing inputs to refine and improve their own capabilities for dealing with future inputs (Michalski, Carbonell, & Mitchell, 1986).Such systems "learn" in the sense that they begin with a naïve model and they improve the performance of the model iteratively by processing additional input data. Anyone who has used structural equation modeling software or another statistical-analysis technique that uses an iterative "fitting" strategy to develop a model is already familiar with this general concept, even though most researchers do not equate such statistical fitting with the ideas of artificial intelligence.

Algorithms that could learn to find and model complex patterns in data became a topic of interest in industry as a response to the broad availability of huge databases of transactional information that organizations began to amass as they became more and more computerized (I. Witten & Frank, 2005). In particular, some managers realized that the transactional data their companies collected provided a representation of consumer behavior, and that data-mining algorithms could reveal nonobvious patterns in these traces of behavior that the organization could use to gain market advantage.

As an example to illustrate the use of such algorithms to mine transactional data, imagine a large supermarket database containing customer transactions, each of which records a list of items purchased in a given shopping session. Using so called "market basket" analysis on such data, a company could unearth patterns of purchases that suggested preferences for a certain item, based on the selection of one or more other items. We frequently see the results of market basket analyses online, when we see a message saying, "Customers who bought this also liked . . .," followed by a list of recommendations for related products. The list of recommendations arises from the application of a so-called *association rules* learning algorithm. One commonly cited example of the results of such an analysis came from a supermarket chain that discovered that a surprising number of shoppers purchased both diapers and beer in the same shopping trip (Padmanabhan & Tuzhilin, 1999; Richins & Dawson, 1992). Figure 7.1 provides a schematic view of how such a pattern might appear.

In Figure 7.1, with a little squinting it is possible to see the diapers–beer pattern by eye, because it occurs in two thirds of the transactions (Customers 1 and 3, but not Customer 2), and because 100 percent of shopping carts that contain diapers also contain beer. In a typical retail database, with thousands of items in the inventory and tens of thousands of shopping cart transactions per month, squinting will not work, and thus one needs an algorithmic method of detecting the patterns. The association rules learning algorithm (also sometimes called affinity analysis) generates and screens a large number of propositions, such as, "if diapers are purchased, then beer is also purchased." The algorithm uses data to evaluate a long list of these rules for a quantity known as *support*,

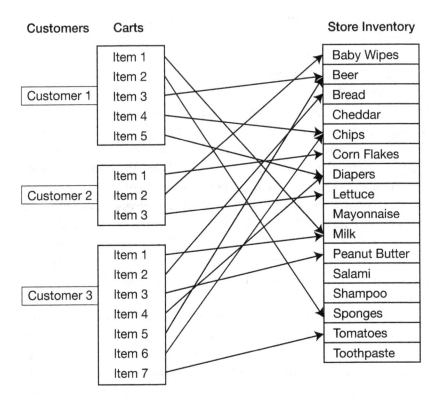

FIGURE 7.1
Schematic view of shopping cart data.

the proportion of times that the pairing occurs across all shopping carts, and another quantity called *confidence*, which is the likelihood that the pairing occurs when the first item is present. In Figure 7.1, we had support of 0.67 (the diapers–beer association occurred in two thirds of the carts) and confidence of 1.0 (the consequent "beer" occurred 100 percent of the time with the antecedent "diapers"). In practice, both support and confidence are generally much lower, but even a rule with low support and moderate confidence can pinpoint purchasing patterns that managers could use to guide pricing, coupon offers, or advertising strategies. From this example, we can see that a search for unknown or unanticipated patterns in a large database might yield pieces of knowledge that could have some commercial or scientific value, even in the absence of theory about consumer behavior.

OVERVIEW OF DATA-MINING TECHNIQUES

The association rules learning technique highlighted in the preceding example is one among a large set of data-mining techniques that researchers have developed over recent decades. In the material below, I provide an overview of machine learning—the algorithmic basis for many data-mining techniques—as well as two key challenges in data mining pertaining to the high dimensionality and the noisiness of data used in many data-mining applications.

Many data-mining techniques fall under the umbrella of machine learning, as described above. Machine learning comprises two distinctive subtopics: supervised learning and unsupervised learning. Supervised learning is parallel in concept to the predictive statistical techniques used by many social-science researchers, such as linear regression, but without the restriction of only exploring linear relationships. When we apply linear regression, we use a straightforward calculation (least squares analysis) to develop an equation for a best-fitting line that relates one or more independent variables (predictors) to a criterion variable. The analysis produces a summary of success—the coefficient of determination, R^2—as well as a complementary value quantifying error, the coefficient of alienation $(1 - R^2)$.

Likewise, with supervised learning techniques, there is always a criterion of some type that the algorithm or system is trying to predict from a set of independent variables. The summary result of the analysis provides an indication of the error rate, which may be the rate of misclassification in a categorical prediction task, or a coefficient of alienation akin to $1 - R^2$. The benefit over linear regression is that, with many supervised learning techniques, neither the independent variables nor the criterion need to be normally distributed interval or ratio data. For example, a supervised learning technique might be used to relate the frequency of co-occurrence of words in a textual database (e.g., "official" close to "bribe") to timings for a particular class of event (e.g., spacing between the occurrence of lawsuits). The former would typically be distributed according to a power law, whereas the latter might follow a Poisson distribution. A supervised learning technique, such as an artificial neural network, could establish a model relating these variables, despite the unusual and heterogeneous distributions in the underlying data. Supervised learning techniques such as neural networks also have no difficulty with prediction or forecasting problems that have multiple simultaneous criteria to be satisfied. For example, in an automotive application, a neural network might use a set of input variables from sensors to predict simultaneously the optimal flow rates of fuel, air, coolant, and other parameters (Alippi, de Russis, & Piuri, 2003).

Unsupervised learning includes a variety of machine-learning techniques that do not use a criterion or dependent variable, but rather look for patterns solely among "independent" variables. Organizational researchers commonly use an unsupervised learning technique in the form of exploratory factor analysis (EFA). EFA unearths a pattern of relations among a set of independent variables without regard for any particular criterion variable. The use of EFA is usually restricted, however, to variables that have linear relationships to one another. In contrast, many unsupervised machine-learning techniques do not require linearly related variables as input. The association rules (market basket) analysis presented earlier in the chapter represented one example of such an unsupervised learning technique. Another common and widely known example of unsupervised learning is clustering: a family of techniques that focuses on gathering observations into groups, such that elements within a group are similar, and elements from different groups are dissimilar (Jain, Murty, & Flynn, 1999).

Both supervised and unsupervised machine-learning techniques are affected by the number of variables used as input to an analysis and, relatedly, by the scope of the models that are developed to represent those data. Researchers in data mining frequently refer to—and develop strategies to address—this so called "curse of dimensionality" (Bellman, 1957). Although an important strength of data-mining techniques is the capability of handling an order of magnitude more input variables than a typical statistical analysis, problems can also arise when the data-mining algorithm requires representation of a resulting model in hundreds of dimensions (Bingham & Mannila, 2001; Indyk & Motwani, 1998).

This dimensionality problem arises because data-mining tasks often begin with a dataset that has hundreds or even thousands of variables and little or no indication of which of the variables are important and should be retained, versus those that can safely be discarded. Analytical techniques used in the model-building phase of data mining depend upon "searching" through a multidimensional space for a set of locally or globally optimal coefficients. Similarly to maximum likelihood and other fitting functions, these are iterative rather than numerical techniques. As the number of variables, and thus the dimensionality of the search space, rises, the computational time required to find an optimal solution often increases exponentially. Likewise, sample size requirements explode as the dimensionality of certain statistical estimation problems rises (Silverman, 1998). For example, a sample of $n = 800$ may suffice for a 5-dimensional estimation problem, but obtaining the same level of accuracy for a 10-dimensional problem might require a sample that is 1,000 times larger.

Finally, the noisiness of variables may also cause havoc in the analysis of high- dimensional data. An apt metaphor for this problem is recognizing shapes in clouds. Stare long enough at a sky full of clouds and you will begin to see discernible shapes among the random billows and swirls. Likewise, in a very large set of variables—even if every variable is pure noise—certain data-mining algorithms (e.g., neural networks) will always detect and report patterns. Machine-learning experts refer to this problem as *overlearning* or *overtraining* (Sjöberg & Ljung, 1995), and there is conceptual similarity to the statistical problem of model overfitting. In effect, a sufficiently powerful machine-learning algorithm can memorize any arbitrary pattern of input data and how it relates to a model's outputs (the criterion variables). The problem is that the model has become so specialized in recognizing the training data that it cannot then generalize to a new dataset. To circumvent this problem, data miners often randomly divide a dataset into a "training sample" and one or more "evaluation samples." By controlling the extent of training or fitting that is used to create a working model with the training sample, researchers can ensure that the model works equally or nearly as well within the evaluation sample.

Because of the difficulties that may arise in high-dimensional data-mining problems, data-mining practitioners routinely put effort into reducing the dimensionality of their data prior to model building. Similar to the procedures used by psychometricians to explore the configuration of measurement scales, common practice in data mining is to look for redundant variables that can be combined to form composites, as well as for variables that can be discarded because they seem unlikely to add to the power of the final model. Reduction of dimensionality can occur both through the use of traditional techniques such as exploratory factor analysis, as well as other tools such as multiple correspondence analysis—conceptually similar to exploratory factor analysis but usable on categorical data.

In the case-study demonstration that follows, I attempt to illustrate the points raised in the foregoing discussion. These include the exploration of a large, archival dataset with tens of thousands of records and hundreds of variables, together with the processes of data cleaning and conditioning, data dimension reduction, model exploration and development, model training, model evaluation, and interpretation of results.

CASE STUDY AND DEMONSTRATION

The data I chose for this case study came from the American Time-Use Survey (ATUS), conducted between 2003 and 2009 by the U.S. Bureau of Labor Statistics (www.bls.gov). The bureau has collected data from more than 98,000 participants, using representative sampling of the U.S. adult population. The ATUS data-collection procedure elicits a broad set of demographic and background variables, information about work (both paid and unpaid), and a wide-ranging profile of time use that paints a picture of how U.S. adults spend their days on different activities, such as commuting, employment, child care, and other life activities. These variables have obvious application to questions of work–life balance, occupational health, and labor-force economics, as well as to other areas. My general research question asked what demographic and background variables accounted for the relative time spent in work versus nonwork activities. Although this question was atheoretical, it is possible that, with a complete exploration of data such as ATUS, new insights might emerge on control or nuisance variables that could benefit future theory or research. I did not intend to undertake such a complete exploration here, but rather to offer the general outline of how such an exploration might take place using data-mining tools.

Having selected a data source, I was now prepared to begin the first of the four processes of data mining, as outlined earlier in the chapter: (1) preprocessing/data preparation, (2) exploratory data analysis/dimension reduction, (3) model exploration and development, and (4) interpretation. To provide an overview of these processes, Figure 7.2 displays a flowchart depicting some of the typical steps and decision points in the data-mining process. It is important to keep in mind that, as with any data-analysis task, progress through the steps is not always as linear as the flowchart would suggest.

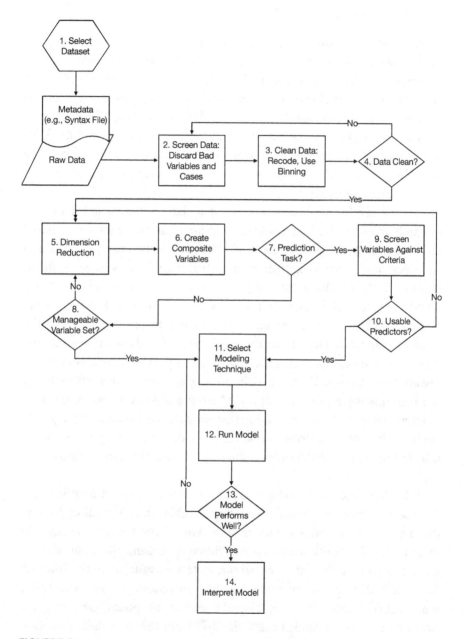

FIGURE 7.2
Flowchart of typical data-mining process.

Data Preparation

Tasks 2 and 3 in Figure 7.2 pertain to cleaning and screening the data prior to the substantive analytical work. For ATUS, the "microdata"—as the government refers to respondent-level data records—were spread across six linked data files (for each year of data) and comprised more than 340 variables, including more than 100 variables representing 17 major time-use categories. Adding additional complexity, the coding of certain fields in the microdata changed for certain variables from year to year. Some variables were abandoned, whereas new ones were adopted for subsequent years of data collection.

Fortunately for the tired, overworked data miner, a grant-funded research group at the University of Maryland has created a server-based software tool that organizes these ATUS data, selects subsets of years and variables, and prepares a custom data dictionary (also known as meta-data) to fit the resulting data output (Abraham, Flood, Sobek, & Thorn, 2008). The tool is known as the American Time-Use Survey extract builder (ATUS-X; www.atusdata.org) and it substantially shortens the cycle of using this large government database for data-mining activity. The existence of this tool underscores an important consideration for researchers and organizations: data mining is rarely a "one-off" activity, but is frequently a process that must be repeatable over time and across different datasets. Any organization that wants to use data mining regularly ought to develop a platform for doing so—a data repository and semi- or fully automated procedures for preparing the data for human analysts to explore.

Individual researchers who want to use data mining on archival data for research purposes should invest considerable effort in finding datasets that are already well prepared for analysis. The ATUS-X is just one example of available databases where an individual or organization has already helped to prepare the data for analysis. Data are available on the Internet for a bewildering variety of topics. Just considering a few examples, journalist Sean Lahman has developed a database of "pitching, hitting, and fielding statistics forMajor League Baseball from 1871 through 2010" (see documentation available at http://baseball1.com/statistics). The Inter-university Consortium for Political and Social Research (ICPSR; www.icpsr.umich.edu) archives hundreds of thousands of files containing social-science research data. A relatively recent addition, entitled WikiPosit (http://wikiposit.com/w), also contains hundreds of thousands of research data files. Data curation experts believe that the supply of freely available datasets—applicable in a wide variety of research fields—will continue to grow indefinitely and at a rapid rate (Hey & Trefethen, 2003). As this expansion continues, the necessity and importance of institutional repositories such as IPCSR will also tend to increase, because of the work that their staff members do to organize, index, and provide metadata for this proliferating collection of available datasets. The most important message, particularly for beginning data miners, is to get the best quality, most carefully curated data that you can access.

Taking advantage of the platform developed by the University of Maryland, I prepared an extract that used several features of ATUS-X. The term "extract" simply refers to a subset of the data (across time, variables, and subjects) that the researcher has specified. I created a rectangular database (the familiar kind, with rows as cases and columns as variables, as typically represented in statistics programs; more complex data shapes are possible, particularly with linked data tables). One example of a less traditional shape of data would be network data that represented the connections among entities such as boards of directors.

My resulting database covered a 7-year period (2003–2009), with field coding harmonized across these years. This harmonization is a particularly important feature of ATUS-X, because it ensures that the response options for any given variable mean the same thing across all years of the data, even if the government had changed the coding scheme partway through the history of the project. I requested the creation of an aggregate employment time variable that integrated across several categories of work activity, including paid work at a primary employer and all secondary employers, time for security procedures related to work, and waiting associated with working. This request was simply a matter of convenience: I could have downloaded the raw variables, recoded them where necessary, and summed them on a common metric myself. Finally, I extracted a subset of available demographic and background variables related to home life, child care, and employment situation. My resulting extract contained 134 variables/columns and $n = 98,778$ data cases, with data in a large text file. ATUS-X provided an SPSS syntax file to guide the process of reading the data into a statistics or data-mining program. The server provided data in a fixed-column format and, in addition to SPSS syntax, could have produced either SAS or Stata code files to read in the data. The use of fixed-column or comma-separated data is very common in data mining, because these formats are universal ones that essentially every program can import and export.

Recall that, in the four-step process described at the beginning of the chapter, I was still in the preprocessing and data-preparation phase (Tasks 2 and 3 in Figure 7.2). Despite the able assistance of ATUS-X in preparing the data, I still had several additional data-preparation tasks to conduct. For example, I reviewed the various exception field codes, such as "Refusal," "Don't know," and "Blank," for each of the nominal and ordinal variables, to ensure that each was treated appropriately as missing data or a legitimate response. I conducted frequency analyses and/or generated basic descriptive statistics for each variable and reviewed the resulting output for anomalous patterns and values. I was primarily looking for out-of-range and undefined values. I was not overly concerned with distributional characteristics, as many data-mining algorithms do not assume normally distributed variables. Although some data-mining algorithms can be configured to handle missing data gracefully, the analyst is well advised to clean and screen the raw data thoroughly, just as with more traditional statistical analysis.

The contrast between working with these data and a dataset with a few hundred cases and a few dozen variables was notable: Every task was time consuming, both in computer-processing time and human time. I liberally used bar charts, frequency histograms, and box plots at this stage to streamline the detection of anomalies, but scanning these was still very much a human process, requiring careful attention to every variable. As with all archival data, because the analyst did not have a hand in gathering the data, there was a substantial time investment necessary just for gaining a basic understanding of what each variable meant and how it was scaled.

During this phase of work, I also detected other variables to be dropped from further analysis, either by dint of large amounts of missing data, or as a result of overlap with logically related variables: Archival government datasets often contain multiple copies of variables that use slightly different coding standards. An example in this category included several of the variables containing minor industry classification codes for secondary jobs. Because some data-mining algorithms (e.g., many implementations of neural-network procedures) require full data or perform listwise deletion, I also used missing data mitigation strategies on a few of the remaining variables.

Finally, I created recoded copies of the time-use variables using "binning" to smooth these data. Binning is a recoding process applied to ordinal, interval, or ratio data to code them into a user-specified set of categories. Data-mining tools provide a range of binning strategies, ranging from an even frequency distribution of responses into a user-determined number of categories to "optimal binning" procedures that establish thresholds for bins, based on minimizing within-bin variance or maximizing covariance with an external criterion. Many of the time-use variables were severely right skewed, with a modal response of zero and a long, sparse tail containing a number of extreme values. Although many data-mining algorithms do not depend on having input data normally distributed, it is still valuable to avoid having dozens of empty categories separating a few sparsely used categories. Further, the classifier algorithms used in data-mining techniques do not care whether the resulting categories are of equally sized intervals.

Considering all of the procedures described above, it is easy to see why many data miners describe the work of data mining as 80 percent preparing the data, and 20 percent involving the fun parts of the process: model exploration, development, training, and evaluation. At the close of the data screening and cleaning process, $n = 60,225$ data records remained in my dataset. The discarded 30,000 cases had missing data on one or more of the key dependent variables—specifically, the discarded cases comprised all of the individuals who reported no weekly time spent in work-related activities, thus making it impossible to create a ratio or contrast between work and nonwork time use. The remaining cases each had at least partially complete data on a set of 17 time-use variables that provided a detailed profile of work versus nonwork activities. I retained 110 background and demographic variables that could potentially serve as inputs to a model that would output an individual's profile of time use and, in particular, the balance between work and nonwork activities. Thinking about conventional predictive models, it is obvious that a useful model cannot use 110 independent variables. As described earlier in the chapter, although somewhat less of a restriction, the same is true of the majority of machine-learning algorithms: The curse of dimensionality inhibits the practicality of a model with such a large number of input dimensions (although, as computational platforms and algorithms get better, this constraint becomes less and less restrictive). Thus, the next task to undertake was dimension reduction.

Dimension Reduction

Tasks 5 and 6 in Figure 7.2 focus on reducing the dimensionality of the data—in effect, looking for ways of working with fewer variables. As with a conventional dataset, there is little value and much danger in retaining a set of variables that are highly interrelated with one another. Survey researchers are aware of the necessity of combining individual items into composite scales, as using all of the individual items in substantive analysis would eat up degrees of freedom and potentially create multicollinearity. In contrast, retaining the best among the items and combining those items worth keeping into composite scores produce more reliable measures and help to maintain parsimony in the configuration of the substantive analysis.

In data-mining applications, similar principles apply, although the variables are often more unruly than typical Likert-type items. In the ATUS-X dataset, there were dozens of variables, none of which was designed in advance to form scales, and many of which were captured using binary or unordered multiple-option scales. One example of this problem came up in a set of 23 variables pertaining to household family configuration. Among these variables were a variety of dichotomous variables indicating the presence of children of various age ranges, as well as separate counts of children for different relational categories (e.g., your "own" children). Data cleaning on these variables indicated that many variables and cases contained "Not in Universe" codes in cells that should have contained a "No" or "0" response. Because EFA would have been a poor choice for data reduction in such data, I turned to multiple correspondence analysis, a technique that parallels EFA but that is suitable for use with categorical variables (Tenenhaus & Young, 1985). Multiple correspondence analysis is one of the most flexible and commonly used tools for data reduction and is a good complement to EFA when working with categorical variables or a mix of variable types. By exploring different solutions with various numbers of dimensions, I was able to reduce the original 23 variables down to two orthogonal dimensions. I configured the analysis to treat missing data on each variable as a distinctive category and to model the correspondence between variables using this new category (thereby preventing the loss of tens of thousands of cases with partially missing data). Output of the multiple correspondence analysis showed that the resulting dimensions had Cronbach's alpha reliabilities of .92 and .74, respectively. An inspection of the discrimination measures (akin to factor loadings) for each variable on the two dimensions showed that the first dimension corresponded to the presence and number of younger children (age < 13 years) in the household, and the second dimension corresponded to the presence of older children. I created object scores (akin to factor scores) to represent these two dimensions and used them in all subsequent analyses.

I performed additional multiple correspondence analysis on other clusters of categorical variables (e.g., 10 occupational classification codes), as well as more conventional EFA on groups of interval and ratio variables (e.g., various measures of hours spent working at primary and secondary places of employment). In all cases where a set of variables was shown to share substantial covariance, I created composite scores reflecting the reduced number of dimensions. In the process of creating composite scores, I also experimented with available missing data imputation techniques—comparing results with and without various imputation strategies—in order to end up with the greatest possible number of usable object or factor scores at the end of each dimension-reduction effort.

The end result of the dimension-reduction phase was a more parsimonious set of 39 variables. The outcome variables—focusing on time use at work and in a variety of other life activities—comprised 16 of the 39 variables, whereas the remaining 23 variables were intended as model inputs. Among the input variables, there was a mix of categorical variables, such as race, numeric variables such as age, and a variety of composite indices derived from the multiple correspondence analysis and EFA procedures described above. Note that, in traditional psychometric applications, an analyst would pay careful attention to the consistent use of interpretable measurement scales and might shudder at an admixture of heterogeneous indices. In contrast, data miners tend to ignore, or at least postpone, these concerns until the interpretation phase of the project. A data miner's primary concern at this point is whether a selected set of variables/indices contains useful "signal" or too much "noise." Also note that these variable sets (23 inputs and 16 outputs) are still somewhat larger than what might be considered optimal, but I erred on the side of inclusion in the hopes of having interesting model results to report in the model development and validation phase. Keeping in mind the exploratory and generative nature of this case study, it made sense to be very liberal in the inclusion of variables. In contrast, when data-mining analyses feed into a "production" system, such as the recommender systems that appear on some retail websites, it makes more sense to try to be parsimonious in variable selection.

Model Development and Validation: Supervised Learning

Two somewhat divergent areas of modeling exist for categorical and numeric data in data mining (Decision Point 7 in Figure 7.2). In the first area, the tasks and goals largely focus on prediction and/or forecasting. These are the so-called supervised learning tasks described at the beginning of this chapter. Supervised learning tasks use a set of inputs to create a model that relates to a set of outputs. Unlike many statistical techniques that focus on multiple predictors for a single criterion, many data-mining methods allow an arbitrary number of inputs and outputs.

Machine-learning researchers nearly always use an analytical strategy that divides data into (at least) two different functional subsets: training data and evaluation data. This division can be as simple as randomly sampling half the data to serve as training data and holding back the remaining cases to serve as evaluation data. In practice, a range of strategies is used, including having multiple training and evaluation datasets. Some of the more sophisticated software platforms for data mining (discussed further at the end of the chapter) automatically manage sub-sampling and the creation of training and holdout samples. When using tools that do not provide such hand holding (e.g., the R open-source statistics program), it is a good idea to have several different training and evaluation sets. As a rule of thumb, if I have sufficient data to do so, I try to make at least a half a dozen sub-samples of at least 1,000 cases each. Note that, with samples of $n = 1,000$ or more, traditional concerns with statistical significance generally do not matter. Two much more important considerations are: (1) can results in one sub-sample be replicated in the other sub-samples, and (2) are the error rates in each evaluation sample sufficiently low for the planned application of the data-mining model?

First considering the training data, both inputs and outputs must be known for each case, and the learning process adjusts internal model values and structures iteratively to create an "optimal" model for relating inputs and outputs. In an evaluation phase, the resulting model uses a new set of data that has both inputs and outputs, the evaluation data, to assess how well the model performs on novel inputs. Finally, when the modeling process is complete, the model can be deployed into a production environment where only model inputs are known and the goal is to predict or forecast outputs. Examples, of supervised learning techniques include neural networks (Bigus, 1996), general additive models (Hastie & Tibshirani, 1990), boosted regression trees (Elith, Leathwick, & Hastie, 2008), and classification and regression tree (CART) models (Breiman, 1984).

To demonstrate supervised learning techniques, I examined the time-use variable pertaining to time spent in work-related activities, in combination with a range of predictors and other time-use variables. The resulting model tried to predict the time spent in work-related activities in light of other time use, together with a set of background demographic variables. I began with a predictor-importance screening—often called "feature selection" by machine-learning researchers—that helped to focus my attention on those predictors that had the greatest likelihood of contributing to the model (Task 9 in Figure 7.2). A "feature" in computer-science terminology is simply an attribute of the object being described—conceptually identical in most cases to what a psychologist thinks of as a variable.

This screening can be accomplished with a tool as simple as stepwise regression. Using forward or backward stepping, it is possible to empirically identify those predictors that have the strongest unique linear relation-ships with the outcome variable (of course, multiple regression is generally limited to exploring linear relationships among variables with jointly normal distributions). As noted above, different results may arise in different samples, and so it is valuable to randomly subdivide the overall available sample and to repeat analyses in several independent segments. Instead of stepwise regression, I used CART feature selection—which works well with both categorical and continuous variables—as my pro-cedure to rank order the predictors by importance. I ran CART in ran-domly sub-sampled sets of n = 1,000 observations. For each run, the output showed a tree-shaped structure with cutoff or option values of particular variables. Figure 7.3 shows a sample of how such trees appear: At each node, the cutoff value on the specified variable does the best job of separating the sample into different levels of the criterion variable. Nodes that are higher (closer to the root of the tree) are better at accurately separating the sample than nodes lower down in the tree. Below each leaf node, you can imagine one segment of the sample that fits the set of criteria between the leaf and the root.

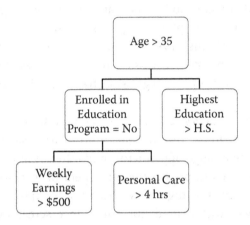

FIGURE 7.3
Sample output of CART analysis.

Examining results across multiple samples suggested that background variables such as the respondent's age, whether they were enrolled in an educational program, weekly earnings, and highest education achieved were likely to function well as predictors. Likewise, competing uses of time, such as household activities, personal care, and socializing, were also likely to serve as good predictors. Overall, I screened 34 variables and found that 20 of these had substantial potential as predictors. These 20 predictors were used in the subsequent supervised learning techniques.

Next, I subjected the variables to five different supervised learning techniques: neural networks, support vector machines (SVMs), boosted trees, random forest, and CART. Neural networks use a computational framework to emulate the activity of biological neurons—the learning process trains the firing threshold of each neuron in a large, interconnected network. Support vector machines (described in greater detail below) project a low-dimensional problem into a higher-dimensional space that can be geometrically divided into regions that represent the different levels of the criterion variable(s). Boosted trees, random forests, and CART each use somewhat different computational strategies toward creating a tree structure similar to that depicted in Figure 7.3. The goal of all of these techniques is the same: Accurately predict the set of outputs provided in training data, given a set of inputs. I suggest that choosing among these techniques should be an empirical matter of which method produces the lowest error rate, given the particular inputs, outputs, and software that are available. Recent "shoot-outs" comparing different machine-learning techniques suggest that the most commonly used contemporary techniques perform similarly across many types of problem, when the algorithms are optimally configured (Caruana & Niculescu-Mizil, 2006). In a typical data-mining situation, however, the analyst must work with whatever algorithms and configuration parameters the available software provides, and these setups are not necessarily commensurate across software packages. Therefore, one should choose the algorithm or method that works best for the data one has, based on a comparison of the success of the different algorithms as implemented in the available data-mining platform.

Recall from the data-screening process that I was now working with "binned" versions of the time-use variables; in the case of work-related time use, the variable comprised six ordered categories. Each learning algorithm was, therefore, attempting to do the best possible job it could at correctly placing each observation in the correct category. The output of each procedure yielded a large set of coefficients that represented the final configuration of the model, along with summary data indicating the number of iterations until a convergence criterion was reached and, most importantly, the error rate in classifications. A completely random process ought to be able choose correctly among six possible outcomes 16.7 percent of the time and would thus be incorrect 83.3 percent of the time. A good algorithm/model should substantially outperform this 83.33 percent error rate. Of the five learning techniques that I screened, CART was the worst, with an error rate of 52.5 percent. In contrast, the SVM model had the best performance, with a 13.1 percent classification error rate. Note that the activities here are represented on the flowchart in Figure 7.1 as Tasks 11 (select modeling technique) and 12 (run model), with the decision about whether to retain a model (Decision Point 13) based on which model provides the best error rate.

An SVM maps a low-dimensional problem into a higher-dimensional space with the goal of being able to describe geometric boundaries between different regions. The input data (the independent variables) from a given case are processed through a "mapping" algorithm called a kernel (the kernel is simply a formula that is run on each case's vector of input data), and the resulting kernel output determines the position of that case in multidimensional space.

A simple 2D–3D mapping example illustrates how this works: Imagine looking at a photograph of a snow-capped mountain photographed from high above the Earth, such that the mountain looks like a small, white circle, completely surrounded by a region of green trees. Using a pair of scissors, there is no way of cutting the photo on a straight line so that all of the white snow is on one side of the cut and all of the green trees are on the other. In other words there is no simple planar (or linear) separation function that could correctly separate or *classify* the white and green points, given their 2D position on the photograph. Alternatively, consider a realistic 3D clay model of the mountain. Now, all the white points occupy a cone at the peak of the mountain, and all of the green points lie at the base of the mountain. It is now easy to imagine inserting a sheet of cardboard through the clay model in a way that cleanly divides the snow-capped peak from the green-tree-covered base. That cardboard is the planar separation function that accurately divides white points from green points. An SVM analysis of this scenario would take the original 2D point data and search for an optimal projection into three dimensions that would maximize the spacing between green points and white points. The result of the analysis would be a mathematical description of the position and orientation of the cardboard plane. Given inputs describing a novel data point, the SVM could then map the data into the higher-dimensional space and then report whether the point was above the cardboard (a white point) or below the cardboard (a green point). The support vectors contain the coefficients that map the input data for each case into the high-dimensional space.

To produce results for the SVM analysis of the time-use data (using a radial basis function kernel), the 20 retained predictors required 750 support vectors. Because this was a multiple classification problem, a separate set of support vectors was generated for each option category in the target variable—a total of 109 sets of support vectors, where each vector has 750 elements (i.e., the output was a rectangular matrix of size 109 × 750). As with neural-network techniques, developing an understanding of the nature and relative importance of predictor variables is not straightforward—researchers designed the algorithms for efficiency and to minimize error rates, rather than to simplify interpretability. Machine-learning researchers are beginning to address this problem by developing visualization techniques (Caragea, Cook, & Honavar, 2001; Caragea, Cook, Wickham, & Honavar, 2008), but the representation of SVM solutions in high multidimensional space makes the interpretation of each predictor's contribution difficult.

Contrast this difficulty with the interpretation of linear regression, where the dependent variable changes in a monotonic function with each independent variable, according to a single coefficient. SVM produces hundreds of support vector coefficients for each variable in the solution, where each coefficient influences the classification outcome in concert with the hundreds of coefficients from every other variable. Figure 7.4 depicts a summary of the ten most "active" variables from the analysis, based on summarizing the variance of coefficients in the support vectors for that variable. The depicted values adequately reflect the proportion of non-zero support vector coefficients for a given variable, and thus provide a relative indication of how many dimensions each variable influences in the multidimensional space.

An interpretation of the support vectors in this case study yielded one or two interesting insights (c.f., Guyon, Weston, Barnhill, & Vapnik, 2002). As suggested by the feature-selection step, age of respondent was a predictor of work time, albeit in a nonlinear way: vectors indicating teen and senior respondents were intermixed as key determinants of work time. Being enrolled in an educational program, having a working spouse, and weekly earnings related to work time. Another intuitively satisfying finding was that time spent in care of household members was related to work time. Interestingly, however, time spent on consumer purchases was

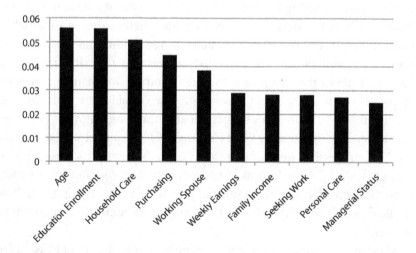

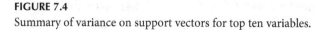

FIGURE 7.4
Summary of variance on support vectors for top ten variables.

more important than a variety of other predictors. A cursory review of the work–family literature suggests that researchers have given minimal attention to consumer activity as a competing time demand to balance with work and family care (Keene & Quadagno, 2004; van der Lippe, Jager, & Kops, 2006), but has rather been lumped in with other domestic tasks. The results of this data-mining model suggest that profiling materialism and consumer values (Richins & Dawson, 1992), as well as time spent in consumer-related activity, might be a fruitful extension to existing models of work–family balance. This finding might thus be considered the most novel insight provided by this data-mining exercise: Consumer behavior, which is not typically considered in the work–family balance literature, appears to relate to the balance of time in work versus nonwork activities. Whether this or any of the other findings have any practical or theoretical importance would require further exploration, but the power of the SVM model to make accurate classifications for a criterion variable based on a diverse range of inputs seems evident from this analysis.

Model Development and Validation: Unsupervised Learning

The other large research area in machine learning and data mining is unsupervised learning. In the flowchart in Figure 7.1, Decision Point 7 shows a bifurcation depending upon whether one is working on a prediction task. Following the "no" path at Decision Point 7 leads to Decision Point 8, where the data miner must decide whether the set of variables that has emerged from Task 5 (dimension reduction) and Task 6 (compositing) is suitable for an unsupervised learning task. In making this judgment, recall that the goal is to understand the intrinsic organization or patterning inside a set of observations or variables, or both, without privileging any of the variables either as inputs or outputs. The most familiar example of unsupervised learning is EFA. Applied statisticians use the EFA processing steps of extraction (e.g., through principal components analysis; PCA), selection of components, and rotation for a variety of applications that we do not normally think of as data mining, but these applications all have in common the detection of nonobvious patterns of association.

Mathematicians have developed a more generalized form of PCA, called independent component analysis (ICA; Comon, 1994), to mathematically separate a set of variables into a minimum set of statistically independent components. A common way of describing this method is to imagine a stereo recording of a person talking while music is playing in the background. Each of the two recording channels thus contains a mix of the voice and the music. Using these two channels as input data, an ICA can separate the recording back into the two independent sources—the voice and the music. Unlike PCA and other EFA techniques, ICA is well suited to work on variables that are not jointly normally distributed, as well as on variables whose relationships to one another are nonlinear (Stone, 2004). Additionally, whereas in PCA the inputs with the highest variance tend to have the most influence on the resulting independent components, this is not true with ICA. As a result, ICA can be applied to variables with unruly distributions (e.g., highly skewed), with the hope of achieving usable results.

In the time-use data for the case study, I found that PCA of the time-use variables was useless, because it produced a large number of components for which each eigenvalue was slightly greater than one. In contrast, fitting the time-use variables from the supervised learning phase above to an ICA revealed two interpretable components, focusing, respectively, on time spent in care of other household members versus other nonwork activities. Interpreting the output of the ICA analysis shares many similarities with interpreting a PCA. There is a matrix of coefficients (the mixing matrix) that relates the component scores back to the original variable data, in a way that is conceptually similar to loadings in the PCA. Examining the matrix revealed which variables loaded highly on each component. An excerpt of the mixing matrix appears in Table 7.1.

Interestingly, the first practical implementation of ICA used neural networks to decompose the data into independent signals (Hyvärinen & Oja, 2000). Neural networks are also used in the unsupervised family of algorithms known as self-organizing maps (Kohonen, 2002). Self-organizing maps are a more sophisticated cousin of simpler clustering techniques used for discovering patterns in data (Kaski, 1997). The goal with all such clustering techniques is to uncover naturally occurring groupings in data (Kaufman & Rousseeuw, 2005).

As a further demonstration of unsupervised learning, I also tried k-means clustering (Jain, Murty, & Flynn, 1999; Berkhin, 2006), a technique that works equally well for continuous, categorical, or mixed sets of variables. For this analysis, my intention was to classify cases (i.e., people) into groups (clusters), where members of a group had similar profiles on

TABLE 7.1

Mixing Matrix From ICA

Time spent	Component 1	Component 2
Care (non-household)	−1.844	0.042
Education	−1.719	−0.004
Care (household)	0.395	−0.006
Shopping	0.376	0.008
Personal care	0.359	−0.288
Professional service	−0.312	−0.036
Other job	−0.304	0.008
Food preparation	−0.245	0.113
Household service	−0.174	0.035
Telephone	0.015	0.323
Travel	−0.010	0.110
Socializing	0.000	0.655

the input variables. The k-means technique requires that the number of clusters be set in advance, and, as a result, most data miners use an iterative process of trying different numbers of clusters to find the most interpretable result. Although researchers have worked on metrics for more systematic selection of the optimal number of clusters (Sugar & James, 2003), it is quick and convenient to try different numbers of clusters. As a result, one practical strategy is to start with two clusters and keep increasing the number until one or more clusters appear that are nearly empty.

For the present analysis, I used the eight time-use variables that the feature-selection algorithm in the supervised learning stage had identified as most promising. This was mainly for expediency. The choice of variables for unsupervised learning is not normally done on the basis of screening against a criterion variable. I experimented with as many as nine clusters and as few as four. A five-cluster solution seemed most interpretable, with the smallest cluster containing 7.7 percent of the cases, and the largest cluster containing 49.4 percent of the cases.

Like the CART output depicted in Figure 7.3, the k-means clustering output provided an overview of the characteristics of the members of each cluster, characterized in terms of their status on the input variables. The first cluster contained individuals who had worked more than a normal workday and who had little time left for other life tasks. Individuals who worked somewhat less than a full day fell into two different clusters, apparently as a result of either having responsibilities for care of household members, or, interestingly, if they spent a lot of time eating. Likewise, those who reported essentially no work time on the day they gave their data also fell into two clusters. Individuals in the first cluster had relatively minimal household activities, but spent a substantial body of time on eating, personal care, travel, and socializing. The second cluster exhibited the opposite pattern.

Summary of the Case Study

To summarize my exploration of this dataset and close the case study, data screening and cleaning revealed a set of about 40 variables and $n = 60,000$ cases, based on an original dataset of over 130 variables and nearly $n = 100,000$ cases. Feature selection led to the choice of 23 input variables, comprising a variety of background characteristics of households, and 16 output variables profiling work and nonwork time. A supervised learning model using the SVM technique yielded a low error rate that highlighted a novel variable for consideration in future work–family research: consumer behavior. An ICA of nonwork time use revealed two meaningful components, one pertaining to care of household members and one pertaining to other nonwork activities. Unsupervised learning using k-means clustering revealed six distinctive profiles of time use in work and nonwork activities, providing a possible basis for segmenting future research populations.

As is typical with data-mining explorations, I spent the great majority of the project effort on conditioning the data and preparing it for data mining, with particular focus on the need to reduce a very large initial set of variables into a more manageable set. Because I had not collected the data myself, understanding the coding of variables, removing redundancy among variables, and mitigating missing data were all time-consuming tasks that had to be accomplished prior to running any machine-learning tasks. Running the models was not particularly difficult or time consuming, although the interpretability of the results varied among procedures and software platforms. An overview of the various options for data-mining software appears in the next section.

OVERVIEW OF AVAILABLE DATA-MINING TOOLS

I conducted the preceding analyses using a combination of different tools, including SPSS, Excel, R, and Statistica. Familiarity with a range of tools was once a key requirement of data mining, because no single tool could perform all of the necessary tasks. This is less true now, with the advent of comprehensive data-mining platforms (described in greater detail below). In my project, the Excel spreadsheet program provided a flexible way to review raw data and prepare comma-separated variable (CSV) files. CSV files are particularly useful when work requires importing and exporting across a variety of programs that use proprietary data formats. I used SPSS for data setup, screening, cleaning, and some data-reduction tasks. I did not have access to the SPSS data-mining package, and so I relied on open-source solutions for most of the substantive data-mining analysis. I used a variety of data-mining tools in R, which has a comprehensive set of analytical methods for data mining, as well as hundreds of other advanced analytical tasks. I also experimented with WEKA (Waikato Environment for Knowledge Analysis; www.cs. waikato.ac.nz/ml/weka) and a trial version of Statistica. Like WEKA, Statistica provides a "workbench" interface that makes data-mining tasks easier for beginners.

The Statistica workbench interface represents one example of highly graphical, semi-automatic data-mining tools that have appeared in the marketplace in recent years. In the usual manifestation, the data miner is presented with a work area organized into the sequential steps involved in data mining—data selection, data preparation, dimension reduction, model building, and model evaluation. Two of the best-known statistical-tool companies, SPSS and SAS, have developed solutions known, respectively, as Clementine and Enterprise Miner. Each of these platforms provides a comprehensive toolkit for all of the major data-mining tasks in an interface that promotes the typical phased approach of data preparation, dimension reduction, model building/evaluation, and interpretation. In the case of SAS Enterprise Miner, which is aimed at a business audience, there is also a well-integrated set of tools for "deploying" data-mining models into commercial usage.

These commercial tools represent just the tip of the iceberg, however. More than a decade ago, Goebel and Gruenwald (1999) conducted a survey and review of data-mining tools that covered 43 different software products. These included both commercial packages and research-focused prototypes. Although other, more recent, reviews have picked leading contenders from among the commercial packages (e.g., Haughton et al., 2003), the number of open-source, free, and/or low-cost packages has proliferated. There are literally hundreds of data-mining tools currently available, at prices ranging from zero to many thousands of dollars, and with specializations in bioinformatics data mining, business data mining, text mining, and numerous other areas.

As with other software tools, each offering has benefits and pitfalls. The open-source, component-based analysis package known as R predominates among open-source offerings (Torgo, 2003). R has an active community of contributors who are constantly adding new features and techniques. However, R lacks the "workbench" orientation of some of the commercial products and requires the data miner to master the command-line capabilities of R (although an increasing number of techniques do have graphical user interfaces available).

A more specialized package in the open-source realm is WEKA, developed by researchers at the University of Waikato in New Zealand. Unlike R, which was designed to be a general statistical package with optional specialized components, WEKA was purpose built for data mining. WEKA offers a workbench interface, as well as a more powerful command line interface (Hall et al., 2009; I. H. Witten, Frank, Holmes, & Hall, 2011). A series of articles and books authored by Ian Witten and Eibe Frank describes both the general techniques of data mining and their use within the WEKA platform (I. H. Witten & Frank, 2002; I. Witten & Frank, 2005; Hall et al., 2009; I. H. Witten et al., 2011). Considering the free, open-source nature of WEKA and the availability of its workbench interface, it is probably the best choice for data-mining beginners who do not have access to a commercial package such as Clementine. Note that the management of the WEKA package has been taken over by a firm that specializes in the maintenance and support of open-source packages.

When choosing a data-mining package, the most important initial consideration is the skill and experience of the analyst. A beginner in this area needs a package that does considerable "handholding"; the expensive, commercial, workbench-focused products are good at this. Similarly to the early days of structural equation modeling, there are dozens of problems that can crop up in the fitting of models, and poorly chosen or poorly conditioned data can lead to unexpected and uninterpretable results. For a more sophisticated and experienced analyst, an open-source package without all the handholding features can provide the opportunity to experiment freely with the full range of algorithmic options. Even in this approach, however, it is good to have a standard statistical-analysis package in the initial stages of a data-mining project, as the same basic data diagnostics, visualizations, and transformations are needed for either traditional statistical analysis or data mining.

CONCLUSION

The demonstration case study in this chapter has shown some of the tedium, some of the complexity, and some of the power of an emerging toolkit of analytical techniques based on supervised and unsupervised machine learning. Although we currently refer to these techniques collectively as data mining (or knowledge discovery in databases, or business intelligence), in the future many of these tools will just be seen as additional analytical techniques in the statistician's array of choices. More importantly, there may be an underlying philosophical difference emerging in the way that we approach data and the way that we think about the relationship of data analysis to other scientific processes.

When experiments were expensive to perform, and it was extremely difficult to create a worthwhile database of indicators and measurements to analyze, many social scientists chose to use their data primarily in a confirmatory mode. Having robust theory prior to data collection was both a necessity and a virtue. In the nascent days of social-science disciplines such as psychology, efforts to emulate the methods and perspectives of the natural sciences led many researchers to take a firmly positivist view of the scientific method (Danziger, 1979). To oversimplify this view somewhat, a strong positivist would neither design a method nor collect and analyze data before having a theoretically guided hypothesis to test. The theory and the hypothesis derived from it framed both the nature of the data to be collected and the form of the analysis to be applied to it. This outlook predominated in psychology throughout much of the twentieth century. Whether strict positivism was a productive approach we will leave to philosophers and historians of science.

As the world has become more wired, however, data have become cheap and terribly plentiful, if not always in the ideal form that we would like. Online social-networking platforms provide a perfect example of this. These sites collect millions of traces of human behavior and communication activity every day, a veritable gold mine of behavioral information collected without regard to theory and with very little consideration for curation or reuse in scientific research (Whitty, 2008). Using data-mining tools and strategies, we can decide to explore these data to look for interesting patterns and relationships that we might never have imagined in the more traditional, confirmatory mode of working. These previously invisible patterns may eventually lead us—after we add back in the hard work of theorizing, explaining, and confirming—into startling new insights.

Although it is possible to view such explorations as a return to the oft-criticized methods of "dustbowl empiricism" (Latham, 2007), it is equally possible to see data mining as a source of ideas and new leads for theory building (Dhar, 1998; Hereth, Stumme, Wille, & Wille, 2000). Dustbowl empiricism was considered objectionable, in part because results were sometimes not reproducible across different samples, and in part because no theory existed to explain empirically derived models. With the availability of massive datasets, a corresponding opportunity to use multiple holdout samples, and explorations of a variety of model-building techniques, however, it is possible to use data mining to detect patterns with both practical and theoretical implications. If you have ever been led to purchase a book or other item that was recommended from the market-basket analysis on a retail website, you are, in a sense, living proof that the patterns detected by a data-mining algorithm reflect some underlying reality in the beliefs and preferences of customers.

Some advocates even make the claim that this highly inductive form of investigation represents a new mode of scientific inquiry that complements standard deductive methods (Goonatilake, 1999; Wachowicz, 2000; Ramakrishnan & Grama, 2002; Wolfram, 2002; Kell & Oliver, 2004; Cai, 2007). When paired with computer simulation—which can be used to configure and run *in silico* experiments to test proposed mechanisms—data mining represents an alternative strategy for inquiring into the emergent properties of complex systems, such as groups, organizations, and societies. Although data mining cannot replace the powerful rigor provided by theoretically driven experimentation, it can provide a new source of ideas and insights for organizational researchers and other scientists to explore. In the future, data mining may also facilitate a transition of some organizational scientists from being designers and conductors of empirical field studies to being explorers of universes of behavioral and social data collected by institutions for other, nonscientific purposes.

REFERENCES

Abraham, K. G., Flood, S. M., Sobek, M., & Thorn, B. (2008). American Time Use Survey Data Extract System: Version 1.0 [Machine-readable database]: Maryland Population Research Center, University of Maryland, College Park, Maryland, and Minnesota Population Center, University of Minnesota.

Alippi, C., de Russis, C., & Piuri, V. (2003). A neural-network based control solution to air–fuel ratio control for automotive fuel-injection systems. *Systems, Man, and Cybernetics, Part C: Applications and Reviews, IEEE Transactions, 33*(2), 259–268.

Bellman, R. E. (1957). *Dynamic programming*. Princeton, NJ: Princeton University Press.

Berkhin, P. (2006). A survey of clustering data mining techniques. *Grouping Multidimensional Data*, 25–71.

Bigus, J. (1996). *Data mining with neural networks*. McGrawHill, USA.

Bingham, E., & Mannila, H. (2001). Random projection indimensionality reduction: applications to image and text data. *Proceedings of the 7th ACM SIGKDD International Conference on Knowledge Discovery and Data Mining*, ACM.

Breiman, L. (1984). *Classification and regression trees*. Boca Raton, FL: Chapman & Hall/CRC.

Cai, Y. (2007). Instinctive computing. In J. G. C. a. J. Siekmann (Ed.), *Artificial intelligence for human computing* (Vol. 4451, pp. 17–46). Heidelberg: Springer.

Caragea, D., Cook, D., & Honavar, V. (2001). *Gaining insights into support vector machine pattern classifiers using projection-based tour methods*. Paper presented at the Proceedings of the 7th ACM SIGKDD International Conference on Knowledge Discovery and Data Mining, San Francisco, CA.

Caragea, D., Cook, D., Wickham, H., & Honavar, V. (2008). Visual methods for examining SVM classifiers. *Visual Data Mining*, 136–153.

Caruana, R., & Niculescu-Mizil, A. (2006, June). An empirical comparison of supervised learning algorithms. In *Proceedings of the 23rd International Conference on Machine Learning* (pp. 161–168), ACM.

Comon, P. (1994). Independent component analysis, a new concept? *Signal Processing, 36*(3), 287–314.

Danziger, K. (1979). The positivist repudiation of Wundt. *Journal of the History of the Behavioral Sciences, 15*(3), 205–230.

Dhar, V. (1998). Data mining in finance: Using counterfactuals to generate knowledge from organizational information systems. *Information Systems, 23*(7), 423–437.

Elith, J., Leathwick, J., & Hastie, T. (2008). A working guide to boosted regression trees. *Journal of Animal Ecology, 77*(4), 802–813.

Fayyad, U., Grinstein, G., & Wierse, A. (2002). *Information visualization in data mining and knowledge discovery*. San Francisco, CA: Morgan Kaufmann.

Goebel, M., & Gruenwald, L. (1999). A survey of data mining and knowledge discovery software tools. *ACM SIGKDD Explorations Newsletter, 1*(1), 20–33.

Goonatilake, S. (1999). *Toward a global science: Mining civilizational knowledge.* Bloomington: Indiana University Press.

Guyon, I., Weston, J., Barnhill, S., & Vapnik, V. (2002). Gene selection for cancer classification using support vector machines. *Machine Learning, 46*(1), 389–422.

Hall, M., Frank, E., Holmes, G., Pfahringer, B., Reutemann, P., & Witten, I. H. (2009). The WEKA data mining software: an update. *ACM SIGKDD Explorations Newsletter, 11*(1), 10–18.

Hastie, T., & Tibshirani, R. (1990). *Generalized additive models.* Boca Raton, FL: Chapman & Hall/CRC.

Haughton, D., Deichmann, J., Eshghi, A., Sayek, S., Teebagy, N., & Topi, H. (2003). A review of software packages for data mining. *The American Statistician, 57*(4), 290–309.

Hereth, J., Stumme, G., Wille, R., & Wille, U. (2000). Conceptual knowledge discovery and data analysis. *Conceptual Structures: Logical, Linguistic, and Computational Issues,* 421–437.

Hey, T., & Trefethen, A. (2003). The data deluge: An e-Scienceperspective. In F. Berman, G. C. Fox, and A. J. G. Hey (Eds.), *Grid computing: Making the global infrastructure a reality,* pp. 809–824. Chichester: Wiley.

Indyk, P., & Motwani, R. (1998, May). Approximate nearest neighbors: Towards removing the curse of dimensionality. *Proceedings of the 30th Annual ACM Symposium on Theory of Computing* (pp. 604–613), ACM.

Jain, A., Murty, M., & Flynn, P. (1999). Data clustering: A review. *ACM Computing Surveys (CSUR), 31*(3), 264–323.

Kaski, S. (1997). *Data exploration using self-organizing maps.* Espoo, Finland: Citeseer.

Kaufman, L., & Rousseeuw, P. (2005). *Finding groups in data: An introduction to cluster analysis.* Hoboken, NJ: WileyBlackwell.

Keene, J., & Quadagno, J. (2004). Predictors of perceived work–family balance: Gender difference or gender similarity? *Sociological Perspectives, 47*(1), 1–23.

Kell, D., & Oliver, S. (2004). Here is the evidence, now what is the hypothesis? The complementary roles of inductive and hypothesis-driven science in the post-genomic era. *Bioessays, 26*(1), 99–105.

Kohonen, T. (2002). The self-organizing map. *Proceedings of the IEEE, 78*(9), 1464–1480.

Latham, G. (2007). *Work motivation: History, theory, research, and practice.* New York: Sage.

March, W., & Gray, A. (1969). Large-scale Euclidean MST and hierarchical clustering. *Statistics, 18*(1), 54–64.

Michalski, R., Carbonell, J., & Mitchell, T. (1986). *Machine learning: An artificial intelligence approach.* San Francisco, CA: Morgan Kaufmann.

Padmanabhan, B., & Tuzhilin, A. (1999). Unexpectedness as a measure of interestingness in knowledge discovery. *Decision Support Systems, 27*(3), 303–318.

Ramakrishnan, N., & Grama, A. (2002). Data mining: From serendipity to science. *Computer, 32*(8), 34–37.

Richins, M., & Dawson, S. (1992). A consumer values orientation for materialism and its measurement: Scale development and validation. *Journal of Consumer Research: An Interdisciplinary Quarterly, 19*(3), 303.

Silverman, B. (1998). *Density estimation for statistics and data analysis.* New York: Chapman and Hall.

Sjöberg, J., & Ljung, L. (1995). Overtraining, regularization and searching for a minimum, with application to neural networks. *International Journal of Control, 62*(6), 1391–1407.

Stone, J. V. (2004). *Independent component analysis: A tutorial introduction.* Cambridge, MA: The MIT Press.

Sugar, C. A., & James, G. M. (2003). Finding the number of clusters in a dataset. *Journal of the American Statistical Association, 98*(463), 750–763.

Tenenhaus, M., & Young, F. (1985). An analysis and synthesis of multiple correspondence analysis, optimal scaling, dual scaling, homogeneity analysis and other methods for quantifying categorical multivariate data. *Psychometrika, 50*(1), 91–119.

Torgo, L. (2003). *Data mining with R: Learning by case studies* (pp. 4–100). Portugal: University of Porto.

van der Lippe, T., Jager, A., & Kops, Y. (2006). Combination pressure: The paid work–family balance of men and women in European countries. *Acta Sociologica, 49*(3), 303–319.

Wachowicz, M. (2000, April). *How can knowledge discovery methods uncover spatio-temporal patterns in environmental data?* Paper presented at Data Mining and Knowledge Discovery: Theory, Tools, and Technology II, Orlando, FL.

Whitty, M. T. (2008). Revealing the real me, searching for the actual you: Presentations of self on an internet dating site. *Computers in Human Behavior, 24*(4), 1707–1723.

Witten, I., & Frank, E. (2005). *Data mining: Practical machine learning tools and techniques.* San Francisco, CA: Morgan Kaufmann.

Witten, I. H., & Frank, E. (2002). Data mining: Practical machine learning tools and techniques with Java implementations. *ACM SIGMOD Record, 31*(1), 76–77.

Witten, I. H., Frank, E., Holmes, G., & Hall, M. A. (2011). *Data mining: Practical machine learning tools and techniques.* San Francisco, CA: Morgan Kaufmann.

Wolfram, S. (2002). *A new kind of science* (Vol. 1). Champaign, IL: Wolfram Media.

Part 2

Research Design and Measurement

8

Use of Conditional Reasoning to Measure the Power Motive

Lawrence R. James, James M. LeBreton, Terence R. Mitchell, Daniel R. Smith, Justin A. DeSimone, Robert Cookson, and Hye Joo Lee

Recent years have brought considerable progress in understanding the implicit or unconscious personality. Psychology now has a better idea of the defensive cognitive processes that people use to create a sense of rationality for what, in truth, are desire-driven behaviors. This knowledge of defensive cognitive processes was used to design a new system for measuring the implicit personality. This new system of personality assessment is referred to as "conditional reasoning." Conditional reasoning was introduced with a test for achievement motivation (James, 1998). A subsequent paper by James et al. (2005) described the development of a conditional-reasoning test for aggression. In this chapter, we introduce a third test for conditional reasoning developed by James and his associates. This test is designed to measure a person's power motive, which we define below as a person's desire to exert his or her will over others.

A strong power motive often sets in motion behaviors toward acquiring and maintaining positions of leadership. However, the relationship between the power motive and how one actually exerts one's will, or one's leadership style, is not direct. There are many ways that the desire to exert oneself can be channeled into a style of leading (e.g., transformational (style), charismatic, empowering, transactional, interpersonal, task oriented, laissez faire, toxic). What direction this channeling takes is largely determined by personality variables other than the power motive. For example, a person with a strong power motive who is also nurturing by disposition is likely to channel his or her desire to lead others into a transformational leadership style. We will refer to the shaping of power by other personality variables as "channeling models."

Our focus in this initial presentation of the power motive is to overview the psychological foundation and content of the conditional-reasoning test that we developed to measure the power motive. Subsequently in this chapter, we will distinguish between the power motive per se and the power motive when it has been channeled into a toxic leadership style by people with both strong power motives *and* strong motives to aggress. Our objective here is to advocate that not all people with a high need for power are toxic. More importantly, we will suggest that power has often been held culpable for toxic leader behaviors that were actually inspired by a desire to harm others (i.e., aggressiveness). We will only briefly discuss other forms of channeling models for the power motive in this paper; these are subjects for later papers. The chapter concludes with a synopsis of our first empirical study in which we related scores for leaders on the conditional-reasoning measure of power motive/toxic leadership to the productivity of their organizations.

A THEORY OF THE CONDITIONAL-REASONING TEST FOR THE POWER MOTIVE

Research findings from a number of scientific studies demonstrate that effective leaders are often socially skilled individuals who strive to be dominant (Winter, 1973, 1992; McClelland, & Boyatzis, 1982; Veroff, 1992; Stricker & Rock, 1998; Judge, Bono, Ilies, & Gerhard, 2002; Foti & Hauenstein, 2007). These individuals want to be leaders (Chan & Drasgow, 2001) and are willing to devote years to attaining the experience and knowledge required to make the strategic decisions that produce effective and successful organizations (Yukl, 2009). As they gain knowledge and experience, effective leaders undergo increasing internal pressures to exert their will on decisions that determine the directions taken by their organizations (Winter, 1973; Veroff, 1992; Resick, Whitman, Weingarden, & Hiller, 2009). They believe that their organizations should follow the most rational and strategic courses of action, and they are increasingly confident that they know what these courses are (McClelland, 1985; Winter, 1992).

In part, these judgments are just what they appear to be. Throughout human evolution, leaders have been responsible for strategic decisions that affect the survival of their social collectives (e.g., family, clan, kingdom, government, military organization, social institution, business—see Finkelstein & Hambrick, 1996; Hambrick, Finkelstein, & Mooney, 2005; Van Vugt, Hogan, & Kaiser, 2008). This broad mission is dependent on leaders' abilities to reason and solve problems in ways that engender the safety and security of the collective (e.g., protect the collective from enemies), assist the collective in acquiring resources (e.g., food, donations, raw materials, financing), promote efficient coordination and cooperation among components of the collective (e.g., design an organizational structure), oversee human-relations issues (e.g., selection, promotion, administration of justice), and provide for effective delivery of a product (e.g., knowledge dissemination, art, health care, warfare, transportation, investments).

In part, these judgments have a motivational component that is far from obvious. The pressure to exert one's will over others comes from a desire to have influence and impact, that is, to attain a position where one can affect courses of events by influencing how people think (e.g., decisions they make), feel (e.g., how stressed are they), and act (e.g., how they perform) (Winter, 1973; McClelland & Boyatzis, 1982; House, Spangler, & Woycke, 1991; Judge et al., 2002; Foti & Hauenstein, 2007). This is the need for power, often referred to as the *power motive* (Winter, 1973).

The power motive can be manifested in any number of ways as one attempts to exert one's will on another person, group, organization, political entity, and so forth (House et al., 1991; Winter, John, Stewart, Klohnen, & Duncan, 1998; Bargh & Alvarez, 2001; Chen, Lee-Chai, & Bargh, 2001). We focus here on the role of the power motive in leadership, where manifesting the power motive is operationally defined as attempting to exert one's will via attaining a position of influence in a hierarchical authority structure (see Overbeck, 2010; Van Vugt et al., 2008).

Hierarchical authority structures are social networks that involve gradations of authority and responsibility. We encounter these hierarchies continuously. Most of us work in hierarchical authority structures, administered by supervisors, managers, and executives. We go to school in hierarchical authority structures, directed by department heads, deans, provosts, and chancellors. We interact with government agencies controlled by bureaucratically designated positions such as administrator, secretary, and director. We seek medical assistance in hospitals administered by heads, supervisors, and medical directors. Supervisors, department heads, and managers run the stores in which we shop. We are protected by a military arranged in tiered levels of authority (e.g., ranging from petty officer to admiral).

We propose that a person's power motive is a primary source of desire to seek positions of significance in one or more hierarchical authority structures and, if so placed, to work intensely and persistently to perform effectively. Stated directly, a strong power motive is *a primary motivating force* for striving to attain positions where one can affect courses of events by influencing how people think, feel, and act.

People with strong power motives are disposed to seek demanding posts, to take initiatives to lead, to work intensely to direct their people to success, and to persevere through setbacks to see that their people finish tasks and meet goals (McClelland, 1985). A key to understanding the power motive is to realize that, for those who wish to influence and control events, the exercise of power is itself intrinsically rewarding. Powerful people *enjoy* seeking and then assuming the responsibilities to make decisions that shape the success and futures of companies, military divisions, government agencies, schools and universities, religious institutions, extended families, and the like (Veroff, 1992; Winter, 1973, 1992).

The full impact of this point requires consideration of the fact that a considerable proportion of people, perhaps the majority, have low or very modest power motives and typically neither seek nor enjoy leadership responsibilities (Winter, 1973, 1992; McClelland, 1985; Chan & Drasgow, 2001). A weak power motive denotes a low need to exercise one's will by attaining a position of significance in a hierarchical authority structure, which indicates that a desire to have impact and influence on others is not especially salient as a work career goal (Winter et al., 1998). In more specific behavioral terms, a weak power motive is often manifested by not taking the initiative to lead groups and avoiding jobs that have supervisory responsibilities (Chan & Drasgow, 2001); never having run for office in school, clubs, or teams (Stricker & Rock, 1998); seldom, if ever, taking strong, forceful actions that affect others (Winter, 1992); avoiding situations that require taking responsibility for the welfare of others (Winter et al., 1998); passing on opportunities to plan and organize projects (Moskowitz, 1994); experiencing discomfort when attempting to persuade others that one's ideas are objectively superior (House et al., 1991); and seldom expressing disagreements with, or criticism of, those in authority (Moskowitz, 1994).

Clearly, not all people want to be leaders (Stricker & Rock, 1998; Chan & Drasgow, 2001). Some of these people not only have low power motives but also desire to be led. That is to say, some people prefer to be dependent on leaders for their survival and social welfare (Winter, 1992; Moskowitz, 1994; Winter et al., 1998). Others have strong desires to be independent or to be unharried by leadership responsibilities in order to pursue other types of objective (e.g., create, write, build). Many additional possibilities exist, but the key is that, as a group, these people share the common attribute of little to no aspiration toward power and leadership. The data support the idea that these people are unlikely to emerge as leaders (Kenny & Zacarro, 1983), and, when placed in leadership positions, these people tend not to perform well, because they lack the motivational and behavioral characteristics required to be effective leaders (Chan & Drasgow, 2001; Foti & Hauenstein, 2007; Judge et al., 2002; McClelland & Boyatzis, 1982; Stricker & Rock, 1998; Yukl, 2009).

Returning to people with strong power motives, it is fair to note the extrinsic rewards that accrue to leaders who hold positions of influence in hierarchical authority structures. Position and power bestow the leader with status, prestige, privilege, access to an unequal distribution of resources, and, frequently, enlarged wealth (Overbeck, 2010). Increases in status and prestige help to satisfy ego needs and to enhance a person's sense of self-worth (Maslow, 1954). The privileges, prestige, and resources that accrue from attaining rank and position in an authority hierarchy are also conducive to feelings of potency, significance, pride, accomplishment, and mastery, and, for some, superiority (Kipnis, 1976; see also Winter, 1973, 1992; McCelland, 1985; McClelland, Koestner, & Weinberger, 1989).

Status, prestige, privilege, unequal distributions of resources, and the like are natural byproducts of the evolutionary proclivity of humans to arrange themselves into hierarchical authority structures (Bargh & Alvarez, 2001; McAdams & Pals, 2006; Van Vugt et al., 2008). Presumably, these incentives came about as means for the group to attract and reward competent and trustworthy people who were willing to step forward and take on the responsibilities of initiating and directing actions that promote group welfare and keep the group safe and secure. The "evolved leader psychology" (Van Vugt et al., 2008, p. 182) is that good leaders are also willing to share their resources generously with their followers. Moreover, they are expected to engage in egalitarian (democratic, delegated, participative) forms of leadership whenever possible. And, they are expected to make strategic decisions that place the welfare of the group ahead of their personal ambitions and gains. It is acceptable to have status and privilege in the evolved leader psychology, as long as one is not ostentatious about it and, perhaps, is even a bit embarrassed by it.

What is not acceptable in the evolved leader psychology model is for leaders to place personal ambitions ahead of group welfare. Leaders' desires for power should be directly proportional to their needs for influence to direct the group toward the needs of the group (Overbeck, 2010). Power should not be sought for the sake of power. It is also the case that status, prestige, privilege, and the like should never be ends in themselves, for, like a fixation on power, this will lead to personal corruption and non-optimal outcomes for the group (Lord Acton, 1865; Russell 1938; Kipnis, 1976).

Unfortunately, the seeking of power is often attributed to leaders' placing their personal ambition ahead of group welfare (see Bargh & Alvarez, 2001). This negative attribution stimulates visions of leaders who are willing to engage in force, threat, and coercion to gain power, privileges, and resources. According to the evolved leader psychology (Van Vugt et al., 2008), when we think leaders are motivated by personal gain, we hark back to domains ruled by chieftains and warlords (still a sizable portion of the world). These domains were (are) often subject to tyranny, threat, exploitation, greed, class warfare, and oppression by aggressive individuals representing soldier classes and narcissistic ruling elites. It is a vision of dominance and oppression that conflicts strongly with our implicit theories of what good leadership is (see Lord, Foti, & DeVader, 1984), and it may fuel a sense of reactance.

We agree with authors such as Bargh and Alvarez (2001) that a general tendency exists, especially in some social-science circles, to denigrate power motives because the motives are thought to be energized *primarily* by personal ambition (e.g., the seeking of status, privilege, and unequal resources, or, worse, by desires to oppress, force, corrupt, and tyrannize). We, however, believe that vilifying the power motive has stifled scientific interest in it and retarded attempts to develop objective ways to measure it. As a result, the field of leadership has done little to advance understanding of a key motivational factor that drives and shapes the reasoning and behaviors of leaders (Hogan & Kaiser, 2005; Vroom & Jago, 2007; Kaiser, Hogan, & Craig, 2008). Indeed, Winter (1992) was one of the first to note that the field of leadership misses the mark when he observed that the seeking of power in the United States is associated with "suspicions, doubts, and denials" (p. 302). Winter (1992, p. 302) went on to say, "Leaders almost never say that their actions are motivated by a desire for power; instead they talk of 'service' or 'duty.' As a result, one might expect Americans to be defensive or unaware of their power motivation."

People with strong power motives may be defensive or unaware of what motivates them, but they nonetheless feel compelled to exert their will over others. How, then, do they deal with the prevailing social stereotype that power should be treated with suspicion because it is associated with exploitation, inevitable corruption, and coercion? The answer is that, like any motive that has garnered social disapproval, the exercise of the motive is protected by defense mechanisms (see Cramer, 2006). We believe that the defense mechanism of rationalization is of particular interest in regard to the power motive. This is because people with strong power motives often justify exerting their wills by embedding their actions in strategic decision-making. The propensity to select their own personal strategies is attributed to the objective merit and rational superiority of these strategies over the strategies proposed by others (see Pfeffer, 1994).

In most cases, someone with a strong power motive does not say or think he/she is seeking or exercising power. Rather, he/she is thinking rationally and arriving at the best strategic decisions, which is the primary evolutionary function of leadership (Van Vugt et al., 2008). This decision-making often does have objective and rational components. In addition, however, it is often molded by unseen forces that serve the defense mechanism of rationalization. This means that the reasoning gives rational support to the release of the power motive. Another way of saying this is that people for whom the power motive directs behavior have developed ways of reasoning that make exerting *their* wills appear to be rational and sensible. These ways of reasoning help to enhance the rational appeal of power and thus will be referred to as *justification mechanisms* (James, 1998; James & LeBreton, 2010; in press).

Basically, justification mechanisms operate from below the level of consciousness (i.e., implicitly) to direct reasoning in predetermined ways (a bias). Reasoning focuses on building logical support and defenses for releasing an underlying desire to use power. It is this desire to exert one's will over others that serves the motivation to lead and gives impetus to achieving significant outcomes as a leader.

UNCOVERING JUSTIFICATION MECHANISMS FOR POWER

Individual differences in desires to exercise power have received comparatively little scientific attention (see Overbeck, 2010). We studied the extant but scant professional literature to gain insights into how people with strong power motives build seemingly objective and rational cases for exercising their wills. We also read a number of autobiographies and biographies by or about leaders. We studied these literatures to uncover (a) the interpretative categories that leaders use to frame (describe) power-based actions by themselves and others, and (b) the subtle and unrecognized biases that they relied on to build rationalizations for their use of power. The search for justification mechanisms involved an attempt to uncover the implicit or unconscious biases that shape the interpretations people with strong power motives place on power activities, and the slants in logic they use to argue for the rationality of strategic decisions that involve a personal use of power.

We indentified four justification mechanisms for power. Each of these mechanisms helps people with strong power motives, hereafter referred to as "POs," build strategic decisions that rationalize their use of power. These four justification mechanisms comprise an initial and, we believe, seminal set of biases that enable the release of the power motive. We make no claim that these four justification mechanisms exhaust the entire set of salient justification mechanisms for power. They do offer a reasonable base on which to begin studies of how to measure the strength of a person's power motive.

Justification Mechanism 1: Agentic Bias

When attempting to think rationally and objectively about strategic decisions, POs instinctively take the perspective of the agents or initiators of actions (see Veroff, 1992; Winter, 1992; Moskowitz, 1994; Overbeck,

2010). Consequently, their thinking often evidences a propensity to confirm (e.g., build logical support for) the agents' ideas, plans, and solutions. These ideas, plans, and solutions are viewed as providing logically superior strategic decisions. Whether others embrace these superior decisions is seen as determined by the agents' personal skills to persuade, convince, and convert people to their ideas (House et al., 1991; Veroff, 1992). The adoption of strategic decisions is thus judged to be contingent on the superiority of the agents' reasoning skills and how effectively they influence others to follow their plans (see Hogan & Kaiser, 2005; Van Vugt et al., 2008; Yukl, 2009).

The key to the Agentic Bias is the perspective from which people frame and reason. POs instinctively look down; that is, they identify with the people (like themselves) who reside in management positions, create strategic plans, and then lead others to carry out the plans. People with weak or nonexistent power motives, whom we will refer to as "NPs," instinctively look up. When thinking about strategic decisions, they take the perspectives of those lower in the organization who are affected by the decisions and actions. They naturally think in terms of the implications and consequences of the decisions on the feelings and actions of followers.

To illustrate, suppose a group of people is told that employee theft usually decreases after surveillance cameras are installed in workplaces. However, the cameras also make many employees nervous and unhappy. Each individual in the group is now asked to draw what she or he thinks is the most salient and reasonable inference based on the information given. The NPs among the group will instinctively see this problem through the eyes of employees, and many will infer that employees are unhappy because surveillance cameras are seen as an invasion of privacy. In contrast, the POs in the group will instinctively see the problem through the eyes of those who must decide whether to install surveillance cameras. To them, the primary issue, based on the information given, is the seriousness of employee theft in a given company.

An implicit bias to think like a PO (or an NP) does not denote error, for one's predisposition to reason from the perspective of those in power, the agents or initiators of action, often engenders a plausible way of looking at the problem. However, a purely rational model calls for dialectics, where the pros and cons of each of several possible points of view are considered (see James, 1998). The connotation of bias here is that one favors the point of view that is consistent with one's latent personality. POs may well subscribe consciously to the idea of multiple points of view, and may even express strong beliefs that the pros and cons of each of these views need to be objectively evaluated. However, when tasked with analyzing specific, real-world problems, POs will instinctively and consistently lean toward seeing the problems through the lens of an agent or initiator/controller of action.

Justification Mechanism 2: Social Hierarchy Orientation

Reasoning from this orientation reflects implicit acceptance of hierarchical authority structures as the primary form of human organization. Reasoning is often based on the unstated and, for many POs, unrecognized premise that disproportionate influence, privilege, and distribution of resources are rational ways of organizing and leading (as opposed to egalitarian power structures—see Sidanius & Pratto, 1999; Buss, 2005; Simon & Oakes, 2006; Overbeck, 2010). As an example of this way of thinking, consider the following premise: Decision-making in most companies is effective when managers are organized in terms of graded levels of authority, where each manager has a sphere of influence in which he or she is responsible for making decisions.

Members of a group of managers are asked to analyze this premise and, individually, identify an unstated assumption on which it is based. POs in the group are predisposed to accept the premise that graded levels of authority and spheres of influence are rational ways of organizing many companies. The unstated assumptions they identify are, thus, likely to be supportive of the premise (e.g., decisions can be made quickly, without lengthy discussion or dissent, in hierarchical authority structures).

NPs, on the other hand, are unlikely to be supportive of the premise, because they do not implicitly accept hierarchical authority structures as the primary and most natural form of human organization (see Bargh & Alvarez, 2001; Van Vugt et al., 2008). In fact, they may well be disposed to reason that power structures that involve disproportionate influence, privilege, and distributions of resources often produce less than optimal decisions. The unstated assumptions they identify are, thus, likely to be critical of the premise. An illustration of subtle and indirect criticism is: The premise assumes that individuals can make better decisions than groups comprised of diverse and knowledgeable individuals. (Place "incorrectly" in front of "assumes" to capture NPs' true meaning.)

NPs are presumably critical because they, like a great many people, subscribe to the evolved leader psychology that leadership is best when it is based on egalitarian (e.g., democratic, participative) forms of decision-making (Lord et al., 1984; Van Vugt et al., 2008). Such thinking evolved from hunter–gatherer societies, where people experienced a sense of "empathetic responsiveness" to one another, a product of having experienced pleasures and suffered pain together (Bandura, 1999, p. 200). This sense of common togetherness and empathy engendered perceptions of similarity and common social obligations (Bandura, 1969), which is to say an egalitarian society. Their preferred leadership pattern also reflected empathetic responsiveness and was characterized by transitory, democratic, consensually appointed leaders whose power was limited to their areas of expertise (see Van Vugt et al., 2008). When necessary for such things as defense of the collective, hierarchical authority structures are viewed as necessary evils that need not have a permanent basis (Van Vugt et al., 2008).

Note that NPs' preferred form of leadership allows people without strong desires to be leaders to be dependent on strong leadership when conditions call for strong leaders (e.g., the group is in peril of being attacked) and to have a voice in decisions that affect them in more stable and tranquil contexts. NPs will be receptive to reasoning that supports this form of leadership. POs, on the other hand, may give explicit recognition to this leveling of the authority structures in stable and tranquil conditions, but their true, unstated, and often unrecognized allegiance is to hierarchically graded systems of power.

Justification Mechanism 3: Power Attribution Bias

Reasoning with this bias reflects a predisposition to logically connect the use of power with positive behavior, values, and outcomes. Acts of power are interpreted in positive terms, such as taking initiative, assuming responsibility, and being decisive (Russell, 1938; Winter, 1973, 1992; McClelland, 1985; Veroff, 1992). These same acts are logically associated with positive outcomes, such as organizational survival, stability, effectiveness, and success. The powerful are viewed as talented, experienced, and successful leaders. In like manner, successful leadership is rationally attributed to the use of power.

The Power Attribution Bias stands in contrast to the tendency of society, including a great many NPs, to correlate the exercise of power with entitlement, corruption, and tyranny (Lord Acton, 1865; Kipnis, 1976). More specifically, the power motive is held culpable for (a) placing personal gain ahead of group welfare; (b) the seeking of influence simply in order to dominate others; (c) the willingness to use threat and coercion in order to gain power, status, and entitlements; and (d) the building of organizations ruled by narcissistic tyrants who oppress, exploit, and victimize subordinates and employees (see Lord Acton, 1865; Kipnis, 1972; Bargh & Alvarez, 2001; Chen et al., 2001; Van Vugt et al., 2008; Resick et al., 2009).

NPs who make attributions that those seeking power are dishonest or corrupt believe their framing and analyses are logical and rational. They often bolster their arguments by pointing to specific examples from history where individuals sought power for corrupt, criminal, or self-serving purposes. Pos, on the other hand, are predisposed to infer that seeking power is necessary for the survival of the collective and the achievement of important goals. They also believe that their framing and analyses are logical and rational, and may point to examples from history that support their inferences (e.g., Abraham Lincoln).

Basically, POs' desire to engage in power clearly places them on the defensive in a culture that tends to frame power in derogatory terms. Justification mechanisms such as the Power Attribution Bias are needed to give POs ostensibly objective and rational reasons for engaging in acts of power (e.g., use of power *is necessary* (in the minds of POs) for organizational survival). It is the apparent objectivity and rationality of this reasoning that deflects the proclivities of NPs to seek less attractive attributions for POs' use of power.

Justification Mechanism 4: Leader Intuition Bias

Decisions and actions appear more reasonable (to POs) when they are based on resources and strategies that confer power to the leader. A great many managers solve problems in much the same way as expert decision-makers, analogous to chess grandmasters who simply look at a chessboard and see potential winning strategies (see Kahneman & Klein, 2009). The experience and training of more mature leaders allow them to see promising strategies quickly. They differ from less experienced and less well-trained leaders in their "unusual ability to appreciate the dynamics of complex [situations] and quickly judge whether a [strategy] is promising or fruitless" (Kahneman & Klein, 2009, p. 515). These "expert" decision-makers often think of this process as reflecting their (leader) intuition (Klein, 1998). What these expert decisionmakers do not realize is that the ones among them who are POs are predisposed to intuitively think of strategies that confer power to themselves (or people like themselves—see Winter, 1973, 1992; McClelland, 1985). NPs among these expert decision-makers will be significantly less prone to intuitively identity these same types of power-conferring strategy as promising.

What has likely happened here is that, over the years, POs selectively attended to patterns and decisions that were not only efficacious but that also involved resources that conveyed power to the leader. Examples of such resources include (a) receiving recognition for such things as being an expert or a first-mover (French & Raven, 1959; Van Vugt et al., 2008; Winter, 1973); (b) being able to inflict pleasure (rewards) or pain (punishment) on subordinates (French & Raven, 1959); (c) being in the nexus of communication or influence structures (French & Raven, 1959); (d) being in control of resources (French & Raven, 1959); (e) functioning in hierarchical authority structures where one has personal responsibility for important decisions (Overbeck, 2010); and (f) working in cultures where the accumulation and exercise of power via forming alliances and coalitions are expected, even encouraged. The result of selective attention and learning is that strategies and actions that allow POs to develop a power base become part of their tacit knowledge structures. This tacit knowledge is accessed automatically (without awareness—Schneider & Schiffrin, 1977), which makes it appear as experience-based intuition of how to solve strategic problems (see Kahneman & Klein, 2009).

NPs may also develop tacit knowledge structures and then rely on experienced-based intuition to make strategic decisions. However, these knowledge structures are unlikely to involve cognitive associations between effective leadership and resources that enhance the NPs' power. This is because NPs have no power motive to direct their perceptual process toward selectively attending to opportunities to exercise power.

CONDITIONAL REASONING

When POs and NPs frame the same events from different perspectives, as illustrated in the Agentic Bias, and use different but rational analyses to arrive at contrasting conclusions about the accumulation and use of power, as indicated in the Leader Intuition Bias, reasoning is said to be "conditional" on the reasoners (James, 1998; James & LeBreton, 2010, in press). By "conditional reasoning," we mean that reasoning is dependent on personality; that is, reasoning is dependent on the strength of the power motives and accompanying justification mechanisms of the reasoners. Conditional reasoning is used in a manner such as the following: Whether reasoning will determine that the use of power is the most rational strategic decision is conditional (i.e., dependent) on whether the person doing the reasoning is a PO or an NP. POs will tend to reason in ways that justify the use of influence and power. NPs will tend to reason in ways that are less accepting of the use of power and may foster the use of more egalitarian methods.

Conditional reasoning is concerned with patterns of individual differences in reasoning about behavior that are unknowingly engendered by underlying personalities. A key feature of conditional reasoning is that, even though POs and NPs come to disparate judgments about what constitutes reasonable behavior, both sets of individuals believe that their reasoning is rational and sensible, as opposed to irrational and inappropriate. A novel contribution of conditional reasoning to the study of personality has been the charting and assessment of the types of reasoning bias—referred to above as justification mechanisms—that POs employ to enhance the rational appeal of seeking, accruing, and using power. We turn now to show how the understanding of justification mechanisms opened the door to a new measurement system for personality.

CONDITIONAL-REASONING MEASUREMENT SYSTEM

Knowledge of justification mechanisms helps us to understand the defensive processes that people use to create a biased sense of rationality for what, in truth, are desire-driven behaviors. People with strong power motives develop justification mechanisms such as the Agentic Bias and the Power Attribution Bias to defend the release of these motives via what, on the surface, appear (to them) to be rational and objective analyses. In contrast, people with weak to modest power motives have no reason to develop justification mechanisms for power, for they have no desire to engage in the use of power. Their lack of justification mechanisms means that they have no biases to enhance the rational appeal of using power. Without these biases to shape their reasoning, they are likely to find reasoning that is based on justification mechanisms to be improbable, implausible, far-fetched, and unlikely.

By definition, we cannot observe the power motive, because it exists primarily in the unconscious (Winter, 1973, 1992; Winter et al., 1998). We can, however, measure the strength of justification mechanisms. We can then use the measures of the justification mechanisms to infer the strengths of the implicit power motives. Specifically, we can infer that people have a strong power motive if their reasoning is strongly influenced by the justification mechanisms for power. Analogously, we infer that people have a weak-to-modest power motive if their reasoning is not influenced by justification mechanisms. Indeed, we expect them to be skeptical of reasoning based on these justification mechanisms.

ASSESSMENT OF JUSTIFICATION MECHANISMS

The assessment of justification mechanisms is based on 20 years of research that shows that people find reasoning that projects their justification mechanisms to be logically compelling (James, 1998; James & LeBreton, 2010, in press). In the present case, we will rely on this research to propose that POs will tend to be logically attracted to reasoning if it is presented from the perspective of the agents or initiators of strategic decisions and managerial actions; is based on acceptance of hierarchical authority structures as the primary and most natural form of human organization; concludes that successful decisions or actions by a leader were because of the use of power; or logically advocates for intuitive decisions and actions that involve resources that confer power on the leader.

A new form of inductive reasoning problem is used to measure the logical attractiveness of reasoning based on justification mechanisms. These problems are referred to as "conditional reasoning problems" to denote that the solutions a person finds to be most logically compelling are dependent on whether the person is primarily a PO or an NP. Table 8.1 contains an illustrative conditional reasoning problem. Respondents are asked to find the most reasonable conclusion based on the information given.

The problem in Table 8.1 is designed to probe for the presence of an Agentic Bias. Respondents are informed that they are about to solve a reasoning problem. No mention is made of the true purpose of the task. This allows us to measure how respondents actually reason when analyzing issues dealing with power.

PO alternative: Alternative (b) is designed to be logically compelling to respondents who instinctively take the perspective of the agents or initiators of strategic decisions and managerial actions. Alternative (b) states that, "The leader is strong and has definite ideas about what should be done," which implies that the leader will define problems, lead group discussions, and have strong persuasive influence on final decisions. This type of reasoning is designed to appeal logically to people who spontaneously assume the perspective of agents, because they instinctively want to be in control (exercise their will), they are convinced that their strategic plans will lead to successful actions, and they believe that the superiority of their

TABLE 8.1

Illustrative Conditional Reasoning Problem for Power

Participative leadership involves inviting subordinates to share in discussions and decision-making with their leader. Together, the leader and subordinates generate and evaluate ideas, and then attempt to reach a consensus about what should be done. Subordinates are often more committed to a course of action when they have had a chance to participate in deciding what it will be.

Based on the above, which one of the following provides the most logical reason for using participative leadership?

(a) The subordinates are independent and prefer to work alone.

(b) The leader is strong and has definite ideas about what should be done.

(c) The subordinates are well informed about the problem at hand.

(d) The subordinates are uncooperative and do not work well together.

---

reasoning is sufficient to persuade others to follow them. We believe that selection of Alternative (b) is indicative of the presence of an underlying Agentic Bias. This, in turn, implies the presence of a strong latent power motive.

We are mindful that empirical research is needed to determine if, in fact, people with a demonstrated history of using power are significantly more likely to select Alternative (b) than people with no such history. Later, we will suggest that the results of early research indicate that this is so. We are also mindful that reasoning on a single problem is not an infallible indicator of a proclivity to make use of the Agentic Bias. Thus, we determine whether a respondent consistently selects reasoning based on an Agentic Bias across a set of reasoning problems that vary in terms of premises, contexts, and conclusions. It is the consistent selection of answers that target this specific justification mechanism that most reliably reveals the presence of an Agentic Bias.

NP alternative: Alternatives based on justification mechanisms are designed to appear as logically plausible and psychologically persuasive to respondents whose reasoning is shaped by the targeted justification mechanisms. In the present case, an attempt was made to capture what POs consider "logical analyses" as they might occur in what Kuhn (1991) refers to as "informal reasoning." Such reasoning focuses less on the strict standards of formal inductive analyses and more on what POs consider reasonable or logical in real, everyday human activity (Galotti, 1989; Haidt, 2001; Hahn & Oaksford, 2007).

NPs, whose reasoning is not guided by power-related justification mechanisms, are expected to be skeptical of the reasoning based on the Agentic Bias. Of greater plausibility to NPs is reasoning that appeals to a spontaneous proclivity to reason from the perspective of followers, and to analyze the problem from what it is about followers that makes participative reasoning reasonable. Alternative (c) is designed to appear as logically plausible and psychologically persuasive to respondents who instinctively reason from this perspective. Selection of Alternative (c) is thus regarded as one indicator of the presence of a weak power motive.

Illogical alternatives: Because conditional-reasoning problems are meant to appear to respondents as traditional reasoning problems, it is necessary to include clearly illogical responses in the problems. The clearly illogical alternatives in this problem are Alternatives (a) and (d). Our intent, and the usual result, is that almost no respondents attempt to solve the problems using clearly incorrect alternatives. On the rare occasion a respondent consistently selects illogical alternatives, our policy is to drop them from the sample.

THE CONDITIONAL-REASONING TEST FOR LEADERSHIP

This approach to assessment is referred to as "conditional reasoning," because how people solve problems is dependent on their personalities (James, 1998). Conditional-reasoning problems, or CR problems, such as illustrated in Table 8.1 are designed to measure whether a person's reasoning is shaped by specific types of bias (i.e., justification mechanisms). The PO answers to the reasoning problems are grounded in the same justification mechanisms that people with strong power motives use to imbue their decisions and behaviors with a sense of rationality. People with strong power motives are drawn to these answers. This is because people who use biases to justify their own decisions and behaviors find reasoning based on the same biases to be logically compelling (James & LeBreton, 2010).

Solving conditional-reasoning problems is an objective process. People with strong power motives perceive that they are taking a reasoning test, which is true (this is also true for NPs). However, the POs have no idea that they find an answer to be logically compelling because it is based on a bias that allows them to justify their own power-based behaviors. Nor are they aware that their solutions reveal their strong motives for power. This is especially salient for power, because, as we discussed earlier, people with strong power motives are seldom aware of the true force of their desires to exert their wills over others. It is also the case that some people who consciously believe that they have strong power motives do not. At least, they fail to have a system of cognitive defenses (i.e., justification mechanisms) to justify the use of power. As noted, absence of a defense system for the use of power implies lack of power motive.

The conditional-reasoning test developed to measure the power motive is referred to as the Conditional-Reasoning Test for Leadership (CRT-L). It contains 25 problems, such as are illustrated in Table 8.1. The majority of problems assess the degrees to which the four justification mechanisms for power affect the reasoning of a respondent. (As discussed shortly, a second type of problem and alternative are also included in the CRT-L.) Respondents are given a "+1" for every PO alternative they select. These scores are summed to furnish a single score. A high score indicates that (a) justification mechanisms are instrumental in guiding reasoning and, thus, that (b) the respondent is implicitly prepared to justify exerting his or her will on others. The respondent is scored as having a strong power motive.

A low score on the CRT-L indicates that the justification mechanisms for power are *not* instrumental in shaping a respondent's reasoning. The lack of a defensive system to justify use of power suggests that respondents have a weak power motive and, thus, are unlikely to engage in power-based decision-making and actions. Scores in the mid range (i.e., between the weak and strong poles) on the CRT-L indicate that implicit defenses for justifying the power motive are not well developed and are invoked sporadically. This suggests the absence of a forceful power motive and an uninspired and inconsistent proclivity to engage in power-based decision-making and behavior.

CHANNELING THE POWER MOTIVE INTO LEADER BEHAVIOR

The desire to exert one's influence over others shapes not only the strategic decisions one makes about what to do, but also how one chooses to do so via leadership. The relationship between one's power motive and leadership style is not direct, however, for there are many ways that the desire to exert oneself can be channeled into a style of leading. What direction this channeling takes is largely determined by personality variables other than the power motive (House et al., 1991; Winter et al., 1998; Bargh & Alvarez, 2001; Chen et al., 2001).

For example, people who want to lead and are also aggressive tend to channel their power motives into abusive and threatening behaviors that create toxic environments for their subordinates (Bargh & Alvarez, 2001). People who are narcissistic tend to channel their power motives into arrogant and imperious forms of leadership (Resick et al., 2009). People who are nurturing, communal, and charismatic are prone to channel their power motives into transformational forms of leadership (House et al., 1991; Bargh & Alvarez, 2001). Extraverted people with strong power motives tend to value relationships with others as they attempt to fulfill their desires for impact. Introverted people with strong power motives tend to place less value on relationships and to avoid impactful careers that require extensive interactions with others (Winter et al., 1998).

We will focus our attention on how aggressive leaders channel their power motives into behaviors that create toxic organizations. We chose aggression as the initial channeling variable for power because we believe that power has been held culpable for abuses that were actually perpetrated by aggression. We note the countless abuses of power documented in papers and books over the history of humankind. We believe power is often not the culprit for these abuses, and, throughout history, people have attributed to power what truly belongs to channeling variables such as aggression and narcissism. As a result, aggression is a particularly worthy candidate for study.

Aggressive people seek and use power in ways that prove to be detrimental to people and to organizations, and both individual and organizational effectiveness suffers accordingly (Kellerman, 2004). These leaders seek and use power in ways that are counterproductive or harmful to organizations, to those around them, or even to themselves (i.e., they are self-destructive; Hogan & Kaiser, 2005; Kaiser et al., 2008). These are leaders who abuse their authority and engage in illegitimate uses of vested powers, often for self-aggrandizing reasons such as the seeking of status and privilege (Bargh & Alvarez, 2001). We will refer to these leaders as "toxic" when their abuses of power unfairly frustrate and hinder the performance, development, and advancement of qualified and motivated individuals, cause short- or long-term harm to the organization, and/or lead to self-destructive behaviors (Van Vugt et al., 2008; Resick et al., 2009).

There are some who believe that access to, and sustained use of, power is corrupting (e.g., Kipnis, 1976). In agreement with Bargh and Alvarez (2001), we believe this implicit theory is unsupportable. If it were valid, then it would follow logically that all leaders who accrue power become corrupt, which is not the case. Toxic leaders are not created by giving people power and allowing them to keep it or to enhance it. Toxic leaders are created by the fact that some people have, not only a high need for power, but also a high need for aggression. The result *of this combination* is that they seek power in aggressive ways, and, if they are successful in attaining power, then they use it in aggressive ways, which is to say, in ways that harm others.

Below, we overview the typical pattern of behaviors and the reasoning that underlies the strategic decision-making of toxic leaders. The discussion then proceeds to how toxic leaders are identified via conditional reasoning.

Toxic Leaders

People who seek and use power in aggressive ways—that is, toxic leaders— often attempt to control others by use of intimidation, threat, force, and bribery. They frequently are viewed as bullies who exploit their followers for personal gain. If they do express interest in, or concern for, their subordinates, it is usually for an ulterior motive such as gaining insight into their subordinates' views in order to better manipulate them. They have little real concern for people, their chief desire being to enhance their own power and entitlements. However, they may appear to be attentive and caring, but this is almost always done to make themselves "look good," so they can enhance their power and status (Winter, 1973; McClelland, 1985). Almost inevitability, their true nature will manifest in a way that harms the development and/or performance of their subordinates.

Toxic leaders evaluate tasks in terms of opportunities to gain recognition and power. Similarly, they evaluate risk in terms of the effects of outcomes on their personal power and reputation. They serve others primarily to extend their own power and status and are often proficient at manipulating and managing impressions of their superiors. They use their power to advance personal interests (e.g., wealth). They evaluate others in terms of their title, status, pedigree, and reputation. They network and form relationships with others in order to enhance their opportunities to take dominant roles, with little consideration given to the effectiveness of their organizations (Winter, 1992).

Toxic leaders often exert their power just for the pleasure of seeing others submit. They tend (a) to set impossible standards and then fire those who fail to satisfy them, (b) to demand unquestioning loyalty and submission, and (c) to claim to be entitled to treatment that exceeds legitimate bounds of leader–subordinate relationships. This toxicity may escalate to the level of hostility, illustrations being leaders who constantly ridicule and degrade subordinates, act as catalysts for dissention and conflict among peers and

254 • *Lawrence R. James et al.*

subordinates, and/or engage in harassment, including sexual harassment (Judge et al., 2006; Rosenthal & Pittinsky, 2006).

The willingness to cause injury and injustice in order to gain or retain power may extend to unethical, if not corrupt, actions such as breaking the law (e.g., financial transgressions) and then demanding that subordinates condone and cover them up. Toxic leaders may also place subordinates in harm's way for selfish gain, such as taking unwarranted and self-interested risks with employee pensions. Toxic leaders' penchant for causing injury may turn inward and engender self-destructive behaviors, such as abuse of drugs and alcohol, excessive spending, sexual escapades, petty larceny (e.g., shoplifting), and increases in serious traffic violations, often the result of road rage (Hogan & Kaiser, 2005; Resick et al., 2009).

The Conditional Reasoning of Toxic Leaders

Toxic leaders think of power and strategic decision-making in terms of their personal potency, that is, their ability to personally dominate, control, intimidate, and instill fear (Winter, 1973). What they want from others is deference and submission, which they (the leaders) often frame as allegiance and respect. This proclivity to think of interactions with others as dominance contests in which the objective is to take control by making others submit is known as a "Potency Bias" (James et al., 2005).

Reasoning shaped by a Potency Bias furnishes toxic leaders with what to them is a rational basis for attaining and using personal power. Toxic leaders often frame people such as themselves as strong, assertive, brave, powerful, bold, and in control. These positive characterizations suggest that attempts to gain control over others by accruing personal power are not only reasonable but also laudatory. Perhaps at least as telling is toxic leaders' framing of leaders who do not seek personal potency. They think of such leaders as weak, impotent, timid, fearful, and not in control (James & Mazerolle, 2002).

Such reasoning suggests that one of the great fears of toxic leaders is being seen as "weak" (Veroff, 1992). It indicates further that, if their quest for dominance is frustrated, and they are at risk of being seen as weak, then toxic leaders are prepared to use injurious and unjust methods to show that they are strong, powerful, bold, and in control (James & Mazerolle, 2002; Baumeister, Campbell, Krueger, & Vohs, 2003). In fact, their pride, honor, and self-respect are tied to their personal potency and status

(Baumeister et al., 2003). Anything that threatens such potency and status is regarded as a form of personal disrespect and dishonor that is deserving of immediate retribution. Losing an argument or not being accorded the office with the greatest status are examples of triggers for retaliation. This proclivity for retaliation is known as the Retribution Bias (James et al., 2005).

Toxic leaders are not interested in sharing or delegating authority. Indeed, they regard questions about their ideas or plans, or any hesitation to implement them, as signs of mutiny (Winter, 1992). Moreover, toxic leaders believe that they are much more able than others to decipher hostility and disrespect in the words and actions of others. They think of themselves as having great skills to see clearly and intuitively into the true nature of human behavior. People with less insight and perceptiveness are thought to be blinded by their naïveté and goodness, and thus fail to discern the dark side of human nature (Hogan & Kaiser, 2005). However, the self-ascribed insight, perceptiveness, and intuitiveness of toxic leaders are illusionary. The true but unrecognized explanation for toxic leaders seeing hostility and disrespect in the actions of others is that they are paranoid, or, in more contemporary terms, suffer from a "Hostile Attribution Bias" (Dodge & Coie, 1987).

Proclivities to see hostile intentions in the actions of others and a desire to dominate relationships with these others often result in callous leadership styles. An authoritarian, dictatorial, domineering style is especially likely if toxic leaders sense disloyalty, for they now feel the need to quell potential rebelliousness and to seek retribution for traitors to the cause. Paranoia, a desire to dominate, and a proclivity to seek retribution can also trigger other forms of unethical behavior, especially if these biases are accompanied by other biases, such as the judgment that one is being unfairly victimized by powerful others, such as government agencies, a competitor, or organized labor (Bandura, 1999; Frost, Ko, & James, 2007).

In sum, toxic leaders are driven by a desire for personal power or potency. Their reasoning is shaped by biases such as the Potency Bias, the Retribution Bias, and the Hostile Attribution Bias. These biases allow them to justify engaging in toxic behaviors to enhance the self-perception that they are not weak but, in fact, are dominant and in control. Their toxicity often takes the form of the four types of unethical leader behavior identified by Kellerman (2004), namely corruption, callousness, evil, and insularity. We illustrated several of these behaviors, to which we would add activities such as misinformation about costs, miscalculation of resources, lying about market demands, sabotage of competitors, exaggeration of earnings, not paying taxes, gambling employee pensions, dissolving healthy companies for short-term profits, and misinforming the public about the safety of a product (Kipnis, 1976). The products of these endeavors are ineffective organizations that are full of alienated and demoralized followers (Van Vugt et al., 2008). That is, over time, toxic leadership produces negative personal and organizational outcomes.

Identifying Toxic Leaders Using the CRT-L

Acts of aggression are protected by a unique set of justification mechanisms. These justification mechanisms differ from those for power. The objective of the aggression justification mechanisms is to create the self-deception that acts of aggression can be justified as self-defense, attempts to restore honor, or legitimate strikes against injustice, disloyalty, or oppression. These rationalizations conceal from awareness the true but unacceptable cause of aggressive actions, namely a willingness to harm others in pursuit of self-centered goals. The aggression justification mechanisms thus protect the aggressive person from realizing that he or she is truly a hostile, malicious, or malevolent person (James et al., 2005; James & LeBreton, 2010).

Over the last 15 years, we have engaged in over 20 studies designed to develop and validate a conditional-reasoning test that identifies aggressive individuals. The Conditional-Reasoning Test for Aggression, or CRT-A, has been the subject of more than 40 peer-reviewed papers and articles in recognized scientific journals. It is now recognized as a leading instrument for identifying aggressive individuals in organizational settings (Landy, 2008)

Aggression components from reasoning problems from the CRT-A were integrated into some of the CR problems in the CRT-L. Basically, we wanted to divide the POs into those who were POs and not aggressive versus those who were POs and aggressive. The result was a PO alternative without aggression (the PO alternative) and an alternative designed for PO respondents who wanted to justify the aggressive use of power (the TX or toxic alternative). The NP alternative remained unchanged (we were not, at this time, interested in differentiating between NPs who are aggressive and NPs who are not aggressive). Finally, a single illogical

TABLE 8.2

Illustrative Conditional-Reasoning Problem for Power and Toxic Leadership

---

After placing surveillance cameras in workplaces, employee theft usually decreases. The cameras also make many employees nervous and unhappy.

Which of the following is the most reasonable conclusion based on the above?

(a) Surveillance cameras are seen as an invasion of privacy.

(b) Many employees have something to hide.

(c) Many companies have serious problems with employee theft.

(d) Surveillance cameras were on sale last year.

---

alternative is included. We also included problems such as illustrated in Table 8.1, with just PO, NP, and illogical alternatives to get pure measures of power.

Table 8.2 illustrates a CR problem that includes PO, TX, and NP alternatives in the same reasoning task, plus one illogical alternative. The PO answer is Alternative (c), which is designed to probe for the presence of an Agentic Bias. The reasoning presented in this alternative is designed to justify installing surveillance cameras from the perspective of management. The TX answer is Alternative (b), which is designed to probe for the combination of an Agentic Bias from power and a Hostile Attribution Bias from aggression. This alternative also attempts to justify installing surveillance cameras from the perspective of the agents of decision-making. However, the alternative also involves an accusatory slant in the form of an attribution involving hostile intent by a large number, perhaps even the majority, of employees. It is anticipated that powerful respondents will be attracted to this answer if they also have a general propensity to sense hostility and malevolent intent in the behavior of people. The NP answer is Alternative (a), which is designed to appear as logically plausible and psychologically persuasive to respondents whose reasoning is *not guided* by a motivational force or desire to influence others via a position of significance in a leadership hierarchy (their behavior may be guided by a number of other motives, including aggression). These respondents should be drawn to reasoning from the perspective of employees that focuses on what it is about surveillance cameras that makes employees nervous and unhappy. Finally, Alternative (d) is meant to be clearly illogical.

RESULTS OF EARLY RESEARCH

We are in the process of conducting validation studies on the CRT-L. At present, we have available only a single study on managers that is best thought of as a pilot study. The objectives of this study were (1) to determine how store managers responded to the CRT-L problems, and (2) to see if these responses correlated with a consequential managerial criterion (store profits). The sample consisted of 101 managers and/or assistant managers of large retail stores associated with a national chain. The criteria consisted of monthly profits adjusted for store size for each of 7 months.

With respect to the first objective, we found variance in the CR problems. The p-values (proportions of respondents selecting an alternative) were modest for the PO alternatives (approximately 15–20 percent of the managers), lower for the TX alternatives (8–12 percent), quite large for the NP alternatives (approximately 70 percent or more of managers), and essentially nonexistent for the illogical alternatives. If these results generalize to larger samples, then we can anticipate that most managers do not have strong needs for power, and, among those who do, there is a small but nontrivial contingent who are toxic.

In regard to the second objective, correlations between responses to the CR problems and the profits criterion were estimated for the month of August. Results demonstrated that these correlations (a) were generally positive and often significant for the PO alternatives, (b) were generally negative and often significant for the TX alternatives, and (c) were generally negative and often significant for NP alternatives if the problem did not have a TX alternative, and low and nonsignificant if the problem included a TX alternative. An empirical scoring key was built based on these results. Alternatives with significant positive correlations with profits were scored +1. Alternatives with significant negative correlations with profits were scored –1. All other alternatives were given a zero. The score on the empirical key was the sum of all the +1 and –1 scores.

The scores on this empirical key were correlated with profits from the months that were *not* used to build the empirical scoring key (i.e., February through July). These are still initial, and not cross, validities, and thus validation in a completely new sample is required for a meaningful statistical inference of validity. The validities provide only a gauge on which to evaluate the promise of the CRT-L in future research studies.

TABLE 8.3

Initial Validities for CRT-L in Predicting Monthly Profits

Month	Criterion	r^a
February	Monthly profits	.350*
March	Monthly profits	.354*
April	Monthly profits	.402*
May	Monthly profits	.404*
June	Monthly profits	.440*
July	Monthly profits	.380*

Notes: n = 101 store managers and assistant managers; * $p < .05$.

a. Pearson correlation, uncorrected for reliability or range restriction.

The validities are reported in Table 8.3. These correlations show a strong consistency over the 6-month period. (The profits criteria were highly correlated over the months, which indicated consistency.) This consistency in validities suggests that the CRT-L has promise as predictor of consequential, real-life managerial criteria. Substantively, the results suggest that nonaggressive managers with strong power motives managed the most profitable retail stores in the sample. The validities also indicate that toxic managers—managers with high power motives coupled with aggressive tendencies—ran retail stores that were significantly less profitable than other stores. Managers with low power needs tended to fall in the middle between these two extremes.

DISCUSSION

The conditional-reasoning technology goes a long way toward solving the problems associated with other measures of the implicit personality (see James & LeBreton, in press). The CRT-L is objective (i.e., people solve reasoning problems) and shows promise for being a reasonable predictor of managerial success. The validities indicate underlying reliability, which has been shown to be acceptable on other conditional-reasoning measures. Also, like other conditional-reasoning measures, it has the benefit of being generally resistant to faking when taken under normal conditions (see LeBreton, Barksdale, Robin, & James, 2007). Finally, the CRT-L is easily and efficiently administered and scored.

Nonetheless, the CRT-L is a work in progress, and much remains to be done. Our primary objective now is to conduct new field tests on the CRT-L. We need to test how well the CRT-L is able to distinguish between leaders and non-leaders, and within leaders, between those driven by power and those driven by both power and aggression. We will use these results to begin the development of an *evidence-based diagnostic system* for identifying individuals who are likely to be effective leaders, as well as those who are likely to be toxic to organizations.

Basic psychometric analyses are also on the horizon. Scales for power and toxic leadership, distributions, reliabilities, factor structures, cutting scores, cross and predictive validities, correlations with alternative personality measures and demographic variables, relationships with assessment center data, and relationships with leadership questionnaires all need to be determined. Channeling models of various types also need to be investigated. The present version leaves unanswered the question of how those high in the power motive but low in aggressiveness channel their needs to exert their wills. New combinations are needed between the CRT-L's measure of the power motive and personality measures such as narcissism and nurturance. These other measures could be assessed implicitly, as here, or explicitly. It would also be interesting to consider relationships between the CRT-L's measure of implicit power and self-perceptions of power. If consistent with prior studies (e.g., Frost et al., 2007), the implicit and explicit measures of power will be uncorrelated but will interact, such that self-perceptions of power guide how implicit desires for power are expressed in leader behavior.

REFERENCES

Bandura, A. (1999). Moral disengagement in the perpetration of inhumanities. *Personality and Social Psychology Review, 3,* 193–209.

Bargh, J. A. & Alvarez, J. (2001). The road to hell: Good intentions in the face of nonconscious tendencies to misuse power. In A. Y. Lee-Chai & J. A. Bargh (Eds.), *The use and abuse of power: Multiple perspectives on the causes of corruption* (pp. 42–55). New York: Taylor & Francis.

Baumeister, R. F., Campbell, J. D., Krueger, J. I., & Vohs, K. D. (2003). Does high self-esteem cause better performance, interpersonal success, happiness, or healthier lifestyles? *Psychological Science in the Public Interest, 4,* 1–44.

Buss, D. M. (2005). *Handbook of evolutionary psychology*. Hoboken, NJ: Wiley.

Chan, K., & Drasgow, F. (2001). Toward a theory of individual differences and leadership: Understanding the motivation to lead. *Journal of Applied Psychology, 86,* 481–498.

Chen, S., Lee-Chai, A. Y., & Bargh, J. A. (2001). Relationship orientation as a moderator of the effects of social power. *Journal of Personality and Social Psychology, 80,* 173–187.

Cramer, P. (2006). *Protecting the self: Defense mechanisms in action.* New York: Guilford Press.

Dodge, K. A., & Coie, J. D. (1987). Social-information-processing factors in reactive and proactive aggression in children's peer groups. *Journal of Personality and Social Psychology, 53,* 1146–1158.

Finkelstein, S., & Hambrick, D. C. (1996). *Strategic leadership: Top executives and their effects on organizations.* Minneapolis/St. Paul, MN: West Educational Publishing.

Foti, R. J., & Hauenstein, N. M. (2007). Pattern and variable approaches in leadership emergence and effectiveness. *Journal of Applied Psychology, 92,* 347–355.

French, J. R., & Raven, B. (1959). The bases of social power. In D. Cartwright (Ed.), *Group dynamics.* New York: Harper & Row.

Frost, B. C., Ko, C. E., & James, L. R. (2007). Implicit and explicit personality: A test of a channeling hypothesis for aggressive behavior. *Journal of Applied Psychology, 92,* 1299–1319.

Galotti, K. M. (1989). Approaches to studying formal and everyday reasoning. *Psychological Bulletin, 105,* 331–351.

Greenwald, A. G. & Banaji, M. R. (1995). Implicit social cognition: Attitudes, self-esteem, and stereotypes. *Psychological Review, 102*(1), 4–27.

Hahn, U., & Oaksford, M. (2007). The rationality of informal argumentation: A Bayesian approach to reasoning fallacies. *Psychological Review, 114,* 704–732.

Haidt, J. (2001). The emotional dog and its rational tail: A social intuitionist approach to moral judgment. *Psychological Review, 108,* 814–834

Hambrick, D. C., Finkelstein, S., & Mooney, A. C. (2005). Executive job demands: New insights for explaining strategic decisions and leader behaviors. *Academy of Management Review, 30,* 472–491.

Hogan, R., & Kaiser, R. B. (2005). What we know about leadership. *Review of General Psychology, 9,* 169–180.

House, R. J., Spangler, W. D., & Woycke, J. (1991). Personality and charisma in the U.S. presidency: A psychological theory of leader effectiveness. *Administrative Science Quarterly, 36,* 364–396.

James, L. R. (1998). Measurement of personality via conditional reasoning. *Organizational Research Methods, 1*(2), 131–163.

James, L. R., & LeBreton, J. M. (2010). Assessing aggression using conditional reasoning. *Current Directions in Psychological Science, 19*(1), 30–35.

James, L. R., & LeBreton, J. M. (in press). *Assessing the implicit personality through conditional reasoning.* Washington, DC: American Psychological Association.

James, L. R. & Mazerolle, M. D. (2002). *Personality in work organizations.* Thousand Oaks, CA: Sage.

James, L. R., McIntyre, M. D., Glisson, C. A., Bowler, J. L., & Mitchell, T. R. (2004). The conditional reasoning measurement system for aggression: An overview. *Human Performance, 17*(3), 271–295.

James, L. R., McIntyre, M. D., Glisson, C. A., Green, P. D., Patton, T. W., LeBreton et al. (2005). A conditional reasoning measure for aggression. *Organizational Research Methods, 1*(1), 69–99.

Judge, T. A., Bono, J. E., Ilies, R., & Gerhardt, M. W. (2002). Personality and leadership: A qualitative and quantitative review. *Journal of Applied Psychology, 87,* 765–780.

Kaiser, R. B., Hogan, R., & Craig, S. B. (2008). Leadership and the fate of organizations. *American Psychologist, 63,* 96–110.

Kahneman, D., & Klein, G. (2009). Conditions for intuitive expertise. *American Psychologist, 64,* 515–526.

Kenny, D.A., & Zaccaro, S.I. (1983). An estimate of variance due to traits in leadership. *Journal of Applied Psychology, 68,* 678–685.

Kellerman, B. (2004). *Bad leadership: What it is, how it happens, why it matters.* Boston, MA: Harvard Business School Press.

Kipnis, D. (1972). Does power corrupt? *Journal of Personality and Social Psychology, 24*(1), 33–41.

Kipnis, D. (1976). *The powerholders.* Chicago, IL: University of Chicago Press.

Klein, G. (1998). *Sources of power: How people make decisions.* Cambridge, MA: MIT Press.

Kuhn, D. (1991). *The skills of argument.* New York: Cambridge University Press.

Landy, F. J. (2008). Stereotypes, bias and personnel decisions: Strange and stranger. *Industrial and Organizational Psychology: Perspectives on Science and Practice, 1,* 379–392.

LeBreton, J. M., Barksdale, C. D., Robin, J., & James, L. R. (2007). Measurement issues associated with conditional reasoning tests: Indirect measurement and test faking. *Journal of Applied Psychology, 92*(1), 1–16.

Lord Acton (1865). Letter to Bishop Mandell Creighton.

Lord, R. G., Foti, R. J., & DeVader, C. L. (1984). A test of leadership categorization theory: Internal structure, information processing, and leadership perceptions. *Organizational Behavior and Human Performance, 34,* 343–378.

Maslow, A. (1954). *Motivation and personality.* New York: Harper.

McAdams, D. P. & Pals, J. L. (2006). A new big five. *American Psychologist, 61*(3), 201–217.

McClelland, D. C. (1985). *Human motivation.* Glenview, IL: Scott, Foresman & Company.

McClelland, D. C. & Boyatzis, R. E. (1982). Leadership motive pattern and long-term success in management. *Journal of Applied Psychology, 67*(6), 737–743.

McClelland, D. C., Koestner, R., & Weinberger, J. (1989). How do self-attributed and implicit motives differ? In F. Halisch & J. H. L. van den Bercken (Eds.), *International perspectives on achievement and task motivation* (pp. 259—289). Lisse, The Netherlands: Swets & Zeitlinger Publishers.

Moskowitz, D. S. (1994). Cross-situational generality and the interpersonal circumjplex. *Journal of Personality and Social Psychology, 66,* 921–933

Meyer, G. J., Finn, S. E., Eyde, L. D., Kay, G. G., Moreland, K. L., Dies, R. R., et al. (2001). Psychological testing and psychological assessment : A review of evidence and issues. *American Psychologist, 56,* 128–165.

Overbeck, J. R. (2010). Concepts and historical perspectives on power, In A. Guinote & T. K. Vescio (Eds.), *The social psychology of power.* New York: Guilford.

Pfeffer, J. (1994). *Managing with power.* Boston, MA: Harvard Business School Press.

Resick, C. J., Whitman, D. S., Weingarden, S. M., & Hiller, N. J. (2009). The bright-side and the dark-side of CEO personality: Examining core self-evaluations, narcissism, transformational leadership, and strategic influence. *Journal of Applied Psychology, 94*, 1365–1381.

Rosenthal, S. A., & Pittinsky, T. L. (2006). Narcissistic leadership. *Leadership Quarterly, 17*, 617–633.

Russell, B. (1938). *Power: A new social analysis.* London: Routledge Classics.

Schneider, W. & Shiffrin, R. M. (1977). Controlled and automatic human information processing: I. Detection, search, and attention. *Psychological Review, 84*, 1–66.

Sidanius, J., & Pratto, F. (1999). *Social dominance: An intergroup theory of social hierarchy and oppression.* New York: Cambridge University Press.

Simon, B. & Oakes, P. (2006). Beyond dependence: An identity approach to social power and domination. *Human Relations, 59*, 105–139.

Stricker, L. J., & Rock, D. A. (1998). Assessing leadership potential with a biographical measure of personality traits. *International Journal of Selection and Assessment, 6*, 164–184.

Van Vugt, M., Hogan, R., & Kaiser, R. B. (2008). Leadership, followership, and evolution: Some lessons from the past. *American Psychologist, 63*, 182–196.

Veroff, J. (1992). Power motivation. In C. P. Smith (Ed.), *Motivation and personality: Handbook of thematic content analysis* (pp. 278–324). New York: Cambridge University Press.

Vroom, V. H. & Jago, A. G. (2007). The role of the situation in leadership. *American Psychologist, 62*, 17–24.

Winter, D. G. (1973). *The power motive.* New York: Free Press.

Winter, D. G. (1992). Power motivation revisited. In C. P. Smith (Ed.), *Motivation and personality: Handbook of thematic content analysis.* New York: Cambridge University Press.

Winter, D. G., John, O. P., Stewart, A. J., Klohnen, E. C., & Duncan, L. E. (1998). Traits and motives: Toward an integration of two traditions in personality research. *Psychological Review, 105*, 230–250.

Yukl, G. A. (2009). *Leadership in organizations* (7th ed.). Boston, MA: Prentice-Hall.

9

Doing Research With Words: Qualitative Methodologies and Industrial/Organizational Psychology

Robert P. Gephart, Jr.

Qualitative research uses linguistic symbols and stories to produce descriptions and interpretations of actual behavior in specific settings. Quantitative research is done with numbers and statistics. Although numbers and quantities appear in qualitative research, and words are essential for quantitative studies, the two forms of research—qualitative and quantitative—are clearly distinguished by their emphases on words and symbols versus numbers and statistics. The general objective of this chapter is to persuade scholars that doing qualitative research with a focus on words has potential to advance I/O psychology and to contribute new insights into issues addressed in I/O psychology, a field where quantification is emphasized.

The chapter begins with an overview of key features of qualitative research. I also discuss how the phenomena and findings uncovered through qualitative methods would differ from those produced through quantitative research. Next, the chapter provides a review of important scholarly worldviews or paradigms in the field of social science. Particular qualitative methods are located in relation to these worldviews, and the ways the intellectual commitments of these worldviews influence the nature, meaning, and use of qualitative methods are addressed. An overview of qualitative methodological approaches that have potential to contribute to I/O psychology research is then provided. These methods include: case studies, interviews, observational approaches, document analysis, computer-aided interpretive textual analysis, and grounded theory. I describe how these approaches have been implemented in past research, explore variations in use of these methods that occur when using different qualitative worldviews, discuss data-analysis strategies used with these approaches, and note benefits and limits of the approaches. The chapter shows how qualitative methods can produce new insights into longstanding concerns in the field and also spur new substantive research. The specific goals of the chapter are thus to: (1) provide an introduction and overview of qualitative methodologies for I/O psychology, (2) show how qualitative methods can contribute to and help advance the field, (3) provide resources for psychologists interested in using qualitative research, or at least becoming better informed about its nature and potential, and (4) persuade readers of the value of qualitative research in I/O psychology.

THE NATURE OF QUALITATIVE RESEARCH

Qualitative research is an "umbrella term" referring to studies that employ a range of interpretive methods to "describe, decode, translate, and otherwise come to terms with the meaning, not frequency, of certain more or less naturally occurring phenomena in the social world" (Van Maanen, 1979, p. 521). Qualitative methods seek to produce historically situated tales or narratives that describe what specific people do in particular places at particular times, and to link these tales to reasoned explanations of what people's conduct means to members themselves (Van Maanen, 1998). The focus is on describing the meaning that concepts have from actors' points of view and the reasoning practices that produce members' points of view (Schutz, 1973; Gephart, 1978, 1997).

It is difficult to specify qualitative work in general owing to its flexibility, emergent character, and the many forms it takes (Van Maanen, 1998, p. xi). Qualitative research tends to be multi-method in focus. It uses an interpretive, naturalistic approach to capture members' meanings in the contexts where they are generated (Denzin & Lincoln, 1994a, 2005). It often uses key experiences of the researcher as data or as events to be understood (Van Maanen, 1979), and it focuses on specific cases and exceptions (Van Maanen, 1998). It thus allows room for unanticipated events or findings.

It also seeks answers to questions about how experience itself is created and given meaning (Denzin and Lincoln, 1994a, p. 4).

The classic Hawthorne Study (Roethlisberger & Dickson, 1939) provides a well-known research investigation that offers an important example of how qualitative research methods can be used to study workplace behavior in a business enterprise. The Hawthorne research helped establish important intellectual bases for industrial psychology, personnel management, and human resources management (Schwartzman, 1993; Zickar & Carter, 2010). This study is one of the most discussed research projects in the history of organizational research (Zickar & Carter, 2010) and may well be the most influential behavioral-science study of a business enterprise ever published (Schwartzman, 1993). It involved three phases: an experimental phase, a large-scale interview phase, and an observational phase. By exploring details of each phase of the study, key features and advantages of each method can be demonstrated. This exploration also demonstrates differences between quantitative and qualitative research regarding documentation of outcomes, as well as the relative benefits of the approaches.

Early experimental studies at the Hawthorne Plant, starting in 1924, attempted to examine the relationship between illumination and productivity (Schwartzman, 1993), but the results were confusing and difficult to interpret. In some cases, increases in illumination were accompanied by an increase in output, but, in other cases, there was no increase and was even a decrease in output. Decreases in illumination led to constant output or increased output, and, in one case, two workers continued to produce at an improved rate even when the light was reduced to the intensity of moonlight.

To understand these puzzling results, a series of experiments that formed the first phase of the Hawthorne Study was designed and implemented in 1927. These experiments addressed the relationship between fatigue and monotony on the one hand and job satisfaction and dissatisfaction on the other. It also sought to assess the impact of varying working conditions (Schwartzman, 1993). The most famous of these experiments involved five female operators who were segregated in a room while they assembled electrical relays for telephones. Baseline data on output were collected. Then, experimental manipulations—rest pauses, shorter workdays, free lunches, small-group incentive plans—were introduced into the setting for 24 experimental periods. The key, controversial finding here was the Hawthorne effect: workers' production of relays rose independently of changes in work conditions and rewards and also rose once rewards were withdrawn.

Investigators began to consider that the study itself might have contributed to the puzzling results. This was hypothesized to occur because investigators listened sympathetically to workers and accorded them special status and attention as they were being studied. In their efforts to keep subjects co-operative and to keep variables in the setting constant for the experiment, the investigators unwittingly altered the total social situation of the group (Roethlisberger and Dickson, 1939, pp. 182–184, in Schwartzman, 1993, p. 7). This realization changed the character of the inquiry. Researchers moved away from testing for effects of single variables or doing a controlled experiment and began to view the work group as a social system of independent elements that included external events, the meanings individuals assigned to the events, and the attitudes of individuals to events. Psychological factors were thus important variables in the situation and not experimental constants.

Researchers thus sought to explore psychological factors and possibilities for improving supervision. To do so, the study shifted from an experimental method to a large-scale interview study involving 30 interviewers and 20,000 workers, conducted between 1928 and 1931. The interview approach was nondirective and focused on matters of interest and concern to employees. It led to the finding that employees were concerned to remain in a specific work group, even if an alternative job paid more, and it demonstrated how workers could "band together" (Schwartzman, 1993, p. 8) to protect themselves against threats to the work group's welfare.

As a result of the interview phase of the study, investigators decided to examine the development of work groups in greater depth, using observational methods (Schwartzman, 1993).

The study was then modified further into an observational study to explore how the work group influenced worker behavior. This involved direct observation of 14 male operators connecting bands of terminals with colored wires and was conducted in the Bank Wiring Observation Room between November 1931 and May 1932—in the midst of the Great Depression. The group was observed in a separate room, and observations were supplemented with interviews to learn what the workers said they did, and to compare this with what workers actually did at work. The observational approach was based on anthropological fieldwork techniques adapted to modern society. Data collection focused on collection of detailed information on workers and their relationships with one another, the meaning of their work (e.g. what is a day's work?), and activities in the work context. Data were collected by two different investigators. A disinterested spectator undertook observations on the group from within the Bank Wiring Observation Room and kept a record of work performance, significant events, conversations, and interactions. An outsider–interviewer who did not go into the room kept contact with the observer and conducted interviews with workers to gain insights into their attitudes, thoughts, and feelings.

At Western Electric, a complex piece-rate work system was used. This included an hourly wage and a sum, based on an amount that total department production exceeded, guaranteed hourly earnings of its members. Management assumed workers would attempt to improve or at least maintain total output, and so a day's work would be defined by the point where fatigue costs balanced the estimate of added monetary rewards, and the group would thus exert pressure on slower workers. However, observers noted the opposite occurred. A day's work became defined by workers as a specific number of units produced, and this number was lower than management anticipated. Anyone who exceeded this standard normative number of outputs was viewed with disfavour, negatively labelled (e.g. "rate-buster"), and sanctioned to bring them in line. For example, after one worker (W6) had met the informal production rate, another worker (W8) encouraged him to stop working: "W8: If you don't quit work I'll bing you" (Roethlisberger and Dickson, 1934, p. 9, quoted in Schwartzman, 1993, p. 12). W8 then struck W6 and chased him around the room.

The influence of workers' informal organization on productivity was discovered in this phase of the research: The group's beliefs affected their output of terminal units. A key finding of the observational research phase was thus to demonstrate the importance of informal relationships (the informal organization) in controlling worker behavior, and to show that these relationships could foster or impede economic objectives (Schwartzman, 1993).

This study demonstrates a number of features of qualitative inquiry (Schwartzman, 1993; Van Maanen, 1998; Gephart & Richardson, 2008). First, the study used multi-method research, including observations and interviews to capture members' meanings and interpretations. Second, it used analytic induction to create explanations of actual observations.

Third, it remained close to data. Fourth, it focused on common behavior in everyday work settings.

Fifth, key decisions made in the Hawthorne Study show how qualitative research that allows research questions to emerge and study design to evolve over time can uncover unexpected findings that conventional quantitative research might fail to uncover (Schwartzman, 1993; Roethlisberger & Dickson, 1939). When researchers found inconclusive experimental results and a peculiar positive result, a conventional follow-up study could have been developed to improve the experimental design and strengthen control variables. However, repeating the experiments with improved designs would miss the fact that the psychological variables thought to be constant were influencing behavior in the original study, and an improved experimental design would fail to uncover grounds for members' actions. Researchers decided instead to chase the positive effect variables, changed the methodology, and undertook an interview study. Second, when researchers found that good data could come from questioning workers in interviews, they could have taken a conventional approach to develop a questionnaire and to use improved sampling techniques. Instead, they sought to develop clinical and interview skills. Thus, through interviewing, researchers were able to uncover information on psychological variables and to gain insights into the nature of the work group and its influence on workers that it would not have been possible to develop using only conventional, quantitative methods. If the interview results had not led to the decision to engage in observation of work groups, the strong influence of informal norms on group output would not have been uncovered. If different choices had been made, the Hawthorne Study would not have turned out to be the pioneering study it is thought to be (Schwartzman, 1993, p. 16). This discussion of the Hawthorne Study thus provides a strong argument for use of qualitative methods in organizational psychology.

COMPARING QUALITATIVE AND QUANTITATIVE RESEARCH

Qualitative research can be further distinguished from quantitative methods. Qualitative research involves collection of qualitative data—

descriptions of phenomena and observations that are rendered through words, linguistic symbols, and texts (Gephart and Richardson, 2008, p. 31). Qualitative analysis interprets qualitative data using nonquantitative techniques and practices, such as an expansion analysis (Cicourel, 1980)—a line-by-line interpretation of how key concepts operate in a passage of data—or writing a case history that describes key events that emerged over time. In contrast, quantitative data are observations recorded in numeric form, and quantitative analysis involves coding, counting, measuring, and statistically analyzing data. Thus qualitative research implies an emphasis on qualities of entities and on processes and meanings not experimentally examined or measured.

Second, qualitative research generally assumes reality can only be approximated, not fully apprehended, and thus it emphasizes the discovery and verification of theory (Denzin & Lincoln, 2005, p. 11). In contrast, quantitative research often assumes a reality "out there" that can be precisely described and understood (Denzin & Lincoln, 2005, p. 11). Third, both qualitative and quantitative research studies seek to understand social actors' points of view, in group contexts and organizational settings. However, qualitative researchers assume they can get close to the actors' perspective only by using sensitive methods such as interviews and observations that capture human action and meanings. They argue that quantitative techniques such as questionnaires are less able to capture the actor's perspective, because they are distant from actual, situated action and require inferences to be interpretable. In contrast, quantitative researchers seem less concerned with capturing actors' perspectives and may regard interpretive methods as unreliable, impressionistic, and subjective (Denzin & Lincoln, 2005). Fourth, qualitative researchers focus on the specifics of particular cases and contexts and seek to inductively develop emic or insider descriptions and explanations that reflect subjects' worldviews and provide insights into specific contexts. Quantitative research often fails to study phenomena directly, but uses measurement instruments to do so and employs etic or outsider explanations to explain data from local contexts. Quantitative studies also use large sample sizes and seek to develop or deduce general models or explanations that generalize across settings. Fifth, qualitative researchers seek thick descriptions of phenomena, view description as a form of research, and tend to uncover a large range of data from a small number of subjects. Quantitative research is less concerned with rich detail, it separates description from analysis and explanation, and it uncovers a smaller set of data points from a large number of subjects.

The main strength of qualitative research is its ability to study phenomena simply not available or accessible elsewhere (Silverman, 2006, p. 43) and thus to allow the "real world" of work to inform and shape research and theorizing (Locke & Golden-Biddle, 2004). Silverman notes (2006) that qualitative work can use naturally occurring data to find situations or sequences of actual behavior where situated meanings are deployed to establish the character of a setting. It can examine how apparently stable phenomena (e.g. work under time pressure) are actually "put together" by participants. Qualitative research also provides insights into processes such as meaning construction that are not readily captured with quantitative methods.

Rynes, Bretz, and Gerhart (1991) undertook a study of the role of recruitment in job choice that shows how qualitative research can provide real-world data on members' meanings to address and resolve contradictory findings from quantitative research. Research done just prior to their study used cross-sectional ratings obtained immediately after screening interviews and revealed that recruiting activities were not important to applicants' job choices. However, earlier research using different methodologies, including interviews, archival data analysis, and longitudinal designs, suggested recruitment might have a substantial impact on job choices. Researchers could not answer definitively whether or not recruitment influences job choice on the basis of evidence available at the time.

Rynes et al. (1991) argue that open-ended longitudinal research is likely to give a more accurate description of applicants' search and choice processes than ratings, because it traces actions over time, allows observation of the full range of search and choice processes, and allows for observation of variations in individuals' job-search strategies. Thus, the researchers sought solid, descriptive findings created by "letting job seekers tell us, in their own words, how they made various decisions leading up to job choice" (Rynes et al., 1991, p. 399). These data allow a better understanding of the underlying psychology of job choice and its relationship to organizational recruiting practices and provided grounds for generating future research questions based on close knowledge of the subjects.

Rynes et al. (1991) used a structured, open-ended interview method with 41 graduating students, from four colleges, at two points in time: early in the second semester and late in the second semester. The first interview sought to understand how applicants formed initial impressions of "fit" with various organizations by, for example, asking subjects to provide examples of a good fit. The second interview focused more on later phases of the search process and general impressions of recruitment practices. Interviews were recorded, transcripts were prepared, and data were content-coded.

As the key objective was to "gain insight into the cognitive processes associated with job search," the analysis emphasized "content-based interpretation" (Rynes et al., 1991, p. 495). After reviewing descriptive statistics for each question (percentage of subjects whose response reflected a surfaced coding category), transcripts were examined "for insight into the incidents, judgements and processes underlying the quantitative results" (Rynes et al., p. 496). In general, the detailed responses and explanations that students provided to questions do not show that ratings of recruitment are "very unimportant" (Rynes et al., p. 510). The importance of recruitment is illustrated by one student who stated, "people do make choices based on how they're treated" (p. 509). Thus, qualitative research can be used to provide rich descriptions of behavior that are not provided by quantitative techniques. These qualitative descriptions can be used as data to understand real work and job-seeking behavior in organizations, and qualitative data from interviews can show how the meanings of phenomena such as recruitment influence subjects' actions. This study thus shows how qualitative research can be used to assess competing theories, and it demonstrates findings that cannot be produced through quantitative research alone.

LIMITATIONS OF QUALITATIVE INQUIRY

Silverman (2006) notes two common features or limitations of qualitative research that often become problems when qualitative research is compared with quantitative research. First, in terms of reliability, some qualitative researchers assert that reliable measures are only needed by positivists, and, as reality unfolds and changes over time, there is no need to worry about the accuracy of measures or the systematic use of methods. Silverman (2006) notes that this argument implicitly assumes that stable properties of phenomena do not exist. If they do not exist, this rules out "any systematic research," whether it is qualitative or quantitative (Silverman, 2006, p. 47). Thus, Silverman argues, following Kirk and Miller (1986), that, if we concede that stable properties of phenomena exist, "why shouldn't other work replicate these properties?" (Silverman, 2006, p. 47). Second, qualitative research is often accused of anecdotalism or exampling (Glaser & Strauss, 1967), as research reports sometimes use only a few telling examples and ignore less clear, contradictory, or deviant examples and cases. Doubts emerge about an explanation of phenomena when samples are selective and not exhaustively analyzed. This limitation can be overcome by use of systematic, theoretical, or other sampling strategies and comprehensive analysis of datasets or observations (Gephart, 2004). However, it erroneously leads many (quantitative) researchers to downplay the value of all qualitative research (Lee, Mitchell, & Sablynski, 1999).

In addition, it is important to point out that there are strong and weak qualitative studies, just as there are strong and weak quantitative studies, and qualitative research per se is not equivalent to "small n" (or poor quality) quantitative research. For example, Perlow (1997) undertook a well-designed and well-conducted qualitative research project that involved a 9-month participant observation study of work–life conflicts and the high-pressure work environment of 17 engineers in a specific software group. The study sought to understand the time pressures faced by engineers, how engineers viewed these issues, and how the issues and views impacted work–life balance. The study used multiple methods, including interviews, job shadowing, an informant protocol wherein informants recorded their activities on randomly selected days, company records on performance, home visits to engineers' residences that included spousal interviews, and an experiment to understand time pressures on engineers and to assess whether or not existing work practices were necessary (Perlow, 1997, p. 115). By systematically analyzing data from multiple sources and tracking engineers' work and nonwork activities across time and settings, Perlow found that time pressures on engineers emerged from people, including other engineers who interrupted their work. The recurrent but seemingly necessary interruptions led to slower work, a crisis mentality in the organization that required long work hours, and negative consequences for the organization.

In contrast, a small-sample, quantitative study would likely involve structured surveys or interviews with (17) engineers using pre-established questions. A quantitative study could be designed to collect standardized measures of time pressure or work stress using previously developed instruments and could attempt to relate the dependent variables (e.g. pressure or stress) to other contextual or psychological variables, e.g. marital status, family size, job satisfaction, or work motivation. A conventional study would also likely produce a more limited range of data and data sources for analysis. It would also be unable to inductively uncover unanticipated features of the work setting, such as interruptions, to use observations to track how interruptions impacted other work activities in actual work settings over time, or to undertake home visits and interviews to describe and understand the impacts that time pressures at work have on home life. Given the small sample size, statistical testing of hypotheses may lack power, and valid inference may be problematic. Thus, a qualitative study would provide a richer description of the research phenomena and contexts than a conventional study, it would describe the phenomena in real contexts as they "actually" exist, it would permit discovery of insights from data via induction, and it would provide rigor through providing multiple data sources on given phenomena. On the other hand, a qualitative study would not be able to provide quantitative measures of the relationships among variables or to quantitatively assess reliability of measures, and hypothesis testing would be more equivocal owing to the lack of quantitative methods. The outcomes of a qualitative study and a small-n quantitative study would thus differ. It seems unlikely, for example, that a small-n quantitative study of work–life conflict would be able to develop and substantiate a model of the vicious work cycle and its impact on work–life balance, or that such a study would have sufficient evidence to form the practical recommendations that Perlow (1997) offers for addressing these problems.

APPROACHES TO QUALITATIVE RESEARCH

There are a number of distinct perspectives or paradigms of qualitative research. Each paradigm makes its own important assumptions about the nature of reality, and each perspective has distinct goals, methodological orientations and practices, and research outcomes (Gephart & Richardson, 2008; see also Denzin & Lincoln, 1994b; Lee et al., 1999; Gephart, 2004;

Locke & Golden-Biddle, 2004; Denzin & Lincoln, 2005). I address four of these views: positivism and post-positivism, interpretivism, critical research, and postmodernism. Common, distinct, and central features that distinguish different paradigms or views are discussed, but the discussion is not exhaustive. Familiarity with these paradigms and their features is needed if researchers are to select and use methodologies in a manner that is consistent with the paradigms and assumptions that are made. In actual practice, the paradigms often overlap and, at times, become indistinct.

Positivism and Post-Positivism

Qualitative positivism and post-positivism tend to make many of the same assumptions as quantitative positivism and post-positivism, but differ insofar as qualitative positivism and post-positivism use qualitative data and not quantitative measures of phenomena (Gephart & Richardson, 2008, p. 32). Positivism uses a realist ontology and assumes the existence of an objective world that can be described and represented in a direct, mirror-like manner if one uses unbiased methods (Silverman, 2006, p. 122). The key focus is on variables that are assumed to compose (or at least represent) real features of the world. The purpose or aim of positivist science is to discover unknown but actual facts (Silverman, 2006). This is done by developing measures or other representations of key constructs, using these measures or representations to uncover deterministic, causal relations among variables (Gephart & Richardson, 2008), and then testing hypotheses that specify the expected relationships anticipated by theory. Post-positivism differs from positivism primarily by assuming the world is probabilistic and not deterministic, and, hence, one can only falsify, not confirm, hypotheses (Gephart & Richardson, 2008, p. 32). The general research process involves identification, operationalization, and measurement of key variables, followed by determining relationships among variables qua facts. These relationships are then compared with hypotheses for confirmation or testing. A key potential limitation of qualitative positivism and post-positivism is the lack of explicit qualitative methods that can be used to establish relationships among qualitative variables or to test or falsify hypotheses involving qualitative variables (Gephart & Richardson, 2008).

Lee et al. (1999) provide a review of qualitative research in organizational and vocational psychology from a positivist perspective. They argue the key value of qualitative methods is to provide "more tools and methods to facilitate our research agenda" (Lee et al., 1999, p. 163). They state that the key purposes of qualitative research are to generate, elaborate, or test theories from organizational psychology. Theory generation occurs when qualitative research "produces formal and testable research propositions" (Lee et al., 1999, p. 164). Theory elaboration occurs when pre-existing conceptual ideas are used, but formal hypotheses or propositions are not present (Lee et al., 1999), and, hence, theory elaboration involves developing explicit hypotheses from relatively simple conceptual models. Theory testing occurs when explicit hypotheses are specified and evaluated in research.

Lee et al. (1999) point out several reservations about qualitative methods that are common among psychologists who subscribe to modernist assumptions and positivist worldviews. First, qualitative methods are seen by psychologists as having too many unconscious biases operating (Lee et al., 1999, p. 182). Second, method descriptions in qualitative articles are seen to "insufficiently describe how they conduct their applications" (Lee et al., 1999, p. 182). Third, there is the view that qualitative methods produce poor-quality research. They argue that, "these tensions . . . derive from differing philosophies of science" (Lee et al., 1999), and that qualitative research may not typically fit with the worldview of traditional I/O psychology research.

Lee et al. (1999) use a conventional positivist view to offer a solution to these limitations that may help qualitative research move beyond "a second-class status" (Lee et al., 1999, p. 184) in industrial psychology. The solution is to

> adopt the conventional and widely accepted ideal for methodological descriptions. Simply put, an article's description of its method must be sufficiently detailed to allow a reader (or our peer reviewers) to replicate that reported study either in a detailed hypothetical or in an actual manner.
>
> (Lee et al., 1999, p. 184)

Although this argument provides one basis for strengthening the role of qualitative methods in I/O psychology, it may not go far enough to be responsive to the range of assumptions made by different paradigms, and a more complete methods discussion does not guarantee that the findings are replicable, meaningful, valid, or important. Thus, it may be important for authors to demonstrate: the appropriateness of methods used in a given study to the questions addressed; the connections with existing theory demonstrated; the reasonableness of criteria used to select cases or subjects; the systematic nature of data collection and analysis; use of accepted procedures for analysis; how themes, concepts, and categories were developed from data; and evidence for and against the researcher's argument; it may also be important to clearly distinguish between data and interpretation (Silverman, 2006).

Lee, Mitchell, Wise, and Fireman (1996) demonstrate the use of qualitative research to provide data for theory testing and elaboration in a situation where quantitative methods alone were not sufficient for testing or elaborating a theory. This study tested a model of voluntary employee turnover (Lee and Mitchell, 1994) that challenged prevailing models of turnover. Conventional models of turnover focused on how job dissatisfaction leads to leaving. In contrast, the Lee and Mitchell (1994) model of turnover was based in image theory and specifies four multiple decision paths of voluntary turnover that are characterized by shocks and by the amount of psychological analysis that precedes a decision to quit. Lee et al. (1996) used a quantitative survey methodology and qualitative interviews to produce data on voluntary turnover among nurses. Semi-structured interview questions were designed to assess the seven major components of the new turnover model, and pattern matching was used to locate features of the model evident in interview responses. For example, Decision Path 1 involves a shock, a matching script, no job search, no evaluation of alternatives, and no offers in hand. Two remaining variables —image violation and disaffection—were not applicable to this path. An example of turnover reflecting this path involved a nurse who quit because her husband planned to move to seek employment. Whereas most traditional turnover models depict quitting to be "the focal and distinct event" (Lee et al, 1996, p. 18), the six cases the authors uncovered that represent Path 1 depict quitting as of secondary importance—a step to a more salient outcome. Traditional models also depict job satisfaction as important to quitting, but the six cases show job satisfaction to be irrelevant.

The study shows that there are new and different ways to conceptualize the turnover process. It uncovered evidence of processes that cannot be explained by traditional turnover theories, and it calls into question some common assumptions in the management literature concerning turnover. Qualitative research was necessary to provide "reliable and valid indicators" to test and thus show the value of the newer turnover model (Lee et al., 1996, p. 28).

The positivistic use of qualitative analysis in I/O psychology research is also evident in Pratt's (2000) ethnographic study of Amway distributors. In this study, Pratt depicted Amway as an organization attempting to manage the identification of its employees with the company. He examined the process of identification through a combination of qualitative data-gathering methods, including participant observation, open-ended interviews, and archival data gathering. Specifically, he worked alongside informants as a normal employee for almost 2 years, sold products, attended formal and informal meetings, and wrote down his observations in a research journal. In addition, a total of 17 current distributors and 16 non-distributors (people who had resisted Amway's practices) were interviewed to gain insights into how individuals viewed their experiences in the organization. Furthermore, the archival data (company books and booklets, audiocassette tapes, stories in magazines, and website) provided the contextual information on the company and on the technical sources that the company used to motivate distributors. The data were reviewed and analyzed iteratively for dominant themes. The results reveal two types of practice used to manage identification: Sensebreaking practices broke down existent meanings, and sensegiving practices provided new meanings. When either practice fails, members may fail to identify with the company or may experience ambivalent identification with the organization. This study is an illustration of the positivistic paradigm in three aspects. First, the researcher's primary consideration was developing theory that reflected the facts of an objective world. Second, language and accounts in this study were used as a resource to provide facts, rather than to understand the worldviews and lives of informants. Last but not least, although there were no specific hypotheses proposed at the outset of the study, the study uncovers and depicts models of identification management and offers several hypotheses at the end of the article that call for future testing and generalization.

Pratt's (2000) study reveals things that can be uncovered and addressed with a good qualitative study, but that cannot be readily uncovered or examined through a good quantitative study. In his study, Pratt sought to illuminate the practices and processes involved in aligning individual and organizational values. Much research has shown that attempts to transform identity tend to fail, but it is not known why. Qualitative research was thus needed to provide more detail on successful and unsuccessful identity-transformation processes (Pratt, 2000), as deep understanding of the processes or dynamics of identification is needed to build theory in this domain. It is difficult to discover social and cognitive processes with quantitative research, whereas one can often observe such processes using qualitative techniques. For example, there is considerable research on "fit," but little on processes that underlie fit.

Pratt (2000) thus used three qualitative methods to explore identification processes and to uncover details that quantitative research could not uncover: semi-participant observation, open-ended interviews, and archival data analysis. Semi-participant observation involved observing distributors and engaging in distribution. These observations and participation were needed to study complex and morally charged processes, such as identity transformation, where natural participation is the best method to get at the phenomenon (Pratt, 2000, p. 460). Natural participation allowed the researcher to gain the trust of employees and to ask questions that might otherwise seem unusual to a co-worker. Open-ended interviews were used to gain insights into how individuals viewed their organizational experiences, and archival data provided insights into Amway's belief system, as well as information about techniques used to indoctrinate members. Rich data on these phenomena as discussed by members themselves would be difficult to produce or capture using quantitative techniques that seek to measure discrete variables at specific points in time. One needs instead to describe in detail how identification as a process occurs in talk and documents and unfolds in specific settings over time.

The unique qualities of rich data collected using multiple methods thus allowed Pratt (2000) to engage in inductive theory building that would be difficult to undertake from quantitative data. First, qualitative findings allow Pratt (2000) to move beyond merely positing identification practices to understand how practices of identification work in processes that lead to multiple forms of identification. Second, Pratt (2000) was able to link motivation to sensemaking in new ways, and to show how the need to create meaning motivates identification when one is confronted with a disparity in identities. Third, the rich data collected over time allowed Pratt (2000) to be the first to show how organizational practices can lead to a wide range of identifications. Fourth, by following identification processes across social actors and situations, Pratt (2000) was able to demonstrate that the process of identification is dynamic and not stable.

The Interpretive Paradigm

Interpretive research seeks to understand the production of meanings and concepts by social actors in real scenes of action (Gephart, 2004). It takes the view that reality is socially constructed (Berger & Luckmann, 1966) and seeks to understand how people create and maintain a sense of shared meaning or intersubjectivity in interaction (Schutz, 1973). In simple form, the social construction of reality is a dialectical process wherein people are born into an objective world, they learn about this world through intersubjective processes that develop subjective meanings for the world, communicate these meanings to others during interaction (intersubjectivity), and use these meanings to create objective realities such as buildings and books. They then give these realities subjective (cognitive or personal) and intersubjective meaning. Intersubjective meaning can be conceived as the sense of shared meaning that is produced in and through social interaction and that exists only during the perishing occasions of social conduct (Schutz, 1973; Cunliffe, in press).

Interpretivists seek to understand the world of lived experience and thus to grasp actors' definition of the situation from the point of view of social actors participating in this world (Schwandt, 1994, p. 118). Interpretive scholars assume that understanding the world of meaning requires interpreting this world of meaning and elucidating processes of meaning construction to understand how meanings become embedded in language and action (Schwandt, 1994). Interpretive research thus assumes that researchers must engage directly with their subjects of study and participate in their worlds (subjective, intersubjective, objective) to understand these worlds and the meanings used to create and sustain them (Locke & Golden-Biddle, 2004). This is done with sensitive methodologies, including observational research and ethnography, that allow researchers to observe and understand members' perspectives and meanings for phenomena, events that are observed, and the actions that flow from these events and meanings (Locke & Golden-Biddle, 2004).

In interpretive research, a relativist stance toward meaning is adopted (Gephart, 2004). It is assumed that different groups or persons may interpret phenomena differently. Interpretive research explores how meanings are created, negotiated, sustained, and modified in specific contexts (Schwandt, 1994, p. 120), and how different interpretations lead to different actions and outcomes (Gephart, 1978). It inductively constructs second-order concepts of social science from first-order or situated concepts of social actors (Schutz, 1973). Interpretive qualitative work thus focuses on language use in social settings and seeks to provide thick descriptions of talk and nonverbal action in such settings (Gephart, 2004, p. 457). The interpretive focus on understanding members' meanings and interpretive processes, rather than on producing qualitative facts, is consistent with the view that what we take to be objective knowledge and truth is the result of perspective. Knowledge and truth are produced in and through social interaction and not merely discovered by the mind (Schwandt, 1994, p. 125). It is important to note that interpretive research does not refer to all forms of research that interpret data. Rather, interpretive research has emerged from specific scholarly domains that address the nature and construction of meaning (Schutz, 1973; Schwandt, 1994).

Interpretive research in I/O psychology provides opportunities to (1) observe and understand actual meanings in the settings in which they are produced, (2) describe and understand how different meanings influence behavior, and (3) explore how context shapes meanings, interpretations, and behavior (Locke & Golden-Biddle, 2004).

Isabella's (1990) study of how managers' interpretations evolve as organizational change unfolds is a classic and award-winning example of research that uses the interpretive perspective.

The study made a number of critical assumptions that reflect the interpretive paradigm. First, organizational members are assumed to create the reality they inhabit. Second, there are shared frames of reference within a collective. Third, managers' interpretations and views are important to organizational change, although they are often made a posteriori, i.e. after events have transpired (Isabella, 1990, p. 10). Isabella thus used an inductive study to explore how managers interpret events over time, and how these interpretations or viewpoints influence change. A sample of 40 managers at all organizational levels was selected for semi-structured interviews that included open-ended questions. The managers were asked to describe and discuss five specific critical events uncovered in a pilot study conducted in the organization, e.g. the acquisition of the company by an international firm. The analysis used a grounded-theory approach, where data were compared with an emerging theory as data collection proceeded, and interview questions were adjusted to respond to emerging insights. Preliminary categories were uncovered by review of data and were used to organize data. Isabella (1990) provides a description of the initial and final categories she used. About 200 excerpts of data were coded inductively into the inductively developed categories. The data revealed that interpretations of key events reflect the stages of anticipation, confirmation, culmination, and aftermath. Each stage is described in detail, using quotations from data to substantiate key points. Then, processes that move individuals from one interpretive stage to the next were recovered from the data, showing the bases for shifts from each stage to the next. A model of evolving interpretations was then inductively constructed. The model reveals several important aspects of changing interpretations, including the importance of cognition and interpretive triggers that accompany the process of change (Isabella, 1990, p. 33).

Isabella's (1990) study shows a number of things that would be missing from a good quantitative study. First, through a pilot study using open-ended interview questions, the researcher was able to get informants to describe in detail the critical events they had experienced. This information made it possible for the researcher to select the five events all informants mentioned, to help structure data-oriented interviews. Second, data-oriented interviews asked informants to describe in detail how each event unfolded, and these interviews provided rich data that described actors' views. The interviews were flexibly undertaken, using questions that covered the same topics for each informant, but the questions were adapted to individual informants to explore areas of specific interest. This flexible approach to adapting interview questions would be unlikely to be used in quantitative studies, where standardization across participants is thought to be critical. Third, an evolving grounded theory was developed from rich data sources by using constant comparisons and contrasting theory and data. Detailed descriptive data are unlikely to be produced in quantitative research, and it would be difficult to inductively uncover substantive patterns or themes from numeric data. Thus, the systematic production of rich qualitative data over time, concerning interpretations of organizational change, allowed Isabella (1990) to see how managers construe events over time and to produce a stage model of change with four analytically discrete stages. The qualitative data and analysis also allowed Isabella to link viewpoints to shifts in interpretive perspectives, to identify cognitive patterns associated with change processes, and to see resistance as an inherent element of the change process, rather than being an obstacle to change, as it is depicted in conventional change literature.

Critical Theory and Research

The critical-research tradition is grounded in the works of Karl Marx and the Frankfurt School in Germany (Morrow, 1994) and has been elaborated by a number of social researchers and philosophers, including, in particular, Jürgen Habermas (1973, 1979) and Claus Offe (1984, 1985). The term "critical" has a range of meanings that include critique oriented toward unveiling ideological manifestations in social relations; critique as methodology that establishes the underlying presuppositions of theories that address the nature of reality, knowledge, and explanation; and critique as a process of self-reflection wherein the investigator is aware of being subject to, or part of, the critique (Morrow, 1994, p. 7). Critical theory provides (a) an approach to the human sciences, (b) a conception of society, and (c) a vision for creating certain social values. As an approach to the human sciences, critical theory insists on analyzing the objective structures that constrain human imagination (Morrow, 1994, p. 9). It is allied with anti-positivist and interpretive approaches in asserting that social facts are qualitatively different from "facts" of nature, because social facts are human creations. Second, as humans create society, the use of social science is not analogous to control of physical nature (Morrow, 1994, p. 9). Thus, critical theorists make a case that social-science research is different from natural-science research. Critical research explores this distinction through a historical approach.

Critical theory can be used to study phenomena and to learn about them—the focus of this chapter. It can also be used to develop political strategies for action (Kincheloe & McLaren, 2005). Further, although power and control are common topics in critical research, critical scholarship has been used to analyze a wide range of topics, including business ethics (Boje, 2008), pedagogy and a range of cultural issues (Kincheloe & McLaren, 2005), and industrial accidents (Gephart & Pitter, 1993). However, the basic focus of critical theory is the historical emergence of capitalism (Gephart, 2004) and the ways that fundamental contradictions in capitalist society play out in social life. A key goal is to create or enhance democracy in society and organizations.

A basic contradiction that is examined by critical theory is that, in a capitalist society, the owners of production have the right to appropriate surplus value from labor and to retain it (Gephart & Richardson, 2008, p. 34). This contradiction produces other contradictions and inequalities in society (Gephart & Pitter, 1993) that often create management and labor relations concerns. These contradictions and capitalist structures emerge historically and may become reified or taken for granted as "immutably concrete and inevitable" natural facts of social life (Gephart & Richardson, 2008, p. 34) that structure social relations in ways that lead certain groups to dominate and oppress other groups. As a result, critical theory is intensely concerned with the ways power operates to dominate and shape consciousness (Kincheloe & McLaren, 2005, p. 309) and to produce alienation that "inhibits the realization of human possibilities" (Morrow, 1994, p. 10). Through critical reflection (Poutanen & Kovalainen, 2010), people can learn to de-reify the taken-for-granted structures and inequalities and thus critique and escape these structures. Recently, critical theory has also addressed the productive aspects of power—the ability to empower, to facilitate democracy (Kincheloe & McLaren, 2005), and to help people become reflectively aware of the social constraints on their lives. Critical theory thus seeks to change the world (Calhoun & Karaganis, 2001).

Critical scholarship is a diverse domain that extends beyond critical theory. It is bounded by Marx on the left and the German social theorist Max Weber (1978) on the right (Morrow, 1994). Critical research uses a dialogic and dialectical methodology involving dialog between the investigator and the subjects of inquiry in an effort to transform ignorance and misapprehensions or false consciousness into more informed or true consciousness (Guba & Lincoln, 1994). However, a variety of methodologies can be used in critical inquiry, and it is arguably the use of critical reflection in conjunction with common qualitative and quantitative methods that produces a critical perspective in research. Indeed, some critical scholars work to build falsifiable theory, some use a more traditional grounded, qualitative approach, and others reject post-positivist and traditional methods altogether (Denzin & Lincoln, 1994b). The validity of critical research is often assessed by scholars in the tradition in terms of the ability of research to produce critical reflexivity that comprehends ideology and transforms repressive structures of domination into democratic structures (Gephart & Richardson, 2008).

Laurie Graham's (1995) covert, ethnographic study of the Japanese model of lean production at work in the Subaru–Isuzu plant in Lafayette, Indiana, provides an example of research from the "left" side of the critical-scholarship domain. She uses a labor-relations perspective and starts by noting a common assumption that the Japanese model "creates a structure that provides for meaningful worker participation in decision making" (Graham, 1995, p. 2). To explore and critique this view, Graham worked as a covert participant observer at Subaru–Isuzu Automotive for about 6 months. She took extensive field notes on workplace events and behavior and developed a detailed case study of her experiences. Her method reflects many aspects of interpretive research, such as seeking workers' views on issues, observing action as it unfolded, and using informal interviews to supplement observations (Graham, 1995, pp. 16–17). Her extensive and detailed data provide thick descriptions of work on the assembly line and the functioning of teams during vehicle assembly. For example, her rich data allow her to describe such common features of Japanese-based work culture as setting and modifying what the company referred to with the unique term "takt time"—the standard time that each worker is allowed to complete a task (Graham, 1995, p. 75).

Graham (1995, p. 98) found that the work team was "the driving structure behind the hegemonic system" that controlled workers. This system used several nested forms and levels of compliance: self-discipline, peer pressure, mutual support, and direct authority. Exploring the theme of domination and alienation, Graham (1995, pp. 136–137) argues that the expressed purpose of the system was to involve workers in managerial decision-making, but this was "not the true purpose of the system." Instead, she notes, "I view its purpose in exactly opposite terms" (Graham, 1995, p. 137). "The intent of this web-like system is to create an inescapable, highly rationalized system of worker compliance" (Graham, 1995, p. 138).

An example from the "right" side of critical scholarship is provided by Barker (1998, originally published in 1993), who used participant observation to explore self-managed work teams at a small manufacturing firm. Barker focuses on concertive control, where workers collaborate to develop their own means of control (Barker, 1998, p. 130). His theoretical context employs concepts of control examined in labor-relations theory and in the social theory of Max Weber. Barker's (1998) focus emerged during the course of fieldwork as he sought to explore how control practices in the research setting differed from the bureaucratic practices in place previously in the setting and prior to the introduction of teams (Barker, 1998, p. 137). He visited the manufacturing facility for one half-day per week for 6 months before beginning extended data collection. Multiple types of data were collected, including in-depth interviews, observations, and documents. The sample of interviews was stratified "as much as possible" (Barker, 1998, p. 137) across teams, employment types (full time, part time), and ethnic and gender lines. A total of 275 research hours were involved in the study, and 37 in-depth interviews were conducted. He found that, although peer pressure was essential to team work, peer pressure and power games were a manifestation of concertive control that rested on the team's values and norms. These team norms became reified and acted as a set of rational rules (Barker, 1998, p. 147). However, the authority to command obedience to rules moved from managers to the team members themselves (Barker, 1998, p. 152), and thus team members became "their own masters *and* their own slaves" (Barker, 1998, p. 152; italics in the original). Barker thus provides a description of work in the new team-based management system that critiques and counters dominant claims that the new system empowers employees and gives them greater control over their work. Referring back to Max Weber's famous idea that bureaucracy can create an iron cage through hierarchical rules, Barker notes an ironic paradox in team-based management: "The iron cage becomes stronger," and "the concertive system creates a new iron cage whose bars are almost invisible to the workers it incarcerates" (Barker, 1998, p. 155). To resist this control, workers "must be willing to risk their human dignity" (Barker, 1998, p. 156). Barker thus exemplifies critical scholarship by using traditional qualitative methods to describe reified structures and taken-for-granted truths about the new team-based structures, to contest these "truths" and show they are false, and to show the hidden managerial and capitalist interests that the contradictions of the workplace serve.

These studies address issues and uncover insights that quantitative research would find it difficult to provide. It is not possible to use quantitative tools such as questionnaire items to describe rich details of factory settings, such as workplace interactions as they unfold, and to do this covertly, as Graham (1995) did. Rich descriptions and in situ observations allow qualitative researchers to record what occurs and to make reasoned interpretations based on complex contextual knowledge and observations of actual experience—those of subjects and of the observer.

Quantitative studies could, however, use questionnaires to explore the nature and correlates of meaningful participation in shop work. For example, one could measure how job satisfaction is related to participation. One could also content-code documents to develop measures of participation to test whether or not a flexible work setting allows participation.

One could also assess which pre-specified forms of participation exist therein. Quantitative studies could also be improved through grounding measurement instruments in the realities of the work setting, e.g. by developing questions about barriers to participation. Clearly, there are real differences in the outcomes of qualitative and quantitative studies of worker participation.

The Postmodern Perspective

Postmodernism is a term with many meanings and a "huge variety of ideas" (Locke & Golden-Biddle, 2004). It is based in philosophy, the humanities, and literature. It can be defined as the era after modernity and as a style of intellectual production (Jameson, 1991). The postmodern perspective on knowledge thus provides a humanistic, rather than a scientific, perspective on organizations and develops research reports that have the character of essays rather than empirical studies. It seeks to re-conceptualize how we experience and explain the world (Rosenau, 1992, p. 4) and to show the "impossibility of establishing" any foundational underpinnings for knowledge (Rosenau, 1992, p. 6). In contrast to modernist research, postmodernism looks to the unique, rather than the general, phenomenon. It examines intertextual relations (how texts become embedded in other texts) rather than causal relations, and explores the unrepeatable rather than the recurrent (Rosenau, 1992, p. 8). From this view, there is no singular reality or truth: There are only multiple realities and multiple truths, none of which is superior to other realities or truths.

Postmodernism offers I/O psychology the opportunity to challenge the content and form of dominant (modernist) models of knowledge, to explore the political and discursive processes that create features of the world that dominate people, and to understand how social categories such as "employee" are produced as totalizing or standardizing tools of control (Locke & Golden-Biddle, 2004). Postmodern scholarship also provides an opportunity to develop "alternative representations" to explore new viewpoints and perspectives (Gephart, Boje, & Thatchenkery, 1996, p. 8). I address important aspects of postmodern scholarship that could help organizational psychologists better understand and critique forms of knowledge in the field, develop new approaches to knowledge formation, and uncover important new questions and topics for study. Given the rapid growth and prevalence of postmodern qualitative research, it is also important for readers to be familiar with the perspective, even if they are not likely to adopt the approach.

Postmodernism assumes that realities are value-laden and that they contain contradictions (Gephart & Richardson, 2008). Postmodern research explores the values and contradictions in organizational life, studies how hidden dichotomies of power operate, and addresses how social categorization is used to control and dominate specific groups and individuals. Reality is seen as a representation created by particular discourses or language systems in specific historical contexts (Locke & Golden-Biddle, 2004). Truth is conceived as an outcome or product of language and power relations in which everyone is embedded. Multiple realities thus exist, and no single reality should be privileged over others (Locke & Golden-Biddle, 2004). Postmodern scholarship challenges the value-free nature of scientific research and asks, "whose interests are being served?"

The focus in postmodern research is often discourse—spoken and written uses of language (Fairclough, 1992) in conversations, stories, and texts that categorize actors (managers, workers) and limit their opportunities for action. Postmodern scholarship explores the political and discursive processes that create features of the world, such as the "employee," and seeks to understand how categories are shaped and used as (often tacit) tools of domination in social life. The goal is to uncover and displace or challenge hidden aspects of communication and discourse (Locke & Golden-Biddle, 2004). Valid or useful postmodern research thus seeks to influence readers' views of the world (Gephart & Richardson, 2008) and to produce "reading effects" that may unsettle a scholarly community such as organizational researchers (Calás & Smircich, 1991). Methodologically, postmodern research tends to focus on texts and to use discourse analysis, narrative analysis, rhetorical analysis, deconstruction, and textual analysis.

Features of postmodern organizational scholarship can be illustrated through an example of deconstruction in organizational research (Martin, 1990). Deconstruction, a perspective on literary criticism developed in the writing of Jacques Derrida (see, e.g., Derrida, 1974; Culler, 1982), uses methods of literary criticism to challenge the consistency and claims of a given text and to uncover underlying literary practices that accomplish meaning in a text (Gephart, 1988, p. 14). For example, Martin (1990) deconstructs a conference speech by a corporation president who claims to be "deeply concerned" about the well-being of employees. Because of an upcoming new product launch, a young woman employee "has arranged to have her Caesarean yesterday in order to prepare for the event" (Martin, 1990, p. 339). Martin deconstructs this story to show how gender conflict is suppressed and thus allowed to continue. In so doing, Martin (1990) examines what is said, what is not said, and how the story could be reconstructed differently to challenge or resist tacitly gendered constructions that de-privilege women at work. The focus of analysis is on "interpretations that lie between the lines" (Martin, 1990, p. 341). Martin dismantles the dichotomy in the story between the public world of work and the private world of the family by exploring silences and disruptions in the story and metaphors that invoke ideological assumptions that de-privilege women. Next, Martin (1990) reconstructs the gender conflicts uncovered by deconstruction by substituting phrases that invert the meaning of the story to reveal how gender inequalities can be discursively alleviated. She concludes by suggesting that some familiar dichotomies and categories in organizational research might need to be abandoned or rethought, and alternatives developed. This research establishes there are important domains of organization, such as gender conflict, that have not been adequately explored or exposed. Through deconstruction, these issues can be uncovered and addressed.

A quantitative study could potentially be designed to content-code the text of the speech that Martin (1990) analyzed or a larger sample of corporate presidents' speeches. Some properties of the text, such as the use of gender-related terms or the presence of textual contradictions, could be counted and, hence, measured, but it would be difficult for quantitative research to provide a line-by-line interpretation of gendered statements in an unfolding speech, to uncover hidden dichotomies, or to propose reconstructed speech acts that avoid producing gender conflict. Thus, many insights into gender conflict in organizations uncovered by Martin (1990) would likely be missed in a good quantitative study.

Comparing Perspectives

Each perspective or paradigm has specific assumptions about the nature of reality. Each has different goals, distinct methodological foci, and different methods and approaches, and each perspective assesses knowledge in different ways. These features are summarized in Table 9.1. A given

TABLE 9.1

Paradigms of Qualitative Research

Dimension	Positivism and post-positivism	Interpretive research	Critical theory	Postmodernism
Nature of reality	Single, objective reality independent of people	Socially constructed reality integrating subjective, inter-subjective, and objective features	Dialectical reality with contradictions that produces power relations, inequities	Multiple, fragmented realities
Goal	Discover facts and interrelationships among facts	Understand how members' meanings and practices in natural contexts create realities	De-reify taken-for-granted meanings; emancipation; social change	Understand how discourses produce social categories and disrupt categorization
Methods foci	Variables, hypotheses, quantification	Language use, communication, meaning	Contradictions, relations of domination and oppression	Discourse, texts
Methods orientation	Ability to mirror reality with reliable and valid measures	Capture meanings and behaviors with linguistic signs and stories	Reflection, critical reflexivity, dialectical methods	Textual analysis
Assessing knowledge	Hypothesis testing, falsification	Capability of scientific interpretations to recover members' knowledge and reasoning processes in actual settings and provide second-level scientific interpretations	Subject knowledge claims to critique; valid knowledge eliminates false consciousness and changes power relations	Ability of analysis to uncover contradictions, expose hidden interests served, critique and displace dominant knowledge claims

methodology can often be used by different paradigms, but the ways that the methodologies are used are shaped by paradigmatic commitments and assumptions.

METHODS FOR COLLECTING AND ANALYZING DATA

This section describes widely used qualitative-research methods that hold promise for I/O psychology. The methods are addressed individually, but the use of multiple methods is common in qualitative research.

Conventional research, including quantitative studies, tends to be described, composed, and enacted through a series of stages where a literature review is completed, hypotheses are developed, measures are selected, data are collected and analyzed, and results and findings are produced. Research designs are thus created in advance of data collection and, generally, are followed with only limited adjustment. In contrast, qualitative research is often open, flexible, and emergent, and may unfold in a nonlinear way (Van Maanen, 1998), and the key foci, purposes and goals, appropriate data, and other design aspects may be determined only late in the research process. Thus, an initial design may guide qualitative research, but many aspects of the design emerge as the research progresses. This section addresses features of specific qualitative methodological approaches, but does not emphasize formal aspects of qualitative-research design.

Case Study

The case study is a widely used method that is difficult to define in a simple manner (Locke & Golden-Biddle, 2004). The qualitative case study "aims to describe a particular phenomenon and how it changed over time in a specific context, emphasizing processes that underlie the phenomenon and respective changes" (Gephart & Richardson, 2008, p. 36). It has three characteristics: (1) a focus on contextual interrelationships that compose a specific research object or entity, e.g. an organization; (2) an analysis of the relationship between contextual factors and the focal entity; and (3) the use of insights about interactions between the contextual factors and the entity to generate or address existing theory (Mills, Durepos, &

Wiebe, 2010, p. xxvii). The object or entity is thus the "case." Case studies can be either qualitative or quantitative or a mix of these approaches (Yin, 1981). For example, Lips-Wiersma and Hall (2007) conducted an in-depth case study to explore whether individuals take more responsibility for their career during times of organizational change. They used the term "case study" to refer to a sample of 50 employees, drawn from a single organization in New Zealand, who were interviewed. The interviews, quantitative information from surveys, and other sources were used to understand how employees manage their careers during significant organizational change.

Different types of case study are possible, including exploratory, descriptive, and explanatory studies (Yin, 1981, p. 59). Case studies can reflect different traditions, such as sociology or anthropology (Hamel, Dufour, & Fortin, 1993). The typical case study is a lengthy description in narrative form (Yin, 1981, p. 64), possibly reflecting the history of specific events. Case studies are often complex, and Yin (1981) recommends that they be organized or built on a clear conceptual framework, so that they can be comprehended more readily. Case studies can thus contextualize phenomena, provide in-depth descriptions and understanding of phenomena, and provide insight into multiple dimensions of phenomena (Yin, 1981; Gephart & Richardson, 2008). Further, although case studies are often conceived to be limited to a single case or instance, Campbell (1975) argues that case studies allow examination of multiple theoretical implications in a single study. Indeed, a case study can recover multiple examples of a given phenomenon, such as employee reactions to organizational change, and can permit comparative analysis of phenomena that recur over the time period in which the case is examined. A variety of qualitative-research methods including ethnography are frequently composed and described as case studies.

The choice of methodology in case-study research is influenced by the paradigmatic and theoretical perspectives used to analyze the case. A positivist case study takes a realist view and examines the facts of a case to recover true descriptions of real-life practices and actors' views. For example, Lips-Wiersma and Hall (2007) used a positivist qualitative approach to determine whether or not individuals do in fact take greater responsibility for career choices when faced with organizational change. An interpretive case, as illustrated by Isabella's (1990) study of managerial interpretations, seeks to describe different perspectives or interpretations among different groups of actors, how these meanings and interpretations evolve or change over time, and their organizational implications. A critical case study often involves examination of views of different actors and contradictory features of meanings and settings that emerge. The accounts of actors are interpreted to reveal how actors' accounts or actions are selectively composed, how they distort or transform meanings, and the ways they privilege certain interests and viewpoints and de-privilege others. For example, Graham's (1995) study of Subaru–Isuzu examines how workers' views differed from management views of work, how management views dominated worker views, and, thus, how problems of work on the shop floor were disguised, hidden, or suppressed in organizational discourse. These factors limited workers' ability to bring about positive changes on the shop floor. A postmodern case study explores values and contradictions in organizational life and attempts to uncover hidden dichotomies of power that operate to control groups and individuals. For example, Boje, Fitzgibbons, and Steingard (1996) undertake a case study of reactive trends evidenced by publications in *Administrative Science Quarterly (ASQ)*. They use textual excerpts from *ASQ* and other sources to show how editors at *ASQ* "used their powers to establish and enforce a structural/functional/rational or systemic modernist knowledge of administrative science" (Boje et al., 1996, p. 87). These authors encourage researchers to reject the dominance of modernist thinking and to use critical postmodernism to "revitalize the organizational discipline by reconnecting them to their pluralist roots" (Boje et al., 1996, p. 91).

Case studies are useful where researchers seek to gain insights into discrete phenomena that change over time, where detailed descriptions of specific phenomena are sought, where there are multiple data sources available, and where processes are a focus for investigation (Gephart & Richardson, 2008, p. 37). Case-study researchers need to (1) bound the case carefully and conceptualize the object of study, (2) select key phenomena to emphasize, (3) find patterns in data, (4) explore different sources of data and find common grounds for interpretations of the data, (5) examine and eliminate alternative explanations for phenomena, and (6) develop generalizations about the case (Stake, 2005, p. 448).

Interviews

Interviews are very common in management and social research and are used as a method in 90 percent or more of reported social-science studies

(Holstein & Gubrium, 1995). An interview is a kind of speech event (Spradley, 1979, p. 55), where a researcher asks questions of an informant, respondent, or subject, and the subject responds to the questions (Gephart, 2004). Interview questions can be either (1) closed-ended or forced-choice questions that force the informant to select a single response from a list or (2) open-ended questions that allow the informant to decide which details to recount. Qualitative interviews can be standardized such that all respondents are given the same questions in the same order (Fontana & Frey, 2005, pp. 701–702), or they can be nonstandardized, where different questions may be asked of different informants (Spradley, 1979). As with other methodologies, the paradigmatic and theoretical commitments of researchers and the questions posed will influence the form the interview takes and the manner in which interview data are interpreted.

Positivist interviews assume: (1) the aim of research is to discover facts, (2) asking questions is an effective and unbiased means to find information on reality that is "out there," (3) respondents have mental structures that match researchers' reasoning and language, and (4) methodological problems of eliciting accurate descriptions of reality are largely technical in nature (Silverman, 2006, p. 122). A conventional interview study develops a sample of subjects by identifying people who are members of a target population and then interviewing them (Gephart & Richardson, 2008). Data are the responses of respondents. Analysis generally involves systematically grouping responses to identify and display key themes. The facts uncovered in interviews thus compose a description of "what happens" in the domain addressed by interview questions. Positivist research thus often uses interview questions to search for the "facts" about behavior and attitudes (Silverman, 2006, p. 119), and such conventional interviews can provide six types of information: facts, beliefs about facts, feelings and motives, standards of action, present or past behavior, and conscious reasons (Silverman, 2006, p. 120).

For example, Rynes et al. (1991) studied the impact of recruitment activities on a job applicant's job choices through use of standardized, open-ended interviews with 41 graduating university students in the U.S. They administered the same questions to all respondents, but used open-ended questions rather than fixed-category-response choices. The interview questions were "designed to elicit information about the reactions to specific companies and specific decisions" (Rynes et al., 1991, p. 494). They thus sought to elicit facts about recruitment, beliefs, feelings and impressions, and other types of information consistent with the conventional interview (see the interview questions used in Rynes et al., p. 521). They used these data to identify a variety of roles that recruitment practices play in job-seeker decisions.

Interpretive, critical, and postmodern forms of scholarship often take an "active" perspective on interviews: scholars assume the interview involves an active process of meaning construction involving the interviewer and informant, rather than a one-sided process that produces meanings that passively reflect reality and constitute facts (Holstein & Gubrium, 1995). Hence, an interview conceived as an active production of reality is analyzed to uncover the practices through which informants and researchers co-construct reality. The ethnographic interview (Spradley, 1979; McCurdy, Spradley, & Shandy, 2005) illustrates an active strategy of interviewing used in interpretive research. Its main objective is to gain insight into features of a culture and how members experience them (Gephart & Richardson, 2008). The term informant is used to refer to a native speaker who can communicate with a researcher and, through informal and unstructured interviews, can teach the researcher about the informant's culture and to help uncover folk concepts informants use to classify experience (Spradley, 1979).

Spradley (1979) outlines a developmental research sequence for producing ethnography. The ethnographic interview is a key aspect of this sequence. Although the ethnographic interview is often an impromptu and informal discussion with informants, a more structured approach can be used by employing five types of descriptive question in ethnographic interviews (Spradley, 1979, pp. 86–91; McCurdy et al., 2005, pp. 33–66). First, grand-tour questions ask for an overview of a domain of cultural knowledge, e.g. "Can you describe a typical day at work?" Second, mini-tour questions are similar to grand-tour questions but deal with a smaller domain of experience, for example a given work task such as taking a call (Spradley, 1979, p. 88). Third, example questions are even more specific and request examples of specific things, e.g. the last call taken. Fourth, experience questions request descriptions of experiences in a given setting. Fifth, native-language check questions are used to identify the key terms that informants use in the interview and to ensure that these terms are actually the terms commonly used in their culture. These questions are used to produce data and allow a structured approach to uncovering themes to be used (Spradley, 1979; McCurdy et al., 2005).

The ethnographic interview is useful where researchers seek to understand features of organizational cultures and settings, to understand what informants know about phenomena, to understand folk theories, and to gain an emic or insider understanding of phenomena (Gephart & Richardson, 2008).

The life-story interview (Atkinson, 1998), a second type of active interview, explores the subjective essence of a person's life (Atkinson, 1998, p. 3) and seeks to produce a narrative of this life that is as complete and honest as possible. It uses mainly open-ended questions and can explore a range of work- and life-related issues. This approach to interviews is appropriate for gaining in-depth insights into a wide range of personal experiences and to understand the lives of a small number of people of interest to the researcher (Gephart & Richardson, 2008). For example, Savishinsky (2000, p. 26) undertook a planned sequence of three rounds of life-history interviews with 26 retirees from Shelby, New York, to explore how they experienced the first 3 years of retirement. He notes the organizational and work relevance of the research by stating that, "studying peoples' feelings about retirement is also to study their attitudes to work" (Savinshisky, 2000, p. 27). Information was gathered on informants' biographies, employment histories and experiences, feelings about jobs they had held, and the formal and informal rituals and ceremonials of retirement. Savinshisky (2000) came to see retirement as a process and not an event. He explores how people prepare for and master retirement and, in so doing, provides a moving narrative of the people's experiences leaving the work force and adjusting to retirement. Although the interpretation of a life story is a highly subjective action, criteria that can be used to assess the method include internal consistency or lack of contradictions in the interview, corroboration on the life story when read by the informant, and the persuasiveness of the story (Atkinson, 1998).

The long interview (McCracken, 1988), another type of active interview, uses an extended interview and a structured interview format to produce focused and intensive interview processes (McCracken, 1988) to take the researcher into the mental worlds of the informant. In this method, interview responses are analyzed to determine "the categories, relationships and assumptions" informing the respondents' view of the world and the specific topic (McCracken, 1988, p. 42). The long interview is useful where in-depth knowledge of a work setting or organizational phenomenon is needed, but where the researcher lacks time or other resources to conduct deep and intensive research. Second, it is useful when rich and abundant data are sought. Third, the method is appropriate where research seeks to develop important details of a phenomenon from a limited number of informants, rather than a large sample. Finally, the long interview can be used to explore important issues, such as consumer behavior, in detail. The unique features of the long interview include the following: (1) it is more efficient and less intrusive than the ethnographic interview, (2) it does not require extensive cultural immersion by the researcher, and (3) it differs from the life-story interview because it explores cultural categories and meanings, rather than individuals' experiences and emotions.

In general, active interviews reflect the interpretive perspective, although they may be used in critical and postmodern studies or even positivist studies. Reliability can be discerned by assessing if the interview information is consistent for a given informant across time. Validity can be assessed in terms of respondents' ability to convey realities in particular settings, rather than through correspondence between claims and objective evidence (Gephart & Richardson, 2008).

Observational Methods and Ethnography

Observational methods immerse the researcher in actual settings, where direct observations of phenomena are undertaken, and a record of the observations can be created. Participant observation (McCall & Simmons, 1969, p. 1) is a blend of methods that involves some extended social interaction with subjects in a study, direct observation of events that occur in the setting, formal and informal interviews, systematic counting of certain features of settings and behavior, and an open approach to determining the direction of the study. In participant observation, the observer's role can vary from full participation in the setting to simply being an observer (Gephart & Richardson, 2008). The researcher can also play either a covert role, by concealing their research identity from subjects, or an overt role, where their research obligations are disclosed to subjects. Overt research is more readily defended from an ethical viewpoint, although covert research may reduce reactivity of subjects to the observer and allow a more "natural" setting to emerge. There are important issues in preparing for entry into the field, and some knowledge of the setting is important before commencing research. Data collection generally includes some form of field notes—written descriptions of observations. Analysis typically includes searching for patterns or themes in field notes and data and may also involve grounded-theory development (Glaser & Strauss, 1967), which is discussed below.

Participant-observation research has been used in many studies in management and human-resource management (Gephart & Richardson, 2008). Classic examples of participant observation include Barker's (1993, 1998) study of self-managing teams and Melville Dalton's *Men who manage* (1959), a covert study of management that sought "to get as close as possible to the world of managers and to interpret this world and its problems from the inside" (Dalton, 1959, p. 1).

Ethnography is a form of participant observation oriented to cultural questions and is perhaps the best known (and mislabelled) observational method (Lee et al., 1999). It is a distinct form of participant observation, owing to its focus on understanding features of culture. We explore ethnography in some detail in this section to illustrate observational strategies that include field research and participant observation.

Ethnography has several distinct features. First, ethnography attempts to understand phenomena using the point of view of group members (Agar, 1980). The goal is to discover and disclose the socially shared understandings necessary to be a member of a specific group or culture (Van Maanen, 1981). Culture is the collective knowledge that is learned, shared, and used to generate behavior and interpret experience (McCurdy et al., 2005). Second, ethnography searches for patterns or schemata that reflect how organizational members organize and interpret events (Agar, 1980). These patterns or schemata, including language used in specific settings, constitute the local culture's system for perceiving, believing, evaluating, and acting (Van Maanen, 1981). Third, ethnography generally involves prolonged contact with group members. An observer becomes an apprentice to an informant who is a group member, so as to learn the culture (Agar, 1980; Van Maanen, 1981). The key assumption is that close and prolonged contact with people allows ethnographers to gain a better understanding of their beliefs, motivations, and behavior than could be gained using any other available approach (Tedlock, 2000). Fourth, ethnographic work produces ethnography—a written representation involving a thick description of features of culture or of a culture as a coherent whole (Van Maanen, 1981, 1988; Tedlock, 2000). Ethnography is thus a "storytelling institution" (Van Maanen, 2006, p. 1) with a literary aspect or emphasis (Van Maanen, 2006; Zickar & Carter, 2010) that uses field-research designs and techniques to produce "historically, politically and personally situated accounts, descriptions, interpretations and representations of human lives" (Tedlock, 2000, p. 455).

Ethnographic methods have three salient features. First, they emphasize "thick descriptions" (Geertz, 1973) of behavior in actual contexts, developed from ongoing involvement by the researcher in these contexts. Second, ethnographic methods examine ideas and practices of members of society that may be taken for granted and unnoticed by them, but that influence how their lives evolve (Schwartzman, 1993). Third, ethnography examines everyday routines and what people say and do, and, hence, ethnography helps us understand and change organizations (Gephart & Richardson, 2008).

Zickar and Carter (2010) note that use of ethnography was important in the early development of I/O psychology. It helped to ground readers in a sense of the reality of the workplace and the actual meanings of workers and managers (Zickar & Carter, 2010). Ethnography declined in use in the 1960s, but, in recent years, there has been a resurgence of ethnography in organizational research (e.g., Agar, 2010; Cunliffe, 2010; Goodall, 2010; Shotter, 2010; Van Maanen, 2010). This may be owing to the fact that many scholars now recognize that any method—quantitative or qualitative—suffers from researcher bias (Zickar & Carter, 2010), and, hence, ethnography is no longer seen as uniquely biased. In addition, the benefits or value of ethnography are now more widely appreciated. Ethnography is consistent with newer interpretive, critical, and postmodern perspectives, it produces insights into contexts and cultures that are hard to obtain with other methods, it grounds researchers in the realities of the workplace, and it thus provides contextual information to support or inform other forms of research, including quantitative scholarship (Zickar & Carter, 2010).

Van Maanen's (1973) study of socialization into a police organization provides a classic example of organizational and occupational ethnography. Van Maanen spent considerable time gaining access to a police department. Once he had secured the opportunity to study police, he spent 3 months undergoing police training and another 4 months riding in patrol cars. He kept field notes on conversations and conducted formal and informal interviews with people involved in, or impacted by, the police world—recruits, vets, administrators, spouses, and others. His observational data were based on his own experiences and experiences that others reported to him. Through this research, he was able to develop a thick or rich description of police activities and worldviews and to understand how they do their work (Van Maanen, 1981). By reviewing his extensive data and uncovering patterns and themes in data, he was able to construct a "paradigm" of the making of police that includes four stages of socialization: pre-entry/choice; admittance/introduction; change/encounter; and continuance/metamorphosis. He describes important features of each stage and illustrates these through important examples recorded in his data. Other, more recent examples of organizational and occupational ethnography include Watson (1994), Graham's study of the Japanese production model (1995), Barker's study of self-managed teams (1988), and Perlow's study of work–life balance (1997).

Document Analysis

Documents are written texts prepared for personal rather than official purposes (Hodder, 2000, p. 703). Documents are distinguished from records, which are prepared to attest to some formal transaction (Hodder, 2000, p. 703). Texts involve documents that consist of words and images that are recorded without the intervention of a researcher (Silverman, 2006, p. 153). Texts and documents in general are composed largely from linguistic data. Documents and texts endure physically, they can be separated across space and time from the author or producer and user, and they produce "mute" evidence, as they often have to be interpreted without the benefit of commentary by the document producers (Hodder, 2000). Documents and texts are particularly important to organizational research, as documents are commonly produced and used in organizations and may describe, reflect, or influence behavior.

Documents and textual data have several important advantages for research (Silverman, 2006, p. 157). First, they are rich sources of data that reveal subtleties. Second, they evidence relevance and effect, as texts often describe important issues and influence how people see and act in the world. Third, texts are naturally occurring phenomena, and, hence, they reveal what participants do without researcher intervention (Silverman, 2006). Indeed, the information provided by documents may differ from other accounts of phenomena, such as interview responses, and some documentary information is not available in spoken form (Hodder, 2000,

p. 704). Finally, documents offer the advantage of availability and can often be accessed by researchers without the need to confront ethics issues (Silverman, 2006).

Procedures used to interpret documents are similar to procedures used to interpret data in case studies, interviews, and observational studies (Hodder, 1994, p. 400). An important limitation to the interpretation and use of documents is that documents provide "mute" evidence. Thus, documents can be read, but meaning does not reside in the materials themselves. Meaning is produced by reading, discussing, and using the materials (Hodder, 1994). Thus, documents cannot be questioned to gain insights into the conditions of their production, interpretation, and use by those who create or use documents. Interpreting documents poses special challenges, including the need to understand contexts where the documents were meaningful, to understand the interpretations and understandings of document producers and users, and to understand how context influences the interpretation of documents (Hodder, 1994).

Different paradigms lead to different approaches to understanding and interpreting documents. For positivist researchers, documents are often treated as a resource for research and are used as sources of facts in some domain. For example, news media articles could be read to determine what organizational leaders say and do about workplace violence. Positivist uses of documents thus often treat documents and records as objective evidence of reality. They seek to uncover the facts disclosed in the documents, and to compare these documented facts to hypotheses or theories (Gephart & Richardson, 2008). Many case studies rely on documents to create a conventional history of the facts of organizational events. A case study may thus organize the facts associated with the events and show how the facts and events unfolded over time.

A key method used to analyze documents from a positivist perspective is content analysis (Silverman, 2006). Content analysis provides a means to quantify qualitative data and is a quantitative rather than a qualitative research method, although it is often misconstrued in this manner. In content analysis, the researcher establishes a set of categories that reflect topics of interest in the document and then counts the number of instances that fall into a category. This process requires selecting texts for research, developing a sample of texts to analyze in detail, constructing a coding frame or categorization scheme, pilot-testing the coding scheme and defining explicit coding rules, testing the reliability of codes, coding the sample, and then statistically analyzing data. Computer-aided text analysis (Kelle, 1995) allows one to use computers for content analysis of texts (Kabanoff, 1997). For example, Palmer, Kabanoff, and Dunford (1997) explored the themes or rationales that managers use to explain and justify downsizing in Australian organizations. To do so, they undertook a computer-aided content analysis of a convenience sample of 87 large Australian organizations for the time period 1986–1992 and sought to determine whether or not there had been a shift in management language and rationales for downsizing during this time period. A computer-based dictionary was created that contained words and phrases that refer to downsizing. Next, the downsizing dictionary was used to analyze the entire dataset to identify all references to downsizing that appeared in the annual reports, and 275 downsizing references were recovered. A coding scheme was then devised based on reading the downsizing references and was used to code these references in terms of explanations, rationales, and justifications. The coded references were then used to formulate nine main downsizing themes, e.g. cost reduction, globalization. Then, each reference was re-read and coded into one of the nine themes. Coding reliability was assessed. The frequency of occurrences of downsizing themes for each organization was used to construct an index to measure actual downsizing activity by organizations. The authors report that the analysis of downsizing showed three languages or interpretations of downsizing: a strategic language, a process language, and a cost-versus-consideration language.

In contrast to positivist document analysis, interpretive researchers use a constructionist perspective to understand how documents are assembled and thus treat documents as topics for analysis in their own right. Questions that interpretive scholars might ask in regard to analysis of documents are: (1) How are documents produced in organized settings? (2) How are documents used by actors in everyday life? (3) How do documents enter into the manufacture of self and identity (Silverman, 2006, p. 155)? Garfinkel (1967) has shown, for example, that there are "good organizational reasons" that many organizational documents and records are incomplete, as these documents are created and produced for particular audiences and purposes. Thus, data are selectively recorded, and this selectivity cannot be easily remedied, as the local conditions and contingencies of work will influence what is recorded and how it is recorded. The task for interpretive scholars is thus to explore how these contextual processes operate in documents.

Interpretive analysis of documents and texts can involve several strategies and perspectives. One approach is *narrative analysis* (Reissman, 1993; Czarniawska-Joerges, 1998; Boje, 2001), which addresses first-person accounts of events or experiences (Reissman, 1993) and uncovers structural and literary aspects of texts. Narrative analysis explores how stories are assembled and uncovers the cultural and linguistic resources used to construct narratives and stories (Reissman, 1993). Narratives provide insight into past actions of people, and analysis of narratives shows us how people interpret and understand these actions. For example, Barry and Elmes (1997) provide a narrative analysis of the discourse of organizational strategy.

A second approach is *rhetorical analysis* (McCloskey, 1985), which explores the art of speaking or communicating and studies how narratives and speech acts persuade readers and listeners about their authenticity (Gephart, 2007, p. 134). From this view, documents are forms of discourse designed and used to persuade readers of their truthfulness and are not "true" accounts. Rhetorical analysis has examined a variety of ways that texts persuade readers, for example, through use of figures of speech that are compelling (McCloskey, 1985). Brown (2000) provides a rhetorical analysis of the Allitt Inquiry report on attacks on children at a hospital in the United Kingdom. The inquiry sought to explain how a nurse could murder young patients and, yet, do so undetected, as these actions challenged the effectiveness of institutions and professionals who worked at these institutions. Brown uncovered rhetorical practices in the inquiry report that made the failure to detect the murders appear sensible. For example, although the nurse in question had exhibited potential disorders, the report described her behavior as unexceptional, and thus it did not signal a problem. By showing how an alternative, demonizing narrative might have been constructed to describe the nurse, Brown (2000) shows that the constructed explanation that things were normal was contestable, and that there were other reasonable interpretations that could also have been made.

A third approach to text analysis is deconstruction, which uses literary techniques to reveal contradictions in a text and thus offer the possibility of other readings of a text (e.g., Culler, 1982). Examples of deconstruction in organizational research include Martin's (1990) study of gender conflict discussed above, Calás and Smircich's (1991) deconstruction of the gendered nature of management texts, Mumby and Putnam's (1992) (re-)reading of bounded rationality, McCloskey's (1985) deconstruction of economic theorizing, and Gephart's (1986) deconstruction of the rhetoric of quantification in social-science methodological research.

Narrative analysis, rhetoric, and deconstruction are three of the major approaches used for interpretive analysis of texts and documents. Gephart (2007) outlines several other useful approaches, including ethnomethodology, conversation analysis, and the analysis of speech acts from a critical (Habermasian) perspective. These approaches are often used in critical and postmodern research as well. The often-subtle differences in paradigm-based uses of these methods relate to the fact that critical studies may focus on ideological features and power implications of texts and address critical-theory topics, whereas postmodern studies tend to emphasize and uncover the fragmented and discontinuous nature of texts, encourage multi-vocal interpretations of texts, and explore postmodern topics and theories.

Computer-Aided Interpretive Textual Analysis

Qualitative computing is often used to understand the meaning of texts and, hence, can be regarded as an additional approach (or set of approaches) to document analysis. However, qualitative computing can also be used for other types of language-based data. The central task of qualitative computing is to understand the meaning of texts using nonmathematical operations to explore data, uncover themes in data, and display data and findings. It is important to note that computers can support routine data-analysis tasks, such as generating lists of key words, attaching codes to segments of text, and searching for and recovering coded text segments (Wolfe, Gephart, & Johnson, 1993). However, computers cannot perform qualitative analysis, as the process is not mechanical or rule-governed, and they cannot interpret data.

Computer-aided interpretive textual analysis (Gephart, 1997, 2010) helps researchers to develop or recover themes from data, to provide thick descriptions of how concepts operate in data, and to ground theory in data (Gephart, 1997, p. 585). In particular, software can be used to compose textual data displays that recover all theoretically meaningful words, phrases, or terms from data and to organize the data in ways that suit researcher needs. Several software programs have been used in qualitative research. These include ATLIS.ti (Bassett, 2010a), Kwatlitan (Peters, 2010), MAXQDA (Humble, 2010), NVIVO (Bassett, 2010b), Ethnograph (www.qualisresearch.com), and TACT (Bradley, 1990). Some programs (e.g. Ethnograph) are oriented to open coding of data files, so that researchers can readily embed codes in data files as they work with the data. Other programs (e.g. TACT) require data be pre-formatted with codes (e.g. speaker, page number, organization), and databases must be compiled, and, hence, it is difficult to add new codes once the database is compiled. Further, some programs provide statistical tools to quantitatively analyse data, as well as to support qualitative-analysis tasks. Furthermore, the functions and capabilities of given programs are subject to ongoing change. Hence, researchers must carefully consider the functions of specific textual-analysis software packages and even specific versions of these packages to determine how these functions fit with the qualitative-research tasks they seek to undertake (Wolfe et al., 1993, p. 654). It is important to emphasize that there is no magic computer button to push to create results and findings from textual data, and computer software does not automate qualitative research. Analysis requires researchers do interpretive work with texts.

Grounded Theory

Grounded theory (Glaser and Strauss, 1967) is arguably the most widely recognized method for collection and analysis of qualitative data. Grounded theory involves the inductive creation of theory from systematically obtained and analyzed data (Glaser and Strauss, 1967). Grounded theory and related techniques are used in positivist and post-positivist, interpretive, and critical research. Grounded theory has been adopted in many fields of scholarship, including education and nursing, and grounded theorizing can use data generated with a range of methods, including interviews, observations, and documents. There is much confusion regarding the meaning of grounded theory, and many uses of the term in organizational research seem distant from primary accounts of the method (Suddaby, 2006). The summary of grounded theory here seeks to offer readers a view of the approach that resonates with foundational conceptions of grounded theory.

Grounded theory emerged as a critique of a priori or grand theory (Glaser and Strauss, 1967), such as Talcott Parson's (1951) general theory of social systems. Grand theory was often developed in abstract spaces using any ideas, evidence, and concepts a theorist might choose to employ. Grand or a priori theory (theory created prior to close examination and analysis of data) thus lacked empirical grounding and created a differentiation between theorists who create deductive theory and empirical researchers who test or seek to confirm theories. A very large number of potential theories can be generated a priori and can provide almost innumerable deductive testing opportunities for researchers. In contrast to a priori theory, grounded theory begins with observations or data and seeks to induce empirical generalizations and concepts that reflect the contours or features of data. It thus provides low-level theory that is data driven and reflective of specific contexts.

There are several steps in doing grounded theorizing: reviewing data to discover or surface and label categories and/or themes in data; comparing incidents or data segments that are applicable to categories; finding properties of categories by comparing incidents; delimiting theory; and writing the theory (Glaser and Strauss, 1967; Locke, 2002). Two important aspects of grounded theory are theoretical sampling and the constant comparative method (Glaser and Strauss, 1967; Strauss and Corbin, 1990, 1994; Charmaz, 2000; Locke, 2001, 2002).

Theoretical sampling involves collecting, coding, and analyzing data and then deciding what data or examples to find next and where to locate them. The next slices of data or incidents are selected because of their important similarities and differences with key categories being studied. For example, in a study of the development of a graduate-student organization (Gephart, 1975, 1978), the researcher observed a series of confrontations and meetings between the leader and critics, where the critics attempted to limit the powers of the leader and, on occasion, threatened to remove him. Later, during a contentious meeting, the leader was removed by the council to which he reported. This was conceptualized as forced removal of the leader and an aspect of leader succession. Past data were reviewed, and a theoretically driven sample of past, partial removal attempts was then noted. Thus, the researcher collected data, developed an initial premise about features of the data, and then used this premise to search through past data and to focus future data collection on features of forced removal. An unfolding process of succession was uncovered that began with criticisms and incomplete attempts to remove the leader, evolved into the successful removal of the leader, and included post-removal meetings. Thus, once the phenomenon of forced removal was identified, it drove theoretical sampling to review past data and search for new data that provided examples of aspects and properties of leadership removal.

In theoretical sampling, selection of incidents or data ceases when no new data are emerging to develop properties of the concepts of interest—a practice called theoretical saturation.

The second key practice is the use of the constant comparative method of analysis (Glaser & Strauss, 1967). In this practice, the researcher compares a given category and its properties with other categories. This is done continuously over the course of research to elaborate properties of categories and anticipate or locate new properties. As described by Locke (2002, p. 25), constant comparison involves (1) naming and comparing data fragments, (2) comparing data fragments with concepts and then comparing concepts with each other, and (3) comparing conceptualizations with each other and with general theoretical perspectives. This process is intended to produce many categories, properties, and hypotheses from data.

The constant comparative method of grounded theory was fundamental to the Gephart studies because it established the existence of forced removal as a distinct form of succession and showed that it involved status degradation of the leader (Gephart, 1978). This important process and interpretation of the process may have been missed without the use of grounded-theory practices. For example, detailed open coding (a grounded-theory technique) of extensive field notes on interactions at the graduate center produced the domain of status-related interactions with the leader. Second, the domain seemed to contain a number of distinct forms of status-related interactions with the leader, including preliminary challenges to the leader's status, more significant removal attempts that took the form of criticisms and calls for resignation, incomplete removal attempts that included at least one formal meeting where forced removal was considered but a decision was never made, and a meeting where the leader was formally removed. Through theoretical sampling, data were reviewed, and new data were collected to develop insights into the different status challenges to the leader. By using the constant comparative method, and reviewing data in an iterative manner, the features of each form of challenge were compared with one another, and a more refined sense of status challenges was developed. When the concept of status degradation was uncovered from reading the sociological literature, it was apparent that the features of leader removal in the present case reflected features of status degradation. Thus, detailed observations of settings, theoretical sampling, constant comparative analysis, and induction—all features of grounded theory—were used to uncover the finding that forced removal of a leader involves status degradation.

A quantitative study would have found it difficult to observe and uncover processes of forced removal in a real setting, to produce comparative data to uncover unique dimensions of forced removal as a form of succession, or to inductively develop hypotheses for future research from case data, as was done in this study. Thus, this approach is data driven and produces substantive theories that address specific contexts (Locke & Golden-Biddle, 2004). Other examples of grounded theory in organizational research include Gephart and Pitter's study of industrial accidents (1993), Sutton's study of emotion expression norms (1991), Kahn's study of organizational caregiving (1993), and Perlow, Okhuysen, and Repenning's study of decision-making and temporal context (2002).

DISCUSSION

Qualitative research has tremendous potential to contribute to I/O psychology. Qualitative methods can be used to explore naturally occurring settings, collect data that are not readily encountered and/or that are difficult to analyze with other methods, and provide insights into real-life settings and the meanings social actors produce and use in these settings. Qualitative methods can be used to study a very wide range of topics in I/O psychology, and they can be used for theory development, theory elaboration, and theory testing. Qualitative methods can also be used in conjunction with quantitative methods to provide broader information and data on phenomena and to overcome the limits of quantitative data.

The chapter has sought to review qualitative research and methods that can be used in I/O psychology. However, it is also useful to point out how qualitative research could be used in the future in the field. First, many, and perhaps most, "qualitative" studies in the I/O psychology literature used mixed qualitative and quantitative methods (e.g. Rynes et al., 1991; Shaffer & Harrison, 2001; Behfar, Peterson, Mannix, & Trochin, 2008), but few use purely qualitative methods. Qualitative methods can continue to be used, hopefully with greater frequency, to complement quantitative methods and data and to answer questions that require rich descriptive information. It is thus recommended that scholars continue to use qualitative and quantitative methods in tandem with one another, and to do so in ways where each type or form of method is used in a manner consistent with its particular research assumptions.

A second opportunity is to combine use of the new technique of systematic self-observation (SSO) concurrently with use of quantitative measures, to capture the naturally occurring meanings of phenomena that are associated with measures. This will allow organizational psychologists to gain a better understanding of the meanings that measures hold for subjects. SSO (Rodriguez & Ryave, 2002) involves training informants to observe and record a selected feature of their everyday experience, for example, feeling job satisfaction or dissatisfaction. Informants are asked to immediately record their experience in a field report as soon as possible after the phenomenon occurs, and they are trained to give a detailed description of actions and speech, to provide background information, thoughts, feelings, and emotion that are associated with the phenomenon, and to describe the situation and the people involved (Rodriguez & Ryave, 2002, p.2). SSO is particularly promising for psychology, as it "gives access to covert, elusive, and/or personal experiences like cognitive processes, emotions, motives, concealed actions, omitted actions, and socially restricted activities" (Rodriguez & Ryave, 2002, p. 3). It is thus most applicable with single, focused phenomena that are natural to a setting, noticeable, intermittent, bounded, and of short duration (Rodriguez & Ryave, 2002, p. 5). Generally, relatively large samples of SSO reports are used.

To illustrate how this might be used, one could have subjects provide an SSO report and also complete a short questionnaire (one or two items) that measure their job satisfaction. Thus, the actual context, statements made, and feelings that emerge when one is satisfied could be systematically linked to the measured levels of job satisfaction. One would know what subjects refer to when they rate their job satisfaction as 4 out of 5; that is, one would know what job satisfaction means, as well as how it is enumerated and measured. This would allow scholars to undertake the difficult task of associating values in psychological scales with naturally occurring meanings in real contexts.

A third opportunity is to use grounded theory for the discovery and validation of new constructs. Grounded-theory techniques can be used to surface new constructs from data in studies conducted in specific settings where constructs of potential interest were likely to be evident (Gephart,

2003). By undertaking grounded-theory development of a construct in a manner somewhat removed from use of prior concepts from the literature, one could investigate if constructs similar to those in the literature naturally emerge from, or are discovered by, the grounded-theory analysis. That is, one can conduct a grounded-theory study from appropriate settings identified by theoretical or other modes of sampling, and examine whether or not the constructs or categories and properties surfaced in the study correspond with existing constructs. As the patterns observed in data are induced from data by grounded theorizing, they will reflect patterns in the actual settings examined, not hypothesized patterns. This process can potentially surface new constructs that can be compared with existing constructs to confirm or contradict prior constructs and dimensions. The value added by using grounded theory is, thus, to uncover true patterns of action or behavior from settings that would not be recovered by deductive, quantitative research.

CONCLUSION

An important issue often raised in discussing qualitative research is how does one assess or evaluate the quality of qualitative studies, such as those addressed above? A variety of criteria have been formulated for assessing qualitative research, including credibility and authenticity (Silverman, 2006). These criteria include fairness, ontological authenticity, educative authenticity, catalytic authenticity, and tactical authenticity and are used to assess the validity of constructionist, critical, and postmodern work (Guba & Lincoln, 2005, p. 207). The view in this chapter is that there are many criteria that are applicable to qualitative research, and no single way to best assess such research (Van Maanen, 1998). Criteria address outcomes of research rather than providing bases for research, and the accounts of researchers can be tailored to emphasize or suggest such qualities, even where they are not internalized into research practices. Thus, this chapter follows Silverman (2006, p. 276) and recommends use of practical criteria that reflect the content of well-conducted research and that allow for flexibility in research activities. Practical issues to emphasize include the appropriateness of the methods to the questions being asked, showing connections to an existing knowledge, clear explanation of criteria used to select cases, and other practical criteria noted earlier in the paper. Second, data should be given in a local context, such as the statements made by an informant before or after. Third, some attempt should be made to show how data extracts represent the entire corpus of data. These criteria are likely as appropriate for quantitative research as for qualitative research, and they thus show that there is no particular reason to prefer any given form of data.

To conclude, there are many good reasons to use qualitative methods in I/O-psychology research. Whether the focus is using qualitative methods as stand-alone methodologies and/or as new tools to complement quantitative methods, I/O psychology can benefit from doing research using words. The intended contribution of this chapter is to describe how to use these methods and to inspire I/O psychologists to use them.

REFERENCES

Agar, M. (1980). *The professional stranger: An informal introduction to ethnography.* New York: Academic Press.

Agar, M. (2010). On the ethnographic part of the mix: A multi-genre tale of the field. *Organizational Research Methods, 13*(2), 286–303.

Atkinson, R. (1998). *The life story interview.* Thousand Oaks, CA: Sage.

Barker, J. R. (1993). Tightening the iron cage: Concertive control in self-managing teams. *Administrative Science Quarterly, 38,* 408–437.

Barker, J. R. (1998). Tightening the iron cage: Concertive control in self-managing teams. In J. Van Maanen (Ed.), *Qualitative studies of organizations* (pp. 126–158). Thousand Oaks, CA: Sage.

Barry, D., & Elmes, M. (1997). Strategy retold: Toward a narrative view of strategic discourse. *Academy of Management Review, 22*(2), 429–452.

Bassett, B. R. (2010a). Computer-based analysis of qualitative data: ATLASti. In A. J. Mills, G. Durepos, & E. Wiebe (Eds.), *Encyclopedia of case study research* (pp. 182–184). Thousand Oaks, CA: Sage.

Bassett, B. R. (2010b). Computer-based analysis of qualitative data: NVIVO. In A. J. Mills, G. Durepos, & E. Wiebe (Eds.), *Encyclopedia of case study research* (pp. 192–194). Thousand Oaks, CA: Sage.

Behfar, K. J., Peterson, R. S., Mannix, E. A., & Trochin, W. (2008). The critical role of conflict resolution in teams: A close look at the links between conflict type, conflict management strategies, and team outcomes. *Journal of Applied Psychology, 93*(1), 170–188.

Berger, P., & Luckmann, T. L. (1966). *The social construction of reality: A treatise in the sociology of knowledge.* New York: Anchor Books.

Boje, D. M. (2001). *Narrative methods for organizational and communication research.* Thousand Oaks, CA., Sage.

Boje, D. (2008). *Critical theory ethics for business and public administration.* Charlotte, NC: Information Age Publishers.

Boje, D. M., Fitzgibbons, D.E., & Steingard, D. S. (1996). Storytelling at *Administrative Science Quarterly*: Warding off the postmodern barbarians. In D. Boje, R. Gephardt, & T. Joseph (Eds.), *Postmodern management and organization theory* (pp. 60–92). Newbury Park, CA: Sage.

Bradley, J. (1990) *T.A.C.T. 1.2 update.* University of Toronto, Toronto, Canada.

Brown, A. D. (2000). Making sense of inquiry sensemaking. *Journal of Management Studies, 37,* 45–76.

Calás, M., & Smircich, L. (1991). Voicing seduction to silence leadership. *Organization Studies, 4,* 567–602.

Calhoun, C., & Karaganis, J. (2001). Critical theory. In G. Ritzer & B. Smart (Eds.), *Handbook of social theory* (pp. 179–200). London: Sage.

Campbell, D. (1975). Degrees of freedom and the case study. *Comparative Political Studies, 8,* 178–185.

Charmaz, K. (2000). Grounded theory: Objectivist and constructivist methods. In N. K. Denzin & Y. S. Lincoln (Eds.), *Handbook of qualitative research* (2nd ed., pp. 509–535). Thousand Oaks, CA: Sage.

Cicourel, A. (1980). Three models of discourse analysis: the role of social structure. *Discourse Processes,* (3), 101–132.

Culler, J. (1982). *On deconstruction: Theory and criticism after structuralism.* Ithaca, NY: Cornell University Press.

Cunliffe, A. L. (2010). Retelling tales of the field: In search of organizational ethnography 20 years on. *Organizational Research Methods, 13*(2), 224–239.

Cunliffe, A. L. (in press). Crafting qualitative research: Morgan and Smircich 30 years on. *Organizational Research Methods,* published online July 26, 2010.

Czarniawska-Joerges, B. (1998). *Narrative approach in organization studies.* Thousand Oaks, CA: Sage.

Dalton, M. (1959). *Men who manage.* New York: Wiley.

Denzin, N. K., & Lincoln, Y. S. (Eds.) (1994a). Introduction: Entering the field of qualitative research. In N. K. Denzin & Y. S. Lincoln (Eds.), *Handbook of qualitative research* (pp. 1–17). Thousand Oaks, CA: Sage.

Denzin, N. K., & Lincoln, Y. S. (Eds.) (1994b). Major paradigms and perspectives. In N. K. Denzin & Y. S. Lincoln (Eds.), *Handbook of qualitative research* (pp. 99–104). Thousand Oaks, CA: Sage.

Denzin, N. K., & Lincoln, Y. S. (Eds.) (2005). Introduction. In N. K. Denzin, & Y. S. Lincoln (Eds.), *The Sage handbook of qualitative research* (3rd ed., pp. 1–32). Thousand Oaks, CA: Sage.

Derrida, J. (1974). *Of grammatology.* Baltimore, MD: The John's Hopkins University Press.

Fairclough, N. (1992). *Discourse and social change.* Cambridge, UK: Polity Press.

Fontana, A., & Frey, J. H. (2005). The interview: From neutral stance to political involvement. In N. K. Denzin & Y. S. Lincoln (Eds.), *The Sage handbook of qualitative research* (3rd ed., pp. 695–727). Thousand Oaks, CA: Sage.

Garfinkel, H. (1967). *Studies in ethnomethodology.* Englewood Cliffs, NJ: Prentice Hall.

Geertz, C. (1973). *The interpretation of cultures.* London: Fontana Press.

Gephart, R. P. (1975). *The development of a graduate students' centre.* Unpublished master's thesis, University of Calgary, Alberta, Canada.

Gephart, R. P. (1978). Status degradation and organizational succession: An ethnomethodological approach. *Administrative Science Quarterly, 23,* 553–581.

Gephart, R. P. (1986). Deconstructing the defense for quantification in social science: A content analysis of journal articles on the parametric strategy. *Qualitative Sociology, 9,* 126–144.

Gephart, R. P. (1988). *Ethnostatistics: Qualitative foundations for quantitative research.* Thousand Oaks, CA: Sage.

Gephart, R.P. (1997). Hazardous measures: An interpretive textual analysis of quantitative sensemaking during crises. *Journal of Organizational Behavior, 18,* 583–622.

Gephart, R.P. (2003). Grounded theory and the integration of qualitative and quantitative research. In F. Dansereau & F. J. Yammarino (Eds.), *Multi-level issues in organizational behavior and strategy* (pp. 133–125). Oxford, UK: Elsevier Science.

Gephart, R. P. (2004). From the editors: Qualitative research and the Academy of Management Journal. *Academy of Management Journal, 47*(4), 454–462.

Gephart, R. P. (2007). Crisis sensemaking and the public inquiry. In C. Pearson, C. Roux-Dufort, & J. Clair (Eds.), *International handbook of organizational crisis management* (pp. 123–160). Thousand Oaks, CA: Sage.

Gephart, R. P. (2010). Computer-based analysis of qualitative data: CAITA. In A. J. Mills, G. Durepos, & E. Wiebe (Eds.), *Encyclopedia of case study research* (pp. 184–186). Thousand Oaks, CA: Sage.

Gephart, R. P., Boje, D., & Thatchenkery, T. (1996). Postmodern management and the coming crises of organizational analysis. In D. Boje, R. P. Gephart, & T. Thathenkery (Eds.), *Postmodern management and organizational theory* (pp. 1–18). Thousand Oaks, CA: Sage.

Gephart, R. P., & Pitter, R. (1993). The organizational basis of industrial accidents in Canada. *Journal of Management Inquiry, 2*(3), 238–252.

Gephart, R. P., & Richardson, J. (2008). Qualitative research methodologies and international human resource management. In M. Harris (Ed.), *Handbook of research in international human resources* (pp. 29–52). Mahwah, NJ: Lawrence Earlbaum Associates.

Glaser, B., & Strauss, A. (1967). *The discovery of grounded theory.* Chicago, IL: Aldine Press.

Goodall, H. L. (2010). From tales of the field to tales of the future. *Organizational Research Methods, 13*(2), 256–267.

Graham, L. (1995). *On the line at Subaru–Isuzu: The Japanese model and the American worker.* Ithaca, NY: Cornell University Press.

Guba, E. G., & Lincoln, Y. S. (1994). Competing paradigms in qualitative research. In N. K. Denzin & Y. S. Lincoln (Eds.), *Handbook of qualitative research* (pp. 105–117). Thousand Oaks, CA: Sage.

Guba, E. G., & Lincoln, Y. S. (2005). Paradigmatic controversies, contradictions, and emerging confluences. In N. K. Denzin & Y. S. Lincoln (Eds.), *Handbook of qualitative research* (3rd ed., pp. 191–215). Thousand Oaks, CA: Sage.

Habermas, J. (1973). *Legitimation crisis.* Boston, MA: Beacon Press.

Habermas, J. (1979). *Communication and the evolution of society.* Boston, MA: Beacon Press.

Hamel, J., Dufour, S., & Fortin, D. (1993). *Case study methods.* Thousand Oaks, CA: Sage.

Hodder, I. (1994). The interpretation of documents and material culture. In N. K. Denzin & Y. S. Lincoln (Eds.), *Handbook of qualitative research* (pp. 393–402). Thousand Oaks, CA: Sage.

Hodder, I. (2000). The interpretation of documents and material culture. In N. K. Denzin & Y. S. Lincoln (Eds.), *Handbook of qualitative research* (2nd ed., pp. 703–715). Thousand Oaks, CA: Sage.

Holstein, J. A., & Gubrium, J. F. (1995). *The active interview.* Thousand Oaks, CA: Sage.

Humble, A. M. (2010). Computer-based analysis of qualitative data: MAXQDA 2007. In A. J. Mills, G. Durepos, & E. Wiebe (Eds.), *Encyclopedia of case study research* (pp. 190–1192). Thousand Oaks, CA: Sage.

Isabella, L. (1990). Evolving interpretation as a change unfolds: How managers construe key organizational events. *Academy of Management Journal, 33,* 7–41.

Jameson, F. (1991). *Postmodernism or the cultural logic of late capitalism.* Durham, NC: Duke UP.

Kabanoff, B. (1997). Introduction. Computers can read as well as count: Computer-aided text analysis in organizational research. *Journal of Organizational Behavior, 18,* 507–511.

Kahn, W. A. (1993). Caring for the caregivers: Patterns of organizational caregiving. *Administrative Science Quarterly, 38,* 539–563.

Kelle, U. (1995). Introduction: An overview of computer-aided methods in qualitative research. In U. Kelle (Ed.), *Computer-aided qualitative data analysis* (pp. 158–166). Newbury Park, CA: Sage.

Kincheloe, J. L., & McLaren, P. (2005). Rethinking critical theory and qualitative research. In N. K. Denzin & Y. S. Lincoln (Eds.), *The Sage handbook of qualitative research* (3rd ed., pp. 303–342). Thousand Oaks, CA: Sage.

Kirk, J., & Miller, M. (1986). *Reliability and validity in qualitative research.* London: Sage.

Lee, T., & Mitchell, T. (1994). An alternative approach: The unfolding model of employee turnover. *Academy of Management Review, 19,* 51–89.

Lee, T., Mitchell, T., Wise, L., & Fireman, S. (1996). An unfolding model of voluntary turnover. *Academy of Management Journal, 39*(1), 5–36.

Lee, T., Mitchell, T., & Sablynski, C. J. (1999). Qualitative research in organizational and vocational psychology, 1979–1999. *Journal of Vocational Behavior, 55,* 161–87.

Lips-Wiersma, M., & Hall, D. T. (2007). Organizational career development is not dead: A case study on managing the new career during organizational change. *Journal of Organizational Behavior, 28,* 771–792.

Locke, K. (2001). *Grounded theory in management research.* Thousand Oaks, CA: Sage.

Locke, K. (2002). The grounded theory approach to qualitative research. In F. Drasgow & N. Schmitt (Eds.), *Measuring and analyzing behavior in organizations* (pp. 17–43). San Francisco, CA: Jossey-Bass.

Locke, K., & Golden-Biddle, K. (2004). An introduction to qualitative research: Its potential for industrial and organizational psychology. In S. G. Rogelberg (Ed.), *Handbook of research methods in industrial and organizational Psychology* (pp. 99–118). Oxford, UK: Blackwell Publishing.

Martin, J. (1990). Deconstructing organizational taboos: The suppression of gender conflict in organizations. *Organization Science, 11,* 339–359.

McCall, G. J., & Simmons, J. L. (1969). The nature of participant observation. In G. J. McCall & J. L. Simmons (Eds.), *Issues in participant observation: A text and reader* (pp. 1–5). Reading, MA: Addison-Wesley.

McCloskey, D.L. (1985). *The rhetoric of economics.* Madison, WI: University of Wisconsin Press.

McCracken, G. (1988). *The long interview.* Thousand Oaks, CA: Sage.

McCurdy, D. W., Spradley, J. P., & Shandy, D. J. (2005). *The cultural experience: Ethnography in complex society* (2nd ed.). Long Grove, IL: Waveland Press.

Mills, A. J., Durepos, G., & Wiebe, E. (Eds.) (2010). *Encyclopedia of case study research* (Vols. I & II). Thousand Oaks, CA: Sage.

Morrow, R. (1994). *Critical theory and methodology.* Thousand Oaks, CA: Sage.

Mumby, D. K., & Putnam, L. (1992). The politics of emotion: A feminist reading of "Bounded Rationality." *Academy of Management Review, 17,* 465–486.

Offe, C. (1984). *Contradictions of the welfare state.* Cambridge, MA: MIT Press.

Offe, C. (1985). *Disorganized capitalism: Contemporary transformations of work and politics.* Cambridge, UK: Polity Press.

Palmer, I., Kabanoff, B., & Dunford, R. (1997). Managerial accounts of downsizing. *Journal of Organizational Behavior, 18,* 623–640.

Parsons, T. (1951). *The social system.* New York: The Free Press.

Perlow, L. A. (1997). *Finding time: How corporations, individuals, and families can benefit from New York practices.* Ithaca, NY: ILR Press.

Perlow, L. A., Okhuysen, G., & Repenning, N. (2002). The speed trap: Exploring the relationship between decision making and temporal context. *Academy of Management Journal, 5,* 931–955.

Peters, V. (2010). Computer-based analysis of qualitative data: Kwalitan. In A. J. Mills, G. Durepos, & E. Wiebe (Eds.), *Encyclopedia of case study research* (pp. 186–190). Thousand Oaks, CA: Sage.

Poutanen, S., & Kovalainen, A. (2010). Critical theory. In A. J. Mills, G. Durepos, & E. Wiebe (Eds.), *Encyclopedia of case study research* (pp. 260–264). Thousand Oaks, CA: Sage.

Pratt, M. (2000). The good, the bad, and the ambivalent: Managing identification among Amway distributors. *Administrative Science Quarterly, 45,* 456–493.

Reissman, C. K. (1993). *Narrative analysis.* Thousand Oaks, CA: Sage.

Rodriguez, N., & Ryave, A. (2002). *Systematic self-observation.* Thousand Oaks, CA.: Sage

Roethlisberger, F. J., & Dickson, W. J. (1939). *Management of the worker.* Cambridge, MA: Harvard University Press.

Rosenau, P. M. (1992). *Post-modernism and the social sciences: Insights, inroads and intrusions.* Princeton, NJ: Princeton University Press.

Rynes, S. L., Bretz, R. D., & Gerhart, B. (1991). The importance of recruitment in job choice: A different way of looking. *Personnel Psychology, 44,* 487–521.

Savishinsky, J. (2000). *Breaking the watch: The meaning of retirement in America.* Ithaca, NY: Cornell University Press.

Schwandt, T. (1994). Constructivist, interpretivist approaches to human inquiry. In N. K. Lincoln & Y. S. Lincoln (Eds.), *Handbook of qualitative research* (pp. 118–137). Thousand Oaks, CA: Sage.

Schwartzman, H. (1993). *Ethnography in organizations.* Thousand Oaks, CA: Sage.

Schutz, A. (1973). Concept and theory formation in the social sciences. In M. Natanson (Ed.), *Collected papers I: The problem of social reality* (pp. 48–66). The Hague, The Netherlands: Martinus Nijho.

Shaffer, M. A., & Harrison, D. A. (2001). Forgotten partners of international assignments: Development and test of a model of spouse adjustment. *Journal of Applied Psychology, 86*(2), 238–254.

Shotter, J. (2010). Situated dialogic action research: Disclosing "Beginnings" for innovative change in organizations. *Organizational Research Methods, 13*(2), 268–285.

Silverman, D. (2006). *Interpreting qualitative data: Methods for analyzing talk, text and interaction* (3rd ed.). Thousand Oaks, CA, London: Sage.

Spradley, J. P. (1979). *The ethnographic interview.* New York: Holt, Rinehart & Winston.

Stake, R. E. (2005). Qualitative case studies. In N. K. Denzin & Y. S. Lincoln (Eds.), *The Sage handbook of qualitative research* (3rd ed., pp. 443–466). Thousand Oaks, CA: Sage.

Strauss, A., & Corbin, J. (1990). *Basics of qualitative research: Grounded theory procedures and technique.* Newbury Park, CA: Sage.

Strauss, A., & Corbin, J. (1994). Grounded theory methodology: An overview. In N. K. Denzin & Y. S. Lincoln (Eds.), *Handbook of qualitative research* (pp. 273–285). Thousand Oaks, CA: Sage.

Suddaby, R. (2006). From the editors: What grounded theory is not. *Academy of Management Journal, 49*(4), 633–642.

Sutton, R. (1991). Maintaining norms about expressed emotions: The case of bill collectors. *Administrative Science Quarterly,* (36), 245–268.

Tedlock, B. (2000). Ethnography and ethnographic representation. In N. K. Denzin & Y. S. Lincoln (Eds.), *The handbook of qualitative research* (2nd ed., pp. 455–486). Thousand Oaks, CA: Sage.

Van Maanen, J. (1973). Observations on the making of policemen. *Human Organization, 32*(4), 407–418.

Van Maanen, J. (1979). Reclaiming qualitative methods for organizational research: A preface. *Administrative Science Quarterly, 24*(4), 520–526.

Van Maanen, J. (1981). *Fieldwork on the beat: An informal introduction to organizational ethnography.* Paper presented at the Workshop on Innovations in Methodology for Organizational Research, Centre for Creative Leadership, Greensboro, NC.

Van Maanen, J. (1988). *Tales of the field: On writing ethnography.* Chicago, IL: University of Chicago Press.

Van Maanen, J. (1998). Different strokes: Qualitative research in the *Administrative Science Quarterly* from 1956 to 1996. In J. Van Maanen (Ed.), *Qualitative studies of organizations* (pp. ix–xxxii). Thousand Oaks, CA: Sage.

Van Maanen, J. (2006). Ethnography then and now. *Qualitative Research in Organizations and Management: An International Journal, 1*(1), 13–21.

Van Maanen, J. (2010). A song for my supper: More tales of the field. *Organizational Research Methods, 13*(2), 240–255.

Watson, T. (1994). *In search of management: Chaos and control in managerial work.* New York: Routledge.

Weber, M. (1978). *Economy and society: An outline of interpretive sociology.* Edited by G. Roth & C. Wittich. Berkeley, CA: Sage.

Wolfe, R., Gephart, R., & Johnson, T. (1993). Computer-facilitated qualitative data analysis: Potential contributions to management research. *Journal of Management, 19*(3), 637–660.

Yin, R. K. (1981). The case study crisis: Some answers. *Administrative Science Quarterly, 26*, 58–65.

Zickar, M. J., & Carter, N. T. (2010). Reconnecting with the spirit of workplace ethnography: A historical review. *Organizational Research Methods, 13*(2), 304–319.

10

Experience Sampling Methodology

*Nikolaos Dimotakis, Remus Ilies, and
Timothy A. Judge*

INTRODUCTION

In the last few years, traditional between-person studies in organizational research have been increasingly complemented by an emerging stream of research that seeks to examine and explain within-person variations[1] in variables of interest (Ilies, Schwind, & Heller, 2007). This line of research, focusing on experienced states, episodic conceptualizations of work, and dynamic and fluctuating factors, investigates research questions that cannot be adequately addressed with between-individual approaches (Alliger & Williams, 1993; Sheldon, Ryan, & Reis, 1996). Because between-individual designs consider variations across time as transient error, they either ignore temporal variations, or consign these within-individual relationships to measurement error. In order to best understand a phenomenon, however, both between- and within-individual conceptualizations and measurements are needed, because each approach leaves considerable variance "on the table" (unexplained by the design). Moreover, a phenomenon can have different manifestations within people compared with between people; see Figure 10.1 for a rather extreme case of cross-level divergence. Thus, within-person designs can provide unique and invaluable insights that stand to make a valuable contribution to the literature.

Within-individual research, of course, is not a new development; according to Scollon, Kim-Prieto, and Diener (2003), the precursor of

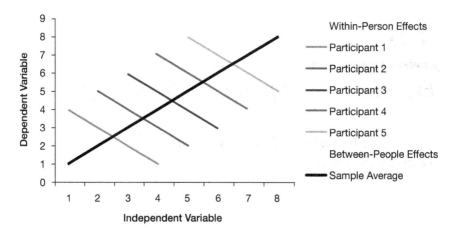

FIGURE 10.1

Graphical representation of effect reversal at the between- versus within-individual level.

today's within-person research streams is Flügel's (1925) study of mood over a 30-day period. However, recent technological and analytical advances have allowed for a wider variety of possible designs and for more easily accessible and statistically robust analysis of within-individual data, thus leading to an increase in interest in such research and a growing body of literature that has begun to highlight dynamic factors and processes.

These advances include the introduction of the experience sampling method (ESM; Larson & Csikszentmihalyi, 1983). ESM aims to examine fluctuations in daily or episodic individual states, and to explain the antecedents and outcomes of these states. In order to accomplish this goal, it involves a frequent sampling of individual experience over a number of days, in order to accumulate a comprehensive and representative understanding of how individuals experience life, of how they react to discrete events, or of transient influences on their feelings, attitudes, or behaviors. This method has allowed for new avenues of research, has facilitated a number of research streams in both basic and applied psychology, and is poised to provide even more significant contributions as the technology and concepts associated with ESM are further developed.

This chapter aims to describe the basic features of ESM, to provide a primer on how ESM can be used in organizational research, and also to introduce the various analytical techniques that are appropriate for analyzing data derived from such designs. We begin by providing an overview of what ESM entails, how EMS studies compare with other research designs, and what typical questions ESM studies seek to answer.

BASIC FEATURES OF ESM

Larson and Csikszentmihalyi (1983) originally defined ESM as a research procedure that requires participants to provide responses to a number of questionnaires delivered to them at random times throughout the day, with such measurement taking place over a number of days—typically a week or longer. The multiple measurements throughout the day involved in ESM designs serve to provide a comprehensive picture of what research participants' daily experience, thoughts, and feelings are like, and the random distribution of surveys seeks to ensure that such sampling is not systematically biased by, for example, consistent sampling of participants at an invariant point of their day that is not representative of the whole day (e.g., lunchtime). Finally, continuing sampling over a number of days aims to provide what Wheeler and Reis (1991) described as a stable and generalizable window on the daily lives of participants.

Depending on the characteristics of the sample, the research context, and the research question, however, some of the features of ESM are more necessary and relevant than others. First, certain research questions might require a nonrandom delivery schedule to be addressed, rather than a random one; for example, an investigation of how positive affect experienced upon waking (i.e., morning positive affect) affects satisfaction with one's behavior at the workplace would require at least one nonrandom survey each day (to assess affect upon waking), and other research questions might require even less randomization. For example, Sonnentag, Binnewies, and Mojza (2008) utilized nonrandom delivery schedules in an investigation of morning mood, and Dimotakis, Scott, and Koopman (2011) utilized nonrandom sampling in order to assess employee job satisfaction at the end of the workday, but used random sampling to assess interpersonal interaction characteristics.

Furthermore, participants in contexts with a high level of task and event variety throughout their typical workday could be sampled with nonrandom surveys, as fixed measurement times in this instance would create fewer concerns about systematically biased measurement compared with contexts in which the workday is less varied. For example, in a professional workplace with a high degree of work variety, nonrandom surveys can provide a reasonably representative sampling of participant experiences across a variety of events and occurrences, whereas, in an organization with highly structured schedules, nonrandom surveys run the risk of sampling individuals at times that are not typical of their daily experience (for example, close to a segment of the workday when workload is always high or low), thus providing an inaccurate picture of employee experience. Similarly, the multiple-daily-measurement requirements might be less applicable to studies that attempt to assess the relationships among different variables throughout the workday. In such studies, certain variables might only be measured once during the day, and such a design could be used to examine the research question in a temporally adequate manner (for example, by testing the relationship between contextual variables measured throughout the workday and attitude variables measured at the end of work or at home; see Ilies, Dimotakis, & De Pater, 2010, and Dimotakis, et al., 2011, for examples of such designs). Finally, although measurements over multiple days are commonly required in order to achieve sufficient statistical power and to ensure a proper sampling of individual experience, measuring participants over consecutive days is not necessarily required and, depending on the specific sample, might actually result in findings that could be less generalizable owing to issues such as seasonality.

Therefore, the exact form that ESM studies ultimately take is influenced by a number of conceptual, empirical, and practical considerations; as with any methodology, researchers need to carefully consider the potential trade-offs to be made when designing an ESM study, in order to ensure that the investigative resources available to them are utilized in an optimal manner, and to guarantee that the research question can be addressed with sufficient methodological rigor.

ESM Designs

In terms of timing of the measurements, three ESM research designs have emerged. These designs differ with regard to the category of research question to which they are best suited and the contexts to which they are most appropriate. These three designs are (a) signal-based, (b) interval-based, and (c) event-contingent. *Signal-based designs* are probably the most frequently utilized format. These studies require participants to respond to questionnaires (or other instruments) delivered to them according to a preselected random or semi-random schedule determined by researchers, thus serving to capture a representative picture of fluctuating variables throughout the participants' day and ultimately enabling the examination of the relationships among these variables. One such example is the study by Ilies, Dimotakis, and Watson (2010), in which participants were randomly signaled to provide measures of affect, blood pressure, and heart rate within their workday. In this context, a signal-based approach enabled these researchers to sample participants' experiences in a comprehensive manner and helped avoid possible systematic biases when examining relationships among these variables.

Other research questions, however, are best addressed by using an *interval-contingent design*, which assesses participants at specific, predetermined points throughout the day. These points might be fixed in time (for example, every 3 hours) or organized around specific daily occurrences (waking up, beginning of the workday, and so on). Such a design is appropriate when recounting the events of the previous period is central to the research question being examined (Alliger & Williams, 1993), and recollection or retrospective bias is not judged to be of concern. Two examples of interval-contingent designs are the study by Daniels, Boocock, Glover, Hartley, and Holland (2009), which requested participants to fill out questionnaires at specific points throughout the day, and the study by Sonnentag and Bayer (2005), which requested participants to fill out questionnaires during specific occurrences in the day (end of the workday and before sleeping). These designs allowed researchers to sample participant information within temporal frames that were optimal for the research questions at hand. This was achieved by initiating measurements at specific points in time, as opposed to an approach that does not take into account between-participant fluctuations in the timeframe of interest (such as the time participants went to sleep).

When the research question concerns the impact of events and experiences that individuals encounter throughout their day, however, such designs are not always optimal. Instead of trying to capture such events using interval- or signal-contingent designs, which could sample individuals at a time that is not close enough to such an occurrence to adequately capture the effects of the occurrence, researchers can utilize an event-contingent ESM design. Event-contingent studies require participants to initiate a measurement themselves, when experiencing the event or episode that is the focus of the study. For example, in an event-contingent study of the effects of workplace incivility, participants could be asked to initiate a survey measurement whenever they encounter such an event during the course of their workday. Depending on the research question and the technological sophistication of the study, the next measurement could then be automatically delayed by some predetermined or random amount of time, to allow for investigations of how the impact of the experienced event might persist over time.

For purposes of clarity, we have thus far described these ESM designs separately. It is also possible to use multiple designs jointly, if the research question requires such an approach. For example, a combined signal- and event-contingent research design could allow for a comprehensive examination of an individuals' typical daily experience, while at the same time ensuring that specific events of interest to the research question are captured with accuracy and timeliness. For example, this approach was followed by Weiss, Nicholas, and Daus (1999), who asked participants to fill out paper questionnaires four times a day, with two of these questionnaires being randomly triggered (within two 1-hour blocks in the morning and afternoon), and two being delivered at set times (when arriving at, and leaving, the workplace). Similarly, Dimotakis et al. (2011) utilized a signal-contingent measurement together with an interval-based signal, in order to examine the relationship between recent workplace interpersonal interactions (assessed with signal-contingent measurement) and job satisfaction at the end of the workday (interval-contingent measurement). This approach thus aims for completeness in assessment, although care must be taken to not oversample individuals during the course of the study (see below for a discussion of such issues).

Comparing ESM Research to Other Methodologies

ESM studies differ in their design, conceptualization, and goals from between-person, cross-sectional, experimental, and even traditional longitudinal designs in a number of ways. Cross-sectional, between-person designs typically seek to examine how a stable individual difference or other stable trait-like characteristic is associated with other stable or trait-like outcomes, whereas ESM studies typically examine how changes in a dynamic, fluctuating state are associated with changes in another state-like outcome. More interestingly, ESM studies have been of use in explaining variation in fluctuating constructs that have previously been mainly examined as stable tendencies. For example, Ilies, Scott, and Judge (2006) used ESM to explain within-person variance in organizational citizenship, prompting Cortina and Landis (2008) to remark that, "these results call into question almost all of the previous research on the topic" (p. 303). Similarly, whereas experimental studies concern the effects of some treatment or manipulation on the outcomes of interest, ESM studies concern the effects of how naturally occurring events and experiences that take place in field settings can influence individuals' feelings, attitudes, and behaviors. Finally, longitudinal designs commonly address growth rates or general trends seen over time, whereas ESM questions are generally concerned more with fluctuations that do not necessarily follow temporal trends[2] (or for which temporal trends are not of central interest).

Thus, each design is optimally positioned to address different types of research question, and this availability of different approaches has the potential to provide the literature with a better-rounded and more comprehensive understanding of the issues being examined. The strength of ESM studies in this context is that they increase our understanding of variability in how people feel, think, and act over the course of their daily lives, and how momentary experiences and events can impact a variety of individual-level outcomes. Next, we discuss some basic considerations when conducting ESM research, including what special issues need to be taken into consideration in terms of research design, and what technological options are available to researchers.

BASIC CONSIDERATIONS WHEN UTILIZING ESM DESIGNS

Design Considerations

As with any research, investigators conducting ESM studies need to carefully consider several issues to guarantee a robust and valid research design. Basic considerations in ensuring the study's internal validity naturally apply, just as with any other research design (see Rosenthal & Rosnow, 1991; Nunnally & Bernstein, 1994; Kerlinger & Lee, 2000), but, in addition, ESM studies require some additional attention to specific issues that are unique to such designs. Below, we discuss these issues and how they can be best addressed.

Perhaps the first consideration is whether an ESM design is best suited for the research question at hand from a cost–benefit perspective. Compared with other research designs, ESM studies generally require a greater investment of time, labor, and monetary resources on the part of the researchers. They also involve much more intensive data collection on the research subjects' part. If the research question could be adequately addressed with a less complex technique, then perhaps ESM might not represent an optimal usage of research resources.

Similar questions have to be addressed when considering the context in which the research will be conducted, as well as the characteristics of the participant sample. For example, ESM studies (especially those with intensive sampling or fully random distribution of surveys) might not be appropriate in organizations in which safety or workload issues would not allow for interruptions or frequent survey delivery (although a modified protocol in which measurement is done by unobtrusive methods could still work in these circumstances). Furthermore, similar issues might apply to specific samples based on occupation or schedule, such as drivers or teachers. To study these occupations, ESM studies might be infeasible or might need to be heavily modified to overcome inherent research-design conflicts.

If ESM is judged to be an appropriate study design option for the research question at hand, a series of decisions then need to be made in outlining the study protocol. The most important of these are the length of the study (how long the data collection will last), the frequency of the sampling (how often research participants will be require to respond to questionnaires), and the question-delivery scheduling (what question sets will be delivered at each sampling period). Below, we briefly discuss these three considerations.

The total length of the study is a common decision to be made when conducting any type of research across time, but is even more important for ESM studies, because of the additional demands placed on participants and the technological limitations that exist in extended data collection. A longer study period can result in greatly enhanced statistical power for the design, which is especially important in day-level designs or analyses that include lagged variables (as lagging scores decrease the number of observations). On the other hand, a lengthy design can result in participant fatigue, especially when each measurement period includes questionnaires of more than minimal length, and can thus jeopardize participant compliance or the quality of the data received. Moreover, the longer the study length, the higher the risk of technological failure due to software crashes, battery depletion, or other similar issues. This is especially true for studies utilizing handheld electronic devices without Internet capabilities (see below for a discussion of technological options). Researchers thus need to balance the potential benefits that a longer data-collection period can provide with the risks associated with the same.

In general, a 2-week period such as the one suggested by Wheeler and Reis (1991) can be seen as a good starting point when designing a study, but, of course, this can vary according to considerations of the research question, the sample, and the technology available. For example, Sonnentag et al. (2008) used a 5-day design in investigating the relationships between recovery activities during leisure time, sleep, and positive affect experienced in the morning, and Ilies, Johnson, Judge, and Keeney (2011) utilized a 10-day design in their investigation of the effects of interpersonal conflict on experienced affect. A more targeted, yet longer, 21-day design was used by Emmons (1986) in an investigation of moods, thoughts, and personal striving.

An issue that is more specific to ESM research compared with other types of design is how frequently to sample the research participants; in other words, how many times a day should questionnaires be delivered to subjects? The two main points in considering this issue are: (1) What are the sample and context constraints? (2) How many daily surveys are required to adequately answer the research questions at hand? In the case of sample and context constraints, there can be objective limits on how many questionnaires can be delivered to participants, as would be the case, for example, if participants had high levels of workload. In addition, as with study-length considerations, sample fatigue and goodwill also need to be taken into consideration when designing a study. Although frequent sampling can provide a high level of power and a very complete picture of research subjects' experience throughout the day, it can also result in frustration on the part of the subjects, ultimately endangering the validity (and perhaps even the successful completion) of the study. Nevertheless, the specifics of the research question being examined need to be carefully considered when making sampling-frequency decisions, in order to ensure that good design principles are followed. For example, when examining a simple mediation design, measuring the independent variable, the mediator, and the dependent variable with separate surveys (for a total of three daily surveys) can help alleviate common methods (source) variance concerns (Podsakoff, MacKenzie, Lee, & Podsakoff, 2003). Similarly, if the research question requires a complete examination of a participant's daily experience, a more frequent sampling schedule containing surveys of shorter length might be more appropriate.

Finally, a related issue concerns the question of delivery schedule. In general, researchers need to ensure that the variables involved in the study are assessed at a time that represents a good fit to the research question being examined. The first issue to be considered is the operationalization of the constructs involved in the study; for example, if the research question involves the outcomes of experienced affect at work, then measuring affect once at the beginning of the workday does not represent a proper operationalization of the affect construct. The same operationalization, however, would be a good fit if the research question involved the outcomes of affect experienced at the beginning of the day at work. That is, the conceptualization of the constructs involved in the study must inform and drive how the variables that model these constructs are delivered to participants. A second issue to be considered is ensuring that the chosen question-delivery schedule guards against threats to the validity of the study. An obvious consideration, for example, is ensuring proper temporal precedence and alleviating common source concerns.

Importantly, these three issues (length, frequency, and scheduling) need to be considered jointly, not in isolation, as they are interrelated. For example, more frequent daily participant sampling might require a shortening of the overall study length to counteract potential subject fatigue, and a delivery schedule that involves longer questionnaires would be in conflict with a more frequent daily sampling of participants (and vice versa). Similarly, frequency decisions directly influence the options available when making scheduling decisions, essentially determining what scheduling options will be available. The key to high-quality ESM research lies in identifying the optimal balance among the aforementioned study characteristics that ensures valid data, in order to effectively test the research question being examined. For example, Foo, Uy, and Baron (2009) utilized a less frequent daily participant-sampling scheme with a longer study duration: although the data collection lasted 28 days, participants were only sampled twice each day. In contrast, Marco and Suls (1993) utilized a shorter study length (8 days) but more frequent daily sampling (8 surveys each day), and a similar approach was followed by van Eck, Nicolson, and Berkhof (1998), who sampled participants very frequently (10 times a day) but for only a short period of time (5 days). A third approach was followed by Kuppens, Oravecz, and Tuerlinckx (2010), who, in assessing participant affect 10 times daily for a period of 2 weeks, utilized a very brief instrument to compensate for the frequent sampling and lengthy data collection involved in their study.

Power Analyses in ESM Designs

In considering the issues described above, an important guiding factor is the statistical power that is needed for testing the hypothesized effects. Although power is naturally an important factor in any type of research (see Cohen, 1992, for an introduction on issues of statistical power), researchers conducting power analyses for ESM designs need to be aware of the multilevel character of their data and the resulting implications for the sample size needed. In general, the multilevel power analyses needed for ESM designs need to take into consideration two different types of sample size: the between-people N (or total number of participants in the study), and the total within-person N (or the total number of within-person observations collected).

Final design decisions can be made based on a variety of factors, such as sample-size availability, study-length constraints, and, of course, the specific research question under examination. In general, a small between-person sample size will result in low statistical power for both between-person (typically of lesser interest in ESM studies) and cross-level analyses (see below for a discussion), whereas a small within-person size resulting from a small study length might result in inadequate power for within-person examinations. A useful tool in such analyses is the *power in two-level designs* program (PINT; Snijders & Bosker, 1993), which can be valuable in estimating statistical power and making trade-offs between the between- and within-sample sizes based on the goals of the specific research project (also see Snijders & Bosker, 1999, for a discussion of power analyses in multilevel contexts).

Technological Considerations

In conducting ESM studies, researchers have a variety of technological options available to them. These options mainly concern what hardware and software (if any) to use in the study. Below, we outline the basic features of several technological options and some of the advantages and disadvantages of each in terms of their cost, reliability, and availability of features.

ESM studies have been conducted using a variety of hardware options. The three basic options include paper formats, portable devices without Internet connection, and Internet-enabled devices. Paper formats involve handing out all the questionnaires involved in the study to subjects in advance (typically in a diary format) and, commonly, some sort of signaling device such as a preprogrammed wristwatch or beeper. Participants are then asked to fill out specific questionnaires by an alarm function in the electronic device, or to fill out questionnaires at specific times if no such device is involved. Studies using paper formats involve the lowest level of fixed costs and, in general, can be economical to conduct. In addition, paper questionnaires have the advantage that they can be used with participants who might not be comfortable with modern technology and have the added benefit of not being subject to electronic glitches, crashes, and battery issues (apart, of course, from the signaling device, if one is used). At the same time, however, they can be impractical when sophisticated variable schedules need to be delivered and can also make it harder to ensure subject compliance with the study design. Although most paper surveys ask subjects to record date and time, subject goodwill is usually the only defense in ensuring that, for example, participants do not fill out a week's worth of questionnaires in one sitting to avoid having to fill them out throughout their workday. Furthermore, complex variable scheduling can become confusing to the participants, unless the directions provided are very clear, and the formatting of the questionnaires is optimized for simplicity and ease of use. Although some researchers can doubtless find creative solutions to alleviate these issues (such as using the signaling device to also record timestamps, if such a feature is available), they are hard to eliminate completely and need to be taken into consideration when deciding to use paper formats for ESM studies. An example of a study utilizing a paper-based format is Marco and Suls' (1993) examination of daily stress and mood trajectories, which requested participants to fill out paper diaries eight times a day, when signaled by a preprogrammed wristwatch provided to them by the researchers.

The second hardware option involves portable devices without an available Internet connection; these include most older personal digital assistant (PDA) devices, as well as any other electronic device used for data collection that does not automatically synchronize with an Internet server (such as blood-pressure monitors; see Ilies, Dimotakis, & De Pater, 2010, for an example). These devices can deliver questionnaires to participants according to a preprogrammed fixed or random schedule, and can hold each participant's data until they are collected at the end of the study, allowing researchers to retrieve the stored data. For example, Bono, Foldes, Vinson, and Muros (2007) utilized portable electronic devices (handheld computers) in an ESM study of the relationship between employee emotional regulation and momentary variations in experienced stress and job attitudes. These devices, although not inexpensive to purchase initially, can enable researchers to deliver highly complex and sophisticated questionnaires to subjects and also allow for compliance checks, as responses are automatically time-stamped. At the same time, however, they are susceptible to programming bugs and hardware crashes, and they depend on participants keeping them in operation by charging them frequently. As such, they can be expected to have a higher rate of failure compared with paper formats, and researchers might not always be able to detect such failures before the completion of the data collection (see Miner, Glomb, & Hulin, 2005, for an example when battery failures resulted in losses in sample size). Therefore, such devices require much testing before the beginning of the study, as well as carefully phrased and delivered instructions to participants about how to maintain the devices, and when and how to inform the researchers about possible technological failures.

Finally, Internet-enabled devices include any method of survey delivery that can communicate with an Internet server automatically, thus enabling researchers to collect and store data in real time. Note that this can include portable (such as smartphones) and non-portable (such as personal computers) devices. In terms of their disadvantages, portable devices are generally quite costly to purchase and to keep online (although, increasingly, as we describe shortly, researchers may have participants complete measures on their own devices, given their increasing availability and use), and personal computers are obviously in a fixed location and can thus be inappropriate in sampling participants who do not spend a large proportion of their day at their desks (although, for employees who have easy access to one, no additional cost is incurred by the researchers). On the other hand, Internet connectivity can provide researchers with a wealth of options in terms of construct measurement and content delivery that are unsurpassed by any other technology. Furthermore, the real-time nature of the data collection allows researchers to quickly discover any faults with the research, enabling them to amend the study design if necessary, before the conclusion of the study. Utilizing this technological option, Song, Foo, and Uy (2008) and Foo et al. (2009) used a Wireless Application Protocol (WAP) technique in order to deliver ESM surveys directly to participants' mobile phones, providing a convenient and immediate way to sample participants. Similarly, in an approach utilizing non-portable, Internet-capable equipment, Judge and Ilies (2004) utilized a web-based survey that was delivered to participants' work computers, using survey programming to ensure that only surveys delivered in a timely manner were accepted.

Finally, there are also a variety of options when deciding what software to use in both Internet-capable and non-Internet-capable devices. In terms of non-Internet-capable devices such as PDAs, the two most popular free programs include the Purdue Momentary Assessment Tool (PMAT; Weiss, Beal, Lucy, & MacDermid, 2004), and the Experience Sampling Program (ESP; Barrett & Barrett, 2001). Both programs are freely available to researchers, and both represent well-established options in conducting this kind of research. Moreover, for Internet-capable devices, there are a variety of free and proprietary survey options that researchers can use in balancing features and technical support versus cost considerations. As with any research, however, care must be taken to avoid compromising basic elements of the research question and study design in exchange for operational convenience and accessibility.

In general, then, there are quite a few options available to researchers who are interested in conducting ESM research; what features one ultimately selects should be a function of the research question being examined, subject to financial, contextual, and sample constraints. Furthermore, increasingly maturing technologies (such as location services) and the decreasing cost of electronic devices that can be used to sample participants will undoubtedly create exciting new opportunities for research, allowing for research designs that were previously impossible or very difficult to implement. However, the basic issues of research design (ESM or otherwise) will still apply, and researchers need to make technology-related decisions with care and attention.

ESM RESEARCH STUDIES

Researchers can design ESM studies that aim to examine a variety of research questions. Although within-person research is the most obvious ESM application, this method can also be successfully utilized to examine between-person and cross-level research questions. We discuss each of these options below, providing some brief examples of each of the three potential ESM applications.

Within-Person Research Questions

Within-person research questions typically concern the effects of dynamic fluctuations in experienced states or of discrete events on state or state-like outcomes (e.g., job satisfaction) at the intraindividual level. That is, within-person designs address the question of how the dependent variable varies *when* the independent variable is higher, *compared with when* the independent variable is lower, and vice versa. In other words, whereas between-person designs seek to explain how individuals behave, feel, or think differently than others, within-person designs seek to explain when individuals behave, feel, or think differently compared with their usual state. An example of such a research question would be whether employees are more helpful when they are in a good mood, compared with when they are not in a good mood; this can be contrasted to a between-person design that seeks to answer the question of whether people who are generally in a good mood help others more, compared with people who are not generally in a good mood.[3] Therefore, within person questions refer to *when*, compared with the between-people consideration of *who*. For example, Ilies and Judge (2002) examined whether individuals reported having higher levels of job satisfaction at times when they reported higher levels of positive affect (or lower levels of negative affect), compared with the times in which they reported having lower levels of positive affect (or higher levels of negative affect).

334 • Nikolaos Dimotakis et al.

The simplest within-person ESM design involves the assessment of two or more variables at various times throughout the day, which are then associated at the momentary measurement level concurrently. For example, apart from the Ilies and Judge (2002) study mentioned above, Ilies, Dimotakis, and Watson (2010), in a 2-week study involving 67 individuals, assessed positive and negative affect and cardiovascular variables at four points throughout the workday, and then used positive and negative affect to predict the cardiovascular responses of individuals at the momentary measurement level, thus investigating the question of how cardiovascular responses fluctuate when individuals experience higher (or lower) levels of positive (or negative) affect, compared with when they do not experience such levels. This study helped demonstrate that cardiovascular responses fluctuated significantly within individuals in response to changes in mood, thus moving beyond simple between-person comparisons of heart-rate and blood-pressure levels.

However, ESM studies can also accommodate variables that are assessed at different times, either owing to the nature of the research question or owing to methodological considerations (for example, to alleviate common source-variance concerns). Such studies can associate variables measured in the first half of the workday to variables measured in the second half, or associate experiences assessed at work with outcomes assessed at the end of work or at home. For example, Sonnentag and Bayer (2005) utilized such a design to examine how work variables (e.g., workload) were associated with psychological detachment; their study collected workplace variables (such as time pressure and work hours), and home-domain variables (such as psychological detachment) with two separate surveys. Similarly, Ilies, Wilson, and Wagner (2009), in an investigation of work–family spillover effects, utilized a design in which affective and satisfaction variables were measured with different surveys throughout the day. Therefore, designs of this type aim to investigate relationships at the level of the day, investigating how the outcome variable fluctuates across days in which an individual experiences higher (or lower) levels of a predictor variable and days in which the individual does not experience such increased (or decreased) levels.

Finally, day-level analyses can also combine elements of the two aforementioned designs, investigating day-level relationships where one or more variables are operationalized as averages of ESM event-level data. For example, Ilies, Dimotakis, and De Pater (2010) utilized this approach

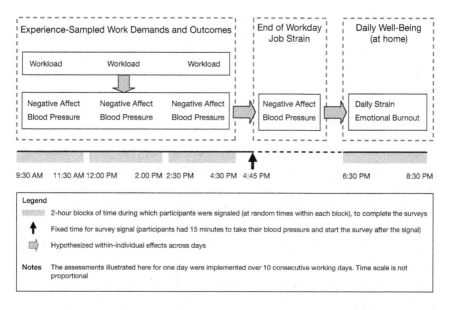

FIGURE 10.2

Graphical representation of the Ilies, Dimotakis, and De Pater (2010) sampling schedule.

in investigating the effects of day-level workload (assessed with randomized surveys at three times throughout the workday and averaged to create a day-level variable) on end-of-work stress outcomes and end-of-day well-being outcomes; both the stress and well-being outcomes were assessed once at the end of the workday and again at the end of the day (with the end-of-day surveys delivered while the study participants were at home). Figure 10.2 provides an illustration of the variable-measurement schedule in this study.

Within-person ESM studies can, of course, address more sophisticated questions involving more than simple univariate or multivariate associations, including moderation and mediation research questions. In these cases, certain within-person designs can be more appropriate than others, depending on the specific research question at hand, and so special attention must be paid during the study-design stage to ensure that the research design selected can be used to test the study hypotheses in a rigorous manner. For example, mediation analyses could utilize a day-level design in which the independent, mediating, and dependent variables are assessed with different surveys to establish within-day temporal precedence and alleviate common method-variance concerns; for example, the Ilies, Dimotakis, and De Pater (2010) article followed this process in separating the measurement of workload, affective stress, and subjective well-being.

Cross-Level Moderator Research

A special case of ESM research design concerns studies in which a between-person variable is proposed to moderate a within-person relationship. For example, the previously mentioned study by Ilies, Dimotakis, and De Pater used such a design to test whether higher levels of job control and perceived organizational support (conceptualized as stable, person-level variables) moderated the within-person relationships of workload, affective stress, and blood pressure at work. That is, this study addressed the question: Do job control and organizational support buffer employees from the day-to-day stressful effects of high workloads on their affect and blood pressure? Similarly, Judge, Scott, and Ilies (2006) followed the same approach in demonstrating that the within-individual relationship between inter-personal justice and state hostility was moderated by participants' trait hostility, such that high-trait-hostility individuals demonstrated a stronger relationship between interpersonal justice and state hostility across days. Finally, Judge, Woolf, and Hurst (2009) used a cross-level approach when examining the within-individual relationship between emotional labor and stress and the moderating role of employees' extraversion.

Such studies generally follow ESM protocols to model the within-person relationships involved in the study (see the section above), and assess the between-person moderator with a separate one-time survey delivered at the beginning or end of the study. It is recommended that special care be taken in assessing the between-person moderator variables, as they are typically only measured once, and inappropriate measurement techniques or time frames chosen for assessment can have a disproportionate impact on study validity. Moreover, in conducting cross-level studies, researchers need to ensure that conceptualizing the between-person moderator as a stable variable is a conceptualization that is appropriate to the construct being assessed; if it is not, then a within-person moderation approach can be utilized instead (see below for a discussion of within-individual moderation issues).

ESM as a Between-Person Research Technique

Apart from the within-person and cross-level research designs described above, ESM studies can also be utilized to address between-person questions in a rigorous fashion. In general, two main approaches can be used in examining between-person questions with ESM techniques. The first one concerns investigating associations between average values of dependent and independent variables. For example, a study investigating how average levels of workload affect average levels of well-being could be conducted by collecting workload and well-being scores with ESM research for a specific period of time, and then aggregating such measures to the level of the person in order to examine whether people who have, on average, higher levels of workload also report, on average, lower levels of well-being. As with between-person surveys, such variables can be assessed at the same time, or with separate daily surveys, and combined during the aggregation process as needed. Although such research can be more resource and labor intensive compared with typical between-person research, it can in turn provide a more stable and reliable assessment of the study variables.

Furthermore, a category of between-person questions that might actually require ESM studies for its examination involves using the *variance* of the dependent variable as a predictor or outcome of some other study variable, something that traditional between-person designs are unable to do. Within-person variance investigations generally seek to explain whether the change or stability in a variable affects some other variable of interest. For example, such research questions could address whether individuals who experience higher levels of variance in their average level of workload report different levels of average well-being, compared with individuals who have lower levels of workload variance, or whether fluctuating levels of daily stress are more or less harmful to individual well-being, compared with stable levels of stress. In other words, these approaches seek to examine whether individuals who exhibit states that fluctuate to a greater degree than others are different in some other regard, or, alternatively, whether individual levels of fluctuation in a variable can be predicted by some other between-individual factor. For example, Fleeson (2001) used such a design, collecting behavioral data to create an index of behavioral variability in an investigation of the nature of personality. In such studies, instead of aggregating variables to the person level, researchers assign individuals a characteristic variance score, based on their reported levels of the variable of interest, and use it as a predictor or antecedent of the other study variables. This approach is still quite novel, however, and could be of use in a variety of areas, such as behavior, motivation, or well-being.

In conclusion, ESM studies can be applied in examinations of a wide variety of research questions, including within-individual, between-individual, and cross-level designs. The exact research questions will determine the exact research design to be utilized, but researchers have a wide variety of options available to them in making such decisions. Next, we turn to a discussion of appropriate analytical techniques that can be used in ESM research, including multilevel modeling and variable-centering considerations.

ANALYTICAL TECHNIQUES

Except for when ESM data are aggregated at the level of the person, ESM data analyses need to contend with some special considerations owing to the nested structure of the data. Owing to this nesting, ordinary least squares (OLS) statistical techniques are inappropriate, because ESM data violate the independence-of-errors assumption of OLS regression. To analyze ESM data, then, as with any other nested data structure, some form of multilevel modeling needs to be utilized. These multilevel modeling techniques consider variance at multiple levels of analysis, adequately address (non)independence issues, and provide a straightforward conceptualization of multilevel data.

Multilevel Modeling

In selecting a statistical software suite to perform these analyses, researchers have a wide variety of available options. Although the most commonly used program is hierarchical linear modeling (HLM) (Raudenbush & Bryk, 2002), other popular statistical-analysis programs, such as SPSS (with the mixed-model option), SAS (with the PROC MIXED analytical approach), Stata (multilevel mixed-model routines), and M-Plus (Muthén & Muthén, 2010), can also offer high-quality, multilevel-modeling solutions. Regardless of the specific choice of analytical software, however, the basic principles of multilevel modeling remain the same.

In general, multilevel modeling requires the simultaneous estimation of regression models at two distinct levels of analysis. At the first level of analysis (e.g., within-individual), the scores for the outcomes of interest are regressed on the within-person scores for the hypothesized predictors. Outcomes and predictors, in this instance, commonly represent day-level or observation-level scores, although any data nested within the individual can be used. In HLM notation, first-level models with no between-person predictors are of the basic form:

Level 1: $\quad Y_{ij} = \beta_{0j} + \beta_{1j}(X) + r_{ij}$

Level 2: $\quad \beta_{0j} = \gamma_{00} + U_{0j}$

$\qquad\qquad \beta_{1j} = \gamma_{10} + U_{1j}$

where γ_{00} represents the mean (pooled) intercept, and γ_{10} represents the mean (pooled) slope. In these equations, the Level-1 residual variance is given by $\text{Var}(r_{ij})$, the variance in the individuals' intercepts is given by $\text{Var}(U_{0j})$, and the variance in their slopes is given by $\text{Var}(U_{1j})$. These models thus estimate the within-person effects of the predictor variable X on the dependent variable Y, while allowing for variance in the Level-1 intercepts and slopes.

When the main effects of a Level-2 (e.g. person-level) variable on the dependent variable need to be accounted for, in addition to the effects of a Level-1 variable, the Level-2 variable is entered in the Level-2 equation predicting the Level-1 intercept β_{0j}. Thus, the HLM equations become:

Level 1: $\quad Y_{ij} = \beta_{0j} + \beta_{1j}(X_{\text{LEVEL-1}}) + r_{ij}$

Level 2: $\quad \beta_{0j} = \gamma_{00} + \gamma_{01}(X_{\text{LEVEL-2}}) + U_{0j}$

$\qquad\qquad \beta_{1j} = \gamma_{10} + U_{1j}$

where γ_{01} represents the effect of the Level-2 predictor on the intercept of the Level-1 variable. Therefore, this approach can provide for dynamic, as well as stable, influences on the dependent variable of interest. An example of this would be the simultaneous estimation of the effects of state positive affect (Level-1 variable) and positive affectivity (a stable Level-2 individual difference) on helping behaviors exhibited in the workplace; such a model examines whether people perform more helping behaviors when they are in a good mood (compared with when they are not), as well as whether people who are generally in a good mood perform more helping behaviors in general (compared with people who are not in a good mood).

Finally, multilevel modeling can be utilized to examine the cross-level moderating effects of a stable person-level variable on the within-individual effects of a dynamic Level-1 variable on the outcomes of interest (see also Hofmann, Griffin, & Gavin, 2000, for a discussion of cross-level modeling issues). The HLM equations for these analyses are represented by:

Level 1: $\quad Y_{ij} = \beta_{0j} + \beta_{1j}(X_{\text{LEVEL-1}}) + r_{ij}$

Level 2: $\quad \beta_{0j} = \gamma_{00} + \gamma_{01}(X_{\text{LEVEL-2}}) + U_{0j}$

$\qquad\qquad \beta_{1j} = \gamma_{10} + \gamma_{11}(X_{\text{LEVEL-2}}) + U_{1j}$

In this model, γ_{11} represents the effects of the Level-2 predictor on the slope of the Level-1 variable. In other words, this model estimates whether the included Level-2 variable affects the magnitude of the relationship between the Level-1 dependent and independent variables, thus providing a formal test of cross-level moderation. Thus, in addition to calculating the magnitude of the within-person relationship being examined (described by the γ_{10} coefficient), this model tests how these slopes might differ across participants based on some between-person variable (whose influence on the Level-1 slope is described by γ_{11}). For example, such an approach could be used to evaluate whether the relationship between state positive affect and helping behaviors is stronger for individuals lower in agreeableness, compared with individuals higher in agreeableness (thus examining whether the behaviors of low-agreeableness individuals are more sensitive to the effects of affective processes). Note that the inclusion of the Level-2 variable in the estimation of the Level-1 intercept (the γ_{01} coefficient in the equations described above) is important in these calculations, as it accounts for the main effects of the Level-2 variable. Omitting this step would be equivalent to including a product term in an OLS regression without the main effect, thus resulting in erroneous estimates.

To illustrate an example of the aforementioned HLM analyses, we present some results from the Ilies, Dimotakis, and De Pater (2010) article, concerning the within-individual effects of workload on systolic blood pressure at work, and the moderating role of perceived organizational support (a between-person variable) on this within-individual relationship (see Table 10.1). The strength of the Level-1 relationship is given by β_{10}, which indicates that, on days in which individuals reported having higher levels of workload, they also demonstrated higher levels of systolic blood pressure ($\beta_{10} = 2.48$, p < .05). In terms of main between-people effects, perceived organizational support was not found to be significantly associated with systolic-blood-pressure scores, indicating that people who perceived themselves as having higher levels of organizational support did not demonstrate blood-pressure levels different than those of people who perceived themselves as having lower levels of organizational support. Finally, perceived organizational support was found to be a significant predictor of the Level-1 workload slope (unstandardized $\gamma_{11} = -4.00$, $p < .01$), thus indicating that the magnitude of the relationship between workload and blood pressure was moderated by perceived-organizational-support levels. Specifically, the unstandardized Level-1 slope for individuals one standard deviation above the study average in perceived organizational support was found to be .32, compared with a 4.65 Level-1 slope for individuals one standard deviation below the study average. In other words, perceived organizational support was found to provide a protective effect for individuals potentially exposed to high levels of workload, in that individuals with high levels of perceived organizational support demonstrated a negligible increase in blood pressure at times when they were operating under conditions of high workload, compared with when they operated under conditions of low workload, whereas individuals with low

TABLE 10.1

Results From Ilies, Dimotakis, and De Pater (2010)

Model/criterion	Blood pressure	T-value
Intercept (γ_{00})	117.16	92.31**
Main effects of perceived organizational support (γ_{01})	.16	1.81*
Main effects of workload (γ_{10})	−1.79	−1.09
Moderating effects of perceived organizational support (γ_{11})	−4.00	−2.85**

Notes: Estimates were obtained using 354 daily data points provided by 64 individuals. Level-1 predictor scores were centered at the individuals' means to eliminate between-individual variance.
* $p < .05$; ** $p < .01$ (directional, one-tailed test).

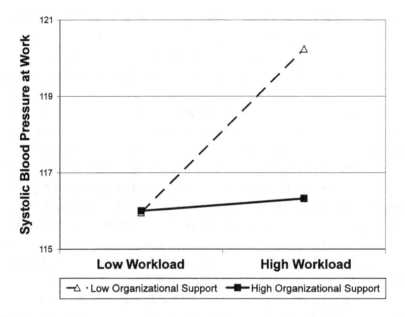

FIGURE 10.3
Graphical representation of the Ilies, Dimotakis, and De Pater (2010) results.

levels of perceived organizational support experienced an increase of approximately 4 blood pressure points at times when they were operating under conditions of high workload, compared with when they operated under conditions of low workload (see Figure 10.3 for a graphical representation of these effects).

Centering in Multilevel Modeling

Multilevel modeling also introduces an additional consideration in terms of how the independent-variable scores are used in the model, in terms of the centering approach used. In general, there are two ways that variable means can be assessed: one is the grand mean, or the average of all observations, and the other is the person (or, in HLM notation, group) mean, an individual-level estimate representing the average of each study participant's scores for that particular Level-1 variable. Therefore, there are two options available to researchers when running multilevel models: grand-mean and person-mean centering.

Grand-mean centering involves subtracting the grand mean from each score and can be useful when running same-level moderation analyses (see

Aiken & West, 1991). On the other hand, person-mean centering involves subtracting the individual participant's mean from each of their observations, which can result in changes in the linear ordering of the variables. Therefore, person-mean centering produces a score that is higher or lower than the one *each* individual reported on average. For example, a positive grand-mean-centered score on a stress scale signifies a time in which an individual is more stressed compared with how *people tend to feel on average*, whereas a positive person-centered score on the same scale signifies that the individual feels more stressed than *she or he* typically feels. Thus, person- and grand-mean centering are neither conceptually nor mathematically equivalent.

Person-mean-centered models are also different in another important fashion, in that they produce estimates that reflect purely within-individual processes, as this type of centering removes all between-person variance from the predictor variables (because the centering results in distributions of scores that all have a mean score of zero for each person). Although this has the benefit of avoiding confounding caused by any possible differences among the individuals in the study (such as personality or rating tendencies), the interpretation of the results is also different than for grand-mean-centered (or uncentered) models, and, as such, person-centering might not be appropriate for all research questions. For example, if the research question is, "how do people behave when they are in a better mood compared with the way they themselves typically feel?", person-mean centering is appropriate. If, however, the research question is, "how do people behave when they are in a better mood compared with the way the average person typically feels?", then grand-mean centering is inappropriate, as between-person variance is included in the research question being examined. Although the distinction is not overt, it affects issues ranging from the interpretation of the research findings to the implications of these findings for research and practice.

Moderation and Mediation Considerations

Finally, there are also some issues relevant to moderation and mediation analyses that need to be considered in multilevel modeling. In terms of moderation analyses, whereas the examples above illustrate cross-level moderation, within-person-research questions can also relate to the moderating role of a Level-1 variable on the effects of another Level-1 variable, and the same can apply to moderation effects within a higher level of analysis. Such analyses can be run as with OLS regression approaches, and either grand- or person-mean centering (or, when appropriate, even a combination of the two) can be used (see Krull & MacKinnon, 2001), as is appropriate for the research question at hand. For example, Dimotakis et al. (2011) used within-level moderation to examine whether the within-individual effects of negative affect on job satisfaction were smaller on days on which participants reported higher levels of positive affect, compared with days on which individuals reported lower levels of positive affect. Similar approaches can be used to model moderation at a higher level (if appropriate), or even to test a three-way interaction concerning the moderating effects of two different between-person variables on a within-individual relationship.

In terms of mediation analyses, the sets of analyses to be conducted to test for mediation in a multilevel setting are not very different from single-level analyses, and such approaches can even be used, with appropriate methodological caution, to test for cross-level mediation as well (that is, to test whether the effects of a between-person variable on a Level-1 outcome are partially or fully mediated through a Level-1 variable). There are, however, some statistical issues that need to be taken into consideration in within-person mediation results, as some traditional single-level mediation analysis tools such as the Sobel test (Sobel, 1982) have been found to demonstrate low levels of power or to provide inaccurate results when used to evaluate outcomes from multilevel models (Krull & MacKinnon, 1999). Although a discussion of all these effects is outside the scope of this chapter, these issues still require some consideration at the data-analysis stage of an ESM project (for treatises on these issues, see Krull & MacKinnon, 1999; MacKinnon, Lockwood, Hoffman, West, & Sheets, 2002; Kenny, Korchmaros, & Bolger, 2003).

CONCLUSION

ESM represents a powerful technique that can be used to examine a variety of within-person research questions, as well as to provide a complementary methodological option to traditional, between-person research techniques. This chapter attempted to describe the basic features of ESM, to examine some issues involved in conducting ESM research, and to provide a primer on the conceptual, technological, and statistical issues that need to be taken into consideration in such research projects.

This method has already been used in facilitating important contributions to a variety of topic areas within the organizational literature, and the role of ESM in conducting research is only expected to increase as improvements in technology and analysis allow for ever more sophisticated studies to be conducted. ESM research has already helped demonstrate that significant within-person fluctuations in a number of factors (such as workload, mood, and citizenship behaviors) exist, and that these fluctuations are not mere transient error but, on the contrary, can represent important independent and dependent variables. With the recent rise of within-person conceptualizations of workplace experiences (see Beal et al., 2005), it seems that the time is ripe for an expansion of such conceptualizations to a number of factors that individuals might encounter throughout their workday, ranging from social and professional interactions with others to positive and negative workplace events, and from individual discretionary behaviors to task performance and workplace attitudes.

Although such increases can provide innovative and novel ways to examine many research questions of interest, care must be taken to ensure that the research questions examined and the study designs utilized do not become the function of the technological options available at the time, but rather that good research-design principles are followed, and imaginative research questions are asked, in order to provide important and impactful contributions to the literature. It is our hope that the information contained in this chapter can provide a useful introduction on how to conduct the latter type of research.

NOTES

1. For our purposes, because within-individual variation only (or mostly) occurs over time, we use the terms within-individual and temporal variation relatively synonymously. So, in experience-sampling designs, observations over time are nested within each individual. Of course, other multilevel designs are not as intimately tied to temporal variation (individuals can be nested within groups at one point in time).

2. Of course, in practice, the differences between ESM and longitudinal designs may be fuzzy (e.g., a researcher studies how monthly performance-feedback meetings affect employees' moods and work attitudes).

3. A third question could ask whether people who are currently in a good mood help others more, compared with people who are not currently in a good mood; questions of that sort, however, involve both between- and within-person sources of variance, thus being less useful for illustration purposes.

REFERENCES

Aiken, L. S., & West, S. G. (1991). *Multiple regression: Testing and interpreting interactions.* Newbury Park, CA, London: Sage.

Alliger, G. M., & Williams, K. J. (1993). Using signal-contingent experience sampling methodology to study work in the field: A discussion and illustration examining task perceptions and mood. *Personnel Psychology, 46,* 525–549.

Barrett, L. F., & Barrett, D. J. (2001). An introduction to computerized experience sampling in psychology. *Social Science Computer Review, 19,* 175–185.

Beal, D. J., Weiss, H. M., Barros, E., & Macdermid, S. M. (2005). An episodic process model of affective influences on performance. *Journal of Applied Psychology, 90,* 1054–1068.

Bono, J. E., Foldes, H. J., Vinson, G., & Muros, J. P. (2007). Workplace emotions: The role of supervision and leadership. *Journal of Applied Psychology, 92,* 1357–1367.

Cohen, J. (1992). A power primer. *Psychological Bulletin, 112,* 155–159.

Cortina, J. M., & Landis, R. S. (2008). When small effect sizes tell a big story, and when large effect sizes don't. In C. E. Lance & R. J. Vandenberg (Eds.), *Statistical and methodological myths and urban legends: Received doctrine, verity, and fable in the organizational and social sciences.* Mahwah, NJ: Lawrence Erlbaum.

Daniels, K., Boocock, G., Glover, J., Hartley, R., & Holland, J. (2009). An experience sampling study of learning, affect, and the demands control support model. *Journal of Applied Psychology, 94,* 1003–1017.

Dimotakis, N., Scott, B. A., & Koopman, J. (2011). An experience sampling investigation of workplace interactions, affective states, and employee well-being. *Journal of Organizational Behavior, 32,* 572–588.

Emmons, R. A. (1986). Personal strivings: An approach to personality and subjective well-being. *Journal of Personality and Social Psychology, 51,* 1058–1068.

Fleeson, W. (2001). Toward a structure- and process-integrated view of personality: Traits as density distributions of states. *Journal of Personality and Social Psychology, 80,* 1011–1027.

Flügel, J. C. (1925). A quantitative study of feeling and emotion in every day life. *British Journal of Psychology, 15,* 318–355.

Foo, M. D., Uy, M. A., & Baron, R. A. (2009). How do feelings influence effort? An empirical study of entrepreneurs' affect and venture effort. *Journal of Applied Psychology, 94,* 1086–1094.

Hofmann, D. A., Griffin, M. A., & Gavin, M. B. (2000). The application of hierarchical linear modeling to organizational research. In K. Klein & S. Kozlowski (Eds.), *Multilevel theory, research, and methods in organizations: Foundations, extensions, and new directions* (pp. 467–511). San Francisco, CA: Jossey-Bass.

Ilies, R., & Dimotakis, N., & De Pater, I. E. (2010). Psychological and physiological reactions to high workloads: Implications for well-being. *Personnel Psychology, 63,* 407–436.

Ilies, R., & Judge, T. A. (2002). Understanding the dynamic relationships among personality, mood, and job satisfaction: A field experience sampling study. *Organizational Behavior and Human Decision Processes, 89,* 1119–1139.

Ilies, R., Dimotakis, N., & Watson, D. (2010). Mood, blood pressure and heart rate at work: An experience-sampling study. *Journal of Occupational Health Psychology, 15,* 120–130.

Ilies, R., Johnson, M. D., Judge, T. A., and Keeney, J. (2011). A within-individual study of interpersonal conflict as a work stressor: Dispositional and situational moderators. *Journal of Organizational Behavior, 32,* 44–64.

Ilies, R., Schwind, K. M., & Heller, D. (2007). Employee well-being: A multi-level model linking work and non-work domains. *European Journal of Work and Organizational Psychology, 16,* 326–341.

Ilies, R., Scott, B. A., & Judge, T. A. (2006). The interactive effects of personal traits and experienced states on intraindividual patterns of citizenship behavior. *Academy of Management Journal, 49,* 561–575.

Ilies, R., Wilson, K. S., & Wagner, D. T. (2009). The spillover of job satisfaction onto employees' family lives: The facilitating role of work–family integration. *Academy of Management Journal, 52,* 87–102.

Judge, T. A., & Ilies, R. (2004). Affect and job satisfaction: A study of their relationship at work and at home. *Journal of Applied Psychology, 89,* 661–673.

Judge, T. A., Scott, B. A., & Ilies, R. (2006). Hostility, job attitudes, and workplace deviance: Test of a multilevel model. *Journal of Applied Psychology, 91,* 126–138.

Judge, T. A., Woolf, E. F., & Hurst, C. (2009). Is emotional labor more difficult for some than for others?: A multilevel, experience-sampling study. *Personnel Psychology, 62,* 57–88.

Kenny, D. A., Korchmaros, J. D., & Bolger, N. (2003). Lower level mediation in multilevel models. *Psychological Methods, 8,* 115–128.

Kerlinger, F. N., & Lee, H. B. (2000). *Foundations of behavioral research.* Forth Worth, TX: Harcourt.

Krull, J. L., & MacKinnon, D. P. (1999). Multilevel mediation modeling in group-based intervention studies. *Evaluation Review, 23,* 418–444.

Krull, J. L., & MacKinnon, D. P. (2001). Multilevel modeling of individual and group level mediated effects. *Multivariate Behavioral Research, 36,* 249–277.

Kuppens, P., Oravecz, Z., & Tuerlinckx, F. (2010, September). Feelings change: accounting for individual differences in the temporal dynamics of affect. *Journal of Personality and Social Psychology.* Advance online publication. doi:10.1037/a0020962

Larson, R., & Csikszentmihalyi, M. (1983). The experience sampling method. *New Directions for Methodology of Social and Behavioral Science, 15,* 41–56.

MacKinnon, D. P., Lockwood, C. M., Hoffman, J. M., West, S. G., & Sheets, V. (2002). A comparison of methods to test mediation and other intervening variable effects. *Psychological Methods, 7,* 83–104.

Marco, C. A., & Suls, J. (1993). Daily stress and the trajectory of mood: Spillover, response assimilation, contrast, and chronic negative affectivity. *Journal of Personality and Social Psychology, 64,* 1053–1063.

Miner, A. G., Glomb, T. M., & Hulin, C. (2005). Experience sampling mood and its correlates at work. *Journal of Occupational and Organizational Psychology, 78,* 171–193.

Muthén, L. K., & Muthén, B. O. (2010). *Mplus User's Guide* (6th ed.). Los Angeles: Muthén & Muthén.

Nunnally, J. C., & Bernstein, I. H. (1994). *Psychometric theory.* New York: McGraw Hill.

Podsakoff, P. M., MacKenzie, S. B., Lee, J. Y., & Podsakoff, N. P. (2003). Common method biases in behavioral research: A critical review of the literature and recommended remedies. *Journal of Applied Psychology, 88,* 879–903.

Raudenbush, S. W., and Bryk, A. S. (2002). *Hierarchical linear models: Applications and data analysis methods.* Newbury Park, CA: Sage.

Rosenthal, R., & Rosnow, R. L. (1991). *Essentials of behavioral research: Methods and data analysis.* New York: McGraw Hill.

Scollon, C. N., Kim-Prieto, C., & Diener, E. (2003). Experience sampling: Promises and pitfalls, strengths and weaknesses. *Journal of Happiness Studies, 4,* 5–34.

Sheldon, K. M., Ryan, R. M., & Reis, H. T. (1996). What makes for a good day? Competence and autonomy in the day and in the person. *Personality and Social Psychology Bulletin, 22,* 1270–1279.

Snijders, T. A. B., & Bosker, R. J. (1993). Standard errors and sample sizes for two-level research. *Journal of Educational Statistics, 18,* 237–259.

Snijders, T. A. B., & Bosker, R. J. (1999). *Multilevel analysis: An introduction to basic and advanced multilevel modeling.* London, UK: Sage.

Sobel, M. E. (1982). Asymptotic confidence intervals for indirect effects in structural equation models. In S. Leinhardt (Ed.), *Sociological methodology* (pp. 290–312). Washington, DC: American Sociological Association.

Song, Z., Foo, M. D., & Uy, M. A. (2008). Mood spillover and crossover among dual-earner couples: A cell phone event sampling study. *Journal of Applied Psychology, 93,* 443–452.

Sonnentag, S., & Bayer, U. (2005). Switching off mentally: Predictors and consequences of psychological detachment from work during off-job time. *Journal of Occupational Health Psychology, 10,* 393–414.

Sonnentag, S., Binnewies, C., & Mojza, E. J. (2008). "Did you have a nice evening?" A day-level study on recovery experiences, sleep and affect. *Journal of Applied Psychology, 93,* 674–684.

van Eck, M., Nicolson, N. A., & Berkhof, J. (1998). Effects of stressful daily events on mood states: Relationship to global perceived stress. *Journal of Personality and Social Psychology, 75,* 1572–1585.

Weiss, H. M., Beal, D. J., Lucy, S. L., & MacDermid, S. M. (2004). Constructing EMA studies with PMAT: The Purdue Momentary Assessment Tool user's manual [Software manual]. Available at www.ruf.rice.edu/~dbeal/PMAT.html

Weiss, H. M., Nicholas, J. P., & Daus, C. S. (1999). An examination of the joint effects of affective experiences and job beliefs on job satisfaction and variations in affective experiences over time. *Organizational Behavior and Human Decision Processes, 78,* 1–24.

Wheeler, L., & Reis, H. T. (1991). Self-recording of everyday life events: Origins, types, and uses. *Journal of Personality, 59,* 339–354.

11

Synthetic Task Environments for Improving Performance at Work: Principles and the Road Ahead

*Aaron S. Dietz, Wendy L. Bedwell,
James M. Oglesby, Eduardo Salas, and
Kathryn E. Keeton*

Synthetic task environments (STEs) have emerged as an increasingly salient methodology to investigate organizational phenomena. They also represent a prominent medium for training essential individual and team competencies, especially when the transfer domain is characterized by dynamic, high-stakes conditions. The value of STEs stems from their capability to abstract critical features from real-world tasks in a setting that is safe, cost-effective, and engaging. Despite these benefits, there remain crucial methodological and logistical factors that researchers and practitioners must consider. STEs encompass a wide range of platforms that vary in fidelity and functionality. These differences, for instance, may ultimately influence the control over experimentation efforts.

The purpose of this chapter is to explain the current state of science and practice surrounding the use of STEs. We begin by contrasting the merits of traditional methodologies (e.g., lab-based and field research) for studying organizational phenomena, highlighting their advantages and disadvantages. This will set the stage for understanding how STEs bridge the gap between traditional methodological approaches. Next, we present principles for effectively utilizing STEs. Finally, we demonstrate how STEs have been used to advance theory, as well as their application as human-resource solutions. We hope to provide researchers and practitioners with a useful conceptualization of STEs to improve their functionality in science and practice and to stimulate future research that will enhance their effectiveness in examining organizational phenomena.

TRADITIONAL APPROACHES TO UNDERSTANDING PERFORMANCE AT WORK

Training and development efforts aimed at performance improvement are critical to successful human-resource management (Jennings, Cyr, & Moore, 1995). As such, research has appropriately focused on investigating various training techniques designed to increase employee knowledge and/or skill or change work-related attitudes that can enhance performance. Selecting the appropriate *context* for research or training implementation, however, can be daunting. Research contexts, for example, have traditionally been dichotomized into two broad categories: those conducted in naturalistic settings and those that rely on contrived laboratory experiments (Driskell & Salas, 1992).

Naturalistic Settings

Naturalistic research seeks to study performance in the field or through the use of high-fidelity simulations that capture the physical essence of that context to a great deal of specificity. Naturalistic research is advantageous because it offers a high degree of realism, which translates into immediate face validity. The issue of face validity is important, because it influences the degree to which policymakers perceive practical benefits of study results. High-fidelity simulations can be especially useful, because they provide an opportunity to practice more dangerous tasks, or low base rate incidents, in a safe environment (e.g., military or aviation training exercises). Further, the high degree of physical fidelity is often thought to curtail skill degradation during transfer of training (Kozlowski & DeShon, 2004).

Naturalistic research contexts, however, do have their challenges. A central concern in naturalistic studies, especially field studies, is the limited experimental control available to researchers (Alluisi, 1967). Maintaining experimental control is critical when assessing performance, as researchers seek to limit the amount of unexplained variance in study results. The effectiveness of a training intervention or influence of a particular construct may be difficult to infer when study variables are not systematically manipulated. A final concern in naturalistic studies relates to external validity. Although the findings are easily applicable to the particular performance environment in which they were collected, the degree to which those findings can be generalized to other contexts may be limited. Essentially, the greater the level of uniqueness in the equipment, task, and team (e.g., NASA spaceflight teams training to use a robotic arm on the International Space Station), the less likely those findings can be related to other performance contexts and teams.

Lab-Based Settings

Unlike naturalistic settings, laboratory research provides greater experimental control over study variables. The results of such studies can be used to communicate theoretical principles to real-world contexts. With respect to external validity, results are typically applicable across a wider variety of work domains and organizational levels, but less can be inferred about a specific domain of interest. Despite such advantages, Driskell and Salas (1992) noted that the utility of this approach has been scrutinized. One particular criticism focused on the artificial nature of lab-based tasks and settings. How can one generalize implications to a real-world operational context, when tasks are systematically manufactured and manipulated under experimentally optimal conditions?

Another obstacle with lab studies relates to the use of older data-collection methods. For example, typical methodologies used to study teams in the 1980s and early 1990s were criticized for being incapable of (1) capturing dynamic processes inherent to teams, (2) assessing complex team performance, and (3) determining relationships among team-level constructs; these are issues that have slowed scientific advances in our understanding of teams and teamwork (Dyer, 1984; Bowers, Salas, Prince, & Brannick, 1992). Accordingly, McGrath (1997) suggested that new methodological tools were required to effectively study teams in context—as complex, dynamic systems, rather than static entities. To address this call, researchers have begun to use different methodologies, such as network analysis and the use of computer-based games to test theories that incorporate some contextual features previously ignored in the study of teams (such as time).

Why Synthetic Task Environments?

STEs seek to optimize the trade-off between "realism" and "control" in research that naturalistic and contrived settings struggle to accomplish alone. They introduce a certain level of realism into the experimental or training task, without sacrificing experimental rigor (Humphrey, Hollenbeck, Ilgen, & Moon, 2004). Thus, STEs are widely used as a methodology for theory building/testing and applying that knowledge to improve individual and team competencies at work. STEs, however, are not a panacea for developing the ideal experimental or instructional paradigm. Appropriate implementation of STEs depends on the careful consideration of a number of theoretical, methodological, and technical factors. Therefore, in the remainder of this chapter, we describe these concerns in greater detail to encourage the appropriate use of STEs. We also provide examples of how STEs have been employed by researchers to study organizational phenomena and by practitioners to deliver effective human-resource solutions.

WHAT ARE SYNTHETIC TASK ENVIRONMENTS?

STEs are now widely used in organizational performance research (Schiflett, Elliott, & Salas, 2004). A review of existing literature, however, revealed an impressive array of terminology associated with STEs. For instance, the term STE describes a number of applications found in the literature, including: synthetic learning environments (e.g., Cannon-Bowers & Bowers, 2008), simulations (e.g., Alessi, 2000), games (e.g., Bowers et al., 1992), virtual worlds (e.g., Boulos, Hetherington, & Wheeler, 2007), microworlds (e.g., Rieber, 1996), and scaled worlds (e.g., Ehret, Gray, & Kirschenbaum, 2000), to name only a few.

In general, STEs refer to special types of simulation, game, or other research or training platform that emphasize the psychological fidelity of the system. Synthetic tasks are abstractions of tasks that occur in the real world (Martin, Lyon, & Schreiber, 1998). An STE, then, provides a medium where multiple synthetic tasks can be employed. A defining feature of STEs is their "task-centric" nature (Cooke & Shope, 2004, p. 264); developers must accurately abstract certain task features of a "real-life" situation in order to provide a psychologically "real" environment where skills can be practiced.

There are several types of fidelity for which any methodology must account: physical, functional, and psychological. Physical fidelity refers to "the degree to which the physical environment of the task is recreated" (Bowers & Jentsch, 2001, p. 294). This is the typical view of fidelity, as to how "realistic" the research environment looks and feels. Functional fidelity refers to the degree to which the environment recreates the purpose, meaning, and other situational or contextual parameters surrounding the actual task (e.g., mission goals, roles, and responsibilities; Elliott, Dalrymple, Schiflett, & Miller, 2004). The third element, psychological fidelity, is perhaps the most difficult to define and create (Bowers & Jentsch, 2001). Kozlowski and DeShon (2004) define psychological fidelity as "the extent to which the training environment [or research platform] prompts the essential underlying psychological processes relevant to key performance characteristics in the real-world setting" (p. 76). Psychological theory is used to guide the development of synthetic tasks that extract the cognitive, behavioral, and affective responses germane to a particular performance context. Taken as a whole, these components of fidelity work in conjunction to create the overall sense of fidelity.

Achieving the appropriate blend of physical, functional, and psycho-logical fidelity is at the heart of selecting or building a testbed for organizational research. Specific STE platforms and scenarios are developed through task analyses to identify the core functional (e.g., goals, roles, and interdependencies) and cognitive characteristics of the target domain (Elliot et al., 2004). Task and work analyses are critical to STE design. These processes help shape specific research and training objectives. With this understanding in mind, task and scenario characteristics can be generated around these dimensions (Elliott et al., 2004). For illustrative purposes, we discuss the cognitive task analysis (CTA) component.

Gugerty (2004) provided a detailed exemplar for collecting and analyzing data based on CTA methods and described how to use those data to generate synthetic tasks. CTA involves two stages: knowledge elicitation and knowledge representation. In general, knowledge-elicitation methods use information gleaned from interviews with subject-matter experts (SMEs) to identify the knowledge and skills required to perform a particular task. Data collected during this first stage of CTA are then represented by techniques that capture the goals, constraints, procedures, and information and knowledge representation requirements for that task. Gugerty (2004) illustrated how multiple synthetic tasks for reconnaissance operations involving uninhabited aerial vehicles (UAVs) could be developed using this approach.

PRINCIPLES FOR USE

Drawing upon the previous section, we present principles for effective STE use. Although many of these principles relate to research in general, there are aspects particularly relevant to STEs that warrant inclusion in the discussion.

Principle 1: Fidelity specifications required for hypothesis testing must be identified.

Fidelity has been discussed previously as a multifaceted and essential consideration in the use of STEs. The degree to which the physical (e.g., hardware and software) and functional (e.g., system behaviors) components reflect the real-world conditions relevant to the task(s), as well as the degree to which psychological fidelity is achieved from the STE as a whole, must be evaluated when selecting an STE. This is largely determined from the intended *purpose*. For example, Bowers and Jentsch (2001) explained that a study examining aircrew communication does not necessarily need to rely on a full-motion flight simulator with a highly realistic cockpit, because these components of physical fidelity are not especially relevant to questions of communication. The type of research question will determine the ways in which the research or training context should mimic real-world conditions.

Principle 2: The merits of custom-built versus commercial-off-the-shelf software should be evaluated before selecting an STE.

STEs can be custom-built or purchased in the form of a commercial-off-the-shelf (COTS) software program. Bowers and Jentsch (2001) observed that a recent trend in research and training has been to use COTS products. These platforms emerged from the computer gaming field and, as such, were designed with the end goal of entertainment rather than knowledge creation. Successful adaptation of COTS products, therefore, usually depends on the psychological fidelity of the platform. For example, the authors described how *Space Fortress* was successfully used to study team processes and decision-making, despite having low levels of physical and functional fidelity. Given the purpose of the research, high levels of physical and/or functional fidelity were not necessary. If, instead, the purpose of the research included physical manipulation of the environment, then *Space Fortress* might not be an appropriate STE, because of its lack of physical fidelity.

Developing custom-made products is an arduous process, but it can yield valuable dividends (e.g., tailored degrees of fidelity, collection of specific outcome and/or process data) for assessing a specific task and environment. This process is described in detail by Cooke and Shope (2004). Developers begin by acquiring an intimate understanding of the performance context in order to constrain initial design. This is accomplished by gathering information for a work context (e.g., through CTA) in light of particular research and training objectives. Other constraints, such as budget and time allowance, will influence the development of an STE as well. Next, developers abstract the aspects of the task that are to be emphasized in the STE. These aspects are then used to develop an initial prototype, which can be as simple as a paper-based mock-up to determine future functional specifications. The actual implementation of the STE involves an iterative process, where developers continually receive feedback from programmers before final implementation.

***Principle 3*: The security of data and individuals must not be compromised during experimentation or training.**

Although this principle is true regardless of the type of experiment, it becomes of paramount importance when using networked systems—a characteristic of some STEs that makes them desirable for team research. STEs that offer multi-user capabilities often rely on computer networks such as the Internet (Bowers & Jentsch, 2001). Research exercises that utilize STEs based on the Internet are able to bring geographically displaced participants together at a relatively low cost. Such added value, however, is not void of potential consequences. Bowers and Jentsch (2001) explained that this open environment might cause disturbances owing to limited bandwidth or server failures. The use of open platforms may also jeopardize the security of data collected or of the individuals who participate in the study. Therefore, researchers should consider using local-area or secured networks to avoid such intrusions.

Principle 4: **Any STE selected for research must allow for investigation of the specific construct of interest.**

The goal of research is to answer questions. Although this statement may seem superficial and obvious to any research endeavor, understanding the relationships between study constructs depends on the careful manipulation of study variables with an appropriate degree of experimental control (Pedhazur & Schmelkin, 1991). Given the impressive array of variables that exist in organizational research, it is unlikely that a universal STE exists that can effectively investigate all constructs of interest (Bowers & Jentsch, 2001). Researchers must, therefore, identify the variable(s) that will help them answer a particular research question and choose the STE that allows for accurate representation of the desired constructs to test their hypothesis. In addition to carefully operationalizing constructs, this requires an understanding of the STE and the constructs that can adequately be examined in that environment. If a researcher is particularly interested in coordinated action, for example, an STE that allows little interdependence among users is not likely the most appropriate tool.

Furthermore, Bowers and Jentsch (2001) explained that researchers must account for extraneous variables that may influence study results. Perhaps the most important extraneous variable to consider in scenario design concerns task difficulty. If a task proves too difficult, or difficulty is not held constant across all study conditions, it may be challenging for researchers to determine whether or not study results were a product of their manipulations or an artifact of scenario difficulty. Replicability of scenarios is also important in this regard. In certain games, there are algorithms that are used to determine what happens when a player makes a decision. Two different players can often make the same decisions, but, if done at slightly different times, the two players can experience dramatically different outcomes. This extraneous condition will cause unwanted outcome variability, creating the potential for erroneous conclusions.

Principle 5: The measurement of dependent variables drives selection of the STE testbed.

Bowers and Jentsch (2001) argued that, although the appropriate manipulation of independent variables and the control of extraneous variables are critical aspects to consider when selecting a testbed, the "measurement of dependent variables must be considered the key characteristic without which a testbed cannot and should not be used" (pp. 302–303). These authors and others (e.g., Cannon-Bowers & Salas, 1997; Salas, Rosen, Held, & Weissmuller, 2009) described important performance-measurement considerations applicable for individual- and team-training testbeds.

The first has to do with whether process or outcome measures are to be used. Whereas outcome measures provide information that indicates what happened as a result of a manipulation, process measures provide information concerning how or why a particular outcome took place. Accordingly, there is a need to utilize, not only outcome measures as dependent variables, but also process measures that illustrate key drivers of performance outcomes. Certain existing COTS games are incapable of capturing process. Others provide limited outcome data, unless the researcher has extensive knowledge of computer programming. Using a game because of familiarity with the product does not ensure the platform can adequately provide the desired data.

Second, performance should be assessed at multiple levels of analysis when team performance is being assessed (e.g., individual- and team-level data). Salas et al. (2009) described how performance can be assessed at the team level. Performance can also be measured as a composition or compilation of individual-level factors to explain how lower-level properties (e.g., individual) manifest or amalgamate over time to influence team performance (Salas et al., 2009). Again, the type of data that any particular STE offers must be considered to determine if it can adequately answer the targeted question. If a research question is focused on understanding variance among team members, STEs that provide aggregated data instead of individual-level data are not appropriate for use. Essentially, consideration must be given to the type of data that an STE can provide to determine if it is appropriate, given the research question(s).

Salas and colleagues (2009) postulated 21 best practices for performance measurement in simulation-based training. Although it is beyond the scope of the present chapter to describe each of these best practices in detail, it is worth mentioning that performance measures should be descriptive, diagnostic, and criterion-based. Further, when STEs are being used for training or instructional purposes, performance measurement should enhance such opportunities to learn. This can be accomplished through scaffolding, after-action reviews, or real-time feedback (see Salas et al., 2009, for a more comprehensive review of performance-based measurement).

TAKING ADVANTAGE OF SYNTHETIC TASK ENVIRONMENTS

With these principles in mind, the current section illustrates how researchers have taken advantage of STEs to explore organizational phenomena. As mentioned earlier in this chapter, a myriad of specific types of STE have been presented in the literature. This discussion will describe four of the most common types: games, simulations, microworlds, and virtual worlds. The sections that follow will (1) define and illustrate each STE, (2) provide a description of potential roadblocks when using each STE, and (3) evaluate areas for future use. When discussing the future use of an STE as a research platform, we consider the role of the STE in aiding the understanding of various strategic human resource management (SHRM) functions (e.g., recruitment, selection, and training/development) where appropriate. We highlight how these tools can be used to inform these areas in both research and practice.

Games/Serious Games and Simulations

Defining Games/Serious Games

Video games have become one of the most profitable and influential forms of entertainment in the world (Squire, 2003). For example, the Sony PlayStation system netted over $150 million in a 24-hour time period when it first debuted in 2001 (Squire, 2003). This sales trend has not slowed. Nintendo's Wii broke the single-month U.S. sales record in December 2009 (Purchese, 2010). Since the dramatic rise in popularity of video games in the 1980s, educators have tried to capitalize on the motivational design of games, wondering if "the magic of *Pac-Man* cannot be bottled and unleashed in the classroom to enhance student involvement, enjoyment, and commitment," (Bowman, 1982, p. 14). To differentiate games used for entertainment, the term "serious games" has been applied to games designed for training and education purposes.

Despite increased attention on the use of games for research, there are issues requiring further clarification. What constitutes a game? That question has been the focus of much research since the early 1980s (e.g., Malone, 1981; Bowman, 1982; Driskell & Dwyer, 1984). A widely cited definition comes from Hays (2005), who defined a game as, "an artificially constructed, competitive activity with a specific goal, a set of rules and constraints that is located in a specific context" (p. 15). Others suggested that games lie on a continuum from humorous to violent (Wilson et al., 2009). Malone (1981) suggested three main elements that make games fun and engaging: challenge, fantasy, and curiosity. Bowman (1982) added the elements of control and feedback, specifically noting that *Pac-Man* players are free to control their own actions and pursue their own goals, within the frame of the overarching goal, and are given clear feedback on performance.

Traditionally, computer games were primarily used in educational settings as a form of drill and practice—essentially, independent study exercises (Thiagarajan, 1998). The majority of these games were drawn from the action genre of video games in order to engage learners. Examples include Alga-Blaster and Reader Rabbit. Drawing upon the training literature, we know that effective training incorporates information, demonstration, practice, and feedback, and these four elements are necessary for effective transfer and, thus, performance improvement (Salas & Cannon-Bowers, 2001; Kraiger, 2003). These early versions of learning tools solely focused on the practice component of effective training. Drill and practice opportunities alone are helpful for problem-based learning (Savery & Duffy, 1995), yet inadequate for other desired learning outcomes.

Educators, trainers, and researchers alike now recognize the power that more sophisticated games hold in providing rich learning contexts (Prensky, 2000; Fletcher & Tobias, 2006; Wilson et al., 2009). Games used in today's learning environment are far removed from what has been termed "integrated learning systems" (i.e., drill and practice games; Oppenheimer, 2003). Technological advancements in both sound and graphics provide a much richer experience than earlier versions (e.g., *Pac-Man*). Additionally, video games now focus on expanded genres, moving beyond action games towards role-playing, strategy, puzzles, sports, and adventure (Squire, 2003).

Serious Games and Organizational Research

The use of computer-based games to research phenomena within organizations abounds. *SimCity* is a COTS game/simulation that is widely known to both game players and researchers. It is a decision-making game in which a player (or players) develops a city (EA Games—*SimCity 4: Deluxe Edition*, 2004). Participants use information such as resident opinion polls to (1) zone or rezone city areas into commercial, residential, and industrial areas; (2) allocate appropriations to city departments (e.g., law enforcement, education, etc.); (3) set the tax rate; and (4) construct buildings, utility plants, bridges/roads, and other structures. Each of these changes ultimately affects the desirability of the city for "residents." The more desirable the city is to live in, the more residents will live there. Performance is generally measured by the total population of the city. This is an example of a low-physical-fidelity game, in that a keyboard and mouse are used to make decisions. A power plant can be built with the click of a button. Alternatively, there is high functional and psychological fidelity. Certain decisions (e.g., law enforcement and taxes) affect citizen attitudes and behaviors much like they do in real life, a characteristic required for functional fidelity. As this creates a sense of purpose with regard to the well-being of a community, players tend to become highly immersed in their "cities," which is indicative of a platform with high psychological fidelity.

Researchers have successfully used this game-based simulation to investigate relationships among constructs. For example, Resick and colleagues (2010) clustered tasks and activities into four roles (Financial Officer—responsible for budget, City Planner—responsible for land zoning and transportation systems, Social Welfare Officer—responsible for education and public health, and Public Works Officer—responsible for utilities and public safety) for a team-based study examining the convergent, discriminant, and predictive validity of various team mental model measurement approaches. *SimCity* was selected because: (1) it can easily be used as a team task (as evidenced in the delineation of the above roles) and (2) the nature of play requires information gathering and processing as well as sharing, which can influence both the sharedness and accuracy of team mental models.

Defining Simulations

Simulations, like games, are artificially constructed activities that (1) are interactive, (2) have a specific purpose designed around the achievement of goals, and (3) have a specific context (Wilson et al., 2009). Unlike games, simulations represent a real phenomenon (Crawford, 1984). Others have suggested the distinction lies in the fact that simulations usually incorporate complex process models that can range from routine to extreme and are driven by a specific algorithm (Randel, Morris, Wetzle, & Whitehead, 1992). These algorithms essentially provide feedback to individuals by "modeling" the results of their decisions (Graesser, Chipman, Leeming, & Biedenbach, 2009). For example, in decision-making simulations such as *SimCity*, players determine a course of action for managing a city through a series of decision points and then watch as the scenario progresses.

Simulations are often used when real systems cannot be used in context (Sokolowski & Banks, 2009), because the context is not available (e.g., testing a moon rover on Earth), is too dangerous to engage (e.g., a nuclear power plant meltdown), and/or has serious—potentially fatal—consequences for failure if engaged without proper training (e.g., flying a plane). Thus, issues relevant to simulations that are not as critical to games include the fidelity and validity of the simulation outcomes. This stems from the rationale behind development of these platforms. Games were originally designed for entertainment, whereas simulations have always sought to reflect an actual phenomenon. Therefore, outcome validity and fidelity were more important than in games. As designers move toward development of games for the purpose of training and development, this trend may change. Most of the research on the effective use of simulations as training tools has focused on either the military or the medical field. However, simulations are now commonly used in businesses and business schools (Faria, 1987, 1998; Summers, 2004).

Simulations and Organizational Research

The medical community frequently relies upon high-fidelity simulations to train medical personnel. High-fidelity simulators (e.g., full-scale mannequins on gurneys connected to intravenous and intensive-care-unit monitors) are used to provide medical students with practice opportunities to diagnose and treat illnesses (Gordon, Wilkerson, Shaffer, & Armstrong, 2001). These are considered high fidelity because they look, feel (physical fidelity), and act (functional fidelity) like real human beings. These characteristics are important for psychological fidelity, as the more functional and physical a simulation is, the more likely the trainees will feel as if they were performing the required tasks in real life.

The medical community has found high-fidelity simulations to provide a good transition between observation of, and actual caring for, live patients (Gordon et al., 2001). Essentially, students are able to put into practice what they have learned from books and observation, without the life-or-death consequences faced when caring for an actual patient. This notion of "safety" is a critical attribute of games/simulations (Wilson et al., 2009) and, thus, makes these tools effective for training complex skills or even performance assessment.

It should be noted, however, that it is not the case that both high physical and functional fidelity are always required for psychological fidelity. As previously described, games such as *SimCity* are highly engaging and replicate actual decision-making, and yet have very low physical fidelity. The degree to which physical and functional fidelity are required in a simulation varies from context to context.

Roadblocks

A major roadblock facing the effective use of games and simulations in any research endeavor is lack of understanding regarding the relationships between game/simulation attributes and learning outcomes (Wilson et al., 2009). Without this knowledge, researchers who seek to understand individual, team, and organizational phenomena through tightly controlled lab studies cannot systematically select a testbed based on the construct of interest. Instead, researchers are left to select testbeds based on whatever they are most familiar with or whatever is most readily available (i.e., platforms of convenience).

Despite the differences between games and simulations, many of the research questions regarding games also apply to simulations. With both types of STE, it is important to determine which attributes (e.g., challenge, rules, goals, and conflict) are relevant for desired outcomes (as is the case with any STE). Researchers are also interested in questions regarding optimal levels of fidelity, as these answers can inform game and simulation development efforts. For example, does the actual task determine the required level of fidelity, or are different levels required depending on the desired learning outcomes? Should the skill level of the learner be taken into consideration when determining the required level of physical, psychological, and functional fidelity, or are these task attributes beneficial to learning regardless of the skills of the trainee? Currently, we do not have answers to these important questions. Today, research is focused, not only on defining what elemental attributes constitute a game, but also on linking those attributes to desired learning outcomes (Cordova & Lepper, 1996; Wilson et al., 2009). This effort should provide evidence-based guidelines to help researchers select more appropriate games and simulations by systematically pairing dependent variables with game/simulation characteristics to most effectively measure (and/or manipulate) the construct(s) of interest.

Future Uses

Despite these roadblocks, games and simulations are more than suitable for understanding organizational phenomena. They are particularly useful for research focused on training and development. Games and simulations have long been used in the military and are making their way into businesses as training tools (Belanich, Sibley, & Orvis, 2004; Smith, Sciarini, & Nicholson, 2007). One reason is that computer games capture audience interest through interaction (Bates, 1997). In an experiment comparing three training conditions—text (i.e., text only), test (i.e., active participation and immediate feedback only), and game (i.e., active participation/dynamic interaction, immediate feedback, goal direction, and competition)—Ricci, Salas, and Cannon-Bowers (1996) found that game-condition trainees not only had significantly greater learning (and retention) than those in the text condition, but also rated training as more enjoyable and effective than did those in either the text or test conditions. The enjoyment factor may indeed be responsible for greater learning and, thus, greater retention, but more research is required to fully explore this relationship.

Another critical aspect of training and development relates to the learning outcomes of training. Training is specifically design to help trainees achieved *desired* learning outcomes. However, we do not currently know what aspects of games and simulations lead to cognitive, affective, or behavioral outcomes. As noted above, research is continuing to investigate these relationships, thanks in large part to the organizational effort of Wilson and colleagues (2009), who created a matrix to identify gaps or conflicting evidence regarding the relationships between attributes and outcomes. A brief glance at the matrix yields a field ripe for research. Investigating these gaps will help provide evidence-based guidelines for the type of game or simulation to use for particular training efforts, based on the desired learning outcomes. This is an area where industrial/ organizational (I/O) psychologists can provide important contributions. First, with a strong background in methods, I/O psychologists can systematically evaluate these relationships using sound methodologies. Second, by applying the science of training to a field largely derived from entertainment (i.e., games), I/O psychologists can improve existing learning efforts by focusing on integrating information, demonstration, practice, and feedback into game and simulation training endeavors.

In addition, organizations that engage in training and development efforts do so because of an anticipated return on investment (ROI). Organizations want to see improved job performance. Unfortunately, little attention is paid to this critical need (Swanson, 2001). Applied research needs to begin to focus on the ROI of games and simulations, compared with face-to-face training techniques. This requires a focus beyond matching game attributes with learning outcomes, or ensuring effective training principles are incorporated into game- or simulation-based training efforts, as described above. Aguinis and Kraiger (2008) suggested evaluating either (1) organizational performance via measures such as profitability, effectiveness, productivity, or operating revenue per employee, or (2) other relevant outcomes, such as reduced costs, improved quality/ quantity of work, employee turnover, organizational reputation, or social capital. Currently, there is a lack of research looking at the effectiveness of training games and simulations in relation to these organizationally relevant outcomes.

Finally, the notion of looking at organizational reputation (e.g., Clardy, 2005) is interesting and can influence other SHRM functions. Consider the impact of training and development efforts on recruiting. U.S. Navy Sea, Air, and Land Teams (SEALs) are known for their intensely rigorous training. As seen in media advertisements, the main goal of SEALs' training is to "construct the reputation of a SEAL as totally dedicated, ruthless, and lethally skilled operators who would be a totally invincible foe" (Clardy, 2005, p. 291). The U.S. Navy can capitalize on this reputation in recruitment efforts, specifically identifying the training as the mechanism by which SEAL members attain this status. Can organizations capitalize on this phenomenon by using their training efforts as a means to recruit? As more and more organizations turn to simulations and games for training, applied researchers should investigate the impact of these STEs on the organizational reputation to determine if there is an opportunity to enhance recruiting efforts.

Microworlds

Defining Microworlds

Microworlds are computer-based platforms that simulate a complex work environment (Di Fonzo, Hantula, & Bordia, 1998; Sauer, 2000; Hoyles, Noss, & Adamson, 2002; Mayer, Dow, & Mayer, 2003). Papert (1980) first coined the term microworld to describe research and training platforms that utilize discovery-based learning paradigms. Essentially, microworlds permit the active exploration of a small environment in the absence of a prescribed rule structure and without consequences for error (Hoyles et al., 2002).

Although microworlds share a number of features with games and simulations, there are several ways in which they are distinct. Simulations and games, for example, are content-driven; participants are instructed to complete a series of tasks/scenarios to meet specified objectives. Conversely, microworlds take a constructivist approach, where learning occurs through one's interaction within the environment (Rieber, 1992). As such, participants define and organize information within the environment to learn autonomously (Miller, Lehman, & Koedinger, 1999; Maier & Grossler, 2000). In addition, simulations and games may require prerequisite knowledge and skills in order to operate the system (e.g., operation of a full-motion flight simulator). Such prerequisite knowledge and skills, however, do not preclude the use of a microworld. Therefore, it is not required to have previous experience within the domain the microworld represents in order to interact with it. It is also worth mentioning that microworlds are most effective when the system emphasizes the connection of new ideas with previously existing knowledge. In other words, although it is not required to have prerequisite knowledge of the domain that is represented by the microworld, the microworld should still tap into one's existing knowledge base to help foster a deep understanding of the relationships and inner working of the system (Rieber, 1992).

Microworlds have some advantages over simulations and games as effective learning tools. They generally cost less to implement and require little training time. Additionally, as the primary learning mechanism is exploratory, microworlds have a wider operational focus than simulations, which are normally designed for one specific purpose. Similar to simulations, these platforms provide a learning environment without the consequences of risking lives and losing resources owing to errors.

Microworlds in Organizational Research

Although microworlds have traditionally been applied within educational contexts (Langley & Morecroft, 1996; Rieber, 1996; Miller et al., 1999), researchers can leverage the unique characteristics of this type of STE to investigate organizational phenomena as well. Romme (2002), for example, evaluated how customer satisfaction was impacted by personnel decision-making using the *Mobile Phone Subscriber Microworld*. This task required participants to build a customer base of subscribers for a mobile-phone service while ensuring the network's capabilities met the demands of the customer. Participants controlled marketing investments and changes to the network in order to attract new customers, and managed cancelled subscriptions as a result of limited network capacity (e.g., dropped calls, loss of signal). Throughout the entire microworld scenario, participants were able to adjust their decisions and test different strategies for maintaining customers based on marketing investments and changes to the network capacity, allowing them to (1) explore multiple approaches to increasing the number of customers and (2) change their theories based on the outcomes of their decisions. Although the *Mobile Phone Subscriber Microworld* is not a comprehensive simulation of a mobile-phone business, it does model a set of basic principles directed at issues regarding customer growth and network capacity, while providing an exploratory learning context in which to learn fundamental skills required for effective customer service.

Granlund (2001) suggested that microworlds, such as *C3 Fire*, could also be utilized to understand team phenomena. In *C3 Fire*, team members share information needed to extinguish a spreading wildfire in the microworld environment, but are not presented with all information about the scenario. This task requires participants to share information and explore a number of possible solutions to control the fire. Such microworlds have been shown to be effective platforms for observing teamwork, communication, and performance in command and control settings—things that are difficult to observe and measure on the job (Johansson, Persson,

Granlund, & Mattsson, 2003). Research has also focused on differences in team-member personalities that may impact team performance and collaboration (Hannen, 2007). Others have utilized microworlds to compare the effectiveness of collaborative tools used by the team, such as communication media (Granlund, 2001) or geographical interface systems (Johansson, Trnka, & Granlund, 2007).

Roadblocks

Perhaps the most challenging roadblock to overcome when utilizing microworlds in research is accounting for individual variability and understanding what impact individual differences have on study outcomes. Because there is no "one right way to perform a task" within a microworld, performance measurement can be more challenging to interpret than is the case for other STEs (Howie & Vicente, 1998, p. 486). Thus, it becomes especially difficult to make comparisons between participants. Additionally, evaluating a participant's true ability on a task from a single trial is complicated, because microworlds permit multiple decision paths to be explored. For example, an individual may commit a minor error during a microworld scenario that leads to a series of events that severely affect the outcome of the scenario. As such, multiple trials are needed in order to effectively measure performance when utilizing microworlds (Brehmer, 2004).

Future Uses

Many organizations have a growing interest in using exploratory learning to gain a competitive advantage (Bell & Kozlowski, 2008; Cabanero-Johnson & Berge, 2009). Microworlds, which rely heavily on such exploratory approaches, have been suggested as one possible training tool to meet the demands associated with critical decision-making in uncertain environments. The U.S. Army, for example, now places greater reliance on resource-management skills and decision-making in military operations (Bondanella et al., 1998). To explore this issue further, we consider the organizationally relevant reasons why the military, in particular, requires effective training that can specifically address uncertain environments, as noted by Bondanella and colleagues. First, the Army deliberately creates a high degree of turnover, with most officers spending no more than

2 years in any given position. This reality creates new challenges for efficient training, because personnel must quickly meet the demands of their new positions. Second, there is a limited opportunity for on-the-job practice to refine and maintain critical teamwork skills needed when personnel are deployed. Through the use of microworlds and proper measurement, command and control personnel can monitor their performance as they acquire and maintain the critical skills needed for optimal decision-making. The characteristics of microworlds provide a well-suited platform for addressing these critical issues in the military and in other organizations with similar training needs.

In addition, microworlds offer the capability of assessing individual differences in decision-making processes for solving complex problems. In this case, microworlds that permit the elicitation of decision-making processes can potentially be used for selection purposes. The very manner in which participants engage with the microworld can provide valuable information regarding their expertise in any given domain (Friel, Thomas, Shanteau, & Raacke, 2001; Shanteau, Weiss, Thomas, & Pounds, 2002). However, as previously mentioned, precautions must be taken when measuring performance in microworlds. Researchers must account for individual differences and how this variability influences decision-making strategies within the microworld (Brehmer, 2004). Future research is needed to detect the relationship between microworld performance and actual task performance, to validate the application of microworlds for selection purposes and ensure there is impact on protected classes.

Although there is great potential for using microworlds to enhance learning processes, research concerning training implementation with this STE is scarce to the point of being practically nonexistent (Sauer, 2000; Jarmasz, 2006). Many proponents argue that microworlds are beneficial in skill and knowledge acquisition, and yet more research is needed to determine exactly which learning outcomes can be successfully achieved. The mapping of a taxonomy of learning outcomes, such as the one provided by Kraiger, Ford, and Salas (1993), to various STEs such as microworlds would be a useful endeavor. Future research should also look at how performance can accurately be measured within microworlds to specifically identify trainee proficiency levels. These issues must be addressed before microworlds can effectively be utilized for training and/or selection purposes.

Virtual Worlds

Defining Virtual Worlds

Virtual worlds, also known as massive multiplayer online role-playing games (MMORPG), are computer environments where a large number of geographically dispersed players can interact and collaborate with one other (Cannon-Bowers & Bowers, 2010). These types of platform are similar to games, as they have established goals and prescribed rules of how to operate within the environment. However, a key distinction is that virtual worlds rely on computer-network servers for multiple players to share the same experience through their own individual computers (Book, 2004). Each player is visually represented in the virtual world through personalized, three-dimensional forms called avatars (McArthur, 2008; Owens, Davis, Murphy, Khazanchi, & Zigurs, 2009). In addition to the physical interaction of avatars, different types of communication medium can be used in virtual worlds, such as auditory communication via microphones or written communication via text chat (Boulos et al., 2007; Messinger et al., 2009). A further distinguishing characteristic between virtual worlds and games is that virtual worlds are perpetual, meaning that activity within the world takes place with or without active involvement of the player—individuals enter and leave the world at any time, while their avatars remain active (Cannon-Bowers & Bowers, 2010).

Virtual Worlds in Organizational Research

This type of STE has markedly changed the strategic landscape in business operations. Organizations are utilizing virtual worlds to help establish a customer base, interact with organizational partners, raise brand awareness, as well as recruit and develop their workforce to optimize performance (Goel & Prokopec, 2009). Consider the process of recruitment and selection. This involves an exchange of information between the organization and the job seeker: a job posting from the organization and a position application from interested candidates, as well as interviews, which require travel time on the part of the job seeker. Virtual worlds allow for these exchanges via avatars and actually provide additional information beyond a company website by enabling a job seeker to explore a virtual representation of an organization, and perhaps interact with existing employees who can provide real-time information. For example, Loiacono, Djamasbi, Tulu, and Pavlov (2011) highlighted that a key drawback to static websites is a lack of commitment to recruitment. Specifically, a visitor to the website who wishes to obtain more information about an organization is typically instructed to click a link that sends them to another static webpage. The authors suggested that the use of live avatars, who are available to interact with potential employees who visit the virtual representation of the organization, can significantly aid in recruitment efforts by providing a "live" interaction, rather than relying solely on text displayed on a webpage. Other researchers have suggested that information presented through a virtual world can increase the attractiveness of an organization and, thus, increase the applicant pool (Howardson & Behrend, 2011). The U.S. Air Force, for example, is reaching out to potential recruits through *Second Life* by informing and educating civilians about military life, as well as providing them with opportunities to participate in activities such as flying planes in the virtual world (Seiler, 2008). This innovative approach to recruitment and selection can decrease costs, as there is no requirement for physical space, with staff on site to conduct face-to-face interviews (Loiacono et al., 2011).

Roadblocks

Although some characteristics associated with virtual worlds are beneficial for research, multiple barriers need to be considered. First, caution is advised when applying research findings outside of the virtual world, as players might not reflect the desired population in terms of demographic characteristics (i.e., researchers should carefully consider whether people who generally play virtual worlds have similar characteristics to the population of interest). Also, the technology medium itself reduces the cues associated with face-to-face interaction. In essence, virtual worlds may not appropriately exhibit the richness of interaction between players that occurs naturally in face-to-face situations (Chesney, Chuah, & Hoffmann, 2009).

There are also technical considerations, similar to those discussed with other STEs. As noted previously, network applications may be vulnerable to limited bandwidth, server failures, and congested traffic (Bowers & Jentsch, 2001). Specific to multiplayer environments, response lags have been reported when a large number of avatars participate in the same area at the same time (Mennecke et al., 2008). With regard to development time, if experimenters plan to develop their own virtual worlds, significant time and monetary investments may be required to fund developers and support staff, as well as to maintain the server (Castranova & Falk, 2008).

Despite the rich and advanced features associated with virtual worlds, it is worth noting that some individuals may not prefer such an environment to traditional methods. For example, Goel and Prokopec (2009) found that a sample of individuals preferred websites, citing them as more descriptive and trustworthy than virtual worlds in raising awareness of company brands. Additionally, members of younger generations—those considered more technologically skilled and accepting of advanced forms of technology—are reluctant to engage in recruitment processes through virtual worlds (Loiacono et al., 2011). The authors suggested that a large portion of the population is unaware of virtual worlds, despite the rising popularity of these STEs for entertainment and even organizational purposes. As such, many may not even consider the possibility of using virtual worlds for recruitment or selection, or even for performance effectiveness for virtual teams. One possible solution is to market the potential of virtual worlds for such uses in order to gain acceptance (Loiacono et al., 2011).

Future Uses

Virtual worlds are increasing in popularity—nearly 12 million *Second Life* avatar accounts and more than 11 million *World of Warcraft* subscriptions were created in 2008 alone (Mennecke et al., 2008). As these platforms have increased the market share for gaming and entertainment, many are looking to apply virtual worlds to aid understanding of performance at work. While organizations are establishing network relationships on a global scale (Townsend, DeMarie, & Hendrickson, 1998), virtual worlds can be utilized for a number of practical applications. For example, organizations can utilize these interactive, virtual media for studying the effectiveness of distributed interactions and the effect of technologically mediated communication.

Further, virtual worlds are starting to play a role in recruitment and selection processes. Organizations have begun to conduct job interviews with potential candidates through avatar interaction (Owens et al., 2009).

Perhaps organizations can gain a competitive advantage by eliminating the need to incur costs associated with recruitment activities, as they can reach a large audience and generate a number of qualified applicants for available positions through effective use of virtual worlds (Jarmon, 2008; Laumer, Von Stetten, Eckardt, & Weitzel, 2009). Research is needed to determine how effective this strategy is, whether it truly opens up the applicant pool, and the estimated cost savings from such an approach.

Organizations are also starting to take interest in virtual worlds for training purposes (Gronstedt, 2007), such as teaching teamwork skills, as these platforms allow players to exhibit critical teamwork competencies, such as leadership and supporting behavior (Bonk & Dennen, 2005; Freeman et al., 2006). Planning, decision-making, and collaboration—skills recognized by the Department of Defense (DOD) necessary to meet the dynamic challenges of military operations—can also be pervasive within online multiplayer platforms such as virtual worlds (Bonk & Dennen, 2005). Although researchers have argued the very nature of virtual worlds allows for systematic training (e.g., Davis, Khazanchi, Murphy, Zigurs, & Owens, 2009), others have reservations regarding the training capabilities of virtual worlds (Taylor & Chyung, 2008). Therefore, more research is needed with regard to the training efficacy of these tools. Future research can look into the factors that influence both the perceived value and the effectiveness of training implementation in virtual worlds (Bonk & Dennen, 2005; Taylor & Chyung, 2008), and the criteria needed for effective training in virtual worlds to ensure transfer, performance improvement, and return on investment.

Finally, organizations are increasing their reliance on virtual teams (Hertel, Geister & Konradt, 2005). Virtual teams are teams (i.e., two or more individuals interacting in a dynamic fashion, interdependently, and adaptively, toward the achievement of mutual goals; Salas, Dickinson, Converse, & Tannenbaum, 1992) whose members are geographically or temporally distributed and interact with each other through a technological medium (Martins, Gilson, & Maynard, 2004). As a defining characteristic of virtual worlds is the ability for multiple players to interact both synchronously and asynchronously through an ever-evolving environment, virtual worlds offer a rich tool with which to study virtual team interactions (Kahai, Carroll, & Jestice, 2007).

THE ROAD AHEAD: ADVANCING THE SCIENCE OF SYNTHETIC TASK ENVIRONMENTS

This chapter has described STEs as an emerging methodological approach for understanding and improving performance. In closing, we return to our previous discussion on lab/field research and practice. Lab research allows for a narrow focus on a specific construct(s) of interest, through tight control of extraneous variables and contextual factors (Shaddish, Cook, & Campbell, 2002). Conversely, field research is "messy," in that there is little control over such factors. However, there is a higher degree of external validity, in that the findings are taken directly from the target population instead of a representative sample (Shaddish et al., 2002).

In this chapter, we have demonstrated the utility of STEs in bridging the lab–field research gap, and we have presented principles to guide researchers and practitioners alike when selecting and designing a research platform. Further, we presented definitions of various subsets of STEs to account for the wide range of applications available to researchers and practitioners. By thoroughly defining various forms and discussing specific examples of STE implementation, we attempt to provide a useful conceptualization of STEs to improve their use and stimulate future research.

To support such methodological advancement, the road ahead can benefit from the establishment of a conspicuous link between the attributes of a particular STE and performance outcomes. Wilson et al. (2009) attempted to answer this question, but limited their review to the gaming literature. Specifically, the researchers sought to uncover the link between game elements (e.g., challenge, control, and fantasy) and learning outcomes. The authors relied on theoretical models of learning (e.g., Kraiger et al., 1993) to evaluate the ways in which game attributes influence cognitive, skill-based, and affective outcomes of learning. Applying a similar method to the evaluation of all STEs will inform our understanding of whether these approaches simply differ along cosmetic/functionality dimensions or along more substantive dimensions that have a bearing on study results.

Our hope is that this effort will enable better selection and design of STEs and spur future research on these methodologies themselves (not just as tools to research psychological constructs of interest). Only then will science and practice be able to effectively tap the power of these tools as both research and training platforms.

ACKNOWLEDGMENT

The work presented here was supported by funding from the National Aeronautics and Space Administration (NASA; Grant# NNX09AK48G). The views expressed in this work are solely those of the authors and not those of NASA or the University of Central Florida.

REFERENCES

Aguinis, H., & Kraiger, K. (2008). Benefits of training and development for individuals and teams, organizations, and society. *Annual Review of Psychology, 60*(1), 451–474. doi:10.1146/annurev.psych.60.110707.163505

Alessi, S. (2000). Simulation design for training and assessment. In H. O'Neil & D. H. Andrews (Eds.), *Aircrew training and assessment* (pp. 197–222). Mahwah, NJ: Erlbaum.

Alluisi, E. A. (1967). Methodology in the use of synthetic tasks to assess complex performance. *Human factors, 9*(4), 375–384.

Bates, A. W. (1997). *Technology, open learning, and distance education.* London: Routledge.

Bedwell, W. L., Pavlas, D., Heyne, K., Lazzara, E. H., & Salas, E. (2012). Toward a taxonomy linking game attributes to learning: An empirical study. *Simulation and Gaming, 43*, 729–760.

Belanich, J., Sibley, D. E., & Orvis, K. L. (2004). *Instructional characteristics and motivational features of a PC-based game* (Technical Report No. 1822). Alexandria, VA: U.S. Army Research Institute for the Behavioral and Social Sciences.

Bell, B. S., & Kozlowski, S. W. (2008). Active learning: Effects of core training design elements on self-regulatory processes, learning, and adaptability [Research Support, U.S. Government, Non-P.H.S.]. *The Journal of Applied Psychology, 93*(2), 296–316. doi: 10.1037/0021-9010.93.2.296

Bondanella, J. R., Lewis, M., Steinberg, P. S., Park, G. S., Levy, D. G., Ettedgui, E., et al. (1998). Microworld simulation for command and control training of theater logistics and support staffs. Washington, DC: RAND.

Bonk, C. J., & Dennen, V. P. (2005). *Massive multiplayer online gaming: A research framework for military training and education.* Available at http://handle.dtic.mil/100.2/ADA431271

Book, B. (2004). *Moving beyond the game: Social virtual worlds.* Paper presented at the State of Play 2 Conference, New York.

Boulos, M. N. K., Hetherington, L., & Wheeler, S. (2007). Second Life: an overview of the potential of 3-D virtual worlds in medical and health education. *Health Information & Libraries Journal, 24*(4), 233–245.

Bowers, C., Salas, E., Prince, C., & Brannick, M. (1992). Games teams play—A method for investigating team coordination and performance. *Behavior Research Methods Instruments & Computers, 24*(4), 503–506.

Bowers, C. A., & Jentsch, F. (2001). Use of commercial, off-the-shelf, simulations for team research. In E. Salas (Ed.), *Advances in human performance and cognitive engineering research* (Vol. 1, pp. 293–317). Amsterdam: Elsevier Science.

Bowman, R. F. (1982). A Pac-Man theory of motivation. Tactical implications for classroom instruction. *Educational Technology, 22*(9), 14–17.

Brehmer, B. (2004). Some reflection on microworld research. In S. G. Schiflett, L. R. Elliott, E. Salas, & M. D. Coovert (Eds.), *Scaled worlds: Development, validation and applications* (pp. 22–36). Aldershot, UK: Ashgate.

Cabanero-Johnson, P. S., & Berge, Z. (2009). Digital natives: Back to the future of microworlds in a corporate learning organization. *The Learning Organization, 16*(4), 290–297.

Cannon-Bowers, J. A., & Bowers, C. A. (2008). Synthetic learning environments. In J. M. Spector, M. D. Merrill, J. v. Merrienboer & M. P. Driscoll (Eds.), *Handbook of research on educational communications and technology* (3 ed., pp. 306–315). New York: Lawrence Erlbaum Associates.

Cannon-Bowers, J. A., & Bowers, C. A. (2010). Synthetic learning environments: on developing a science of simulation, games, and virtual worlds for training. In S. W. J. Kozlowski & E. Salas (Eds.), *Learning, training, and development in organizations* (pp. 229–262). New York: Taylor & Francis Group.

Cannon-Bowers, J. A., & Salas, E. (1997). A framework for developing team performance measures in training. In M. Brannick, E. Salas, & C. Prince (Eds.), *Team performance assessment and measurement* (pp. 45–62). Mahwah, NJ: Erlbaum.

Castranova, E., & Falk, M. (2008). Virtual worlds as petri dishes for the social and behavioral sciences. *Social Science Research Network*. Retrieved from http://papers.ssrn.com/sol3/papers.sfm?abstract_id=1445340

Chesney, T., Chuah, S. H., & Hoffmann, R. (2009). Virtual world experimentation: An exploratory study. *Journal of Economic Behavior & Organization, 72*(1), 618–635.

Clardy, A. (2005). Reputation, goodwill, and loss: Entering the employee training audit equation. *Human Resources Development Review, 4*, 279–304.

Cooke, N. J., & Shope, S. M. (2004). Designing a synthetic task environment. In S. J. Schiflett, L. R. Elliott, E. Salas, & M. D. Coovert (Eds.), *Scaled worlds: Development, validation, and applications* (pp. 263–278). Aldershot, UK: Ashgate.

Cordova, D. I., & Lepper, M. R. (1996). Intrinsic motivation and the process of learning: Beneficial effects of contextualization, personalization, and choice. *Journal of Educational Psychology, 88*, 715–730.

Crawford, C. (1984). *The art of computer design.* Berkeley, CA: Osborne/McGraw-Hill.

Davis, A., Khazanchi, D., Murphy, J., Zigurs, I., & Owens, D. (2009). Avatars, people, and virtual worlds: Foundations for research in metaverses. *Journal of the Association for Information Systems, 10*(2), 90–117.

Di Fonzo, N., Hantula, D. A., & Bordia, P. (1998). Microworlds for experimental research: Having your (control and collection) cake, and realism too. *Behavior Research Methods, Instruments, & Computers, 30*(2), 278–286.

Driskell, J. E., & Dwyer, D. J. (1984). Microcomputer videogame based training. *Educational Technology*, 24(2), 11–15.

Driskell, J. E., & Salas, E. (1992). Can you study real teams in contrived settings? The value of small group research to understanding teams. In R. W. Swezey & E. Salas (Eds.), *Teams: Their training and performance* (pp. 101–124). Norwood, NJ: Ablex Publishing Corporation.

Dyer, J. (1984). Team research and team training: State-of-the-art review. In F. A. Muckler (Ed.), *Human factors review* (pp. 258–323). Santa Monica, CA: Human Factors Society.

Ehret, B. D., Gray, W. D., & Kirschenbaum, S. S. (2000). Contending with complexity: Developing and using a scaled world in applied cognitive research. *Human factors*, 42(1), 8–23.

Elliott, L. R., Dalrymple, M. A., Schiflett, S. G., & Miller, J. C. (2004). Scaling scenarios: Development and application to C4ISR sustained operations research. In S. G. Schiflett, L. R. Elliott, E. Salas, & M. D. Coovert (Eds.), *Scaled worlds: Development, validation, and applications* (pp. 119–133). Aldershot, UK: Ashgate.

Faria, A. J. (1987). A survey of the use of business games in academia and business. *Simulation & Games*, 18, 207–224.

Faria, A. J. (1998). Business simulation games: Current usage levels—A ten year update. *Simulation & Gaming*, 29, 207–224.

Fletcher, J. D., & Tobias, S. (2006, February). *Using computer games and simulations for instruction: A research review.* Paper presented at the Society for Advanced Learning Technology Meeting, Orlando, FL.

Freeman, J., MacMillan, J., Haimson, C., Weil, S., Stacy, W., & Diedrich, F. (2006, February). *From gaming to training.* Paper presented at the Society for Advanced Learning Technology, Orlando, FL.

Friel, B. M., Thomas, R. P., Shanteau, J., & Raacke, J. (2001). CWS applied to an air traffic control simulation task (CTEAM). *2001 International Symposium on Aviation Psychology.* Columbus, OH: Ohio State University.

Goel, L., & Prokopec, S. (2009). If you build it will they come?—An empirical investigation of consumer perceptions and strategy in virtual worlds. *Electronic Commerce Research*, 9, 115–134.

Gordon, J. A., Wilkerson, W. M., Shaffer, D. W., & Armstrong, E. G. (2001). "Practicing" medicine without risk: Students' and educators' reponses to high-fidelity patient simulation. *Academic Medicine*, 76, 469–472.

Graesser, A. C., Chipman, P., Leeming, F., & Biedenbach, S. (2009). Deep learning and emotion in serious games. In U. Ritterfeld, M. Cody, & P. Vorderer (Eds.), *Serious games: Mechanisms and effects* (pp. 81–100). New York: Routledge, Taylor & Francis.

Granlund, R. (2001). Web-based micro-world simulation for emergency management training. *Future Generation Computer Systems*, 17(5), 561–572. doi: 10.1016/s0167-739x(00)00039-x

Gronstedt, A. (2007). *Second Life produces real training results.* Retrieved November 29, 2012 from www.gronstedtgroup.com/pdf/T_D_Magazine_secondlife_article_07.pdf.

Gugerty, L. (2004). Using cognitive task analysis to design multiple synthetic tasks for uninhabited aerial vehicle operation. In S. G. Schiflett, L. R. Elliott, E. Salas, & M. D. Coovert (Eds.), *Scaled worlds: Development, validation and applications* (pp. 240–262). Aldershot, UK: Ashgate.

Hannen, T. W. (2007). *The effect of personality styles and team organization in team performance.* Unpublished master's thesis, Naval Postgraduate School, Monterey, CA.

Hays, R. T. (2005). *The effectiveness of instructional games: A literature review and discussion* (Technical Report No. 2005–004). Orlando, FL: Naval Air Warfare Center Training Systems Division.

Hertell, G., Geister, S., Konradt, U. (2005). Managing virtual teams: A review of current empirical research. *Human Resource Management Review, 15,* 69–95.

Howardson, G. N., & Behrend, T. S. (2011). *Internet job seekers' information expectations predict organizational attraction.* Paper presented to the 26th Annual Meeting of the Society for Industrial and Organizational Psychology, Chicago, IL.

Howie, D. E., & Vicente, K. J. (1998). Measures of operator performance in complex, dynamic microworlds: Advancing the state of the art. *Ergonomics, 41*(4), 485–500.

Hoyles, C., Noss, R., & Adamson, N. (2002). Rethinking the microworld idea. *Journal of Educational Computing Research, 27,* 29–53.

Humphrey, S. E., Hollenbeck, J. R., Ilgen, D. R., & Moon, H. (2004). The changing shape of large-scale programs for research: MSU-DDD as an illustrative example. In S. G. Schiflett, L. R. Elliott, & M. D. Coovert (Eds.), *Scaled worlds: Development, validation and applications.* Aldershot, UK: Ashgate.

Jarmasz, J. (2006). *Accelerated training with microworlds for command dynamic decision making* (DRDC Toronto TR 2006–239). Toronto: Defence Research and Development Canada.

Jarmon, L. (2008). Pedagogy and learning in the virtual world of Second Life. In P. Rogers, G. A. Berg, M. Hricko, & C. Howard (Eds.), *Enyclopedia of distance and online learning* (2nd ed., Vol. 3, pp. 1610–1619). Hershey, PA: IGI.

Jennings, P. D., Cyr, D., & Moore, L. F. (1995). Human resource management on the Pacific Rim: An integration. In L. F. Moore & P. D. Jennings (Eds.), *Human resource management on the Pacific Rim: Institutions, practices, and attitudes* (pp. 351–379). New York: DeGruyter.

Johansson, B., Persson, M., Granlund, R., & Mattsson, P. (2003). C3Fire in command and control research. *Cognition, Technology, and Work, 5,* 191–196.

Johansson, B., Trnka, J., & Granlund, R. (2007). The effect of geographical information systems on a collaborative command and control task. In B. Van Den Walle, P. Burghardt, & C. Nieuwenhuis (Eds.), *Proceedings of the 4th International Conference on Information Systems for Crisis Response and Management (ISCRAM)* (pp. 191–200). Delft, The Netherlands.

Kahai, S. S., Carroll, E., & Jestice, R. (2007). Team collaboration in virtual worlds. *The Data Base for Advances in Information Systems, 38*(4), 61–68.

Kozlowski, S. W. J., & DeShon, R. P. (2004). A psychological fidelity approach to simulation-based training: Theory, research, and principles. In E. Salas, L. R. Elliott, S. G. Schiflett, & M. D. Coovert (Eds.), *Scaled worlds: Development, validation, and applications.* Burlington, VT: Ashgate.

Kraiger, K. (2003). Perspectives on training and development. In W. C. Borman, D. R. Ilgen, & R. J. Klimoski (Eds.), *Comprehensive handbook of psychology* (Vol. 12, pp. 171–192). Hoboken, NJ: Wiley & Sons.

Kraiger, K., Ford, J. K., & Salas, E. (1993). Application of cognitive, skill-based, and affective theories of learning outcomes to new methods of training evaluation. *Journal of Applied Psychology, 78*(2), 311–328.

Langley, P. A., & Morecroft, J. D. W. (1996). Learning from microworld environments: A summary of the research issues. In G. P. Richardson & J. D. Sterman (Eds.), *System dynamics '96*. Cambridge, MA: System Dynamics Society.

Laumer, S., Von Stetten, A., Eckardt, A., & Weitzel, T. (2009). Online gaming to apply for jobs: The impact of self- and e-assessment on staff recruitment. *42nd Hawaii International Conference on System Sciences*. Waikoloa, HI: IEEE.

Loiacono, E., Djamasbi, S., Tulu, B., & Pavlov, O. (2011). Why virtual job recruitment is not well accepted by generation Y?—A case study of Second Life. In J. A. Jacko (Ed.), *Human-computer interaction, PartIV* (pp. 245–254). Berlin: Springer-Verlag.

Maier, F. H., & Grossler, A. (2000). What are we talking about?—A taxonomy of computer simulations to support learning. *System Dynamics Review, 16*(2), 135–148.

Malone, T. W. (1981). Toward a theory of intrinsically motivating instruction. *Cognitive Science, 4*, 333–369.

Martin, E., Lyon, D. R., & Schreiber, B. T. (1998). Designing synthetic tasks for human factors research: An application to uninhabited air vehicles. *Human Factors and Ergonomics Society 42nd Annual Meeting*. Santa Monica, CA: Human Factors and Ergonomics Society.

Martins, L. L., Gilson, L. L., & Maynard, M. T. (2004). Virtual teams: What do we know and where do we go from here? *Journal of Management, 30*(6), 805–835.

Mayer, R. E., Dow, G. T., & Mayer, S. (2003). Multimedia learning in an interactive self-explaining environment: What works in the design of agent-based microworlds? *Journal of Educational Psychology, 95*(4), 806–812.

McArthur, V. (2008). Real ethics in a virtual world. In *CHI 2008 extended abstracts on human factors in computing systems*. Florence, Italy: ACM.

McGrath, R. G. (1997). A real options logic for initiating technology positioning investments. *Academy of Management Review, 22*, 974–996.

Mennecke, B. E., McNeill, D., Roche, E. M., Bray, D. A., Townsend, A. M., & Lester, J. (2008). Second life and other virtual worlds: A roadmap for research. *Communication of the Association for Information Systems, 22*(20), 371–388.

Messinger, P. R., Stroulia, E., Lyons, K., Bone, M., Niu, R., Smirnov, K., et al. (2009). Virtual worlds—past, present, and future: New directions in social computing. *Decision Support Systems, 47*, 204–228.

Miller, C. S., Lehman, L. F., & Koedinger, K. R. (1999). Goals and learning in microworlds. Cognitive Science. *Cognitive Science, 23*(3), 305–336.

Oppenheimer, T. (2003). *A flickering mind: The false promise of technology in the classroom*. New York: Random House.

Owens, D., Davis, A., Murphy, J. D., Khazanchi, D., & Zigurs, I. (2009). Real-world opportunities for virtual-world project management. *IT Professional, 11*(2), 34–41.

Papert, S. (1980). *Mindstorms: Children, computers, and powerful ideas*. New York: Basic Books.

Pedhazur, E. J., & Schmelkin, L. P. (1991). *Measurement, design, and analysis: An integrated approach*. New York: Psychology Press.

Prensky, M. (2000). *Digital game-based learning*. New York: McGraw Hill.

Purchese, R. (2010, January). Wii and DS thrash competition in US. *Eurogamer*. Retrieved September 13, 2010, from www.eurogamer.net/articles/wii-and-ds-thrash-competition-in-us

Randel, J. M., Morris, B. A., Wetzle, C. D., & Whitehead, B. V. (1992). The effectiveness of games for educational purposes: A review of recent research. *Simulation and Gaming, 23*, 261–276.

Resick, C. J., Murase, T., Bedwell, W. L., Sanz, E., Jiménez, M., & DeChurch, L. A. (2010). Mental model metrics and team adaptability: A multi-facet multi-method examination. *Group Dynamics: Theory, Research, & Practice, 14*, 332–349.

Ricci, K. E., Salas, E., & Cannon-Bowers, J. A. (1996). Do computer-based games facilitate knowledge acquisition and retention? *Military Psychology, 8*, 295–307.

Rieber, L. P. (1992). Computer-based microworlds: A bridge between constructivism and direct institution. *Educational Technology Research and Development, 40*(1), 93–106.

Rieber, L. P. (1996). Seriously considering play: Designing interactive learning environments based on the blending of microworlds, simulations, and games. *Educational Technology Research and Development, 44*(2), 43–58.

Romme, A. G. L. (2002). *Microworlds for management education and learning.* Tilburg, The Netherlands: Tilburg Univeristy.

Salas, E., & Cannon-Bowers, J. A. (2001). The science of training: A decade of progress. *Annual Review of Psychology, 52*, 471–499.

Salas, E., Dickinson, T. L., Converse, S. A., & Tannenbaum, S. I. (1992). Toward an understanding of team performance and training. In R. W. Swezey and E. Salas (Eds.), *Teams: Their training and performance* (pp. 3–29). Norwood, NJ: ABLEX.

Salas, E., Rosen, M. A., Held, J. D., & Weissmuller, J. J. (2009). Performance measurement in simulation-based training: A review and best practices. *Simulation & Gaming, 40*(3), 328–376.

Sauer, J. (2000). The use of micro-worlds for human factors research in extended spaceflight. *ActaAstronautica, 46*(1), 37–45.

Savery, J. R., & Duffy, T. M. (1995). Problem based learning: An instructional model and its constructivist framework. *Educational Technology, 35*(5), 31–37.

Schiflett, S. G., Elliott, L. R., & Salas, E. (Eds.) (2004). *Scaled worlds: Development, validation and applications.* Aldershot, UK: Ashgate.

Seiler, J. (2008). *MyBase launches in Second Life.* Retrieved September 6, 2011, from www.engagedigital.com/blog/2008/12/02/mybase-launches-in-second-life

Shaddish, W. R., Cook, T. D., & Campbell, D. T. (2002). *Experimental and quasi-experimental design for generalized causal inference.* Boston, MA: Houghton-Mifflin.

Shanteau, J., Weiss, D. J., Thomas, R. P., & Pounds, J. C. (2002). Performance-based assessment of expertise: How to decide if someone is an expert or not. *European Journal of Operational Research, 136*, 253–263.

SimCity 4: Deluxe Edition. (2004). Emeryville, CA: EA Games.

Smith, P., Sciarini, L., & Nicholson, D. (2007). The utilization of low cost gaming hardware in conventional simulation. *Interservice/Industry Training, Simulation, & Education Conference* (pp. 965–972). Orlando, FL: National Defense Industrial Association.

Sokolowski, J. A., & Banks, C. M. (2009). *Principles of modeling and simulation: A multidisciplinary approach.* Hoboken, NJ: John Wiley & Sons.

Squire, K. D. (2003). Video games in education. *International Journal of Intelligent Games & Simulation, 2*, 49–62.

Summers, G. J. (2004). Today's business simulation industry. *Simulation & Gaming, 35*, 208–241.

Swanson, R. A. (2001). *Assessing the financial benefits of human resource development.* Cambridge, MA: Perseus.

Taylor, K. C., & Chyung, S. Y. (2008). Would you adopt Second Life as a training and development tool? *Performance Improvement, 47*(8), 17–25.

Thiagarajan, S. (1998). The myths and realities of simulations in performance technology. *Educational Technology, 38*(5), 35–41.

Townsend, A. M., DeMarie, S. M., & Hendrickson, A. R. (1998). Virtual teams: Technology and the workplace of the future. *The Academy of Management Executive, 12*(3), 17–29.

Wilson, K. A., Bedwell, W. L., Lazzara, E. H., Salas, E., Burke, C. S., Estock, J., et al. (2009). Relationships between game attributes and learning outcomes: Review and research proposals. *Simulation & Gaming, 40*(2), 317–266.

12

Petri Nets: Modeling the Complexity of Modern Jobs

Michael D. Coovert

The world contains many interesting and sometimes unusual phenomena. Some of the more fascinating are organizations and the individuals who work the various jobs found therein. During a typical week, it would not be unusual to cross paths with a schoolteacher, a cobbler (or other skilled trade person), a musician, and a pilot. Many psychologists and human-resource specialists are interested in the problem of describing these jobs and the task processes that are performed as an incumbent interacts with a series of tools and work aids. We also often need to make useful descriptive statements about the jobs. For example, is it possible to create a model of what gets done? That is, can the flow of information and tasks through the job be represented? Is the model executable? In other words, can the model be run, and can changes to its states be identified and measured? Finally, can the model provide evaluative information of the type that allows for the analysis of the job or its incumbents?

This chapter describes a methodological tool that can be helpful to those interested in describing and modeling jobs, as well as those developing training aids and evaluation systems for incumbents in those jobs. The technique is Petri nets, and it has a storied history and successful application in several domains, including: informatics, engineering, and computer science. This chapter is a high-level overview of the technique, presenting the basic building blocks. Many advances in the methodology are not mentioned for space consideration, and also as they are more directly applicable to other disciplines (e.g., modeling distributed computational systems). My hope is to inform the reader and perhaps pique his or her interest in utilizing it for problems commonly faced in research and applications when modeling is appropriate. If found useful, additional information is easily gleaned through perusing the references provided here.

OVERVIEW OF PETRI NETS

One story places an initial cut at the development of this representational technique with a young 14-year-old named Carl Adam Petri who, desiring a representation for understanding chemical interactions, began working on the approach. He formally proposed the Petri net methodology in his dissertation "Communication with automata" (1962). Initially, it was not widely adopted; however, the work was eventually recognized as a general tool with capabilities for modeling systems with many different properties, such as concurrency, parallel action, conflict, and so forth. Subsequently, its use spread throughout computer science, informatics, engineering, and related disciplines. The IEEE awarded Carl Petri the Computer Pioneer Award for establishing Petri net theory and noted that his work has not only been "cited by hundreds of thousands of scientific publications, but significantly advanced the fields of parallel and distributed computing" (Greengard, 2010).

Petri proposed his method as a general-purpose modeling tool for asynchronous systems (e.g., systems in which there is no timing requirement or time dependency). Applications that have been successfully modeled by Petri nets have such diverse characteristics as being: distributed, asynchronous, concurrent, hierarchical, and stochastic. For our purpose of developing models of workers, the approach is especially useful, as individuals at work often perform tasks in an asynchronous fashion, with stochastic properties. Furthermore, as we have the capability of modeling hierarchical structures with parallel activities (and conflict) with this methodology, aggregates of individuals (sub-teams and teams) can also be modeled.

Psychologists and engineers often employ job analysis when describing work or workers. Traditional job-analysis techniques are helpful for providing static descriptions of jobs and workers. Furthermore, conventional tools such as flow diagrams, narrative descriptions, and time-line analysis are useful for a variety of modeling problems; however, they impose constraints on the representation and are often not powerful enough to capture all the complexities of the work domain. Specifically, those tools make it difficult to expose critical time dependencies, task concurrencies, and behavior that is event-driven.

Petri nets are a very useful and powerful modeling tool and overcome these aforementioned shortcomings. Petri nets have both graphical and mathematical properties. The graphical aspect provides a useful tool for representing a system in a visual manner, making it an excellent communication medium. As a mathematical tool, algebraic equations, state equations, or other mathematical parameters are established that control the behavior of the system. The mathematical underpinning of the nets allows for rigorous analyses. My focus is to provide an overview of Petri nets and describe two applications. Readers specifically interested in the mathematics of Petri nets are referred to Reutenauer (1990).

The basic Petri net is a place/transition (P/T) net and is useful for general modeling problems. There are, however, many elaborations and extensions to the basic structure. For example, elaborations include Petri nets with time (c.f., Artifex, INA, ORIS, see Petri Nets World, 2010), stochastic Petri nets (c.f., ExSpect, F-net, PACE), and colored or high-level Petri nets (c.f., ALPHA/Sim, CPN Tools, Kontinuum), among others.If you would like a full treatment, a good overview of developments and extensions can be found in the book edited by Jensen and Rozenberg (1991). Readers interested in special issues are encouraged to explore the literature (cf., Peterson, 1981; Jensen & Rozenberg, 1991; Reisig, 1992) on the topic of interest, and to employ various software packages for the analysis of their models (cf., Alphatech, 1990; Chiiola, 1989; Metasoftware, 1992; Perceptronics, 1992). The website: Petri Nets World (2011) is a valuable source of information on software and features/requirements. Thus, we consider the basic structure here, and I have pointed you toward some sources for further information.

Perhaps the best-known dynamic modeling approach is Markov chain analysis. Although very useful in many situations, it does, however, have at least two common shortcomings. First, the model can quickly grow in size and out of control as the complexity of the modeled system increases (Melnyk, 2004). Second, Markov chain analysis is typically restricted to modeling probabilities with exponential distributions (Trivedi et al., 1995).

Distributions associated with modeling human performance are stochastic systems but often non-Markovian. Stochastic Petri nets (SPNs) have been developed to fulfill this need, along with deterministic stochastic Petri nets (DSPNs), which incorporate both generally distributed and deterministic firing distributions.

Current Applications

To date, the primary disciplines utilizing Petri nets are computer science, informatics, and engineering. Petri nets have applications, however, in other areas where modeling states, events, parallel activities, dependencies, and conflict are appropriate. For example, our prior work has utilized them for modeling individuals and teams performing different jobs, from a lab simulation of supplying ships at sea to actual operators in combat information centers aboard U.S. Naval warships (Coovert, Salas, & Cannon-Bowers, 1990, 1991; Coovert & Dorsey, 1994; Coovert, Craiger, & Cannon-Bowers, 1995; Coovert & Craiger, 1997; Coovert & Dorsey, 2000) and teams onboard U.S. Air Force AWACS platforms, an example of which is provided below. Most recently, we have modeled operators of micro-unmanned aerial vehicles (MUAVs) (Yagoda & Coovert, 2009), also described below. Other areas likely to be of interest to work psychologists include: workflow models (Salimifard & Wright, 2001; Feller, Wu, Shunk, & Fowler, 2009; van Hee, Hidders, Houben, Paredaens, & Thiran, 2009; Xu, Liu, Wang, & Wang, 2009), manufacturing systems (Aized, 2009; Dai, Li, & Meng, 2009), learning and tutoring systems (Heh, Chang, Li, & Chang, 2008; Huang, Kuo, Lin, & Cheng, 2008; Tung, Huang, Keh, & Wai, 2009), construction simulations (Biruk & Jaskowski, 2008); workplace risk analysis (Vernez, Buchs, Pierrehumbert, & Besrour, 2004), and human activity detection in video (Albanese et al., 2008).

As one can see, the methodology is widely applied to a variety of problems. This is owing to the fact that it is both a very general modeling tool and is very powerful. In its most elemental form, however, it can be quite simple. I now describe the basic components of Petri net models.

Basic Components

The basic elements of a Petri net are few; however, we can use these limited building blocks to construct very complex and powerful models. There are three elements in a Petri net, the first being the representation of an active component of the system. Active components, called *transitions*, are depicted as rectangles or squares and are used to represent agents or events. Depicted with circles, *places* are the second building-block type, and are used to represent passive components such as: channels, preconditions, enabling states, post conditions, or termination states. Connections between the active and passive system components are represented by *directed arcs* (arrows), with the direction of the head of the arc indicating the direction of the relationship (e.g., the flow of information; readers familiar with path diagrams where arrows indicate the direction of influence will be comfortable with the notation). As an example, an active component connected to a passive component and the passive connected to a subsequent active one are represented as rectangle–arc–circle–arc–rectangle. Table 12.1 presents the basic components and their descriptions. Two additional components include a weight function (W), which can be use to assign probabilities (or likelihoods) to an arc, and a marking associated with the places (M) to denote the current state of the net.

Owing to their graphical nature, Petri nets are a very helpful tool for communication. This is similar to the function of the path diagram used in structural equation modeling (Coovert, Penner, & MacCallum, 1990). Through the incorporation of tokens, however, these nets go beyond

TABLE 12.1

Basic elements of a Petri net

Element	Description	Visual depiction
Place	Passive element that represents the beginning and ending "states" of an activity	◯
Transition	Active element that represents an activity	▢
Token	Represents an entity, the state, or marking of the net	●
Arc	Shows directionality of the flow of information	⟶
Inhibiter arc	Prevents a transition from firing	⟶●

flowcharts and block diagrams and are useful for representing and simulating the dynamic and concurrent activities of a system. Tokens reside in places and move throughout the net as the transitions "fire." The firing of a transition is controlled by rules associated with the transition. In the simplest case, a transition is enabled and fires as soon as a token resides in the place that precedes it. Tokens are used to represent abstract or non-abstract entities within a model and are depicted with a solid circle.

Formally, the structure of a Petri net is a bipartite directed graph, $G = [P, T, F, W, M]$, where $P = \{p_1, p_2, \ldots, p_n\}$ is a set of finite places, $T = \{t_1, t_2, \ldots, t_m\}$ is a set of finite transitions, and $F = \{P \times T\} \cup \{T \times P\}$ is a set of directed arcs. The set of input places of a transition (t) is given by $I(t) = \{p \mid (p, t) \in F\}$, and the set of output places of transition (t) is given by $O(t) = \{p \mid (t, p) \in F\}$. The weights are specified as W:F $\{1, 2, 3, \ldots\}$ delineating the weight function for each arc. Finally, the marking of the places with tokens and the number of tokens is given by M:P $\{1, 2, 3, \ldots\}$.

Figure 12.1 provides examples of common connections. Let us consider what is presented in Figure 12.1 for a moment. The left panel depicts *OR-split*, a situation in which an operator, having reached the place labeled *a*, can proceed down one of two paths where transition 1 or transition 2 will fire. If transition 1 fires first, the sequence of tasks beginning with place *b* will follow, whereas, if transition 2 fires, the sequence of *a* beginning with place *c* will be enabled. *OR-join* depicts a situation in which two or more task lines become combined into one subsequent stream of behaviors. Once a token resides in place *a*, and another token resides in place *b*, transitions 1 and 2 will fire, placing one token in place *c* and thus enabling the subsequent tasks in that line to then be executed. The *AND-split* depicts a situation in which a token residing in place *a* will follow either path *b* or *c*, depending upon how the enabling state in transition 1 is executed. The *AND-join* is similar to the *OR-join* in that tokens residing in *a* and *b* will be combined by the operation in transition 1, resulting in the placing of a token in place *c*. The difference is one transition enables this in the *AND-join* operation, whereas it takes two transitions with the *OR-join* operator.

Reachability is an important topic in the analysis of Petri nets. It deals with the ability of a token to flow through the system and encounter or reach a desired state. Owing to complexity, it is not always evident when one looks at a net if any state is or is not reachable. As an example, consider

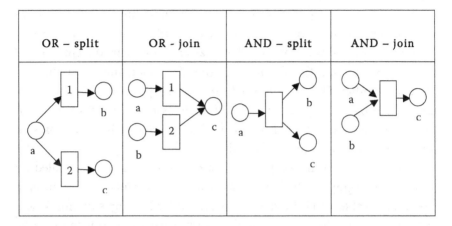

OR – split	OR - join	AND – split	AND – join

FIGURE 12.1
Common operations represented as Petri nets.

a net representing individuals working in a team. A token represents a piece of information that needs to flow from one individual in the team to another. Reachability analysis would verify that the information could (or could not) reach the intended teammate. Reachability also specifies a *state-space* (Kristensen, Christensen, & Jensen, 1998), as a directed graph can be constructed that has a node for each reachable marking. This is an important feature, given the complexity of any particular net and the desire to prove a unique state can be achieved. More on reachability can be found in Christensen and Kristensen (1997), Jensen (1997), and Pinzon, Jafari, Hanisch, & Zhao (2004).

Basic Elements

As mentioned, in the simplest case, only three elements are used to construct a Petri net model. Transitions reflect active model components, places represent passive components, and directed arcs add structure in terms of all linkages between: places-to-transitions and transitions-to-places. Tokens represent the current state of the system (e.g., where a token resides, that activity is being performed or that place is being occupied). A somewhat richer representation, with weight functions and markings, is often required. The weight functions are useful as a way to control behavior within a net when more than one arc can be traversed at any particular decision point. Consider a net modeling the behavior of individuals who can go down two different aisles after entering a store. One aisle contains dairy and the other pharmacy products. Weights applied to the arcs represent the likelihood of an individual going down one aisle versus the other. Hence, a .6 weight on the dairy arc would represent a preference over the pharmacy aisle (.4). Nets constructed of behavior typical of expert versus trainee can employ different weights to represent the performance of individuals in the two groups.

Another type of arc keeps a transition from firing and is called an inhibitor arc (graphically depicted as an arc with a solid circle on the end; see, again, Table 12.1). Inhibitor arcs are utilized in any situation where we do not want the activity ascribed with a particular transition to be executed. The markings of a net allow us to determine properties of the net (e.g., the amount of workload; the statistical distribution associated with a transition) at any particular time.

Some Common Examples

Table 12.2 contains some useful components for constructing graphs to represent an individual performing various aspects of a job. For example, the *fixed sequence* illustrates a situation in which a task is carried out in the order specified by the net. In this case, the token beginning in place *a* cannot be deposited in place *b* until the operations specified in transition 1 are carried out. Similarly, a token in place *b* cannot move to place *c* until it's been operated on by transition number 2. *Explicit choice* is a useful example whereby a situation exists with the token in place *a*, and rules _ are specified by the two linkages connecting it to transitions 1 and 2. As an example, consider a pilot who has two choices of action. Transition 1 specifies lowering the landing gear, and transition 2 specifies trimming the aircraft. Rules are embedded on the linkages connecting place *a* with transition 1 that would ensure the pilot completes a pre-landing gear-lowering checklist. In a similar fashion, rules embedded on the link connecting place *a* with transition 2 would ensure the pilot checks critical aircraft readings, such as: aircraft attitude, air speed, the vertical descent rate, altitude, and so forth, in order to properly trim the aircraft. Therefore, these rules and the mathematical structure really contain a good deal of the richness of the model. These specifics often underlie the more graphical nature that we see specified in the places, transitions, and directed arcs. The *probabilistic choice* block shows how we can easily constrain the firing of the transition according to statistical properties of the model. For example the linkageα might contain a probability level of .2, and the linkage from place a to transition 2 via the arc labeled β might contain the value .8. In this case, it would be much more likely that transition 2 would fire than would transition 1 (.8 versus .2). This type of probabilistic modeling can be very helpful, for example, in instances in which we are specifying models of novice versus normative versus expert behavior, and we see that, as skill is acquired, the relative probabilities change in the execution of certain behaviors over others. In our example, the .2 might increase to .8, whereas the original .8 decreases to a .2, depicting the evolution from novice to expert behavior. Another example reflecting increasing complexity of modeled behavior is the *interleaved sequence* block. Examination of that portion of the figure shows how tasks can be performed in parallel, but the upper task is actually broken into two task elements, and a delay Δ is built in before the onset of task 2. Finally, there are situations in which we may need to keep one event from occurring if something else is going on in a model. For example, pilots are taught to maintain a sterile cockpit environment during two critical phases of flight— takeoff and landing. In our example of an *inhibitor arc*, two different chains of behavior are represented. Beginning with place a, our example would represent the phase of flight for takeoff. The lower portion of that network, beginning with place d, represents pilot–cockpit communications. Once the pilot has begun the critical phase of beginning the takeoff, depicted by the firing of transition 1, the token then moving to place b would inhibit the communications within the cockpit. This would be represented by transition 2. Until the critical phase of flight of being clear of the ground and well established in the climb, there would be no talking in the cockpit, and then the inhibitor arc would be freed once the token passed from place b through the firing of transition 3.

With the basic elements specified, I encourage the reader to begin experimenting with the technique. Many useful tools exist in the software world for implementing Petri nets. The reader is encouraged to grab one of the tools and to construct a model of a problem they currently face. As with many tools, the best way to become comfortable is to utilize it, for that often brings both understanding and insight into its potential.

TABLE 12.2

Useful representations in many real-world models

Representational goal	Description	Graph
Fixed sequence	Two or more tasks are carried out in a specified order	a → 1 → b → 2 → c
Explicit choice	A selection is made between two tasks, according to conditions specified in ∂	a → ∂ → 1 → b; a → ∂ → 2 → c
Probabilistic choices	The selection between tasks is made according to probabilities specified in α and β. This allows for nondeterministic descriptions of task sequences	a → ∂ → 1 → b; a → ∂ → 2 → c
Interleaved sequences	Tasks are done in sequence, but overlap for a period of time. The upper task (1) is broken down into two elements (1a and 1b), and the lower task (2) starts after 1a is executed and a delay Δ has elapsed	a → 1a → b → 1b → c; Δ Delay; d → 2 → e
Inhibitor	If transition 1 fires prior to transition 2, a token in place *b* inhibits the firing of transition 2. Once transition 3 fires and removes the token from place *b*, inhibition on the arc is removed, and transition 2 is free to fire	a → 1 → b → 3 → c; d → 2 → e

TWO EXAMPLES

The overview of the technique complete, I now provide two real-world examples to illustrate how Petri nets can be utilized. I want to emphasize, however, that the examples I provide here are just the tip of the iceberg for modeling organizational phenomena. A strength of the technique is that the components (e.g., places, transitions, arcs) can be employed to model at various levels of abstraction. At a low level, a transition might be utilized to represent a user's mouse click, and, at a high level of abstraction, it might represent an entire component of a manpower planning system. Similarly, the mathematics embedded on the arcs might be simple weight functions or more complex equations. The level of abstraction and complexity chosen by the modeler needs to be appropriate to suit the purpose at hand.

Mission Specialist

The first example is a high-level representation of one individual in a three-member team that operates MUAVs for search and rescue. High level refers to the notion that the model focuses on major aspects of the job, such as at the duty level, as opposed to a low-level (or detailed) perspective, such as modeling task elements.

A pilot, flight director, and mission specialist are the three individuals in our team. The pilot focuses on flying the helicopter; the flight director ensures the safety of the team; and the mission specialist interprets information from an onboard camera. Petri nets were developed to represent each of the individuals in this team. To construct models, job-analysis information for each position was examined, as well as videotapes of the teams during search and rescue operations following Hurricane Katrina. Further details on this team task can be found in Yagoda and Coovert (2009).

Figure 12.2 presents the Petri net representation of the MUAV mission specialist. Transitions in the model represent behavior at a job duty level, and so this is a macro perspective of what the operator does. A more detailed model could be built by utilizing subnets depicting job tasks or job-element activities and embedding them within the duty-level transitions of the figure, but, for our purposes, we will model the operator at this macro level.

The uppermost sequence of places and transitions in Figure 12.2 illustrates the mission specialist preparing for flight. Major duties include rehearsing and completing communications and preflight payload check prior to takeoff. The next sequence represents the operation of the payload. The mission specialist is ensuring safety and flight statuses and checks communication with the pilot, capturing and interpreting video feeds, and so forth. Following that, the payload specialist continues communicating

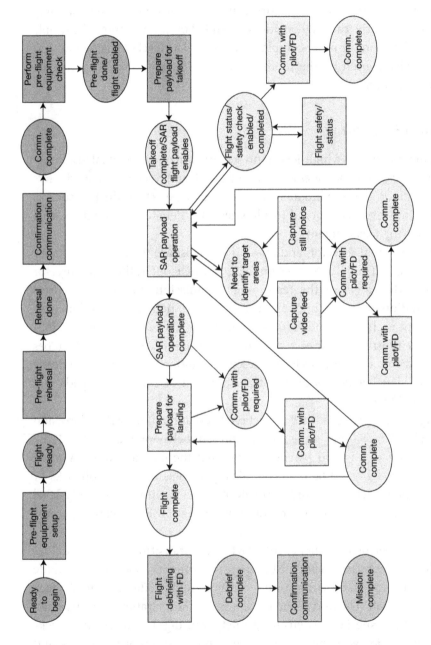

FIGURE 12.2
Petri net representation of a mission specialist operator who is part of a three-person team operating a micro aerial vehicle for search and rescue operations.

TABLE 12.3

Micro Air Vehicle Mission Specialist Major Job Duties

Mission specialist

1. Task is completely mediated
2. SM expertise and training before entering field
3. Preflight rehearsal
4. Preflight equipment check
5. Operate payload camera on board MUAV via handheld remote
6. Target views of damaged/interesting areas
   - Capture video feed
   - Capture still photos
7. Provide mission confirmation communication to pilot and FD
8. Provide relevant warning communication to pilot and FD
9. Flight debriefing with FD
   - Check to make sure all target views/images were captured

with the pilot and prepares the payload component for landing. Upon landing, a debriefing occurs, and the mission is complete. The specific tasks associated with the MUAV network in Figure 12.2 are presented in Table 12.3.

This represents a high-level perspective of the mission-specialist job. It is useful for communicating and describing the tasks or duties performed by this operator. The high-level (macro perspective) representation is employed for training purposes and also communicating with individuals with little experience or expertise in the area depicted by the Petri net. An advantage of Petri nets, compared with a representation built from a flowchart, is that the net can be executed and utilized to answer various questions about operator performance. These are dynamic models of a system and can be utilized to evaluate the behavior and/or overall performance of a system. Structural equation models, although useful, tend to deal with static components as well. The measurement model depicts how well the constructs are represented by indicators, whereas the structural model depicts the influence of one latent variable on another, but it is not a dynamic representation of the system in that it is not executable. Much can be learned about the behavior of a nondeterministic system by running simulations.

I have already mentioned the usefulness of this type of representation for training purposes. It has also proven most helpful for various purposes in discussions with subject-matter experts. Being able to point to and discuss a particular part of the network facilitates discussion on all sides. Petri nets can also be useful to simulate a reconfiguration of the job in terms of tasks completed or the sequence in which tasks are accomplished. Showing an incumbent how they took path A–C–F–G and it took them 94 seconds, whereas experts follow A–B–L–T and it takes only 61 seconds can be most illuminating. Finally, the technique often facilitates traditional analyses. Yagoda and Coovert (2009) present data whereby analyses of communication between team members are facilitated by this type of representation.

AWACS Team

A second example describes three individuals working as a team aboard an Air Force AWACS. The three team members are *combat air patrol* (CAP), *strike* (STK), and *high-valued asset* (HVA) *protector*. In one possible configuration, CAP serves as a leader of the team and typically provides a defensive role for the forces in the airspace. STK is an offensive player in this team, charged with pulling together strike packages (e.g., radar jammer, weapons platform). HVA protector directs assets that are often unable to protect themselves, such as tankers and intelligence platforms. A cognitive task analysis of these jobs revealed nine major job duties or categories. These categories are *pre-mission planning, a priori knowledge, directing, situational awareness, resource management, dynamic operational planning and prioritizing, individual internal cognitions (reminders), communications*, and *team issues*. Within these nine major categories are 31 primary duties. These categories and duties are listed in Table 12.4. There are approximately 260 tasks associated with these 31 primary job duties. Details of the cognitive task analysis are in Gordon, Coovert, & Elliot (2012).

A Petri net depiction of this three-member team and their duties is shown in Figure 12.3. The figure is a model of the team performing the duties on the job (e.g., in the aircraft), and so the duties in the *pre-mission planning* category are not represented as they have already taken place. This depiction is somewhat different from the example provided earlier. In the MUAV mission specialist example, the tasks and duties associated with each team member are unique. The AWAC team is different in that

TABLE 12.4

Major Categories of AWACS Weapons Director Performance

1. **Pre-mission planning**
   - Mission specific directives (devise external to the team)
   - Contracting (team planning phase)
   - Individual objectives (tasks carried out by individual WDs during mission planning)

2. **A priori knowledge**
   - Knowledge obtained through training and experience
   - Knowledge received during pre-mission briefing

3. **Directing**
   - Routine events
   - High demand routine events
   - Non-routine critical events

4. **Situational awareness**
   - Remain aware of the Big Picture
   - Monitor aircraft in the area of operations
   - Be aware of potential conflicts
   - Track weather conditions

5. **Research management (goal)**
   - Cognitive actions: attend and track data; identify timing of task execution
   - Physical actions: gather resources for use; use resources
   - High-level goals

6. **Dynamic operational planning and prioritizing**
   - Reassess the situation and prioritize events
   - Reclassification
   - Miscellaneous

7. **Individual internal cognitions (reminders)**
   - Maintain awareness of job knowledge
   - Attend to and track data
   - Interpret data
   - Operational problem solving and decision-making

8. **Communications**
   - During pre-mission planning
   - During dynamic operational planning and prioritizing
   - During directing
   - Expressly for team issues
   - To maintain situational awareness

9. **Team issues**
   - Member communication
   - Problem solving
   - Communication of tasks
   - Cooperation

each member can perform all of the tasks in the nine cognitive/behavioral categories and will do so depending upon permission assignments. So, instead of a separate net for each operator, we employ a hierarchical representation, where each operator can perform any cognitive/behavioral categories, duties, and tasks specified therein. To accomplish this, each operator is denoted by a separate token. The readings cited earlier on colored Petri nets are a good overview for further details and examples of this type of representation. For this type of team job, representing each operator as a separate token allows for the clear presentation of individuals performing separate duties, tasks, and activities concurrently (in parallel) with one another. The center of the figure contains a "holding pen" or initial place for the three operators.

Let us consider as an example the three-member team taking action after receiving an intelligence warning ("Pigpen, Ajax. Possible Prithvi at estimated zero niner twenty north, seventy-eight east"). The warning provides the location of a fleeing ground target posing an immediate threat to a high-valued asset. The target must be attacked and requires coordinated action on the part of the three members of the team. STK must immediately engage in five cognitive/behavioral categories (*a priori knowledge, individual internal cognition, situational awareness, dynamic planning and prioritizing, communicating*); CAP engages in two (*dynamic planning and prioritizing, communication*); HVA protector engages in two (*team issues, directing*). An animation of the network executing can be viewed at http://dl.dropbox.com/u/12291204/Animation%20of%20a%20 Petri%20Net%20Representation%20of%20a%20team.pptx.mp4.

To provide a thorough example, refer to the tasks for the AWACS operator presented in Morehouse (1997). These are tasks associated with the *directing routine events* category in which the weapons directors engage. Each of these specific tasks can be represented as a small Petri net that is part of the larger hierarchical structure (Figure 12.3). Consider the entire stream of behaviors that need to be completed upon receiving the intelligence warning. These cognitions and behaviors are represented as a sequence of hierarchical nets and elaborations. By considering the information presented in Figures 12.3 and 12.4, we can get a feel for the full scope of behaviors performed by the HVA team member when engaged in one of the possible behaviors for directing routine events. Here is what happens. First, the communication comes into the team, and each team member understands the appropriate behaviors that must be executed. For our

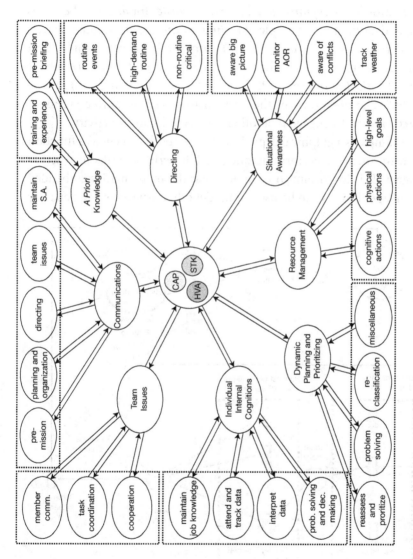

FIGURE 12.3

A three-member team aboard an AWACS. Eight major job categories and their duties are depicted. As a hierarchical network, each place within the broken-outlined box can be further elaborated into the tasks associated with that duty.

example, the HVA weapons director will execute a *directing* task; see Figure 12.4. (For clarity purposes, the entire state space is not illustrated. Dashed arcs present possible paths, whereas the solid arcs depict the path taken in our example. The dashed outlined boxes represent subnets in our representation.) The *cognitive and behavioral cluster* for *directing* becomes instantiated, and, in our example, *directing routine events* becomes active. From the routine tasks, *request and interpret track ID (F)* is enabled and completed. As part of that, the *request and interpret track ID* subnet number 8—*display/interpret PDS remote emitter tabular display*—is completed. The operator can then return to *directing routine events* or (depicted) return to engage in another behavioral-cluster activity.

This example is a graphical depiction of the steps that occur as a function of one team member performing one possible series of tasks in reaction to a trigger. It is important to recognize that the mathematics embedded in the linkages or arcs can be used to model other aspects of the behavior

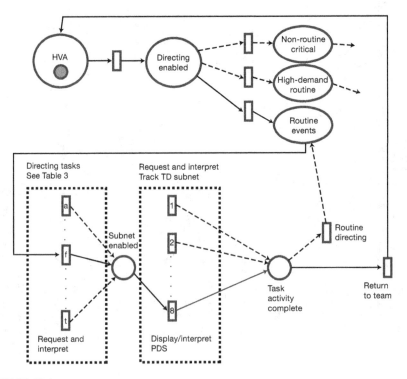

FIGURE 12.4
This network is an elaboration depicting the HVA team member performing the directing task, including subnet tasks and activities.

of the system. For example, at any place where more than one directed arcs leaves that place, a probability can be associated with the arc, and that probability and the distribution can be used to model the behavior of the individuals. As another example, consider the behavior of an expert performing this series of tasks, versus the behavior of a novice. Similarly, times can be placed within the network as well. In our example, the execution of this series of tasks and activities would take on the order of 35 seconds for a trained WD, whereas a novice may take upwards of a minute or more.

As in the earlier example, the representation of this team could be put to other purposes as well, such as finding an optimal organizational structure of the team. Another would be to simulate the impact of a change in the weapons-director system interfaces and note the impact of completion time, errors, false alarms, and so forth. In sum, modeling a team in this fashion provides many advantages not provided in other techniques.

SUMMARY

This chapter serves as an introduction to a technique for modeling simple, moderate, and complex relationships. The method has been widely applied in other disciplines, and it is equally applicable to constructs and relationships found in the world of work. These relations exist between individuals, individuals interacting with devices, and individuals interacting within and across teams.

In the case of traditional statistical and methodological approaches, we start simple and build models. For example, we might begin to build a model in an area by examining the relationship between two variables with a simple correlation. As understanding increases, we add variables to create constructs and utilize methodologies such as regression, factor analysis, path analysis, and structural equations. However, these methods are often still deficient for modeling and testing—especially via simulation —some real-world complexities, such as parallelism, concurrency, conflict, as well as others mentioned in the introduction of this chapter.

In a similar fashion, with Petri nets, we begin with a simple representation and build, often adding layers of hierarchical complexity and specifying relations via mathematical equations or statistical distributions.

Our basic elements in Petri nets consist of: transitions, places, and directed arcs. Beginning with very simple, straightforward models, these become elaborated through the incorporation of mathematical and statistical relations that facilitate the development of networks of various sorts, often representing increased complexity, hierarchical structures, and distributed parallel components.

For those interested in studying organizational phenomena, the method can be applied to a host of problems. Consider, for example, job analysis, especially when behavioral sequences or time need to be represented and modeled. Job design/redesign is another natural application for the technique. Application allows for the reconfiguration of individuals or devices, or the sequence in which tasks are done. By incorporating the probability of one part of the net being traversed versus another, along with the element of time to completion, we can build models of performance. Sometimes, likelihood estimates (as in fuzzy sets) or prior probabilities (as in Bayesian models) can also be utilized if appropriate. This typically means having access to, or being able to compute, these estimates. Manpower planning systems can also be constructed with this technique. Organizational structures of varying types (e.g., hierarchical, organic) can be constructed, and individuals can be represented as tokens that move throughout the system. Training systems can be enhanced through the use of this technique. The ability to graphically depict the process of work that needs to be done is often a greater advantage to a novice trying to understand complex work relations. It can also facilitate the description of that evolution of cognition's behaviors as a novice evolves to expert performance. Traditional performance measurement and diagnostic systems can also be impacted through the application of this methodology.

In conclusion, managers and I/O psychologists often face problems where the typical methods they apply, although helpful, are deficient for addressing the issue at hand. If you encounter such a situation, try sketching the problem using the basic components of a Petri net, specifying the constructs with places and transitions and the relationships among them with an appropriate type of arc. You will find this exercise most helpful. When ready, take the next step by putting it into one of the available software programs and watch your model come to life! Push the boundary conditions of your understanding by changing parameters and relationships. You might just see the issue facing you in a new light, while simultaneously discovering there is a new and powerful tool for your use.

ACKNOWLEDGMENT

The nets describing the MUAV operators were developed by Rosemarie Yagoda under my direction, as part of her senior honors thesis at the University of South Florida. Rosemarie is now in the Human Factors Ph.D. program at North Carolina State University.

REFERENCES

Aized, T. (2009). Modeling and performance maximization of an integrated automated guided vehicle system using coloured Petri Nets and response surface methods. *Computers & Industrial Engineering, 57*(3), 822–831.

Albanese, M., Chellappa, R., Moscato, V., Picariello, A., Subrahmanian, V. S., Turaga, P. et al. (2008). Constrained probabilistic Petri Net framework for human activity detection in video. *IEEE Transactions on Multimedia, 10*(6), 982–996.

Alphatech, Inc. (1992). *Modeler.* Burlington, MA: Author.

Biruk, S., & Jaskowski, P. (2008) Simulation modeling construction project with repetitive tasks using Petri Nets theory. *Journal of Business Economics and Management, 9*(3), 219–226.

Chiiola, G. (1989). *GreatSPN.* Torino, Italy: University di Torino.

Christensen, S., & Kristensen, L. M. (1997). State space analysis of hierarchical Coloured Petri Nets. In B. Farwer, D. Moldt, & M. O. Stehr (Eds.), *Proceedings of Workshop on Petri Nets in Systems Engineering—Modeling, Verification, and Validation* (Department of Computer Science Report no. 205, pp. 32–43). Germany: University of Hamburg,.

Coovert, M. D., & Craiger, J. P. (1997). Modeling performance and establishing training criteria in training systems. In K. Ford, S. Kozlowski, K. Kraiger, E. Salas, & M. Teachout (Eds.), *Improving training effectiveness in work organization* (pp. 47–71). Hillsdale, NJ: Lawrence Erlbaum Associates.

Coovert, M. D., Craiger, J. P., & Cannon-Bowers, J. A. (1995). Innovations in modeling and simulating team performance: Implications for decision making. In R. Guzzo & E. Salas (Eds.), *Team effectiveness and decision making in organizations: Frontiers of industrial and organizational psychology* (pp. 149–203). San Francisco, CA: Jossey-Bass.

Coovert, M. D., Cannon-Bowers, J. A., & Salas, E. (1990). Applying mathematical modeling technology to the study of team training and performance. *Proceedings of the National Security Industrial Association's 12th Interservice/Industry Training Systems Conference* (pp. 326–333). Orlando, FL: PM TRADE.

Coovert, M. D., & Dorsey, D. (1994). Simulating individual and team expertise in a dynamic decision making environment. In A. Verbraeck, H. G. Sol, & P. W. G. Bots (Eds.), *Proceedings of the Fourth International Working Conference on Dynamic Modeling and Information Systems* (pp. 187–204). Noordwijkerhout, The Netherlands: Delft University Press.

Coovert, M. D., & Dorsey, D. W. (2000). Computational modeling with Petri nets: Solutions for individual and team systems. In D. R. Ilgen & C. L. Hulin (Eds.), *Computational modeling of behavior in organizations: The third scientific discipline* (pp. 163–181). Washington, DC: American Psychological Association.

Coovert, M. D., Penner, L., & MacCallum, R. C. (1990). Covariance structure modeling in personality and social psychological research: An introduction. In C. Hendrick & M. Clark (Eds.), *Review of personality and social psychology: Research methods in personality & social psychology* (Vol. II, pp. 291–330). Newbury Park, CA: Sage.

Coovert, M. D., Salas, E., & Cannon-Bowers, J. A. (1990). Modeling team performance with Petri nets. *Proceedings of the 1990 Symposium on Command and Control Research* (pp. 288–296). McLean, VA: Science Applications International Corporation.

Coovert, M. D., Salas, E., & Cannon-Bowers, J. A. (1991). Process models of team behavior. *Proceedings of the American Control Conference*. IEEE Press.

Coovert, M. D., Salas, E., Cannon-Bowers, J. A., Craiger, P., & Takalkar, P. (1990). Understanding team performance measures: Application of Petri nets. *Proceedings of the 1990 IEEE International Conference on Systems, Man, and Cybernetics* (pp. 387–393). Washington, DC: IEEE Computer Society Press.

Dai, X., Li, J., & Meng, Z. (2009). Hierarchical Petri net modeling of reconfigurable manufacturing systems with improved net rewriting systems. *International Journal of Computer Integrated Manufacturing, 22*(2), 158–177.

Feller, A. L., Wu, T., Shunk, D. L., & Fowler, J. (2009). Petri Net translation patterns for the analysis of eBusiness collaboration messaging protocols. *IEEE Transactions on Systems Man and Cybernetics: Part A—Systems and Humans, 39*(5), 1022–1034.

Gordon, T.G., Coovert, M. D. & Elliott, L. R. (2012). Integrating cognitive task analysis and verbal protocol analysis: A typology for describing jobs. In M. A. Wilson, W. Bennett, Jr., S. G., Gibson, & G. Michael (Eds.), *The handbook of work analysis: Methods, systems, applications, and science of work measurement in organizations.* New York, NY: Routledge Academic.

Greengard, S. (2010). Obituary Carl Adam Petri, 1926–2010. *Communications of the ACM, 53*(9), 14.

Heh, J. S., Chang, J. C., Li, S. C., & Chang, M. (2008). Providing students hints and detecting mistakes made by students in a virtual experiment environment. *IEEE Transactions on Education, 51*(1), 61–68.

Huang, Y. M., Kuo, Y. H., Lin, Y. T., Cheng, S. C. (2008). Toward interactive mobile synchronous leaning environment with context-awareness service. *Computers & Education, 51*(3), 1205–1226.

Jensen, K. (1997). *Coloured Petri Nets. Basic concepts analysis methods and practical Use. Vol. 2, Analysis Methods* (Monographs in Theoretical Computer Science, 2nd corrected printing). Berlin: Springer-Verlag.

Jensen, K., & Rozenberg, G. (Eds.) (1991). *High-level Petri nets: Theory and application.* Berlin: Springer-Verlag.

Kristensen, L. M., Christensen, S., & Jensen, K. (1998). The practitioner's guide to coloured Petri nets. *International Journal on Software Tools for Technology Transfer, 2,* 98–132.

Melnyk, R. V. (2004). Petri Nets: An alternative to Markov Chains. *Archives of the Reliability Information Analysis Center,* First Quarter.

Metasoftware. (1992). *Design CPN.* Boston, MA: Author.

Morehouse, J. W. (1997). *E-3 Weapons director task list.* Department of the Air Force, Air Combat Command.

Perceptronics (1992). *Percnet/hsi user's manual.* Woodland Hills, CA: Author.

Peterson, J. L. (1981). *Petri nets and the modelling of systems.* Englewood Cliffs, NJ: Prentice Hall.

Petri, C.A. (1962). *Kommunikation mit automaten.* Schriften des IIM Nr. 2, Institute fur Instrumentelle Mathematik, Bonn. English translation: Communicating with automata. Technical Report RADS-TR-65-377 (1966). New York: Griffiss Air Force Base.

Petri nets (2010, June). 31st International Conference on Application and Theory of Petri Nets and Other Models of Concurrency. Braga, Portugal.

Petri nets (2011). 32nd International Conference on Application and Theory of Petri nets and Concurrency. Tyne, UK.

Pinzon, L., Jafari, M. A., Hanisch, H. M., & Zhao, P. (2004). Modeling admissible behavior using event signals. *IEEE Transactions on Systems Man and Cybernetics: Part B—Cybernetics, 34*(3), 1435–1448.

Reisig, W. (1992). *A Primer in Petri net design.* Berlin: Springer-Verlag.

Reutenauer, C. (1990). *The mathematics of Petri nets.* Hartford, England: Prentice Hall.

Salimifard, K., & Wright, M. (2001). Petri Net-based modeling of workflow systems: An overview. *European Journal of Operational Research, 134*(3), 664–676.

Trivedi, K. S., Bobbio, A., Ciardo, G., German, R., Puliafito, A., & Telek, M. (1995). Non-Markovian Petri Nets. In *SIGMETRICS '95*, pp. 263–264.

Tung, M. C., Huang, J. Y., Keh, H. C., & Wai, S. S. (2009). Distance learning in advanced military education: Analysis of joint operations course in the Taiwan military. *Computers & Educations, 53*(3), 653–666.

van Hee, K., Hidders, J., Houben, G. J., Paredaens, J., & Thiran, P. (2009) On the relationship between workflow models and document types. *Information Systems, 34*(1), 178–208.

Vernez, D., Buchs, D. R., Pierrehumbert, G. E., & Besrour, A. (2004). MORM—A Petri Net based model for assessing OH&S risks in industrial processes: Modeling qualitative aspects. *Risk Analysis, 24*(6), 1719–1735.

Yagoda, R., & Coovert, M. D. (2009). Modeling human–robot interaction with Petri-nets. *Proceedings of the Human Factors and Ergonomics Society,* San Antonio, TX, 1413–1417.

Xu, L. D., Liu, H. M., Wang, S., & Wang, K. L. (2009). Modeling and analysis techniques for cross-organizational workflow systems. *Systems Research and Behavioral Science, 26*(3), 367–389.

13

A Brief Primer on Neuroimaging Methods for Industrial/Organizational Psychology

Cory S. Adis and James C. Thompson

Before the 1980s, few researchers in cognitive psychology consulted with researchers interested in understanding the brain. Similarly, few brain researchers were interested in how the mind works. This state of affairs led philosopher Mario Bunge to make the statement that the study of cognition had been brainless, and the study of the brain had been mindless. More than 30 years later, and despite remarkable improvements in neuroimaging technology, the same criticisms that were leveled against cognitive psychology could be applied to I/O psychology. I/O psychology has been a brainless science. Despite the emergence of areas such as social cognition (Fiske & Taylor, 1991) and social cognitive neuroscience (Lieberman, 2007) that begin to span the distance between our field and neuroscience, in I/O psychology, we have yet to pay serious attention to the importance of the brain.

Neuroscientists are laying the foundation by investigating how the brain is wired for social living (Ochsner & Lieberman, 2001; Adolphs, 2003, 2009; Lieberman, 2007). In fact, many neuroscientists are actively investigating the "social brain hypothesis," which posits that the human brain has evolved from a quarter of its volume to its current size because of the survival advantages of our social nature (Byrne & Whiten, 1988; Allman, 1999; Barrett & Henzi, 2005; Dunbar & Schultz, 2007). Many of the findings produced by social neuroscience could have implications for I/O psychology, which has its major dealings in social-level phenomena.

Neuroscientific insights into areas such as cooperation (Rilling et al., 2002), deception (Spence et al., 2001; Langleben et al., 2002; Lee et al., 2002), and trust (Winston, Strange, O'Doherty, & Dolan, 2002; Yamagishi et al., 2003) are just a few of the ways in which I/O psychology can benefit from expanding its borders.

In this chapter, we describe some commonly used technologies in neuroscience and discuss how they may be applied to central research domains in I/O psychology. Our purpose is not to provide a lengthy technical guide, but rather a primer to promote neuroscientific literacy within the I/O community. The techniques we describe are a small subset of all the measurement approaches used in the many branches of neuroscience. We limit our focus to a few methodologies within the following technologies:

- structural magnetic resonance imaging (MRI) for creating structural pictures of the brain;
- functional magnetic resonance imaging (fMRI) for creating mappings of brain activity; and
- electroencephalography (EEG) for measuring the electrical output of the brain.

In the remainder of the chapter, we explain these measurement techniques and encourage two means of enriching I/O psychology with brain-based data. First, neuroimaging provides a means of testing the psychological theories at the level in which they are ultimately constrained —the physiological level. Although not all theories will be easily tested with neuroimaging data, there should be some recognition that the mental phenomena we study must ultimately be produced by the brain of one or more individuals. Second, technological advances in neuroimaging equipment and methods are making it possible to use these measurement techniques in applied settings to address actual organizational issues.

Throughout the chapter, we suggest research directions for brain-based approaches to studying I/O topics. We also describe recent examples of studies using these technologies and discuss their immediate implications. From a purely epistemological perspective, it is no longer possible to have a comprehensive theory of psychology without incorporating some reference to the brain (e.g., Marr, 1982). Our purpose is to increase awareness of neuroimaging research within the I/O community, so that I/O psychologists might draw more heavily from the fields of neuroscience.

STRUCTURAL MRI

The technique of MRI is used for taking images of tissue, including that of the brain. This technique provides static images that can be used for discerning the structural anatomy of the brain. As MRI is similar to the simpler technique of computed tomography (CT), we will explain the use of CT as a primer for structural MRI.

Both CT and MRI construct 3D images from many 2D scans or *slices*. Much as a digital image is made up of pixels, each one of these slices is made up of a 2D matrix of data points. The size of the overall matrix, together with the number of elements within the matrix, determines the resolution of the image. Most research MRI scanners can yield a resolution of around 1 mm^2. To get a complete scan, multiple slices are acquired and reconstructed into a 3D volume. The 3D data points that make up the volume are called *voxels*, and these voxels are the basic unit of analysis in most MRI research.

CT is a good analogy for structural MRI, because it makes use of X-rays, with which most readers will be familiar. CT uses X-ray absorption properties to differentiate between bone, brain tissue, and cerebrospinal fluid (CSF). The bones of the skull absorb more X-rays than the other tissues and appear a different color on the photographic plates that capture the image. Likewise, the tissues of the brain absorb more X-rays than the fluid-filled ventricles. The scanner works by rotating around the head and imaging two dimensions in one slice. It repeats this process in the dimension perpendicular to its rotation to collect multiple slices and, hence, a 3D X-ray image of brain densities.

When taking structural images of brain tissue, one of the things researchers might be interested in doing is distinguishing between white and gray matter. Gray matter is composed mainly of dendritic branches and cell bodies where incoming signals are received and responses are processed. The response of a cell is either to produce an electrical pulse—an action potential—or not. White matter is composed mainly of axons —the part of the cell that carries the electrical pulse from the cell body to synapses with other cells. Axons tend to run in bundles called tracts and are white in appearance because of the fatty myelin sheath that insulates the electrical pulse in the axon, similar to how plastic coating insulates electrons in a copper wire.

Being able to differentiate between white matter and gray matter allows researchers to compare the volume of these brain tissues in specific areas of the brain, or to quantify the thickness of gray matter on the brain's outer surface (i.e., the cerebral cortex). Gray-matter volumes and cortical-thickness measurements allow researchers to infer the amount of brain tissue available to process information and perform cognitive tasks. Although this "more is better" assumption discounts the possibility that smaller volumes of gray matter could be acting more efficiently than larger volumes, there is evidence that this assumption is correct. For example, cortical volumes have been meta-analytically found to relate positively with intelligence in children and adults (McDaniel, 2005). Moreover, improved performance after training is positively correlated with brain volume in relevant areas (Boyke, Driemeyer, Gaser, Buchel, & May, 2008). In any case, whether it requires more volume or less volume of different brain tissues to produce better brain function is an empirical question, and one that is uniquely answered by structural MRI.

CT scans cannot distinguish between white and gray matter very well, because these tissues have similar densities and absorb similar amounts of X-rays. Though gray matter and white matter do not differ dramatically in their relative densities, they do have noticeable differences in their relative water concentrations. Magnetic resonance technology, which capitalizes on the inherent magnetic properties of various molecules, can detect small differences in water concentrations in different areas and can easily distinguish between gray matter and white matter, as well as the bones of the skull and the CSF.

A critical difference between MRI and CT is that, unlike CT, MRI does not use X-ray radiation, which is considered harmful. Moreover, unlike earlier imaging technologies (e.g., positron emission tomography (PET)), MRI does not image radioactive tracer molecules, which can also be harmful in large doses, prohibiting repeated or prolonged brain scans. To understand what is actually measured with MRI, take the example of the commonly imaged water molecule. Water is the most abundant molecule in the human body, making it highly useful for MR scanning.

Recall that water molecules contain two positively charged hydrogen ions (i.e., two H^+ cations) and one negatively charged oxygen ion (i.e., one O^{+2} anion). These two hydrogen cations naturally spin around a specific axis. Because these ions are charged, the spinning motion generates a small electrical current and a magnetic field on the ion's surface. A spinning magnetic field will exert a force (magnetic moment) on surrounding electric or magnetic fields, and the direction of this force changes with the orientation of the spin axis. The magnetic pulling of spinning ions creates a measurable quantity that is used for MRI.

The magnetic pull of any one ion is slight, and MRI requires a very powerful electromagnet to function. Even then, MRI measures the net magnetization of a large number of ions in one local area. The electromagnet exerts a powerful magnetic field around the head that interacts with the field of the spinning hydrogen cations in water molecules. Although the molecules remain in place, the positively charged hydrogen atoms shift the orientation of their spin and come into alignment, like millions of compass needles.

Once the hydrogen atoms are aligned, a radio-wave pulse is fired at the brain tissue, and the hydrogen atoms are momentarily knocked 90 degrees off their spin axes. When they return back to alignment, they release electromagnetic energy, which is picked up by detectors. Tissues with more hydrogen protons release more energy when the protons realign.

In sum, MRI makes use of a magnetic field that is sensitive to small perturbations, such as that caused by the position of electromagnetically charged particles such as the single positive hydrogen ions of water molecules. More water molecules mean more hydrogen cations and a greater perturbation in the magnetic field. In this way, MRI can be used to assess the water density of different areas and distinguish between gray and white matter.

These images of gray and white matter acquired using MRI can inform the study of cognition in several ways, but we will focus on one: voxel-based morphometry (VBM), which makes use of MRI's ability to distinguish between white and gray matter. As mentioned earlier, cortical gray matter is made up of dendrites and cell bodies, which are considered to be the major computational unit in the brain. In contrast, white matter is comprised of the myelinated fibers that connect brain regions (Figure 13.1). It is argued that the density of gray matter in a particular brain region, as measured using MRI, is related to the number and organization of neurons within that region (Fischl & Dale, 2000). Cortical gray-matter density might thus reflect how well a particular brain region is able to perform its role in cognitive or behavioral processes. VBM involves initially segmenting MRI images into those voxels that contain gray matter, those that contain white matter, and those that contain CSF. This segmentation is usually

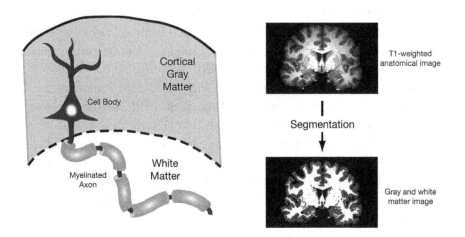

FIGURE 13.1
The anatomical basis of VBM. Cortical gray matter is made up primarily of dendrites and cell bodies (left). In contrast, the white matter is made up of neuronal fibers that are insulated with a fatty substance called myelin (left). The differences in the relative content of water and fat between gray and white matter leads to contrast on an MRI image (right). An imaging technique known as T1-weighting optimizes the contrast between these two tissue types. Post-acquisition segmentation algorithms can then be used to segment the T1-weighted image into a gray- and white-matter image. One can then examine the density of gray and white matter in these images.

based on image-intensity values: in a typical anatomical MRI image, white matter appears white, gray matter appears gray, and CSF appears black.[1] Gray and white matter images have been used as neurophysiological correlates of pathological conditions, such as Alzheimer's Disease (for a meta-analytic review, see Ferreira, Diniz, Forlenza, Busatto, & Zanetti, 2011). However, VBM has also been used extensively to study cognition and behavior. Recently, VBM has been used to study central areas in I/O, such as personality or creativity.

Personality and VBM

In recent years, the term "personality neuroscience" (Canli, 2008; DeYoung & Grey, 2009; DeYoung et al., 2010) has been added to the list of burgeoning brain-based research domains. The purpose of personality neuroscience is to develop causal models describing how biological mechanisms produce the psychological tendencies captured by traits. Personality traits are stable, structural constructs, and should be reflected in brain structure.

DeYoung and colleagues (DeYoung & Grey, 2009; DeYoung et al., 2010) used VBM to test the relationship between personality as measured by the Big Five and gray-matter density in hypothesized brain areas. For example, they reasoned that people draw positive emotion from being social, and that being social is more rewarding to extroverts than it is to introverts. They tested individual differences in gray-matter density in areas associated with reward sensitivity (the nucleus accumbens, amygdala, and orbitofrontal cortex). In the DeYoung et al. (2010) study, differences in brain structure in the medial orbitofrontal cortex were related to scores on the extroversion scale. Similarly, DeYoung et al. obtained significant relationships between gray-matter density in hypothesized areas and neuroticism, conscientiousness, and agreeableness scores. The only personality dimension that was not associated with individual differences in hypothesized brain areas was openness.

Evidence that there are recognizable differences in individuals' brains that relate to personality differences suggests that behavioral differences associated with personality dimensions can be traced to structural brain differences between individuals. By identifying the brain areas where gray-matter densities consistently covary with personality, we can build brain-based theories of personality, as demonstrated by DeYoung and colleagues (DeYoung & Grey, 2009; DeYoung et al., 2010). Knowing how brain differences contribute to the expression of different traits opens numerous doors for future research in both brain structure and personality.

Creativity and VBM

Human creativity is well within the purview of I/O psychology and has continued to attract recent attention (e.g., Baer & Oldham, 2006; Choi, Anderson, Veillette, 2009; Byron, Khazanchi, & Nazarian, 2010; Unsworth & Clegg, 2010; Zhang & Bartol, 2010). It has also been studied in the neurosciences through EEG (Dietrich, 2003; Fink & Neubauer, 2006; Jausovec, 2000; Jausovec & Jausovec, 2000), fMRI (Carlsson, Wendt, & Risberg, 2000; Bechtereva et al., 2004; Howard-Jones, Blakemore, Samuel, Summers, & Claxton, 2005; Asari et al., 2008), and through structural MRI techniques (Jung et al., 2009; Takeuchi et al., 2010).

Within structural MRI, Takeuchi et al. (2010) recently found VBM evidence of brain areas associated with creativity. Takeuchi et al. draw from biological evidence that tied creativity to dopaminergic circuitry and, in particular, the part of the dopamine system residing in the prefrontal cortex (e.g., Flaherty, 2005; Folley & Park, 2005; Geake & Hansen, 2005;

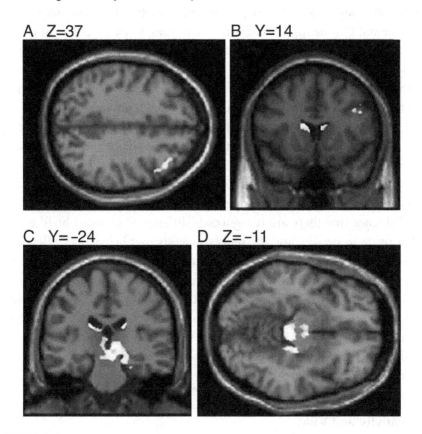

FIGURE 13.2

Regions of correlation between gray-matter volume and creativity test scores (p < 0.05 corrected for multiple comparisons. (A) Axial view. Regions of significant correlation are shown in the right DLPFC. (B) Coronal view. Regions of significant correlations are shown in the bilateral striata, together with a significant cluster in the right DLPFC. (C) Coronal view. Regions of significant correlations are shown in the regions of the bilateral striata, together with a significant anatomical cluster in the midbrain. (D) Axial view. An anatomical cluster with significant correlations is shown in the regions in the midbrain, extending into the parahippocampal gyrus. The anterior part of the cluster includes the substantia nigra and ventral tegmental area. The posterior part of the cluster includes architectures such as the PAG and the reticular formation.

Source: Adapted from Takeuchi et al., 2010.

Heilman, Nadeau, & Beversdorf, 2003). The prefrontal cortex is purported to produce novelty-seeking behavior and has a role in goal-directed thoughts and problem solving (Dietrich, 2004; Flaherty, 2005; Duch, 2007). This makes the prefrontal cortex a key area to look for individual differences in brain structure that relate to creativity.

Takeuchi et al. (2010) found that gray-matter volume of the dorsolateral prefrontal cortex is positively related to creativity, as measured by a divergent thinking task. Moreover, they found significant relationships with gray-matter density and creativity in other dopaminergic areas extending from the prefrontal cortex, such as bilateral striata, the precuneus, and midbrain areas (see Figure 13.2). These findings reveal insights into the underlying circuitry behind creative thought and the creative process and might someday be used to predict creativity based on structural brain images.

FUNCTIONAL MRI

Whereas structural MRI uses the magnetic properties of water in different brain tissues, fMRI is a neuroimaging technique that can take advantage of the differences in the magnetic properties of various chemicals or molecules, most commonly, differences in oxygen-rich blood (oxygenated hemoglobin (Hb)) and oxygen-poor blood (deoxygenated hemoglobin or (dHb)). Hb is diamagnetic (i.e., non-magnetic), as it has no unpaired electrons and zero magnetic moment, whereas dHb is paramagnetic (i.e., magnetic), as it has both unpaired electrons and a significant magnetic moment (for a detailed explanation, we refer the reader to the excellent textbook by Huettel, Song, & McCarthy, 2009). These differences in Hb and dHB cause them to respond differently to the MR pulse and therefore appear different under the MRI scanner.

The "functional" in functional MRI means this measurement approach examines the brain in action. Neuronal activity requires aerobic metabolism, which means that cells require the presence of oxygen to efficiently convert glucose into usable energy. The oxygen is delivered to the cells by Hb. The taking in of oxygen by active cells results in a local decrease in the amount of Hb and an increase in dHb in the capillaries and venous beds of the activated cortex. In response to the oxygen metabolism, there is a large increase in regional cerebral blood flow, bringing in new Hb and reducing the local concentration of dHb. It is the decrease in paramagnetic dHb that leads to an increase in magnetic signal, producing a response that is called the blood oxygen level-dependent (BOLD) response (Malonek & Grinvald, 1996). This signal is the source of data for most fMRI studies.

The hemodynamic activity underlying the BOLD response takes several seconds to develop and peaks at 6–8 seconds after stimulus onset. It then returns to baseline approximately 15–16 seconds following stimulus onset. The 6–8-second delay is known as the *hemodynamic lag*. This means that, if a hemodynamic brain response occurs, it will occur 6–8 seconds after the cognitive task begins. The hemodynamic lag has important implications for study design, as described below.

It is important, when reading fMRI studies, to remember that this technique is an indirect measure of neuronal activity. The precise nature of the coupling between neuronal activity and the hemodynamic response is not completely understood, although recent findings suggest that it is a combination of inputs to a cell and intracellular processing, rather than the spiking output of neurons (Logothetis, Pauls, Augath, Trinath, & Oeltermann, 2001). However, the interpretation of results from fMRI studies in terms of underlying neuronal activity should be done with caution. For example, an increase in BOLD signal in a particular region could be a result of excitatory activity, inhibitory activity, or some combination of both (Logothetis et al., 2001). It also means that, as we gain a further understanding of neurovascular coupling, we may be able to develop methods sensitive to selective aspects of neuronal activity (e.g., excitatory versus inhibitory inputs; Lee et al., 2010).

The great advantage of fMRI, as compared with other functional neuroimaging techniques such as EEG or PET, is the ability to both localize activity with high spatial precision and provide coverage of the entire brain in a non-invasive manner. In most typical research settings, the spatial resolution of each *voxel* is around 3 mm^3, although newer techniques have pushed the resolution to around 1.5 mm^3. At this resolution, it is most likely that fMRI is measuring BOLD changes resulting from the activity of populations of thousands of neurons, rather than single neurons. However, techniques that provide better spatial resolution, such as single-cell recordings, are both highly invasive (i.e. require neurosurgery) and only able to record from an extremely limited spatial area. EEG, which will be described later, can provide excellent temporal resolution, but is very limited in the spatial resolution it can provide. In contrast, during a typical fMRI acquisition, one collects signal from upwards of 20,000 voxels, covering the whole brain, with an acquisition approximately every 1–3 seconds. The benefit of this coverage is that one can gather information about the functioning of multiple brain regions together, rather than treating each region as a separate entity (Christoff & Owen, 2006).

Designing fMRI Studies

fMRI studies typically take a block design, an event-related design, or a combination of these two designs. The block design is used to make simple comparisons between two (or more) conditions, often an experimental condition and a control condition. Each participant will typically experience both conditions, such that they will be given one block of experimental stimuli lasting a predetermined duration, followed by a block of equal duration of the other condition (or conditions). By comparing images of the brain in these different conditions, researchers infer the involvement of brain areas in a task. This information could provide evidence for one theory or another. Henson (2006, p. 64) summarizes the logic by saying,

> If one can design experimental conditions that differ in the presence of a cognitive process according to one theory, but not according to another, then the observation of distinct patterns of brain activity associated with those conditions constitute evidence in favour of the first theory.

The timing and duration of these blocks must take into consideration the hemodynamic lag and the time it takes for blood oxygenation to return to baseline. Stimuli from the second conditions cannot be presented sooner than the return to baseline after the first condition, or else the effects of the conditions will be indistinguishable. However, the BOLD response to stimuli presented faster than this lag does add linearly. As blood oxygenation does not return to baseline for 15–16 seconds, the response to multiple stimuli presented with a consistent inter-event interval of less than about 10–15 seconds will reach a steady-state level. The block design, then, takes advantage of this steady-state response by presenting a sequence of stimuli from the same condition, and then a sequence of stimuli from another condition. For example, in an examination of subtle racial biases, an experimenter might present a series of faces of outgroup members followed by a series of faces of ingroup members. The block design yields the highest BOLD increase of any fMRI design—approximately 0.5–1 percent change in BOLD signal (Huettel et al., 2009).

The problem with the block design is that stimulus order becomes predictable, such that participants begin to anticipate the stimuli that will occur in the next block, and they show brain responses prematurely. This will diminish the difference between conditions and weaken any effect of the experimental condition that may be present. In addition, as the block design takes advantage of the steady-state BOLD response, it is not possible to resolve individual events within a block, making analysis strategies such as sorting fMRI responses based on performance (e.g., accuracy, nature of decision) impossible.

Some of the drawbacks of block designs are ameliorated by the event-related design. Rather than present blocks of stimuli from one condition, then blocks of stimuli from another, event-related designs randomize the presentation of stimuli such that stimulus order and time between stimuli are variable. The underlying assumption in event-related designs is that brain responses can be associated with individual stimuli, rather than steady-state activation being connected with a stream of the same stimuli. Each brain response is time-locked to the onset of a stimulus, and multiple responses to the same kind of stimulus can be averaged to reveal a typical brain response to that type of stimulus. If stimuli are presented in rapid succession, but with a randomized inter-stimulus interval, the linear summation of overlapping responses means that it is possible to use methods such as linear deconvolution to resolve responses to individual stimuli (Dale & Buckner, 1997). One can then also randomize stimulus order, reducing predictability, as well as sort events based on how people respond behaviorally to them. This design is known as a *rapid event-related* design.

The main drawback with this design is that it generally yields low BOLD increases—only 0.05–0.2 percent change in BOLD signal (Huettel et al., 2009). This slight change in blood oxygenation might be difficult to detect, resulting in Type II error. However, unlike block designs, event-related designs offer more flexibility in the way they are analyzed. For instance, event-related designs allow trials to be sorted based on performance data (accuracy, response latency), so that degree of brain response can be regressed on performance (as is typical of research designed to identify the brain regions involved in performing cognitive tasks).

Neuroimaging studies typically employ the subtraction method in order to make inferences about the sensory, cognitive, or motor contributions to the local BOLD response (Huettel et al., 2009). Ideally, the goal of the subtraction method is to have an active task and a control task that are identical but for the isolated component of interest. For example, in the first studies to demonstrate that the BOLD response increases as a function of sensory stimulation, Kwong and colleagues (1992) compared the MR response from the occipital cortex of participants under two conditions: lying in the scanner with the room lights on for 60 seconds, and lying in the scanner for the same length of time but with the room lights off. Using this design, Kwong et al. demonstrated activity in the brain resulting from the processing of visual inputs. Since that time, fMRI designs have become increasingly more sophisticated, but the majority of studies still rely on the comparison (or *contrast*) between two or more conditions.

To illustrate the subtraction method, consider the topic of conflict. In I/O research, there is substantial discussion of the antecedents and consequences of cognitive conflict, as opposed to affective conflict (for a review, see De Dreu & Weingart, 2003). When determining the relationship of various antecedents and consequences of these two constructs, we must typically rely on subjective ratings of the amount of each conflict type felt, or perceptions of the amount of conflict that exists in a group. With fMRI, it might be possible to distinguish between cognitive and affective conflict in brain scans and derive an index of the amount of each type that is experienced by the individual. For example, much research points to the amygdala (a small nucleus located deep beneath each temporal lobe) as the gateway to emotion. The degree to which the amygdala becomes activated during conflict processing should indicate the degree to which affective conflict is induced. In addition, whereas the rostral medial prefrontal cortex (the area underlying the middle of the forehead) is involved in resolving affective conflict, resolving cognitive conflict appears to require the ventrolateral prefrontal cortex (Ochsner, Hughes, Robertson, Cooper, & Gabrieli, 2009). This evidence demonstrates that affective and cognitive conflict are handled differently in the brain. Evidence such as this might allow us to assess the type of conflict the participant might be feeling without asking them. When antecedents are correlated with this index, we get a clearer picture of the types of stimulus that produce each type of conflict. When consequences are examined, we can be more confident that outcomes are the result of the correct type of conflict.

In the above example, fMRI is used to demonstrate that the brain responds differently to one type of conflict than to another. This provides evidence for the distinction between cognitive and affective conflict. An important consideration for the application of fMRI methodology in I/O is the logic of an experiment that showed distinct brain responses. We must build upon prior data establishing the selectivity of brain regions to a particular cognitive task. This is because activation of one brain area during one type of task does not mean that same area will not be activated by dissimilar tasks. Only after selectivity has been (probabilistically) established can we infer psychological states or cognitive operations based on activity in specific brain regions (Poldrack, 2006). Once a critical mass of data linking brain areas to cognitive tasks has accumulated, we can look at the amount of response from one brain area and infer the mental process occurring as an individual engages in a task. Fortunately, large bodies of evidence have been accumulating in the neurosciences, and much of it is being catalogued in databases. Since fMRI's introduction in neuroimaging in 1993, the number of studies using this technology has been growing steadily (see Figure 13.3 for a year-by-year publication count). Now is an opportune time to capitalize on what neuroscientists have learned.

In the traditional approach to functional-imaging research, activation levels of brain regions in experimental groups are compared with those of control groups; within-group differences are attributed to error (Underwood, 1975; Lamiell, 1981; Kosslyn et al., 2002). More recently, neuroimaging studies have begun utilizing predictive, between-person designs and regression analyses, instead of between-group designs and ANOVA (Kosslyn et al., 2002). According to Kosslyn et al. (2002), this shift in focus allows researchers to form more powerful theories by utilizing natural variation between people. For example, such an approach has been used to predict dispositional negative affectivity from activity in the right prefrontal lobe (Tomarken, Davidson, Wheeler, & Doss, 1992; Sutton & Davidson, 1997). Thus, if one can infer a causal relationship between activation and a cognitive task, one can predict cognitive performance from brain activation. In the section that follows, we detail how accumulated evidence from fMRI studies can be used to study leader performance from brain activation.

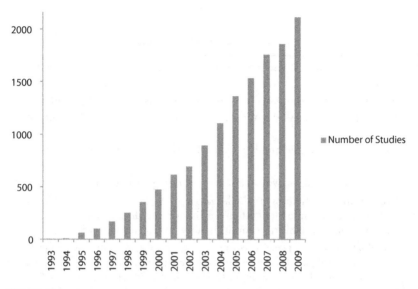

FIGURE 13.3

fMRI publications, year by year, since the technique's inception in 1993.

Source: Pubmed search of fMRI methodology by year.

Leadership and fMRI

The psychological study of leadership has progressed through many different perspectives, from individual-focused to situation-focused, and back to an intermediate state (Zaccaro, 2007). Along the way, leadership researchers have approached the topic from a multitude of directions (Yammarino, Dionne, Chun, & Dansereau, 2005). Additionally, there are many new leadership directions on the horizon, as the field becomes more differentiated (see Avolio, Walumbwa, & Weber, 2009, for a review). In a newer direction, researchers are turning to the brain as a source of data about leaders or leadership (e.g., Rock & Schwartz, 2006; Klein & D'esposito, 2007; Goleman & Boyatzis, 2008; Peterson, Balthazard, Waldman, & Thatcher, 2008;). Although leadership scholars have begun applying neuroscientific knowledge to the leadership domain, we are not aware of any studies directly using fMRI to study leadership. One way this could be accomplished is to relate activation in brain regions involved with leadership activities to leader performance. Table 13.1 depicts a multi-stage process for linking leadership to the brain using fMRI.

TABLE 13.1

A Research Plan Connecting Leader Cognition to fMRI Brain Scans

1. Identify important leadership processes (see Zaccaro, 2001, for an integrative framework).
2. Break processes down to cognitive (information-processing) components.
3. Identify brain areas linked to those cognitive processes in neuroscience literature and databases.
4. Design tasks that would mimic/resemble leader activities involving leader processes.
5. Collect data on brain activity of leaders performing those activities.
6. Use activation levels during multiple tasks as multiple predictors of leader performance (e.g., amount of activity in visual cortex during imagery task, amount of activity in mirror neuron circuitry during empathy task, etc.).
7. Reevaluate concept of leader performance—a complete definition will require a complex conceptualization of performance across multiple roles (see behavioral complexity; Hooijberg & Quinn, 1992; Denison, Hooijberg, & Quinn, 1995; Hooijberg, 1996; Hooijberg, Hunt, & Dodge, 1997; Boal & Hooijberg, 2000; Hooijberg & Schneider, 2001)

As an example, take a leader's potential to accurately perceive the motives and problems faced by individuals or groups of individuals—a quality described as social perceptiveness (Zaccaro, Gilbert, Thor, & Mumford, 1991). Social perceptiveness also has an analog in cognitive psychology—the process of mentalization (Frith, Leslie, & Morton, 1991; Frith & Frith, 1999; Blakemore, Winston, & Frith, 2004; see also Premack & Woodruff, 1978; Dennett, 1987). Mentalization is the process of inferring and manipulating the mental states of others (Frith & Frith, 1999). The mental states of other people are inherently unobservable, and so coming to understand what others are thinking or feeling can be difficult to accomplish. Neuroscientific work in this area might lead to insights into how social perceptiveness and mentalizing are accomplished.

Current theory maintains that people use their own mental states as a model for inferring how others feel (Blakemore et al., 2004; Mitchell, 2008). This is accomplished through mental simulation in which an individual is believed to mentally project him or herself into an alternative perspective (Buckner & Carroll, 2007; Mitchell, 2009). First, observers simulate how they would feel if they were placed in similar situations, and then assume that others feel the same way. In regard to how mentalization is accomplished in the brain, evidence from neuroimaging consistently finds the same brain regions activating when a person experiences a psychological state as when a person infers the psychological state of others (Blakemore et al., 2004; Mitchell, 2008). For example, one region involved with feeling physical pain, the anterior cingulate cortex, is also activated when that person watches a video of another experiencing pain (Singer et al., 2004). Similarly, when people estimate the preferences of another, they use the same brain region as when they self-report their own preferences (Mitchell, Macrae, & Banaji, 2004).

Interestingly, the areas of the brain that mediate this self-projection overlap greatly with areas of the brain used to recall autobiographical memories (Spreng, Mar, & Kim, 2009), suggesting that self-projection into another person's perspective for social perceptiveness is similar to self-projection into one's own personal past.

In a recent study, St. Jacques, Conway, Lowder, and Cabeza (2011) took a closer look at the brain areas involved with self-projection. Participants in this study wore a specially designed camera that continuously takes pictures, without input from the participant. As participants went through the course of their day, the camera took a stream of thousands of pictures from their perspective. One week later, participants were scanned in an MRI machine while viewing their own pictures and other participants' pictures. A block design was used such that an individual's own pictures and others' pictures were presented in alternating blocks. While viewing these pictures, participants were told to relive their own events or to understand the events depicted in others' pictures. Following stimuli presentation, participants made ratings of the extent to which they were able to relive events in the reliving condition, and the extent they were able to understand the events in the understanding condition.

The results of this experiment help to distinguish brain areas that are involved with reliving autobiographical memories from brain areas involved with understanding someone else's perspective. For instance, although both reliving and understanding used the medial prefrontal cortex (mPFC; an area along the midline between the two hemispheres in the very front of the brain), the ventral mPFC was more heavily recruited for reliving personal events, whereas the dorsal mPFC was more heavily recruited for understanding others' experiences. Perhaps most interestingly, participants' subjective reports of their reliving and understanding moderated the activity in these areas. In other words, in the reliving condition, participants showed greater activation in the ventral mPFC for trials upon which they reported better ability to relive the experience. In the understanding condition, participants showed greater activation in the dorsal mPFC for trials in which they reported better ability to understand others' experiences.

For both conditions, the level of activation varied with the ability of the participant to engage in cognitive processing (either recalling autobiographical memories or understanding another person's perspective). Although more research is necessary to further examine and replicate the results of St. Jacques et al. (2011), their findings offer preliminary evidence that may be useful in applied settings. In particular, activation levels in the dorsal mPFC might one day be used to make (reverse) inferences about an individual's social perceptiveness. If level of activation in the dorsal mPFC depends on the degree to which an individual is able to understand another person's perspective, then it is reasonable to look for stable individual differences in dorsal mPFC activation levels in order to predict individual differences in social perceptiveness.

Frith and Frith (1999) identify a system of three brain areas involved with mentalizing: the superior temporal sulcus detects goals of others, the inferior frontal regions represents those goals, and the medial prefrontal cortex represents mental states of the self for comparison with that of others. In fact, according to Mitchell (2008), some of the most consistent findings in cognitive neuroscience pertain to how inferences about other people are formed (see also, Blakemore et al., 2004). Since Frith and Frith's (1999) review, neuroimaging studies on social inference have consistently indicated activity in specific brain regions: the mPFC, inferior frontal cortex, temporoparietal junction, precuneus/posterior cingulate, amygdala, superior temporal sulcus, and the temporal pole (some of these areas are depicted in Figure 13.4; Mitchell, 2008).

By taking fMRI scans of leaders while they engage in a mentalizing task, researchers can relate activation in the above areas to mentalizing performance. If one, or all, of these areas is integral to the functioning of leaders, activation levels can be used to predict leader performance and aid in the assessment of leadership skills. In this manner, brain-scan assessments might one day be used to select leaders for hire or promotion, or to evaluate the effectiveness of leader-development programs. If the program is effective at inducing a certain use of the brain, we should expect pretest/ posttest differences in brain activation in areas involved with producing certain skills.

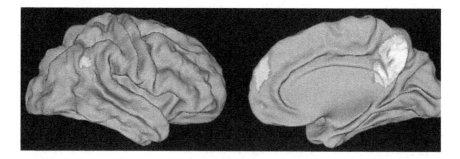

FIGURE 13.4

Three brain regions commonly modulated by tasks that require inferences about the mental states of other people. The image isolates the right hemisphere, showing the outer (lateral) view on the left, and the inner (medial) view on the right. Highlighted in the left panel is a region of the temporo-parietal junction, toward the back of the right hemisphere. Highlighted on the left side of the right panel is the medial prefrontal cortex—situated at the front of the brain's medial surface—and, toward the right (posterior) portion, the precuneus/posterior cingulate.

Source: Mitchell, 2008.

Of course, this is but one example of a cognitive function that would be necessary for leader effectiveness. A full fMRI assessment would look for activation patterns that indicate more cognitive functions, such as occipital lobe activity for its association with simulation of mental imagery (Kosslyn et al., 2004; Zacks, 2008), which might predict complex problem solving (Taylor, Pham, Rivkin, & Armor, 1998; Christensen & Schunn, 2009). One could also observe orbitofrontal activity for its association with planning (Wallis, 2007), which might predict a leader's skill at forming a strategy.

Organizational Citizenship Behavior and fMRI

The above discussion of fMRI in leadership research is just one example of how this technology can be used in I/O psychology. As another example, consider the area of organizational citizenship behaviors (OCBs). OCBs can be defined as behaviors of individuals outside of formal reward systems that facilitate effective organizational operations (Organ, 1988). One question regarding OCBs that I/O psychology is just beginning to address is that of the intentions of employees to produce these behaviors. However, there is little that is known about the motivational antecedents of OCBs, because current theory and methods have little to say about underlying intent behind these behaviors (Bolino, Turnley, & Niehoff, 2004).

As behaviors involved in task performance are specified by role requirements, we rarely concern ourselves with questions about what motives drive task performance. People engage in performance to obtain various outcomes (Vroom, 1964); the motives are simply to do the job that needs to be done. Although Campbell and colleagues (Campbell, 1990; Campbell, McCloy, Oppler, & Sager, 1993) included motivation, along with knowledge and skill, as determinants of performance, this construct does not explain what we mean by motive. Motivation is commonly conceptualized as a function of choice to perform, level of effort, and persistence of effort (Schmitt et al., 2003). As a good constitutive definition, this approach to motivation describes *what* it is, but not *why* it occurs. What is missing is the reason behind a certain choice.

Compared with task performance, the behaviors involved with contextual performance are less formalized and specified. These behaviors have been said to "shape the organizational, social, and psychological context that serves as the catalyst for task activities and processes" (Borman & Motowidlo, 1997, p. 100). They are outside the formalized role requirements and, therefore, done at the employee's discretion. As these are voluntary behaviors, researchers have greater reason to be concerned with, not only *what* is done, but also *why* it is done. Whereas motives to engage in task performance are fairly limited, motives to engage in contextual performance can be numerous.

Bolino et al. (2004; see also, Podsakoff, MacKenzie, & Hui, 1993) highlight the underrepresented role of motives in OCB research. They argue that researchers typically assume that OCBs are motivated by altruistic, or at least unselfish, goals. This assumption has been reinforced, in part, because OCBs have been found to relate to positive attitudes, such as high job satisfaction (Bateman & Organ, 1983) and positive affect (Kaplan, Bradley, Luchman, & Haynes, 2009). People are motivated to engage in positive behaviors because, not only do they help out someone else or the organization, but it also makes one feel good to perform OCBs.

However, as Bolino et al. (2004) point out: the potential dark side of OCB is rarely examined. In the way of examples of negatively motivated OCBs, Bolino et al. (2004, p. 234) offer, "self-serving motives, transgressions, [making] others look bad, dissatisfaction with or disinterest in one's in-role responsibilities, [and] dissatisfaction with one's personal life."

For example, self-serving motives for committing an OCB might be to manage one's image or influence a supervisor's performance ratings. Disinterest with in-role responsibilities might lead to seeking extra-role tasks to get out of more menial work. These negative motives are not typical, and Bolino et al. do not claim that these motives are the true drivers of OCBs. Instead, they argue that current theory and methods are unable to address these alternative motives and rule them out. Perhaps neuroimaging can be used to address the question of motives behind OCBs (or other contextual performance).

One of the advantages of fMRI is that it allows researchers to observe otherwise unobservable brain activity. Intentions are difficult to determine, because they are unobservable and internal to the actor. Some intentions might not be known by the actor. Other intentions that are known might be reported inaccurately, for example for self-preserving or self-aggrandizing reasons. With the appropriate theory, researchers might be able to detect something about intentions based on fMRI pictures of the brain in action.

No fMRI studies currently exist investigating OCB, although an exploratory experiment could easily be devised. For example, researchers could have a participant recount the most recent, or a recent and significant, OCB while in the scanner and observe the areas of the brain that are used to reflect on this occasion. Although little is known about what brain areas are active when a person thinks about engaging in OCB, one might suspect basic differences based on the original intentions behind the action. For example, Bolino et al. (2004) suggested positively and negatively motivated types of OCB. There are likely to be differences in the brain between the "feel-good," intrinsic motivation of helping someone out and the more calculative, extrinsic motivation of gaining favor.

Little is known about the difference between positive and negative intentions in the brain, although there is research that investigators might draw from in order to frame hypotheses. For example, the processing of empathy in the brain has been examined in past brain research (e.g., Farrow et al., 2001; Singer et al., 2004; Botvinick, et al., 2005) and might provide clues to why one might engage in OCBs. Empathy has been linked to helping behaviors both with (Preston & de Waal, 2002; Marsh, Kozak, & Ambady, 2007) and without neuroimaging (e.g., Batson, 1991). Based on past findings, Rameson, Morelli, and Lieberman (2012) recently predicted brain activity in a region of the mPFC in association with a task that required empathizing with photographs of people described in short scenarios. The mPFC would be a good candidate to examine in the present hypothetical study.

Given expectations for the involvement of the mPFC in empathic OCBs, we can devise a task that might let us differentiate between positively motivated OCBs and negatively motivated OCBs. Perhaps researchers could obtain photographs of co-workers prior to an MRI scanning session that could be shown to the participant while in the scanner. One option for a task could be to ask the participant to imagine that the featured co-worker asks for help meeting an approaching deadline. The participant can either decide to provide help or not. This can be repeated a few times with a few different co-workers of varying organizational level (i.e., peers, superiors, subordinates, etc.). After the scanning session, researchers could ask participants to reflect upon their decisions whether or not to help, and to report on the reasons behind these decisions. Based on reported reasoning, the researchers could classify the intent according to type and compare the brain responses elicited by each type. Assuming substantial differences between brain activity of positive intent and that of negative intent, subsequent researchers would be able to interpret the brain activity of later participants as they engage in helping decisions, and predict the intent behind those decisions.

At this point, it is important to remind the reader of the problem of reverse inference that must be taken into consideration any time brain function is linked to cognitive function. As discussed above, a good body of research is desirable before one can confidently say that a brain area produces a specific cognitive operation. The question of the origin of positively motivated and negatively motivated OCBs is a new area of research, and so selectivity of the mPFC cannot be established a priori. In other word, although we may be able to say that this brain area is implicated in OCBs that have empathetic origins, we cannot say that the mPFC produces empathy, or that activation of the mPFC means that empathy is occurring. The reader is referred to Poldrack (2006) for an insightful discussion of the reverse-inference problem and its resolution.

Real-Time fMRI

One very interesting advancement in fMRI technology is the ability to display brain scans in real-time. Whereas typical fMRI scans are averaged across multiple trials and used to show differences between experimental and control groups, real-time fMRI (rtfMRI) allows participants to see the activity in their own brains as they engage in cognitive operations. This feedback mechanism can be used to train individuals to willfully control activation in their own brains. Recently, it has been used to successfully train individuals to control the activation in a number of brain areas (see deCharms, 2007, 2008, for reviews). For example, deCharms et al. (2005) used rtfMRI to train participants to increase and decrease a number of areas responsible for modulating pain intensity (e.g., rostral anterior cingulate cortex, secondary somatosensory cortex, the insula, supplemental motor cortex, superior cerebellum, and superior temporal gyrus). Importantly, the participants' subjective responses to pain intensity decreased when they were actively focused on decreasing activation in these areas and increased when they were actively focused on increasing activation.

Although reduction in pain sensitivity is not the objective of most I/O psychologists, this technology might be utilized with promising results in other kinds of training as well. If rtfMRI can be used to control other brain regions, it may be used to make certain cognitive or affective states prepotent. For example, in the above section on leader mentalizing, we described the role of key brain areas that contribute to detecting the needs and motives of others. Perhaps biofeedback about control of activity in those regions could make a person prepotently sensitive to others' needs. Alternatively, this form of biofeedback could be used to boost baseline activity in areas of the dorsolateral prefrontal cortex associated with creativity (e.g., Takeuchi et al., 2010), or in the area of the inferior parietal lobe known as Broca's area. It is possible that practice activating the former could contribute to greater creativity, whereas practice activating the latter could contribute to greater verbal fluency.

ELECTROENCEPHALOGRAPHY/ MAGNETOENCEPHALOGRAPHY

Although structural MRI can provide details about the volume of different brain tissue, and fMRI can provide high-spatial-resolution information about hemodynamic changes associated with cognitive function, neither of these techniques can match the temporal resolution afforded by EEG

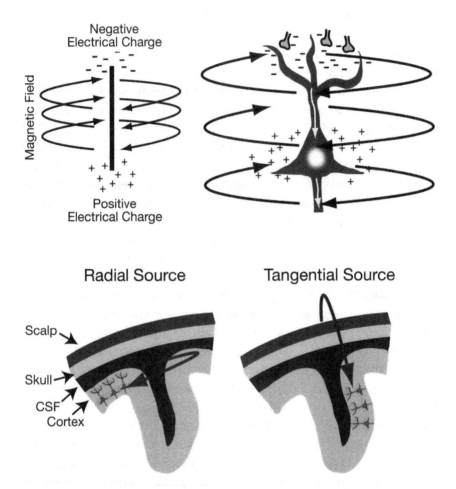

FIGURE 13.5

The basis of electro- and magneto-encephalographic signals. With the flow of any electrical current, an electrical dipole is produced, as is a magnetic field in the orthogonal direction to the dipole (top left). When inputs from a neighboring neuron, in the form of excitatory neurotransmitters, are released into the extracellular space, a current flows into the apical dendrites of the receiving neuron. This results in a net negative charge in this region of the neuron (top right). As the current flows through and out the neuron, a net positive charge occurs at the basal dendrites of the neuron. At the same time, a magnetic field is formed. If enough neurons fire at the same time, these currents (and fields) sum together to produce a source and can be observed from the scalp surface. If the neuronal sources are in the gyrus, and perpendicular to the scalp surface, the magnetic field cannot be detected (bottom left). If the neuronal sources are in the sulcal walls, and thus parallel to the scalp surface, the magnetic field can be detected outside the scalp (bottom right). In both cases the electrical activity would be able to be detected.

or magnetoencephalography (MEG). These techniques measure the electrical (EEG) or magnetic (MEG) signal associated with the synchronous activity of large populations of neurons (Figure 13.5). When there is excitatory input into a neuron, current flows from the presynaptic extracellular space into the cell body. This yields a net negative charge outside the neuron and a positive charge within the neuron, creating a *dipole*. When this dipole is created, a magnetic field tangential to the direction of the dipole is also created. Although recordings from outside the skull would not be able to measure the activity of a single dipole, if thousands to millions of dipoles of the same orientation fire at the same time, an electrical potential can be measured from the scalp. If the dipole is oriented tangentially to the cortical surface, the magnetic field can be measured as well.

EEG and MEG measure largely the same neural phenomena, although there are some differences: for one, MEG can only measure tangential sources, whereas EEG measures radial and tangential sources; second, the location of EEG sources is blurred owing to the resistivity of the scalp, whereas the MEG signal is more sensitive to the distance between sources and sensors. These factors all act to greatly reduce the spatial resolution of EEG/MEG. However, what these two techniques lack in the ability to spatially localize activity, they make up for in the ability to resolve processes in time. EEG/MEG can be measured as fast as systems can write the data—usually between 500 Hz and 1 kHz. Given that most of the neural activity that these techniques are sensitive to occurs at frequencies below 200 Hz, this is more than adequate. EEG is recorded from electrodes placed on the outside of the scalp. There is no need to shave the hair in order to maintain contact, as contact between the electrode and the scalp is maintained through the use of an electrolytic gel or saline fluid. MEG is measured using highly sensitive magnetometers, which sit at some small distance from the scalp.

EEG/MEG Data Analysis

There are two main approaches to analyzing EEG/MEG data: frequency-domain analysis of the power of different EEG/MEG rhythms in the 1–70 Hz range, and time-domain analysis of *event-related potentials/fields* (ERPs/ERFs). We will focus our discussion here on studies that apply time-domain analysis to ERPs/ERFs. The assumption with this technique is that the brief, synchronous activity of thousands to millions of neurons produces the potential/field that can be measured outside the skull/scalp. On a trial-by-trial basis, this synchronous firing is assumed to be time-locked to some cognitive/behavioral event, and any temporal variance of firing, as well as any background activity, is assumed to be random. Under this assumption, one can average together many experimental trials of a particular task to yield a potential/field that contains positive and negative polarity deflections that reflect the neural activity associated with cognitive/behavioral events. These positive and negative polarity deflections are known as ERP/ERF *components*. ERP/ERF components are usually named after the serial position in which they occur (e.g., P1/N1/P2/N2/P3), or the latency, in milliseconds, at which they occur (e.g., P100/N170). However, components that have been linked to particular cognitive events are sometimes given a label that reflects that event (e.g., contralateral delay activity (CDA), or error-related negativity (ERN)—see below).

EEG in I/O Psychology

EEG technology can be useful in I/O psychology for providing cognitive-reaction time data and measuring time-dependent responses to stimuli. One use for this is to identify brain responses occurring immediately or implicitly, which would not otherwise be detected. For example, numerous studies have documented a specific component, known as ERN, that occurs when a person commits an error while performing an experimental task (Dehaene, Posner, & Tucker, 1994; Gemba, Sasaki, & Brooks, 1986). This negative electrical potential begins simultaneously with committed errors and reaches its maximum within a tenth of a second of an incorrect response (Gehring, Goss, Coles, Meyer, & Donchin, 1993).

As this ERN occurs so quickly, it is likely to precede conscious awareness of one's mistakes. Indeed, researchers have found that, although recognition of an error is not necessary for the negativity to occur, what is important is the individual's motivation to avoid errors. Gentsch, Ullsperger, and Ullsperger (2009) found that task instruction could affect the amplitude of the negative peak, such that instructions that emphasized committing few errors generated higher-amplitude ERNs than instructions that emphasized speed in performance. Similarly, Pailing and Segalowitz (2004) found that participants offered payment commensurate with a lack of mistakes showed stronger ERN responses. These findings support the perspective that the ERN is generated in response to actions that conflict with goals. In certain situations, errors in performance are encouraged (e.g., during error-based training). It would be interesting to evaluate ERN under such conditions. Perhaps ERN can be used as an indicator of trainees' motivations, allowing trainers to more easily identify trainees' orientation toward mistakes.

Recently, researchers have examined the ERP/ERF activity that occurs when one person observes the actions (Sebanz, Knoblich, Prinz, & Wascher, 2006) and mistakes of another person (van Schie, Mars, Coles, & Bekkering, 2004). van Schie et al. argue, from an observational-learning perspective, that participants should be able to process others' mistakes in the same way as they process their own mistakes, and therefore should show the same error-recognizing response. Using an experimental task requiring coacting dyads, they found that electrical brain responses thought to originate in the medial frontal lobe and motor cortex depended on the correctness of partners' behavioral responses (see Figure 13.6). They concluded that monitoring the performance of one's partner occurs in a similar way as monitoring one's own performance.

These findings have immediate implications for teams and teamwork. As the ERN is strongest when participants are highly motivated not to commit errors, and the ERN occurs when participants observe errors committed by others, it stands to reason that error responses of one team member to the errors committed by other team members should be moderated by the observer's motivation to meet team goals. If true, this methodology could provide a new direction for research on task cohesion and team dynamics. We would expect higher ERN in observers of errors, when those observers are cohesive and motivated to perform well as a team. If evidence substantiates this connection, ERN might one day be used to index task cohesion in teams.

Alternatively, if task motivation is known to be high, the ERN might be related to the participants' understanding of the teammates' tasks. As the ERN occurs when individuals do something that conflicts with intentions, it is likely that intentions must be known for the negativity to occur. Therefore, ERN might be used as an indicator of team members' knowledge of each others' knowledge, or the team's transactive memory system (TMS; Wegner, 1986, 1995; Wegner, Erber, & Raymond, 1991). TMSs are composed of an individual's own knowledge and his or her knowledge of what team members know. These two types of knowledge

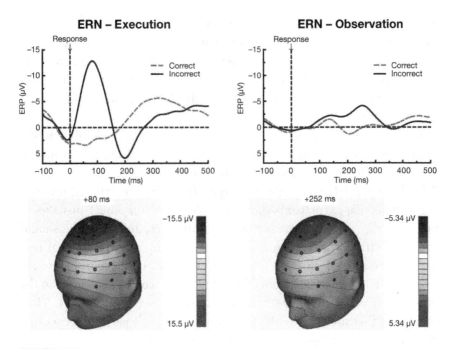

FIGURE 13.6

Error-related negativities. Top, response-locked averages at electrode Cz for correct and incorrect responses in the execution condition (left) and the observation condition (right). Dashed gray lines indicate correct, and solid black lines indicate incorrect response trials. Bottom, spline maps showing the topography of the ERN difference wave in the execution condition and the observation condition, taken at the peak where correct and incorrect ERP differed maximally—80 ms and 252 ms after the response, respectively. The Cz electrode at the vertex is marked in light blue for reference.

Source: van Schie et al., 2004.

can be used by a team to reduce information redundancy and increase information diversity. As the team develops, each team member becomes more specialized, which reduces the cognitive demands on any one team member, while expanding the resources of the team as a whole (Wegner, 1986, 1995). Through these mechanisms, TMSs have been found to correlate with team performance in laboratory settings (Liang, Moreland, & Argote, 1995) and field settings with existing teams (Austin, 2003; Lewis, 2003). Within the ERN paradigm, we might expect different patterns of electrical brain responses, depending on the state of TMSs within a team. Team members that accurately represent the intentions of their teammates should show greater ERNs in response to errors. Errors committed by team members that do not elicit strong ERN in observers should indicate a lack of understanding of intentions. This latter case implies that the team might need further practice time together before they are ready to perform at an optimal level.

Hyperscanning

The above sections detail how social processes can begin to be explored through neuroimaging techniques. However, although neuroscience data can be applied to investigations of team and interpersonal dynamics, owing to the restrictive nature of the equipment used for neuroimaging, direct investigations of interpersonal interactions have been limited. In EEG studies using the most widely available equipment, individuals are tethered in place and discouraged from unnecessary movement. Studies using MRI and fMRI are even more restrictive, as participants are required to lie motionless, with their heads in the claustrophobic bore of the machine. Recently, however, researchers have begun connecting data from multiple MRI machines or multiple EEG recorders running simultaneously, via a technique that has been dubbed "hyperscanning."

Hyperscanning has been utilized in fMRI research to record brain activity of two individuals interacting socially (Montague et al., 2002) and engaging in economic exchange (King-Casas et al., 2005). In EEG research, hyperscanning has been used to measure the synchronicity of neuro-electrical activity from the brains of up to four individuals engaged in a card game (Urbano et al., 1997, 1998; Babiloni et al., 2001, 2005; Astolfi et al., 2010). The studies that used card games as tasks are interesting, because these games typically utilize two teams of two members, playing against one another. This allows the researchers to examine cooperation and competition in the brains of individuals and teams at the same time. These techniques could offer a wealth of information for future researchers.

CONCLUDING REMARKS

The purpose of this chapter was to begin a discussion of neuroimaging techniques and their applications in I/O psychology. We hope we have convinced the reader that the neurosciences offer a valid and informative approach to the study of behavior at work. Other areas of social science, such as economics, advertising (e.g., du Plessis, 2008), and marketing (e.g., Lindstrom, 2008), are already turning to the brain for answers or as a data source to support theories. What is more, the U.S. Army, traditionally one of I/O psychology's biggest customers, has shown active interest in the potential of neuroscience. In a recent study and report, the National Research Council reviewed potential areas where neurosciences could support and facilitate military needs (National Research Council, 2009). One of its chief conclusions was that these technologies, "have great potential to improve soldier performance and enable the development of technologies to increase the effectiveness of soldiers on the battlefield" (National Research Council, 2009, p. 1). The first three recommendations to come from this report were to incorporate neuroscience for developing training programs, improving training evaluation methods, and to improve the selection of individuals for training programs and careers. These areas are well within the purview of I/O psychology, and I/O psychology should have a seat at the table. To do so, however, we must be able to collaborate with neuroscientists and understand their methods and their language. We hope this chapter has inspired some first steps in this direction.

Despite the advantages and opportunities offered by neuroimaging techniques, we recognize that neuroimaging cannot (yet) be used to replace traditional methods in I/O psychology. To see this, we computed a quick, "back of the napkin" utility analysis (using the Brogden, Cronbach, Glaser model; Cabrerra & Raju, 2001) to compare the value of fMRI with paper-and-pencil self-report methods in selection contexts. If one assumes that a standard-deviation increase in performance on a particular job is associated with a $30,000 increase in value to an organization, and the organization selects 10 out of 100 applicants, then the utility of fMRI (estimated to cost $500 per applicant) prevails over the utility of a $10 paper-and-pencil questionnaire only when the validity of fMRI exceeds that of the questionnaire by at least .82. Under the same assumptions, a selection method that costs $300 will lose out to fMRI when the validity coefficient associated with the latter is .34 higher than that of the former. This is more within the realm of possibility.

As an alternative view, if we wished for an improvement of .10 over a $10 paper-and-pencil test, fMRI would be a cost-effective method, if the brain-scan price came down to around $70 per applicant. Versus a selection strategy that costs $300 dollars per applicant, the cost of fMRI would have to come down to around $360 per applicant to be cost effective at an increase of 0.10 in predictive validity. Given the high costs of fMRI and the low costs of traditional measures, it is unlikely that fMRI will be used to replace traditional forms of selection for mundane roles, but the use of fMRI to select for high-stakes roles is much more appealing. Even with the high costs of MRI (and recognizing EEG costs are much lower), neuroimaging techniques hold great promise for building and testing theories in I/O psychology.

NOTE

1. VBM is not without its limitations. Difficulties in this segmentation can occur at the boundary between white and gray matter. From an anatomical perspective, the boundary between gray and white matter is not uniform, as myelinated fibres can project to different cortical layers, depending on their origin (Braak, 1984). Second, even if there were a sharp boundary between gray and white matter, there would always be voxels that cover both sides of this boundary and thus contain both tissue types (a problem known as *partial voluming*). As segmentation requires that a voxel be classified as gray, white, or CSF, the issue of misclassification can arise around the boundaries of the different tissues. Several methods have been developed to try and address the problem of partial voluming, with the most successful methods employing prior spatial or anatomical knowledge about tissue classification in order to help determine to which tissue category a particular voxel belongs (Ashburner & Friston, 2000).

REFERENCES

Adolphs, R. (2003). Cognitive neuroscience of human social behavior. *Nature Reviews Neuroscience, 4*, 165–78.

Adolphs, R. (2009). The social brain: Neural basis of social knowledge. *Annual Review of Psychology, 60*, 693–716.

Allman, J. M. (1999). *Evolving brains.* New York: Scientific American Library.

Asari, T., Konishi, S., Jimura, K., Chikazoe, J., Nakamura, N., & Miyashita, Y. (2008). Right temporopolar activation associated with unique perception. *NeuroImage, 41*, 145–152.

Ashburner, J., & Friston, K. J. (2000). Voxel-based morphometry: The methods. *NeuroImage, 11*, 805–821.

Astolfi, L., Toppi, J., Gallani, F. D., Vecchiato, G., Salinari, S., Mattia, D., et al. (2010). Neuroelectrical hyperscanning measures of simultaneous brain activity in humans. *Brain Topography, 23*, 243–256.

Austin, J. R. (2003). Transactive memory in organizational groups: The effects of content, consensus, specialization, and accuracy on group performance. *Journal of Applied Psychology, 88*(5), 866–878.

Avolio, B. J., Walumbwa, F. O., & Weber, T. J. (2009). Leadership: Current theories, researches, and future directions. *Annual Review of Psychology*, *60*, 421–449.

Babiloni, C., Babiloni, F., Carducci, F., Cincotti, F., Rosciarelli, F., Rossini, P. M., et al. (2001). Mapping of early and late human somatosensory evoked brain potentials to phasic galvanic painful stimulation. *Human Brain Mapping*, *12*(3), 168–179.

Babiloni, F., Cincotti, F., Babiloni, C., Carducci, F., Mattia, D., Astolfi, L., et al. (2005). Estimation of the cortical functional connectivity with the multimodal integration of high resolution EEG and fMRI data by Directed Transfer Function. *NeuroImage*, *24*(1), 118–131.

Baer, M., & Oldham, G. R. (2006). The curvilinear relation between experienced creative time pressure and creativity: Moderating effects of openness to experience and support for creativity. *Journal of Applied Psychology*, *91*(4), 963–970.

Barrett, L. & Henzi, P. (2005). The social nature of primate cognition. *Proceedings Biological Sciences*, *272*, 1865–1875.

Bateman, T. S., & Organ, D. W. (1983). Job satisfaction and the good soldier: The relationship between affect and employee "citizenship." *Academy of Management Journal*, *26*(4), 587–595.

Batson, C. D. (1991). *The altruism question: Toward a social psychological answer.* Hillsdale, NJ: Erlbaum.

Bechtereva, N. P., Korotkov, A. D., Pakhomov, S. V., Roudas, M. S., Starchenko, M. G., & Medvedev, S. V. (2004). PET study of brain maintenance of verbal creative activity. *International Journal of Psychophysiology*, *53*, 11–20.

Blakemore, S. J., Winston, J., & Frith, U. (2004). Social cognitive neuroscience: Where are we heading? *Trends in Cognitive Science*, *8*, 215–222.

Boal, K. B., & Hooijberg, R. (2000). Strategic leadership research: Moving on. *Leadership Quarterly*, *11*, 515–549.

Bolino, M. C., Turnley, W. H., & Niehoff, B. P. (2004). The other side of the story: Reexamining prevailing assumptions about organizational citizenship behavior. *Human Resource Management Review*, *14*, 229–246.

Borman, W. C., & Motowidlo, S. J. (1997). Task performance and contextual performance: The meaning for personnel selection research. *Human Performance*, *10*(2), 99–109.

Botvinick, M., Jha, A. P., Bylsma, L. M., Fabian, S. A., Solomon, P. E., & Prkachin, K. M. (2005). Viewing facial expressions of pain engages cortical areas involved in the direct experience of pain. *NeuroImage*, *25*, 312–319.

Boyke, J., Driemeyer, J., Gaser, C., Buchel, C., & May, A. (2008). Training-induced brain structure changes in the elderly. *Journal of Neuroscience*, *28*(28), 7031–7035.

Braak, H. (1984). Architectonics as seen by lipofuscin stains. In A. Peters & E. G. Jones (Eds.), *Cerebral cortex: Cellular components of the cerebral cortex* (Vol 1.). New York: Plenum Press.

Buckner, R. L., & Carroll, D. C. (2007). Self-projection and the brain. *Trends in Cognitive Sciences*, *11*, 49–57.

Byrne, R., & Whiten, A. (Eds.) (1988). *Machiavellian intelligence: Social expertise and the evolution of intellect in monkeys, apes, and humans.* Oxford, UK: Clarendon.

Byron, K., Khazanchi, S., & Nazarian, D. (2010). The relationship between stressors and creativity: A meta-analysis examining competing theoretical models. *Journal of Applied Psychology*, *95*(1), 201–212.

Cabrera, E. F., & Raju, N. S. (2001). Utility analysis: Current trends and future directions. *International Journal of Selection and Assessment, 9*(1-2), 92-102.

Campbell, J., McCloy, R., Oppler, S., & Sager, C. (1993). A theory of performance. In N. Schmitt & W. Borman (Eds.), *Personnel selection in organizations* (pp. 35-71). San Francisco, CA: Jossey-Bass.

Campbell, J. P. (1990). Modeling the performance prediction problem in industrial and organizational psychology. In M. D. Dunnette & L. M. Hough (Eds.), *Handbook of industrial and organizational psychology* (Vol. 1, 2nd ed., pp. 687-732). Palo Alto, CA: Consulting Psychologists Press, Inc.

Canli, T. (2008). Toward a "molecular psychology" of personality. In O. P. John, R. W. Robins, & L. A. Pervin (Eds.), *Handbook of personality: Theory and research* (pp. 311-327). New York: Guilford Press.

Carlsson, I., Wendt, P. E., & Risberg, J. (2000). On the neurobiology of creativity. Differences in frontal activity between high and low creative subjects. *Neuropsychologia, 38*, 873-885.

Choi, J., Anderson, T. A., & Veillette, A (2009). Contextual inhibitors of employee creativity in organizations: The insulating role of creative ability. *Group & Organization Management, 34*(3), 330-357.

Christensen, B. T., & Schunn, C. D. (2009). The role and impact of mental simulation in design. *Applied Cognitive Psychology, 23*, 327-344.

Christoff, K., & Owen, A. M. (2006). Improving reverse neuroimaging inference: Cognitive domain versus cognitive complexity. *Trends in Cognitive Sciences, 10*(8), 352-353.

Dale, A. M., & Buckner, R. L. (1997). Selective averaging of rapidly presented individual trials using fMRI. *Human Brain Mapping, 5*, 329-340.

De Dreu, C. K. W., & Weingart, L. R. (2003). Task versus relationship conflict, team performance, and team member satisfaction: A meta-analysis. *Journal of Applied Psychology, 88*(4), 741-749.

deCharms, R. C., Maeda, F., Glover, G. H., Ludlow, D., Pauly, J. M., Soneji, D., et al. (2005). Control over brain activation and pain learned by using real-time functional MRI. *Proceedings of the National Academy of Sciences, 102*(51), 18626-18631.

deCharms, R. C. (2007). Reading and controlling human brain activation using real-time functional magnetic resonance imaging. *Trends in Cognitive Science, 11*, 473-481.

deCharms, R. C. (2008). Applications of real-time fMRI. *Nature Review: Neuroscience, 9*, 720-728.

Dehaene, S., Posner, M. I., & Tucker, D. M. (1994). Localization of a neural system for error detection and compensation. *Psychological Science, 5*(5), 303-305.

Denison, D. R., Hooijberg, R., & Quinn, R. E. (1995). Paradox and performance: A theory of behavioral complexity in managerial leadership. *Organization Science, 6*(5), 524-541.

Dennett, D. C. (1987). *The intentional stance.* Cambridge, MA: MIT Press.

DeYoung, C. G., & Grey, J. R. (2009). Personality neuroscience: Explaining individual differences in affect, behavior, and cognition. In P. J. Corr & G. Matthews (Eds.), *The Cambridge handbook of personality psychology* (pp. 323-346). New York: Cambridge University Press.

DeYoung, C. G., Hirsh, J. B., Shane, M. S., Papademetris, X., Rajeevan, N., & Grey, J. R. (2010). Testing predictions from personality neuroscience: Brain structure and the Big Five. *Psychological Science, 21*(6), 820–828.

Dietrich, A. (2003). Functional neuroanatomy of altered states of consciousness: The transient hypofrontality hypothesis. *Consciousness and Cognition, 12*, 231–256.

Dietrich, A. (2004). The cognitive neuroscience of creativity. *Psychonomic Bulletin & Review, 11*, 1011–1026.

du Plessis, E. (2008). *The advertised mind: Groundbreaking insights into how our brains respond to advertising.* Philadelphia: Millward Brown.

Duch, W. (2007). Creativity and the brain. In A. G. Tan (Ed.), *A handbook of creativity for teachers* (pp. 507–530). Singapore: World Scientific Publishing.

Dunbar, R. I., & Schultz, S. (2007). Evolution in the social brain. *Science, 317*, 1344–1347.

Farrow, T. F., Zheng, Y., Wilkinson, I. D., Spence, S. A., Deakin, J. F., Tarrier, N., et al. (2001). Investigating the functional anatomy of empathy and forgiveness. *NeuroReport, 12*, 2433–2438.

Ferreira, L. K., Diniz, B. S., Forlenza, O. V., Busatto, G. F., & Zanetti, M. V. (2011). Neurostructural predictors of Alzheimer's disease: A meta-analysis of VBM studies. *Neurobiology of Aging, 32*(10), 1733–1741.

Fink, A., & Neubauer, A. C. (2006). EEG alpha oscillations during the performance of verbal creativity tasks: Differential effects of sex and verbal intelligence. *International Journal of Psychophysiology, 62*, 46 –53.

Fischl, B., & Dale, A. M. (2000). Measuring the thickness of the human cerebral cortex from magnetic resonance images. *PNAS, 97*(20), 11050–11055.

Fiske, S. T., & Taylor, S. E. (1991). *Social cognition* (2nd ed.). New York: McGraw Hill.

Flaherty, A. W. (2005). Frontotemporal and dopaminergic control of idea generation and creative drive. *The Journal of Comparative Neurology, 493*, 147–153.

Folley, B. S., & Park, S. (2005). Verbal creativity and schizotypal personality in relation to prefrontal hemispheric laterality: A behavioral and near-infrared optical imaging study. *Schizophrenia Research, 80*, 271–282.

Frith, C. D., & Frith, U. (1999). Interacting minds—A biological basis. *Science, 286*, 1692–1695.

Frith, U., Leslie, A. M., & Morton, J. (1991). *Trends in Neuroscience, 14*, 433.

Geake, J. G., & Hansen, P. C. (2005). Neural correlates of intelligence as revealed by fMRI of fluid analogies. *NeuroImage, 26*, 555–564.

Gehring, W. J., Goss, B., Coles, M. G. H., Meyer, D. E., & Donchin, E. (1993). A neural system for error detection and compensation. *Psychological Science, 4*, 385–390.

Gemba, H., Sasaki, K., & Brooks, V. B. (1986). "Error" potentials in limbic cortex (anterior cingulate area 24) of monkeys during motor learning. *Neuroscience Letters, 70*, 223–227.

Gentsch, A., Ullsperger, P., & Ullsperger, M. (2009). Dissociable medial frontal negativities for a common monitoring system for self and externally caused failure of goal achievement. *NeuroImage, 47*(4), 2023–2030.

Goleman, D., & Boyatzis, R. (2008). Social intelligence and the biology of leadership. *Harvard Business Review, 86*(9), 74–81.

Heilman, K. M., Nadeau, S. E., & Beversdorf, D. O. (2003). Creative innovation: Possible brain mechanisms. *Neurocase, 9*, 369–379.

Henson, R. (2006). Forward inference using functional neuroimaging: dissociations versus associations. *Trends in Cognitive Sciences, 10*(2), 64–69.

Hooijberg, R. (1996). A multidirectional approach toward leadership: An extension of the concept of behavioral complexity. *Human Relations, 49*(7), 917–946.

Hooijberg, R., Hunt, J. G., & Dodge, G. E. (1997). Leadership complexity and development of the leaderplex model. *Journal of Management, 23*, 375–408.

Hooijberg, R., & Quinn, R. E. (1992). Behavioral complexity and the development of effective managerial leaders. In R. L. Phillips & J. G. Hunt (Eds.), *Strategic management: A multiorganizational-level perspective* (pp. 161–176). New York: Quorum.

Hooijberg, R. & Schneider, M. (2001). Behavioral complexity and social intelligence: How executive leaders use stakeholders to form a systems perspective. *The Nature of Organizational Leadership*, S. J. Zaccaro and R. Klimoski (Eds.), pp. 104–131. San Francisco, CA: Jossey-Bass, series by the Society of Industrial Organization Psychologists (SIOP).

Howard-Jones, P. A., Blakemore, S. J., Samuel E. A., Summers, I. R., & Claxton, G. (2005). Semantic divergence and creative story generation: An fMRI investigation. *Brain Research/ Cognitive Brain Research, 25*, 240–250.

Huettel, S. A., Song, A. W., & McCarthy, G. (2009). *Functional magnetic resonance imaging* (2nd ed.). Sunderland, MA: Sinauer Associates, Inc.

Jausovec, N. (2000). Differences in cognitive processes between gifted, intelligent, creative, and average individuals while solving complex problems: An EEG study. *Intelligence, 28*, 213–237.

Jausovec, N., & Jausovec, K. (2000). Differences in resting EEG related to ability. *Brain Topography, 12*, 229 –240.

Jung, R. E., Gasparovic, C., Chavez, R. S., Flores, R. A., Smith, S. M., Caprihan, A., et al. (2009). Biochemical support for the "threshold" theory of creativity: A magnetic resonance spectroscopy study. *The Journal of Neuroscience, 29*(16), 5319–5325.

Kaplan, S., Bradley, J. C., Luchman, J. N., & Haynes, D. (2009). On the role of positive and negative affectivity in job performance: A meta-analytic investigation. *Journal of Applied Psychology, 94*, 162–176.

King-Casas, B., Tomlin, D., Anen, C., Camerer, C. F., Quartz, S. R., Montague, P. R. (2005). Getting to know you: Reputation and trust in a two-person economic exchange. *Science, 308*(5718), 78–83.

Klein, H. E., & D'esposito, M. (2007). Neurocognitive inefficacy of the strategy process. *Annals of the New York Academy of Science, 1118*, 163–185.

Kosslyn, S. M., Cacioppo, J. T., Davidson, R. J., Hugdahl, K., Lovallo, W. R., Spiegel, D., et al. (2002). Bridging psychology and biology: The analysis of individuals in groups. *American Psychologist, 57*(5), 341–351.

Kosslyn, S. M., Thompson, W. L., Shepard, J. M., Ganis, G., Bell, D., Danovich, J., et al. (2004). Brain rCBF and performance in visual imagery tasks: Common and distinct processes. *European Journal of Cognitive Psychology, 16*, 696–716.

Kwong, K. K., Belliveau, J. W., Chesler, D. A., Goldberg, I. E., Weisskoff, R. M., Poncelet, B. P., et al. (1992). Dynamic magnetic resonance imaging of human brain activity during primary sensory stimulation. *PNAS, 89*, 5675–5679.

Lamiell, J. (1981). Toward an idiothetic psychology of personality. *American Psychologist, 36*, 276–289.

Langleben, D. D., et al. (2002) Brain activity during simulated deception: An event-related functional magnetic resonance study. *Neuroimage, 15*, 727–732.

Lee, J. H., Durand, R., Gradinaru, V., Zhang, F., Goshen, I., Kim, D. S., et al. (2010). Global and local fMRI signals driven by neuronsdefined optogenetically by type and wiring. *Nature, 465,* 788–792.

Lee, T. M., Liu, T. M., Tan, L. H., Chan, C. C., Mahankali, S., Feng, C. M., et al. (2002) Lie detection by functional magnetic resonance imaging. *Human Brain Mapping, 15,* 157–164.

Lewis, K. (2003). Measuring transactive memory systems in the field: Scale development and validation. *Journal of Applied Psychology, 88*(4), 587–604.

Liang, D. W., Moreland, R., & Argote, L. (1995). Group versus individual training and group performance: The mediating factor of transactive memory. *Personality & Social Psychology Bulletin, 21*(4), 384–393.

Lieberman, M. D. (2007). Social cognitive neuroscience: A review of core processes. *Annual Review of Psychology, 58,* 259–289.

Lindstrom, M. (2008). *Buyology: Truth and lies about why we buy.* New York: Doubleday.

Logothetis, N. K., Pauls, J., Augath, M., Trinath, T., & Oeltermann, A. (2001). Neurophysiological investigation of the basis of the fMRI signal. *Nature, 412*(6843), 150–157.

McDaniel, M. A. (2005). Big-brained people are smarter: A meta-analysis of the relationship between in vivo brain volume and intelligence. *Intelligence, 33,* 337–346.

Malonek, D., & Grinvald, A. (1996). Interactions between electrical activity and cortical microcirculation revealed by imaging spectroscopy: Implications for functional brain mapping. *Science, 272,* 551–544.

Marr, D. (1982). *Vision: A computational investigation into the human representation and processing of visual information.* New York: Henry Holt & Co., Inc.

Marsh, A. A., Kozak, M. N., & Ambady, N. (2007). Accurate identification of fear facial expressions predicts prosocial behavior. *Emotion, 7,* 239–251.

Mitchell, J. P. (2008). Contributions of functional neuroimaging to the study of social cognition. *Current Directions in Psychological Science, 17*(2), 142–146.

Mitchell, J. P. (2009). Inferences about mental states. *Philosophical Transactions of the Royal Society of London, Series B, Biological Sciences, 364,* 1309–1316.

Mitchell, J. P., Macrae, C. N., & Banaji, M. R. (2004). Encoding-specific effects of social cognition on the neural correlates of subsequent memory. *Journal of Neuroscience, 26,* 4912–4917.

Montague, P. R., Berns, G. S., Cohen, J. D., McClure, S. M., Pagnoni, G., Dhamala, M., et al. (2002). Hyperscanning: Simultaneous fMRI during linked social interactions. *Neuroimage, 16,* 1159–1164.

National Research Council (2009). *Opportunities in neuroscience for future army applications.* Washington, DC: National Academy Press.

Ochsner, K. N., Hughes, B., Robertson, E. R., Cooper, J. C., & Gabrieli, D. E. (2009). Neural systems supporting the control of affective and cognitive conflict. *Journal of Cognitive Neuroscience, 21*(9), 1841–1854.

Ochsner, K. N., & Lieberman, M. D. (2001). The emergence of social cognitive neuroscience. *American Psychologist, 56,* 717–734.

Organ, D. W. (1988). *Organizational citizenship behavior: The good soldier syndrome.* Lexington, MA: LexingtonBooks.

Pailing, P. E., & Segalowitz, S. J. (2004). The error related negativity as a state and trait measure: Motivation, personality, and ERPs in response to errors. *Psychophysiology, 41,* 84–95.

Peterson, S. J., Balthazard, P. A., Waldman, D. A., & Thatcher, R. W. (2008). Neuroscientific implications of psychological capital: Are the brains of optimistic, hopeful, confident, and resilient leaders different? *Organizational Dynamics, 37*(4), 342–353.

Podsakoff, P. M., MacKenzie, S. B., & Hui, C. (1993). Organizational citizenship behaviors and managerial evaluations of employee performance: A review and suggestions for future research. In G. R. Ferris & K.M. Rowland (Eds.), *Research in personnel human resources management* (Vol. 11, pp. 1–40). Greenwich, CT: JAI Press.

Poldrack, R. A. (2006). Can cognitive processes be inferred from neuroimaging data? *Trends in Cognitive Sciences, 10*, 59–63.

Premack, D., & Woodruff, G. (1978). Does the chimpanzee have a theory of mind? *Behavioral and Brain Sciences, 1*, 515–526.

Preston, S. D., & de Waal, F. B. (2002). Empathy: Its ultimate and proximate bases. *Behavioral and Brain Sciences, 25*, 1–20; discussion, 20–71.

Rameson, L. T., Morelli, S. A., & Lieberman, M. D. (2012). The neural correlates of empathy: Experience, automaticity, and prosocial behavior. *Journal of Cognitive Neuroscience, 24*(1), 235–245.

Rilling, J. K., Gutman, D. A., Zeh, T. R., Pagnoni, G., Berns, G. S., & Kilts, C. D. (2002). A neural basis for social cooperation. *Neuron, 35*, 395–405.

Rock, D., & Schwartz, J. (2006). The neuroscience of leadership.*Strategy + Business, 43*, 72–83.

Sebanz, N., Knoblich, G., Prinz, W., & Wascher, E. (2006). Twin peaks: An ERP study of action planning and control in coacting individuals. *Journal of Cognitive Neuroscience, 18*(5), 859–870.

Schmitt, N., Cortina, J. M., Ingerick, M. J., Wiechmann, D., Borman, W. C., Ilgen, D. R., et al., (2003). Personnel selection and employee performance. In *Handbook of psychology: Industrial and organizational psychology* (Vol. 12., pp. 77–105). John Wiley & Sons, Inc.

Singer, T., Seymour, B., O'Doherty, J., Kaube, H., Dolan, R. J., & Frith, C. D. (2004). Empathy for pain involves the affective but not sensory components of pain. *Science, 303*(5661), 1157–1162.

Spence, S. A., Farrow, T. L., Herford, A. E., Wilkinson, I. D., Zheng, Y., & Woodruff, P. W. (2001). Behavioural and functional anatomical correlates of deception in humans. *Neuroreport, 12*, 2849–2853.

Spreng, R. N., Mar, R. A., & Kim, A. S. (2009). The common neural basis of autobiographical memory, prospection, navigation, theory of mind, and the default mode: A quantitative meta-analysis. *Journal of Cognitive Neuroscience, 21*, 489–510.

St. Jacques, P. L., Conway, M. A., Lowder, M. W., & Cabeza, R. (2011). Watching my mind unfold versus yours: An fMRI study using a novel camera technology to examine neural differences in self-projection of self versus other perspectives. *Journal of Cognitive Neuroscience, 23*(6), 1275–1284.

Sutton, S. K., & Davidson, R. J. (1997). Prefrontal brain asymmetry: A biological substrate of the behavioral approach and inhibition systems. *Psychological Science, 8*, 204–210.

Takeuchi, H., Taki, Y., Sassa, Y., Hashizume, H., Sekiguchi, A., Fukushima, A., et al. (2010). Regional gray matter volume of dopaminergic system associate with creativity: Evidence from voxel-based morphometry. *NeuroImage, 51*, 578–585.

Taylor, S. E., Pham, L. B., Rivkin, I. D., & Armor, D. A. (1998). Harnessing the imagination: Mental simulation, self-regulation, and coping. *American Psychologist, 53*(4), 429–439.

Tomarken, A. J., Davidson, R. J., Wheeler, R. E., & Doss, R. C. (1992). Individual differences in anterior brain asymmetry and fundamental dimensions of emotion. *Journal of Personality and Social Psychology, 62*, 676–687.

Underwood, B. J. (1975). Individual differences as a crucible in theory construction. *American Psychologist, 30*, 128–134.

Unsworth, K. L., & Clegg, C. W. (2010). Why do employees undertake creative action? *Journal of Occupational and Organizational Psychology, 83*(1), 77–99.

Urbano, A., Babiloni, F., Babiloni, C., Ambrosini, A., Onorati, P., & Rossini, P. M. (1997). Human short-latency cortical responses to somatosensory stimulation. A high resolution study. *NeuroReport, 8*(15), 3239–3243.

Urbano, A., Babiloni, C., Carducci, F., Fattorini, L., Onorati, P., & Babiloni, F. (1998). Dynamic functional coupling of high resolution EEG potentials related to unilateral internally triggered one-digit movements. *Electroencephalography in Clinical Neurophysiology, 106*, 477–487.

van Schie, H. T., Mars, R. B., Coles, M. G. H., & Bekkering, H. (2004). Modulation of activity in medial frontal and motor cortices during error observation. *Nature Neuroscience, 7*(5), 549–554.

Vroom, V. H. (1964). *Work and motivation.* New York: Wiley.

Wallis, J. D. (2007). Orbitofrontal cortex and its contribution to decision making. *Annual Review of Neuroscience, 30*, 31–56.

Wegner, D. M. (1986). Transactive memory: A contemporary analysis of the group mind. In B. Mullen & G. R. Goethals (Eds.), *Theories of group behavior* (pp. 185–205). New York: Springer-Verlag.

Wegner, D. M. (1995). A computer network model of human transactive memory. *Social Cognition, 13*, 319–339.

Wegner, D. M., Erber, R., & Raymond, P. (1991). Transactive memory in close relationships. *Journal of Personality and Social Psychology, 61*(6), 923–929.

Winston, J. S., Strange, B. A., O'Doherty, J., & Dolan, R. J. (2002). Automatic and intentional brain responses during evaluation of trustworthiness of faces. *Nature Neuroscience, 5*(3), 277–283.

Yamagishi, T. et al. (2003). You can judge a book by its cover: Evidence that cheaters may look different from cooperators. *Evolution and Human Behavior, 24*, 290–301.

Yammarino, F. J., Dionne, S. D., Chun, J. A., & Dansereau, F. (2005). Leadership and levels of analysis: A state-of-the-science review. *Leadership Quarterly, 16*, 879–919.

Zaccaro, S. J. (2001). *The nature of executive leadership: A conceptual and empirical analysis of success.* Washington, DC: American Psychological Association.

Zaccaro, S. J. (2007). Trait-based perspectives of leadership. *American Psychologist, 62*(1), 6–16.

Zaccaro, S. J., Gilbert, J. A., Thor, K. K., & Mumford, M. D. (1991). Leadership and social intelligence: Linking social perceptiveness and behavioral flexibility to leader effectiveness. *Leadership Quarterly, 2*(4), 317–342.

Zacks, J. M. (2008). Neuroimaging studies of mental rotation: A meta-analysis and review. *Journal of Cognitive Neuroscience, 20*(1), 1–19.

Zhang, X., & Bartol, K. M. (2010). The influence of creative process engagement on employee creative performance and overall job performance: A curvilinear assessment. *Journal of Applied Psychology, 95*(5), 862–873.

14

Advances in Knowledge Measurement

Nikki Dudley-Meislahn, E. Daly Vaughn,
Eric J. Sydell, and Marisa A. Seeds

Organizational researchers have long recognized knowledge as a critical predictor of job performance. Numerous studies have documented support for the importance of knowledge in the prediction of task performance and in the explanation of variance in ratings of overall performance (e.g., Hunter, 1983, 1986; Pulakos, Borman, & Hough, 1988; Borman, White, & Dorsey, 1995). In structural job performance models, knowledge is typically included as a critical mediator between other predictors, such as cognitive ability, and job performance (e.g., Hunter, 1983; Schmidt, Hunter, & Outerbridge, 1986; Borman, White, Pulakos, & Oppler, 1991; Campbell, McCloy, Oppler, & Sager, 1993). Despite the critical role of knowledge in performance models, there has been limited research on knowledge-measurement methodologies in organizational research. In this chapter, our primary goal is to generate increased interest in knowledge measurement by identifying methodologies from literatures outside organizational research that we believe will enhance our ability to assess knowledge.

This chapter is not intended to be a comprehensive review of all possible measurement methodologies outside organizational research; rather, we offer two methodologies that have been particularly effective in other fields of research and thus hold promise for organizational research. The chapter is structured as follows: First, we define knowledge and then discuss possible reasons why there have been limited advances in knowledge measurement. Next, we offer a review of measurement approaches that have been used to date to assess knowledge in organizational research. Understanding current measurement procedures gives insight into how we may benefit from integrating additional methodologies into this work. Following this, we detail two methodologies for knowledge measurement from outside organizational research and how these could be leveraged. Finally, we discuss how recent advances in technology may be utilized to increase knowledge-measurement efficiency.

DEFINING KNOWLEDGE

Knowledge is a schematic, meaningful organization of key facts, principles, and other information pertaining to a particular domain (Fleishman & Mumford, 1989; Costanza, Fleishman, & Marshall-Mies, 1999). Knowledge forms a foundation for performance (Ericsson & Charness, 1994), and, in most domains, improving relevant knowledge is related to performance improvements (Chi, Glaser, & Rees, 1982; Greeno & Simon, 1988; Ward, Byrnes, & Overton, 1990; Anderson, 1993; Ericsson & Charness, 1994). There are two overarching types of knowledge: declarative and procedural knowledge. Declarative knowledge is knowledge about facts and things (Campbell, 1990) and has been defined in cognitive psychology as, "factual information that is somewhat static in nature which is usually describable" (Best, 1989, p. 7). Examples of declarative knowledge include facts, attributes, goals, and self-knowledge (Best, 1989; Campbell, 1990). By contrast, procedural knowledge refers to "the dynamic information underlying skillful actions" (Best, 1989, p. 7); that is, the knowledge of rules and procedures for taking action (Brucks, 1986). Procedural knowledge has also been referred to as behavioral scripts, which contain information about the sequences of behavior appropriate to particular situations (Gioia & Manz, 1985).

Knowledge can be acquired formally, such as through instruction from others, or informally, through an individual's experience or observations over time. Procedural knowledge that is acquired through everyday experiences is also known as tacit knowledge, which is a central component of practical intelligence (Wagner & Sternberg, 1985; Sternberg, 1988; Sternberg, Wagner, Williams, & Horvath, 1995). Tacit knowledge has been defined as, "action-oriented knowledge, acquired without direct help from others that allows individuals to achieve goals they personally value" (Sternberg et al., 1995, p. 916). Tacit knowledge is not formally taught and, as such, it is hard to articulate, because it is not formalized in explicit procedures and rules (Lievens & Chan, 2010).

As mentioned previously, knowledge has been extensively utilized within models of performance as a key performance predictor (Campbell et al., 1993). Organizational research has also demonstrated the criticality of knowledge and its advancement in models of training success (Goldstein & Ford, 2002), leadership effectiveness (Janson, 2008), as well as career success (Dreher & Bretz, 1991). With its prominence as a predictor and criterion, it is surprising how rarely researchers have considered ways to advance its measurement.

FACTORS CONTRIBUTING TO LIMITED KNOWLEDGE RESEARCH

There are several potential reasons why knowledge assessment has been underutilized. First, during the past 30 years, there has been a substantial expansion within the literature of the job-performance domain, from task performance to a broader view of performance. As a result, researchers have focused more on noncognitive predictors in examining these other performance dimensions. Second, because knowledge measurement is complex, resources have been devoted to measuring other, more readily discernible factors. Third, knowledge is malleable and can generally be taught, making it seem less critical to assess. Fourth, owing to limitations in available technology, knowledge measurement has traditionally been considered very time and resource intensive. However, improvements in technological capabilities have ameliorated many of these concerns. We now expand upon the four reasons identified for the limitations in knowledge-measurement research.

Expansion of Performance Domain

During the last several decades, organizational research has shifted to a more holistic view of performance that goes well beyond task proficiency. The performance domain has expanded to include areas such as citizenship performance (Bateman & Organ, 1983; Smith, Organ, & Near, 1983; Brief & Motowidlo, 1986; Organ, 1990; Borman & Motowidlo, 1993;

Coleman & Borman, 2000; Borman & Penner, 2001; Borman, Penner, Allen, & Motowidlo, 2001) and adaptability (Campbell, 1999; Hesketh & Neal, 1999; Pulakos, Arad, Donovan, & Plamondon, 2000), as well as focusing more on how individuals perform within social systems and settings (Carpenter, 2003). Until recently, this shift seemed to drive a decrease rather than an increase in knowledge assessment. This decrease may have been due to the fact that early knowledge research focused on predicting task performance. In that vein, knowledge was positioned as a proximal predictor, often between cognitive ability and task performance, and was typically conceptualized as technical proficiency operationalized using job-knowledge tests (e.g., series of multiple-choice questions assessing technical know-how) or performance-based methodologies (e.g., work samples evaluated by one or more assessors). The expansion of the performance domain drove an increased focus on noncognitive predictors, such as personality, motives, attitudes, affect, and culture fit. In fact, early literature on citizenship performance emphasized that its correlation with volitional and personality variables, rather than knowledge variables, differentiated it from task performance (Borman & Penner, 2001).

In more recent job-performance models, knowledge has been included as a critical mediator between distal predictors, such as personality traits and motives, and the less technical aspects of job performance such as citizenship performance (see Dudley & Cortina, 2008; Motowidlo, Borman, & Schmit, 1997). In addition, Dudley and Cortina (2009) found that several knowledge variables predicted the personal-support dimension of citizenship performance above and beyond other noncognitive predictor variables. Similarly, adaptability researchers have identified knowledge as critical to effective performance (Mitchel & Daniels, 2003; Chen, Thomas, & Wallace, 2005; Ployhart & Bliese, 2006; Schmitt & Chan, 2006), although, as mentioned previously, research supporting this relationship is limited. In our view, the expansion of the performance domain should drive an increased rather than a decreased focus on knowledge predictors, especially those relevant to these less technical performance domains.

Complexity of Knowledge Measurement

Another reason for limited focus on knowledge to date may be the fact that knowledge is challenging to measure. First, it tends to be domain-specific, which requires an in-depth analysis of a particular domain and limits some of the resulting measures to a fairly narrow, specific type of knowledge. Knowledge measures also tend to be lengthy and, therefore, ill suited for assessment sessions that have time constraints. Additionally, the methodologies often employed in organizational research to assess knowledge, such as situational judgment tests (SJTs), interviews, work samples, and simulations, are not always based on a construct approach, and, hence, it is not always clear what they are measuring (Christian, Edwards, & Bradley, 2010).

Perception of Knowledge Trainability

The third posited reason why organizational researchers have done less to advance knowledge measurement is the general belief that candidates, once hired, can advance their knowledge deficiencies through training and experience. However, the wisdom of the assumption that job applicants can learn job-relevant knowledge after being hired has come into question for two reasons. First, sometimes, new hires will not or cannot be trained in the job-relevant knowledge. Second, training is costly and time consuming; as such, a job applicant who possesses the requisite knowledge will, all other things being equal, be superior to a candidate who does not possess the knowledge. If it is possible to hire people who are already equipped with the knowledge bases required for a job, then on-boarding costs could decrease substantially.

Limitations in Technological Capabilities

In addition to the previously cited reasons for limited advances in knowledge measurement, impediments related to available technology have curtailed many forms of organizational assessment, but particularly data-intensive assessments such as knowledge. More specifically, two limitations in traditional assessment include the following:

1. The primary testing modality has been paper-and-pencil tests. In the past several decades, computerized tests have become more ubiquitous, and yet the vast majority of these tests are simple conversions of existing paper tests that do little to exploit the available technology.
2. Applied datasets have been scarce and difficult to find. Before computers became commonplace, organizations did not track job

performance thoroughly or as often. As a result, little relevant data were available to validate new psychological measures.

Fortunately, organizational researchers and practitioners are beginning to incorporate the rapidly advancing technological capabilities available. As a result, the above limitations are beginning to be abated, and an exciting new period in the development of psychometric assessments is emerging.

MEASUREMENT APPROACHES IN ORGANIZATIONAL RESEARCH

In this section, we provide an overview of the approaches that have been used most frequently in organizational research and personnel selection to measure knowledge. These approaches include (a) self- and other-reports, (b) interviews, (c) knowledge tests, and (d) performance-based methodologies (e.g., simulations, work samples).

Self- and Other-Reports

The self-report approach to measuring knowledge asks individuals to evaluate the extent to which the respondent agrees or disagrees with one or more statements related to their level of knowledge. There are variations of this approach as well, in both practice and research. For example, instead of asking to what extent individuals agree with a statement, the item(s) may explicitly ask the individual and/or the individual's supervisor or peer to evaluate his/her level of knowledge using a response scale, such as from novice to expert. There are numerous studies in the organizational-research literature that have employed self- and/or other-reports to gain insight into one's knowledge level (e.g., Bar-On, 1997; Bettencourt, Gwinner, & Meuter, 2001).

Although organizational researchers have employed self- and other-report measures because they are easy to build and take little time to complete, they do not directly tap the cognitive processes that make up one's knowledge. In lieu of measuring actual knowledge, self- and other-report measures assess *perceptions* of the individual's knowledge, which, although valuable in their own right, do not provide an unequivocal assessment of knowledge (Stone et al., 2000; Donaldson & Grant-Vallone, 2002). For example, it is likely that one's perceptions are related to other variables, as well including personality characteristics, such as self-efficacy and social confidence.

Interviews

Interviews are another methodology that has been used, typically in a hiring context, to assess a candidate's knowledge level. Huffcutt, Conway, Roth, and Stone (2001) reviewed the constructs most commonly assessed in interviews and found that applied social skills and accumulated knowledge and skills were measured in 27.8 percent and 9.8 percent of interviews, respectively. Within accumulated knowledge, frequently assessed constructs to determine what candidates know and can do included: technical knowledge, job knowledge, product knowledge, use of tools, budgeting, experience, work history, exposure, education, and academic achievement (Huffcutt et al., 2001).

Depending on the interview techniques used, it may be possible to directly tap into knowledge during the interview process. However, some knowledge may be particularly difficult to evaluate during an interview process. Thus, the use of the interview methodology would be dependent on the particular knowledge one is trying to assess. Additionally, interviews are subjective measures and, even with structured questions and rating scales, can be impacted by interviewee personal characteristics, self-presentation tactics, as well as interviewer impressions and biases (Posthuma, Morgeson, & Campion, 2002; Levashina & Campion, 2007; Barrick, Shaffer, & DeGrassi, 2009). Thus, although interviews can be a useful tool to tap into knowledge level, they are not pure measures of one's knowledge, and they are time and resource intensive for both the candidate and the interviewer.

Knowledge Tests

Knowledge tests can take many forms. Three types of test that have been used in organizational research to assess knowledge include: job knowledge tests, SJTs, and tacit knowledge tests. Job knowledge tests are used to assess the level of knowledge one has within a specific knowledge domain relevant to job requirements (e.g., a phlebotomy knowledge test for a phlebotomist). Job knowledge tests can take many forms, the most common being to display information (e.g., written passage, numerical chart) and pose a multiple-choice question with one right answer, and, thus, are not influenced by test-taker impression management.

Job knowledge tests have a long history in organizational research. This measurement methodology has documented substantial validities in the prediction of job performance. For example, in their meta-analytic work, Hunter and Hunter (1984) report a validity of .51 between job knowledge and performance. Additionally, Schmidt and Hunter (1998) found that conventional job knowledge tests showed a 14 percent increase in validity beyond general mental ability tests in the prediction of overall job-performance ratings. Job knowledge tests have been primarily used to evaluate technical or professional expertise and knowledge required for specific jobs or professions. As such, these measures are often limited by the fact that the respondents must have previous experience in the job or have received education or training relevant for the job (Hunter & Hunter, 1984; Schmidt & Hunter, 1998). These tests can also be developed to assess a knowledge domain more broadly based on an analysis of the tasks essential to the job and built at a level such that life experiences, school experiences, and/or training from other types of job may provide the foundation needed to perform well on the test (e.g., general mechanical knowledge tests). Unfortunately, generic knowledge measures have been associated with poorer prediction (Dye, Reck, & McDaniel, 1993) and limited face validity. Also, job knowledge tests can be costly and time consuming to build and, depending on the consistency of the knowledge domain, could require relatively frequent updates to remain aligned with job content. Additionally, they may also be less appropriate for jobs in which the required technical expertise can be trained fairly quickly.

SJTs also have a lengthy history in organizational research and employee selection (e.g., File, 1945; File & Remmers, 1971; Motowidlo, Dunnette, & Carter, 1990; Weekley & Jones, 1997, 1999; Clevenger, Pereira, Wiechmann, Schmitt, & Harvey, 2001; Whetzel, McDaniel, & Nguyen, 2008; Christian et al., 2010; Motowidlo & Beier, 2010). Broadly considered, situational judgment testing is a measurement methodology that presents a candidate with a job-related situation and then provides several response options, each representing a different course of action to take in the particular situation. Typical instructions ask what one should do (effectiveness instructions) or what one would do in the situation (would do instructions) (for more information on types of instruction, see McDaniel & Nguyen, 2001; Ployhart & Ehrhart, 2003; Lievens, Sackett, & Buyse, 2009). How the candidate responds to the item provides insight into his/her relevant knowledge, skills, abilities, or other characteristics (KSAOs) (Gessner & Klimoski, 2006; Ployhart & MacKenzie, 2010). Candidate responses are typically scored using theory, subject matter expert judgment, empirical keying, or some combination of these methods (Weekley, Ployhart, & Holtz, 2006).

In the organizational-research literature, SJTs have been used to measure numerous knowledge constructs, such as team role knowledge (Mumford, Van Iddekinge, Morgeson, & Campion, 2008), negotiation knowledge (Phillips, 1993), interpersonal knowledge (Weekley & Jones, 1999), and adaptability knowledge (Grim, 2010). However, even with an overarching construct focus, SJTs are inherently multidimensional (Lievens & Chan, 2010; Ployhart & MacKenzie, 2010). Within an SJT, there are a range of situations, all with different content elements to which people respond. As such, there has been an extensive debate in the research literature on what SJTs truly are—method or construct—and what they measure. Individual responses to SJTs are likely the result of a combination of ability, experience, knowledge, skills, and personality (McDaniel & Nguyen, 2001; McDaniel & Whetzel, 2005; Gessner & Klimoski, 2006; Ployhart & MacKenzie, 2010).

Owing to this complexity, much of the challenge has been determining what underlying factors a particular SJT measures. Recently, Motowidlo and colleagues developed a theory of SJTs that starts with the premise that SJT scoring methods produce a measure of procedural knowledge (see Motowidlo, Hooper, & Jackson, 2006a, 2006b; Motowidlo & Beier, 2010, for additional information). They define procedural knowledge as, "how much a person knows about effective behavior in situations like those described in an SJT" (Motowidlo et al., 2006a, p. 62). Their theory suggests that the procedural knowledge captured by an SJT includes implicit trait policies (ITPs), as well as job-specific knowledge. ITPs are beliefs that people hold about the relationship between the expression of certain personality traits and effectiveness in job situations (Motowidlo & Beier, 2010).

Although the constructs measured are unclear, SJTs have numerous strengths that promote their use in organizational research and personnel selection. Research has documented that SJTs can predict diverse dimensions of job performance, including both task and citizenship performance, and that they have incremental validity above and beyond traditional predictors of job performance, including cognitive ability, personality, and job experience (Chan & Schmitt, 2002; Weekley & Ployhart, 2005). In addition, SJTs tend to produce highly favorable applicant reactions and have fairly low subgroup differences (Weekley, Ployhart, & Harold, 2004). Also, in contrast to most of the work on knowledge, Motowidlo and Beier (2010) emphasize that ITPs, when accurate, represent general-domain knowledge (versus job-specific knowledge); as such, they may apply to a wider range of jobs than other knowledge measures.

Tacit knowledge tests are a third type of knowledge measure. Although tacit knowledge tests could be viewed as a subset of SJTs, the research and theoretical basis for tacit knowledge tests develops novel ideas and approaches that merit their own consideration. As previously mentioned, tacit knowledge is a type of procedural knowledge—an action-oriented, context-specific knowledge about what to do in a specific situation or class of situations—that is acquired through everyday experiences. Or, as Stemler and Sternberg (2006) explain, tacit knowledge is "the kind of knowledge that people possess even if they are not able to articulate the principles guiding their behavior or to explain where this knowledge was acquired" (p. 110).

Similar to SJTs, tacit knowledge situational judgment tests (TKSJTs) present a scenario followed by a question, and then a series of response options. Sternberg and Stemler (Stemler & Sternberg, 2006; Sternberg, 1997) specified a set of seven strategies around which response options can be based, in line with the theory of practical intelligence. Typically, responses are scored against an expert-response profile. Individuals' responses are evaluated in terms of their distance from the expert-response average. These test items share similar weaknesses to SJTs, including lack of clarity on precise knowledge measured. Additional information on TKSJTs, as well as their pros and cons, can be found in Stemler and Sternberg (2006) and Sternberg and Horvath (1999).

Performance-Based Measures

Performance-based measures are those assessments of procedural knowledge and skills that require candidates to perform tasks or activities similar to those found on the job (Ployhart, Schneider, & Schmitt, 2006). There are numerous types of performance-based methodology used to assess procedural knowledge, including work sample tests and simulations. In fact, SJTs conceptually overlap and have even been called work samples or simulations themselves (Bauer & Truxillo, 2006). Additionally, although assessment centers have also been used to assess knowledge—and exercises within an assessment center are typically simulations or other performance-based measures—at present, our focus is on the individual measures themselves.

Work sample tests and simulations can take on many different forms, as they are built to have a high level of fidelity between the test and the work itself (Guion, 1998). Even so, similar to SJTs and TKSJTs, work samples and simulations can vary in their level of fidelity and, with the technology that exists today, these measurement methodologies can be highly sophisticated in bringing to life the psychological and physical aspects of work settings. One example of this is a simulation that uses virtual-reality technology in which the individual feels as though he/she is present in an environment created by a computer (see Pierce & Aguinis, 1997). More conventional work sample and simulation methodologies can involve anything from role-playing to video-based methods to computer-simulated experiences.

Performance-based methodologies have been used extensively in organizational research, starting as early as Münsterberg's (1913) work sample tests to select drivers and ship pilots. They are generally thought to be some of the most valid predictors of job performance (Schmidt & Hunter, 1998), having achieved impressive validities in prior meta-analytic work (e.g., .54 between work samples and supervisor ratings of job performance; Hunter & Hunter, 1984). In addition to these high validities, many researchers assert that work samples and simulations tend to have lower group differences than cognitive-ability measures (e.g., Callinan & Robertson, 2000; Schmitt & Mills, 2001; Cascio, 2003). However, an emerging consensus in the selection literature is that any measurement methodology can be associated with small or large group differences; it depends on the nature of the construct(s) being measured (see Bobko, Roth, & Buster, 2005).

When used as selection tests, a significant benefit of work sample and simulation methodologies is that they tend to generate very positive applicant reactions (Cascio & Aguinis, 2005). They have high levels of face validity as they resemble the job itself and have the additional benefit of serving as a realistic job preview for the candidate applying for the position. Although work samples and simulations have numerous positive characteristics, the constructs they measure are quite complex and diverse. By their very nature, work samples/simulations require individuals to demonstrate mastery of a specific job-relevant task in a high-fidelity setting, which, by implication, assesses individuals' requisite procedural knowledge necessary to perform that task. Although this direct link to job performance does provide evidence of knowledge relevance, it is not always completely clear what specific knowledge(s) are being assessed by the methodology and when the individual's other attributes may also impact performance.

MEASUREMENT APPROACHES FROM OTHER FIELDS

In the previous section, we discussed the current methodologies most commonly used in organizational research and employee selection to assess knowledge. We now turn our attention to two methodologies that have promise as alternatives to our traditional knowledge measures. These methodologies are *construct generation*, or the free-form listing of attributes, and *idea generation*, or the free-form listing of strategies or ideas. As we review these methodologies, keep in mind that we are not advocating either should replace current knowledge-measurement methodologies. Instead, we hope these methods will serve to stimulate research and innovation to advance knowledge measurement. Additionally, although the reviewed methodologies may have been developed to assess specific knowledge, skills, or other variables, we believe that, when considered more broadly, they may serve as building blocks to assess other knowledge constructs.

Construct Generation Measures

Overview

Construct generation measures are based on the fusion of two early lines of research, George Kelly's (1955) work in personal construct psychology and Heinz Werner's (1957) structural–developmental theory. Kelly (1955) asserts that each individual has a certain number of personal constructs, or basic cognitive structures, through which he or she interprets, anticipates, evaluates, and understands aspects of the world. The guiding assumption of Kelly's theory is that people construct the meaning of their own lives by creating, testing, and continually revising personal theories about the world around them. These personal theories can also be called construct systems, because they include an indefinite number of personal constructs that the individual uses to understand, differentiate, integrate, and predict life events (Delia, 1976; Applegate & Delia, 1980).

Werner's (1957) structural–developmental theory suggests that people's personal construct systems develop according to the orthogenetic principle, in which a global, undifferentiated construct becomes increasingly differentiated, articulated, and hierarchically integrated. As such, individuals with greater construct development in a particular domain possess more differentiated, articulated, and integrated systems of relevant personal constructs, leading to greater information-processing capacity in that domain (Burleson & Caplan, 1998; Waltman, 2002; Griffin, 2006). Put another way, the complexity of someone's knowledge domain varies by the quantity of personal constructs he/she has within the domain, how abstract these constructs are, and how elaborately they relate to one another. Both Kelly's (1955) and Werner's (1957) theories are at the core of constructivist theory, which suggests that people use their existing knowledge systems or personal constructs to understand and interpret new information. People with more highly developed systems of domain-relevant constructs will be better able to acquire, understand, store, retrieve, organize, and generate information and ideas related to this domain (Burleson & Caplan, 1998). Therefore, understanding the complexity of one's personal constructs in a particular domain will aid in the prediction of one's behaviors in that domain.

Description of Methodology

The goal in construct-generation measurement is to ascertain the complexity of one's knowledge structure within a particular construct domain (Burleson & Caplan, 1998). The methodology includes acquiring one or more samples of domain-relevant knowledge via free-response written descriptions. Typically, respondents are asked to generate as many unique constructs as possible that are relevant to the domain of interest within a specified timeframe. Each response generated represents a construct within his/her knowledge domain (Crockett, 1965; O'Keefe & Sypher, 1981; O'Keefe, Shepherd, & Streeter, 1982; Burleson & Waltman, 1988; Burleson, Applegate, & Delia, 1991; Burleson & Caplan, 1998). The set of constructs elicited in the free-response written descriptions are a sample of the individual's overall construct system within that domain (see O'Keefe & Delia, 1979; Burleson et al., 1991). This set is evaluated on various attributes and, from this evaluation, a knowledge-complexity score is obtained for the particular construct domain.

Based on prior research, the response attributes most often coded are differentiation, abstractness, organization, and content (Burleson & Caplan, 1998). Of these, differentiation of constructs is generally the primary basis for scoring, because it tends to be the most efficient scoring approach and is moderately-to-highly correlated with abstractness and organization scores (Burleson & Caplan, 1998; O'Keefe & Sypher, 1981). Differentiation coding includes counting the number of distinct constructs embedded in a response (Applegate, 1990; Burleson & Waltman, 1988; Crockett, Press, Delia, & Kenny, 1974). Coding procedures for differentiation are fairly straightforward; hence, generally high levels of intercoder reliability are obtained (Burleson & Waltman, 1988). Specific rules to follow for determining what constitutes a construct can be found in Burleson and Waltman (1988).

One may also evaluate the written descriptions on the abstractness of the constructs included (see Delia et al., 1974; Applegate, 1980, 1990; Burleson, 1984) and estimate the degree of organization among constructs (see Crockett, 1965, 1982; Crockett et al., 1974). In addition to differentiation, abstractness, and organization, content analysis is also feasible with qualitative data. For example, Neimeyer and Neimeyer (2002) developed a classification system for the content analysis of personal constructs that includes 45 content categories divided into six basic areas, including moral, emotional, relational, personal, intellectual/operational, and values/interests.

There has been some debate on how construct-generation measures are scored, particularly regarding what the construct-differentiation score represents. Although the prevailing theory is that high scores on construct differentiation are a result of having a large number of highly integrated constructs in a particular knowledge domain, some researchers have suggested alternative explanations. For example, O'Keefe and Delia (1982) and Sypher and Applegate (1984) suggested that a person may score highly on this type of measure, not because they have a large number of constructs available, but because they can more easily access the constructs they do have in this knowledge domain. Other researchers (e.g., Beatty & Payne, 1985; Allen, Mabry, Banski, Stoneman, & Carter, 1990) have suggested that construct generation is driven by an individual's motivational characteristics, rather than the cognitive constructs they have available, although most research has found construct complexity to be independent from general personality traits (O'Keefe & Delia, 1982; Samter & Burleson, 1984; Burleson & Waltman, 1988).

Still other researchers (e.g., Powers, Jordan, & Street, 1979; Beatty & Payne, 1984) have suggested that construct-complexity scores may be influenced by the individual's verbal skills and/or the wordiness of his/her responses. However, numerous studies have found little relationship between the construct complexity and measures of loquacity, such as the number of words used to express a construct or used in an informal conversation (Burleson, Applegate, & Neuwirth, 1981; Burleson, Waltman, & Samter, 1987). Providing additional support that one's wordiness does not appear to be a major driver of construct-complexity scores, construct-differentiation scores have also been found to be unrelated to assessments of talkativeness (Angell, 2000), verbal fluency, verbal intelligence, general intelligence, vocabulary and intellectual achievement, writing speed, and narrative writing skill (see Burleson et al., 1981; Burleson & Rowan, 1985; Burleson & Waltman, 1988).

Research Using the Methodology

Construct complexity methodology has garnered extensive conceptual, empirical, and practical support in fields outside organizational research. An early measure based on this methodology, which is still used today, is the role category questionnaire (RCQ; Crockett, 1965). The RCQ has been used extensively to assess the breadth, complexity, and articulation of one's cognitive schemata in the interpersonal domain (e.g., O'Keefe & Delia, 1979; Sypher & Zorn, 1986; Applegate, Coyle, Seibert, & Church, 1989; Samter, Burleson, & Basden-Murphy, 1989; Sypher, Bostrom, & Seibert, 1989; Applegate, Kline, & Delia, 1991; Kline, 1991; Burleson & Caplan, 1998).

Research on the RCQ provides support for the construct complexity methodology more broadly, as it is the most common construct-complexity measure used in the research literature.

The RCQ asks participants to provide free-response written descriptions of two peers whom they know, one liked and one disliked (Crockett, 1965). Participants are asked to list all the adjectives, characteristics, or other attributes (e.g., beliefs, habits, ways of treating others, mannerisms, etc.) that describe each of these individuals. They are generally given 5 minutes to complete each description. The constructs elicited by the RCQ are a sample of the total number and type of interpersonal constructs the individual has available within his/her cognitive schemata. Those who have a more differentiated, complex, and integrated construct system have more abstract, interconnected interpersonal constructs available to them and will express a greater number of these constructs on the RCQ (Delia, 1976; Applegate & Delia, 1980; Burleson & Caplan, 1998).

Even today, the RCQ is the most common application of the free-form construct generation methodology. Its success in other fields has been largely due to its extensive reliability and validity evidence (see reviews by O'Keefe & Sypher, 1981; Delia, O'Keefe, & O'Keefe, 1982; Burleson, 1987; Burleson & Waltman, 1988; Sypher & Sypher, 1988; Burleson et al., 1991; Burleson & Caplan, 1998). In terms of reliability, the RCQ has obtained strong test–retest reliabilities across multiple studies (e.g., O'Keefe, Shepherd, & Streeter, 1982; Adams-Webber, 2001). Additionally, the RCQ has demonstrated discriminant validity with general intellectual ability and verbal intelligence, while showing convergent validity with measures of construct abstractness and organization (see O'Keefe & Sypher, 1981; Burleson, Waltman, & Samter, 1987; Burleson & Waltman, 1988; Applegate, 1990). Research has also empirically linked the RCQ's interpersonal construct complexity with numerous interpersonally relevant skills, capabilities, and outcomes, including better communication skills (e.g., Burleson & Caplan, 1998), perspective-taking ability (e.g., Kline, Pelias, & Delia, 1991), nonverbal decoding ability (e.g., Woods, 1996), and social perception skills (e.g., Burleson, 1994).

Although the majority of the research using the RCQ has assessed general interpersonal construct knowledge, researchers have documented support for the notion that there are multiple systems of interpersonal constructs (see Coopman, 1998). Researchers have argued that, although the RCQ is useful for assessing interpersonal constructs in general (a liked and disliked peer), it might not be as useful for gaining insight into the complexity of knowledge structures in other knowledge domains, including other interpersonal knowledge domains (e.g., Daly, Bell, Glenn, & Lawrence, 1985; Martin, 1991, 1992; Wilson, Cruz, & Kang, 1992). As a result, when assessing other knowledge domains, researchers have employed a methodology similar to the RCQ, but tailored to the specific knowledge domain of interest.

For example, Daly et al. (1985) developed a measure to assess the complexity of constructs one has for conversational interactions. Their measure of conversational complexity only had a moderate relationship with interpersonal cognitive complexity, as assessed by the RCQ. In other research, Martin (1991, 1992) demonstrated that his measure of the complexity of constructs for personal relationships functioned independently of RCQ-based interpersonal cognitive complexity. Additionally, several researchers have shown that people typically develop distinct interpersonal construct systems for co-workers (e.g., Meyer & Sypher, 1993; Zorn, McKinney, & Moran, 1993; Zimmermann, 1994; Zimmermann, Hart, Allen, & Haas, 1998). These findings suggest that people may develop several differentially elaborated and integrated systems of interpersonal constructs, and that, although construct generation may be viable, the methodology needs to elicit constructs from the particular domain of interest.

Within an organizational context, limited research has applied this free-form construct generation methodology. However, in the research that has been conducted, construct complexity has been related to effectiveness on the job, particularly for those in management-level positions (e.g., Sypher, 1984; Walton, 1985; Streufert & Swezy, 1986; Coopman, 1998). More recently, Dudley and Cortina (2009) applied this construct generation methodology to assess interpersonal construct knowledge specific to ROTC cadets. Their hypothesis was that those cadets who had greater knowledge of peer cadet characteristics would be more effective helpers, because cadets could leverage their insight into their peers' attributes to determine the optimal approach for helping and adapting to peer cadets.

To assess interpersonal construct complexity specific to the ROTC environment, Dudley and Cortina (2009) used an approach similar to the RCQ. However, instead of asking respondents to describe peers, they were asked to describe fellow cadets, one most liked and one least liked, to assess interpersonal construct complexity within that domain, which follows examples set by previous work in which the term "peer" had been changed to reflect the population (see Sypher & Zorn, 1986; Applegate et al., 1989; Sypher et al., 1989). As in prior research, cadets were given 5 minutes to complete each description and asked to be as detailed as possible, paying particular attention to the fellow cadet's beliefs, ways of treating others, traits, mannerisms, and similar attributes. The number of constructs generated was used to determine each cadet's interpersonal construct-complexity score, termed "target knowledge." Findings provided evidence for the incremental validity of cadet interpersonal construct complexity, above and beyond other key predictors of helping behaviors in the citizenship literature, including both motivational attributes and personality characteristics (Dudley & Cortina, 2009).

Opportunity in Organizational Research

We envision several steps for using construct-complexity measures in organizational research. First, researchers will need to identify the specific knowledge construct they seek to measure. Some knowledge variables may be more amenable to measurement via this methodology than others. As interpersonal knowledge and its variants have been studied in some depth, these knowledge constructs offer a good basis from which organizational researchers could employ this methodology.

Second, if the specific knowledge construct has not already been assessed in the literature, items would need to be designed to gather samples of the domain-relevant knowledge via free-response written descriptions. If assessing an interpersonal knowledge, items typically ask the participant to think of a specific person or category of person, and think of all the adjectives, characteristics, or other attributes they can think of to describe these individuals. Examples of interpersonal knowledge include leadership knowledge, co-worker knowledge, and customer knowledge. Importantly, knowledge constructs beyond interpersonal knowledge may also be assessed with this technique. For example, if one wished to assess someone's knowledge of a specific data program or knowledge of a new technology, the question posed could be to list all attributes associated with the target phenomenon. Unfortunately, at present, we are not aware of any research that has looked at using construct generation this way; however, it is an opportunity for future research. Respondents should be given a time limit per construct-complexity item. In prior research, this has typically been 5 minutes for interpersonal knowledge measurement (e.g., Dudley & Cortina, 2009). Future research can determine the number of items and time limit required to obtain a reliable measure of specific knowledge constructs.

Third, researchers must determine the optimal scoring procedure to use, given the specific knowledge construct they are measuring and the research question being asked. As mentioned previously, there are three knowledge attributes most commonly computed from the type of data gathered via construct generation: differentiation, abstraction, and organization (see Burleson & Caplan, 1998, for details). Content analysis has also been used in previous research (see Neimeyer & Neimeyer, 2002). However, as there has been limited organizational research applying this methodology, optimal scoring procedures to reflect job-relevant knowledge domains have yet to be determined. Consequently, we recommend exploring these methods and, at a minimum, including differentiation coding, as it has been used the most frequently with the most consistent results in prior research.

Last, organizational researchers will need to consider the best method for collecting construct-complexity data. Written responses have typically been coded by hand. Although this method works, other methods should be explored, as hand coding is extremely time consuming and likely impractical for use in many applied contexts. Before discussing the implications of technology for construct-complexity measurement, however, we present another alternative approach to knowledge measurement.

Idea Generation Methodology

Overview

Idea generation involves asking respondents to generate ideas in response to stimuli. Although conceptually similar to the construct complexity methodology, we introduce it separately in this chapter owing to distinctions in the methodology, response set, scoring, prior research, and potential application as a knowledge measure. Idea generation is divergent from construct complexity in that the stimuli are not individuals or roles, and responses are not descriptors or constructs. Instead, the stimuli are hypothetical scenarios or questions, and responses are typically ideas, associations, or strategies generated in response to the particular stimuli.

Another term often used for idea generation is ideation, which is defined as the process of generating ideas that could be useful for achieving some desired state or outcome (Reinig, Briggs, & Nunamaker, 2007).

The idea generation methodology has foundations both in Guilford's structure-of-intellect model and constructivist theory (e.g., Guilford, 1956, 1967; Guilford & Hoepfner, 1971). Guilford's model describes the cognitive process underlying the methodology, whereas constructivist theory provides an understanding of how the methodology samples one's underlying knowledge. Guilford's (1956) structure-of-intellect model differentiates between two processes, convergent and divergent thinking, both of which are ways one generates additional information from what is given. Convergent thinking aligns with the intelligence-testing notion of integrating information to determine a right answer, such as in numeric or verbal reasoning tests. On the other hand, divergent thinking involves generating multiple options or possibilities based on current information, which is the cognitive process underlying idea generation.

As mentioned previously in relation to the construct complexity methodology, constructivist theory suggests that people react to the world around them through their own interpretive schemas or knowledge systems, also referred to as personal constructs, cognitive structures, cognitive schemata, or cognitive templates (O'Keefe, Delia, & O'Keefe, 1980; Delia et al., 1982; Nicotera, 1995). Prior experience and learning impact the processing of scenario cues, as well as the responses to the scenarios via interpretive cognitive schemas. Interpretive cognitive schemas are generated and evolve over time as individuals break their experiences into usable units of interpreted beliefs and corresponding behaviors about the world; these influence, create, and control activities such as strategies one might use in different types of situation (Delia, O'Keefe, & O'Keefe, 1982; Nicotera, 1995). Thus, when a hypothetical scenario is posed, and an individual is asked to produce multiple responses, the ideas and/or strategies listed in response are based on existing knowledge structures that have been developed and stored over time, through previous interactions and experiences with similar stimuli and/or learned knowledge (Sypher & Higgins, 1989).

This methodology of asking one to produce multiple responses to a specific prompt in a stream-of-consciousness fashion is sometimes called a divergent thinking task (Plucker & Renzulli, 1999). People with more highly developed systems of domain-relevant strategies and ideas will be better able to adapt their approach within a domain, as they have multiple options available to them. Thus, understanding the complexity of one's cognitive schemas in a particular domain will aid in the prediction of one's behaviors in that domain, and in the prediction of one's ability to adapt within that domain.

Description of Methodology

Consistent with construct-complexity measurement, the goal of the idea generation methodology is to estimate the extent of one's knowledge of a particular domain by acquiring samples of knowledge from within that domain. Instead of thinking of individual constructs or descriptors, idea generation involves presenting individuals with a stimulus, typically a verbal or figural prompt, and asking them to think of as many ideas, approaches, or actions they could take in response to this stimulus as possible, within a specified timeframe (Guilford, 1950; Christensen, Merrifield, & Guilford, 1953; Wallach & Kogan, 1965; Meeker, 1969; Michael & Wright, 1989; Kim, 2006).

Using this methodology to assess one's level of knowledge in a domain is based on the assumption that individuals differ in the structural complexity or elaboration of cognitions relevant to the domain. Accordingly, the ideas or strategies elicited by this methodology constitute a sample of the total ideas or strategies the participant has available. Responses are evaluated on various attributes, and a knowledge score is obtained for the individual for the particular domain.

Idea generation tasks can vary extensively by the specific prompts and/or the type of response(s) requested of the individual being changed. These variations have implications for precisely what a particular idea generation task is measuring, as well as for the criteria to which performance on the task is most likely to be linked (Mumford, Marks, Connelly, Zaccaro, & Johnson, 1998; Baer & Kaufman, 2005; Reiter-Palmon, Illies, Cross, Buboltz, & Nimps, 2009). For example, divergent thinking tasks that ask the respondent to generate as many uses of a brick as possible have been linked to creativity (Wallach & Kogan, 1965), whereas divergent thinking tasks that ask the respondent to generate strategies he/she could use to help a colleague have been linked to ratings of helping behaviors (Dudley & Cortina, 2009). If the prompt and/or question driving the participant response are focused on a specific knowledge domain, such as different sales strategies one could use in a situation, then the responses generated are reflective of the individual's knowledge in this domain.

Historically, most idea generation tasks have been built with an eye toward predicting creativity. One example is the alternate uses task, in which participants are asked to list as many uses as they can think of for three common objects—a brick, shoe, and newspaper (Wallach & Kogan, 1965). Another example is a consequences or implications task, in which participants are asked to list as many consequences as they can think of to hypothetical events, such as what would happen if people no longer needed to sleep (Christensen, Merrifield, & Guilford, 1953; Goff & Torrance, 2002).

Outside creativity research, idea generation tasks have been used to assess knowledge. For example, in the sales and marketing literature under the cognitive selling paradigm (Weitz, Sujan, & Sujan, 1986; Leong, Busch, & John, 1989; Leigh & McGraw, 1989; Szymanski & Churchill, 1990), idea generation tasks have been used to assess salesperson knowledge. An example task from this literature includes the free-form listing of sales strategies given a particular customer type and/or sales situation (e.g., Sujan, Sujan, & Bettman, 1988). Additionally, in the organizational-research literature, divergent thinking tasks have involved providing respondents with domain-specific hypothetical scenarios and asking that they list the actions or strategies they might employ in a particular situation (e.g., Mumford et al., 1998; Dudley & Cortina, 2009). In some studies, the idea generation methodology is called a problem-solving task, in that issues or challenges are presented, and the participant is asked to list possible solutions (e.g., Reiter-Palmon et al., 2009).

In addition to the task itself, instructions can vary in terms of how much direction they provide to the respondent. Instructions may simply ask for one to think of as many ideas as possible, or they may ask the individual to be creative and think of things that they believe others will not (Torrance, 1966; Goff & Torrance, 2002). As the latter is particularly relevant for creativity research, we hypothesize the former would be most relevant in assessing knowledge; however, research is needed to verify what instructions would be optimal in assessing knowledge in various domains.

Although specific idea generation tasks can vary substantially, all are open-ended tasks to which a respondent may give numerous responses (Runco & Acar, 2010). Response attributes provide insight into the depth and articulation of one's knowledge in the particular domain. Similar to construct complexity response evaluation, as these are open-ended, qualitative data, there are numerous attributes on which responses can be scored. Fluency, or the number of ideas, is the most commonly used metric; however, there are numerous other metrics including: uniqueness (number of unique responses), originality (number of statistically infrequent ideas), cleverness (creativity level of responses), flexibility (different categories of ideas, the variety of ideas), elaboration (level of detail or expansion on the basic idea), and resistance to premature closure (the degree of psychological openness) (for detailed information on various scoring methodologies, see Kim, 2006, 2008; Silvia, 2008; Torrance, 2008). The quality or effectiveness of the ideas or strategies generated is still another option for evaluating responses (Burleson & Caplan, 1998).

Despite the potential for advancement of knowledge measurement provided through idea generation tasks, some of the more traditional scoring methodologies have recently been challenged (e.g., Runco, 2008; Silvia et al., 2008). Researchers, primarily focused on creativity, have been considering and developing additional methodologies, such as the Top 2 index (which asks respondents to pick their two most creative responses; see Silvia et al., 2008), snapshot scoring (which provides a single holistic rating of a set of responses; see Silvia, Martin, & Nusbaum, 2009), the consensual scoring technique (which provides scoring based on ratings of independent raters; see Amabile, 1982, 1996), and the creativity quotient (which accounts for ideation fluency and flexibility in one score; see Bossomaier, Harré, Knittel, & Snyder, 2009). However, even with recent advances and alternative metrics, methods of scoring divergent-thinking tasks have changed little since the 1960s (Wallach & Kogan, 1965; Torrance, 1967), and still no agreed-upon best practice exists. Therefore, additional research would be beneficial to further understand scoring methodologies and their impact on measured constructs.

Research Using the Methodology

The idea generation methodology has a lengthy history and extensive research surrounding its use. Although we propose this methodology as a tool that can be used to assess knowledge, as previously mentioned, divergent-thinking tasks have been used extensively as measures of creativity (Guilford, 1950; Merrifield, Guilford, Christensen, & Frick, 1962; Barron & Harrington, 1981; Batey & Furnham, 2006; Kim, 2006).

The specific divergent-thinking tasks used in creativity research do not necessarily align with the types of task one would use to assess an individual's knowledge of a domain. We feel this is a critical point to make, because the relationship between idea generation and various outcomes is likely impacted by the type of task. Thus, given the scope of the current chapter, we focus on research that has utilized the idea generation methodology to examine a particular knowledge.

The primary research utilizing idea generation tasks to assess particular knowledge is found within the sales and marketing literature. This line of inquiry is called the "cognition selling paradigm"; its focus is on linking sales behaviors to underlying knowledge structures. This research has employed idea generation and similar methodologies, such as free-response elicitation, to assess salesperson knowledge (Sujan et al., 1988). The theory is that salespeople acquire and comprehend information based on how the current sales situation relates to their recollection of past sales situations and results (Morgan & Stoltman, 1990). These recollections are contained in the form of knowledge structures that include both declarative knowledge, such as client categories or products, and procedural knowledge, such as selling scripts. Salespeople utilize these knowledge structures to identify customer needs and determine their sales approach (Szymanski, 1988; Szymanski & Churchill, 1990). Generally, this research has found that more effective salespeople have richer, more interrelated knowledge structures than less effective salespeople, both in terms of customer traits and strategies for selling to customers. More effective salespeople also tended to list more specific, problem solving-oriented strategies for selling, whereas less effective salespeople used more global, relationship-oriented strategies (Sujan et al., 1988, 1991). This research provides additional support for the use of idea generation as a methodology for estimating underlying knowledge structures.

Within the organizational-research literature, studies implementing idea generation to assess knowledge are currently very limited. Mumford et al. (1998) looked at leadership knowledge assessed via idea generation and found that performance on the idea generation tasks was positively related to leadership performance. These results were maintained even after controlling for intelligence and expertise. In addition, Dudley and Cortina (2009) used an idea generation methodology to assess the helping-strategy knowledge (which they termed helping-strategy richness) of ROTC cadets. Their hypothesis was that those cadets who had greater helping-strategy knowledge (i.e., more helping strategies available to them) would be rated as more effective helpers by their peers. To assess helping-strategy knowledge specific to the ROTC environment, Dudley and Cortina (2009) asked participants to review three scenarios in which a peer required assistance, and they were given 3 minutes to list all the different approaches or strategies they could think of to help the peer in each situation. Cadets' responses were evaluated based on the number of strategies identified. They found that the cadets who generated more, unique helping strategies were rated as better helpers than those who generated fewer strategies. Findings also confirmed the incremental validity of a cadet's helping-strategy knowledge above and beyond other helping-behavior predictors in the prediction of helping-behavior effectiveness (Dudley & Cortina, 2009).

Opportunity in Organizational Research

As detailed in the previous section, although the idea generation methodology has most commonly been used in studies of creativity, it has also been adapted to assess knowledge in several key domains, including salesperson knowledge, helping-strategy knowledge, and leader knowledge. In line with our suggestion for using the construct complexity methodology, we recommend several steps for using idea generation in organizational research.

First, researchers need to identify the knowledge they seek to measure and determine if it makes sense to assess the particular knowledge via idea generation. Owing to its promise in previous research, we recommend organizational researchers consider knowledge of strategies or approaches that underlie key performance behaviors, such as Dudley and Cortina's (2009) helping-strategy richness.

Second, items need to be developed to gather samples of the relevant knowledge via free-response written descriptions. If strategy knowledge is being assessed, items typically present the participant with a situation to which he/she must respond by listing all the possible strategies or approaches he/she can think of to address the situation. Respondents should be given a time limit per idea generation item. In prior research, this has typically been 3 minutes for strategy-knowledge measurement (e.g., Dudley & Cortina, 2009).

Third, as with the construct complexity measure, researchers must determine the optimal scoring procedure to use, given the specific knowledge construct and research question. As mentioned previously, numerous attributes may be used to evaluate idea generation responses, such as fluency (number of ideas), flexibility (different categories of idea, the variety of ideas), originality (number of statistically infrequent ideas), cleverness (creativity level of responses), and elaboration (level of detail or expansion on the basic idea). However, as with construct complexity, the methodology is currently limited, owing in part to the paucity of organizational research using the idea generation methodology. As a result, optimal scoring procedures have yet to be determined. In general, we recommend starting with the most commonly used metric, fluency, or the number of ideas. Research would also benefit from the examination of other metrics, such as flexibility and originality, to acquire additional insight into the breadth of one's knowledge.

Last, organizational researchers will need to consider the best method for collecting idea generation data. Consistent with construct complexity research, typically, idea generation responses are coded by hand, counting and evaluating the various ideas generated by the respondent. Although feasible, this method is rather time consuming and potentially impractical in some applied contexts. As with construct complexity measures, idea generation measures stand to benefit from advances in technology that could allow for a more efficient scoring process.

INTEGRATION OF TECHNOLOGY ADVANCEMENTS

The rapid rate of technology advancement has already created an impact on all aspects of how organizational researchers gather, track, analyze, and disseminate data. Prior to advancements in personal computing and programming capabilities, most research in psychological assessment was conducted using paper-based formats to capture information on constructs of interest. Using a paper-based format naturally limits the methods one can use to measure a construct to the familiar item types (forced choice, multiple choice, Likert-type, etc.). Furthermore, conducting studies reliant upon qualitative data could be an arduous and time-intensive undertaking.

In the early days of personal computers and the Internet, most tests were built to mimic their paper-based counterparts (Couper, 2008). Modern technology allows researchers and practitioners many advantages over traditional, paper-based assessments, including increased data-tracking capabilities, better integration of auditory or video stimuli, high-resolution imagery, animation, and/or simulation (Trull, 2007; Greene, 2011). In addition to capturing participants' responses to items or events, many computer programs available to researchers now also track response latencies, errant mouse clicks, changed answers, and more (Hornke & Kersting, 2006). From an assessment standpoint, this offers researchers an opportunity to capture constructs in innovative and unprecedented ways. Provided these technological advancements, our discipline is well positioned to explore new measurement methodologies in greater depth, breadth, and efficiency than ever before.

In regard to the two knowledge assessment methodologies described in the current chapter, in the past, the qualitative nature of the responses would have raised significant barriers to the adoption of these measurement methodologies, particularly in a selection setting or when using large sample sizes. However, improved technological capabilities and statistical packages, specifically with respect to interpreting answers, make evaluating free-form answers easier, less subjective, and more efficient. In one well-known example, essays for the GMAT are now graded automatically by a computer software program (Rudner, Garcia, & Welch, 2006). This system can evaluate responses based on a host of criteria, including content and grammatical fluency.

To assess knowledge with a construct complexity or idea generation methodology, the researcher or practitioner now has a wide range of technological options to efficiently and effectively interpret the data, from automatically counting the number of responses to evaluating the quality of the individual responses alone and in relation to the rest of the respondents' answers. Altogether, technological improvements have opened the door to open-ended response measurement methodologies that were previously impractical options for organizational research.

CONCLUSION

The goal of this chapter was to provide insight into knowledge measurement methodologies. After reviewing the measures that are currently used in organizational research, we introduced and highlighted two methodologies that have been developed in other disciplines to assess knowledge. These measures both utilize free-form responses to a stimulus. Construct complexity measures elicit descriptors, and idea generation assessments prompt a listing of actions or ideas. As discussed, these methodologies have been used to assess various types of knowledge, and yet have received little attention within organizational research. In the past, free-form-response methodologies have been considered cumbersome owing to the manual effort required to code and score responses; however, technological improvements can ease both data collection and interpretation. For example, computer programs can now code free-form responses to the specifications of a measure, greatly reducing the amount of time needed to evaluate a response. We suggest that these methodologies could be further adapted and positioned by organizational researchers to offer alternatives for direct knowledge measurement.

Although we recognize that the two measurement methodologies described in this chapter are not the only methodologies that could be implemented to better assess individuals' knowledge in organizational settings, we do believe they hold great promise. Additionally, we advocate these approaches in hopes that they can serve as an impetus for additional research and exploration of knowledge measurement. Through methods enabling direct and efficient assessment of knowledge, organizational researchers will be better equipped to understand the relationship between knowledge and other critical constructs, such as prior work experience, ability, personality, and job performance.

REFERENCES

Adams-Webber, J. R. (2001). Cognitive complexity and role relationships. *Journal of Constructivist Psychology, 14,* 43–50. doi:10.1080/10720530125762

Allen, M., Mabry, E. A., Banski, M., Stoneman, M., & Carter, P. (1990). A thoughtful appraisal of measuring cognition using the Role Category Questionnaire. *Communication Reports, 3,* 49–57.

Amabile, T. M. (1982). Social psychology of creativity: A consensual assessment technique. *Journal of Personality and Social Psychology, 43,* 997–1013. doi:10.1037/0022-3514.43.5.997

Amabile, T. M. (1996). *Creativity in context: Update to "The Social Psychology of Creativity."* Boulder, CO: Westview Press.

Anderson, J. R. (1993). Problem solving and learning. *American Psychologist, 48,* 35–44. doi:10.1037/0003-066X.48.1.35

Angell, L. R. (2000). Further exploring the relationship between loquacity and construct differentiation. *Journal of Constructivist Psychology, 13*, 321–326. doi:10.1080/10720530050130139

Applegate, J. L. (1980). Person- and position-centered teacher communication in a day care center: A case study triangulating interview and naturalistic methods. *Studies in Symbolic Interaction, 3*, 59–96.

Applegate, J. L. (1990). Constructs and communication: A pragmatic integration. In G. Neimeyer (Ed.), *Advances in personal construct psychology* (Vol. 1, pp. 203–230). Greenwich, CT: JAI Press.

Applegate, J. L., Coyle, K., Seibert, J. H., & Church, S. (1989). Interpersonal constructs and communicative ability in a police environment: A preliminary investigation. *International Journal of Personal Construct Psychology, 2*, 385–399.

Applegate, J. L., & Delia, J. G. (1980). Person-centered speech, psychological development, and the contexts of language usage. In R. St. Clair & H. Giles (Eds.), *The social and psychological contexts of language* (pp. 245–282). Hillsdale, NJ: Erlbaum.

Applegate, J. L., Kline, S. L., & Delia, J. G. (1991). Alternative measures of cognitive complexity as predictors of communicative performance. *International Journal of Personal Construct Psychology, 4*, 193–213.

Baer, J., & Kaufman, J. C. (2005). Whence creativity? Overlapping and dual-aspect skills and traits. In J. C. Kaufman & J. Baer (Eds.), *Creativity across domains: Faces of the muse* (pp. 313–320). Mahwah, NJ: Lawrence Erlbaum Associates Publishers.

Bar-On, R. (1997). *The Bar-On Emotional Quotient Inventory (EQ-i): A test of emotional intelligence.* Toronto: Multi-Health Systems.

Barrick, M. R., Shaffer, J. A., & DeGrassi, S. W. (2009). What you see may not be what you get: Relationships among self-presentation tactics and ratings of interview and job performance. *Journal of Applied Psychology, 94*, 1394–1411. doi:10.1037/a0016532

Barron, F., & Harrington, D. M. (1981). Creativity, intelligence, and personality. *Annual Review of Psychology, 32*, 439–476. doi:10.1146/annurev.ps.32.020181.002255

Bateman, T. S., & Organ, D. W. (1983). Job satisfaction and the good soldier: The relationship between affect and employee "citizenship." *Academy of Management Journal, 26*, 587–595. doi:10.2307/255908

Batey, M., & Furnham, A. (2006). Creativity, intelligence, and personality: A critical review of the scattered literature. *Genetic, Social, and General Psychology Monographs, 132*(4), 355–429. doi:10.3200/MONO.132.4.355-430

Bauer, T. N., & Truxillo, D. M. (2006). Applicant reactions to situational judgment tests: Research and related practical issues. In J. A. Weekley & R. E. Ployhart (Eds.), *Situational judgment tests: Theory, measurement, and application* (pp. 233–249). Mahwah, NJ: Lawrence Erlbaum Associates Publishers.

Beatty, M. J., & Payne, S. K. (1984). Loquacity and quantity of constructs as predictors of social perspective-taking. *Communication Quarterly, 32*, 207–210.

Beatty, M. J., & Payne, S. K. (1985). Is construct differentiation loquacity? A motivational perspective. *Human Communication Research, 11*, 605–612.

Best, J. B. (1989). *Cognitive psychology* (2nd ed.). New York: West Publishing.

Bettencourt, L. A., Gwinner, K. P., & Meuter, M. L. (2001). A comparison of attitude, personality, and knowledge predictors of service-oriented organizational citizenship behaviors. *Journal of Applied Psychology, 86*, 29–41. doi:10.1037/0021-9010.86.1.29

Bobko, P., Roth, P. L., & Buster, M. A. (2005). Work sample selection tests and expected reduction in adverse impact: A cautionary note. *International Journal of Selection and Assessment, 13,* 1–10. doi:10.1111/j.0965-075X.2005.00295.x

Borman, W. C., & Motowidlo, S. J. (1993). Expanding the criterion domain to include elements of contextual performance. In N. Schmitt & W. Borman (Eds.), *Personnel selection in organizations* (pp. 71–98). New York: Jossey-Bass.

Borman, W. C., & Penner, L. A. (2001). Citizenship performance: Its nature, antecedents, and motives. In B. W. Roberts & R. Hogan (Eds.), *Personality psychology in the workplace* (pp. 45–61). Washington, DC: American Psychological Association. doi:10.1037/10434-002

Borman, W. C., White, L. A., & Dorsey, D. W. (1995). Effects of ratee task performance and interpersonal factors on supervisor and peer performance ratings. *Journal of Applied Psychology, 80,* 168–177. doi:10.1037/0021-9010.80.1.168

Borman, W. C., White, L. A., Pulakos, E. D., & Oppler, S. H. (1991). Models of supervisory job performance ratings. *Journal of Applied Psychology, 76,* 863–872. doi:10.1037/0021-9010.76.6.863

Borman, W. C., Penner, L. A., Allen, T. D., & Motowidlo, S. J. (2001). Personality predictors of citizenship performance. *International Journal of Selection and Assessment,* 9(1–2), 52–69.

Bossomaier, T., Harré, M., Knittel, A., & Snyder, A. (2009). A semantic network approach to the Creativity Quotient (CQ). *Creativity Research Journal, 21*(1), 64–71. doi:10.1080/10400410802633517

Brief, A. P., & Motowidlo, S. J. (1986). Prosocial organizational behaviors. *Academy of Management Review, 11,* 710–725. doi:10.2307/258391

Brucks, M. (1986). A typology of consumer knowledge content. *Advances in Consumer Research, 13,* 58–63.

Burleson, B. R. (1984). Age, social-cognitive development, and the use of comforting strategies. *Communication Monographs, 51*(2), 140–153. doi:10.1080/03637758409390190.

Burleson, B. R. (1987). Cognitive complexity. In J. C. McCroskey & J. A. Daly (Eds.), *Personality and interpersonal communication* (pp. 305–349). Newbury Park, CA: Sage.

Burleson, B. R. (1994). Friendship and similarities in social-cognitive and communication abilities: Social skill bases of interpersonal attraction in childhood. *Personal Relationships, 1,* 371–389.

Burleson, B. R., Applegate, J. L., & Delia, J. G. (1991). On validly assessing the validity of the Role Category Questionnaire: A reply to Allen et al. *Communication Reports, 4,* 113–119.

Burleson, B. R., Applegate, J. L., & Neuwirth, C. M. (1981). Is cognitive complexity loquacity? A reply to Powers, Jordan, and Street. *Human Communication Research, 7,* 212–225.

Burleson, B. R., & Caplan, S. E. (1998). Cognitive complexity. In J. C. McCroskey, J. A. Daly, M. M. Martin, & M. J. Beatty (Eds.), *Communication and personality: Trait perspectives* (pp. 230–286). Cresskill, NJ: Hampton Press.

Burleson, B. R., & Rowan, K. E. (1985). Are social-cognitive ability and narrative writing skill related? *Written Communication, 2,* 25–43.

Burleson, B. R., & Waltman, M. S. (1988). Cognitive complexity: Using the Role Category Questionnaire measure. In C. H. Tardy (Ed.), *A handbook for the* study of human communication: Methods and instruments for observing, measuring, and assessing communication processes (pp. 1–35). Norwood, NJ: Ablex.

Burleson, B. R., Waltman, M. S., & Samter, W. (1987). More evidence that cognitive complexity is not loquacity: A reply to Beatty and Payne. *Communication Quarterly, 35*, 317–328.

Callinan, M., & Robertson, I. T. (2000). Work sample testing. *International Journal of Selection and Assessment, 8*, 248–260. doi:10.1111/1468-2389.00154

Campbell, J. P. (1990). Modeling the performance prediction problem. In M. D. Dunnette & L. M. Hough (Eds.), *Handbook of industrial and organizational psychology* (2nd ed., Vol. 1, pp. 687–732). Palo Alto, CA: Consulting Psychologists Press.

Campbell, J. P. (1999). The definition and measurement of performance in the new age. In D. R. Ilgen & E. D. Pulakos (Eds.), *The changing nature of performance: Implications for staffing, motivation, and development* (pp. 399–430). San Francisco, CA: Jossey-Bass.

Campbell, J. P., McCloy, R. A., Oppler, S. H., & Sager, C. E. (1993). A theory of performance. In N. Schmitt & W. C. Borman (Eds.), *Personnel selection in organizations*. San Francisco, CA: Jossey-Bass.

Carpenter, T. (2003). *Toward a comprehensive taxonomy of interpersonal performance in organizations.* Unpublished doctoral dissertation. George Mason University, Fairfax, VA.

Cascio, W. (2003). *Managing human resources: Productivity, quality of work life, and profits* (6th ed.). Boston, MA: McGraw-Hill.

Cascio, W. F., & Aguinis, H. (2005). *Applied psychology in human resource management* (6th ed.). Englewood Cliffs, NJ: Prentice Hall.

Chan, D., & Schmitt, N. (2002). Situational judgment and job performance. *Human Performance, 15*, 233–254. doi:10.1207/S15327043HUP1503_01

Chen, G., Thomas, B., & Wallace, J. C. (2005). A multilevel examination of the relationships among training outcomes, mediating regulatory processes, and adaptive performance. *Journal of Applied Psychology, 90*, 827–841. doi:10.1037/0021-9010.90.5.827

Chi, M. T. H., Glaser, R., & Rees, E. (1982). Expertise in problem solving. In R. J. Sternberg (Ed.), *Advances in the psychology of human intelligence* (Vol. 1). Hillsdale, NJ: Erlbaum.

Christian, M. S., Edwards, B. D., & Bradley, J. C. (2010). Situational judgment tests: Constructs assessed and a meta-analysis of their criterion-related validities. *Personnel Psychology, 63*, 83–117. doi:10.1111/j.1744-6570.2009.01163.x

Christensen, P. R., Merrifield, P. R., & Guilford, J. P. (1953). *Consequences form A-1.* Beverly Hills, CA: Sheridan Supply.

Clevenger, J., Pereira, G. M., Wiechmann, D., Schmitt, N., & Harvey, V. S. (2001). Incremental validity of situational judgment tests. *Journal of Applied Psychology, 86*, 410–417. doi:10.1037/0021-9010.86.3.410

Coleman, V. I., & Borman, W. C. (2000). Investigating the Underlying Structure of the Citizenship Performance Domain. *Human Resource Management Review, 10*(1), 25-44. doi:10.1016/S1053-4822(99)00037-6

Coopman, S. Z. (1998). Personal constructs and communication in interpersonal and organizational contexts. In G. Neimeyer & R. Neimeyer (Eds.), *Advances in personal construct psychology* (Vol. 4). Greenwich, CT: JAI Press.

Costanza, D. P., Fleishman, E. A., & Marshall-Mies, J. (1999). Knowledges. In N. G. Peterson, M. D. Mumford, W. C. Borman, P. R. Jeanneret, & E. A. Fleishman

(Eds.), *An occupational information system for the 21st century: The development of O*NET* (pp. 71–90). Washington, DC: American Psychological Association. doi:10.1037/10313-005

Couper, M. P. (2008). *Designing effective web surveys.* Cambridge, UK: Cambridge University Press.

Crockett, W. H. (1965). Cognitive complexity and impression formation. In B. A. Maher (Ed.), *Progress in experimental personality research* (Vol. 2, pp. 47–90). New York: Academic Press.

Crockett, W. H., Press, A. N., Delia, J. G., & Kenny, C. T. (1974). *Structural analysis of the organization of written impressions.* Unpublished manuscript, University of Kansas, Lawrence, KS.

Crockett, W. H. (1982). The organization of construct systems. In J. C. Mancuso & J. R. Adams-Webber (Eds.), *The construing person* (pp. 62–95). New York: Praeger.

Daly, J. A., Bell, R. A., Glenn, P. J., & Lawrence, S. (1985). Conceptualizing conversational complexity. *Human Communication Research, 12,* 30–53.

Delia, J. G. (1976). Change of meaning processes in impression formation. *Communication Monographs, 43,* 142–157. doi:10.1080/03637757609375926

Delia, J. G., Clark, R. A., & Switzer, D. E. (1974). Cognitive complexity and impression formation in informal social interaction. *Speech Monographs, 41*(4), 299–308. doi:10.1080/03637757409375854

Delia, J. G., O'Keefe, B. J., & O'Keefe, D. J. (1982). The constructivist approach to communication. In F. E. X. Dance (Ed.), *Human communication theory: Comparative essays* (pp. 147–191). New York: Harper & Row.

Donaldson, S. I., & Grant-Vallone, E. J. (2002). Understanding self-report bias in organizational behavior research. *Journal of Business and Psychology, 17,* 245–260. doi:10.1023/A:1019637632584

Dreher, G. F., & Bretz, R. D. (1991). Cognitive ability and career attainment: Moderating effects of early career success. *Journal of Applied Psychology, 76*(3), 392–397. doi:10.1037/0021-9010.76.3.392

Dudley, N. M., & Cortina, J. M. (2008). Knowledge and skills that facilitate the personal support dimension of citizenship. *Journal of Applied Psychology, 93,* 1249–1270. doi:10.1037/a0012572

Dudley, N. M., & Cortina, J. M. (2009). *Knowledge and skills that facilitate effective helping.* Unpublished manuscript.

Dye, D. A., Reck, M., & McDaniel, M. A. (1993). The validity of job knowledge measures. *International Journal of Selection and Assessment, 1*(3), 153–157. doi:10.1111/j.1468-2389.1993.tb00103.x

Ericsson, K. A., & Charness, N. (1994). Expert performance: Its structure and acquisition. *American Psychologist, 49,* 725–747. doi:10.1037/0003-066X.49.8.725

File, Q. W. (1945). The measurement of supervisory quality in industry. *Journal of Applied Psychology, 29,* 323–337. doi:10.1037/h0057397

File, Q. W., & Remmers, H. (1971). *How supervise? Manual.* San Antonio, TX: Psychological Corporation.

Fleishman, E. A., & Mumford, M. D. (1989). Abilities as causes of individual differences in skill acquisition. *Human Performance, 2,* 201–223. doi:10.1207/s15327043hup0203_4

Gessner, T. L., & Klimoski, R. J. (2006). Making sense of situations. In J. A. Weekley & R. E. Ployhart (Eds.), *Situational judgment tests: Theory, measurement, and application* (pp. 13–38). Mahwah, NJ: Lawrence Erlbaum Associates Publishers.

Gioia, D. A., & Manz, C. C. (1985). Linking cognition and behavior: A script processing interpretation of vicarious learning. *Academy of Management Review, 10*, 527–539.

Goff, K., & Torrance, E. P. (2002). *Abbreviated Torrance test for adults.* Bensenville, IL: Scholastic Testing Service.

Goldstein, I. L., & Ford, J. K. (2002). *Training in organizations* (4th ed.). Belmont, CA: Wadsworth/Thomson Learning.

Greene, R. L. (2011). Some considerations for enhancing psychological assessment. *Journal of Personality Assessment, 93*(3), 198–203. doi:10.1080/00223891. 2011.558879

Greeno, J. G., & Simon, H. A. (1988). Problem solving and reasoning. In R. C. Atkinson, R. J. Herrnstein, G. Lindzey, & R. D. Luce (Eds.), *Stevens' handbook of experimental psychology* (Rev. ed.). New York: John Wiley & Sons.

Griffin, E. (2006). *A first look at communication theory* (6th ed.). New York: McGraw-Hill.

Grim, A. M. (2010). *Use of situational judgment test to measure individual adaptability in applied settings.* Master's thesis, George Mason University. Retrieved from http://hdl.handle.net/1920/5793

Guilford, J. P. (1950). Creativity. *American Psychologist, 5*, 444–454.

Guilford, J. P. (1956). The structure of intellect. *Psychological Bulletin, 53*, 267–293. doi:10.1037/h0040755

Guilford, J. P. (1967). *The nature of human intelligence.* New York: McGraw-Hill.

Guilford, J. P., & Hoepfner, R. (1971). *The analysis of intelligence.* New York: McGraw-Hill.

Guion, R. M. (1998). *Assessment, measurement, and prediction for personnel decisions.* Mahwah, NJ: Erlbaum.

Hesketh, B., & Neal, A. (1999). Technology and performance. In D. R. Ilgen & E. D. Pulakos (Eds.), *The changing nature of performance: Implications for staffing, motivation, and development* (pp. 21–55). San Francisco, CA: Jossey-Bass.

Hornke, L. F., & Kersting, M. (2006). Optimizing quality in the use of web-based and computer-based testing for personnel selection. In D. Bartram & R. K. Hambleton (Eds.), *Computer-based testing and the Internet: Issues and advances* (pp. 149–162). New York: John Wiley & Sons.

Huffcutt, A. I., Conway, J. M., Roth, P. L., & Stone, N. J. (2001). Identification and meta-analytic assessment of psychological constructs measured in employment interviews. *Journal of Applied Psychology, 86*, 897–913. doi:10.1037/0021-9010.86.5.897

Hunter, J. E. (1983). A causal model of cognitive ability, job knowledge, job performance, and supervisor ratings. In F. Landy, S. Zedeck, & J. Cleveland (Eds.), *Performance measurement and theory* (pp. 257–266). Hillsdale, NJ: Lawrence Erlbaum.

Hunter, J. E. (1986). Cognitive ability, cognitive aptitudes, job knowledge, and job performance. *Journal of Vocational Behavior, 29*, 340–362.

Hunter, J. E., & Hunter, R. F. (1984). Validity and utility of alternative predictors of job performance. *Psychological Bulletin, 96*, 72–98. doi:10.1037/0033-2909.96.1.72

Janson, A. (2008). Extracting leadership knowledge from formative experiences. *Leadership, 4*(1), 73–94. doi:10.1177/1742715007085770

Kelly, G. A. (1955). *The psychology of personal constructs* (Vol. 1). Oxford, UK: W. W. Norton.

Kim, K. H. (2006). Can we trust creativity tests? A review of the Torrance Tests of Creative Thinking (TTCT). *Creativity Research Journal, 18*, 3–14. doi:10.1207/s15326934crj1801_2

Kim, K. H. (2008). Meta-analyses of the relationship of creative achievement to both IQ and divergent thinking test scores. *Journal of Creative Behavior, 42*(2), 106–130.

Kline, S. L. (1991). Construct differentiation and person-centered regulative messages. *Journal of Language and Social Psychology, 10*, 1–27.

Kline, S. L., Pelias, R., & Delia, J. G. (1991). The predictive validity of cognitive complexity measures on communication-relevant abilities. *International Journal of Personal Construct Psychology, 4*, 347–357.

Leigh, T. W., & McGraw, P. F. (1989). Mapping the procedural knowledge of industrial sales personnel: A script-theoretic investigation. *Journal of Marketing, 53*, 16–34. doi:10.2307/1251522

Leong, S., Busch, P. S., & John, D. R. (1989). Knowledge bases and salesperson effectiveness: A script-theoretic analysis. *Journal of Marketing Research, 26*(2), 164–178. doi:10.2307/3172603

Levashina, J., & Campion, M. A. (2007). Measuring faking in the employment interview: Development and validation of an interview faking behavior scale. *Journal of Applied Psychology, 92*, 1638–1656. doi:10.1037/0021-9010.92.6.1638

Lievens, F., & Chan, D. (2010). Practical intelligence, emotional intelligence, and social intelligence. In J. L. Farr & N. T. Tippins (Eds.), *Handbook of employee selection* (pp. 339–359). New York: Routledge/Taylor & Francis Group.

Lievens, F., Sackett, P. R., & Buyse, T. (2009). The effects of response instructions on situational judgment test performance and validity in a high-stakes context. *Journal of Applied Psychology, 94*, 1095–1101. doi:10.1037/a0014628

Martin, R. (1991). Examining relationship thinking: The relational cognition complexity instrument. *Journal of Social and Personal Relationships, 8*, 467–480.

Martin, R. (1992). Relational cognition complexity and relational communication in personal relationships. *Communication Monographs, 59*, 150–163.

McDaniel, M. A., & Nguyen, N. T. (2001). Situational judgment tests: A review of practice and constructs assessed. *International Journal of Selection and Assessment, 9*, 103–113. doi:10.1111/1468-2389.00167

McDaniel, M. A., & Whetzel, D. L. (2005). Situational judgment test research: Informing the debate on practical intelligence theory. *Intelligence, 33*, 515–525. doi:10.1016/j.intell.2005.02.001

Meeker, M. N. (1969). *SOI: Its interpretation and its uses.* Columbus, OH: Charles Merrill.

Merrifield, P. R., Guilford, J. P., Christensen, P. R., & Frick, J. M. (1962). The role of intellectual factors in problem solving. *Psychological Monographs, 76*, 1–21.

Meyer, J. C., & Sypher, B. D. (1993). Personal constructs as indicators of cultural values. *Southern Communication Journal, 58*, 227–238.

Michael, W. B., & Wright, C. R. (1989). Psychometric issues in the assessment of creativity. In J. A. Glover, R. R. Ronning, & C. R. Reynolds (Eds.), *Handbook of creativity* (pp. 33–52). New York: Plenum Press.

Mitchell, T. R., & Daniels, D. (2003). Observations and commentary on recent research in work motivation. In L. Porter, G. Bigley, & R. Steers (Eds.), *Motivation and work behavior* (7th ed.). New York: McGraw Hill.

Morgan, F. W., & Stoltman, J. J. (1990). Adaptive selling—Insights from social cognition. *Journal of Personal Selling & Sales Management, 10*, 43–54.

Motowidlo, S. J., & Beier, M. E. (2010). Differentiating specific job knowledge from implicit trait policies in procedural knowledge measured by a situational judgment test. *Journal of Applied Psychology, 95*, 321–333. doi:10.1037/a0017975

Motowidlo, S. J., Borman, W. C., & Schmit, M. J. (1997). A theory of individual differences in task and contextual performance. *Human Performance, 10,* 71–83. doi: 10.1207/s15327043hup1002_1

Motowidlo, S. J., Dunnette, M. D., & Carter, G. W. (1990). An alternative selection procedure: The low-fidelity simulation. *Journal of Applied Psychology, 75,* 640–647. doi:10.1037/0021-9010.75.6.640

Motowidlo, S. J., Hooper, A. C., & Jackson, H. L. (2006a). A theoretical basis for situational judgment tests. In J. A. Weekley & R. E. Ployhart (Eds.), *Situational judgment tests: Theory, measurement, and application* (pp. 57–81). Mahwah, NJ: Lawrence Erlbaum Associates Publishers.

Motowidlo, S. J., Hooper, A. C., & Jackson, H. L. (2006b). Implicit policies about relations between personality traits and behavioral effectiveness in situational judgment items. *Journal of Applied Psychology, 91,* 749–761. doi:10.1037/0021-9010.91.4.749

Mumford, M. D., Marks, M. A., Connelly, M., Zaccaro, S. J., & Johnson, J. F. (1998). Domain-based scoring of divergent-thinking tests: Validation evidence in an occupational sample. *Creativity Research Journal, 11,* 151–163.

Mumford, T. V., Van Iddekinge, C. H., Morgeson, F. P., & Campion, M. A. (2008). The team role test: Development and validation of a team role knowledge situational judgment test. *Journal of Applied Psychology, 93,* 250–267. doi:10.1037/0021-9010.93.2.250

Münsterberg, H. (1913). *Psychology and industrial efficiency.* Boston, MA: Houghton, Mifflin and Company. doi:10.1037/10855-000

Neimeyer, R. A. & Neimeyer, G. J. (Eds.) (2002). *Advances in personal construct psychology* (Vol. 5). New York: Praeger.

Nicotera, A. M. (1995). The constructivist theory of Delia, Clark, and associates. In D. P. Cushman & B. Kovacic (Eds.), *Watershed research traditions in human communication theory* (pp. 45–66). Albany, NY: SUNY Press.

O'Keefe, B. J., & Delia, J. G. (1979). Construct comprehensiveness and cognitive complexity as predictors of the number and strategic adaptation of arguments and appeals in a persuasive message. *Communication Monographs, 46,* 231–240.

O'Keefe, B. J., & Delia, J. G. (1982). Impression formation and message production. In M. E. Roloff & C. R. Berger (Eds.), *Social cognition and communication* (pp. 33–72). Beverly Hills, CA: Sage.

O'Keefe, B. J., Delia, J. G., & O'Keefe, D. J. (1980). Interaction analysis and the analysis of interactional organization. In N. K. Denzin (Ed.), *Studies in symbolic interaction* (Vol. 3, pp. 25–57). Greenwich, CT: JAI Press.

O'Keefe, D. J., Shepherd, G. J., & Streeter, T. (1982). Role category questionnaire measures of cognitive complexity: Reliability and comparability of alternative forms. *Central States Speech Journal, 33,* 333–338.

O'Keefe, D. J., & Sypher, H. E. (1981). Cognitive complexity measures and the relationship of cognitive complexity to communication. *Human Communication Research, 8,* 72–92.

Organ, D. W. (1990). The motivational basis of organizational citizenship behavior. *Research in Organizational Behavior, 12,* 43–72.

Phillips, J. F. (1993). Predicting negotiation skills. *Journal of Business and Psychology, 7,* 403–411. doi:10.1007/BF01013754

Pierce, C. A., & Aguinis, H. (1997). Using virtual reality technology in organizational behavior research. *Journal of Organizational Behavior, 18,* 407–410. doi:10.1002/(SICI)1099-1379(199709)18:5<407::AID-JOB869>3.0.CO;2-P

Ployhart, R. E., & Bliese, P. D. (2006). Individual adaptability (I-ADAPT) theory: Conceptualizing the antecedents, consequences, and measurement of individual differences in adaptability. In S. Burke, L. Pierce, & E. Salas (Eds.), *Understanding adaptability: A prerequisite for effective performance within complex environments.* Oxford, UK: Elsevier.

Ployhart, R. E., & Ehrhart, M. G. (2003). Be careful what you ask for: Effects of response instructions on the construct validity and reliability of situational judgment tests. *International Journal of Selection and Assessment, 11*, 1–16. doi:10.1111/1468-2389.00222

Ployhart, R. E., & MacKenzie, W. I. (2010). Situational judgment tests: A critical review and agenda for the future. In S. Zedeck (Ed.), *APA handbook of industrial and organizational psychology.* APA Books.

Ployhart, R. E., Schneider, B., & Schmitt, N. (2006). *Staffing organizations: Contemporary practice and theory* (3rd ed.). Mahwah, NJ: Lawrence Erlbaum Associates Publishers.

Plucker, J. A., & Renzulli, J. S. (1999). Psychometric approaches to the study of creativity. In R. J. Sternberg (Ed.), *Handbook of creativity.* New York: Cambridge University Press.

Posthuma, R. A., Morgeson, F. P., & Campion, M. A. (2002). Beyond employment interview validity: A comprehensive narrative review of recent research and trends over time. *Personnel Psychology, 55*, 1–81. doi:10.1111/j.1744-6570.2002.tb00103.x

Powers, W. G., Jordan, W. J., & Street, R. L. (1979). Language indices in the measurement of cognitive complexity: Is complexity loquacity? *Human Communication Research, 6*, 69–73.

Pulakos, E. D., Borman, W. C., & Hough, L. M. (1988). Test validation for scientific understanding: Two demonstrations of an approach to studying predictor-criterion linkages. *Personnel Psychology, 41*, 703–716. doi:10.1111/j.1744-6570.1988.tb00648.x

Pulakos, E. D., Arad, S., Donovan, M. A., & Plamondon, K. E. (2000). Adaptability in the workplace: Development of a taxonomy of adaptive performance. *Journal of Applied Psychology, 85*(4), 612–624. doi:10.1037/0021-9010.85.4.612

Reinig, B. A., Briggs, R. O., & Nunamaker, J. F. Jr. (2007) On the measurement of ideation quality. *Journal of Management Information Systems, 23*(4), 143–161.

Reiter-Palmon, R., Illies, M., Cross, L., Buboltz, C., & Nimps, T. (2009). Creativity and domain specificity: The effect of task type on multiple indexes of creative problem-solving. *Psychology of Aesthetics, Creativity, and the Arts, 3*(2), 73–80. doi:10.1037/a0013410

Rudner, L. M., Garcia, V., & Welch, C. (2006). An evaluation of the IntelliMetric [SM] essay scoring system. *Journal of Technology, Learning, and Assessment, 4*(4). Available from http://ejournals.bc.edu/ojs/index.php/jtla/article/view/1651.

Runco, M. A. (2008). Commentary: Divergent thinking is not synonymous with creativity. *Psychology of Aesthetics, Creativity, and the Arts, 2*(2), 93–96. doi:10.1037/1931-3896.2.2.93

Runco, M. A., & Acar, S. (2010). Do tests of divergent thinking have an experiential bias? *Psychology of Aesthetics, Creativity, and the Arts, 4*(3), 144–148. doi:10.1037/a0018969

Samter, W., & Burleson, B. R. (1984). Cognitive and motivational influences on spontaneous comforting behavior. *Human Communication Research, 11*, 231–260.

Samter, W., Burleson, B. R., & Basden-Murphy, L. (1989). Behavioral complexity is in the eye of the beholder: Effects of cognitive complexity and message complexity on impressions of the source of comforting messages. *Human Communication Research, 15*, 612–629.

Schmidt, F. L., & Hunter, J. E. (1998). The validity and utility of selection methods in personnel psychology: Practical and theoretical implications of 85 years of research findings. *Psychological Bulletin, 124*, 262–274. doi:10.1037/0033-2909.124.2.262

Schmidt, F. L., Hunter, J. E., & Outerbridge, A. N. (1986). Impact of job experience and ability on job knowledge, work sample performance, and supervisory ratings of job performance. *Journal of Applied Psychology, 71*, 432–439. doi:10.1037/0021-9010.71.3.432

Schmitt, N., & Chan, D. (2006). Situational judgment tests: Method or construct? In J. A. Weekley & R. E. Ployhart (Eds.), *Situational judgment tests: Theory, measurement, and application* (pp. 135–155). Mahwah, NJ: Lawrence Erlbaum Associates Publishers.

Schmitt, N., & Mills, A. E. (2001). Traditional tests and job simulations: Minority and majority performance and test validities. *Journal of Applied Psychology, 86*, 451–458. doi:10.1037/0021-9010.86.3.451

Silvia, P. J. (2008). Creativity and intelligence revisited: A latent variable analysis of Wallach and Kogan (1965). *Creativity Research Journal, 20*(1), 34–39. doi:10.1080/10400410701841807

Silvia, P. J., Martin, C., & Nusbaum, E. C. (2009). A snapshot of creativity: Evaluating a quick and simple method for assessing divergent thinking. *Thinking Skills and Creativity, 4*(2), 79–85. doi:10.1016/j.tsc.2009.06.005

Silvia, P. J., Winterstein, B. P., Willse, J. T., Barona, C. M., Cram, J. T., Hess, et al. (2008). Assessing creativity with divergent thinking tasks: Exploring the reliability and validity of new subjective scoring methods. *Psychology of Aesthetics, Creativity, and the Arts, 2*(2), 68–85. doi:10.1037/1931-3896.2.2.68

Smith, C. A., Organ, D. W., & Near, J. P. (1983). Organizational citizenship behavior: Its nature and antecedents. *Journal of Applied Psychology, 68*, 653–663. doi:10.1037/0021-9010.68.4.653

Stemler, S. E., & Sternberg, R. J. (2006). Using situational judgment tests to measure practical intelligence. In J. A. Weekley & R. E. Ployhart (Eds.), *Situational judgment tests: Theory, measurement, and application* (pp. 107–131). Mahwah, NJ: Lawrence Erlbaum Associates Publishers.

Sternberg, R. J. (1988). *The triarchic mind: A new theory of human intelligence.* New York: Penguin.

Sternberg, R. J. (1997). The concept of intelligence and its role in lifelong learning and success. *American Psychologist, 52*, 1030–1037. doi:10.1037/0003-066X.52.10.1030

Sternberg, R. J., & Horvath, J. A. (Eds.) (1999). *Tacit knowledge in professional practice.* Mahwah, NJ: Lawrence Erlbaum Associates, Inc.

Sternberg, R. J., Wagner, R. K., Williams, W. M., & Horvath, J. A. (1995). Testing common sense. *American Psychologist, 50*, 912–927. doi:10.1037/0003-066X.50.11.912

Stone, A., Turkkan, J., Bachrach, C., Jobe, J., Kurtzman, H., & Cain, V. (Eds.) (2000). *The science of self-report: Implications for research and practice.* Mahwah, NJ: Lawrence Erlbaum Associates Publishers.

Streufert, S., & Swezey, R. W. (1986). *Complexity, managers, and organizations.* Orlando, FL: Academic Press.

Sujan, H., Sujan, M., & Bettman, J. R. (1988). Knowledge structure differences between more effective and less effective salespeople. *Journal of Marketing Research, 25*, 81–86. doi:10.2307/3172927

Sujan, H., Sujan, M., & Bettman, J. R. (1991). The practical know-how of selling: Differences in knowledge content between more effective and less effective performers. *Marketing Letters, 2*, 367–378.

Sypher, B. D. (1984). The importance of social-cognitive abilities in organizations. In R. N. Bostrom (Ed.), *Competence in communication* (pp. 103–127). Beverly Hills, CA: Sage.

Sypher, H. E., & Applegate, J. L. (1984). Organizing communication behavior: The role of schemas and constructs. In R. N. Bostrom (Ed.), *Communication yearbook 8* (pp. 310–329). Beverly Hills, CA: Sage.

Sypher, B. D., Bostrom, R. N., & Seibert, J. H. (1989). Listening, communication abilities, and success at work. *Journal of Business Communication, 26*, 293–303.

Sypher, H. E., & Higgins, E. (1989). Social cognition and communication. *Communication Research, 16*(3), 309–314.

Sypher, H. E., & Sypher, B. D. (1988). Cognitive differentiation and communication behavior: The Role Category Questionnaire. *Management Communication Quarterly, 2*, 283–294.

Sypher, B. D., & Zorn, T. E. (1986). Communication-related abilities and upward mobility: A longitudinal investigation. *Human Communication Research, 12*, 420–431.

Szymanski, D. M. (1988). Determinants of selling effectiveness: The importance of declarative knowledge to the personal selling concept. *Journal of Marketing, 52*(1), 64–77. doi:10.2307/1251686

Szymanski, D. M., & Churchill, G. A. (1990). Client evaluation cues: A comparison of successful and unsuccessful salespeople. *Journal of Marketing Research, 27*(2), 163–174. doi:10.2307/3172843

Torrance, E. P. (1966). *The Torrance tests of creative thinking–Norms—Technical manual research edition—Verbal tests, forms A and B—Figural tests, forms A and B*. Princeton NJ: Personnel Press.

Torrance, E. P. (1967). The Minnesota studies on creative behavior. *Journal of Creative Behavior, 1*, 137–154.

Torrance, E. P. (2008). *Torrance tests of creative thinking: Norms—technical manual, verbal forms A and B*. Scholastic Testing Service.

Trull, T. J. (2007). Expanding the aperture of psychological assessment: Introduction to the special section on innovative clinical assessment technologies and methods. *Psychological Assessment, 19*(1), 1–3. doi:10.1037/1040-3590.19.1.1

Wagner, R. K., & Sternberg, R. J. (1985). Practical intelligence in real-world pursuits: The role of tacit knowledge. *Journal of Personality and Social Psychology, 49*, 436–458. doi:10.1037/0022-3514.49.2.436

Wallach, M. A., & Kogan, N. (1965). *Modes of thinking in young children: A study of the creativity–intelligence distinction*. New York: Holt, Rinehart, & Winston.

Waltman, M. S. (2002). Developments in constructivist work in communication studies, psychology, and education: Introduction to the special section in constructivism. *American Communication Journal, 5*, 1–6.

Walton, E. (1985). The relevance of personal construct theory to management. In F. Epting & A. W. Landfield (Eds.), *Anticipating personal construct psychology* (pp. 95–108). Lincoln: University of Nebraska Press.

Ward, S. L., Byrnes, J. P., & Overton, W. F. (1990). Organization of knowledge and conditional reasoning. *Journal of Educational Psychology*, 82, 832–837. doi:10.1037/0022-0663.82.4.832

Weekley, J. A., & Jones, C. (1997). Video-based situational testing. *Personnel Psychology*, 50, 25–49. doi:10.1111/j.1744-6570.1997.tb00899.x

Weekley, J., & Jones, C. (1999). Further studies of situational tests. *Personnel Psychology*, 52, 679–700. doi:10.1111/j.1744-6570.1999.tb00176.x

Weekley, J. A., & Ployhart, R. E. (2005). Situational judgment: Antecedents and relationships with performance. *Human Performance*, 18, 81–104. doi:10.1207/s15327043hup1801_4

Weekley, J. A., Ployhart, R. E., & Harold, C. M. (2004). Personality and situational judgment tests across applicant and incumbent settings: An examination of validity, measurement, and subgroup differences. *Human Performance*, 17, 433–461. doi:10.1207/s15327043hup1704_5

Weekley, J. A., Ployhart, R. E., & Holtz, B. C. (2006). On the development of situational judgment tests: Issues in item development, scaling, and scoring. In J. A. Weekley & R. E. Ployhart (Eds.), *Situational judgment tests: Theory, measurement, and application* (pp. 157–182). Mahwah, NJ: Lawrence Erlbaum Associates Publishers.

Weitz, B. A., Sujan, H., & Sujan, M. (1986). Knowledge, motivation, and adaptive behavior: A framework for improving selling effectiveness. *Journal of Marketing*, 50(4), 174–191. doi:10.2307/1251294

Werner, H. (1957). *Comparative psychology of mental development* (Rev. ed.). Oxford, UK: International Universities Press.

Whetzel, D. L., McDaniel, M. A., & Nguyen, N. T. (2008). Subgroup differences in situational judgment test performance: A meta-analysis. *Human Performance*, 21, 291–309. doi:10.1080/08959280802137820

Wilson, S. R., Cruz, M. G., & Kang, K. H. (1992). Is it always a matter of perspective? Construct differentiation and variability in attributions about compliance gaining. *Communication Monographs*, 59, 350–367.

Woods, E. (1996). Associations of nonverbal decoding ability with indices of person-centered communicative ability. *Communication Reports*, 9, 13–22.

Zimmermann, S. (1994). Social cognition and evaluations of health care team communication effectiveness. *Western Journal of Communication*, 58, 116–141.

Zimmermann, S., Hart, J., Allen, M., & Haas, J. (1998). Detecting cultural knowledge in organization members' personal construct systems. *Journal of Constructivist Psychology*, 10, 117–134.

Zorn, T. E., McKinney, M. M., & Moran, M. M. (1993). The structure of interpersonal construct systems: One system or many? *International Journal of Personal Construct Psychology*, 6, 139–166.

Index

References to Figures or Tables will be in *italics*. I/O psychology stands for industrial/organizational psychology.

490 • *Index*